The Complete Encyclopedia of Horses

M. E. ENSMINGER

The busy professional horseman has need for a book that contains, under one cover, in concise, quick, and easy-to-find form, scientific, yet practical, information about the gamut of the horse business—from vitamins to saddlery, from breeding to showing or racing. Also, most people—horse lovers all—have found at one time or another, their dreams filled with stallions and stagecoaches, cossacks and circus ponies, and race-tracks and steeplechasers. But lack of know-how frequently prevented these dreams from coming true.

The horse industry merits a complete, in-depth, equine encyclopedia. In support of this assertion, the following facts and figures relative to the United States horse industry are noteworthy:

- There are approximately 10 million horses in the United States.
- Horses represent an investment of $13 billion.
- A total of more than 250,000 4-H Club members have horse or pony projects, 100,000 more than have beef cattle projects.
- Annual expenditures for horse feed, drugs, tack, and equipment average about $750 per horse, for a total of $7.3 billion annually.
- Annual wages paid in the horse industry exceed $1 billion.
- Horse racing makes for America's leading spectator sport; about 75 million people go to races each year, 30 million more than wit-

...ng pro and col-

...ot tell the whole ...ture about the ...nd in any other ...values in back ...need for a book ...ach values and ...oyment in the

...Ensminger, says ...is encyclopedia: ...write a book; ...work any more ...e. Rather, as a ...ceaselessly away ...ny writings and ...ched the stage ...to abandon it ...them make a ...ell I succeeded ...jective—every- ...quick and easy ...ppropriately ti- *...ncyclopedia of*

...pedia of Horses ...contains every- ...bortion to zoo- ...ditionally, it is ...more than 400 ...many of which ...complete, in-

depth encyclopedia. It covers more items, has more scientific yet practical information, and offers more illustrations that tell a story than any other book of its kind.

The Complete Encyclopedia of Horses

OTHER BOOKS BY M. E. ENSMINGER

The Stockman's Handbook
Animal Science
Beef Cattle Science
Dairy Cattle Science
Sheep and Wool Science
Swine Science
Poultry Science
Horses and Horsemanship
The Complete Book of Dogs
China—The Impossible Dream

THE COMPLETE ENCYCLOPEDIA OF HORSES

M.E. Ensminger
B.S., M.A., Ph.D.

(Photo by Mr. Frank Turgent; courtesy, Mrs. Garvin E. Tankersley, Al-Marah Arabians, Washington, D.C.)

SOUTH BRUNSWICK AND NEW YORK: A. S. BARNES AND COMPANY
LONDON: THOMAS YOSELOFF LTD

© 1977 by A. S. Barnes and Co., Inc.

A. S. Barnes and Co., Inc.
Cranbury, New Jersey 08512

Thomas Yoseloff Ltd
Magdalen House
136–148 Tooley Street
London SE1 2TT, England

Library of Congress Cataloging in Publication Data
Ensminger, M   Eugene.
    The complete encyclopedia of horses.

    Bibliography: p.
    1. Horses—Dictionaries.   I.   Title.
SF278.E57   636.1'003   74-9282
ISBN 0-498-01508-4

to

JANET MARTSON

—my longtime secretary,
  who made me look good professionally.

Contents

Preface

"Everything about horses; and quick and easy to find." Such was the need; and out of this need arose—

THE COMPLETE ENCYCLOPEDIA OF HORSES

The busy professional horseman has need for a book which contains, under one cover, in concise, quick, and easy-to-find form, scientific—yet practical, information about the whole gamut of the horse business—from vitamins to saddlery, from breeding to showing or racing. Also, most folks—horse lovers all, have, at one time or another, found their dreams filled with stallions and stagecoaches, cossacks and circus ponies, and race tracks and steeplechasers. But lack of know-how frequently prevented these dreams from coming true.

The horse industry merits a complete, in-depth, equine encyclopedia. In support of this assertion the following facts and figures relative to the U.S. horse industry are noteworthy:

● There are an estimated 8 million horses in the U.S.

● Horses represent a $13 billion investment.

● A total of 320,767 4-H Club members had horse and pony projects in 1974; double the number that had beef cattle projects.

● Annual expenditures for horse feed, drugs, tack and equipment average about $1,000 per horse, for a total of $8.0 billion annually.

● Annual wages paid in the horse industry exceed $1 billion.

● Horse racing makes for America's leading spectator sport; 79 million people went to the races in 1974, 31 million more than went to automobile racing, the second ranking spectator sport.

But figures alone do not tell the whole story.

The unique thing about the horse industry, not found in any other business, is the human values back of it. Thus, in addition to increasing profit, there was need for a book that would enhance the human values and make for greater enjoyment in the grandest sport of all.

I didn't just set out to write a book; nor do I consider this work any more finished than my lifetime. Rather, as a perfectionist, I worked ceaselessly away at it until, following many writings and reams of paper, I reached the stage where I was willing to abandon it to the readers and let them make a judgment as to how well I succeeded in meeting my major objective—everything about horses; and quick and easy to find—in this book appropriately entitled, *The Complete Encyclopedia of Horses*.

I express my deep appreciation to all those who participated in this mountainous task—to my staff, who worked long and diligently, especially to Audrey Ensminger, for her inspiration, encouragement, and assistance; to the two artists who were responsible for most of the drawings—Professor Richard F. Johnson, Head, Department of Animal Science, California Polytechnic State University, San Luis Obispo, California; and Ruth Geary, of my staff; to all the breed associations, magazines, and individuals who responded so liberally to my call for pictures and information; and to Ernst Peterson, professional photographer, and Margit Sigray Bessenyey, Hungarian Horse Breeder, both of Hamilton, Montana, for the attractive colored jacket picture of Hungarian Horses.

M. E. ENSMINGER

Clovis, California

The Complete Encyclopedia of Horses

Thoroughbred mare and foal. (Courtesy, The Jockey Club)

American White mares on White Horse Ranch, Naper, Nebr. (Courtesy, American Albino Association, Inc., Crabtree, Oregon)

ABORTION, EQUINE (PREMATURE EX-PULSION OF THE FETUS).—The causes of abortion may be grouped under five headings as follows:

● *Salmonella abortivoequina abortion* occurs most frequently in the last half of pregnancy.

● *Streptococcic abortion* usually occurs early in pregnancy—prior to the fifth month.

● *Virus, or epizootic abortion* (rhinopneumonitis), generally occurs late in pregnancy—after the fifth month. Some foals are born alive and die at 2 to 3 days of age.

● *Viral arteritis* is caused by a virus. It produces fever, inflammation of the mucosa in the respiratory tract, and edema of the eyelids and legs. As many as 50 to 80 percent of pregnant mares may abort.

● *Miscellaneous causes of abortion* may be due to such things as accidents, faulty feeds, or twins.

TREATMENT.—Quarantine animals that have aborted and give them good feed and care.

CONTROL.—Burn or bury the bedding and fetus of mares that have aborted. Disinfect contaminated premises. Isolate newly introduced animals to the farm.

PREVENTION.—Prevent abortion caused by *Salmonella abortivoequina* by vaccinating all pregnant mares with a bacterin every year where premises are infected with the organism.

Prevent streptococcic abortion by mating only healthy. animals and observing scrupulous cleanliness at mating.

Prevent rhinopneumonitis by intranasal inoculation with hamster-adapted virus, a modified live virus vaccine. Inoculate all horses of both sexes and all ages in July and October of each year.

Prevent viral arteritis by quarantining affected animals, and isolating new horses brought to the farm. Use vaccine in problem areas.

DISCUSSION.—It is estimated that for the United States as a whole, one-half of all pregnant mares either abort or produce weak foals. Sanitation and herd health are important factors in lessening the number of abortions regardless of kind. Consult a veterinarian whenever abortion occurs. Cattle abortion on the premises will not affect pregnant mares and cause them to abort.

(Also see DISEASES AND PARASITES; and HEALTH PROGRAM.)

Fig. A-1. Born and born alive are the two most important factors in breeding horses. This Hungarian foal has a good start in life at Bitterroot Stock Farm, Hamilton, Montana, owned by Margit Sigray Bessenyey. (Photo by Ernst Peterson, Hamilton, Montana.)

ACCIDENT.—A sudden event or change occurring without intent, usually through carelessness, unawareness, lack of information, or a combination of causes, and resulting in a person, horse, or object getting hurt. In most horse accidents, the rider is to blame. Either he has been reckless or uninformed, or he is not a good enough horseman for the mount that he is using.

Most accidents result from a failure of the horseman to communicate with the horse. The aids (see AIDS) are a mutual language between horse and horseman; hence they should be understood and used properly. But an accomplished horseman does more—he communicates with the horse so that each understands and anticipates the other. A horseman understands the sight and sound of the horse that he is leading; he has a feel for the horse that he is riding or driving; and he interprets the stance of the horse, or the movement of his ears, eyes, and/or muscles. Until such time as communication of this type exists, accidents can best be avoided by the horseman entrusting himself only to a well-trained, mature horse.

ACCOUNTS, ENTERPRISE.—When one has a diversified horse enterprise—for example when producing yearlings for sale, having a racing or showing stable, standing stallions for public service, and growing corn—enterprise accounts should be kept; in this case four different accounts for four different enterprises. The reasons for keeping enterprise accounts are:

● It makes it possible to determine which enterprises have been most profitable, and which least profitable.

● It makes it possible to compare a given enterprise with competing enterprises of like kind, from the standpoint of ascertaining comparative performance.

● It makes it possible to determine the profitableness of an enterprise at the margin (the last unit of production). This will give an indication as to whether to increase the size of a certain enterprise at the expense of an alternative existing enterprise when both enterprises are profitable in total.

ACROSS THE BOARD.—See COMBINATION (BET).

ACTINOBACILLOSIS.—See NAVEL INFECTION.

ACTION.—This refers to the movement of the feet and legs.

Although the degree of action of the horse will vary somewhat with the type (speed, show, and saddle), the usefulness of all horses is dependent upon their action and their ability to move in various types of racing, driving, hunting, riding, polo, etc. In all types and breeds, the motion should be straight and true with a long, swift, and elastic stride.

(Also see GAITS.)

AGE.—The life-span of horses averages about 22 years. Horses generally are at their best between 3 and 12 years of age. This may vary because of individual differences in animals or because of differences in the kind of work they do.

The age of horses is, therefore, important to breeder, seller, and buyer.

HOW TO DETERMINE AGE.—The approximate age of a horse can be determined by noting the time of appearance, shape, and degree of wear of temporary and permanent teeth. Temporary, or milk, teeth are easily distinguishable from permanent ones because the former are smaller and whiter.

The best way to learn to determine age in horses is by examining the teeth of individual horses of known ages.

A mature male horse has 40 teeth and a mature female has 36, as shown in Table A-1. Quite

Fig. A-2. How to look a horse in the mouth. With the tongue held in one hand and the lower jaw grasped with the other hand, you can look at the teeth for as long as you like.

TABLE A-1

TYPES AND NUMBER OF TEETH IN HORSES

Types of Teeth	Number of Teeth		
	Mature Male	Mature Female	Young Animal, Either Sex
Molars or grinders	24	24	12
Incisors or front teeth	12	12	12
The 2 central incisors are known as centrals or nippers; the next 2, 1 on each side of the nippers, are called intermediates or middles; and the last, or outer pair, are the corners.			
Tushes or pointed teeth	4	0	0
These are located between the incisors and molars in males. Females do not have tushes as a rule.			
Total teeth	40	36	24

commonly, a small, pointed tooth, known as a "wolf tooth," may appear in front of each molar in the upper jaw, thus increasing the total number of teeth to 42 in the male and 38 in the female. Less frequently, two more wolf teeth in the lower jaw increase the total number of teeth in the male and female to 44 and 40, respectively. A foal of either sex has 24. The mare does not have tushes (canine teeth) as a rule.

Figs. A-3 to A-18 are guides for determining the age of horses by their teeth.

Even experienced horsemen cannot determine the age of an animal accurately after it is 12 years old. After this age, the teeth change from oval to triangular and they project or slant forward more and more as the horse becomes older.

Side views of the mouths of 5, 7, and 20-year-old horses are shown in Fig. A-18.

An animal's environment can affect wear on the teeth. Teeth of horses raised in dry sandy areas, for example, will show more than normal wear; a 5-year-old western horse may have teeth that would be normal in a 6 to 8-year-old horse raised elsewhere. The teeth of cribbers also show more than normal wear. The age of such animals is hard to determine, and the age of a horse with a parrot mouth also is difficult to estimate.

(Also see TEETH, STRUCTURE OF.)

Fig. A-3. Temporary incisors to 10 days of age: First or central upper and lower temporary incisors appear.

Fig. A-4. Temporary incisors at 4 to 6 weeks of age: Second or intermediate upper and lower temporary incisors appear.

Fig. A-5. Temporary incisors at 6 to 10 months: Third or corner upper and lower temporary incisors appear.

Fig. A-6. Temporary incisors at 1 year: Crowns of central temporary incisors show wear.

Fig. A-7. Temporary incisors at 1½ years: Intermediate temporary incisors show wear.

Fig. A-8. Temporary incisors at 2 years: All show wear.

Fig. A-9. Incisors at 4 years: Permanent incisors replace temporary centrals and intermediates; temporary corner incisors remain.

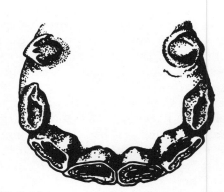

Fig. A-10. Incisors at 5 years: All permanent; cups in all incisors.

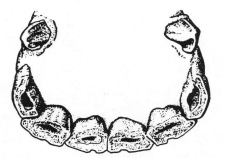

Fig. A-11. Incisors at 6 years: Cups worn out of lower central incisors.

Fig. A-12. Incisors at 7 years: Cups also worn out of lower intermediate incisors.

Fig. A-13. Incisors at 8 years: Cups worn out of all lower incisors, and dental star (dark line in front of cup) appears on lower central and intermediate pairs.

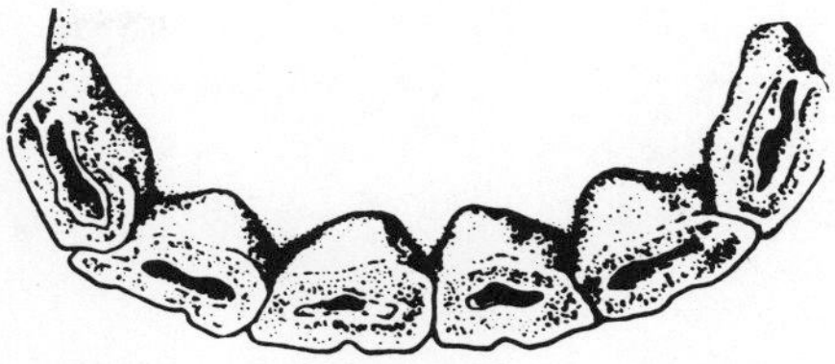

Fig. A-14. Incisors at 9 years: Cups worn out of upper central incisors; dental star on upper central and intermediate pairs.

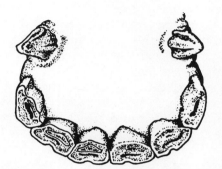

Fig. A-15. Incisors at 10 years: Cups also worn out of upper intermediate incisors, and dental star is present in all incisors.

Fig. A-16. Incisors at 11 or 12 years: Cups worn in all incisors (smooth mouthed), and dental star approaches center of cups.

Fig. A-17. Characteristic shape of lower incisors at 18 years.

Fig. A-18. Side view of 5, 7, and 20 year-old mouth. Note that as the horse advances in age, the teeth change from nearly perpendicular to slanting sharply toward the front.

AGED HORSE.—Correctly speaking, a horse eight years of age or over; but the term is often used to indicate a horse that is smooth-mouthed; that is, twelve years of age or older.

AGE OF OLDEST HORSE.—Authentic records of very old horses are hard to come by. Old Bill, a horse owned throughout his lifetime by Mr. Petrie, of Edinburgh, Scotland, is reputed to have lived to age 62.

An Italian Army horse, Topolino, was foaled on February 24, 1909, and died in February, 1960, at the age of 51.

Old Nellie, a black mare of draft breeding, raised by a Missouri farmer, was 53 years and 8 months old when she died in 1969.

Since the average life-span of a horse is about one-third the life expectancy of a person in the United States, in terms of human life a 50-year-old horse would be equivalent to a 150-year-old man.

AGORAPHOBIA.—A term used to describe a horse that has an abnormal fear of being in open spaces—contrasted with claustrophobia. This state sometimes develops in a horse that is kept continuously in a stable and never ridden outside a ring. Such an animal is frightened by the great outdoors, and will shy at everything and anything. With patience, the condition can usually be corrected. Prevention, which is the wisest course, consists in allowing the animal the run of a pasture or corral, or in leading or riding in open space.

AGRICULTURAL USE.—See USES OF HORSES.

AIDS.—After the rider is properly mounted, he is ready to put the horse in motion. This is accomplished by means of the "aids," which are really the only mutual language between the horse and rider. There are two kinds of aids—(1) natural and (2) artificial.

THE NATURAL AIDS.—The natural aids to retaining equilibrium and controlling the horse's movements are the legs, the hands and reins, the weight of the rider, and the voice. When necessary, these may be assisted by the artificial aids: spurs and crop. For a finished performance, all of the natural aids must be invoked in unison, and the artificial aids must be used sparingly, if at all.

ACTION OF THE LEGS.—The rider's legs are used primarily for the purposes of producing impulsion (forward movement) and increasing the gait. These results are obtained by a simple pressure on the horse by the inner calf muscles of the rider. Should this prove inadequate, the use of spurs or the whip may be resorted to. One of the rider's legs may be used with greater force than the other, thus displacing the horse's hind quarters laterally to prevent it from side stepping, to straighten the horse, or to change direction in a cramped space.

ACTION OF THE REINS.—The reins are an intermediary between the rider and the mount; they afford direct contact between the hands and the horse's mouth. The reins regulate the impulsion—slowing, stopping, or backing the horse. The reins, acting through the mouth and the neck, are also used to change direction of travel or to turn the horse to either the right or the left.

ACTION OF THE WEIGHT.—By shifting the position of his body from the hips up—a weight of approximately one hundred pounds in the average person—the rider can contribute materially to variations in the balance of the horse. When moving, stopping, or turning, the rider may facilitate and hasten the obedience of the mount by slightly displacing his weight in the direction of desired movement.

THE ARTIFICIAL AIDS.—Ingenious man has devised many artificial aids which, when judiciously used by an experienced horseman, may supplement effectively the natural aids. In addition to the whip and spur, the following equipment may be listed under this category: longeing whip, link straps, martingales, nosebands, various types of reins, and innumerable types of bits.

Such artificial aids should be used sparingly—particularly the spur and whip. Perhaps for the most part, they should be used only when there has been disobedience to the natural aids.

AIRS, CLASSICAL.—See DRESSAGE.

AIR TRANSPORTATION.—Plane shipments are a specialty, the details of which had best be left in the hands of an experienced person or agency, such as an importing or exporting company. At the present time, such shipments are largely confined to race-horses, valuable breeding animals, and polo ponies.

(Also see TRANSPORTING . HORSES.)

Fig. A-19. An Appaloosa loaded in a jet cargoliner, ready for flight. With this arrangement, loading in the stall is accomplished on the ground. The stall containing the horse is then lifted into the airplane door by forklift, maneuvered into position, and tied down by the loading crew. (Courtesy, Western Horseman)

AKHAL-TEKE.—A breed of light horses found in the U.S.S.R. It is a very old breed; it was one of the first to have its own stud book. Bay, gray, and a golden shade, with black points, are the only colors.

ALBINO HORSE, AMERICAN.—See BREED(S).

AL BORAK.—The mythical winged horse of Mohammed. The animal was supposed to be white in color, to have a human head, and to possess dazzling splendor and incredible speed.

ALFALFA (LUCERNE).—An important, perennial, leguminous forage plant with trifoliate leaves and bluish purple flowers. It is grown widely, principally for hay. Alfalfa is capable of surviving dry periods because of its extraordinarily long root system, and it is adapted to widely varying conditions of climate and soil. It yields the highest tonnage per acre and has the highest protein content of the legume hays.

Good quality alfalfa hay is excellent for horses. It averages 15.3 percent protein, which is of high quality; and it is a good source of certain minerals and vitamins. In addition to being used as a hay, alfalfa is an ingredient of most all-pelleted feeds.

ALLERGY.—A severe reaction, or sensitivity, which occurs in some individuals following the introduction of certain antigens into their bodies.

ALLOWANCE RACE.—The theory of an allowance race is to bring together horses whose recent performances are similar. The conditions are usually very simple. First, they specify a base weight to be carried by all eligible horses. Then, certain weight reductions are given to the horses with the poorest records. While races of most types make allowances of this nature, an "allowance race" as such, is the common term for all small purse events which are not claiming races, handicaps, or maiden special weight races. Conditions for a typical allowance race late in the summer of 1975 might read as follows:

"Seventh Race. Purse $4,000. For three-year-olds which have not won two races other than maiden or claiming in 1975. Three-year-olds 114 lbs.; older 122 lbs. Nonwinners of $3,500 once since March 8th allowed 3 lbs.; a race other than maiden or claiming at one mile or over, since June 14, 6 lbs.; such a race in 1975, 9 lbs., a race of any kind in 1975, 11 lbs. One mile."

Thus, a four-year-old whose last win was worth $3,500 and who won it in a six-furlong allowance race on March 1st, would go to the post carrying 113 lbs.—9 lbs. allowed off because of his record. An eligible three-year-old who had won $3,500 in a one-mile allowance race on July 1st would go to the post at the base weight of 114 lbs.

ALLOWANCES, NUTRITIVE.—See NUTRITIVE NEEDS.

ALSO-RAN.—A racehorse that finishes behind the first three, or out of the money.

ALTER.—To castrate a horse; to geld.

AMATEUR.—One who rides or drives for the love of the sport and not as a profession. An amateur must not deal (trade) in horses as a vocation, and he must not allow his picture to be used in advertising in connection with the sport.

The wife, and the children if they are over thirteen years of age, are considered professional if they assist in the husband's (father's) profession.

AMATEUR CLASS.—An amateur class in a horse show is one which requires an amateur (see AMATEUR) to ride or drive.

AMBLE.—An easy four-beat gait with lateral motion. It is a form of the stepping pace. At the ordinary pace, the horse's legs on the same side move together, as opposed to the trot in which the diagonal legs are raised and planted simultaneously. In the amble, there is a slight break so that the lateral legs (the legs on the same side) do not move at exactly the same time, but are planted one after the other with a slight pause between. The amble is the natural, slow gait of the donkey.

AMERICAN ALBINO ASSOCIATION, INC.—Box 79, Crabtree, Oregon 97335. (See Appendix for complete breed registry association list.)

AMERICAN ALBINO HORSE.—Renamed American White; American Creme. See BREED (S).

AMERICAN ANDALUSIAN ASSOCIATION.—Box 1290, Silver City, New Mexico 88061. (See Appendix for complete breed registry association list.)

AMERICAN ASSOCIATION OF OWNERS AND BREEDERS OF PERUVIAN PASO HORSES.—P. O. Box 2035, California City, California 93505. (See Appendix for complete breed registry association list.)

AMERICAN ASSOCIATION OF VETERINARY PRACTITIONERS.—The veterinary practitioners of America are banded together in the American Association of Equine Practitioners.

ADDRESS: American Association of Equine Practitioners, Route 5, 14 Hillcrest Circle, Golden, Colorado 80401.

AMERICAN BASHKIR CURLY.—Curly-haired horses have long been known in the Ural Mountains; hence, the name Bashkir. History also records that the nomadic Mongols rode curly horses.

However, the modern history of curly horses began in Nevada, where the breed registry was formed. The most distinctive characteristic of the breed is the curly coat, with corkscrew mane and wavy tail.

AMERICAN BASHKIR CURLY REGISTRY. —Box 453, Ely, Nevada 89301. (See Appendix for complete breed association list.)

AMERICAN BUCKSKIN.—See BREED (S).

AMERICAN BUCKSKIN REGISTRY ASSOCIATION.—Box 1125, Anderson, California 96007. (See Appendix for complete breed registry association list.)

AMERICAN CONNEMARA PONY SOCIETY. —R.D. 1, Hoshiekon Farm, Goshen, Connecticut 06756. (See Appendix for complete breed registry association list.)

AMERICAN CREAM DRAFT HORSE ASSOCIATION.—Hubbard, Iowa 50122. (See Appendix for complete breed registry association list.)

AMERICAN CREAM HORSE.—See BREEDS.

AMERICAN CREME HORSE.—Pale cream horses have been around a very long time. However, they were not accorded breed status until recently. The most distinctive characteristic of the breed is their color; they range from ivory white to sooty cream, with pale cream being most common. Both the American Creme Horse and the American White Horse are registered by the American Albino Association, Inc., Crabtree, Oregon, with separate divisions provided for each.

AMERICAN DONKEY AND MULE SOCIETY, INC.—2410 Executive Drive, Indianapolis, Indiana 46241. (See Appendix for complete breed registry association list.)

AMERICAN DRESSAGE INSTITUTE, THE. —The American Dressage Institute, a nonprofit, tax deductible corporation, was founded in 1967. Its stated purposes are to further classical riding in the United States and to provide instruction in dressage, both as a form of national and international competition and as a form of performing art. It offers dressage instruction at all levels and conducts annual dressage training and judging seminars.

ADDRESS.—The American Dressage Institute, Round Hill Road, Greenwich, Conn. 06830.

AMERICAN GOTLAND HORSE.—See BREED(S)

AMERICAN GOTLAND HORSE ASSOCIATION.—R. R. #2, Box 181, Elkland, Missouri 65644. (See Appendix for complete breed registry association list.)

AMERICAN HACKNEY HORSE SOCIETY.— P. O. Box 174, Pittsfield, Illinois 62363. (See Appendix for complete breed registry association list.)

AMERICAN HANOVERIAN SOCIETY.—809 W. 106th Street, Carmel, Indiana 46032. (See Appendix for complete breed registry association list.)

AMERICAN HORSE COUNCIL, INC.—The American Horse Council, which represents all sectors of the U.S. horse industry, was formed in 1969. It is dedicated to the development of the American equine industry. It seeks a fair tax consideration for horse producers (farmers) and develops educational programs and activities designed to meet the needs of the horse industry.

ADDRESS.—American Horse Council, Inc., Twelfth Floor, 1700 K Street, N.W., Washington, D.C. 20006.

AMERICAN HORSE SHOWS ASSOCIATION (A.H.S.A.).—The American Horse Shows Association was organized in 1917. At the invitation of Mr. Reginald C. Vanderbilt, fifty delegates representing twenty-six shows met in New York City for the purpose of electing officers, adopting a schedule of dates, and appointing a committee to formulate rules.

Today, the American Horse Shows Association formulates rules governing the running of shows, the types of competition, and the judging. Also, it lists approved judges and stewards and publishes an annual *Rule Book*.

ADDRESS.—The American Horse Shows Association, Inc., 527 Madison Avenue, New York, N.Y. 10022.

AMERICAN LIPIZZAN HORSE REGISTRY.—P. O. Box 415, Platteville, Wisconsin 53818.

AMERICAN MORGAN HORSE ASSOCIATION, INC.—Box 29, Hamilton, New York 13346. (See Appendix for complete breed registry association list.)

AMERICAN MUSTANG.—See BREED (S).

AMERICAN MUSTANG ASSOCIATION, INC.—P. O. Box 338, Yucaipa, California 92399. (See Appendix for complete breed registry association list.)

AMERICAN PAINT HORSE.—See BREED (S).

AMERICAN PAINT HORSE ASSOCIATION.—Box 13486, Fort Worth, Tex. 76118. (See Appendix for complete breed registry association list.)

AMERICAN PART-BLOODED HORSE REGISTRY.—4120 S. E. River Drive, Portland, Ore. 97222. (See Appendix for complete breed registry association list.)

AMERICAN PASO FINO HORSE ASSOCIATION, INC.—Room 3018, 525 William Penn Place, Pittsburgh, Penn. 15219. (See Appendix for complete breed registry association list.)

AMERICAN QUARTER HORSE ASSOCIATION.—Box 200, Amarillo, Tex. 79105. (See Appendix for complete breed registry association list.)

AMERICAN REMOUNT ASSOCIATION.—(The Half-Thoroughbred Registry), Box 1066, Perris, Calif. 92370. (See Appendix for complete breed registry association list.)

AMERICAN SADDLEBRED PLEASURE HORSE ASSN.—801 S. Court Street, Scott City, Kansas 67871.

AMERICAN SADDLE HORSE.—See BREED(S).

AMERICAN SADDLE HORSE BREEDERS' ASSOCIATION.—929 S. Fourth St., Louisville, Ky. 40203. (See Appendix for complete breed registry association list.)

AMERICAN SHETLAND PONY CLUB.—Box 435, Fowler, Ind. 47944. (See Appendix for complete breed registry association list.)

AMERICAN SHIRE HORSE ASSOCIATION.—6960 Northwest Drive, Ferndale, Washington 98248. (See Appendix for complete breed registry association list.)

AMERICAN SOCIETY FOR THE PREVENTION OF CRUELTY TO ANIMALS (A.S.P.C.A.).—The A.S.P.C.A. was first chartered by the New York State Legislature on April 10. 1866. Today, there are more than 800 humane organizations of varying names and areas of work scattered throughout the United States, but all with a common goal: Kindness to animals. Representatives of A.S.P.C.A. inspect stables and horse shows and investigate cases of misuse or cruelty to horses.

There is no national A.S.P.C.A. as such. Rather, the American Humane Association (AHA) is a loosely organized federation composed of most of the state and local A.S.P.C.A. societies, working toward common ideals, but the local A.S.P.C.A. groups are not bound or governed by the A.H.A.

(Also see the HUMANE SOCIETY OF THE UNITED STATES.)

AMERICAN SUFFOLK HORSE ASSOCIATION, INC.—672 Polk Blvd., Des Moines, Iowa 50312. (See Appendix for complete breed registry association list.)

AMERICAN TRAKEHNER ASSOCIATION, INC.—P. O. Box 268, Norman, Oklahoma 73069.

AMERICAN VETERINARY MEDICAL ASSOCIATION.—Most American veterinarians are members of the American Veterinary Medical Association.

ADDRESS: American Veterinary Medical Association, 600 S. Michigan Avenue, Chicago, Ill. 60605.

AMERICAN WALKING PONY.—See BREED(S).

AMERICAN WALKING PONY ASSOCIATION.—Route 5, Box 88, Upper River Road, Macon, Georgia 31201.

AMERICAN WHITE; AMERICAN CREME.—See BREEDS.

ANATOMY OF THE HORSE.—Anatomy refers to the structure of the animal body and the relation of its parts.

Broadly speaking, one type of animal is required for slow, heavy, draft purposes, and quite another for recreation and sport. This is really the distinction between draft and light horse breeds. However, further and very fundamental differences in structure fit the respective types and breeds for more specific purposes. Thus, the Thoroughbred running horse possesses certain hereditary structural characteristics which better fit him for speed and endurance than for usage as a five-gaited saddle horse. For the same reason, hunters are seldom obtained from among American Saddle Horses. In general, these structural differences between different types of horses are as marked as the fundamental differences between beef-type and dairy-type cattle. Yet, it must be pointed out that, regardless of the usage to which the animal is put, horsemen universally emphasize the importance of a good head and neck, short coupling, strong loin, and good feet and legs.

(Also see SKELETON OF THE HORSE; FOOT; PELVIC LIMBS; RIBS; SKULL; STERNUM; THORACIC LIMBS; and VERTEBRAL COLUMN.)

ANDALUSIAN.—See BREED (S).

ANEMIA, EQUINE INFECTIOUS.—See EQUINE INFECTIOUS ANEMIA

ANEMIA, NUTRITIONAL.—A condition of the blood characterized by lack of red cells or hemoglobin.

CAUSE.—Commonly an iron deficiency, but may be caused by a deficiency of copper, cobalt, and/or certain vitamins (riboflavin, pyridoxine, pantothenic acid, and/or folic acid).

SYMPTOMS.—Loss of appetite, poor performance, progressive emaciation, and death.

DISTRIBUTION AND LOSSES.—Worldwide. Losses consist of retarded growth and deaths.

TREATMENT.—Provide dietary sources of the nutrient or nutrients the deficiency of which is known to cause the condition.

CONTROL AND ERADICATION.—When nutritional anemia is encountered in horses, it can usually be brought under control by improving the ration.

PREVENTION.—Supply dietary sources of iron, copper, cobalt, and certain vitamins. Keep confinement of suckling foals to a minimum, and provide supplemental feeds at an early age.

REMARKS.—Anemia is a condition in which the blood is either deficient in quality or quantity (a deficient quality refers to a deficiency in hemoglobin and/or red cells). Levels of iron in most feeds are believed to be ample, since most feeds contain 40 to 400 mg/lb.

ANGLO-ARAB.—This refers to Thoroughbred X Arabian crosses, along with subsequent recrosses. Animals having any blood other than Thoroughbred and Arabian in their pedigrees, cannot be called Anglo-Arabs.

ANIMAL UNITS.—An animal unit is a common animal denominator, based on feed consumption. It is assumed that one mature horse or one mature cow represents an animal unit. The comparative (to a mature horse or a mature cow) feed consumption of other age groups or classes of animals determines the proportion of an animal unit which they represent. For example, it is generally estimated that the ration of one mature horse or one mature cow will feed five hogs raised to 200 pounds. For this reason, the animal unit/head on this class and age of animals is two-tenths. Table A-2 gives the animal units for different classes and ages of livestock and poultry.

TABLE A-2

ANIMAL UNITS

Type of Livestock	Animal Unit per Head
Horse	1
Cow	1
Bull	1.25
Young cattle, one year old	0.5
Calf	0.25
Foal	0.5
Brood sow or boar	0.4
Hogs raised to 200 pounds	0.2
Ewe or ram	0.14
Lamb	0.07
Chickens, layers or breeders (75)	1
Chickens, replacement pullets (325 to 6 Mo. of age)	1
Chickens, broilers (650 to 8 Wks. of age)	1
Turkeys, breeders (per 35)	1
Turkeys, raised (per 40)	1
Turkeys, raised (75 to 6 Mo. of age)	1

ANKLE *(leg mark).*—White extending from the coronet to and including the fetlock.

(Also see COLORS AND MARKINGS OF HORSES—Fig. C-10.)

ANKLE BOOTS.—A number of different types of protective boots, designed to protect the ankles or fetlocks from being bruised. Ankle boots are used on both the front and hind legs.

ANTHELMINTIC (VERMIFUGE).—A product which removes worm parasites.

ANTHRAX (SPLENIC FEVER, CHARBON).—An acute, infectious disease caused by *Bacillus anthracis,* a large, rod-shaped organism.

SYMPTOMS.—This disease has a history of sudden deaths. Sick animals are feverish, excitable, and later depressed. They carry the head low, lag behind the herd, and breathe rapidly. Swellings appear over the body and around the neck region. Milk secretion may turn bloody or stop entirely, and there may be a bloody discharge from all body openings.

TREATMENT.—Isolate all sick animals. At the first sign of any of the above symptoms, a veterinarian should be called at once. The veterinarian may give large quantities of antibiotic (3 to 12 million units of penicillin). In the early stages of the disease, 50 to 100 milliliters (ml.) of antianthrax serum may also be helpful. Provide good nursing care.

CONTROL.—Quarantine infected herds. All carcasses and contaminated material should be burned completely or buried deeply and covered with quicklime, preferably on the spot. Vaccinate all exposed but healthy animals, rotate pastures, and initiate a rigid sanitation program. Spray both sick and healthy animals with an insecticide to avoid fly transmission of the infection.

PREVENTION.—In infected areas, vaccination should be repeated each year, usually in the spring. Provide fly control by spraying animals during the insect season.

DISCUSSION.—The disease is general throughout the world in so-called anthrax districts. Cattle are more susceptible to anthrax than horses. A horseman should never open the carcass of a dead animal suspected of having died from anthrax. Instead, a veterinarian should be summoned at the first sign of an outbreak. Control measures should be carried out under the supervision of a veterinarian. The bacillus that causes anthrax can survive for years in a spore stage, resisting all destructive agents.

(Also see DISEASES AND PARASITES; and HEALTH PROGRAM.)

ANTIBIOTIC.—A chemical substance, produced by molds or bacteria, which has the ability to inhibit the growth of or to destroy other microorganisms.

Certain antibiotics, at stipulated levels, are approved by FDA for growth promotion and for the improvement of feed efficiency of young equines up to one year of age. Unless there is a disease level, however, there is no evidence to warrant the continuous feeding of antibiotics to mature horses. Such practice may even be harmful. Hence, where antibiotics are needed for therapeutic purposes, it is best to seek the advice of a veterinarian.

BROAD-SPECTRUM ANTIBIOTIC.—An antibiotic which attacks both gram-positive and gram-negative bacteria, and which may also show activity against other disease agents.

MEDIUM-SPECTRUM ANTIBIOTIC.—An antibiotic which attacks a limited number of gram-positive and gram-negative bacteria.

NARROW-SPECTRUM ANTIBIOTIC.—An antibiotic whose activity is restricted to either gram-negative or gram-positive bacteria. For example, penicillin is active primarily against gram-positive organisms, whereas streptomycin attacks only gram-negative organisms.

ANTIBODY.—A substance that opposes the action of another substance.

ANTIGEN.—A foreign substance which, when introduced into the body, stimulates formation of protective antibodies.

ANTISEPTIC.—A compound that inhibits the growth of microorganisms, and which is usually applied to the skin.

ANTITOXINS.—See TOXOIDS.

ANVIL.—See SHOEING—Table S-5.

APPALOOSA.—See BREED (S) .

APPALOOSA HORSE CLUB, INC.—Box 8403, Moscow, Ida. 83843. (See Appendix for complete breed registry association list.)

APPETITE.—The immediate desire to eat when feed is present. Loss of appetite in a horse is usually caused either by illness or bad condition of the teeth. When a horse does not clean up his regular ration, he should be examined to determine the cause.

APPETITE, DEPRAVED.—See DEPRAVED APPETITE.

APPETIZERS.--See TREATS.

APPLES AND OTHER FRUITS.—An apple a day is good for a horse, especially when used as a tidbit or reward. They are very palatable because of their sugar content. However, the feeding of apples can be overdone; many a case of colic, or even death, has resulted from old dobbin's stolen visit to the orchard.

Also, peaches, plums, and pears are occasionally used as treats for the horse. The seeds of stone fruits should always be removed prior to feeding.

(Also see TREATS.)

APPOINTMENTS.—The clothes, equipment, and tack required for riders and horses in certain horse show "appointment classes." The details of appointments are much too voluminous to cover in this book. Instead, the reader wishing information relative to correct appointments for a specific class is referred to the *Rule Book* of the American Horse Shows Association, which is revised annually.

(Also see CLOTHES FOR RIDERS; and SHOWING A HORSE.)

APPRENTICE ALLOWANCE.—Asterisks by the names of jockeys in an entry column ("bugs") indicate that the jockey is an apprentice and thereby entitled to a weight allowance to compensate for his inexperience. According to JOCKEY CLUB rules, a rider may claim (in overnight races—those not filled by advance nominations) a weight allowance of seven pounds until he has ridden 20 winners. After 20 winners, the apprentice is allowed five pounds off until the first anniversary of his first victory or until he has won 40 races—whichever period is longer.

APPUYER.—A French term meaning to move in two directions at the same time, usually forward and to the side. In the U.S., it is commonly referred to as "two-tracking" or "traveling on two paths."

APRON.—See SHOEING—Table S-5.

ARAB.—Used interchangeably with Arabian; hence, a breed of horses.

ARABIAN.—See BREED (S).

ARABIAN HORSE REGISTRY OF AMERICA. —One Executive Park, 7801 Belleview Avenue, Englewood, Colo. 80110. (See Appendix for complete breed registry association list.)

ARM.—The area back of and below the point of the shoulder and above the forearm. The arm should be well muscled.

(Also see PARTS OF A HORSE—Fig. P-4.)

ARMY HORSES.—See WARFARE, HORSES IN.

Fig. A-20. West Frieze of the Parthenon, "Youth and Bearded Man," built between 447 and 406 B.C. This work of art united two objects particularly venerated by the Greeks, youth and horse, in the wonderful unity which real horsemanship creates between a horse and his rider. As shown, riding was different in that day. The Athenian mounted bare-legged without saddle or stirrups. He used a bridle, but no bit.

ART, HORSES IN.—The contribution of horses has extended far beyond their utility value. Prior to recorded history, they were accorded a conspicuous place in the art of the day and made the chief object of myths.

In 2000 B.C., in models and on pottery vases, the Egyptians were showing stallions hitched to chariots and used in the military, religious, and ceremonial occasions of the Pharaohs.

Next to the human figure, the ancient Greeks used the horse as their most constant art subject. In the Parthenon Frieze of the Acropolis, built between 447 and 406 B.C., a procession of Athenians is depicted mounted and in chariots.

In 1969, China unearthed one of the greatest art-horse cultural treasures of all time—the bronze horses and chariots of Eastern Han Dynasty (A.D. 25–A.D. 220). The find was discovered in a large brick tomb of a high official who had an army. The author of this book was accorded the rare privilege of visiting China and of studying and photographing these artifacts now in a museum in Peking.

Outstanding among the finds is a big group of bronzes including 39 horses, 1 ox, 14 vehicles (7 chariots, 6 carts, and 1 ox cart), 17 armed warriors on horseback with lances in hand, and 20 male and female slaves. On the backs of some of the figurines are inscriptions such as "The Chang's male slave" or "The Chang's female slave." The horses of five of the horse-drawn chariots have inscriptions on their chests giving the official title of their owner and the number of his chariot attendants.

This is the most complete set of bronze chariots, horses, and figurines ever found in China. The chariots are finely modeled. One exquisite chariot is covered with a round canopy, has a covered front to protect the lower part of the occupant's body, and is pulled by fully harnessed horses with foreheads jauntily decorated. Another chariot, more cart-like, has a rectangular box-like frame with a door at the back for convenience in getting in and out.

All thirty-nine of the horses are handsome and almost prance with vitality and strength. One of them, the Galloping Horse, is unique. It is literally floating through the air, with three of its feet off the ground. But the right back foot is on a bird. The horse is neighing, while the poor startled bird looks backward, as if to see what has happened. The bird not only supports the full weight of the horse, but conveys the message that the horse gallops faster than a bird can fly.

By the Roman era, the horse had become synonymous with military might, and was often symbolized artistically by immense size.

In Renaissance art, fine horses and elegant horsemanship served as a status symbol.

Thus, down through the ages, art has portrayed the people-horse relationship—how they have contributed to each other with each advancing step in civilization. Even today, in an era of sophisticated mechanization, the horse still contributes richly to the works of many artists.

Fig. A-21. Part of a find of 230 artifacts, including 39 bronze horses, taken from a large brick tomb discovered in October, 1969; thought to have belonged to a high official, who had an army, in the late Eastern Han Dynasty (A.D. 25–A.D. 220). Now on display in the Exhibit of Cultural Relics, in Peking.

A. Bronze horse with one foot on a swallow, to indicate its swiftness. This horse is literally floating through the air, with head up and tail high, and three feet off the ground.

B. Bronze horse-drawn cart, with umbrella over the man.

Fig. A-22. TRIUMPH OF LOVE. Cupid holding a bow and arrow stands on a flaming urn placed on a triumphal car. Before him sits a naked youth, his hands tied behind his back. The car is drawn by two white stallions mounted by winged cupids. On the left, a man with upraised hand attempts to stop them. On either side are people forming a procession: Mercury playing on a pipe, a young warrior with a staff, and a group led by a young woman. In the background is a view of a walled town at the foot of a hill. (Courtesy, Kress Collection, National Gallery of Art, Washington, D.C.)

ARTHRITIS.—An ailment of the joints, similar to rheumatism. It occurs fairly frequently in old horses, developing very slowly. There is no known treatment.

ARTIFICIAL AIDS.—See AIDS.

ARTIFICIAL INSEMINATION (A.I.).—Artificial insemination is, by definition, the deposition of spermatozoa in the female genitalia by artificial rather than by natural means.

Legend has it that artificial insemination had its origin in 1322, at which time an Arab chieftain used artificial methods to impregnate a prized mare with semen stealthily collected by night from the sheath of a stallion belonging to an enemy tribe. There is no substantial evidence, however, to indicate that the Arabs practiced artificial insemination to any appreciable degree.

The Russian physiologist, Ivanoff, began a study of artificial insemination of farm animals, particularly horses, in 1899; and, in 1922, he was called upon by the Russian government to apply his findings in an effort to reestablish the livestock industry following its depletion during World War I. Crude as his methods were, his work with horses must be considered the foundation upon which the success of the more recent work is based.

The shifting of the large-scale use of artificial insemination to cattle and sheep, two decades after it was first introduced for horses, was not caused by the fading importance of the horse and the increased demand for cattle and sheep. Rather, it was found that progress was quicker and more easily achieved with these animals, because the physiological mechanism of reproduction in cattle and sheep is more favorable than in horses.

Today, there is renewed interest in artificial insemination of horses, as a result of a successful method of freezing stallion semen in 1964. Stallion semen is now being collected, processed, and frozen somewhat similarly to bull semen.

Mares are inseminated by (1) using a syringe and catheter arrangement with a speculum, (2) placing a gelatin capsule, holding 10 to 25 milliliters of extended semen, in the cervix by hand, or (3) introducing a rubber catheter by hand into the cervix and injecting the semen by means of a syringe attached to the opposite end of the tube.

ADVANTAGES OF ARTIFICIAL INSEMINATION:

● It increases the use of outstanding sires.
● It alleviates the danger and bother of keeping a sire.
● It makes it possible to overcome certain physical handicaps to mating.
● It lessens sire costs.
● It reduces the likelihood of costly delays through using infertile sires.
● It makes it feasible to prove more sires.
● It creates large families of animals.
● It increases pride of ownership, when a better stallion can be used.
● It may lessen and control certain diseases.
● It increases profits.

LIMITATIONS OF ARTIFICIAL INSEMINATION:

● It must conform to physiological principles.
● It requires skilled technicians.
● It necessitates considerable capital to initiate and operate a cooperative breeding program.
● It is not always possible to obtain the services of a given sire.
● It may accentuate the damage of a poor sire.
● It may restrict the sire market.
● It may increase the spread of disease.
● It may be subject to certain abuses.

SOME A.I. PROBLEMS NEED TO BE SOLVED.—Until recently, stallion semen could not be stored for any length of time. It is viable for only one to two days in the liquid state. However, stallion semen has now been frozen successfully, and its use will grow. This development may write a new chapter in horse breeding, especially in breeding grade mares.

But before wide-scale use can be made of artificial insemination of horses, solutions to additional problems must be found. These include the following needs:

● The ability to breed more mares per stallion.
● The ability to detect when mares are ready for breeding.
● The ability to bring mares in heat at will.

REGISTRATION OF FOALS PRODUCED THROUGH ARTIFICIAL INSEMINATION.—Although artificial insemination was first practiced with horses, many American registry associations now frown upon or forbid the practice. Moreover, there is little unanimity of opinion among them so far as their rules and regulations apply to the practice.

SUMMARY OF ARTIFICIAL INSEMINATION.—Today, artificial insemination is taking on a new look. Stallion semen is being frozen and stored, with the result that these "King Tuts" may be in production long after death.

Without doubt, from a technical standpoint, the wide-scale use of artificial insemination in horses only awaits the time when a few of the remaining problems are overcome. To be sure, there is and will continue to be resistance on the part of some horse registry associations and some breeders, with the result that research in the area of artificial insemination of horses will continue to lag. But progress cannot be stopped! Artificial insemination will expand in horses, especially with grade mares, just as it has in the dairy industry as soon as the remaining barriers are removed.

Who would not like to use a valuable stallion as widely as possible, and long after death? Imagine being able substantially to increase the number of offspring per year from a syndicated stallion whose stud fee is $5,000 or $20,000! Also, through the wide-scale use of artificial insemination in horses, many stallions could be eliminated (one stallion is now kept for each 7.3 foals produced), thereby effecting a considerable saving in keep.

The knowledge of the reproductive processes gained from artificial insemination can contribute materially to the increased efficiency of animal production. Perhaps, among its virtues, therefore, artificial insemination does offer some promise of assuring a higher conception rate in horses.

Fig. A-23. Ascarids (large roundworms) taken from a 6-month-old Shetland Pony. (Courtesy, Dr. V. S. Myers, Jr., V.M.D., Department of Veterinary Surgery and Radiology, University of Minnesota, St. Paul, Minn.)

ASCARIDS OR LARGE ROUNDWORMS.— (Parascaris equorum) The female varies from 6 to 22 inches long and the male from 5 to 13 inches. When full grown, both are about the diameter of a lead pencil.

SYMPTOMS.—The injury caused by ascarids ranges from light infections producing moderate effects to heavy infections that may cause death. Death usually is due to a ruptured intestine. Serious lung damage caused by migrating ascarid larvae may result in pneumonia. More common are retarded growth and development manifested by a potbelly, rough haircoat, and digestive disturbances. Ascarids affect foals and young animals, but rarely affect horses over five years old; older animals develop immunity from early infections.

TREATMENT.—Veterinarians most commonly use one of the following compounds for the treatment of this parasite: carbon disulfide, piperazine compounds, trichlorfon, dichlorvos, thiabendazole, or mebendazole.

PREVENTION AND CONTROL.—Keep the foaling barn and paddocks clean; store manure in a pit two to three weeks, allowing the spontaneously-generated heat to destroy the parasites; provide clean feed and water; and place young foals on clean pasture.

DISCUSSION.—Ascarids attack horses throughout the United States. The presence of ascarids results in loss of feed to feeding worms, lowered work efficiency, retarded growth in young animals, lowered breeding efficiency, and death in severe infections.

(Also see DISEASES AND PARASITES; HEALTH PROGRAM; and PARASITES OF HORSES.)

ASS.—The ass, along with horses and zebras, belongs to the genus Equus. They are native to Asia and Northern Africa. In comparison with the horse, the ass is smaller, has a shorter mane and shorter hair on the tail, has longer ears, and does not have the chestnuts on the inner surface of the hind limbs. Asses are hardy, gregarious, sure-footed, rugged, and patient, but somewhat stubborn.

ASSOCIATIONS, BREED REGISTRY.—See

Appendix for complete list of breed registry associations.

ASTERISK.—1. Used in front of a horse's name, an asterisk (*) indicates "imported."

2. Used in front of a jockey's name, it indicates that he is an apprentice rider.

ASTHMA.—Asthma is generally thought to be caused by spasm of the small circular muscles that surround the bronchial tubes. The continued existence of this affection of the muscles leads to their paralysis, and the forced breathing leads to emphysema, which always accompanies heaves.

(Also see HEAVES.)

ASTRINGENT.—A drug, such as tannic acid, alum, and zinc oxide or sulphate, that causes contraction of tissues.

AT THE END OF THE HALTER.—Sold with no guarantee except title.

AUCTIONS.—Auctions are trading places where animals are sold by public bidding to the buyer who offers the highest price. This method of selling is very old; it was first started in Great Britain many centuries ago.

AUTOMATION VS. MUSCLE POWER.—A century ago, muscles provided 94% of the world's energy needs; coal, oil, and waterpower provided the other 6%. Today, the situation is reversed in the developed nations. They now obtain 94% of their energy needs from coal, oil, natural gas, and waterpower, and only 6% from the muscle power of men and animals.

AUTOPSY.—Inspection, and partial dissection, of a dead body to determine the cause of death.

Fig. A-24. Horse auction in progress—the 1973 Keeneland Summer Sales. The highest priced Thoroughbred yearling ever sold at public auction is in the ring. This colt, by Bold Ruler–*Iskra, by LeHaar, was consigned by Claiborne Farm and purchased by a Japanese syndicate. In this auction 350 yearlings brought a total of $19,885,000, for an average price of $56,514. (Courtesy, The Thoroughbred Record, Lexington, Ky.)

AVOIRDUPOIS WEIGHTS AND MEASURES.—Avoirdupois is a French word, meaning "to weigh." The old English system of weights and measures is sometimes referred to as the "Avoirdupois System," to differentiate it from the "Metric System."

(Also see METRIC SYSTEM.)

AZOTURIA (HEMOGLOBINURIA, MONDAY MORNING DISEASE, BLACKWATER).—This is a condition which occurs in horses following idleness.

CAUSE.—Associated with faulty carbohydrate metabolism and with work following a period of idleness in the stall on full rations.

SYMPTOMS.—Profuse sweating, abdominal distress, wine-colored urine, stiff gait, reluctance to move, and lameness. Finally, animal assumes a sitting position, and eventually falls prostrate on the side.

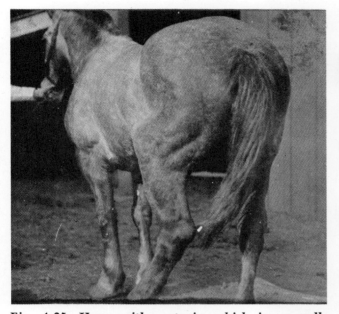

Fig. A-25. Horse with azoturia, which is generally attributed to faulty metabolism. Note paralysis of the thigh and signs of pain. Prevention lies in restricting the ration and providing daily exercise when the animal is not at work. (Courtesy, Pitman-Moore, Indianapolis, Ind.)

DISTRIBUTION AND LOSSES.—Worldwide, but the disease is seldom seen in horses at pasture and rarely in horses at constant work.

TREATMENT.—Absolute rest and quiet. While awaiting the veterinarian, apply heated cloths or blankets, or hot-water bottles to the swollen and hardened muscles.

CONTROL AND ERADICATION.—Azoturia is noncontagious. When trouble is encountered, decrease the ration and increase the exercise on idle days.

PREVENTION.—Restrict the ration and provide daily exercise when the animal is idle. Give a wet bran mash the evening before an idle day or turn the idle horse to pasture.
(Also see **FIRST AID FOR HORSES.**)

B

BABBLER.—A hunting term referring to a hound which throws its tongue too much, either when it is not sure of the scent or when it is very far behind the leading hound.

BABESIASES.—See EQUINE PIROPLASMOSIS.

BACK.—1. The command to move backward.
2. The part of the body which is behind the withers, in front of the loin, and above the ribs. In riding horses, it is the part of the top that holds the weight of the rider. In all horses, the function of the back is to transmit to the front end of the body the efforts of propulsion which are communicated to it from the back legs through the loin.
(Also see PARTS OF A HORSE—Fig. P-4.)

BACKING.—To cause a horse to move backward. A foal should be taught to back at an early age. At whatever age a horse is taught to back, he should not be required to take more than one or two steps at the first lesson. An excellent way in which to teach a mature horse to back is to ride him directly in front of a gate, then have an attendant open the gate toward him so as to force him backward, while the rider pulls lightly on the reins and gives the command "back." When the horse is backing, the direction is controlled by the use of leg pressure and the indirect rein.

BACKING RACE.—In a backing race, the horses are lined up with their tails toward the finish line, which for beginners is usually about fifty feet away. They must back all the way, and the winner must cross the line tail first, with both hind feet crossing before either front foot crosses. For advanced riders, the distance may be greater than fifty feet and the course for each contestant may be laid out with rails far enough apart so that a horse can back between them. A backing race can be an interesting event in a gymkhana (a contest designed to test skills).

BACTERIA.—Bacteria are one of the smallest and simplest known forms of plant life. They possess just one cell, vary in size and shape, multiply by transverse fission, and possess no chlorophyll. Bacteria are exceedingly numerous in nature, and the majority of them are beneficial; for example, those that create the fermentation processes used in the manufacture of vinegar and the ripening of cheese. The few that cause disease are referred to as pathogens.

GRAM-NEGATIVE BACTERIA.—Those bacterial species which are decolorized by acetone or alcohol.

GRAM-POSITIVE BACTERIA.—Those bacterial species which retain a crystal-violet color even when exposed to alcohol or acetone.

BACTERICIDE.—A product which kills bacteria.

BACTERINS.—Bacterins are standardized suspensions of bacteria (and their products) that have been killed by heat or chemical means and are unable to produce disease. When introduced into the body, they stimulate the production of protective antibodies which act against subsequent attacks of organisms of the kind contained in the bacterin. They produce an active immunity.

Theoretically, bacterins should be useful in the prevention of every infectious disease in which the causative agent is known. Unfortunately, they do not always give the desired results, especially in diseases of a chronic nature.

Often a product may be a mixed bacterin; that is, it may contain more than one organism. This usually includes secondary invaders when the true causative agent is unknown.

BACTERIOSTAT.—A product which retards bacterial growth.

BALANCED (*horse*).—A balanced horse is one with a pleasing relationship of the parts to each other. Such an animal is said to be nicely balanced, or to possess symmetry and balance.

BALANCED ACTION.—This refers to the shifting of the horse's center of gravity to fit his motions. A horse running free has perfect natural balance. At a fast gallop (such as in a running race), a horse stretches out his head and neck and puts his weight in front. This frees his hindquarters, from which comes the power of propulsion.

Normally, the center of gravity is just behind the withers. However, if the horse at liberty decides to turn suddenly, pivoting on one hind leg, he shifts his weight back and the center of gravity moves to the rear, thereby freeing his front end.

When riding, the experienced horseman shifts his balance to coincide with that of the horse, thereby helping him to readjust himself and compensate for the added weight of a rider on his back. Thus, the monkey seat—the ultra-short stirrups and crouched position of the jockey—places his center of balance over the horse's withers because the running horse's center of balance is far forward.

BALANCED RATION.—A ration which provides an animal with proper proportions and amounts of all the required nutrients for a period of 24 hours. Needs differ according to age and use.

[Also see RATION (S).]

BALANCED SEAT.—This refers to a shifting of the center of gravity of the rider to fit the action.

(Also see BALANCED ACTION and HORSEMANSHIP.)

BALD (*head mark*).—A bald face, or white face, including the eyes and nostrils, or a partially white face.

(Also see COLORS AND MARKINGS OF HORSES—Figs. C-9 and C-10.)

BALK.—A horse that stands still—refuses to go. This vice was not uncommon in the draft horse and horse-and-buggy era. The causes of balking are numerous; among them, too severe punishment when overloaded, and sore shoulders. The legendary cures (none recommended by the author) included (1) pounding on one shoe to divert the balky horse's attention; (2) pouring sand in one ear, which was supposed to shake the idea of balking out of his head; and (3) building a fire under him. The author recalls the incident of a neighboring farmer who tried the "fire cure," only to have the singed team move forward just enough to burn up the load of hay which they were pulling.

In the old days, when selling a balky horse at auction it was generally announced that he "sells at halter." Belatedly, some uninformed buyer learned that this meant that the horse was prone to balk, and that he wouldn't pull the hat off your head.

BALLASTING.—The rider's weight serves as ballast. Shifting of the weight of the rider to signal the horse and to help him perform as the rider desires is known as "ballasting the horse." The movable ballast (rider) on a horse works much like the ballast (such as kegs) on a small cargo boat, with the kegs shifted to balance the list of the ship caused by the wind. Correct ballasting aids in achieving a rhythmic relationship between horse and rider.

BALLET, HORSE.—See HORSE BALLET.

BANDAGES.—There are several different kinds of bandages, and each kind is used for a different purpose. Tail bandages are used on the tail for protection and to keep the hair in place. Stable bandages are used on the legs of sick or lame horses for warmth, to reduce the heat or inflammation, and as protection against sprains. Exercise bandages are used during fast work. Various materials are used for the different purposes, including flannel, cotton, stockinette.

BANDAGES, PRESSURE.—If properly applied, pressure bandages may be used with benefit on horses with weak or injured tendons or on horses that tend to "stock up." First apply a thick layer of dry cotton, then wrap spirally with even pressure.

BANGED.—Hair of the tail cut off in a straight line.

BANGTAIL.—1. Slang term for a racehorse passed down from the old days when running horses usually had banged tails, often banged close to the dock, or docked and banged.
2. Also, a wild horse.

BARB.—The Barb is the native horse of the Barbary States, which include Algeria, Tunisia, Morocco, Tripoli, and Fez. In comparison with the Arabian, it is larger, more docile, less spirited, and less refined.

BAREBACK BRONC RIDING (a rodeo event).—The bronc wears no halter or bridle. The cowboy must secure himself to the horse with one hand only on the handle of a rigging going around the animal approximately where the saddle girth would fit. In order to qualify, the contestant must stay on the bronc for 8 to 10 seconds, depending on the event.

BAREBACK RIDING.—Riding without a saddle. The ancient Greeks, who were accomplished horsemen, rode bareback. Likewise, the American Indian either rode bareback or seated on a blanket. The expert bareback rider is graceful and balanced on his mount; and is able to ride with arms folded and without reins, and without grip except when absolutely necessary.

The hazards of learning to ride bareback are: (1) using the reins to help hang on, with the result that it may be difficult ever to develop good hands; and (2) overuse of the leg grip.

BAREFOOT.—Unshod.

BARLEY.—The Arab, who was a good horseman, fed barley exclusively. Also, it is the leading horse grain in Western U.S.

Compared with corn, barley contains somewhat more protein (crude protein: barley 13%; corn 10%) and fiber (due to the hulls) and somewhat less carbohydrate and fat. Like oats, the feeding value of barley is quite variable, due to the wide spread in test weight per bushel. Most horsemen feel that it is preferable to feed barley along with more bulky feeds; for example, 25% oats or 15% wheat bran.

When fed to horses, barley should always be steam rolled or ground coarsely.

BARN RAT (BARN-SOUR, OR STABLE HOUND).—A horse that will not leave the sta-
ble willingly unless in the presence of another horse is called a "barn rat." The vice is man-made, not foaled; and is the result of bad handling. Among the severe measures taken to break a barn rat of the habit are extreme whipping and spurring, throwing the animal, and shooting a blank shotgun shell. Administering such remedies should be left to the professional horseman.

BARNS.—Needs for housing horses and storage of materials vary according to the intended use of the buildings.

TYPES AND SIZES OF HORSE BARNS.— Broadly speaking, horse barns are designed to

Fig. B-1. A small two-stall barn, typical of many found in suburban areas today. The stalls open directly into a corral to the back of the barn. (Courtesy, **The Western Horseman**)

serve either (1) small horse establishments that have one to a few animals, (2) large horse breeding establishments, or (3) riding, training, and boarding stables.

Various types and sizes of stalls and sheds are used in horse barns. However, in all types except the breeding shed, ceilings should be 9 feet high and doors should be 8 feet high and 4 feet wide. The breeding shed should have a ceiling 15 to 20 feet high and a door wide enough to permit entrance of vehicles.

The recommended plans for different kinds of horse barns are as follows:

SMALL HORSE ESTABLISHMENTS.—These horse barns are for housing pleasure horses or ponies, or for raising a few foals (Fig. B-1). Box stalls should be 12 feet square and tie stalls should be 5 feet wide and 10 or 12 feet long.

Build the stalls in a row and provide a combination tack and feed room for units with one or two stalls. Use separate tack and feed rooms for units with three or more stalls. Generally, not more than a one-month supply of feed is stored at a time. The use of all-pelleted feed lessens storage space requirements.

LARGE HORSE-BREEDING ESTABLISHMENTS.—Large establishments need specially designed buildings for different purposes. They are as follows:

● *Broodmare and foaling barn.*—This can be a rectangular building either (a) with a central aisle and a row of stalls along each side, or (b) of the "island" type with two rows of stalls back to back surrounded by an alley or runway. Most broodmare stalls are 12 feet square, although they may be up to 16 feet square. A stall 16 feet square is desirable for foaling. A broodmare barn needs an office for records; toilet facilities; hot water supply; veterinary supply room; tack room; and storage space for hay, bedding, and grain.

Until foaling time, broodmares are usually housed in an open shed (see Fig. B-2).

● *Stallion barn.*—This barn provides quarters for one or more stallions. It should have a small tack and equipment room, and it may or may not have feed storage. The stalls should be 14 feet square, or larger (see Fig. B-3).

Provide a paddock near the barn or, if possible, adjacent to it. The paddock can be any shape but each side should be at least 300 feet long.

Fig. B-2. Broodmare loafing sheds on the Hungarian Horse breeding establishment of Bitterroot Stock Farm, Hamilton, Montana, owned by Margit Sigray Bessenyey. (Photo by Ernst Peterson, Hamilton, Montana.)

Fig. B-3. Stallion barn at Westerly Stud, Santa Ynez, Calif. It is comprised of three stalls, each 16 feet by 16 feet in size; and it is insulated and equipped with an overhead sprinkler system and infrared lamps. It faces three large stallion paddocks, each in permanent pasture.

● *Barren mare barn.*—Use an open shed or rectangular building that has a combination rack and trough down the center or along the wall. Provide storage space for hay, grain, and bedding. Allow each animal 150 square feet of space.

● *Weanling and yearling quarters.*—Either an open shed (Fig. B-4) or a barn with stalls may be used. Both weanlings and yearlings may be kept in the same building, but different age and sex groups should be kept apart. When stalls are used, two weanlings or two yearlings may be kept together. Stalls should be 10 feet square.

Fig. B-4. An open shed for weanlings. This type of building furnishes a desirable place in which to winter young stock and idle horses unless the weather becomes too severe. (Courtesy, USDA)

● *Breeding shed.*—This should be a large, roofed enclosure that has a laboratory for the veterinarian. hot water facilities, and stalls for preparing mares for breeding and for holding foals. The shed should be 24 feet square.

● *Isolation quarters.*—These quarters are for sick animals and animals new to the farm. Use a small barn that has feed and water facilities and an adjacent paddock. Stalls should be 12 feet square (see Fig. B-5).

RIDING, TRAINING, AND BOARDING STABLES.—For this purpose, the quarters may consist of (1) stalls constructed back to back in the center of the barn with an indoor ring around the stalls, (2) stalls built around the sides of the barn with the ring in the center, or (3) stalls on either side of a hallway or alleyway and the ring outdoors. Box stalls should be 10 to 12 feet square and tie stalls should be 5 feet wide and 10 to 12 feet long.

REQUISITES OF HORSE BARNS.—Whether a new horse layout is built or an old one is altered, all buildings, fences, corrals, and trees should be placed according to a master plan, for once established, they usually are difficult and expensive to move. The arrangement should make the best possible use of land and should require little walking by attendants when caring for horses.

All horse barns should meet the following requisites:

● *Accessibility.*—They should be on an all-weather roadway or lane to facilitate the use of horses, delivery of feed and bedding, and removal of manure.

● *Dryness.*—They should be on high ground so water will drain away from them.

● *Expandable design.*—They should be designed so that they may be enlarged easily if and when the time comes. Often a building can be lengthened provided no other structures or utilities interfere.

● *Water and electricity.*—Water and electricity should be available and convenient to use.

● *Controlled environment.*—Barns should be built to modify winter and summer temperatures, maintain acceptable humidity and ventilation, minimize stress on the horse's nerves, and protect horses from rain, snow, sun, and wind.

● *Reasonable cost.*—Initial cost is important but durability and maintenance should be considered, as well as such intangible values as pride and satisfaction in the buildings and the advertising value.

● *Adequate space.*—Too little space may jeopardize the health and well-being of horses, but too much space means unnecessary expense.

● *Storage areas.*—Storage space for feed, bedding, and tack should be provided in the building where they are used.

● *Attractiveness.*—An attractive horse barn increases the sale value of the property. A horse barn will have aesthetic value if it has good proportions and is in harmony with the natural surroundings.

Fig. B-5. Isolation barn at Gem State Stables, Tipton, Calif. Each stable opens into a small turnout area. (Courtesy, Velma V. Morrison)

● *Minimum fire risk.*—The use of fire-resistant materials gives added protection to horses. Also, fire-retarding paints and sprays may be used.

● *Safety.*—Projections that might injure horses should be removed. Feeding and watering equipment should be arranged so attendants need not walk behind horses.

● *Labor saving construction.*—This requisite is a must in any commercial horse establishment. Also, where horses are kept for pleasure, unnecessary labor should be eliminated in feeding, cleaning, and handling.

● *Healthful living conditions.*—Healthy horses are better performers; therefore, barns should be easy to keep clean so they will provide healthful living conditions.

● *Rodent and bird control.*—Feed and tack storage areas should be rodent and bird proof.

● *Suitable corrals and paddocks.*—Horse barns should have well-drained, safe, fenced corrals or paddocks adjacent to them. If this is not possible, the corral or paddock should be nearby.

● *Flexibility.*—Possible changes in use make it desirable for horse barns to be as flexible as possible, even to the point that they can be cheaply and easily converted into cabins, garages, storage buildings, or buildings for other uses. Also, for suburbanites and renters, permanent, portable barns are advantageous.

MATERIALS.—When building materials for horse barns are bought, the factors to be considered are initial cost, durability and maintenance, attractiveness, and fire resistance.

Some of the materials available and being used are wood, including plywood; metal; masonry, including concrete, concrete block, cinder, pumice block, brick and stone; and plastics. Also, preengineered and prefabricated horse barns are being used more often, especially on smaller horse establishments.

PLANS.—Building plans for a small horse barn are shown in Fig. B-6. Complete working drawings may be obtained through county agricultural agents or from extension agricultural engineers at most State agricultural colleges. There is usually a small charge.

If working drawings of this plan are not available in your State, write to the U. S. Department of Agriculture, Agricultural Engineering Research Division, Plant Industry Station, Beltsville, Md. 20705. The U. S. Department of Agriculture does not distribute drawings but will direct you to a State that does distribute them.

(Also see BUILDINGS; ENVIRONMENTAL CONTROL; and EQUIPMENT.)

BARREL RACING *(a rodeo event).*—This is the only woman's event in rodeo. It is an excellent test of combined speed and agility of horseflesh, for it is a race against time coupled with ease of maneuverability. Each contestant must ride a cloverleaf pattern around three barrels. Women and girls are particularly suited to barrel racing; in colorful attire, they contribute much to spectator appreciation of the sport.

BARREN.—A mare that is not in foal.

BARS *(of foot).*—See FOOT—Parts of the foot.

BARS *(of mouth).*—Space (where the gums are devoid of teeth) between tushes and molar teeth on which the bit rests in the mouth.

BASE NARROW.—Standing with front or rear feet close together, yet standing with legs vertical.

BASE WIDE.—Standing with front or rear feet wide apart, yet with legs vertical.

BASKETBALL *(on horseback).*—The game originated with the Cossacks, who were expert horsemen. They played with a sheepskin, which they forward passed—throwing it ahead while a member of the team raced and caught it at a gallop.

In the days of the United States Cavalry, the game was played with a regulation basketball. With virtually no holds barred, it was pretty rough stuff.

BAY.—See COLORS AND MARKINGS OF HORSES.

BEACH, BELL.—Famous horsewoman whose book, *Riding and Driving for Women,* was published in 1912. True to the custom of the day, Miss Beach was a strong advocate of the side saddle. She predicted that riding astride would never become popular with women. On her death in 1933, the leading newspapers of America reported that on occasion Bell Beach went hunting with reins of No. 50 cotton thread.

BEANING.—A coined word referring to the cleaning out of the sheath of stallions and geldings. If not removed, the hard concretions will, in time, make it difficult for the horse to urinate.

BEAUTY.—This refers to the attractiveness and pleasing appearance with which the horse displays himself at all times.

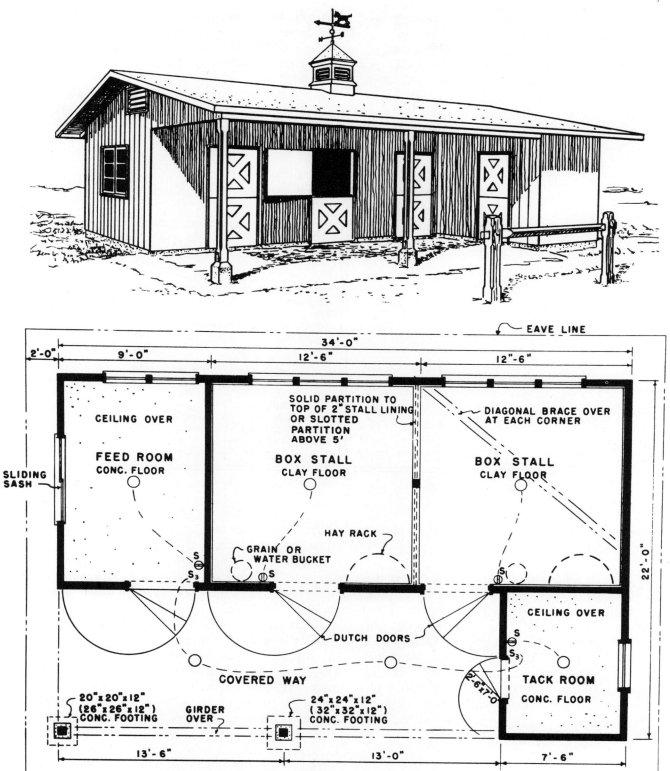

Fig. B-6. Horse barn exterior and interior floor plan. The barn has two box stalls, a feed room, and a tack room.

BEDDING.—The term "bedding" refers to materials used to make a bed for animals.

The horseman should select bedding material according to availability and price, absorptive capacity, and potential value as a fertilizer. Bedding should not be dusty, too coarse, or too easily kicked aside. Cereal grain straw or wood shavings generally make the best bedding material for horses.

A soft, comfortable bed will insure proper rest. The animal will be much easier to groom if his bedding is kept clean. A minimum daily allowance of clean bedding is 10 to 15 pounds per animal.

Table B-1 shows that bedding materials differ considerably in their relative capacities to absorb liquid.

TABLE B-1

WATER ABSORPTION OF BEDDING MATERIALS

Material	Lbs. of Water Absorbed per Cwt. of Air-Dry Bedding	Material	Lbs. of Water Absorbed per Cwt. of Air-Dry Bedding
Barley straw	210	Rye straw	210
Cocoa shells	270	Sand	25
Corn stover (shredded)	250	Sawdust (top quality pine)	250
Corncobs (crushed or ground)	210	(run-of-the-mill hardwood)	150
Cottonseed hulls	250	Sugar cane bagasse	220
Flax straw	260	Tree bark (dry, fine)	250
Hay (mature, chopped)	300	(from tanneries)	400
Leaves (broadleaf)	200	Vermiculite[1]	350
(pine needles)	100	Wheat straw (long)	220
Oat hulls	200	(chopped)	295
Oat straw (long)	280	Wood chips (top quality pine)	300
(chopped)	375	(run-of-the-mill hardwood)	150
Peanut hulls	250	Wood shavings (top quality pine)	200
Peat moss	1,000	(run-of-the-mill hardwood)	150

[1] This is a mica-like mineral mined chiefly in South Carolina and Montana.

Other facts of importance, relative to certain bedding materials and bedding uses, are:

1. *Wood products (sawdust, shavings, tree bark, chips, etc.).*—The suspicion that wood products will hurt the land is rather widespread but unfounded. It is true that shavings and sawdust decompose slowly, but this process can be expedited by the addition of nitrogen fertilizers. Also, when plowed under, they increase soil acidity, but the change is both small and temporary.

Softwood (on a weight basis) is about twice as absorptive as hardwood, and green wood has only fifty percent the absorptive capacity of dried wood.

2. *Cut straw.*—Cut straw will absorb more liquid than long straw; cut oats or wheat straw will take up about twenty-five percent more water than long straw from comparable material. But there are disadvantages to chopping; chopped straws may be dusty.

From the standpoint of the value of plant food nutrients per ton of air dry material, peat moss is the most valuable bedding and wood products the least valuable.

The minimum desirable amount of bedding to use is the amount necessary to absorb completely the liquids in manure. For twenty-four-hour confinement, the minimum daily bedding requirements of horses, based on uncut wheat or oats straw, is 10 to 15 pounds. With other bedding materials, these quantities will vary according to their respective absorptive capacities (see Table B-1). Also, more than minimum quantities of bedding may be desirable where cleanliness and comfort of the horse are important.

In most areas, bedding materials are becoming scarcer and higher in price, primarily because (1) geneticists are breeding plants with shorter straws and stalks, (2) there are more competitive and numerous uses for some of the materials, and (3) the current trend toward more confinement rearing of livestock requires more bedding.

Horsemen may reduce bedding needs and costs as follows:

● *Chop bedding.*—Chopped straw, waste hay, fodder, or cobs will go further and do a better job of keeping horses dry than long materials.

● *Ventilate quarters properly.*—Proper ventilation lowers the humidity and keeps the bedding dry.

● *Provide exercise area.*—Where possible and practical, provide for exercise in well-drained, dry pastures or corrals, without confining horses to stalls more than necessary.

(Also see BUILDINGS—Space requirements for feed and bedding, Table B-11.)

BEEFY HOCKS.—Thick, meaty hocks, lacking in quality.

BEHAVIOR OF HORSES.—Each animal species has characteristic ways of performing certain functions and rarely departs therefrom. The horse is no exception. Some noteworthy horse behavior patterns follow:

● *Communication.*—The signals consist of patterns of sound, produced by motions of the respiratory and upper alimentary tract. A *snort* is a danger signal to the whole herd; a *neigh* is a distress call; a *nicker* is a sign of relief; and a *whinny* is a call of pleasure and expectancy.

● *Courtship.*—The sight of a mare elicits characteristic courtship by the stallion, including smelling the external genitalia and groin of the mare, extending his neck with an upcurled upper lip, and pinching the mare with his teeth by grasping the folds of her skin near the croup.

Heat (estrus) in mares is marked by the mare allowing the stallion to smell and bite her, frequent urination in small quantities, mucous discharge from the vulva, spreading the hind legs, and lifting the tail sideways.

● *Dominance.*—Any group of horses develops a hierarchical structure, or "peck order," in which each animal assumes a position of relative dominance. This order is maintained by sounds and gestures; challenging is kept to a minimum.

Fig. B-7. Dominance being developed by "horse judo." (Photo by Dave Smith, Mesa, Ariz.)

● *Fighting.*—Under wild conditions, natural enemies are avoided by flight or fight, according to the situation. The teeth and hind feet are used for fighting.

● *Hearing.*—Horses hear over a great range in frequencies, and they can pick up sounds too slight for man to hear.

● *Leadership.*—In wild bands, there is always a stallion leader.

● *Look-out.*—During the day, it is rare to see all members of a herd lying down together. One horse is almost always on the look-out.

● *Pawing.*—The modern domestic horse paws the ground when excited in much the same way as did Przewalsky's Horse.

● *Vision.*—In its natural habitat, the adult horse keeps a sharp look-out for its natural enemies, even while grazing. Also, it is noteworthy that the eye of the horse is adapted in several ways for darkness, as in nocturnal animals. Also, its eyes are set on the sides of the head so that each eye receives a very wide and largely different scene. The lens of the horse's eye is non-elas-tic, but the retina is arranged on a slope, the bottom part being nearer the lens than the top part. Thus, in order to focus on objects at different distances, the horse has to raise or lower his head so that the image is brought on to that part of the retina at the correct distance to achieve a sharp image. This arrangement is advantageous to wild horses because, while the head is down grazing, both near objects on the ground and distant ones on the horizon are in focus simultaneously.

Color vision in horses has not been established. (Also see INTELLIGENCE OF HORSES.)

BELGIAN.—See BREED (S).

BELGIAN DRAFT HORSE CORPORATION OF AMERICA.—P. O. Box 335, Wabash, Indiana 46992. (See Appendix for complete breed registry association list.)

BELLEROPHON.—A Prince of Corinth in Greek mythology who tamed the winged horse, Pegasus. According to legend, Bellerophon used a golden bridle to coax the curious animal from his favorite meadow, then made him captive and rode him off to destroy the dragon-like monster, the Chimera. Success encouraged him to try to fly to Olympia to live with the gods. However, Zeus, angered by this mortal's ambition, sent a gadfly to sting Pegasus, causing him to unseat his venerable and conceited master, who fell to earth crippled and blinded.

BENDING RACE.—A bending race calls for a row of jump standards set ten to twelve feet apart. Then each contestant leaves the starting line, weaves in and out among the stakes, and returns to the starting line—racing against time. Obviously, speed plus changing leads handily are requisites for a winner.

BET.—Among horsemen this generally refers to wagering on a horse race.

BIG HITCH.—A "heavy hitch" of draft horses in fours, sixes, eights, or even more.

BIGHT OF THE REINS.—The part of the reins passing between thumb and fingers and out the top of the hand.

BIKE.—See VEHICLES—Horse drawn.

BILLET.—A strap that enters a buckle (as the ends of harness reins, the cheek pieces that buckle on the bit, or on a saddle).
(Also see SADDLES, ENGLISH—Fig. S-2.).

BIOLOGICS.—Biologics may be defined as medicinal preparations made from microorganisms (bacteria, protozoa, or viruses) and their products. They include various vaccines, bacterins, serums, and similar preparations. These agents are one of the most valuable contributions to animal health, and they are constantly being improved. They are used essentially for rendering animals immune to various infections.

It is noteworthy, however, that not all attempts to confer immunity by biologics are successful. In some cases, it seems impossible to create an immunity against infection. The common cold in humans is a case in point. In other cases, the animal may die from the disease or its complications, in spite of an inoculation, because of a biologic of poor quality, infection before the treatment is begun, or improper administration of the biologic.

BIRTH DATE.—Regardless of when a foal is born, its birth date is always considered as January 1. Thus, a foal born May 1, 1970, will be fifteen years old on January 1, 1985. This is done from the standpoint of racing and showing. As a result, horsemen who race or show make every effort to have foals arrive as near January 1 as possible, thereby getting the advantage of more growth than animals born later in the year. This is especially important in the younger age groups; for example, when racing or showing a two-year-old.

A shift of the date of birth (the January 1 birthday, for purposes of racing and showing) to somewhere between March 1 and May 1 would improve conception rate and foaling percentage, simply because mares would be bred under more natural and ideal spring conditions. Thus, it would have considerable virtue from the standpoint of the horse producer. On the other side of the ledger, however, it would create problems in racing and in registrations, both here and abroad. Also, such a deep-rooted tradition would be difficult to change; in fact, much consideration has been given to this matter from time to time. In the final analysis, therefore, stepping-up breeding research is the primary avenue through which the deplorably low percentage foal crop may be improved.

BISHOPED TEETH.—See TEETH, TAMPERED (OR "BISHOPED").

BITER.—See NIPPING.

BITING.—See VICES—Biting.

BITS.—The bit is the most important part of the bridle. In fact, the chief use of the other parts of the bridle is to hold the bit in place in the horse's mouth. The bit provides communication between the rider or driver and the horse.

The snaffle bit, which is still the most widely used of all varieties, was the first type of bit to which historians make reference, having been developed by the early Greek horsemen.

The author of this book, who was accorded the rare privilege of studying and photographing the cultural relics of China, was fascinated with a horse bit that he saw on display in a Peking museum. This bit was used in 113 B.C. in the Western Han Dynasty. It's a gilded snaffle bit with cheek bars (see Fig. B-8).

Figs. B-9, B-10, and B-11 show the most common types of bits. There are many variations on each of these types.

The proper fit and adjustment of the bit is very important. It should rest easily in the mouth and be wide enough so that it will not pinch the cheeks or cause wrinkles in the corners of the mouth. As a rule, a curb-type bit rests lower in the mouth than a snaffle. All bits should

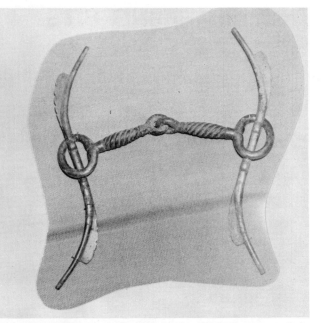

Fig. B-8. Gilded snaffle bit with cheek bars, used in 113 B.C., in the Western Han Dynasty. (Photo by Audrey Ensminger)

have large rings or other devices to prevent them from passing through the mouth when either rein is drawn in turning the horse.

The following points about bits should be remembered:

● Usually, the snaffle bit is used when a horse is started in training.

● The hunting, or egg butt, snaffle is used on hunters and jumpers.

● The curb bit is a more severe bit than the snaffle. It may be used either alone or with the snaffle.

● The Pelham bit is one bit that is used with two reins and a curb chain. It is a combination of a snaffle and a curb bit and is used in park or pleasure riding and hunting.

● The Weymouth bit combined with a snaffle bit is known as a bit and bridoon.

● Western bits are similar to the curb bit but they have longer shanks and are larger. Usually, they are used with a solid leather curb strap but sometimes they have a small amount of chain in the middle of the leather curb strap.

ENGLISH RIDING BITS

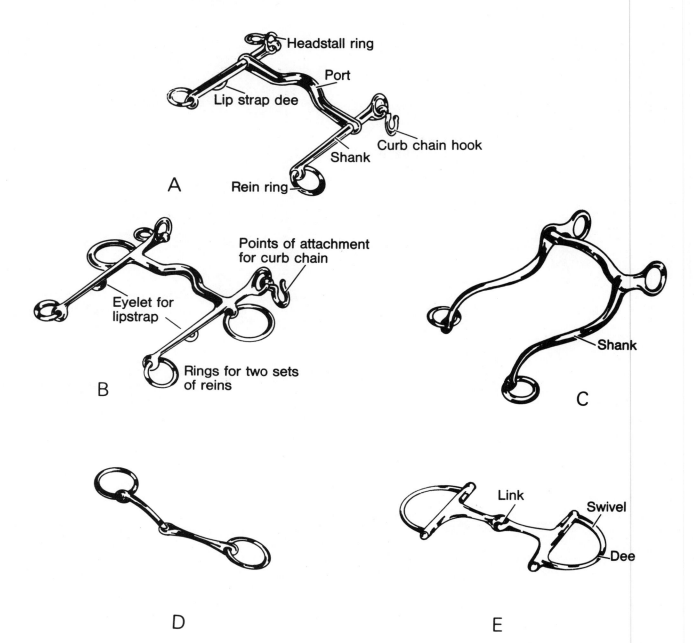

Fig. B-9. Five common types of English riding bits. *(a) Weymouth curb bit: a bit used along with a snaffle bit in a Weymouth bridle for three- and five-gaited horses; (b) Pelham curb bit: a bit used in a Pelham bridle for hunters, polo ponies, and pleasure horses; (c) Walking horse bit: a bit often used on Walking Horses; (d) Snaffle bit: the most widely used of all bits; (e) Dee race bit: a bit often used on Thoroughbred racehorses.*

WESTERN RIDING BITS

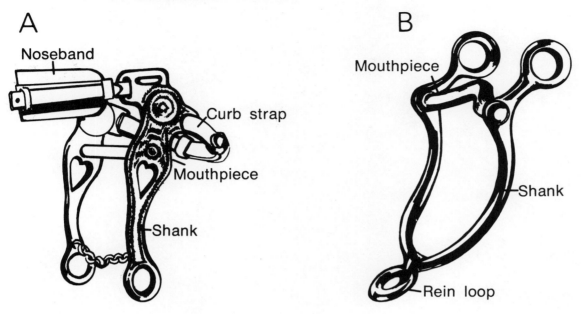

A

Noseband

Curb strap

Mouthpiece

Shank

B

Mouthpiece

Shank

Rein loop

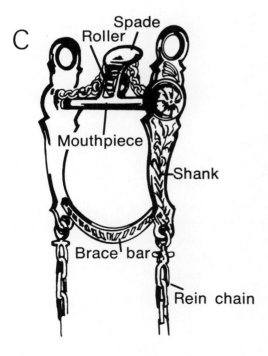

C

Spade

Roller

Mouthpiece

Shank

Brace bar

Rein chain

Fig. B-10. Three common types of Western riding bits. (a) Hackamore bit: a bit used on most cow ponies; (b) Roper curved cheek bit: a bit used on many roping horses; (c) Spade mouth bit: a bit used on many stock horses.

DRIVING BITS

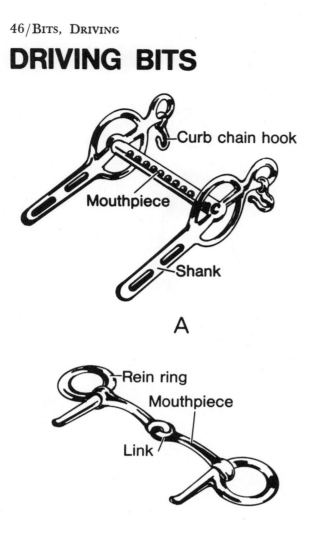

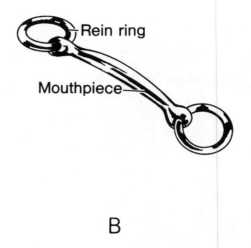

Fig. B-11. Three common types of driving bits. (a) Liverpool bit: a curb bit used on heavy harness horses; (b) Bar Bit: a bit used on trotting harness horses that carry check reins and are driven with a strong hand; (c) Half-cheek snaffle bit: a bit used on harness racehorses, roadsters, and fine harness horses.

BITTING.—The term "bitting" refers to the process of teaching the horse to accept the bit and obey its commands. There are as many ways of accomplishing this as there are horsemen. However, in general, the English method consists of using a snaffle bit and some kind of bitting rig, and working a horse on a longe line with this bitting rig on it; then working the horse carefully after he is first mounted, with a snaffle bit or a full bridle, using only the snaffle reins. Western horsemen use both the bosal hackamore and the hackamore bit bridle as training devices.

BITTING RIG.—This device is used in teaching the horse the meaning of the bit and how to hold his head correctly. When properly used, the bitting rig is excellent; when improperly used, the mouth may be spoiled or the neck made rigid.

There are about as many variations of the bitting rig as there are horsemen. But, in its simplest form it consists of a surcingle or roller; fitted with rings at the top, sides, and bottom for reins, overcheck, and tie-down; attached to a crupper by a backstrap.

Some trainers use the bitting rig when the horse is being worked on a longe line. Others, including those who work on the longe line, put the horse in a bitting rig, then turn him loose in a paddock, corral, or stall. Those who follow the latter procedure can work several horses at one time.

BLACK.—See COLORS AND MARKINGS OF HORSES.

BLACK BEAUTY.—The name of a book (first published in 1877) by Anna Sewell, in which the main character was a horse, Black Beauty. *Black Beauty* is a favorite children's story.

BLACK HAWK FAMILY.—A noted early-day family of Morgan horses, tracing to Vermont Black Hawk—a grandson of Justin Morgan. They were longer legged, faster, and more handsome than most of the Morgans of the day.

BLACK POINTS.—The term "black points" refers to the black mane, tail, and generally lower legs of all bay horses and some duns and buckskins.

BLAZE *(head mark)*.—A broad, white marking covering almost all the forehead but not including the eyes or nostrils.

(Also see COLORS AND MARKINGS OF HORSES—Fig. C-9.)

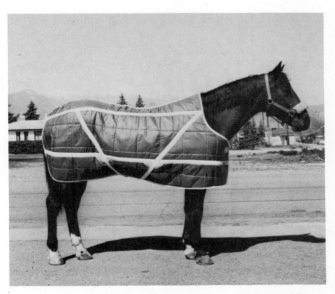

Fig. B-12. A blanket. (Courtesy, **The Western Horseman.)**

BLANKETS.—Blankets come in many designs, materials, and colors. Many show horses of all breeds and types are kept blanketed the year-round, for blanketing helps keep the hair coat slick and shiny.

The size of horse blankets is measured in inches from the center of the breast, where the blanket fastens, to the rear end of the blanket.

(Also see SADDLE BLANKET.)

BLEEDER.—1. A racehorse that bleeds at the nose, from unknown cause, is called a bleeder.

(Also see FIRST AID FOR HORSES.)

2. A horse that is kept at a laboratory and used for the production of serum is known as a "bleeder."

BLEMISHES AND UNSOUNDNESSES.—An integral part of selecting a horse lies in the ability to recognize common blemishes and unsoundnesses and the ability to rate the importance of each.

A thorough knowledge of normal, sound structure makes it easy to recognize imperfections.

Any deviation from normal in the structure or function of a horse constitutes an unsoundness. From a practical standpoint, however, a differentiation is made between abnormalities that do and those that do not affect serviceability.

Blemishes include abnormalities that do not affect serviceability, such as wire cuts, rope burns, nail scratches, or capped hocks.

Unsoundnesses include more serious abnormalities that affect serviceability.

Fig. U-1 shows the location of common blemishes and unsoundnesses.

A buyer should consider the use to which he intends to put the animal before he buys a blemished or unsound horse.

(Also see UNSOUNDNESSES.)

BLINDERS.—See BLINKER.

BLINDNESS.—Partial or complete loss of vision is known as blindness. Either or both eyes may be affected. A blind horse usually has very erect ears and a hesitant gait. Frequently, blindness also can be detected by the discoloration of the eye. Further and more certain verification can be obtained by moving the hand gently in close proximity to the eye, and watching the horse's reaction.

(Also see UNSOUNDNESSES.)

BLIND STAGGERS (MEGRIMS).—This is an old-fashioned term for a common horse ailment in the horse-and-buggy era. The condition was most prevalent in harness horses, particularly those used for draft purposes. Cases of blind staggers are still encountered.

The modern view is that it is due to heart disease, and that the brain symptoms are secondary. Attacks invariably occur while animals are at work. Too tight a collar or throatlatch appear to trigger the ailment.

First-aid consists in idling the animal, and applying cold compresses to the head. The veterinarian, who should be called at once, will usually give a heart tonic.

BLINKER (BLINDERS OR WINKERS).—An attachment to the bridle or hood, designed to re-

Fig. B-13. Racing blinkers—a hood with leather cups.

strict the vision of the horse from the sides and rear and to focus the vision forward. Driving blinkers (or winkers) are made of leather, often with a crest or embellishment on the outside. Racing blinkers are in the form of a hood with leather cups that act as shields.

BLISTER.—An irritant applied as a treatment for unsoundnesses and blemishes.

BLOOD.—Blood accounts for approximately $\frac{1}{80}$th of a total weight of a horse. It is carried by arteries from the heart to all parts of the body, thence it returns through veins, with the heart acting as a pump.

BLOOD HEAT.—This refers to the normal temperature of a horse, which is 100.5° F.

BLOOD-HORSE.—A pedigreed horse. To most horsemen, the term is synonymous with the Thoroughbred breed.

BLOOD SPAVIN.—Blood spavin is a varicose vein enlargement which appears on the inside of the hock but immediately above the location of bog spavin. No successful treatment for blood spavin is known.

(Also see UNSOUNDNESSES.)

BLOOD STOCK.—Horses of Thoroughbred breeding; animals whose highest and best use is for racing.

BLOOD TESTING HORSES (HEMATOLOGY).—All body cells require oxygen. With strenuous exercise, as in racing, the oxygen requirement increases.

Oxygen is transported by hemoglobin, the protein-iron coloring matter in blood.

It follows that any reduction in the hemoglobin content, or in total blood volume, will lower the oxygen-carrying capacity of the blood. When this condition is marked, anoxia, or anemia, develops, fatigue sets in, and there is lowered stamina and endurance.

Anoxia may be caused by many conditions. Usually it is due either to (1) nutritional deficiency, or (2) blood worms—both of which may be aggravated by the stress and strain of racing, endurance trials, and showing.

Most trainers accept one or more of the following as indicative of the lack of fitness: loss of appetite, loss of weight, excessive blowing following work, a dry, harsh cough, rough coat, dull eye, watery instead of beady sweating, and "blowing up" over the loins. In an effort to be more exacting, some veterinarians who attend racing stables, endurance trials, and show strings now use blood examinations as a means of evaluating physical fitness.

It appears that, although there are breed differences, most horses which show consistent, good racing form have hemoglobin levels between 14 and 16 grams per milliliter, red cell counts between 9 and 11 million per cubic millimeter, and packed cell volumes between 40 and 45 percent. Also, other blood determinations are sometimes made. The blood testing approach is interesting and appealing. However, much more information on the subject is needed. Proof of this assertion becomes evident when it is realized that all horses whose blood pictures fall within the above range are not necessarily good performers; neither are horses with blood pictures outside this range incapable of winning. Some horses do respond to treatment, but, generally, the results have been inconsistent and disappointing. One needs to know if horses which have lower blood values, but which do not respond to treatment, carry all of the red cells and hemoglobin that they are capable of developing—whether they have less potential for racing. Even more perplexing is the fact that this blood count can be too high, producing polycythemia. A horse with polycythemia frequently loses appetite, fails to thrive in the stable, performs unsatisfactorily, and may show cyanosis (dark bluish or purple coloration of the skin and mucous membrane due to lack of oxygen). It is also noteworthy that absolute polycythemia occurs at high altitudes or when there is heart disease or fibrosis of the lungs.

Racehorses with anemia are sometimes treated either by (1) injecting iron and/or vitamin B_{12}, or (2) giving orally (in the feed or water) one of several iron preparations. Sometimes vitamin C (ascorbic acid), and folic acid and the other B-complex vitamins are added.

At this time, there is insufficient knowledge of equine anemia, or of ways of stimulating hematopoiesis, to make a winner. The true role of therapy, if any, remains unknown.

The most that can be said at this time is that prevailing treatments usually satisfy the owner or trainer who insists that his charges "get the works." Most scientists are agreed, however, that "quickie" miracle shots or concoctions will never replace sound nutrition and parasite control on a continuous basis.

BLOOD TYPING.—Blood typing involves a study of the components of the blood, which are inherited according to strict genetic rules that have been established in the research laboratory. By determining the genetic "markers" in each sample and then applying the rules of inheritance, parentage can be determined. To qualify as the offspring of a given mare and stallion, an animal must not possess any genetic markers not present in his alleged parents. If he does, it constitutes grounds for illegitimacy.

Blood typing is used for the following purposes:

● To verify parentage. The test is used in instances where the offspring may bear some unusual color or markings or carry some undesirable recessive characteristic. It may also be used to verify a registration certificate.

● To determine paternity when a mare has been served by two or more stallions during one breeding season.

● To provide a permanent blood type record for identification purposes.

Two samples of blood are required for each animal to be studied; and the samples must be taken in tubes and in keeping with detailed instructions provided by the laboratory. In parentage cases, this calls for blood samples from the foal and both parents; in paternity cases, samples must be taken from the foal, the mare, and all the stallions.

Through blood typing, parentage can be verified with ninety percent accuracy. Although this means that ten percent of the cases can't be settled, it's not possible to do any better than that in human blood typing.

Two laboratories in the U.S. are capable of determining horse parentage.

ADDRESSES.—1. Serology Laboratory, School of Veterinary Medicine, University of California, Davis, California.

2. Department of Animal Science, Texas A & M University, College Station, Texas.

BLOODWORMS.—See STRONGYLES.

BLOOM.—Hair that is clean and of a healthy texture.

BLOW.—To blow wind after strenuous exercise.

BLOWFLY.—See FLIES.

BLOW OUT.—To walk or exercise a horse either to loosen its muscles for further exercise, or to prevent chilling and stiffening after a hard workout.

BLUE EYE.—An unsound eye with a blue appearance; the sight may or may not be entirely gone.

BLUEGRASS COUNTRY.—This refers to the great horse breeding area in Kentucky, the center of which is around Lexington. This area is characterized by luxuriant bluegrass pastures and fertile soils, conditions ideal for horse breeding.

BOARDING AGREEMENT.—Boarding Agreements should always be in writing, rather than verbal, "gentlemen's agreements."

From a legal standpoint, a Boarding Agreement is binding to the parties whose signatures are affixed thereto. Thus, it is important that the agreement be carefully filled out, read, and fully understood before signing. (See sample Boarding Agreement, pages 51–52.)

BOG SPAVIN.—Bog spavin is a filling of the natural depression on the inside and front of the hock. A bog spavin is much larger than a blood spavin. Treatments usually include some combination of cold packs, antiphlogistic applications (clay, mud, cooling lotions, etc.), stimulating liniments, mild to severe blisters, the aspiration or withdrawal of the fluid from the joint, and injections of hydrocortisone. Some equine veterinarians prefer patient daily massage with an absorbent type liniment for two to three weeks. Treatment consists of applying a special bog spavin truss or of applying tincture of iodine. Blistering or firing is seldom successful.

(Also see UNSOUNDNESSES.)

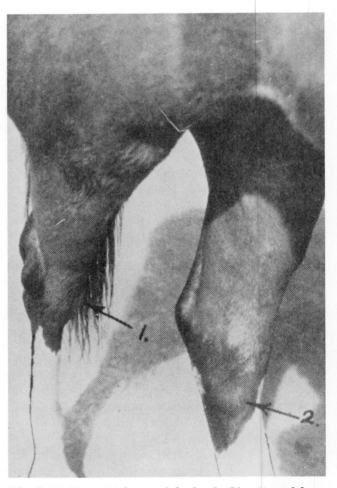

Fig. B-14. Bog spavin on right hock (No. 1) and bone spavin on left hock (No. 2). Bog spavin is a filling of the natural depression on the inside and front of the hock. Bone spavin is a bony enlargement that appears on the inside and the front of the hock at the point where the base of the hock tapers into the cannon part of the leg. (Courtesy, USDA)

```
*********************************************************************************

                        BOARDING AGREEMENT

(To be executed in duplicate; one copy to be retained by each party.)

This agreement made and entered into by and between _____,
                                              (owner of horse)
_____, hereinafter designated "Horse Owner," and
      (address)
_____, _____,
   (owner of stable)              (address)
hereinafter designated, "Stable Owner."  This agreement covers the horse

described as follows:

_____        _____    _____    _____
       (Name)                     (Sex)      (Age)       (Color)


Stable Owner agrees that ---

    1.  He will keep the horse in a stall and/or paddock described as follows:


    2.  He will feed, water, and care for the horse in a good and husbandlike

manner; feeding horse as follows:

Kind of Feed _____ _ _ _ _ Amount of Feed _ _ _ _ _ _
                                   Morning        Noon        Night
                                    (lbs)         (lbs)        (lbs)


    3.  He will perform the following additional services:

        a.  Grooming (specify): _____

        b.  Exercising (specify): _____

        c.  Parasite treatments (specify): _____

            _____

            _____

        d.  Others (list): _____

            _____

            _____
```

Horse Owner agrees that ---

　　1.　He will make all arrangements for the periodic shoeing of the horse, and assume the cost thereof.　Any exception to this shoeing arrangement shall be given in the space that follows:

　　2.　He will pay Stable Owner (a) for the foregoing facilities, feed, and services the sum of $____per month, payable on the _____day of each month in advance; and (b) for drugs and medications, at cost, the first of each month following invoicing.

　　3.　Stable Owner shall be entitled to a lien against the boarded horse for the value of services rendered, and shall be entitled to enforce said lien according to the appropriate laws of the state, provided (a) Stable Owner performs the services herein specified, and (b) Horse Owner fails to make a scheduled payment.

Horse Owner and Stable Owner mutually agree that ---

　　1.　In the event the horse shall require the services of a Veterinarian, Stable Owner will immediately contact Horse Owner.　In the event Horse Owner cannot be reached, Stable Owner is hereby authorized, as agent for Horse Owner, (a) to call Dr. _____,DVM; and, should he be unavailable, (b) to call any other licensed veterinarian of his choice.　All fees charged by said veterinarian shall be the sole and exclusive responsibility of the Horse Owner, with no liability whatsoever on the part of Stable Owner for such fees.

　　2.　This document constitutes the entire agreement between the parties and there are no other agreements between them except as noted below.

_____　　_____
　　　　(Signature of Horse Owner)　　　　　　　　　　(date)
_____　　_____
　　　　(Signature of Stable Owner)　　　　　　　　　　(date)

BOLTING.—1. A horse breaking out of control or trying to run away is said to be bolting.

2. A horse that eats too rapidly.

(Also see VICES—Bolting.)

BONE.—The measurement of the circumference around the cannon bone about halfway between the knee and fetlock joints. Eight inches of bone is average for the Thoroughbred. "Flat bone" indicates that the cannon and the back tendon are parallel, with the tendon clean-cut and standing well away from the cannon bone. The word "flat" refers to the appearance of the cannon, which is wide and flat when viewed from the side although narrow from the front; and does not mean that the bone itself is flat.

(Also see MEASURING HORSES.)

BONE MEAL (STEAMED BONE MEAL).— this is a mineral supplement sometimes fed to horses. It is produced by cooking fresh bones under steam pressure, followed by pressing, drying, and grinding the residue.

Bone meal has the following composition:

	%
Crude protein	12.1
Crude fat	3.2
Crude fiber	2.0
Total Ash	71.8
Calcium	28.98
Iron	.08
Magnesium	.64
Phosphorus	13.59
Potassium	.13
Sodium	.46
Chlorine	.06
Sulphur	.3
Manganese, mg./lb	13.8
Copper, mg./lb	7.4

With the exception of iodine, bone meal contains all the minerals needed by horses under most conditions. Of course, iodine can easily be provided in the form of iodized salt.

BONE SPAVIN (JACK SPAVIN).—Bone spavin (or jack spavin) is a bony enlargement that appears on the inside and front of the hock at the point where the base of the hock tapers into the cannon part of the leg. It is one of the most destructive conditions affecting the usefulness of a horse. The lameness is most evident when the animal is used following rest. A hereditary weak-

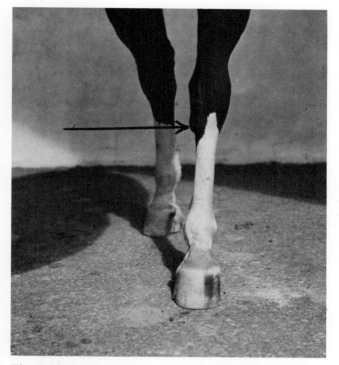

Fig. B-15. Bone spavin on left leg (they are always on a hind leg). Note that it is on the inside and front of the hock and where the base of the hock tapers into the cannon part of the leg. (Courtesy, USDA)

ness—together with such things as bruises, strains, and sprains—appears to cause bone spavin. Rest seems to be the most important treatment. Counterirritants, iodine, liniments, and blistering agents have all been used with varying degrees of success. Surgery or firing by a qualified veterinarian may be in order.

(Also see UNSOUNDNESSES.)

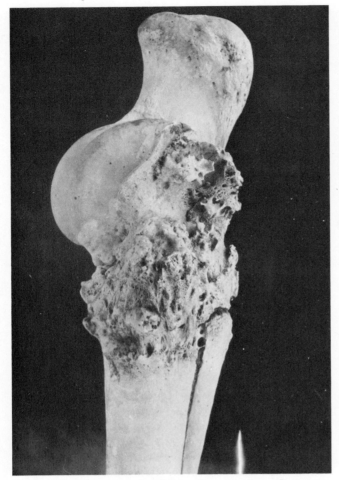

Fig. B-16. Bone (or jack) spavin, showing the extra bone formation (exostosis) of the metatarsal and tarsal bones. This is a medial, or inside, view of the hock area. (Photo by J. C. Allen & Son, West Lafayette, Ind.)

BOOKMAKER.—A person who, on or off the racetrack, accepts bets and lays agreed odds against any horse winning a race.

BOOKS, HORSE.—See Appendix III.

BOOTS (for horses).—Boots are used to protect the legs or feet against injuries. The most common injuries requiring such protection are those caused (1) by brushing when the inside of the leg, usually on or in the region of the fetlock joint, is knocked by the opposite foot, (2) by over-reaching when the hind toes strike into the

rear of the foreleg, or (3) by speedy cutting when the inside of the leg is struck high above the joint, usually under the hock. The shins (either front or hind) may also be endangered as a result of striking an obstacle when jumping.

Various types of boots are available to protect the horse from the different kinds of injuries listed above; among them, the quarter boots to prevent bruising of a front heel from a hind toe, worn by five-gaited Saddle Horses, Tennessee Walking Horses, and harness horses (see HARNESS—Figs. H-4 and H-5); the shin boots worn by the polo pony to guard cannons from injury by the mallet; and many others.

(Also see QUARTER BOOTS.)

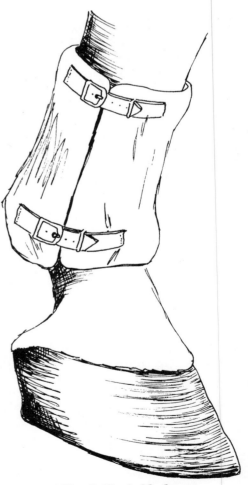

Fig. B-17. Ankle boot.

BOOTS, WESTERN *(for people).*—Western boots are more than a handsome trademark of the range. They're practical. The high heel is designed to give the wearer protection against losing his stirrups at critical moments; it prevents the foot from slipping through when pressure is applied for quick stops and turns. The top protects the ankles and calves of the legs against inclement weather, brush, insects, and snakes.

Modern Western boots possess two added features; namely, (1) comfort, and (2) adaptation for walking, so that the wearer can walk without it being a painful experience.

BOSAL.—The braided rawhide or rope noseband of a bosal hackamore. The bosal is knotted under the horse's jaw.

(Also see HACKAMORES.)

BOTS *(Gastrophilus spp.).*—Four species of bots have been found in the United States but only three are serious pests of horses.

Fig. B-18. Adult bot fly, Gastrophilus hemorrhoidalis. *(Courtesy, USDA)*

SYMPTOMS.—Animals attacked by the bot fly may toss their heads in the air, strike the ground with their front feet, and rub their noses on each other or any convenient object. Animals infected with bots may show frequent digestive upsets and even colic, lowered vitality and emaciation, and

reduced work output. Bots may penetrate the stomach wall and cause death.

Fig. B-19. Stomach of a horse opened to show bot larvae attached to the lining. (Courtesy, USDA)

TREATMENT.—Use of carbon disulfide, trichlorfon, or dichlorvos under the direction of a veterinarian is recommended.

PREVENTION AND CONTROL.—Frequent grooming, washing, and clipping help prevent bot attacks. Prevention of reinfection is best assured through community campaigns in which all horses within the area are treated. Fly nets and nose covers offer some relief from the attacks of bot flies.

DISCUSSION.—Bots are worldwide. The presence of bots results in loss of feed to feeding worms, itching and loss of tail hair from rubbing, lowered work efficiency, retarded growth of young animals, lowered breeding efficiency, and death in severe infections.

(Also see DISEASES AND PARASITES; HEALTH PROGRAM; and PARASITES OF HORSES.)

Fig. B-20. Eggs of the bot fly attached to hairs on the leg of a horse. (Courtesy, Dr. V. S. Myers, Jr., V.M.D., Department of Veterinary Surgery and Radiology, University of Minnesota, St. Paul, Minn.)

BOTTOM—1. A term applied to horses that possess vigorous physical qualities combined with stamina, the capacity to endure strain, and spirit.

2. A hunting term. It denotes either (a) a fence with a big and deep, though jumpable, ditch in it, or (b) a quite unjumpable ditch or brook running at the bottom of a deep gully or ravine.

BOWED TENDONS.—Enlarged tendons behind the cannon bones, in both the front and hind legs, are called bowed tendons. Descriptive terms of "high" or "low" bow are used by horsemen to denote the location of the injury; the high bow appears just under the knee and the low bow just above the fetlock. This condition is often brought about by severe strains, such as heavy training or racing. When bowed tendons are pronounced, more or less swelling, soreness, and lameness are present. Treatment consists of blistering or firing. The object of blistering and firing is to convert a chronic into an acute inflammation. This hastens nature's processes by bringing more blood to the part, thus inducing a reparative process which renders the animal suitable for work sooner than would otherwise be the case.

Blisters consist of such irritating substances as Spanish fly and iodide of mercury (one common preparation consists of 15 parts Spanish fly, 8 parts iodide of mercury, and 120 parts of lard). Before applying a blister, the hair should be closely clipped from the affected area, the scurf brushed from the skin, and the animal tied so that it cannot rub, lick, or bite the treated area. The blistering agent is then applied by rubbing it into the pores of the skin with the palm of the hand. Three days later the blistered area should be bathed with warm water and soap, dried, and treated with sweet oil or vaseline to prevent cracking of the skin. Firing, which is used for about the same purposes as blistering, consists of the application of a hot iron or the use of thermocautery to the affected area. Recently, there has been a growing interest in the surgical treatment of bowed tendons, which has been tried on a limited scale with varying degrees of success.

(Also see UNSOUNDNESSES.)

BOWEL MOVEMENT *(foal)*.—See FOAL—Bowel movement.

BOWING.—Bowing or kneeling is a pretty trick, and easily taught—provided the trainer is patient and intelligent. Trainers use different methods. But the following procedure is most common: The first lessons are given by stationing the horse near a wall, with the trainer standing on the near side. Then, the step by step procedure is: (1) make the horse stretch or camp slightly; (2) hold the reins quite short, pick up the near front foot at the pastern and carry it back until the knee touches the ground, and, simultaneously, pull back on the reins until the horse's nose also touches the ground; and (3) reward the horse with a carrot or a bit of sugar. Repeat this procedure until the horse is sure of what is wanted.

Next, induce the horse to carry his foot back on signal. This is accomplished by the trainer pulling back on the reins, and, at the same time, tapping the front of the knee with his whip. When the horse has mastered this, the trainer mounts and continues the schooling from above. The horse is made to stretch by touching him on the leg just back of the knee. Because the signals are now coming from above (rather than on the ground), and the horse has the rider's weight to balance, it is usually best to have the help of an assistant standing on the ground.

Some horsemen make use of the Rarey strap (a strap used to keep one foreleg off the ground —similar to the strap sometimes used instead of breeding hobbles for mares) to teach a horse to bow or kneel.

The horse should be taught to bow with either leg, and he should always be rewarded for his willingness.

BOWLEGGED.—Wide at the knees, close at the feet.

BOX *(of rodeo)*.—A rodeo term used to designate the pen beside the chute (a pen confining the calf or steer to be released for roping). The ropers must remain in the box until the instant specified for release by the rules governing the event in which they are competing.

BOX STALL.—See STALL.

BRACE BANDAGES.—Resilient bandages on the leg of horses worn in some cases in an effort to support lame legs, and worn in other cases to protect a horse from cutting and skinning its legs while racing.

(Also see HARNESS—Fig. H-4.)

BRAIDING (PLAITING).—Braiding, or plaiting, is the interlacing of three or more strands of hair. Custom decrees different "hair do's" for horses used for different purposes. The mane of the Hackney is braided with yarn and "sewn" into about fourteen small rosettes along the crest. The mane of the hunter is braided into about seven braids, which fall along the side of the neck. Braiding similar to the hunter is often accorded the Thoroughbred, hack, polo pony, and riding pony. With Tennessee Walking Horses, the foretop and first lock are braided.

(Also see GROOMING A HORSE—Fig. G-3.)

BRAN.—See WHEAT BRAN.

BRAND.—A mark used as a means of identification. On the Western range, hide branding is primarily a method of establishing ownership. Also, it is a powerful deterrent to rustling (stealing). In purebred horses, it may be used as a means of ascertaining ancestry or pedigree.

Until recently, the hot iron was the preferred method of branding. In this method, the irons are heated to a temperature that will burn sufficiently deep to make a scab peel, but which will not leave deep scar tissue.

Today, a new method known as "cold branding" is becoming popular. It consists in using a super-chilled (by dry ice or liquid nitrogen) branding iron, which is applied to the closely clipped surface for about 20 seconds, following which the hair grows out white. On horses, the brand may be applied under the mane should it be desired that it not be conspicuous.

(Also see Fig. B-21 IDENTIFICATION; and LAW AND HORSES—Brands and brand inspection.)

BREAKING *(gait)*.—A horse's leaving its gait and "breaking" into a gallop. A trotter or pacer must remain on gait in a race. If a harness horse makes a break, the driver must immediately pull him back to his gait.

BREAKING *(training)*.—Teaching a young horse to obey commands and accept direction and control is known as breaking. A foal will not need breaking if it has been trained properly. When a young horse can be saddled or harnessed with satisfactory ease, it is because a good training program has been followed. Saddling and harnessing are just additional steps. A good time to harness and work the horse for the first time is during the winter as a coming two-year old.

BREAKING CART.—The usual breaking cart is characterized by low wheels and long shafts on which there are special metal attachments to hold the tugs so that breeching is unnecessary. Sometimes it has an extension at the back to prevent the horse that is being broken from rearing and coming over backwards.

(Also see VEHICLES, HORSE-DRAWN.)

Fig. B-21. Horses cold branded (freeze branded on the right shoulder). (Courtesy, Louisiana State University)

BREAKING TACKLE.—The term "breaking tackle" refers to those items of equipment used in the early stages of training. Although varying somewhat, the complete breaking tackle usually consists of a cavesson breaking head collar with metal nose part and ring and padded noseband, a bridle for later use, a roller-adjustable on each side, side reins, crupper, driving reins and longeing reins (about 35 feet long), and a whip.

BREAST PLATE; THE BREAST COLLAR.—The breast plate usually consists of a short, wide strap that passes over the neck in front of the withers, two adjustable straps that run from each end of the short strap back to the saddle, two adjustable straps that run down the shoulders to a ring on the breast plate, and another adjustable strap that runs from this ring and attaches to the girth after passing between the forelegs. Sometimes this type is equipped with a strap that runs from the ring on the breast plate to

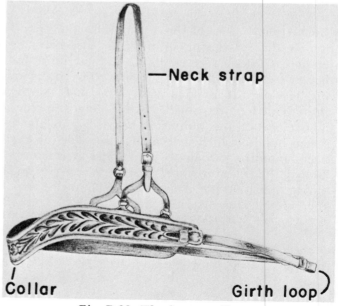

Fig. B-22. The breast collar.

the neckband, and acts as a martingale.

The breast collar serves the same purpose as the breast plate. Fig. B-22 shows a breast collar. (Also see HARNESS—Fig. H-4.)

Either the breast plate or the breast collar is frequently used on slender-bodied horses and on horses which require some special security to prevent the saddle from slipping to the rear (such as racehorses). With both articles, it is important that they be adjusted as loosely as possible consistent with holding the saddle in place, with proper allowance made for motion and movement of the horse's neck.

BREATHING RATE.—Normal breathing rate for the horse is 8 to 16 times per minute; meaning that the animal inhales that many times per minute, and exhales a like number of times.

The breathing rate can be determined by placing the hand on the flank, by observing the rise and fall of the flank, or, in the winter, by watching the breath condensate in coming from the nostrils. Rapid breathing due to recent exercise, excitement, hot weather, or poorly ventilated buildings should not be confused with disease. Respiration is accelerated in pain and in febrile (feverish) conditions.

BREECHING.—The broad leather band on harness that goes behind the horse's quarters. It is for the purpose of facilitating backing or going down a hill.

BREED (S).—A breed of horses may be defined as a group of horses having a common origin and possessing certain well-fixed, distinctive, uniformly-transmitted characteristics that are not common to other horses.

There is scarcely a breed of horses that does not possess one or more distinctive breed characteristics in which it excels all others. Moreover, any one of several breeds is often well adapted to the same use. To the amateur, this is most confusing, and he is prone to inquire as to the best breed. Certainly, if any strong preference exists, it should be an important factor, though it is recognized that certain breeds are better adapted to specific purposes.

It is noteworthy that most of the U. S. breeds of light horses are American creations. There are two primary reasons for this: (1) the diverse needs and uses for which light horses have been produced, and (2) the fact that many men of wealth have bred light horses.

Table B-2 is a summary of the breeds of horses and ponies, and their characteristics. (Also, see the accompanying pictures of each of the breeds.)

BREED RECOGNITION.—No person or department has authority to approve a breed. The only legal basis for recognizing a breed is contained in the Tariff Act of 1930, which provides for the duty-free admission of purebred breeding horses provided they are registered in the country of origin. But this applies to imported animals only. In this book, therefore, no official recognition of any breed is intended or implied. Rather, every effort has been made to present the factual story of the breeds. In particular, information about the new or less widely distributed breeds is needed and often difficult to obtain.

BREED REGISTRY ASSOCIATIONS.—A Breed Registry Association consists of a group of breeders banded together for the purposes of: (1) recording the lineage of their animals, (2) protecting the purity of the breed, (3) encouraging further improvement of the breed, and (4) promoting interest in the breed. A list of the horse breed registry associations is given in Appendix I.

BREED MAGAZINES.—See Appendix II.

*Note: Breed illustrations Fig. B-23 through Fig. B-46 appear in color between pages 64 and 65.

BREEDS OF LIGHT HORSES, PONIES, AND DRAFT HORSES, AND THEIR CHARACTERISTICS

Breed	Place of Origin	Color	Other Distinguishing Characteristics	Primary Uses	Disqualifications
Light Horses and Ponies:					
American Buckskin	United States.	Buckskin, red dun. gruella.	Dorsal stripe, and usually zebra stripes on the legs and transverse stripes over the withers and shoulders.	Stock horses. Pleasure horses. Show purposes.	White markings above knees and hocks. White spots on body.
American Gotland Horse	Baltic Island of Gotland, a part of Sweden.	Bay, brown, black, dun, chestnut, palomino, roan, and some leopard and blanket markings.	Average about 51″ high, with a range of 12 to 14 hands.	Harness trot racing. Pleasure horses. Jumpers. Suitable for children and moderate sized adults.	Pintos and animals with large markings are disqualified.
American Mustang	North Africa Barbary Coast; thence taken to Spain by the conquering Moors; propagated in Andalusia; thence brought to America by the Conquistadores. American Mustang Assoc. formed in 1962.	Any color.	Must be between 13-2 and 15 hands at the withers Short back.	Pleasure riding. Show. Trail riding. Endurance trials. Stock horses. Jumping.	
American Paint Horse	United States.	White plus any other color. Must be a recognizable paint.	No discrimination is made against glass, blue, or light-colored eyes.	Stock horses. Pleasure horses. Show purposes. Racing.	Lack of white markings above knees or hocks except on face; Appaloosa color or blood; adult horses under 14 hands; 5-gaited horses.
American Saddle Horse	United States; in Fayette County, Ky.	Bay, brown, chestnut, gray, or black. Gaudy white markings are frowned upon.	Ability to furnish an easy ride with great style and animation. Long, graceful neck, and proud action.	Three- and five-gaited saddle horses. Fine harness horses. Pleasure horses. Stock horses.	
American Walking Pony	Macon, Georgia, in 1968.	No color stipulation. It's a cross between Welsh Pony and Tennessee Walking Horse; hence, the colors of both parent breeds occur.	Must perform the running-walk gait. Height from 13 to 14-2 hands.	Pleasure riding. Mount for children or small adults.	

(Continued)

TABLE B-2 (CONTINUED)

BREEDS OF LIGHT HORSES, PONIES, AND DRAFT HORSES, AND THEIR CHARACTERISTICS

Breed	Place of Origin	Color	Other Distinguishing Characteristics	Primary Uses	Disqualifications
American White; American Creme (American Albino) Both breeds are registered by the American Albino Assoc., Inc., Crabtree, Ore.	American White: United States; on White Horse Ranch, Naper, Nebraska. American Creme: United States, primarily in Washington and Oregon.	Snow-white hair, pink skin, and light blue, dark blue (near black), brown, or hazel eyes. American Creme: pale cream.	Ranges from 32 inches to 17 hands; hence, it includes both horses and ponies.	Riding and utility. Their snow-white color makes them attractive as trained horses for exhibition purposes, parade horses, and flag bearer **horses.**	
Andalusian	Spain.	White and bay.		Bull fighting. Parade. Dressage. Jumping. Pleasure riding.	Andalusian animals not tracing to the Spanish Registry, which is supervised by the Army in Spain.
Appaloosa	United States; in Oregon, Washington, and Idaho; from animals originating in Fergana, Central Asia.	Variable, but usually white over the loin and hips, with dark round, or egg-shaped spots thereon.	The eye is encircled by white, the skin is mottled, and the hoofs are striped vertically black and white.	Stock horses. Pleasure horses. Parade horses. Race horses.	Animals not having Appaloosa characteristics, and animals of draft horse or pony, Albino, or Pinto breeding; cryptorchids; and animals under 14 hands at maturity (5 yrs. or older).
Arabian	Arabia.	Bay, gray, and chestnut with an occasional white or black. White marks on the head and legs are common. The skin is always dark.	A beautiful head, short coupling, docility, great endurance, and a gay way of going.	Saddle horses. Show horses. Pleasure horses. Stock horses. Racing.	
Chickasaw	Developed by the Chickasaw Indians of Tennessee, North Carolina, and Oklahoma, from horses of Spanish extraction.	Bay, black, chestnut, gray, roan, sorrel, and palomino.	Short head and ears; short back; short neck; square, stocky hips; low set tail; wide chest; very wide between the eyes.	Cow pony.	

(Continued)

TABLE B-2 (CONTINUED)

BREEDS OF LIGHT HORSES, PONIES, AND DRAFT HORSES, AND THEIR CHARACTERISTICS

Breed	Place of Origin	Color	Other Distinguishing Characteristics	Primary Uses	Disqualifications
Cleveland Bay	England; in the Cleveland district of Yorkshire.	Always solid bay with black legs.	Larger than most light horse breeds; weighs from 1150 to 1400 pounds.	Today, it is used chiefly as a general utility horse; for riding, driving, and doing all kinds of farm work. Also, used in cross-breeding to produce heavyweight hunters.	Any color other than bay, although a few white hairs on the forehead are permissible.
Connemara Pony	Ireland; along the west coast.	Gray, black, bay, brown, dun, cream, with occasional roans and chestnuts.	Range in height from 13 to 14-2 hands.	Jumpers, showing under saddle and in harness; for medium-sized adults and children.	Piebalds and skewbalds not accepted.
Galiceno	Galicia, a province in north-western Spain.	Solid colors prevail. Bay, black, chestnut (sorrel), dun (buckskin), gray, brown, and palomino are most common.	Intermediate in size. At maturity, they stand 12 to 13 hands and weigh 625 to 700 pounds.	Riding horses.	Albinos, pintos, paints, cryptorchids, and monorchids.
Hackney	England; on the eastern coast, in Norfolk and adjoining counties.	Chestnut, bay, and brown are most common colors, although roans and blacks are seen. White marks are common and are desired.	In the showring, custom decrees that heavy harness horses be docked and have their manes pulled. High natural action.	Heavy harness or carriage horses. For cross-breeding purposes to produce hunters and jumpers.	
Hungarian Horse	Hungary.	All colors; either solid or broken.	A unique combination of style and beauty with ruggedness.	Stock horses. Cutting horses. Pleasure horses. Trail riding. Hunters. Jumpers.	Cryptorchids; glasseyed.
Lipizzan	Lipizza, Yugoslavia, the town from which the breed takes its name.	White. But Lipizzan foals are born dark (brown or gray), then turn white at 4 to 6 years of age. About 1 in 600 remains black or brown throughout life. When the latter happens, it is considered good luck.	Elastic walk, with knee action. Without a peer as dressage horses.	Dressage. Harness horses. Pleasure horses. Hunters. Jumpers. Parade horses.	Glass eyes; extreme Roman nose; deformed or crooked limbs.

(Continued)

TABLE B-2 (CONTINUED)

BREEDS OF LIGHT HORSES, PONIES, AND DRAFT HORSES, AND THEIR CHARACTERISTICS

Breed	Place of Origin	Color	Other Distinguishing Characteristics	Primary Uses	Disqualifications
Missouri Fox Trotting Horse	United States; in the Ozark hills of Mo. and Ark.	Sorrels predominate, but any color is accepted.	The fox trot gait.	Pleasure horses. Stock horses. Trail riding.	If animal cannot fox trot.
Morgan	United States; in the New England states.	Bay, brown, black, and chestnut; extensive white markings are uncommon.	Easy keeping qualities, endurance, and docility.	Saddle horses. Stock horses.	Wall-eye (lack of pigmentation of the iris), or natural white markings above the knee or hock except on the face.
Morocco Spotted Horse	United States.	Spotted. Secondary color: White, which must comprise not less than 10%, not including legs or white on the face.		Parade horses. Saddle horses. Stock horses. Pleasure horses. Harness horses.	Must not be under 14-2 hands, and must not be of draft or pony breeding or show such characteristics.
National Appaloosa Pony	United States; Rochester, Indiana.	All colors, with the following most popular: Leopard, blanket type, snowflake, or roan.	Mottled skin or nose and around eyes. White sclera encircling the eyes.	Working pony, show pony, trail riding, jumping, and racing.	Albino, pinto, or paint.
Palomino	United States; from animals of Spanish extraction.	Golden (the color of a newly minted gold coin or 3 shades lighter or darker), with a light colored mane and tail (white, silver, or ivory, with not more than 15% dark or chestnut hair in either). White markings on the face or below the knees are acceptable.		Stock horses. Parade horses. Pleasure horses. Saddle horses. Fine harness horses.	Animals of draft horse or pony breeding, and the offspring of piebald or albino breeding not eligible for registration.
Paso Fino (Continued)	Peru, Puerto Rico, Cuba, and Colombia.	Any color, although solid colors are preferred.	The paso fino gait, which may be described as a broken pace.	Pleasure horses. Parade horses. Endurance rides.	Animals not possessing the paso fino gait.

TABLE B-2 (CONTINUED)

BREEDS OF LIGHT HORSES, PONIES, AND DRAFT HORSES, AND THEIR CHARACTERISTICS

Breed	Place of Origin	Color	Other Distinguishing Characteristics	Primary Uses	Disqualifications
Peruvian Paso Horse	Peru.	Any color, but solid colors are preferred.	These horses are naturally five-gaited—walk, paso, trot, huachano (broken pace), and canter.	Pleasure. Parade. Endurance horses.	Light forequarters, coarseness, or extreme height.
Pinto	United States; from horses brought in by the Spanish Conquistadores.	Preferably half color or colors and half white, with many spots well placed. The two distinct pattern markings are: Overo and Tobiano.	Glass eyes are not discounted. Association has separate registry for ponies and/or horses under 14 hands.	Any light horse purpose, but especially for show, parade, novice, pleasure purposes, stock horses.	
Pony of the Americas	United States; Mason City, Iowa.	Similar to Appaloosa; white over the loin and hips, with dark, round or egg-shaped spots.	Happy medium of Arabian and Quarter Horse in miniature, ranging in height from 46 to 54 inches, with Appaloosa color.	Child's western type using pony.	Ponies not within the height range; or not having the appaloosa color, including mottled skin and much exposed sclera of the eye. Pinto markings and loud-colored roans.
Quarter Horse	United States.	Chestnut, sorrel, bay and dun are most common; although they may be palomino, black, brown, roan, or copper-colored.	Well-muscled and powerfully built. Small alert ear; sometimes heavily-muscled cheeks and jaw.	Stock horses. Racing. Pleasure horses.	Pinto, appaloosa, and albino colors are ineligible for registry; also white markings on the underline.
Shetland Pony	Shetland Isles.	All colors, either solid or broken.	Small size. Two classes recognized by registry: (1) 43" and under, and (2) 43" to 46". Good disposition.	Children's mounts. Harness. Roadster. Racing.	Over 46" in height.
Spanish-Barb	United States. Descended from Barb-Andalusian horses brought to America by the Spaniards in the 1500s and 1600s.	All colors. Dun, gruella, sorrel, and roan are most common. Most animals are solid colored.	Small (13-3 to 14-1), short-coupled, deep-bodied, with good action. Without extreme muscling.	Cow ponies. Western riding. English riding. Pack horses.	

(Continued)

Fig. B-23. American Buckskin stallion, Apple Cash, the first ABRA Champion. Owned by Dr. Kenneth G. Ormiston D.V.M., Rialto, Calif. (Courtesy, American Buckskin Registry Association, Inc.)

Fig. B-24. American Creme stallion, Polar Bar, owned by Edward Bales, Prineville, Ore. (Courtesy, American Albino Association, Inc.)

Fig. B-25. American Gotland Horse stallion, *Amiral, Bred by K. E. Everz, Hemse, Gotland, Sweden, and imported by Admiral Robert C. Lee. Owned by Leeward Farm, Elkland, Mo. (Courtesy, Leeward Farm)

Fig. B-26. American Mustang stallion, Knight's Excaliber, owned by Rosalind Nuetzel, Wild Rose, Wisc. (Courtesy, American Mustang Assn., Inc.)

Fig. B-27. American Paint Horse stallion, Dual Image. APHA champion and many other winnings, owned by Mr. C. E. Swain, San Antonio, Tex. (Courtesy, American Paint Horse Assn.)

Fig. B-28. American Walking Pony stallion, BT Golden Splendor, owned by Mrs. Joan Hudson Brown, Browntree Stables, Macon, Ga. (Courtesy, Mrs. Brown)

Fig. B-29. American White stallion, White Wings, bred by White Horse Ranch, Naper, Neb., and owned by Ingabord Swenson, Aurora, Ohio. (Courtesy, American Albino Association, Inc., Crabtree, Oregon)

Fig. B-30. Appaloosa stallion, Navajo Breeze, owned by Terlingua Appaloosas, Murrieta, Calif. (Courtesy, Appaloosa Horse Club, Inc.)

Fig. B-31. Arabian stallion, *Aramus; imported from Poland. In 1970, *Aramus was named U. S. and Canadian National Champion Stallion. Owned by Burton and Lowe Arabians and Wayne Newton, Rice Lake, Wisc. (Courtesy, International Arabian Horse Association)

Fig. B-32. Chickasaw gelding, Johnny Reb, nation[al] high point Chickasaw horse, owned by Mr. and Mr[s.] Roy Hughes, Clarinda, Iowa. (Courtesy, Mr. and Mr[s.] Hughes)

Fig. B-33. Hackney champion pair, Cassilis Venus an[d] Cassilis Sovereign; bred, owned, and driven by Mr[s.] J. Macy Willets, Cassilis Farm, Great Barringto[n,] Mass. (Courtesy, Mrs. Willets)

Fig. B-34. Hungarian Horse stallion, Hungarian Kallo. Sire of many notable winners in the Hungarian breed. Owned by Mrs. Margit Sigray Bessenyey, Hamilton, Mont. (Photograph by Ernst Peterson, Hamilton, Mont.; Courtesy, Hungarian Horse Association)

Fig. B-35. Morgan mare, UVM Treasure, owned by Mr. and Mrs. John G. Hagan, Rapidan River Farm, Lignum, Va. (Courtesy, A. C. Drowne, American Morgan Horse Assoc., Inc.)

Fig. B-36. Morocco Spotted Horse stallion, Chief Wauconda. Many times champion, owned by George Larsen, Kingston, Ill. (Courtesy, Morocco Spotted Horse Co-operative Association of America)

Fig. B-37. Palomino stallion, Yellow Straw. This attractive horse was sculptured by Doris Lindner, well-known English sculptor of horses, owned by Mr. and Mrs. Willard Beanland, Hidden Hills, Calif. (Courtesy, Mr. and Mrs. Beanland)

Fig. B-38. Paso Fino stallion, Mar de Plata Lace, grand champion of the breed. Owned by Paso Fino Farms, Valdosta, Ga. (Courtesy, Rosalie MacWilliam, Lorton, Va.)

Fig. B-39. Pinto Horse, Ja-Mar's Brandy. A champion pleasure type gelding, owned by James Boswell, Jr., Farmington, Mich. (Courtesy, The Pinto Horse Association of America, Inc.)

Fig. B-40. Pony of the Americas mare, SD's Flashy Maiden. Sold by Golden Rod Farms, Chariton, Iowa, for the price of $2,500, to Dr. James Colyer, Hays, Kan. (Courtesy, Keith E. Stone, Golden Rod Farms)

Fig. B-41. Quarter Horse stallion. (Courtesy, American Quarter Horse Association)

Fig. B-42. Spanish Mustang mare, Spring Lamb, and her stud colt, Utah Cal, owned by Jeff Edwards, Brislawn-Edwards Spanish Barb Wild Horse Research Farm, Porterville, Calif. (Courtesy, Mr. Edwards)

Fig. B-43. *Standardbred stallion, Nevele Pride, fastest trotter of all time at 1:54–4/5 for the mile; Stanley Dancer driving. (Courtesy, Stanley Dancer Stables, New Egypt, New Jersey)*

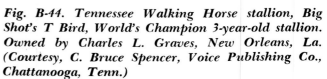

Fig. B-44. *Tennessee Walking Horse stallion, Big Shot's T Bird, World's Champion 3-year-old stallion. Owned by Charles L. Graves, New Orleans, La. (Courtesy, C. Bruce Spencer, Voice Publishing Co., Chattanooga, Tenn.)*

Fig. B-45. Thoroughbred stallion, Secretariat, bred by Helen (Penny) Tweedy, Meadow Stud, Doswell, Virginia. In 1973, Secretariat was syndicated by Seth Hancock, Claiborne Farm, Lexington, Ky., for a world record price of $6,080,000; 32 shares at $190,000 each. (Photograph by Tony Leonard. Picture courtesy of Mrs. Tweedy)

Fig. B-46. Welsh Pony stallion, Liseter Shooting Star. Many times champion and fine breed representative, owned by Mrs. J. Austin duPont, Liseter Hall Farm, Newtown Square, Pa. (Courtesy, Mrs. duPont)

BREEDS OF LIGHT HORSES, PONIES, AND DRAFT HORSES, AND THEIR CHARACTERISTICS

Breed	Place of Origin	Color	Other Distinguishing Characteristics	Primary Uses	Disqualifications
Spanish Mustang	United States. Beginning about 1925, Robert E. Brislawn, Sr., began gathering them on his ranch at Oshoto, Wyo.	They run the gamut of equine colors, including all the solid colors, and all the broken colors.	Only 5 lumbar vertebrae (most breeds have 6). Short ears; low-set tail; and round leg bones.	Cow ponies. Trail riding.	
Standardbred	United States.	Bay, brown, chestnut, and black are most common, but grays, roans and duns are found.	Smaller and less leggy and with more substance and ruggedness than the Thoroughbred.	Harness racing, either trotting or pacing. Harness horses in horse shows.	
Tennessee Walking Horse	United States; in the Middle Basin of Tennessee.	Sorrel, chestnut, black, roan, white, bay, brown, gray, and golden. White markings on the face and legs are common.	The running walk gait.	Plantation Walking Horses. Pleasure horses. Show horses.	
Thoroughbred	England.	Bay, brown, chestnut, and black; less frequently, roan and gray. White markings on the face and legs are common.	Fineness of conformation. Long, straight and well-muscled legs.	Running races. Stock horses. Saddle horses. Polo mounts. Hunters.	
Welsh Pony	Wales.	Any color except piebald and skewbald. Gaudy white markings are not popular.	Small size; intermediate between Shetland Ponies and other light horse breeds. The American Welsh Stud Book height stipulations are: "A" Div.—cannot exceed 12-2 hands. "B" Div.—over 12-2 and not more than 14 hands.	Mounts for children and small adults. Harness show ponies. Racing. Roadsters. Trail riding. Parade. Stock cutting. Hunting.	Piebald or skewbald.
Ysabella, named after Queen Isabella of Spain. (Continued)	United States; McKinzie Rancho, Williamsport, Ind. Foundation animals were American Saddlers.	Gold, white, or chestnut; with flaxen, silver or white mane and tail.	There may be white markings on face and legs.	Pleasure riding and exhibition horses.	Bay color, spots, black mane and tail.

TABLE B-2 (CONTINUED)

BREEDS OF LIGHT HORSES, PONIES, AND DRAFT HORSES, AND THEIR CHARACTERISTICS

Breed	Place of Origin	Color	Other Distinguishing Characteristics	Primary Uses	Disqualifications
Draft Horses:					
American Cream Horse	United States.	Cream, with white mane and tail and pink skin. Some white markings.	Medium size. Good disposition.	Farm work horses. Exhibition purposes.	
Belgian	Belgium.	Bay, chestnut, and roan are most common, but browns, grays, and blacks are occasionally seen. Many Belgians have a flaxen mane and tail and a white-blazed face.	Lowest set and most massive of all draft breeds.	Farm work horses. Exhibition purposes.	
Clydesdale	Scotland; along the River Clyde.	Bay and brown with white markings are most common, but blacks, grays, chestnuts, and roans are occasionally seen.	Superior style and action. Feather or hair on the legs.	Farm work horses. Exhibition purposes.	
Percheron	France, in the northwestern district of La Perche.	Mostly black or gray, but bays, browns, chestnuts, and roans are seen.	In comparison with other draft breeds, noted for its handsome clean-cut head.	Farm work horses. Exhibition purposes.	
Shire	England; primarily in the east central counties of Lincolnshire and Cambridgeshire.	Common colors are bay, brown, and black with white markings; although grays, chestnuts, and roans are occasionally seen.	Taller than any other draft breed. Feather or hair on the legs.	Farm work horses. Exhibition purposes.	
Suffolk	England; in the eastern county of Suffolk.	Chestnut only.	They are the smallest of the draft breeds. Close-to-the ground and chunky build.	Farm work horses. Exhibition purposes.	Any color other than chestnut.

(Continued)

TABLE B-2 (CONTINUED)

BREEDS OF LIGHT HORSES, PONIES, AND DRAFT HORSES, AND THEIR CHARACTERISTICS

Breed	Place of Origin	Color	Other Distinguishing Characteristics	Primary Uses	Disqualifications
Asses:					
Jacks and Jennets	Domesticated in Egypt.	Black with a white nose; red; gray.	Compared to horse, the ass is smaller; has shorter hair on the mane and tail; does not possess the chestnuts on the inside of the hind legs; has much longer ears; has smaller, deeper hoofs; has a louder and more harsh voice—called a bray; is less subject to founder or injury; and is more hardy.	For crossing on horses to produce mules.	
Donkeys, Miniature Mediterranean	Sardinia and Sicily.	Mouse color to almost black.	Dorsal stripe, forming a cross with stripe over withers and down shoulders.	Children's pet.	Over 38" high. Without cross.

Fig. B-47. American Saddle Horse stallion, Gallant Guy O'Goshen, World's Champion Stallion six times, 1955-56-57-58-59-60. Owned by Mrs. H. G. Wittenberg, Louisville, Ky. (Courtesy, American Saddle Horse Breeders Association)

Fig. B-48. Cleveland Bay stallion, Cleveland Farnley. (Courtesy, Mr. A. Mackay-Smith)

Fig. B-49. Connemara Pony stallion, Camus John's Gladiator, owned by Alvin M. Mavis, Mavis Connemara Farm, Rochester, Ill. (Courtesy, Mr. Mavis)

Fig. B-51. Lipizzan stallion, Maestoso Brezova II. This stallion was High School Dressage—trained at the Spanish Riding School, Vienna, Austria, and exhibited at the 1962 World's Fair in Seattle, Washington. Owned by Raflyn Farms, Snohomish, Wash. (Courtesy, Evelyn L. Dreitzler)

Fig. B-50. Galiceno stallion, Gray Badger. Champion at the Southwestern Exposition and Fat Stock Show, Fort Worth, Tex. (Courtesy, Galiceno Horse Breeders Association)

Fig. B-52. Missouri Fox Trotting mare, Bay Jeannie. (Courtesy, Missouri Fox Trotting Horse Breeders Association)

Fig. B-53. Peruvian Paso stallion, Broche del Oro. (Courtesy, American Association of Owners and Breeders of Peruvian Paso Horses)

Fig. B-54. Shetland Pony filly, Oh Oh's Star of the Show, owned by Dr. and Mrs. R. L. Malcolm, Jr., Middletown, Ohio and Mrs. R. L. Malcolm, Richmond, Ind. (Courtesy, Dr. R. L. Malcolm, Jr.)

Fig. B-57. Clydesdale mare, Howford Classic Lady, Champion at the Royal Highland Show, Lanark, Scotland. (Courtesy, Horse Association of America)

Fig. B-55. American Cream Horse stallion, Bavender's King No. 15. (Courtesy, American Cream Horse Association)

Fig. B-56. Belgian stallion, Conquest. Grand Champion at the American Belgian Show, the National Belgian Show, and the Chicago International, owned by Meadow Brook Farms, Rochester, Mich. (Courtesy, Belgian Draft Horse Corp.)

Fig. B-58. Percheron stallion, La Donald. Many times Grand Champion Percheron stallion, owned by Ray H. Bast, Richfield, Wisc. (Courtesy, Mr. Bast)

Fig. B-59. Shire stallion, winning two-year-old, exhibited by Lou Shattuck, Horseshoe Ranch, Toppenish, Wash. (Courtesy, Mr. Shattuck)

BREED NUMBERS.—Table B-3 shows the 1971 and total registrations to date of the various breeds of horses.

BREEDER.—Owner of the dam at the time of service who was responsible for the selection of the sire to which she was mated.

BREEDING.—An attempt to regulate the progeny through intensive selection of the parents.

BREEDING CLASSES.—Classes in which the entries are always shown in hand, which means that they are led by the groom or owner, without tack other than a halter or a bridle. Breeding classes may be for stallions, mares, broodmares (in which case the foal may be at foot), and stallions with get.

Entries in breeding classes are judged on breed type, conformation, quality, substance, and soundness.

BREEDING CONTRACT *(stallion).*—See STALLION, STALLION BREEDING CONTRACT.

BREEDING FARM *(horse).*—A farm that specializes in breeding horses.

(Also see BREEDING HORSES; and INCENTIVE BASIS FOR THE HELP.)

Fig. B-60. Suffolk mare, imported from England. (Courtesy, American Suffolk Horse Association)

1971 (OR AS SHOWN) AND TOTAL REGISTRATIONS OF HORSES IN UNITED STATES BREED ASSOCIATIONS

Class	Breed	1971 Registrations	Total Registrations (since Breed Registry started)
Light Horses and Ponies:	Quarter Horse	73,594	800,000
	Thoroughbred	25,000	700,000
	Half-Breds[1]	192	41,580
	Arabian		
	Purebreds	9,300	78,500
	Half Arabians and		
	Anglo Arabs[2]	12,585	101,054
	Appaloosa	18,008	160,252
	Standardbred	11,654	368,785
	Tennessee Walking Horse . . .	8,000	130,000
	American Saddle Horse	3,972	140,629
	American Paint Horse	3,053	19,053
	Morgan	2,766	45,071
	Pinto	2,000	16,000
	Palomino[3]	1,738	38,222
	Pony of the Americas	1,435	14,481
	Shetland Pony	1,045	128,196
	Welsh Pony	850	23,185
	Hackney	551	18,311
	American Part-Blooded[4]	439	8,408
	Paso Fino	269	1,344
	American Buckskin	239	1,848
	American White; American Creme .	169	4,292
	Connemara Pony		
	Purebred	123	1,235
	Halfbred	26	125
	Peruvian Paso	105	1,050
	Chickasaw Horse	78	1,200
	Galiceno	65	1,852
	American Mustang	55	907
	Morocco Spotted Horse	45	1,787
	Hungarian Horse	25	300
	American Walking Pony	25	52
	Spanish Barb	13	303
	American Gotland Horse	11	219
	Lipizzan	4	62

Class	Breed	Latest Annual Registrations Year	Latest Annual Registrations No.	Total Registrations (since Breed Registry started) Through Year	Total Registrations (since Breed Registry started) No.
Draft Horses:	Belgian	1966	617	1966	69,641
	Percheron	1971	223	1971	251,099
	Clydesdale	1965	17	1965	25,698
	Suffolk	1971	16	1971	2,756
	Shire	1971	15	1971	22,081
	American Cream Horse	1971	——	1971	199
Donkeys and Jacks:	Miniature Donkeys	1966	50	1966	2,500
	Jacks and Jennets	1971	28	1971	37,440

[1] Half-bred Thoroughbreds registered by the American Remount Association, Inc., P. O. Box 1066, Perris, Calif. 92370.
[2] Registered in the International Arabian Horse Association, 224 East Olive Avenue, Burbank, California.
[3] Includes registrations in both the Palomino Horse Association, Inc., and the Palomino Horse Breeders of America.
[4] Half-bloods, grades and crosses of all light horse breeds, except Arabian and Thoroughbred; registered in American Part-Blooded Horse Registry, 4120 S. E. River Drive, Portland, Oregon 97222.

Fig. B-61. Mare and foal. (Courtesy, Margit Sigray Bessenyey. Photo by Ernst Peterson, Hamilton, Mont.)

BREEDING HOBBLES.—See HOBBLES.

BREEDING HORSES.—In the wild state, each band of 30 to 40 mares was headed by a stallion leader who sired all of the foals in that band. With plenty of outdoor exercise on natural footing, superior nutrition derived from plants grown on unleached soils, regular production beginning at an early age, little possibility of disease or infection, and frequent services during the heat period, 90% or higher foaling rates were commonplace. The low fertility usually encountered under domestication must be caused to a large extent by the relatively artificial conditions under which horses are mated.

Horse owners who plan to breed one or more mares should have a working knowledge of heredity and know how to care for breeding animals and foals. The number of mares bred that actually conceive varies from about 40 to 85%, with the average running less than 50%. Some mares that do conceive fail to produce living foals. This means that, on the average, two mares are kept a whole year to produce one foal, and even then, some foals are disappointments from the standpoint of quality.

(Also see HEREDITY IN HORSES.)

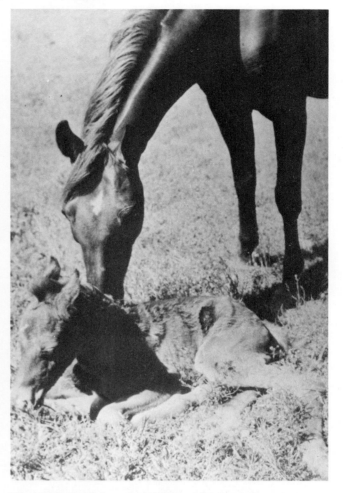

Fig. B-63. A mare and her newborn foal on pasture. When the weather is warm, the most natural and ideal place for foaling is a clean open pasture away from other livestock. Under these conditions, there is less danger of either infection or mechanical injury to the mare and foal. (Courtesy, National Cottonseed Products Association, Inc.)

Fig. B-62. A mare (left) and a stallion (right) on the range.

HEALTH PROGRAM FOR BREEDING AND FOALING.—

1. Mate only healthy mares to healthy stallions and observe scrupulous cleanliness at the time of service and examination. Never breed a mare that has any kind of discharge.

2. Provide plenty of exercise for the stallion and pregnant mare in harness, under saddle, or by turning them loose in a large pasture where plenty of shade and water are available.

3. During spring and fall when the weather is warm, allow the mare to foal in a clean, open pasture away from other livestock. During bad

weather, keep the mare in a roomy, well-lighted, well-ventilated box stall that is provided with clean bedding. Before using the stall, thoroughly disinfect it with a lye solution made by adding one can of lye to 12 to 15 gallons of water. After the foal is born, remove all wet, stained, or soiled bedding and dust the floor lightly with lime. Do not use too much lime because it irritates the eyes and nasal passages of foals. When the afterbirth has been completely discharged, it should be buried in lime or burned. The mare should be kept isolated until all discharges have stopped.

Fig. B-64. A healthy start in life! Hungarian mare and foal on a clean pasture at Bitterroot Stock Farm, Hamilton, Montana, owned by Margit Sigray Bessenyey. (Photo by Ernst Peterson, Hamilton, Montana)

4. To lessen the danger of navel infection, promptly treat the navel cord of the newborn foal with tincture of iodine.

5. As a precaution against foaling diseases and other infections, a veterinarian may administer antibiotics to both the mare and foal on the day of foaling.

SYSTEMS OF BREEDING.—Systems of breeding, whether planned or by chance, have made it possible to produce horses specially adapted to riding, racing, or driving. There is no one best system of breeding or secret of success for all conditions. Each breeding program is an individual case, requiring careful study. The choice of the system of breeding should be determined primarily by the size and quality of the herd, by the finances and skill of the operator, and by the ultimate goal ahead.

The systems of breeding from which the horseman may select are:

● *Purebreeding* is the system in which the lineage, regardless of the number of generations removed, traces back to the foundation animals accepted by the breed or to animals that have been subsequently approved for infusion. Purebreeding may be conducted as either inbreeding or outcrossing, or part of each.

● *Inbreeding* is the mating of animals more closely related than the average of the population from which they came. It may be done either by closebreeding or linebreeding.

   ● *Close breeding* is breeding closely related animals such as sire to daughter, son to dam, or brother to sister.
   ● *Linebreeding* is breeding related animals so as to keep the offspring closely related to some highly admired ancestor such as half brother to half sister, female descendent to grandsire, or cousin to cousin.

● *Outcrossing* is the mating of animals that are members of the same breed but that show no relationship in the pedigree for at least four to six generations.

● *Grading up* is breeding a purebred sire of a given breed to a native, or grade, female.

● *Crossbreeding* is mating animals of different breeds.

HAND BREEDING, CORRAL BREEDING, AND PASTURE BREEDING.—No phase of horse production has become more unnatural or more complicated with domestication than the actual breeding operations. Hand mating, in which the animals are coupled under supervision, is undoubtedly the best way in which to breed mares; it is the accepted practice in the better breeding establishments throughout the world. It guards against injury to both the stallion and the mare.

Although leaving much to be desired, corral breeding is next best to hand breeding. In this system, after first ascertaining that the mare is in heat, she and the stallion are turned loose together in a small, well-fenced corral. The attendants should remain out of the corral, where they can see but not be seen by the animals, until service is completed, following which the stallion and the mare are returned to their respective quarters.

Pasture breeding simply consists of turning the stallion into a pasture with the band of mares which it is intended that he serve. Except on the ranges of the far West, this method of breeding is seldom practiced with domestic horses. With valuable animals, both corral and pasture breeding are too likely to cause injury, and the practices should be condemned. In pasture breeding, a stallion will handle fewer mares because of the repeated services of a mare, and he may even become sterile toward the end of the breeding season. Moreover, in pasture breeding, accurate breeding records are impossible.

FERTILIZATION.—Generally, the egg is liberated during the period of one day before to one day after the end of heat. Unfortunately, there is no reliable way of predicting the length of heat nor the time of ovulation; although an expert technician can predict the time of ovulation by feeling the ovary (follicle) with the hand through the rectum wall.

Fig. B-65. Teasing a mare, using a solid fence for separation. Breeding a mare that is not in season is a wasteful practice, and more important, it may result in damaging the future breeding efficiency. (Courtesy, Washington State University)

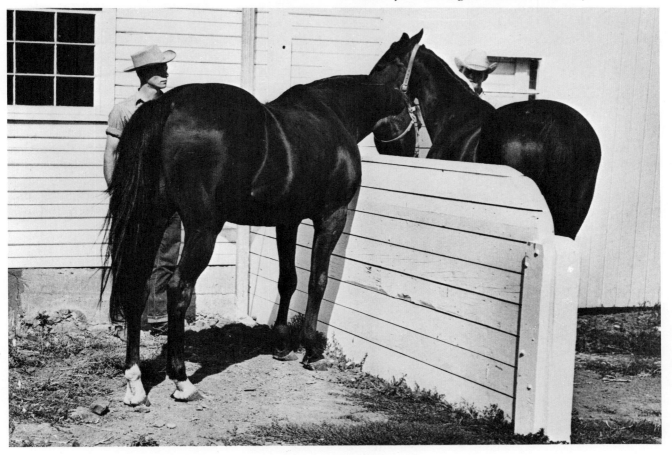

The sperm (or male germ cells) are deposited in the uterus at the time of service and from there ascend the reproductive tract. Under favorable conditions, they meet the egg, and one of them fertilizes it in the upper part of the oviduct near the ovary.

A series of delicate time relationships must be met, however, or the egg will never be fertilized. The sperm cells live only 24 to 30 hours in the reproductive tract of the female, and it probably requires 4 to 6 hours for them to ascend the female reproductive tract. Moreover, the egg is viable for an even shorter period of time than the sperm, probably for not more than 4 to 6 hours after ovulation. For conception, therefore, breeding must take place within 20 to 24 hours before ovulation.

As mares usually stay in heat from 4 to 6 days, perhaps the highest rate of conception may be obtained by serving the mare daily or every other day during the heat period, beginning with the third day. When many mares are being bred and heavy demands are being made upon a given stallion, this condition may be obtained by reinforcing a natural service with subsequent daily artificial inseminations as long as heat lasts. In no case should the mare be bred twice the same day.

HOW TO INCREASE THE PERCENT FOAL CROP.—Recognition of the following facts and pointers may help to increase the percentage of foals produced:

1. Mares bred in the late spring of the year are more likely to conceive. If mares are bred out of season, spring conditions should be duplicated as nearly as possible.

2. Mares bred as three- and four-year-olds and kept in regular production thereafter are more likely to conceive and produce living foals.

3. Infections or other unhealthy conditions of either the mare or stallion are not favorable for production.

4. More conceptions will occur if the mare is bred at the proper time within the heat period. Usually mares bred just before going out of heat are more likely to conceive.

5. Returning the mare to the stallion for retrial or rebreeding is important.

6. Mares in foal should be fed and cared for properly so as to develop the young. Balance of proteins, minerals, and vitamins is important.

7. It must also be remembered that old mares, overfat mares, or mares in a thin, run-down condition are less likely to be good breeders. Unfortunately, these conditions frequently apply to mares that are bred following retirement from the racetrack or the show-ring.

In the final analysis, improved management and increased research are the primary avenues through which improved reproduction in horses —a higher percentage foal crop—can be achieved.

(Also see BIRTH DATE; FEED; FEEDING HORSES; MARE; and STALLION.)

BREEDING *RECORD FORMS.*—An important requisite in any horse breeding program is the keeping of relatively simple but meaningful records. Tables B-4a, -4b, -5a, and -5b are record forms developed by the author. One is for the broodmare, and the other is for the stallion. These record forms may be modified somewhat to suit individual needs and desires.

BREEDING MARES BY THE MOON.—Early horse breeders were much influenced by the moon. Gervase Markham, in his *Masterpiece* (1584), gave the following directions:

"To get a colt foal, cover before the full of the moon, and when the sign is female. To get mare colts, cover over the full of the moon in the male sign. To know which of your mares be with foal, about Christmas pour a little water in her ear. If she only shakes her head, she is with foal. But if she shakes both head and body, she is not in foal."

It is interesting to note in the foregoing that the word "colt" is used indiscriminately for foals of either sex.

BREED TYPE.—The combination of characteristics which distinguish a breed, such as color, height at maturity, shape of body and head, and action.

BREEDY.—Smart and trim about the head and front part of body.

TABLE B-4-A

INDIVIDUAL LIFETIME BROODMARE RECORD

Name of mare _____

Number or other identity _____

Birth date _____

Show or performance record _____

_____

Temperament _____ (gentle, nervous, cross)

Bred by _____ (name and address)

Purchased: from _____ (name and address)

Date _____ Price _____

Disposal: Sold to _____ (name and address)

Date _____ Price _____

Remarks _____

Photo

Production Record of Mares

Year	Sire of foal	Birth date of foal	Temperament of mare at foaling (gentle, nervous, cross)	Foaling (normal, requiring assistance, ret. placenta)	Vigor foal at birth (deform-ities)	Sex of foal	Iden-tity of foal	Date foal was weaned	Score of foal				Disposal of foal				Remarks
									Under 1 year	Yearling	2-year-old	3-year-old	Sold to Name and Address	Date	Price	Reasons	

(See Table 4b for reverse side of record form.)

TABLE B-4-B

INDIVIDUAL LIFETIME BROODMARE RECORD

Health Record

Date	Immunization			Type of parasite treatment	Other veterinary treatment	Remarks
	Encephal-omyelitis	Tetanus	Abortion			

(This is the reverse side of Table 4-a)

INDIVIDUAL YEARLY STALLION BREEDING RECORD

Name of stallion _____

Number or other identity _____

Birth date _____

Show or performance record _____

_____

For breeding year of _____

For foaling year of _____

Total number of services _____

No. services/conception _____

Photo

Mares in Foal to Stallion

Name of mare	Date mare was bred	Date foaled	Vigor of foal at birth	Sex of foal	Disposal of foal				Remarks
					Sold to (name and address)	Date	Price	Reasons	

(See Table 5-b for reverse side of record form.)

TABLE B-5-B

INDIVIDUAL YEARLY STALLION BREEDING RECORD

Health Record

Date	Immunization		Other				Type of parasite treatment	Semen Test	Veterinary Treatment	Remarks
	Encephal-omyelitis	Tetanus								

(This is the reverse side of Table 5-a)

BREEZING.—A race term used to explain a speed in a workout where a horse is running at a controlled speed.

BRIDA, À LA.—A term used by the conquistadores, meaning to ride with long stirrups—the "forked-radish" seat. The conquistadores and other sixteenth-century caballeros prided themselves on being able to ride "in both seats"; the "forked-radish" seat for parade and other purposes, and the seat with short stirrups, invented by the Moors and useful for fighting, known as riding *à la gineta*.

BRIDLE(S).—Lightweight bridles and bits usually indicate competent horsemen and well-mannered horses. Bridles may be either single or double. A single bridle is equipped with one bit, whereas a double bridle is ordinarily equipped with both a snaffle bit and a curb bit, two headstalls, and two pairs of reins. Only one rein is used with Western bridles.

All bridles should be properly fitted, and the headstall should be located so that it neither slides back on the horse's neck nor pulls up against his ears. The cheek straps should be adjusted in length so the bit rests easily in the mouth without drawing up the corners. And the throatlatch should be buckled loosely enough to permit the hand, when held edgeways, to pass between it and the horse's throat.

The kind of bridle used will depend on the horse's training and intended use. Fig. B-66 shows the most common types of bridles.

BRIDLING.—Bridling is easy if the following procedure is followed:

Take the crownpiece of the bridle in the left hand and the reins in the right. Approach the horse from the left side opposite the shoulder. With your right hand slip the reins over his head, allowing them to rest on the crest directly behind the ears. Remove the halter—if there is one. Place yourself just behind the horse's head, facing front. Then, step by step, bridle him as follows (see Fig. B-67):

● *Step 1.*—Take the crownpiece of the bridle in your right hand and slip the horse's nose between the cheek pieces (and in the cavesson or noseband, if the bridle is so equipped). Raise the bridle with the right hand, until the crownpiece of headstall is just in front of the ears and the bit is dangling against the teeth. With your left hand, cup the horse's chin firmly, holding the bar of the bit across the palm and keeping it against the teeth with your thumb.

● *Step 2.*—Slip the ends of your fingers between the horse's lips on the far side and into the animal's mouth. Thereupon, he will open his mouth and curl back his lips.

● *Step 3.*—With a quick pull on the crownpiece, bring the bridle into position; that is, the bit in his mouth and the crownpiece slipped over his ears.

● *Step 4.*—Buckle the throatlatch.

From these steps and the accompanying figure the novice should not get the impression that in bridling a horse each step is so distinct and different as to be marked by intermittent pauses. Rather, when properly executed, bridling is a series of rhythmic movements, and the entire operation is done so smoothly and gracefully that it is difficult to discern where one stage ends and the next one begins.

BRIDLES

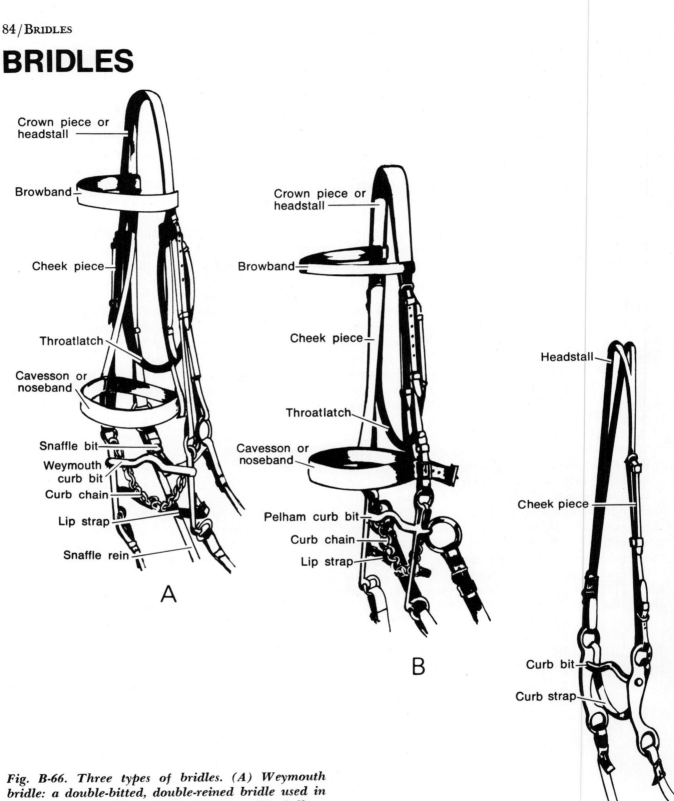

Crown piece or headstall

Browband

Cheek piece

Throatlatch

Cavesson or noseband

Snaffle bit

Weymouth curb bit

Curb chain

Lip strap

Snaffle rein

A

Crown piece or headstall

Browband

Cheek piece

Throatlatch

Cavesson or noseband

Pelham curb bit

Curb chain

Lip strap

B

Headstall

Cheek piece

Curb bit

Curb strap

C

Fig. B-66. Three types of bridles. (A) Weymouth bridle: a double-bitted, double-reined bridle used in showing three- and five-gaited horses; (B) Pelham bridle: a single-bitted, double-reined bridle used on hunters, polo ponies, and pleasure horses; (C) one ear, or split ear, bridle: a bridle often used on working stock horses.

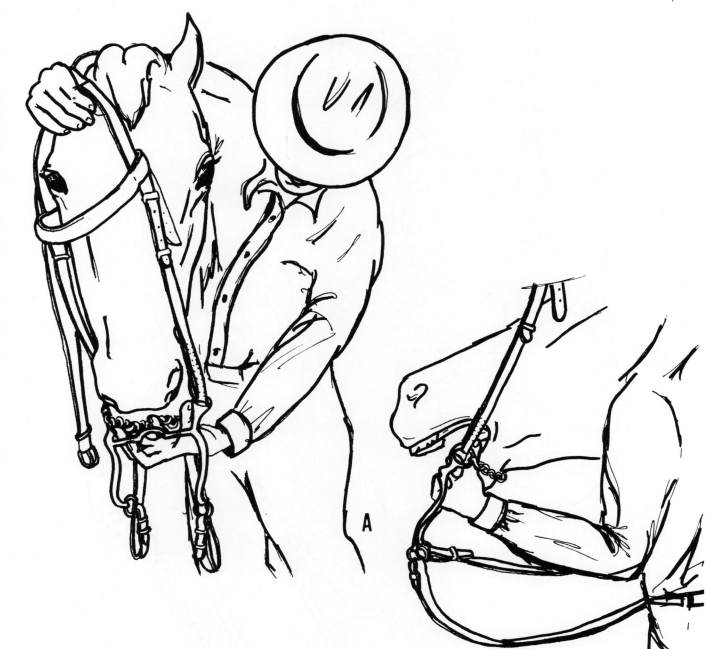

Fig. B-67. Steps in bridling a horse:

A. Step 1.—*Bridle in position—with the nose between the cheek pieces, the crownpiece in front of the ears, and the bit dangling against the teeth.*

B. Step 2.—*Mouth open.*

C. Step 3.—*Bridle on, with bit in mouth and crownpiece over ears.*

D. Step 4.—*Throatlatch buckled.*

BRIDOON.—The British term for a snaffle bit. A bridoon usually refers to a snaffle bit with large rings and a mouthpiece that is somewhat larger than normal snaffles. Such a bit is ideal for the rider who hangs on to the bit or maintains his balance by pulling on the reins.

BRISKET.—That part of the horse's body between the forelegs.

BRITTLE HOOFS.—Hoofs that are abnormally dry and fragile.

BROKE.—1. Tamed and trained to a particular function, as halter-broke.
2. Also, to leave or alter gait; e.g., the trotter broke stride.

BROKEN AMBLE.—The term for one of the "slow" gaits in which there are four irregularly cadenced beats.

BROKEN CREST.—A heavy neck which breaks over and falls to one side.

BROKEN-KNEES.—Knees with scars on them, indicating that the horse has fallen. Often scars are an indication that the horse is awkward and inclined to stumble. So beware when buying a knee-scarred horse.

BROKEN WIND.—See WINDY.

BRONCO (BRONCHO, BRONC).—An unbroken or imperfectly broken range horse of western United States. Sometimes the term is used to refer to a vicious or unbreakable horse, or to a horse that is trained to buck.

BROODMARE.—A mare kept for breeding or reproductive purposes.
(Also see MARE.)

BROOM POLO.—A game, suitable for intermediate riders, which is similar to indoor polo. However, a soft ball, such as a basketball, is used, and brooms take the place of mallets. Little danger is involved, and no head gear is necessary.

Fig. B-68. Broom polo. (Courtesy, Byron H. Good, Michigan State College)

BROOMTAIL.—A wild and untrained western range horse of inferior quality.

BROTHERS (OR SISTERS).—A male horse related to another horse having the same parents or one parent in common.

FULL BROTHERS.—By the same sire and out of the same dam.

HALF BROTHERS.—Out of the same dam, by different sires. This is one of the most frequently misused terms. Horses by the same sire and out of different dams are referred to as "by the same sire", or else the name of the sire is used, as "by Man O' War." This distinction is for a definite purpose, for only a few horses can be half brothers (or half sisters) to a famous horse, but hundreds can be by the same sire. This restricted definition tends to give a little of the credit to good broodmares instead of leaving the meaning ambiguous.

BROTHERS IN BLOOD.—By the same sire out of full sisters; or by full brothers out of the same dam, or any combination of exactly the same blood.

THREE-QUARTER BROTHERS.—For example, horses having the same dam and whose sires have identical sires but different dams.

SEVEN-EIGHTS BROTHERS.—The progeny of a horse and his son produced by the same mare, or similar combinations of lineage.

BROUGHAM.—The most popular closed carriage of its day. This vehicle was first built about 1839 by Lord Brougham, of England, after whom it was named. The original Brougham was built to be drawn by one horse and to carry two people. Later they were made to be pulled by two horses and seat four people.

Fig. B-69. The Brougham. This vehicle was enclosed and suitable for winter use.

BROWN.—See COLORS AND MARKINGS OF HORSES.

BRUCE LOWE SYSTEM.—This system, which was originated at the beginning of the twentieth century by an Australian from whom it takes its name, is a means of tracing descent through the mares listed in the *GENERAL STUD BOOK.* Thirty families have been evaluated. These "taproot mares" were allotted values according to the

number of times their descendents had won classic races. All of these families trace their origin to one of the three foundation Thoroughbred sires—the Byerly Turk (foaled 1679), the Darley Arabian (foaled 1700), and the Godolphin Arabian (foaled 1724).

BRUISES AND SWELLINGS.—See FIRST AID FOR HORSES.

BRUSH.—To force a horse to top speed over a short distance.

BRUSHES *(for grooming).*—See GROOMING EQUIPMENT—How To Groom.

BRUSH-FENCE.—An obstacle, either natural or artificial, composed of brushwood, or of some other suitable hedging plant.

BRUSHING.—Striking the fetlock with the other hoof. It may be caused by faulty conformation, poor shoeing, or fatigue. Sometimes it can be corrected by shoeing.

BUCEPHALUS.—The horse of Alexander The Great. Bucephalus was his mount through the Asian campaigns. The horse died in India in 326 B.C. and was buried by the Jhelum River.

BUCKAROO (BUCKEROO).—A Western term referring to a hard-riding cowboy who usually spends most of his time breaking broncs. Sometimes, the term is applied to rodeo riders, also.

BUCKED SHINS.—Bucked shins refers to a temporary racing unsoundness. For the most part, it is peculiar to two-year-olds, although occasionally a three-year-old that did little campaigning at two will fall victim to the condition. It usually strikes early in the final stages of preparation to race or early in the racing career. It is a very painful inflammation of the periosteum (bone covering) along the greater part of the front surface of the cannon bone, caused by constant pressure from concussion during fast works or races. Afflicted horses become very lame and are very sensitive when the slightest pressure is applied about the shins; many horses will almost lie down to keep a person from touching the sore area.

Fig. B-70. Bucked shins on an Arabian. Treatment varies, but rest and cooling out are always required. (Reproduced with permission of Haileybury Farm and Tampa Tracings, 1971: Courtesy, The Wickes, Newville, Pa.)

When a horse begins to develop bucked shins, most experienced trainers feel that it is wise to continue rather vigorous exercise until the acute form is produced; following which the routine treatment consists in cooling the shins out with antiphlogistic treatment (and time) and applying a good blister. When a pronounced case of shin-buck is treated in this manner, the condition will not likely return. However, if exercise is discontinued at the first indication that the horse is about to "buck" and treatment is given, he will often develop the condition again about the time he is ready to start racing. It is not uncommon for a two-year-old to buck two or three times before he can race successfully.

BUCKING.—See VICES—Bucking.

BUCKING HORSE.—A rodeo term for a horse that bucks violently, with or without the stimuli of bucking straps, hot shots, etc. Rodeo contractors are willing to pay a good price for a bucking horse that will buck for repeated performances, and year after year. Most horses can be made to buck by use of the bucking straps or hot shots, but only a few will buck hard enough to put on a good show; and most horses will quit bucking and start running if spurred too hard.

BUCKING STRAP.—This is a leather strap which is applied around the flanks of the horse to pinch and irritate him in order to make him buck in a rodeo.

BUCK-KNEED (KNEE-SPRUNG; OVER AT THE KNEES).—Standing with the knees too far forward.

BUCKSKIN, AMERICAN.—See BREED (S).

BUDGET.—A budget is a projection of records and accounts and a plan for organizing and operating ahead for a specific period of time. A short-time budget is usually for one year, whereas a long-time budget is for a period of years. The principal value of a budget is that it provides a working plan through which the operation can be coordinated. Changes in prices, droughts, and other factors make adjustments necessary. But these adjustments are more simply and wisely made if there is a written budget to use as a reference.

HOW TO SET UP A BUDGET—.It's unimportant whether a printed form (of which there are many good ones) is used or one made up on an ordinary ruled 8½" x 11" sheet placed sidewise. The important things are that (1) a budget is kept, (2) it be on a monthly basis, and (3) the operator be "comfortable" with whatever form or system is to be used.

An important part of any budget, or any system of accounting, is that there shall be a listing, or chart, of classifications or categories under which the owner wants the transactions accumulated. In a horse operation that both breeds and races, there may be 150 or more such classifications. From the standpoint of facilitating record keeping, each classification is usually given a number for identification purposes. Then the farm bookkeeper, or the farm manager, codes or classifies each transaction into the proper category.

No budget is perfect. But it should be as good an estimate as can be made—despite the fact that it will be affected by such things as droughts, diseases, markets, and many other unpredictables.

A simple, easily kept, and adequate budget can be evolved by using forms such as those shown in Tables B-6, B-7, and B-8.

The Annual Cash Expense Budget (see Table B-6) should show the monthly breakdown of various recurring items—everything except the initial loan and capital improvements. It includes labor, feed, supplies, fertilizer, taxes, interest, utilities, etc.

The Annual Cash Income Budget (see Table B-7) is just what the name implies—an estimated cash income by months.

The Annual Cash Expense and Income Budget (see Table B-8) is a cash flow chart obtained from the first two forms. It's a money "flow" summary by months. From this, it can be ascertained when money will need to be borrowed, how much will be needed, and the length of the loan along with a repayment schedule. It makes it possible to avoid tying up capital unnecessarily, and to avoid unnecessary interest.

TABLE B-6

ANNUAL CASH EXPENSE BUDGET

_____ For _____
(name of farm)   (date)

Item	Total	Jan.	Feb.	Mar.	Apr.	May	June	July	Aug.	Sept.	Oct.	Nov.	Dec.
Labor hired													
Feed purchased													
Stud fees													
Gas, fuel, grease													
Taxes													
Insurance													
Interest													
Utilities													
etc.													
Total													

TABLE B-7

ANNUAL CASH INCOME BUDGET

For _____

		(name of farm)										(date)	

Item	Total	Jan.	Feb.	Mar.	Apr.	May	June	July	Aug.	Sept.	Oct.	Nov.	Dec.
30 yearlings													
30 stud fees, @ $500 each													
490 bu. wheat													
etc.													
Total													

TABLE B-8

ANNUAL CASH EXPENSE AND INCOME BUDGET (CASH FLOW CHART)

For _____

		(name of farm)										(date)	

Item	Total	Jan.	Feb.	Mar.	Apr.	May	June	July	Aug.	Sept.	Oct.	Nov.	Dec.
Gross income	25,670					1,000	1,000	etc.					
Gross expense	13,910					575	2,405	etc.					
Difference	11,760					425	1,405	etc.					
Surplus (+) or Deficit (−)	+					+	−						

BUG BOY.—An apprentice jockey. In an entry column, asterisks by the names of jockeys indicate that the jockey is an apprentice.

BUGGY.—A light one-horse carriage. In the U.S., it is made with four wheels; in England, it is made with two wheels.

BUILDING DEPRECIATION.—See DEPRECIATION ON HORSE BUILDINGS; and TAXES, INCOME.

BUILDINGS.—Properly designed, constructed, and arranged horse buildings give increased animal comfort and performance, greater efficiency in the use of feed, and less expenditure of labor in the care of horses. Also, attractive barns add to the beauty of the landscape. In serving these purposes, barns need not be elaborate or expensive.

The primary reasons for having horse buildings are (1) to provide a place in which to confine horses and store feed and tack and (2) to modify the environment by controlling temperature, humidity, and other factors.

Fig. B-71. A practical and attractive open shed at Bitterroot Stock Form (home of Hungarian Horses), Hamilton, Montana, owned by Margit Sigray Bessenyey. (Photo by Ernst Peterson, Hamilton, Mont.)

(Also see BARNS; ENVIRONMENTAL CONTROL; and EQUIPMENT, FEED, AND WATER.)

SPACE REQUIREMENTS.—One of the first, and frequently one of the most difficult, problems confronting the horseman who wishes to construct a building is that of arriving at the proper size or dimensions.

● *Space requirements for horse barns.*—Some conservative average figures of barn space requirements of horses are presented in Table B-9.

● *Space requirements for service passages.*—These are given in Table B-10.

● *Space requirements for feed and bedding.*—Table B-11 gives the storage space requirements for feed and bedding. This information may be helpful to the individual operator who desires to compute the barn space required for a specific horse enterprise. Also, this table provides a convenient means of estimating the amount of feed or bedding in storage.

BULLDOGGING (STEER WRESTLING).—This refers to throwing a steer by seizing the horns and twisting the neck. In rodeo competi-

tion, the cowboy leaps off his horse, grasps the steer by the horns and endeavors to throw him in the shortest possible time by twisting his head to one side.

BULLFINCH.—A high thick fence which cannot be jumped over except through some holes that may be in it. Such fences are rather common in England, and are occasionally seen in hunter trials in America.

BULL PEN.—Auction ring.

BULL RIDING *(a rodeo event)*.—This is the most dangerous of the rodeo riding events. The cowboy must secure himself to the bull's back by using a loose rope wrapped around the animal's middle and held in place with one hand. The contestant must stay on the bull for 8 to 10 seconds, depending on the event, in order to qualify.

BUN-EATING CONTEST.—A game played by mounted horsemen. The requirements are: a starting line; at the opposite end of the course, a rope or wire from which rolls or buns are suspended on strings; and a group of eager contestants. Experienced riders may play the game standing in the saddle; beginners sit in the saddle. Contestants must eat the buns without touching them with their hands.

BURNS (SCALDS).—Burns on a horse should be treated much like they are on humans. If they are minor, an ointment will usually suffice. If they are severe, professional help should be sought.
(Also see ROPE BURNS.)

BURRO.—A donkey.
(Also see DONKEYS.)

BUSINESS ASPECTS OF HORSE PRODUCTION.—In the present era, many horse enterprises are owned and operated as businesses, with a profit motive—just as other stockmen have

Kinds, Uses, and Purposes	Recommended Plan	Box Stalls or Shed Areas				Tie Stalls (size)
		Size	Height of Ceiling	Height of Doors	Width of Doors	
Smaller Horse Establishments: Horse barns for pleasure horses, ponies, and/or raising a few foals.	12′ x 12′ stalls in a row; combination tack-feed room for 1- and 2-stall units; separate tack and feed rooms for 3-stall units or more. Generally, not more than a month's supply of feed is stored at a time. Use of all-pelleted rations (hay and grain combined) lessens feed storage space requirements.	Horses: 12′ x 12′ Ponies:1 10′ x 10′	8′–9′	8′	4′	5′ wide; 10′–12′ long
Larger Horse Breeding Establishments: The following specially designed buildings may be provided for different purposes:						
Broodmare and Foaling Barn	A rectangular building, either (1) with a central aisle, and a row of stalls along each side, or (2) of the "island" type, with two rows of stalls, back to back, surrounded by an alley or runway. Ample quarters for storage of hay, bedding, and grain. A record or office room, toilet facilities, hot water supply, veterinarian supply room, and tack room are usually an integral part of a broodmare barn.	12′ x 12′ to 16′ x 16′	9′	8′	4′	
Stallion Barn	Quarters for one or more stallions, with or without feed storage. A small tack and equipment room. Stallion paddocks, at least 300 ft. on a side, adjacent to or in close proximity.	14′ x 14′	9′	8′	4′	
Barren Mare Barn	An open shed or rectangular building, with a combination rack and trough down the center or along the wall. Storage space for ample hay, grain, and bedding.	150 sq. ft. per animal	9′	8′	4′	
Weanling or Yearling Quarters	Open shed or stalls. The same type of building is adapted to both weanlings and yearlings; but different ages and sex groups should be kept separate. When stalls are used, two weanlings or two yearlings may be placed together.	10′ x 10′	9′	8′	4′	
Breeding Shed	A large roofed enclosure with a high ceiling; should include laboratory for the veterinarian, hot water facilities, and stalls for preparing mares for breeding and holding foals.	24′ x 24′	15′–20′	8′	9′	
Isolation (quarantine) Quarters	Small barn, with feed and water facilities and adjacent paddock; for occupancy by new or sick animals.	12″ x 12′	9′	8′	4′	

(Continued)

1 Even for ponies, a 12′ x 12′ stall is recommended since (1) it costs little more than a 10′ x 10′, and (2) it affords more flexibility—it can be used for bigger horses when and if the occasion demands.

TABLE B-9 (CONTINUED)

SPACE REQUIREMENTS FOR HORSE BARNS; KINDS AND PLANS

For Riding Academies and Training and Boarding Stables	Either (1) stalls constructed back to back in the center of the barn, with an indoor ring around the outside; (2) stalls around the outside and a ring in the center; or (3) stalls on either side of a hallway or alleyway, and an outdoor ring.	12' x 12'	9'	8'	4'	5' wide; 10'–12' long

TABLE B-10

RECOMMENDED MINIMUM WIDTHS FOR SERVICE PASSAGES

Kind of Passage	Use	Minimum Width
Feed alley	For feed cart	4'
Driveway	For wagon, spreader, or truck	9'–12'
Doors and gate	Drive-through	8'– 9'

TABLE B-11

STORAGE SPACE REQUIREMENTS FOR FEED AND BEDDING

Kind of Feed or Bedding	Pounds per Cubic Feet (approx.)	Cubic Feet per Ton (approx.)	Pounds per Bushel of Grain	Cubic Feet per Bushel
Hay—				
Timothy, loose	3	625–640		
Wild hay, loose	3–4	450–600		
Alfalfa, loose	4	470–485		
Clover, loose	4	500–512		
Chopped hay	10	210–225		
Baled hay (closely stacked) . .	10	150–200		
Straw and Shavings—				
Straw, baled	10	200		
Straw, loose	2–3	600–1,000		
Shavings, baled	20	100		
Silage—				
Corn or sorghum silage in tower silos	40	50		
Corn or sorghum silage in trench silos	35	57		
Mill Feed—				
Bran	13	154		
Middlings	25	80		
Linseed or soybean meal . . .	35	57		
Grain—				
Corn, shelled	45	45	56	1.25
Corn, ear	28	72	70	2.50
Corn, snapped	25	81	80	3.25
Oats	26	77	32	1.25
Barley	39	51	48	1.25
Wheat	48	42	60	1.25
Rye	45	44	56	1.25
Grain sorghum	45	44	56	1.25

cattle, sheep, or swine enterprises. These horsemen must treat their operations as businesses and become more sophisticated; otherwise, they won't be in business very long. Other horsemen keep horses as a hobby—for much the same reason that some folks play golf, hunt, fish, or go boating. When kept for the latter purpose, their cost should be looked upon much like that of any other hobby or an evening's entertainment; that is, decide in advance how much they can afford to spend, then stop when that amount has been spent.

(Also see INCENTIVE BASIS FOR THE HELP; TAXES, INCOME.)

BUTTOCKS, POINT OF.—See PARTS OF A HORSE—Fig. P-4.

BUYING A HORSE.—In addition to desirable qualities in conformation and action, there should be style and beauty, balance and symmetry, an abundance of quality, an energetic yet manageable disposition, freedom from vices, good wind, suitable age, freedom from disease, and proper condition. The buyer should also be on the alert for possible misrepresentations.

The amateur should enlist the help of a competent horseman when buying a horse.

(Also see SELECTING AND JUDGING HORSES.)

B VITAMINS.—The addition of the B vitamins to the ration of horses is in the nature of good insurance, especially for horses that are under stress as in racing and showing. It is known that the horse needs some of the B vitamins. However, it is less clear as to which ones are needed, in what quantities they are needed, and their status from the standpoints of synthesis and absorption in the horse. Thiamine, riboflavin, niacin, pantothenic acid, and B_{12} must be considered.

(Also see VITAMINS.)

BYE DAY.—A hunting term meaning an unscheduled hunt.

BYERLY TURK.—The Byerly Turk was imported into England in 1689 by Captain Byerly. He became one of the three foundation sires of the Thoroughbred breed. The Herod line traces to him.

C

CABALLERO.—The Spanish word for horseman.

CABALLO.—The Spanish word for horse.

CADENCE.—The beat, time, measure, or sequence of a horse's gait.

CALCIUM—.See MINERALS.

CALF-KNEED.—Standing with knees too far back, directly opposite to buck-kneed or knee-sprung, is called calf-kneed.

(Also see UNSOUNDNESSES.)

CALF ROPING (a rodeo event).—Calf roping is the time-honored job of the ranch horse. The horse must measure the speed of the calf being roped and time his approach with maximum exactness to give the rider the best opportunity possible to throw his loop to greatest advantage. Also, the horse must keep a tight rope on the calf as the rider dismounts to tie the animal; and he must continue to hold a tight rope until the tie-down is completed.

In the rodeo, calf roping is done as follows: The calf is roped by a mounted contestant; the horse comes to a sliding stop when the rider lays an arm on his neck in preparation for leaving the saddle; the rider runs to the calf to hog-tie its legs; and the horse, facing the calf, keeps the rope on the calf taut until its legs are hog-tied. A calf roping horse must be trained to come to a sliding stop quickly and to keep the rope taut while facing the calf. He must hold this position until the rider returns and mounts him.

Fig. C-1. Calf roping. (Courtesy, Palomino Horse Breeders of America)

CALGARY STAMPEDE.—One of North America's largest rodeos. It is an annual event held each July, in Calgary (Alberta, Canada), featuring a rodeo, horse racing, fireworks, and other types of entertainment.

CALICO-PINTO.—A multicolored or spotted pony.

CALK.—Grips on the heels and the outside of the front shoes of horses, designed to give the horse better footing and prevent slipping.

CALKING.—Injury to the coronary band by the shoe of the horse. Usually incurred by horses whose shoes have calks, or by horses that are "rough-shod," as for ice.

CALORIE.—Two methods of measuring energy are commonly employed in the United States: (1) the newer calorie system, and (2) the older total digestible nutrient (TDN) system. Terms common to these two systems follow:

1 calorie (c) = the heat required to raise the temperature of one gram of water one degree centigrade.

    1 kilocalorie (kc) = 1000 calories.

    1 megacalorie or therm (mcal) = 1000 kcal.

    1 lb. TDN = 2000 kcal or 2 megacalories.

To determine the caloric value of feed (or other substance), an instrument known as the bomb calorimeter is used in which the feed (or other substance) tested is placed and burned with the aid of oxygen (see Fig. C-2).

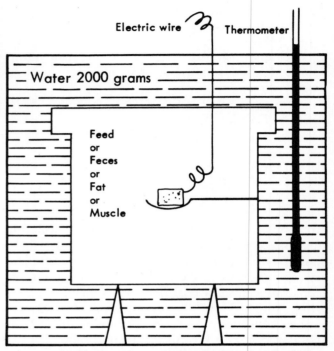

Fig. C-2. Diagrammatic sketch of a bomb calorimeter used for the determination of the gross energy value (caloric content) of various materials, including horse feed.

Briefly stated, the procedure is as follows: An electric wire is attached to the material being tested, so that it can be ignited by remote control; 2,000 grams of water are poured around the bomb; 25 to 30 atmospheres of oxygen are added to the bomb; the material is ignited; the heat given off from the burned material warms the water; and a thermometer registers the change in temperature of the water. For example, if one gram of material is burned and the temperature of the water is raised one degree centigrade, 2,000 cal. are given off. Hence, the material contains 2,000 cal./gram.

CAMP OUT (CAMP).—A horse is said to camp out when the forelegs stretch out to the front while the back legs hold in position. This stance was first used on horses in ladies' harness classes. The reason: While camping out, a horse cannot move forward until he first collects himself. Later, this stance was adopted by horse show people, both for driving and saddle horses.

(Also see POSING.)

CANADIAN CUTTING HORSE ASSOCIATION.—10123 112th St., Edmonton, Alberta, Canada.

CANADIAN MOUNTED POLICE, THE ROYAL.—See POLICE HORSE.

CANNON.—See PARTS OF A HORSE—Fig. P-4.

CANTER.—A slow, restrained, three-beat gait. Two diagonal legs are paired and produce a single beat that falls between the successive beats of the two unpaired legs. The canter imposes a special wear on the leading forefoot and its diagonal hindfoot. It is important, therefore, to change the lead frequently.

Fig. C-3. The canter.

CANTLE.—See SADDLES—Figs. S-2 and S-3.

CAPITAL.—Horsemen who are in business to make a profit should never invest money, either their own or borrowed, unless they are reasonably certain that it will make money. Capital will be needed for land, buildings, machinery and equipment, horses, feed, supplies, labor, and miscellaneous items.

Whether establishing or enlarging a horse enterprise, the most common question, a two-pronged one, is—how much money will it take, and how much will it make? This information is needed by both horsemen and lenders. Unfortunately, a simple answer cannot be given.

CAPITAL GAIN.—See TAXES, INCOME.

CAPPED ELBOW.—An enlargement of the elbow, usually caused by contact with the shoe when the horse is lying down. The best way to prevent capped elbow is to use shoes with short heels. Except in the early inflammatory stages, treatment is ineffective.

(Also see UNSOUNDNESSES.)

CAPPED HOCK.—Capped hock is an enlargement at the point of the hock; it is usually caused by bruising. Daily painting of the enlargement with tincture of iodine may help to diminish it. Though it may be unsightly, capped hock need not be considered serious unless it interferes with the work of the horse. Successful reduction of the swelling depends on prompt and persistent treatment, with antiphlogistic applications, before the fluid has a chance to form the fibrinous tissue in the sheath or bursa. Once the "cap" has set or become fibrinous, all that can be done is to remove any inflammation present, and then, by a series of blisters, attempt to cause resorption (reduction in size).

(Also see UNSOUNDNESSES.)

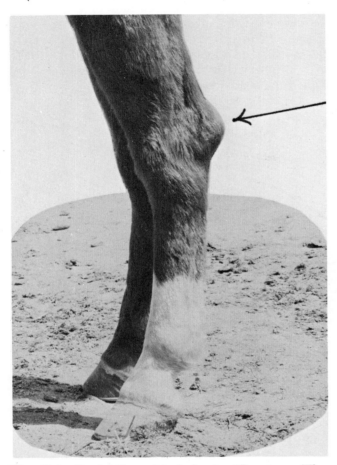

Fig. C-4. Unsightly capped hock. (Courtesy, **The Western Horseman.**)

CAPPING FEE.—The fee contributed by a non-member of a hunt when he rides to hounds at the invitation of a member. In the old days, it was customary for the hunt secretary, after the field had collected, to go among them with his cap held out for donations from nonmembers; hence, the origin of the name.

CAPRIOLE.—An intricate movement performed by the Lipizzan horses in the Spanish Riding School in Vienna. It is considered the ultimate of all high-school and classical training. The horse leaps into the air, and, while in the air,

kicks out with the hind feet. The Capriole also, like so many other forms of high-school work, belongs to the Medieval methods of combat, in which, by means of such jumps by the horse, the surrounded rider could rid himself of adversaries. By kicking out with the hind legs, the horse prevented the enemy from getting within striking distance with sword and lance. (See Fig. C-5.)

CARBOHYDRATES—.The carbohydrates are organic compounds composed of carbon, hydrogen, and oxygen. This group includes the sugars, starch, cellulose, gums, and related substances. They are formed in the plant by photosynthesis as follows:

$$6CO_2 + 6H_2O + \text{energy from sun} =$$
$$C_6H_{12}O_6 \text{ (glucose)} + 6O_2$$

On the average, the carbohydrates comprise about three-fourths of all the dry matter in plants—the chief source of horse feed. They form the woody framework of plants as well as the chief reserve food stored in seeds, roots, and tubers. When consumed by horses, carbohydrates are used as a source of heat and energy, and any excess of them is stored in the body as fat, or, in part, secreted.

CARCASS DISPOSAL.—In the disposal of carcasses, it is a safe rule to assume that all are a source of some infection, then subsequently to adopt the proper sanitary precautions.

The most sanitary method of destroying a carcass is to burn it, preferably at the site of death in order to prevent the contamination of surrounding ground. A trench of sufficient size should be prepared, a fire built, and the animal placed on top so that it will be consumed in its entirety.

The most common method of horse carcass disposal is by burial. So that this method will be effective, the carcass should be buried deep and covered with quicklime. The top of the carcass should be at least 4 feet below the surface of the ground and in soil from which there is no danger of contamination by drainage. Burial should not be near a flowing stream, for this will only serve to spread the disease downstream.

Near large centers of population, rendering

Fig. C-5. Lipizzan stallion doing the Capriole without the rider. (Courtesy, Spanish Riding School, Wels, Austria.)

plants will take carcasses, and they afford the easiest method of disposal.

When an animal dies, it is recommended that a veterinarian be called immediately to perform a post-mortem examination. This is done in an attempt to determine the cause of death and study the abnormal conditions present. It is never safe for one who is uninformed about specific disease lesions to open an animal carcass. Such practice may not only serve to spread a very highly contagious disease but may also expose the operator to a dangerous infection.

CAREERS WITH HORSES.—The author receives numerous letters from boys and girls asking about training and job placement in horse work. Here is what he tells them:

The first and most important requisite for a successful career in the equine field is that the person must possess a great love for horses. This appears to be an inborn trait, for some people never acquire a natural ability to work with horses—no matter how long or how hard they try. When such love for horses exists, the animals are more docile and easier to handle, for the caretaker's feelings are relayed to his charges. Also, a great love for horses appears to be essential if the caretaker is to feed them regularly and cheerfully, with enjoyment and without regard to long hours and Sundays or holidays; if he is to provide clean, dry bedding, despite the fact that a driving storm may make it necessary to repeat the same operation the next day; if he is to serve as nursemaid to a newborn foal or a sick horse, though it may mean loss of sleep and working with cold, numb fingers; and if he is to remain calm and collected, though striking an animal or otherwise giving vent to his feelings might at first appear to be warranted.

Next to having a great love for horses, to be successful in the equine field it is important that the person have adequate knowledge, both scientific and practical. Also, owners and managers of large operations, must have skill in money management and knowledge of the business aspects. A college education is important. If they are good students, serious consideration should also be given to completing a veterinary or Ph.D. degree. Additionally, those who have not grown up with horses should learn the rudiments of the business by working two years on a good horse establishment. Most young folks entering the horse field aspire higher than being a groom and mucking out stalls. Nevertheless, this is a good place to start.

Finally, industry and good judgment are very necessary requisites for success in the horse business. These words carry the same connotation in all industries and are self-explanatory.

When it comes to hiring girls for horse work, some employers still think Victorian and side saddle. But if girls meet the requisites outlined above, they should be able to find, or to make, employment opportunities.

Among the professional opportunities in the multi-million dollar horse industry are the following:

● Owning, managing, or working on a horse breeding establishment.

● Training horses.

● Operating a boarding stable.

● Veterinarians in private practice, or with drug manufacturers, or with large horse establishment.

● In research, sales, and public relations with companies that manufacture and distribute feed, tack, and other products for the horse industry.

● As farriers (horseshoers).

● On the staffs of horse magazines and breed registry associations.

● In college teaching.

● As riding school instructors.

● With racing stables; and as racing officials and jockeys.

● With hunt clubs.

● With summer camps.

● Horse shows.

● Buying and selling horses.

● Rodeo riding.

● As secretaries, office managers, and executive assistants, to administrators and associations engaged in the horse field.

● Consultants.

CAROTENE.—Carotene is the yellow-colored, fat-soluble substance that gives the characteristic color to carrots and to butterfat (vitamin A is nearly a colorless substance). Carotene derives its name from the carrot, from which it was first isolated over 100 years ago. Although its empirical formula was established in 1906, it was not until 1919 that Steenbock discovered its vitamin A activity. Though the yellow color is masked by the green chlorophyll, the green parts of plants are rich in carotene and thus have a high vitamin A value. Also, the degree of greenness in a roughage is a good index of its carotene content, provided it has not been stored too long. Early-cut, leafy green hays are very high in carotene.

Aside from yellow corn, practically all of the cereal grains used in horse feeding have little carotene or vitamin A value. Even yellow corn has only about one-tenth as much carotene as well-cured hay. Dried peas of the green and yellow varieties as well as carrots are also valuable sources of carotene.

Studies by the New Jersey station indicate that the carotene content of alfalfa hay may be more available to the horse and more efficiently converted into vitamin A than the carotene of timothy hay.

CAROTENE CONVERSION.—Vitamin A is not synthesized in the cecum; thus, it must be provided in the feed, either (1) as vitamin A per se, or (2) as carotene, the precursor of vitamin A.

It is now known that cattle are only about 25 percent as efficient as rats in converting carotene to vitamin A. As a result, many beef cattle nutritionists are adding sufficient vitamin A per se to meet all the needs for this particular vitamin and completely disregarding the carotene present in the ration. It seems prudent that the same thinking apply in formulating horse rations.

The International Standards for vitamin A activity based on vitamin A and beta-carotene are as follows: One International Unit (I.U.) of vitamin A = one U.S.P. unit = vitamin A activity of 0.300 mcg of crystalline vitamin A alcohol, corresponding to 0.344 mcg of vitamin A acetate or 0.550 mcg of vitamin A palmitate. Beta-carotene is the standard for pro-vitamin A. One International Unit of vitamin A activity is equivalent to 0.6 mcg of beta-carotene or 1 mg of beta-carotene = 1667 I.U. of vitamin A. International Standards for vitamin A are based on the utilization by the rat of vitamin A and/or beta-carotene.

The vitamin A equivalent for carotene was calculated by assuming that 0.6 mcg of beta-carotene = one I.U. of vitamin A.

Because the various species do not convert carotene to vitamin A in the same ratio as rats, it is suggested that the conversion rate given in Table C-1 be used.

Individual feed samples may vary widely in carotene content from indicated averages because of such influencing factors as crop, variety, harvesting and storage conditions, and climate and soil pertinent to the locality where the feed was produced. Therefore, book values of carotene should be used with judgment, often in conjunction with more specific information on hand about the feed.

TABLE C-1

CONVERSION OF BETA-CAROTENE TO VITAMIN A FOR DIFFERENT SPECIES [1]

Species	Conversion mg beta-carotene to I.U. Vitamin A		I.U. Vitamin A Activity (calculated from carotene)
	(mg)	(I.U.)	(%)
Standard	1 =	1,667	100
Horses			
Growth	1 =	555	33.3
Pregnancy	1 =	333	20.0
Sheep	1 =	400–500	24.0–30.0
Swine	1 =	500	30.0
Beef cattle	1 =	400	24.0
Dairy cattle	1 =	400	24.0
Poultry	1 =	1,667	100.
Rat	1 =	1,667	100.
Man	1 =	556	33.0

[1] W. M. Beeson, "Relative Potencies of Vitamin A and Carotene for Animals," *Federation Proc.* 24 (1965) : 924–926.

CAROUSEL.—A riding exhibition performed to music in dance-like patterns by a group on horseback. The performance is designed to resemble old-fashioned formal dances such as the Quadrille or the Lancers. Such rides are frequently done in fancy dress and make a most attractive spectacle.

CARRIAGES.—Man made much use of saddle and packhorses before the carriage came into general use. Also, primitive sliding vehicles preceded the use of wheels. The coming of the wheel made as big an impact on civilization as did the internal combustion engine years later. The Egyptians are believed to have been the original makers of wheels; the first vehicles were probably the wagons and chariots referred to in the Old Testament.

The earliest carriage, still in perfect condition, to be found today is the State Chariot of Tutankhamen (1361–1352 B.C.) in the Cairo Museum, Egypt. The first known carriage to be built in Great Britain was made by William Rippon for the second Earl of Rutland in 1555.

The golden age of the carriage arrived in the eighteenth century. Many different styles of vehicles were built. The high phaeton was a popular vehicle of the period. Later, it was succeeded by the pony phaeton—a long, low vehicle.

The names of different types of carriages often came from the name of the builder or the place in which they were made. Although carriages were built throughout the world, it was generally accepted that French and British carriage builders were the masters of their craft.

(Also see VEHICLES, HORSE-DRAWN.)

CARROTS AND OTHER ROOTS.—Carrots are relished by horses. Additionally, they're succulent, and high in carotene and minerals. Carotene, known as the precursor of vitamin A because the animal body can convert it into the vitamin, derives its name from the carrot from which it was first isolated over 100 years ago. Carotene is the yellow-colored substance that imparts the characteristic yellow color to carrots. Each pound of fresh carrots contains 48 milligrams of carotene, which can be converted into 26,640 I.U. of vitamin A by the young equine. This is sufficient vitamin A to furnish half the daily allowance of a 1,000-pound horse. By contrast, 1 pound of timothy hay (mature) provides only 2.1 milligrams of carotene, or 1,165 I.U., which is only $\frac{1}{43}$rd of the daily vitamin A requirement for a 1,000-pound horse. Also, carrots are a good source of minerals; on a dry basis one pound contains 0.42% calcium and 0.34% phosphorus, whereas mature timothy hay as fed contains 0.17% and 0.15% of these elements, respectively. Additionally, carrots are high in sugar; on a dry basis they contain 40% sugar (invert), which explains their sweetness.

Horsemen have long fed carrots, especially during the winter months when green feeds are not available, and to horses that are stabled much of the time. They report that one to two pounds of carrots per horse per day will stimulate the appetite, increase growth, assist in reproduction, make for normal vision, and improve the health, coat, and attractiveness of the animal.

Carrots should be cleaned, sliced from end to end in small strips, so as to avoid choking; then mixed with the grain.

Other roots such as parsnips, rutabagas, turnips, potatoes, and sugar beets may be fed to horses in small amounts, provided they are first cut finely enough to avoid choking.

(Also see TREATS—For Horses.)

CART.—Any two-wheeled vehicle which may be drawn by a horse or pony.

(Also see VEHICLES, HORSE DRAWN.)

CART, TRAINING.—See VEHICLES, HORSE-DRAWN.

CAST.—A horse that has fallen or lain down close to a wall or fence so that it cannot get up without assistance.

CASTRATION.—The operation in which the testes (or ovaries) are removed is called castration.

(Also see FOAL.)

CATARACT.—An opacity of the lens of the eye. The lens becomes gray and opaque and does not allow the light to pass through. Fortunately, cataract is rare in horses, although it can occasionally be congenital and can affect one or both eyes. There is no effective treatment for the condition.

CATCHWEIGHT.—In a "catchweight" race, no horse is required to carry a specific weight. Instead, each horse may carry what his trainer chooses.

CAT-HAMMED.—Said of a horse having long, relatively thin thighs and legs.

CAVALLETTI.—This refers to a series of timber jumps that are adjustable in height and spacing for schooling horses. The popularization of the Cavalletti is attributed to the great Italian horseman, Major Piero Santini, author of forward-seat riding, who died in 1912.

Often a series of differently spaced bars set at different heights are permanently placed in the schooling area and horses are trotted or cantered over them as part of their daily training. For work at the trot, the bars are usually from ½ to 1½ feet in height and centered 4 feet apart. For work at the canter, they may run from 1½ to 3½ feet high. If it is desired that the horse take them in succession without an intervening stride, they are set 8 feet apart. If a stride between bars is desired, they may be set at from 11 to 12 feet apart, depending on the length of stride of the horse being schooled. For two strides apart, a distance of 24 feet apart is usually used.

The heights of, and distances between, bars are not rigid for every young horse destined for the hunting field or show jumping. The Cavalletti may be used to lengthen or shorten stride; in connection with the standards to control habits of takeoff; or as an aid in correcting faults in spoiled, mature hunters and jumpers—rushing, running out, refusing, etc. Of course, no training device is better than the skill of the trainer.

Fig. C-6. Cavalletti. A series of jumps of adjustable, or different, height and spacing for schooling horses.

CAVALRY.—Army mounted on horseback.
(Also see WARFARE, HORSES IN.)

CAVESSON.—A cavesson is a nosepiece or noseband, which is often quite large. It may be either a breaking cavesson or a cavesson noseband.

A breaking, or longeing, cavesson is used in the training of the young horse and is a superior form of head collar, having a padded nosepiece onto which usually is set a metal plate fitted with three swiveling rings, to any one of which the longe rein may be fastened.

Today, most full bridles or double bridles are equipped with a cavesson or noseband, an inch or so in width, held in place by a narrow strap that goes over the horse's nose. In the show-ring, five-gaited and walking horse classes wear nosebands that are broad across the nose and of bright color or colors. On show horses whose mouths have been spoiled in training, the cavesson is worn very tight so as to keep the horse's mouth shut.
(Also see BRIDLES.)

CAVVY (*Cavayard*).—A herd of riding horses used by cowboys in their work.

CAYUSE.—1. An Indian pony.
2. Also, this term is applied to a native range horse.

CECUM SYNTHESIS.—In the case of ruminants (cattle and sheep), there is tremendous bacterial action in the paunch. These bacteria build body proteins of high quality from sources of inorganic nitrogen that nonruminants (humans, rats, chickens, swine, poultry, and dogs) cannot use. Farther on in the digestive tract, the ruminant digests the bacteria and obtains good proteins therefrom. Although the horse is not a ruminant, apparently the same bacterial process occurs to a limited extent in the cecum—that greatly enlarged blind pouch of the large intestine of the horse. However, it is much more limited than in ruminants, and the cecum is located beyond the small intestine, the main area for digestion and absorption of nutrients. This points up the fallacy of relying on cecum synthesis in the horse; above all, it must be remembered that little cecum synthesis exists in young equines.

In recognition of the more limited bacterial action in the horse, most state laws forbid the use of such nonprotein nitrogen sources as urea in horse rations. For such an animal, high-quality proteins in the diet are requisite to normal development.

The limited protein synthesis in the horse (limited when compared with ruminants), and the lack of efficiency of absorption due to the cecum's being on the lower end of the gut (thereby not giving the small intestine a chance at the ingesta after it leaves the cecum), clearly indicate that horse rations should contain high-quality proteins, adequate in amino acids.
(Also see DIGESTIVE SYSTEM.)

CENTAUR.—The centaurs were an ancient mythical Greek race of people dwelling in the mountains of Thessaly. They were imagined as men with the bodies of horses and half-bestial natures.

CERTIFICATION.—The act of certifying a hunter; i.e., a guarantee that he has hunted for a season with a registered pack and is eligible to compete in qualified hunter classes. A certificate to this effect, signed by the Master of a recognized hunt, may be demanded by the secretary of the show before a horse is accepted in qualified hunter classes.

CHALLENGE TROPHY.—A cup, or other similar article, donated with certain stipulations under which it is to be won. Usually, the original trophy remains the perpetual property of a show, club, or association, with the name of each successive winner engraved thereon, and with the winner each year given a duplicate trophy. Frequently, the rules specify that the trophy will become the permanent property of the winner after having been won a designated number of times (usually three) by the same contestant.

CHAMPING.—A term that describes the horse's playing with the bit. Its development is encouraged in bitting a young horse by using a bit with "keys" attached to the mouthpiece, which tends to make the saliva flow and keep the mouth moist—an aid in producing a "soft" mouth.

CHAMPION.—1. The show animal declared to be the best when two or more first place winners of preceding classes compete.
2. The mount of Gene Autry, Western singer and actor.
(Also see MOTION PICTURE HORSES.)

CHAMPIONSHIP CLASSES.—In addition to providing competition within classes, major horse shows also have championship classes, or competition between class winners. Since the rules governing championship classes may change slightly from year to year, the competitor is admonished to study the latest annual *Rule Book* of the American Horse Shows Association.

CHAMPIONSHIP, GRAND.—In the hunter-jumper division, Grand Championships may be awarded to:
1. *Place winners.*—The first place (blue ribbon) winners are eligible to compete. The Grand Championship is awarded by the judge(s) to the horse which in his opinion has shown the most consistent performance throughout the show and which has the best way of going and the best conformation, quality, and substance.
2. *Point winners.*—Grand Championship and Reserve Championship ribbons are awarded on the basis of points only.

CHAPS.—Leather leggins which resemble trousers without a seat. Often they are decorated by fringes and extensions. Chaps are worn over regular pants by western ranch hands as leg protection and for riding through brush.

CHARBON.—See ANTHRAX.

CHARGER.—A horse suitable for cavalry use. The officer's charger was usually a little larger than the regulation cavalry mount; he had to be capable of carrying weight, and he had to be handy, speedy, and able to change leads on a full gallop at every second stride in order to support the officer as he swung his saber from side to side.

CHARIOT.—Refers to two different kinds of vehicles. One type of chariot is a vehicle for conveying persons in state affairs, with only two seats inside. Another type of chariot is a two-wheeled vehicle, usually drawn by two horses, and used in ancient warfare, in processions, and in races.

CHECK.—Short for checkrein.

CHECKREIN (OVERCHECK).—A strap coupling the bit of a bridle to the harness back band to keep the head up and in position. There are two types of checkreins: (1) the overhead type, in which the strap runs between the ears; and (2) the side type, in which a strap on either side of the horse's head is run from the bit through the Dees or metal loops that hang from the crownpiece, back to the terret of the harness pad. The overhead checkrein is the most severe.
When properly adjusted, checkreins are not uncomfortable, and they prevent such vices as kicking, bolting, etc. Checkrein may be used with a bitting rig to teach the young horse to hold

his head properly. Also, checkreins may be used on a pony or horse when a child is learning to ride, to keep the mount from putting his head down to eat grass everytime he stops.

Checkreins that are too tight cause the horse great discomfort and may engender bad habits.

(Also see HARNESS.)

CHEEK.—See PARTS OF A HORSE—Fig. P-4.

CHEEK PIECE (CHEEK STRAP).—The cheek piece, or cheek strap, is that part of the bridle which lies against the horse's cheek. On the lower end it fastens to the bit, on the upper end it fastens to the crownpiece.

(Also see BRIDLES.)

CHELATED TRACE MINERALS.—See MINERALS.

CHEMICAL ANALYSIS OF FEED.—See FEED.

CHEST.—The area lying at the top of and between the forelegs. It should be deep and wide. Ample chest, along with a large, full heart-girth and a good middle, provide needed space for the vital organs and indicate a strong constitution and good feeding and staying qualities.

(Also see PARTS OF A HORSE—Fig. P-4.)

CHESTNUT (SORREL).—See COLORS AND MARKINGS OF HORSES.

CHESTNUTS (MALLENDERS).—The horny growth on the inside of the horse's legs, above the knees and below the hocks. Hind limb chestnuts are absent in the donkey and very small in the mule. They are regarded as vestiges of the first toe of prehistoric horses.

CHICKASAW HORSE.—See BREED (S).

CHICKASAW HORSE ASSOCIATION, INC., THE.—P. O. Box 8, Love Valley, North Carolina 28677. (See Appendix for complete breed registry association list.)

CHICKEN COOP.—A type of jump used in horse shows. It is a replica of a panel that is used to cover a wire fence in hunting country so that the fence may be jumped safely. A chicken coop is usually a little over four feet high.

(See JUMPS—Fig. J-5.)

CHINESE TAG.—See TAG.

CHIN STRAP.—A chin strap has the same placement and function as a curb chain (see Curb Chain). The only difference is that one is a leather strap whereas the other is a steel chain. Chin straps are used on both driving and riding horses. Either a chin strap or a curb chain is satisfactory if properly adjusted and cared for. A curb strap will stretch, whereas a chain will not. Also, a strap is more difficult to keep clean than a chain.

(Also see CURB CHAIN.)

CHISHOLM TRAIL.—This was the most famous of all early-day trails. It was marked by Jesse Chisholm and opened in 1867. It stretched hundreds of miles, from Texas to Abilene, Kansas.

CHUCK WAGON.—A wagon that is equipped with a stove and food, and which is taken out with the cowboys on the range.

CHUKKAR (CHUKKER).—A seven-and-one-half-minute period in a polo game. (From the Hindu language, meaning "a circle.")

(Also see POLO.)

CHUNKS, FARM.—See FARM CHUNKS.

CHUTE.—A narrow, high-walled passageway for

holding or restraining animals. In rodeos, a chute is the place in which horses are saddled, bridled, and mounted before entering the ring for competition. On the range, the chute is used for branding, saddling green horses, etc.

CINCH.—Girth of a Western saddle.

CINCINNATUS.—The mount of General U.S. GRANT. He was a giant of a horse, standing over 17½ hands high.

CIRCUS HORSE.—A circus horse is a horse that performs in the circus, of which there are the following three kinds:

1. *Vaulting horse, or resinback.*—These animals are generally white or light gray in color, of draft type—usually Percheron breeding (although animals of other draft breeds are used), weigh approximately 1,500 to 1,600 pounds, are broad-backed and of good temperament, and have a smooth, easy canter. Resin is applied to their backs to keep the barefoot performers from slipping; hence, the term "resinback" for circus horses that are used by bareback riders. As the animal canters around the ring, the rider(s) stands on its back and leaps on and off.

2. *High-School horse.*—This refers to light horses which usually perform solo, with a velvet-clad female rider putting her mount through various dressage steps and causing him to waltz, cakewalk, or tango to the music. High-School horses may be of any color.

3. *Liberty horses.*—These are the circus horses which do their tricks and go through their routines without a rider. They are generally bedecked with colored harness and ostrich-feather plumes and shown in groups where they heel, bow, pirouette, find their place in line by number, etc. Training of liberty horses is achieved by cues and voice.

The circus horse should not be confused with classic dressage. The performance of the circus horse includes artificial movements designed to entertain, whereas classic dressage is based on the natural movements of the horse.

CLAIMING RACE.—A race in which all the horses are entered at stated prices and may be claimed (purchased) by any other owner of a starter in the race. In effect, all horses in a claiming race are offered for sale.

CLASSES OF HORSES.—See TYPES AND CLASSES OF HORSES.

CLASSIC RACES.—There are five English classic races: the 2000 Guineas (founded in 1809; 1 mile, or 1.6 km), the 1000 Guineas (founded in 1814; 1 mile, or 1.6 km), the Derby (founded in 1780; 1½ miles, or 2.4 km), the Oaks (founded in 1780; 1½ miles, or 2.4 km), and the St. Leger (founded in 1776; 1¾ miles, or 2.9 km). All the Classic Races are for three-year-olds. No horse has ever won all five races, but Sceptre won all but the Derby in 1902.

The United States classics, which may be considered as counterparts to the English models, and which are also for three-year-olds, are: the Kentucky Derby (founded in 1875; 1¼ miles, or 2.0 km); the Preakness Stakes (founded in 1873; 1 3/16 miles, or 1.9 km); and the Belmont Stakes (founded in 1867; 1½ miles, or 2.4 km). Nine horses have won the Triple Crown (the Kentucky Derby, Preakness, and Belmont), the most recent being Secretariat in 1973.

CLEAN.—A term indicating that there are no blemishes or unsoundnesses on the legs.

CLEVELAND BAY.—See BREED(S).

CLEVELAND BAY ASSOCIATION OF AMERICA.—Middleburg, Virginia 22117. (See Appendix for complete breed registry association list.)

CLEVER.—A term used by horsemen to indicate that the animal performs well, with agility and promptness.

CLICKING (FORGING).—Striking the forefoot with the toe of the hind foot on the same side. Also known as forging.
(Also see FORGING.)

CLINCH CUTTER.—See SHOEING—Table S-5.

CLIP.—A triangular upward projection at the front (toe clip) or at the side (quarter clip) of a horseshoe over the outside of the hoof, used for attachment purposes. Usually there is one clip on the front shoe and one or two clips on the hind shoe, depending upon the nature of the work required of the horse. Horseshoes are fastened by means of nails plus clips.

CLIPPING.—The removal, by hand or machine, of the coat or the mane. The dual objective of clipping the coat is to facilitate drying after excessive work and to improve the appearance. The entire coat may be clipped, or the body and legs may be clipped down to or slightly above the knees and hocks. With hunters, the hair is not generally clipped under the saddle or on the legs, so that the hair on the back may serve as a pad and the hair on the legs may protect the horse from such objects as thorns and brush. Clipped horses should be kept stabled in winter.

(Also see GROOMING A HORSE—Clipping and Shearing.)

CLOSE ORDER DRILL.—Riding in formation with the stirrups of riders in close proximity to each other is called Close Order Drill. Such a drill is of great value in teaching control of horses.

CLOTHES FOR RIDERS.—In general, riding clothes seldom change in style. Moreover, they are utilitarian. Peg-top breeches, for example, provide plenty of seat room. Close fitting legs eliminate wrinkles that might cause chafing. Chamois leather linings inside the knees and calves keep the muscles of the legs from pinching under the stirrup leathers and increase the firmness of the leg grip. Boots or jodhpurs protect the ankles from the stirrup irons. And high boots also keep the breeches from snaring on objects along the trail, shield the trouser legs from the saddle straps and the horse's sides, and protect the legs from rain and cold. For the most comfortable ride, wear either regulation or jodh-

pur-type breeches made to order.

The time of day, the kind of riding horse, and the class in which shown at horse shows determine the riding attire. In addition to selecting proper clothes, well-groomed and experienced riders place emphasis on fine tailoring, good materials, and proper fit. Also, when riding a saddle horse, do not wear gaudy colors, excess jewelry, or sequins, except in parade classes.

For information on clothes for riders for specific show classes see the official *Rule Book* of the American Horse Shows Association.

Appropriate riding clothes for the most common occasions are as follows:

ENGLISH RIDING.—

1. Informal park or school riding, morning or afternoon classes.

■ *Coat.*—Any conservative color, tweeds or checks.

■ *Jodhpurs or breeches.*—Jodhpurs of gabardine, whipcord, or cavalry twill in colors to match or to contrast with the coat; Kentucky-style breeches with bell bottoms and no flare at the hips.

■ *Vest.*—Optional; light, solid color or tattersall check.

■ *Shirt.*—Man's shirt, white or colored, broadcloth or oxford cloth.

■ Neckwear.—Four-in-hand tie or bow tie.

■ *Hat.*—Saddle derby to match jodhpurs or coat.

■ *Boots.*—Black or brown strap or elastic jodhpur boots.

■ *Gloves.*—Optional; leather gloves to blend with habit.

■ *Jewelry and other accessories.*—Cuff links, tie pin, belt; spurs of unrowelled type and whip or crop optional.

2. Semiformal, afternoon or evening classes.

■ *Coat.*—Gabardine, wool gabardine, dress

Fig. C-7. Proper riding attire. (Drawings by Ethel Gadberry.)

ENGLISH RIDING, Semi-Formal.   **WESTERN RIDING, with coat.**

ENGLISH RIDING, Formal.

WESTERN RIDING, without coat.   **HUNTING.**

JUMPING.

worsted, or other men's-wear materials; inverted pleats in back; dark colors preferred; in summer, linen or tropical worsted.

■ *Jodhpurs or breeches.*—Jodhpurs of same material as coat to make a matching riding habit; Kentucky-style breeches with bell bottoms, no flare at the hips, and no cuff.

■ *Vest.*—Solid color or tattersall check.

■ *Shirt.*—Man's shirt in white or light color to match suit.

■ *Neckwear.*—Man's four-in-hand tie to match or contrast with the coat.

■ *Hat.*—Saddle derby to match suit.

■ *Boots.*—Black or brown jodhpur boots.

■ *Gloves.*—Optional; leather in a natural shade or to match suit.

■ *Jewelry and other accessories.*—Tie clasp, cuff links, belt; spurs and riding whip optional.

3. Formal evening riding.—

a. *Five-gaited horse:*

■ *Coat.*—Black or midnight blue tuxedo-style riding coat with one button in front and inverted pleats; men usually wear a dark suit instead of a tuxedo.

■ *Jodhpurs or breeches.*—Material and color to match coat.

■ *Vest.*—Any solid color to match habit.

■ *Shirt.*—Man's shirt.

■ *Neckwear.*—Four-in-hand or bow tie.

■ *Hat.*—Saddle derby.

■ *Boots.*—Black jodhpur boots with tuxedo; brown or black with a suit.

■ *Gloves.*—Leather gloves to match habit.

■ *Jewelry and other accessories.*—Cuff links and tie pin; gaited riding whip, crop, and spurs optional.

b. *Three-gaited horse:*

■ *Coat.*—Tuxedo model in black or midnight blue; shawl collar with satin lapels; soft pastel colored coats also can be worn; white coat in summer. Equitation classes must wear a dark tuxedo-style coat with a silk top hat in the evening and a matched suit with a derby in the daytime.

■ *Jodhpurs or breeches.*—Material and color to match coat; satin stripe down outside of jodhpurs.

■ *Vest.*—Optional; white pique vest or cummerbund.

■ *Shirt.*—Formal style, white, stiff-front tuxedo; shirt with wing collar and pleated front.

■ *Neckwear.*—Black, white, or midnight blue bow tie.

■ *Hat.*—Silk top hat.

■ *Boots.*—Black leather or patent leather jodhpur boots.

■ *Gloves.*—Leather gloves to match habit.

■ *Jewelry and other accessories.*—Formal shirt studs; walk-trot stick optional.

WESTERN RIDING.—

■ *Coat.*—Coats and jackets usually not worn except in bad weather; tailored equitation suits may be worn (matching shirt and pants).

■ *Pants.*—Western cut pants of gabardine, cotton twill, cavalry twill, or wool worn with chaps, shotgun chaps, or chinks; conservative color and well tailored.

■ *Vest.*—Optional; leather or cloth.

■ *Shirt.*—Western type; color to match or contrast with western pants; solid or patterned fabric acceptable; long-sleeved.

■ *Neckwear.*—Knotted kerchief, dogger-type tie, choker, or silk scarf tied ascot style and tucked into open neck of shirt.

■ *Hat.*—Western hat, felt or straw.

■ *Boots.*—Western boots.

■ *Gloves.*—Optional; leather.

■ *Jewelry and other accessories.*—Hand carved belt and western belt buckle; carry a rope or riata; if closed reins are used in trail and pleasure horse classes, carry hobbles; spurs optional.

HUNTING AND JUMPING.—

1. Hunting (informal).

■ *Coat.*—Black oxford or tweed.

■ *Jodhpurs or breeches.*—Jodhpurs with peg and cuff or breeches; colors of brick, tan, buff, or canary.

■ *Vest.*—Optional; hunting yellow or tattersall.

■ *Shirt.*—Stock shirt or ratcatcher.

■ *Neckwear.*—Choker, stock, or ratcatcher tie.

■ *Hat.*—Brown or black hunting derby; hunting cap if 18 years old or less.

■ *Boots.*—Black or brown boots; high or jodhpur.

■ *Gloves.*—Brown leather gloves or rain gloves of string.

■ *Jewelry and other accessories.*—Stock or choker pin, hunting crop, and spurs with straps that match boots.

2. Hunt seat equitation.

■ *Coat.*—Oxford or tweed hunt coat; black or other conservative color.

■ *Jodhpurs or breeches.*—Buff, brick, or canary breeches.

■ *Vest.*—Optional; canary with black coat.

■ *Shirt.*—Stock shirt.

■ *Neckwear.*—White stock or choker.

■ *Hat.*—Hunting derby; hunting cap if 18 years old or less.

■ *Boots.*—Black or brown hunt boots.

■ *Gloves.*—Optional.

■ *Jewelry and other accessories.*—Stock pin worn straight across on a stock tie or choker; spurs of unrowelled type and crop or bat optional.

3. Member of a hunt (formal).

■ *Coat.*—Black hunt coat of melton or heavy twill; may wear a black coat of shadbelly or other cutaway-type scarlet hunt livery; collar should be same material and color as the coat unless the rider has been invited to wear hunt-club colors, in which case the collar should conform to hunt livery.

■ *Jodhpurs or breeches.*—Buff, brick or canary with black coat; men wear white breeches if they wear a scarlet coat.

■ *Vest.*—Buff or yellow; hunt colors if hunt-club member.

■ *Shirt.*—White stock shirt.

■ *Neckwear.*—White stock fastened with a plain gold safety pin worn straight across stock.

■ *Hat.*—Silk hunting hat; hat guard required with scarlet coat or black shadbelly; staff members and juniors wear hunt caps; adults wear a derby with a hat guard when a black coat is worn.

■ *Boots.*—Regular hunting boots of black calf with tabs; black patent leather tops permissible for women; brown tops for men on the staff.

■ *Gloves.*—White or yellow string rain gloves or brown leather gloves.

■ *Jewelry and other accessories.*—Sandwich case, flask, and regulation hunting whip; spurs of heavy pattern with a moderately short neck, preferably without rowels and worn high on the heels.

■ *Boot garters.*—Plain black or black patent leather with patent leather boot tops; brown with brown boot tops; white with white breeches.

4. Jumping.

■ *Coat.*—Any color of hunt coat in solid or check; jumping coat may be of any informal forward seat type.

■ *Jodhpurs or breeches.*—Breeches of a color contrasting to coat.

■ *Vest.*—Checkered or solid color.

■ *Shirt.*—Man's shirt; ratcatcher shirt when stock is worn.

■ *Neckwear.*—Stock or four-in-hand tie.

■ *Hat.*—Hunting derby or hunt cap.

■ *Boots.*—Black or brown hunting boots.

■ *Gloves.*—Optional.

■ *Jewelry and other accessories.*—Stock pin and belt; jumping bat and spurs optional.

OTHER RIDING OCCASIONS.—

1. *Side saddle forward seat for hunting.*—Silk hunting hat; hat guard required; dark melton habit with matching skirt; black boots without tops; spurs are optional; white or colored rain gloves, neckwear, coat collar, vest, sandwich case, and flask are the same as for a member of a formal hunt.

2. *Side saddle show seat.*—Habit of dark blue, black, or oxford gray with matching or contrasting skirt; black jodhpur boots; four-in-hand or

bow tie; white shirt; hard derby; white or pigskin gloves.

3. *Plantation walking horse (Tennessee Walking Horse).*—Clothes should be the same as those worn for riding three- or five-gaited horses; men can wear a soft felt hat; women seldom wear a hat.

CLOVER HAY.—A legume hay, of which there are several varieties, sometimes fed to horses. If well cured, and free from dust and mold, a clover-timothy mixed hay is excellent for horses.

CLUB, 4-H.—See "F" 4-H CLUB.

CLUCK.—To move the tongue in such a way as to produce clucks. The command to go, proceed; the signal to increase speed. Clucking in public or in the presence of other riders is frowned upon.

CLYDESDALE.—See BREED (S).

CLYDESDALE BREEDERS' ASSOCIATION OF THE UNITED STATES.—Route 3, Waverly, Iowa 50677. (See Appendix for complete breed registry association list.)

COACH.—A large four-wheeled carriage, usually enclosed, with doors on each side and generally a front and a back seat inside and an elevated seat outside and in front for the driver. It takes its name from a small town in Hungary where it was first made.

COACH DOGS.—Coach dogs were formerly used to run in attendance to coaches. The Dalmatian breed was used for this purpose.

COARSE.—Lacking in quality—shown in texture of hair, hairy fetlocks, all-over lack of refinement, common head; flat and shelly feet, and coarse legs.

COAT.—The external growth of hair on a horse. Fineness of coat denotes high quality. Also, a smooth, silky appearance is indicative of a healthy animal, whereas a rough, dull coat is a warning signal that something is wrong—that there may be nutritional deficiencies and/or parasites.

COAT DRESSING.—"Trifles make perfection, but perfection is no trifle," is an old and well-known adage among horsemen. This philosophy prompts experienced caretakers to use a good coat dressing to achieve the all-important "bloom" or eye appeal in show, parade, and sale animals. Also, they use a coat dressing because they take pride in the every-day appearance of their charges, for how the horses look is indicative of the kind of caretakers back of them.

A coat dressing will not take the place of the natural conditioning of the horse, which can be achieved only through proper feeding, health, grooming, and shampooing.

Proper grooming should always precede the use of coat dressing. Coat dressing is best applied by means of a heavy cloth (preferably terry cloth). Moisten the rag with the dressing and rub the coat vigorously in the direction of the natural lay of the hair; then brush to bring out the bloom.

Coat dressing should always be used following washing, and for show, parade, or sale. It is best to apply a heavier application of coat dressing 12 to 24 hours ahead of the event, then go over the horse with a lightly dressed rag just ahead.

COB.—A close-knit horse, heavy-boned, short-coupled and muscular, but with quality, and not so heavy or coarse as to be a draft animal. A cob is usually small, standing under 15 hands.

COBALT.—See MINERALS.

COBBY.—Close-coupled, stoutly built. Like a cob.

COCKED ANKLES.—Cocked ankles refers to horses that stand bent forward on the fetlocks in a cocked position. This condition can be cor-

rected by proper trimming, allowing the toes to grow out while keeping the heels trimmed. However, where cocked ankles are of nutritional origin (as a result of the rickets syndrome), they should be treated by correcting the causative nutritional deficiency or imbalance.

[Also see UNSOUNDNESSES; and FEET (of horses).]

COCK HORSE.—An extra horse used with English stage coaches, ridden behind the coach in ordinary going, but hitched before the team for added draft when coming to steep hills or heavy going.

COFFIN BONE (PEDAL BONE).—The largest of the three bones which constitute the bony base of the horse's foot, about which the other supporting structures are arranged. It resembles a miniature foot in shape and is so porous in structure as to resemble pumice stone in appearance and density. Racehorses sometimes fracture this bone, which is a great disaster.

(Also see FOOT—Fig. F-20. Parts of the Foot.)

COLD-BACKED.—Describes a horse that humps his back and does not settle down until the saddle has been on a few minutes. Some "cold-backed" horses will merely tuck their tails and arch their backs when first mounted, but others will take a few crow hops until warmed up.

COLD BLOOD.—A horse of draft horse breeding.

COLD-JAWED.—A tough-mouthed horse.

COLDS.—Horses are subject to colds very similar to that in man. Colds are caused by a virus and, as in humans, there are various strains of the horse cold virus. The symptoms are: loss of appetite, shivering, a rise in temperature to 103° F. or 104° F., and an increased pulse rate to around 50 or 60. Usually, a discharge develops, but the glands are not affected. Afflicted horses often develop a sore throat and a nasty cough.

Colds are highly contagious and can spread rapidly through an entire stable. Therefore, affected animals should be isolated immediately. A veterinarian should be called, who will generally administer an antibiotic to prevent secondary infection. Good nursing will help. The latter includes keeping the horse warm and dry in a well-ventilated but not drafty place and giving him a bran mash.

COLD-SHOEING.—Shoeing a horse without heating and shaping the shoe before nailing it on.

COLIC.—The term "colic" refers to a set of symptoms which indicate severe abdominal pain. Colic is more common in horses than in other animals, which is attributed to the small size of the stomach, the inability to vomit or unload the stomach, the great size of the intestines, the puckerings of the large intestine which allow food or foreign bodies to lodge there, the great range in movement allowed to the intestines within the abdomen, the frequency with which the horse is affected with internal parasites, and the fact that the horse has to work at the direction of his master.

CAUSE.—A digestive disturbance which may be caused by a variety of conditions: feed to which the animal is unaccustomed, sudden changes in the ration, rapid eating, imperfectly cured or damaged feeds, the horse being worked too soon or too hard after feeding, or gorging on water—especially when the animal is warm.

SYMPTOMS.—Excruciating pain; and, depending on the type of colic, other symptoms are: distended abdomen, increased intestinal rumbling, violent rolling and kicking, profuse sweating, constipation, and refusal of feed and water.

DISTRIBUTION AND LOSSES.—Colic occurs worldwide. Insurance companies specializing in horse coverage report that the major cause of death to horses is colic.

TREATMENT.—Call a veterinarian. To avoid danger of inflicting self-injury, (1) place the animal in a large, well-bedded stable, or (2) take it for a slow walk.

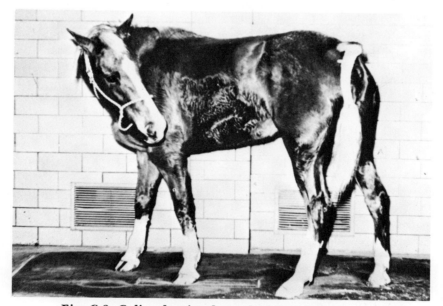

Fig. C-8. Colic; showing horse looking at flank, profuse sweating, and tail switching—characteristic symptoms. (Courtesy, Dr. V. S. Myers, Jr., V.M.D., Department of Veterinary Surgery and Radiology, University of Minnesota, St. Paul, Minn.)

Most veterinarians use the stomach tube in the treatment of colic.

CONTROL AND ERADICATION.—Proper feeding, working, watering, and parasite control.

REMARKS.—Colic is also a symptom of abdominal pain that can be caused by a number of different conditions. For example, bloodworms cause a colic due to damage in the wall of blood vessels. This results in poor circulation to the intestine.

(Also see FIRST AID FOR HORSES.)

COLLECTED.—A term denoting a horse in good form when in action. A collected horse is up to its bit, with its neck flexed, jaw relaxed, and hocks well under it; it has full control of its limbs at all gaits; and it is ready and able to respond to the aids of its rider.

COLLECTED GAIT (S).—A horse may perform in either a collected or extended manner. Thus, the slow canter is a collected form of the gallop. When collected, the horse arches his neck, brings his head back, and drives his hocks well under the body. At a collected gait, the stride is shortened, and the action is more elevated, more showy, and more animated. Good horsemen generally change frequently from the collected to the extended forms of the various gaits, and back again.

COLORADO RANGER HORSE ASSOCIATION, INC.—7023 Eden Mill Road, Woodbine, Maryland 21797.

COLORS AND MARKINGS OF HORSES.—Within certain breeds, some colors are preferred or required, and others are undesirable or constitute disqualifications for registration. A good horseman needs a working knowledge of horse colors and patterns because they are the most conspicuous features by which a horse can be described or identified.

BODY COLORS.—The five basic body colors of horses are as follows:

● BAY.—Bay is a mixture of red and yellow. It includes many shades, from a light yellowish tan (light bay) to a dark, rich shade that is almost brown (dark bay). A bay horse usually has a black mane and tail and black points.

● BLACK.—A black horse is completely black, including the muzzle and flanks. If in doubt whether the horse is dark brown or black, note the color of the fine hairs on the muzzle and the hair on the flanks; tan or brown hairs at these points indicate the horse is not a true black, but a seal brown.

● BROWN.—A brown horse is almost black but can be distinguished by the fine tan or brown hairs on the muzzle or flanks.

● CHESTNUT (SORREL).—A chestnut horse is basically red. The shades vary from light washy yellow (light chestnut) to a dark liver color (dark chestnut). Between these come the brilliant red-gold and copper shades. Normally, the mane and tail of a chestnut horse are the same shade as the body, although they may be lighter. When they are lighter, the coloring is called flaxen mane and tail. Chestnut color is never accompanied by a black mane and tail.

● WHITE.—A true white horse is born white and remains white throughout life. White horses have snow-white hair, pink skin, and brown eyes (rarely blue).

Besides the five basic colors, horses have five major variations to these coat colors. The variations are as follows:

● DUN (BUCKSKIN).—Dun is a yellowish color of variable shading from pale yellow to a dirty canvas color. A dun horse has a stripe down the back.

● GRAY.—This is a mixture of white and black hairs. Sometimes a gray horse is difficult to distinguish from a black horse at birth, but gray horses get lighter with age.

● PALOMINO.—This is a golden color. Palomino horses have a light colored mane and tail of white, silver, or ivory.

● PINTO (CALICO OR PAINT).—Pinto is a Spanish word that means painted. The pinto color is characterized by irregular colored and white areas in either piebald or skewbald patterns. Piebald horses are black and white, and skewbald horses are white and any other color except black.

● ROAN.—Roan is a mixture of white hairs with one or more base colors. White with bay is red roan; white with chestnut is strawberry roan; and white with black is blue roan.

HEAD MARKS.—When identifying an individual horse, it is generally necessary to include more identification than just body color. For example, it may be necessary to identify the dark sorrel as the one with the blaze face. Some common head markings are shown in Fig. C-9.

LEG MARKS.—Leg marks are often used, along with head marks, to describe a horse. The most common leg marks are shown in Fig. C-10.

COLORS, RACING.—The colored jacket and cap worn by jockeys in a race. Colors must be registered by owners; and they cannot be used by any other person.

COLOSTRUM.—The milk secreted by the mare for the first few days after foaling. It is nature's product, designed to give young a good start in life. Colostrum is higher than normal milk in dry matter, protein, vitamins, and minerals. Additionally, it contains antibodies that give newborn foals protection against certain diseases.
(Also see FOAL.)

COLT.—A young stallion under three years of age; in Thoroughbreds, the age is extended to include four-year-olds.

COMBINATION BET (ACROSS THE BOARD).—A combination pari-mutuel (race) ticket on a horse is known as "across the board," meaning that the bettor collects something if his horse finishes first, second, or third. This type of bet is the equivalent of making three bets at once on the same horse. A combination bet of $6.00 is the same as a $2.00 win, $2.00 place and $2.00 show, bet all in one ticket.

COMBINATION HORSE.—One used for both saddle and driving purposes. In the show-ring, custom decrees that a combination horse be brought into the ring in harness and be shown as directed. Then he is unhitched in the ring and put under saddle to be shown again as directed. Three-gaited combination classes are common in horse shows of the United States.

COMBINED TRAINING.—See THREE-DAY-EVENT.

COME A CROPPER.—A term meaning to fall off a horse.

COMMERCIAL FEED.—See FEED.

COMPETITIVE RIDES.—See ENDURANCE TRIALS (Rides).

COMPUTERS IN THE HORSE BUSINESS.—Accurate and up-to-the-minute records and controls have taken on increasing importance in all agriculture, including the horse business, as the investment required to engage therein has risen. Today's successful horsemen must have, and use, as complete records as any other business. Also, records must be kept current.
Big and complex enterprises have outgrown hand record keeping. It's too time consuming, with the result that it doesn't allow management enough time for planning and decision making. Additionally, it does not permit an all-at-once consideration of the complex interrelationships which affect the economic success of the business. This has prompted a new computer technique known as linear programming.
Linear programming is similar to budgeting, in that it compares several plans simultaneously and chooses from among them the one likely to yield the highest returns. It is a way in which to analyze a great mass of data and consider many

Star   Stripe   Blaze

Star, stripe,
and snip   Snip   Bald

Star and stripe

Fig. C-9. The head marks of horses. Star is any white mark on the forehead located above a line running from eye to eye; stripe is a narrow white marking that extends from about the line of the eyes to the nostrils; blaze is a broad, white marking covering almost all the forehead but not including the eyes or nostrils; star, stripe, and snip includes all three marks; snip is a white mark between the nostrils or on the lips; bald is a bald face, or white face, including the eyes and nostrils, or a partially white face; star and stripe includes both star and stripe.

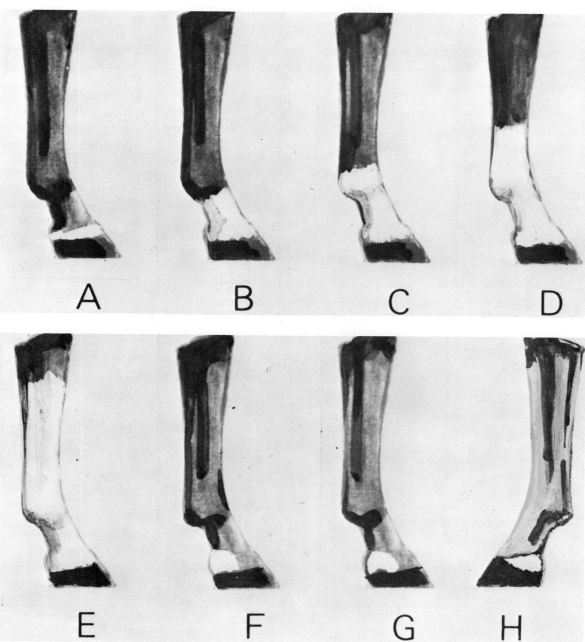

Fig. C-10. The leg marks of horses. (A) Coronet, *a white stripe covering the coronet band; (B)* Pastern, *white extends from the coronet to and including the pastern; (C)* Ankle, *white extends from the coronet to and including the fetlock; (D)* Half stocking, *white extends from the coronet to the middle of the cannon; (E)* Stocking, *white extends from the coronet to the knee, and when the white includes the knee the mark is called a full stocking; (F)* White heels, *both heels are white; (G)* White outside heel, *outside heel only is white; (H)* White inside heel, *inside heel only is white.*

alternatives. It is not a managerial genie, nor will it replace decision-making managers. However, it is a modern and effective tool in the present age, when just a few dollars per head or per acre can spell the difference between profit and loss.

There is hardly any limit to what computers can do if fed the proper information. Among the difficult questions that they can answer for a specific horse operation are:
- How is the entire operation doing so far?
- What enterprises are making money; which ones are freeloading or losing?
- Is each enterprise yielding maximum returns?
- How does this operation stack up with its competition?
- How can you plan ahead?
- How can income taxes be cut to the legal minimum?
- What is the least-cost ration formulation and the best buy in ingredients?

For providing answers to these questions, and many more, computer accounting costs an average of one percent of the gross income.

There are three requisites for linear programming a horse establishment, namely:
1. Access to a computer.
2. Computer know-how, so as to set up the program properly and be able to analyze and interpret the results.
3. Good records.

The pioneering computer services available to farmers were operated by universities, trade associations, and government; most of them were on an experimental basis. Subsequently, others have entered the field, including commercial data processing firms, banks, machinery companies, feed and fertilizer companies, and farm suppliers. They are using it as a "service sell," as a replacement for the days of "hard sell."

Programmed farming is here to stay, and it will increase in the horse business.

COMPUTERS IN HORSE BREEDING OPERATIONS.—In the past, the biggest deterrent to adequate records on a horse breeding establishment has been the voluminous and time-consuming record keeping involved. Keeping records as such does not change what an animal will transmit, but records must be used to locate and propogate the genetically superior animals if genetic improvement is to be accomplished.

Computers can be used in performance testing. Also, computerized records can be used for breeding record purposes—as a means of keeping management up to date and as an alert on problems to be solved or work to be done. Each animal must be individually identified. Reports can be obtained at such intervals as desired, usually monthly or every two weeks. Also, the owner can keep as complete or as few records as desired. Here are several of the records that can be kept by computer:
- Pedigrees.
- Records of animals that need attention, such as:
  - Animals four months old that are unregistered.
  - Animals ready for inspection or scoring.
  - Mares that have been bred two consecutive times.
  - Mares that have not conceived two months after foaling.
  - Mares due to foal in thirty days.
  - Foals seven months of age that haven't been weaned.
  - Animals that have not received their seasonal vaccinations; for example, that have not been vaccinated against sleeping sickness by May 1.
  - Animals that have not been treated for parasites at the scheduled time.
- A running or cumulative inventory of the herd, by sex; including foals dropped, foals due, and purchases and sales—in number of animals and dollars.
- The depreciation of purchased animals according to the accounting method of choice.

CONCENTRATE.—See FEED.

CONCEPTION.—The act of becoming pregnant is known as conception.
(Also see BREEDING HORSES.)

CONDITION.—The state of fitness.

CONDITIONING.—Good condition is produced by proper attention to details of management, correct feeding, proper exercise, care of teeth, and good grooming. No matter how superior the genetics and conformation of a horse may be, proper conditioning is requisite to winning a show or race, or topping a sale.

CONESTOGA HORSES.—The early-day colonist farmers of Pennsylvania used large horses that were hitched to enormous wagons for transporting freight overland to and from river flat boats and barges along the Ohio, Cumberland, Tennessee, and Mississippi Rivers. Both the horses and wagons were given the names Conestoga after the Conestoga Valley, a German settlement in Pennsylvania.

CONFORMATION.—Body shape or form. See Fig. C-11 for ideal type versus common faults.

(Also see JUDGING HORSES—Table J-1; and SCORE CARD.)

CONGENITAL.—Acquired during development in the uterus and not through heredity.

CONNEMARA PONY.—See BREED (S).

CONQUISTADORS.—Any one of the leaders in the Spanish conquest of America, especially of Mexico and Peru, in the sixteenth century.

CONSTIPATION.—When the feces of any horse, especially an old one, is in the form of hard balls which cannot be easily disintegrated with the toe of a shoe, the animal should be treated with laxative feeds such as bran mashes, with a little Glauber salts or Epsom salts added. In severe cases, an enema may be necessary.

Newborn foals are sometimes constipated. (See FOAL—Bowel Movement.)

CONTRACTED FEET *(contracted heels)*.— This condition, known as contracted, most often occurs in the fore feet and is characterized by a

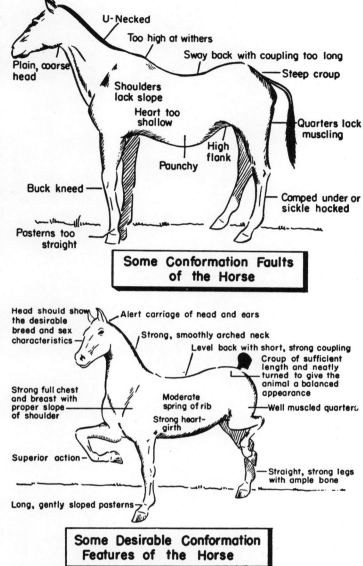

Fig. C-11. Ideal type versus common faults. Regardless of type or breed, certain desirable characteristics should be present in all horses. The successful horse judge must be able to recognize both the desirable characteristics and the common faults, and the relative importance of each. (Drawings by R. F. Johnson)

drawing in or contracting at the heels (see Fig. C-12). A tendency toward contracted feet may be inherited, but improper shoeing usually aggravates the condition. Paring, removal of shoes, or use of special shoes constitutes the best treatment.

[Also see UNSOUNDNESSES; and FEET (of horse).]

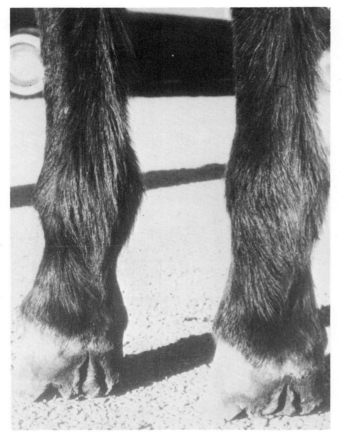

Fig. C-12. Contracted heels on forefeet. (Courtesy, **Western Horseman,** *Colorado Springs, Colo.)*

CONTRACTS (STALLION).—See STAL-LION—Breeding Contract.

CONTROL OF THE HORSE.—The horse has whims and ideas of his own. Always, however, the rider should be the boss, with the mount promptly carrying out his wishes. With the experienced horseman, this relationship is clear-cut, for the rider is able to relay his feelings to the horse instantly and unmistakably.

A well-mannered horse may be said to be the combined result of desirable heredity, skillful training, and vigilant control. Once conception has taken place, it is too late to change the genetic make-up of the animal. However, the eventual training and control of the horse are dependent upon how well the horseman understands equine mental faculties as well as methods of utilizing these faculties so that the desired performance may be obtained.

Purebred horse breeding establishments have long been aware, consciously or unconsciously, of equine mental faculties. As a result, most breeders have substituted gradual and early training programs for the so-called breaking of animals at three to five years of age. Even on some of the more progressive ranches, the cowboy and the bucking bronco are fast passing into permanent oblivion.

For complete control and a finished performance, the horse should have a proud and exalted opinion of himself; but at the same time he should subjugate those undesirable traits that make a beast of his size and strength so difficult to handle by a comparatively frail and small man. Complete control, therefore, is based on mental faculties rather than muscular force.

The faculties of the horse that must be understood and played upon to obtain skillful training and control at all times are summarized briefly.

MEMORY.—To a considerable degree, the horse's aptitude for training is due to his memory; for he remembrs or recognizes the indications given him, the manner in which he responded, and the rewards or punishments that followed his actions. These facts must be taken into consideration both in training the young horse and in retaining control of the trained animal.

Discipline and reward must be administered very soon after the act (some competent horsemen say that it should be within three seconds) in order for the horse to associate and remember.

CONFIDENCE AND FEAR.—In the wild state, the horse was his own protector; and his very survival was often dependent upon rapidity of escape. In a well-mannered horse, it is necessary that confidence in the rider replace fear. Thus, it is best to approach the horse from the front. He should be spoken to in a quiet, calm voice and should be stroked by using comparatively slow movement of the hands to avoid exciting him. Above all, when one is approaching a horse, he should make certain that the animal knows of his presence. Startling a horse often causes accidents for which the animal is blameless.

During moments of fright, the good horseman utilizes the means by which the horse is calmed.

However, when the horse is voluntarily and knowingly disobedient, the proper degree of punishment should be administered immediately.

ASSOCIATION OF IDEAS.—Horses are creatures of habit; for example, when the grain bin door is heard to open, the horse regularly anticipates his feed. For this reason, the schooling of a horse should be handled by the same competent horseman, who allows the animal an opportunity to associate the various commands with the desired response. A well-trained horse may become confused and ill-mannered when poorly handled by several persons.

WILLINGNESS.—A willing worker or performer is to be desired. Some animals submit to the horseman's subjugation with little trouble and hesitation, whereas others offer resistance to the point of being stubborn. Complete control over the mount at all times is achieved through the judicious employment of rewards and punishments.

REWARDS.—The two most common rewards given horses are a praising voice and a gentle stroking with the hand. Satisfying the horse's greediness for such things as a lump of sugar is also most effective, but this may make for great disappointment if the reward is not available at all times. To be effective, rewards must not be given promiscuously but only when deserved. It is also important that the same word always be used for the same thing and that the horseman means what he says.

PUNISHMENT.—The two common types of equine punishment are the spur and the whip. Punishment should be administered only when the horseman is certain that the animal is being disobedient and not when the horse lacks sufficient training, has not understood some command, or has done something wrong because of the rider. When necessary, however, the punishment should be administered promptly, so that the animal understands why it is given; and it should be given with justice and with the horseman retaining a cool head at all times. Following punishment, the animal should be made to carry out the original command that he failed to follow, and then he should be properly rewarded.

COOL OUT.—To cause a horse to move about quietly after heavy exercise. Failure to cool out a horse following heavy exercise may result in stiffness or laminitis (founder). Cooling out is generally accomplished by very quickly removing the tack and scraping excess sweat from the horse's body with scrapers; covering him with a cooler (blanket); and walking slowly. As soon as the respiration and heartbeat approach normal, he may be crosstied and rubbed with dry linen or Turkish towels and allowed a few swallows of water. After vigorous rubbing and sponging of the head and nostrils, the horse may be walked by the groom or mechanical walker until respiration and pulse are completely normal. When cooling out, a sip of water should be given at intervals until the thirst is completely quenched.

COON FOOTED.—Having long low pasterns and shallow heels.

COPENHAGEN.—The charger ridden by the Duke of Wellington in the battle of Waterloo.

COPPER.—See MINERALS.

CORINTHIAN.—A Corinthian horse show class is one in which the riders and horses are required to appear in proper hunting appointments.

CORN (MAIZE).—Corn ranks second to oats as a horse feed. It is palatable, nutritious, and rich in energy-producing carbohydrate and fat, but it has certain very definite limitations. It lacks quality (being especially low in the amino acids, lysine and tryptophan) and quantity of proteins (it runs about 9%), and it is deficient in minerals, particularly calcium.

Corn may be fed to horses on the cob, shelled, cracked, as corn-and-cob meal, or flaked.

CORNS.—A bruise to the soft tissue underlying the horny sole of the foot—which manifests itself in a reddish discoloration of the sole immediately below the affected area—is known as a corn. Fast work on hard and rough roads, flat soles, weakened bars, and poor shoeing may cause corns. Paring, special shoeing, poulticing, sanitation, and rest constitute the best treatment.

(Also see UNSOUNDNESSES.)

CORONA.—See SADDLE BLANKET.

CORONET.—1. The top of a horse's hoof, just below the hairline.

2. A white stripe covering the coronet band.

(Also see PARTS OF A HORSE—Fig. P-4; COLORS AND MARKINGS OF HORSES—Fig. C-10).

CORRAL.—An enclosure for confining horses. Usually it is built with a high, stout fence.

CORRAL BREEDING.—See BREEDING HORSES.

COST TO KEEP A HORSE.—For the U.S. as a whole, the average cost to keep a horse is $1,000 per year. A breakdown of expenses follows:

	$
Feed (grain, hay, and pasture)	450
Tack, shoes, trailer, clothes, and miscellaneous equipment . . .	450
Drugs	100
Total	$1,000

Since there are an estimated 8 million horses in the U.S. today, from vitamins to saddlery the nation's horses make for an 8.0 billion dollar per year business.

COTTONSEED MEAL.—Among the oilseed meals, cottonseed meal ranks second in tonnage to soybean meal.

The protein content of cottonseed meal can vary from about 22% in meal made from undecorticated (unhulled) seed to 60% in flour made from seed from which the hulls have been removed completely. Thus, in screening out the residual hulls, which are low in protein and high in fiber, the processor is able to make a cottonseed meal of the protein content desired—usually 41, 44 or 50%.

Cottonseed meal is low in lysine and tryptophan and deficient in Vitamin D, carotene (vitamin A value), and calcium. Also, unless glandless seed is used, it contains a toxic substance known as gossypol, varying in amounts with the seed and the processing. But, it is rich in phosphorus.

Some prejudices to the contrary, good grade cottonseed meal is satisfactory for horses. It may be fed in the amounts necessary to balance ordinary rations.

COUGH.—When a horse coughs, the horseman should listen. A hard, dry cough accompanied by breaking wind is indicative of heaves. Persistent coughing, accompanied by a nasal discharge and a temperature above 102° F., is cause to call the veterinarian. Any horse with a cough should have his hay wetted down and his corral sprinkled with water.

COUPE.—A four-wheeled, closed horse-drawn carriage for two persons inside, with an outside seat for the driver in front.

COUPLING (SHORT COUPLED).—The section between the point of the hip and the last rib. A short-coupled horse is considered to be an easy keeper, while a long-coupled horse is said to "take a bale of hay a day." The width of four fingers is considered to constitute a short coupling.

(Also see PARTS OF A HORSE—Fig. P-4.)

COURTESY (on horseback).—Courtesy on horseback does not differ in principle from courtesy anyplace else. Horsemen should always show consideration for other riders.

(Also see HORSEMANSHIP—Rules of Good Horsemanship.)

COVERT (pronounced "Cover").—A hunting term indicating a brush or thicket in which hounds search for fox or scent of fox.

COWBOY.—One who tends and drives cattle, particularly on the western range. Also, rodeo riders are called cowboys.

Fig. C-13. *The pause that refreshes! Cowboy and cow pony having a refreshing drink in the high country. (Courtesy,* **The Western Horseman;** *photo by Charles J. Belden, Pitchfork, Wyoming)*

COWGIRL.—A girl who tends cows; the counterpart of the cowboy.

COW HOCKS, COW-HOCKED.—Standing with the joints of the hocks bent inward, with the toes pointing outward.

COWPOKE.—A man who makes his living caring for cattle on the western range.

COW PONY.—The horse used by a cowboy.

CRAB BIT.—Bit with prongs extending at the horse's nose. Purpose is to tip the horse's head

Fig. C-14. *Margit Sigray Bessenyey sits tall in the saddle, astride a Hungarian horse, as she rounds up cattle on her Bitterroot Stock Farm, Hamilton, Montana. (Photo by Ernst Peterson, Hamilton, Montana)*

up and help prevent him from ducking his head, bowing his neck, and pulling hard on the rein.

CRACKED HEEL.—See SCRATCHES.

CRADLE.—A device designed to prevent a horse from biting himself, particularly when he has some irritation which is under treatment. The cradle consists of several lengths of rounded wood fastened at intervals (by leather straps or other material) to form a neck piece which goes

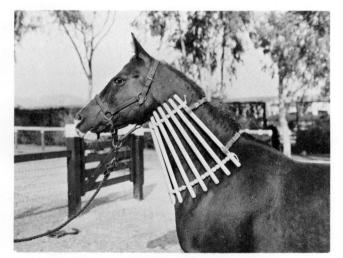

Fig. C-15. *Cradle. (Courtesy, USDA)*

around the horse's neck from throat to shoulder. Sometimes cradles are padded, thereby making for greater comfort to the horse.

CREDIT IN THE HORSE BUSINESS.—Credit is an integral part of today's horse business. Wise use of it can be profitable, but unwise use of it can be disastrous. Accordingly, horsemen should know more about it. They need to know something about the lending agencies available to them, the types of credit, how to go about obtaining a loan, and methods of computing interest.

The common lending sources of farm credit are: commercial banks, production credit associations, Federal land banks, individuals and other private lenders, life insurance companies, merchants and dealers, and the Farm Home Administration.

TYPES OF CREDIT.—Following are the three general types of agricultural credit to consider, based on length of term and type of collateral needed:

1. *Short-term or production credit.*—This is for up to one year. It is used for purchase of feed and operating expenses.

2. *Intermediate credit.*—This type of credit may be for one to seven years. It is used for the purchase of breeding stock, machinery, equipment, and semipermanent investments. Repayment is made from the profits over several production periods.

3. *Long-term credit.*—This type of credit is used for land and major farm building, and for physical plant construction. Repayment is made over several years, from profits.

HELPFUL HINTS FOR BUILDING AND MAINTAINING A GOOD CREDIT RATING. —Horsemen who wish to build up and maintain good credit are admonished to do the following:

● Keep credit in one place, or in few places.
● Get the right kind of credit.
● Be frank with the lender.
● Keep complete and accurate records.
● Keep annual inventory.
● Repay loans when due.
● Plan ahead.

CREEP, FOAL.—By definition, a creep is an enclosure for feeding purposes, accessible to sucklings but through which their dams cannot pass.

For best results, the following guides should be observed when building a foal creep:

1. *Location.*—The creep should be located at a spot where the mares are inclined to loiter—near water and shade, close to salt, and on high ground.

2. *Enticing.*—It is important that the creep attract sucklings—that they want to enter and remain in it, rather than be curious from the outside. This means that it should be high and dry, and in warm areas it should be shaded. Additionally, and most important, it should be of adequate size, for foals fear too close confinement. Of course, the greater the number of foals, the larger the creep. But even with one or two foals, the creep should be a minimum of 16' x 16' to avoid "equine claustrophobia." Over and above this minimum base size, a safe rule of thumb is to allow 30 square feet of creep area per foal. Thus, if 14 foals are to be accommodated, the size creep is computed as follows:

16' x 16'	=	256 sq. ft., minimum base size
30 sq. ft. x 14 =		420 sq. ft., to be added
Total		676 sq. ft.

676 sq. ft. = 26' x 26', the size creep necessary for 14 foals.

3. *The enclosing fence.*—The creep fence may be of board, pole, or pipe construction. It should be 60 inches high; with three boards, rails, or pipes on 20-inch centers from the top; and on posts centered 8 feet apart.

4. *The opening.*—The opening should be sufficiently wide and high that foals can go in and out without hitting, but narrow and low enough to keep the mares out. For most breeds, an opening 20 inches wide and 52 inches high is about right. The opening may be constructed of two round posts or pipes set at the proper distance apart, with a cross arm about 6 inches lower than the shortest mare at the withers. Thus, if the shortest mare is 14-2 hands (or 58 inches), the

cross arm should be 52 inches from the ground. Avoid projections or sharp corners on the creep opening.

Where mares and foals are on pasture, particularly when they're some distance from the barn, creep-feeding is usually the most practical way to facilitate supplementing mare's milk and grass.

Fig. C-16. A foal creep. With this arrangement the foal can be fed separately from the dam.

5. *Feed container.*—The ration container may feed from one or both sides. With a group of foals, it is usually best that the feeder be placed in the center of the creep and feed from both sides. If it feeds from one side, it should be 18 inches wide; if it feeds from both sides, it should be 30 inches wide. Allow about 1½ linear feet of feeder space per animal. Thus, a 10 to 12 ft. trough feeding from both sides (30 inches wide) will accommodate fourteen foals.

The height of the feed container from the ground will vary according to the breed and height of the animals. A rule of thumb is that it should be about ⅔ the height (at withers) of foals. A foal that will develop into a 15 hand (60 in.) horse at maturity will be about 50 inches high at weaning time; hence, the feed container for such an animal should be 32 to 34 inches from the ground.

SOME CAUTIONS.—Like most good things, a creep can be misused. For example, when foals are creep-fed, rather than stall-fed twice daily, it's easier to neglect them. As a result, one or more of them may be off feed without being no-

ticed, at which time the others may overeat. Also, sometimes a foal knocks a hip down, or injures the top of his head, when going through the creep opening. Then there's the occasional mare that seems to squeeze through any opening, with the result that she may overeat and founder. However, round posts, plus padding if necessary, will usually alleviate the former hazard; and even the most crafty mare can usually be kept out of a creep by limiting both the height and width of the opening. Besides, it is recognized that there are injury hazards with other methods of feeding. For example, a foal is frequently bitten or kicked by its own dam who objects to junior putting his nose in the grain box with her.

CREST.—The top part of the neck. This is very well developed in stallions.

(Also see PARTS OF A HORSE—Fig. P-4.)

CRIBBER.—See VICES—Cribber.

CRICKET (ROLLER).—A copper roller, rollers, or other loose copper in the port of a spade mouth bit.

(Also see BITS—Fig. B-10)

CRIOLLO.—The cow pony of South America. The Criollos are descendants of imported Spanish horses, with infusion of Arabian and Barb breeding. Dun and skewbald are the most common colors, although they are of many and bizarre colors. Most of them range in height from 13-3 to 14-3 hands. The Criollos are tough, fast, and well suited to the work that they are required to do; but they are not beautiful according to our standards of horseflesh. They are heavier boned than our light horse breeds; they have Roman noses; and most of them have small eyes.

CRITTER.—Refers to any cattle.

CROP.—A whip with a straight stock and a loop. Crops vary according to use. The riding crop is usually made of leather and has a short, straight stock of whalebone, hawthorne (wood), or rawhide. The racing bat is a crop with leather tags along each side. The hunting whip, or thong (incorrectly called a hunting crop), is made of steel, cane, or fiberglass, which may be covered with braided nylon, gut, or plaited Kangaroo hide. It has a thong and a silk or cord lash attached to the top end, and a buckhorn handle at the lower end for opening gates.

CROP-EARED.—Refers to an animal which has had the tips of its ears either cut off or frozen off.

CROPPER.—A rider who falls is said to "come a cropper."

CROSSBRED.—The progeny of a sire and dam of different breeds.

Fig. C-17. Three Arabian-Percheron crossbred fillies. (Courtesy, Prof. Byron H. Good, Michigan State University, East Lansing, Mich.)

CROSS-COUNTRY EVENTS.—See THREE-DAY EVENT.

CROSS-FIRING.—Cross-firing, a defect in the way of going, is generally confined to pacers and consists of a scuffing on the inside of the diagonal fore and hind feet.

CROUP.—The topline from the hips back. The croup should be long, wide, nicely turned, and heavily muscled.
(Also see PARTS OF A HORSE—Fig. P-4.)

CROW HOP.—Mild or playful bucking motion.

CROWNPIECE (of bridle).—The crown piece of a bridle is the part that goes over the head and rests just back of the ears.
(Also see BRIDLES—Fig. B-66.)

CRUPPER.—A leather strap with a padded semicircular loop. The loop end goes under the tail and the strap end is affixed at the center of the back band of a harness or the cantle of a saddle to prevent the saddle from slipping over the withers.
(Also see HARNESS.)

CRYPTORCHID.—A stallion with one or both testicles retained in the abdomen. Such undescended testicles are usually sterile because of the high temperature in the abdomen. This condition appears to be heritable. Thus, it is recommended that animals so affected not be retained for breeding purposes.

CUBBING (CUB HUNTING).—The prehunting-season training of young hounds and young foxes. The objects are to teach young hounds to hunt, and young foxes to run rather than to hide and be routed out. Clothes are informal. Young horses and riders are usually welcome at cubbing time, but they should not interfere with the serious business of educating hounds and foxes.

CULTURE.—The propagation of microorganisms, or of living tissue cells, in special media conducive to their growth. By taking a culture from the infected site and growing it on such media, it is possible to make tests, including microscopic examination, and thus identify the type of organism causing the infection.

CURB.—Curb is the name given to the condition in which there is a fullness at the rear of the leg and below the point of the hock. This fullness is due to enlargement of the ligament or tendon. The condition is caused by anything that brings about a thickening in the ligament, tendon, or skin of this region so as to cause a deviation in the straight line that normally extends from the point of the hock to the fetlock. Firing and blistering are the usual treatments.

(Also see UNSOUNDNESSES.)

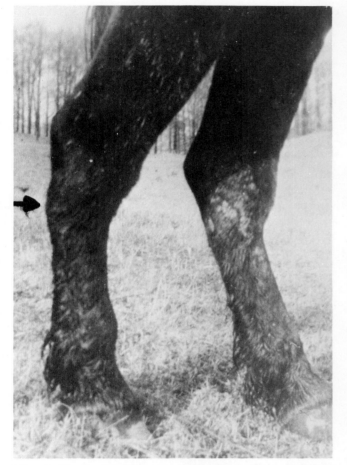

Fig. C-18. Curb. (Courtesy, Michigan State University)

CURB BIT.—A bit mouthpiece, designed to bring pressure to bear on the horse's bars.

(Also see BITS.)

CURB CHAIN.—A series of links of steel of different shapes and sizes, usually single-linked, sometimes double. The links gradually increase in size from the extremities of the chain to the middle, where in riding bits a plain round pendant ring is suspended at right angles to the chain proper. Through this pendant ring the lip strap runs. The curb chain should lie flat in the

groove of the chin. A curb chain should be adjusted so that it applies no pressure when the reins are loose but tightens up as soon as the rider pulls up on the reins. It is properly adjusted if you can slip two fingers under it when it is loose. Its function is to provide mechanical attachment for the bit against the jaw and to subject the head and neck (and hence the whole body) to the control of the hand. Pressure on the lower jaw pulls the lower jaw and chin inward toward the body. This causes the horse to arch his neck, get his legs beneath him, pull himself together, and be ready for the command.

(Also see CHIN STRAP.)

CURRY.—Cleaning or grooming with curry comb, dandy brush, body brush, sponge, rub rag, hoof pick, etc.

CUT-OUT.—The cutting out of certain animals in a herd in order to examine, castrate, brand, etc.

CUTTER, CLINCH.—See SHOEING—Table S-5.

CUTTING HORSE (a sporting event).—This event is designed to test the "cow sense" of a horse, by cutting cattle from the herd. The horse

Fig. C-19. Cutting horse, Lucky Penny, shown working without a bridle. Lucky Penny is a registered Quarter Horse, owned by Clem Boettcher, East Bernard, Texas. (Courtesy, Western Horseman, Colorado Springs, Colo.)

is on his own to out-think and out-perform the cows assigned to him. The person astride a cutting horse merely goes along for the ride. Cutting horse judges penalize riders who rein or signal their horses.

D

DAILY DOUBLE, THE.—The Daily Double is a popular form of betting on both the first and second races of the day with a single wager. In betting on the Daily Double the bettor attempts to pick the winner of both the first and second races before the first race begins and he collects only if both horses win. This, of course, is more difficult than picking a single winner—and pay-offs reflect this. These tickets are sold in $2.00 and $10.00 denominations at a few selected windows with appropriate Daily Double signs.

DAISY-CUTTER.—A horse that seems to skim the surface of the ground at the trot. Such horses are often predisposed to stumbling.

DALLY.—The act of taking a turn around the saddle horn with a lariat to hold a roped animal. Some ropers tie the rope securely to the saddle horn; others carry it in their hand until an animal is roped, then take up the slack and "take a dally around the horn."

DAM.—The female parent of a horse.

DANDY BRUSH.—See GROOMING A HORSE—Table G-1.

DAN PATCH.—Dan Patch's exploits took place soon after the turn of the century, from 1902 to 1910. In 1906, he paced the fastest mile ever, in 1:55, at the Minnesota State Fair. That record stood until 1938. It was not recognized, however, because a windshield was pulled in front of the sulky to break the wind. But to the 93,000 rabid fans who witnessed the feat, and to his worshippers everywhere, the record stood.

The great horse's owner, Will Savage, was a fabulous and colorful character. Will and Dan belonged to each other—even in death. Mr. Savage made headlines of a sort when he paid $60,000 for the six-year-old Standardbred pacer in 1902. Even his friends referred to the deal as "Savage's folly." But subsequent events proved how wrong they were.

Dan Patch brought fame and fortune to his master, and to himself. A railroad line, The Dan Patch Line, was named after him. There were also Dan Patch sleds, coaster wagons, cigars, washing machines (a two-minute performer like Dan), and shoes for kiddies. And Mr. Savage built the great horse an empire, surroundings befitting his station in life. The stable was equipped with modern living quarters for sixty caretakers. Two race tracks were constructed; the best mile strip ever built, and a covered half-miler with 8,400 panes of glass. Even during a Minnesota blizzard, Dan and his stable mates could train in comfort and style.

Dan Patch was the idol of his day—the Babe Ruth, the Bing Crosby, and the Beatles. People came to see him, as they do any other notable. Lili Langtry, the famous actress, arranged to have her train stopped near Dan's so that she could go to his private car for a visit. Men vied for his shoes, women fought to pluck hair from his mane and tail, small boys played Dan Patch in the backyard, and people wept when he became ill.

The town of Hamilton changed its name to Savage, in honor of the man who had put it on the map.

But there was more than a platonic relationship between horse and owner—there was something almost supernatural between Dan and Will. On July 4, 1916, Dan Patch and Will Savage both took ill on the same day. Those keeping vigil over the horse saw him snuff out his last race—the race with life itself—on July 11. He died at age twenty. Thirty-two hours later, Dan's master, Will Savage, was dead at age fifty-seven. Both were buried at the same hour; Mr. Savage in Lakewood cemetery, and Mr. Patch under the shade of an oak tree on the bank of the Minnesota River.

Fig. D-1. *The fabulous Dan Patch, flawless early-day performer and great attraction on tracks throughout the U.S. (Courtesy, United States Trotting Association, Columbus, Ohio)*

Fig. D-2. *A rare "triple dead heat" of Quarter Horses, which occurred at the Alameda Country Fair Grounds, Pleasanton, Calif. (Photo by Photo-Patrol, Inc., San Mateo, Calif.; courtesy, American Quarter Racing Association, Tucson, Ariz.)*

DAPPLE.—Small spots, patches, or dots contrasting in color or shade with the background, such as dapple-gray.

DARK HORSE.—A racehorse whose ability and chances of success in a race are not known outside his own stable.

DARLEY ARABIAN.—Darley Arabian was imported into England in 1706 by Richard Darley, a Yorkshire squire. He was a purebred Arabian of the Managhi strain. He became the most famous of all the Thoroughbred foundation sires and had a profound influence on the Thoroughbred breed.

DASHBOARD.—A screen of wood or leather placed on the forepart of a horse-drawn carriage or other vehicle, to prevent water, mud, or snow being thrown up by the heels of the horse(s).

DASH RACE.—A race short enough to allow the horses to cover the entire distance at top speed.

DEAD HEAT.—A race in which two or more horses tie—there is no single winner.

DEBILITATING.—Weakening.

DEERFLY.—See FLIES.

DENMARK.—Denmark (foaled in 1839) was a four-mile Thoroughbred race stallion, and the horse to which most modern American Saddle Horses now trace. Although this horse did not achieve great fame on the track, his races were said to be characterized by unusual stamina and gameness. Denmark left numerous progeny, but his most notable offspring was Gaine's Denmark.

DENTAL STAR.—A marking on the incisor teeth of horses, used in judging their age. It first appears on the lower central and intermediate incisors when the horse is about eight years of age.

(Also see TEETH, STRUCTURE OF; and see AGE, Figs. A-3 to A-18.)

DEPRAVED APPETITE (PICA).—Equines, particularly those confined to stalls or small corrals, frequently consume such materials as dirt, sand, hair, bones, and feces. Such a depraved appetite is known as "pica." This condition is usually caused by one or both of the following conditions:

● *Boredom*—because they have time on their hands. If this condition prevails, step up the exercise.

● *Nutritional deficiencies*—which may be due to (1) a deficiency of one or more nutrients, or (2) an imbalance between certain nutrients. Nutritional deficiencies are more apt to occur during the latter third of pregnancy, because the fetus is growing more rapidly at that time.
(Also see WOOD CHEWING.)

DEPRECIATION ON HORSE BUILDINGS AND EQUIPMENT.—In 1962, the Treasury issued "useful life" guidelines. If a horseman follows them, he will not be challenged. For buildings, it's twenty-five years; for machinery and equipment, it's ten years.
(Also see TAXES, INCOME.)

DERBY.—The word "derby" stems from a classic race exclusively for three-year-olds which was initiated at Epsom Downs, in England, in 1780, by the 12th Earl of Derby. This race became so famous that, today, the word "derby" is considered synonymous with any well-known race; hence, there is the Kentucky Derby, the Japan Derby, etc. In England, the word is pronounced "darby," whereas in the U.S. it is pronounced "derby."

DIAGNOSTIC AGENTS.—Some biological products, usually injected, which are used solely for the diagnosis of diseases. Tuberculin, which is used in the diagnosis of tuberculosis, is an example of such an agent.

DIAGONAL.—Refers to the forefoot's moving in unison with its opposite hindfoot at the trot. If it is the left forefoot, it is called the left diagonal.

DIARRHEA.—See SCOURING.

DIGESTIVE SYSTEM.—The alimentary canal includes the entire tube extending from the mouth to the rectum. Table D-1 and Fig. D-4 show the comparative structures and sizes of the digestive tracts of farm animals, whereas Fig. D-3 shows the location of the digestive system in the horse. As noted, the digestive tract of a horse is anatomically and physiologically quite different from that of a ruminant. The digestive tract of horses is much smaller, with the result that horses cannot eat as much roughage as cattle. Also, the primary seats of microbial activity in ruminants and horses occupy different locations in the digestive system in relation to the small intestine. In cows and sheep, the rumen precedes the small intestine; in horses, the cecum follows it.

TABLE D-1

CAPACITIES OF DIGESTIVE TRACTS OF HORSE, COW, AND PIG [1]

Parts of digestive tract	Horse	Cow	Pig
	(quarts)	(quarts)	(quarts)
Stomach	8 to 16	(200)	6 to 8
Rumen (paunch)	—————	160	—————
Reticulum (honeycomb)	—————	10	—————
Omasum (manyplies)	—————	15	—————
Abomasum (true stomach of cow) . . .	—————	15	—————
Small intestine	48	62	9
Cecum	28 to 32	—————	—————
Large intestine	80	40	10

[1] Values are for average-size horses of 1,000 to 1,200 lb.

Both the amount of bacterial synthesis and the efficiency of absorption of nutrients synthesized by the microorganisms are likely to be lower in a horse than in a ruminant. In comparison to a cow, therefore, a horse should be fed less roughage, more and higher quality protein (no urea), and added B vitamins. Actually, the nutrient requirements of a horse appear more nearly parallel to those of a pig than a cow.

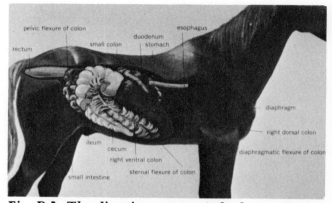

Fig. D-3. The digestive system of the horse. (Reproduced with permission of Haileybury Farm and Tampa Tracings, 1971; Courtesy, The Wickes, Newville, Pa.)

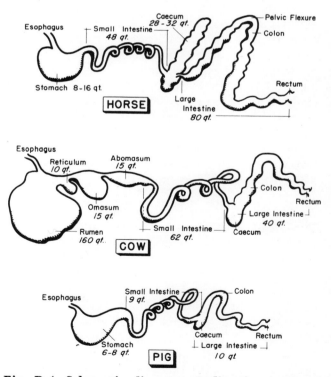

Fig. D-4. Schematic diagram of digestive tracts of horse, cow, and pig.

DIGGING.—This refers to the stable vice characterized by the horse digging a hole in his stall, usually just inside the entrance. The only effective way in which to prevent this vice is to stable the horse on a hard surface.

(Also see VICES—Stall pawing.)

DIRECTION (change of).—When a horse is worked entirely, or almost entirely, in a ring, especially if he is cantered or galloped any length of time, it is advisable to change direction frequently. In so doing, the lead or diagonal is also changed and the horse is able to rest himself by shifting the bulk of his weight from one pair of legs to another. In the show-ring, the judge(s) always asks for at least one change of direction so that he may see the rider from both sides and so that he may see the horse on both leads. In a horsemanship class, the rider should make a half-turn towards the wall (half-turn in reverse). In a saddle horse or hunter class, he should reverse toward the center. In both cases, the order from the ringmaster will be, "Reverse, please."

(Also see LEAD.)

DISEASES AND PARASITES OF HORSES.—Horse owners and caretakers have a responsibility for the horses in their care. They must protect their animals from diseases and parasites.

In general, disease is defined as any departure from the state of health. Beyond a doubt, the most serious menace threatening the horse industry is equine ill-health. There are many degrees of ill-health, but by far the largest loss is a result of the diseases that are due to a common factor transmitted from animal to animal. These disorders are classed as infectious, contagious, and parasitic diseases and are considered theoretically controllable. Today, with the modern rapid transportation facilities and the dense horse population centers, the opportunity for animals to become infected are greatly increased compared with a generation ago.

Few people realize the extent of losses caused by diseases and parasites. One is inclined to consider only those costs due to death or depreciation, but actual animal disease losses are far more extensive. For example, considerable cost is involved in keeping out diseases that do not exist in the United States. Also, quarantine of a diseased area may cause depreciation of land values, or may even restrict whole agricultural programs.

The fact that many animal diseases are transmissible to man is well known, and, as a result, the ever-present human danger adds to the economic loss. Approximately ninety different types of infectious and parasitic diseases can be spread from animals to human beings.

Although it is difficult to estimate the actual death loss due to parasites, it is even more difficult to make a proper appraisal of the losses due to unthriftiness and stunting that invariably result from parasitic invasions.

Despite all these disturbing factors, it is satisfying to know that the United States is regarded as the safest country in the world for a flourishing horse industry. In order to insure further progress, however, thousands of workers—including scientists with the U.S. Department of Agriculture, colleges, pharmaceutical houses, practicing veterinarians, and others—are constantly striving to make this country even healthier for both man and beast.

For information on each of the major horse diseases and parasites, see their alphabetical listing in this book.

(Also see HEALTH PROGRAM.)

CAUSES OF DISEASE.—Any agent that may bring about an abnormal condition of any or all tissues of the body is a disease-producing entity. Among the chief causes may be listed infectious agents, such as bacteria, viruses, and parasites; and noninfectious agents, including chemicals, poisons of various types, faulty nutrition, and injuries. In addition to the actual causative agent, any of the following conditions may predispose disease: overwork, exposure to cold, and long shipments—especially in cold weather.

The activity of disease in the animal body results in a change in the tissues invaded. It is usually marked by inflammation, which is manifested by increased blood supply to the part affected and by heat, redness, swelling, and pain in the affected part.

Diseases are often named after the part affected with the suffix "itis" (meaning inflammation) attached—for example, conjunctivitis (inflammation of the conjuctiva of the eye) or enteritis (inflammation of the intestines, or entrails).

The infection of a tissue and the production of a disease by a living agent is not always easily accomplished. The agent must first gain entrance to the animal by one of the body openings (respiratory, digestive, or genital tract) or through the skin. It then usually multiplies and attacks the tissues. To accomplish this, it must be sufficiently powerful (virulent) to overcome the defenses of the animal body. The defenses of the animal body vary and may be weak or entirely lacking, especially under conditions of a low nutritional plane and poor management practices.

DISH-FACED.—A term used if the face is concave below the eyes, and, especially in Arabians, if the profile shows a definite depression below the level of the eyes. This term is also applied to some horses and many ponies that have flat or concave foreheads with prominent temples, but this type is the absolute opposite to the "dish" of the Arab, which has a prominent forehead.

DISHING.—When moving, each foot of the horse should move forward in a straight line, without the feet being thrown either inward or outward. Any deviation from this action is indicated by one of three terms: dishing, paddling, or winging. There is not complete agreement among horsemen in the use of these terms, especially in the use of the word, "dishing." To some authorities, dishing means that the hocks are thrown in and the hind feet thrown out. To others, it refers to any foot (front or hind) thrown outward. To still others, it means that a horse turns his feet inward.

DISINFECTANTS.—A disinfectant is an agent which is intended to destroy microorganisms on inanimate surfaces. It should be distinguished from an antiseptic, which is intended for destruction or reduction of microorganism populations on living tissue. (Two common antiseptics—boric acid and iodine—are listed in Table D-2.)

Under ordinary circumstances, proper cleaning of barns removes most of the microorganisms present, along with the filth. However, those remaining may be capable of causing an outbreak of disease. Therefore, a good disinfectant should

(Chemical agents should not be relied upon to destroy spores; controlled and prolonged heat is required for this purpose.)

Kind of Disinfectant	Usefulness	Strength	Limitations and Comments
Alcohol	Effective against the less resistant disease germs provided there is adequate exposure.	70% alcohol—the content usually found in "rubbing" alcohol.	Limited application. Not recommended for general use. Often used as a local antiseptic in obtaining blood samples or making hypodermic injections. Not reliable for sterilization of instruments.
Boric Acid1	As wash for eyes, and other sensitive parts of the body.	1 oz. in 1 pt. water (about 6% solution).	It is a weak antiseptic. It may cause harm to the nervous system if absorbed into the body in large amounts. For this and other reasons, antibiotic solutions and saline solutions are fast replacing it.
Cationic Bactericides (Many commercial products available, including QAC, i.e., quaternary ammonium compounds)	Primarily detergents but some are actively bactericidal. Use only as recommended by a sanitarian.	Concentration varies with different products and under different conditions. Follow authoritative recommendations.	They have only a slight toxicity and are non-irritant and odorless. They are neutralized by soap, anionic detergents and even by mineral content of some waters. Superior to chlorine compounds in the presence of organic matter. They are not effective against TB organisms and spores.
Cresols (Many commercial products available)	A generally reliable class of disinfectant. Effective against brucellosis, and tuberculosis.	4 oz. per gal.; or according to the directions found on the container.	Cannot be used where odor may be absorbed. Do not use on or around animals (carcinogenic).
Heat (by steam, hot water, burning, or boiling)	In the burning of rubbish or articles of little value, and in disposing of infected body discharges. The steam "Jenney" is effective for disinfection if properly employed—particularly if used in conjunction with a phenolic germicide.	10-min. exposure to boiling water is usually sufficient.	Exposure to boiling water will destroy all ordinary disease germs, but sometimes fails to kill the spores of such diseases as anthrax and tetanus. Moist heat is preferred to dry heat, and steam under pressure is the most effective. Heat may be impractical or too expensive.
Hypochlorites (chlorine compounds)	For deodorizing manure, sewers and drains.	200 parts available chlorine per million of water. Unstable; replace solution frequently as recommended.	Excellent for disinfection, but with following limitations: Not effective against the TB organism and spores. Its effectiveness is greatly reduced in presence of organic matter, even in small quantities. Hypochlorites deteriorate rapidly when exposed to air.
Iodine1	Extensively used as skin disfectant, for minor cuts and bruises.	Generally used as a tincture of iodine 2% or 7%.	Never cover with a bandage. Clean skin before applying iodine.
Iodophor (iodine complexed with a detergent which releases free iodine at a controlled rate)

(Continued) | For area disinfection where large quantities of organic soil are not present. | 75 parts available iodine per million is minimum under ideal circumstances. 150 ppm. is recommended for most practical uses. Unstable —replace solution frequently. | An excellent disinfectant but with the following practical limitations: Germicidal agent rapidly consumed by organic matter, necessitating frequent replacement. Functions best in a highly acid range. Solution strength must be increased to get necessary available iodine when mixture is made with alkaline water. Iodine slowly volatilizes from solution. Considerable control should be exercised. |

Kind of Disinfectant	Usefulness	Strength	Limitations and Comments
Lime (quicklime; burnt lime; calcium oxide)	As a deodorant when sprinkled on manure and animal discharges; or as a disinfectant when sprinkled on the floor or used as a newly-made "milk of lime" or as a whitewash.	Use as a dust; as "milk of lime"; or as a white-wash but use fresh.	Not effective against organism of TB and the spore formers. Wear goggles when adding water to quicklime.
Lye (sodium hydroxide or caustic soda)	On concrete floors; and against microorganisms of brucellosis. In strong solution (5%) effective against anthrax.	1 can (13-oz.) to 12 to 15 gals. water. To prepare a 5% solution, add 5 cans (13-oz.) to 10 gals. water.	Damages fabrics, aluminum, and painted surfaces. Be careful, for it will burn the hands and face. Not effective against organisms of TB, or strangles, or most spores. *Diluted vinegar can be used to neutralize lye.*
Phenolic Germicides, Synthetic (those containing odorless nontoxic phenols such as orthophenyl phenol or orthobenzyl parachlorophenol)	A very reliable class of disinfectants effective against all disease-producing fungi and bacteria including the TB organism.	Varies with different formulations; follow directions on manufacturer's label.	Excellent for disinfection. They are not inactivated by soap, anionic detergents, hard water or organic matter. They are effective against all bacteria and fungi including the TB organism but not the spores of anthrax and tetanus.
Sal Soda	It may be used in place of lye against foot-and-mouth disease and vesicular exanthema.	10.5% solution (13½ ozs. to 1 gal. water).	
Soap	Its power to kill germs is very limited. Greatest usefulness is in cleansing and dissolving coatings from various surfaces, including the skin, prior to application of a good disinfectant.	As commercially prepared.	Although indispensable for sanitizing surfaces, soaps should not be used as disinfectants. They are not regularly effective; staphylococci and the organisms which cause diarrheal diseases are resistant.
Soda Ash (or sodium carbonate)	It may be used in place of lye against certain diseases.	5% solution (1 lb. to 3 gals. water). Most effective in hot solution.	Commonly used as a cleansing agent, but has disinfectant properties, especially when used as a hot solution.

[1] Sometimes loosely classed as a disinfectant but actually an antiseptic and practically useful only on living tissue.

be employed in the cleaning program as a preventive measure. In case of a disease outbreak, the premises must be thoroughly disinfected.

In choosing a chemical disinfectant it should be realized that not all disease-producing bacteria are subject to the same chemical agents. Of the many chemical disinfectants available, the synthetic phenolics have generally been considered most practical and most broadly effective, followed by the cresols, the quaternary ammonium compounds, and the hypochlorites.

Table D-2 gives a summary of the limitations, usefulness, and strength of some common disinfectants.

DISMOUNTING.—See HORSEMANSHIP.

DISPOSITION.—See SELECTING AND JUDGING HORSES.

DISTAFF SIDE.—The female side of the pedigree.

DISTANCE *(between horses)*.—This refers to the space between the nose of one horse and the tail of the horse in front of him. Traditionally, that distance was supposed to be the length of the horse; any less distance than that was considered unsafe. For ordinary ring riding and close-order mounted drill and music rides the normal distance is four feet. This is sufficient space to avoid danger of the lead horse kicking the horse behind, and of the horse in the rear stepping on the heels of the horse in front. In the hunt field, greater distances between horses are necessary, so that if a horse refuses a jump or falls at a jump the next rider will not crash headlong into him. Likewise, on a trail with steep ascents and descents considerable distance between horses must be kept.

DISTEMPER (STRANGLES).—A widespread contagious disease caused by *Streptococcus equi*, a bacterium.

SYMPTOMS.—Sick animals show depression, loss of appetite, high fever, and a discharge from the nose. By the third or fourth day of the disease, the glands under the jaw start to enlarge, become sensitive, and eventually break open and discharge pus. A cough is present.

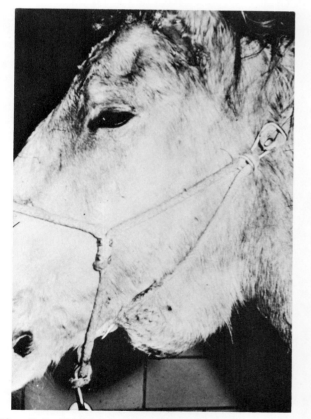

Fig. D-5. Distemper; showing the enlarged glands under the jaw—a characteristic symptom. (Courtesy, Dr. V. S. Myers, Jr., V.M.D., Department of Veterinary Surgery and Radiology, University of Minnesota, St. Paul, Minn.)

TREATMENT.—Good nursing is the most important treatment. This includes clean, fresh water, good feed, uniform temperature, and shelter away from drafts. A veterinarian may prescribe one of the sulfas or antibiotics, or both.

CONTROL.—Put affected animals in strict quarantine. Clean and disinfect contaminated quarters and premises.

PREVENTION.—Prevention consists of avoiding contact with infected animals or contaminated feeds, premises, and equipment. The injection of animals with bacterin containing killed *Streptococcus equi* will help raise the level of immunity and may prevent the disease. However, the use of bacterins is not always beneficial.

DISCUSSION.—The disease is worldwide and it attacks animals of any age, but it is most common in young stock. Death losses are low. Affected animals are usually immune for the remainder of life.

(Also see DISEASES AND PARASITES; and HEALTH PROGRAM.)

DISTILLERS PRODUCTS.—This includes a number of by-products obtained from the manufacture of alcohol and distilled liquors from corn, rye, grain sorghum, wheat, molasses, and potatoes. Although the products are similar, the name of the product from which each by-product was made is always included. For example, where corn is used, the by-product is correctly known as corn distillers dried solubles.

Distillers products contain from 25 to 30 percent protein, but the protein is not of good quality, being deficient in the amino acids lysine and tryptophan. They are of particular value for horses as a vitamin supplement in rations, because of their high content of the B-complex vitamins.

DISUNITED.—Said of a horse that uses its legs in the wrong sequence when cantering or galloping. In a disunited horse, the feet on the same side, instead of the diagonal pair, strike the ground simultaneously when the animal canters or gallops.

DOCK.—The solid portion of the tail. It contains the end vertebrae of the spine.

DOCKED AND SET.—A tail which has had part of the dock removed. Also, at the same time, the two large muscles that are used to pull the tail down are cut or "nicked" and the tail "set" to make the horse carry it high.

(Also see SET-TAIL.)

DOG.—A slang term for a sluggish horse which has constantly to be urged along.

DOG CARTS.—Dog carts were so named because they were used for carrying sporting dogs, under the seat. They carried four passengers, back to back, plus the hounds. At first they were two-wheeled. Later, they were built with four wheels. Usually they were driven by one horse, but the bigger four-wheeled dog carts sometimes required two horses.

DOGGIE.—A motherless calf in a range herd. Also, the term "doggie" is sometimes used to refer to poor or inferior mature cattle.

DOMESTICATION AND EARLY USE (of horse).—The horse was probably the last of present-day farm animals to be domesticated by man. According to early records, after subduing the ox, the sheep, and the goat, man domesticated the ass and then the camel; and, finally, the horse became his servant.

Horses appear to have been domesticated first in Central Asia or Persia more than 3,000 years B.C., for they spread westward through southern Europe in the time of the Lake Dwellers. They were reported in Babylonia as early as 2000 B.C., perhaps coming into the country via neighboring Persia.

Although the Egyptians—the most advanced civilization of the day—had domesticated and used the ass from the earliest times, horses were wholly unknown to them until the dynasty of the Shepherd Kings, who entered Egypt from Asia in 1680 B.C. It is reported that, thereafter, the horse was much favored in Egypt.

Presence of the horse seems to have prompted the invention of the chariot, a type of vehicle drawn by horses that the Egyptians used in war

Fig. D-6. The four-wheeled dog cart.

and other pursuits. The Bible also relates (Genesis 50:9) that when Joseph took his father's remains from Egypt back to Canaan "there went up with him both chariots and horsemen." It is probable that the Egyptians were largely responsible for the spread of domesticated horses to other countries.

Certainly, Greece was not even peopled, and there were no horses in Arabia during the early period when they were flourishing in Egypt. But horses and chariots were used in Greece at least a thousand years before Christ, to judge from the account of their use in the siege of Troy. It is also interesting to note that the first and most expert horsemen of Greece, the Thessalonians, were colonists from Egypt. As evidence that the Greeks were accomplished horsemen, it might be pointed out that they developed the snaffle bit at an early period. Also, one of their number is said to have originated the axiom "No foot, no

Fig. D-8. Distinguished young Greek in fashionable riding habit. Bowl painting, 500 B.C. Though the Greeks were accomplished horsemen, at this time the use of the saddle and stirrups appears to have been unknown. (Courtesy, The Bettmann Archive)

Fig. D-7. Joseph using horses in his move to Egypt (about 1500 B.C.), from a miniature painting in the Bible of the Counts of Toggenburg, 16th century. (Courtesy, The Bettmann Archive)

horse." Yet the use of the saddle and stirrups appears to have been unknown at this time.

From Greece, the horse was later taken to Rome and from there to other parts of Europe. The Romans proved to be master horsemen. It was they who invented the curb bit. According to historians, when Caesar invaded Britain, about 55 B.C., he took horses with him. Although there were other horses in Britain at the time of the Roman occupation, Eastern breeding was probably greatly infused at this time—thus laying the foundation for the Blood Horse of today.

The Arabs, strangely enough, did not use horses to any extent until after the time of Mohammed (A.D. 570 to 632), depending on camels before that time. As evidence of this fact, it is noted that in the seventh century after Christ, when Mohammed attacked the Koreish near Mecca, he had but two horses in his whole army; and at the close of his murderous campaign, although he drove off 24,000 camels and 40,000 sheep and carried away 24,000 ounces of silver, not one horse appeared in his list of plunder. This would seem to indicate rather conclusively that Arabia, the country whose horses have done so much to improve the horses of the world, was not the native home of the horse and that the Arabs did not use horses until after the time of Christ.

Of course, it seems incredible that all the various breeds, colors, and types of draft, light, and pony horses should have descended from a common, wild ancestor. Rather, there were probably many different wild stocks giving descent to domestic horses.

(Also see HISTORY OF HORSES IN UNITED STATES.)

DOMINANT AND RECESSIVE FACTORS.— Some genes have the ability to prevent or mask the expression of others, with the result that the genetic makeup of such animals cannot be recognized with accuracy. This is called dominance. The gene that is masked is recessive. Thus, black is dominant to chestnut; hence when a pure black stallion is crossed on a chestnut mare, all of the offspring will be black. The resulting black is not genotypically pure, however; it is Bb, where B stands for the dominant black and b for the recessive chestnut. This black animal will produce germ cells carrying black and chestnut genes in equal proportion. Then if an F_1 stallion is crossed on F_1 mares, the F_2 population will, on the average, consist of three blacks to one chestnut. The chestnut, being a recessive, will be pure for color; that is, the mating of two chestnut horses will produce chestnut offspring, which is the situation in the Suffolk breed of draft horses where all animals of the breed are chestnuts. Of the three blacks, in the F_2, however, only one is pure for black (with the genetic constitution BB). The other two will be Bb in genetic constitution, and will produce germ cells carrying B and b in equal proportion.

As can be readily understood, dominance often makes it difficult to identify and discard all animals carrying an undesirable recessive factor. Also, in some cases dominance is neither complete nor absent, but incomplete or partial and expressed in a variety of ways. The best known case of this type in horses is the Palomino color. The dilution gene D is incompletely dominant over d. In the heterozygous condition, the dilution of chestnut produces palomino.

(Also see HEREDITY IN HORSES.)

DONKEYS *(Equus asinus).*—This refers to small asses or burros. The males are known as jacks, and the females as jennets. Compared with the horse, the ass is smaller; has shorter hairs on the mane and tail; does not possess the "chestnuts" on the inside of the hind legs; has much longer ears; has smaller, deeper hoofs; possesses a louder and more harsh voice, called a bray; is less subject to founder or injury; is more hardy; and has a longer gestation period—jennets carry their young about 12 months.

Donkeys should be fed and cared for in the same manner as horses, lessening their feed and space requirements in keeping with their smaller size.

The American Donkey and Mule Society is a non-profit organization devoted to the welfare and perpetuation of the donkey and mule and the best interests of their owners. The Society maintains a registry for donkeys, mules, and hinnys at the following address: 2410 Executive Drive, Indianapolis, Indiana 46241. Also, the Society publishes a quarterly, appropriately called *Mr. Longears.*

(Also see BREED (S).)

Fig. D-9. Donkeys at Bitterroot Stock Farm, Hamilton, Montana, owned by Margit Sigray Bessenyey. (Photo by Ernst Peterson, Hamilton, Montana)

DOOR (STABLE).—The space through which a horse passes upon entering or leaving his stall. It should be wide enough to allow a horse to pass through easily without bumping his hips, and it should be high enough to avoid the horse hitting his head. Doors 4 feet wide and 8 feet high meet these requirements.

Doors should always be equipped with a device by which they can be fastened open securely (as well as fastened shut), thereby alleviating the hazard of a hip getting knocked as a result of wind blowing a door against him as he is entering his stall.

(Also see BUILDINGS—Table B-9.)

DOPING.—Administering a drug to a horse to increase or decrease his speed in a race is known as doping. Race course officials run saliva tests, urine tests (urinalyses), etc., in order to try to detect any horses that have been doped. Usually such tests are conducted on the winners of every race and on the first three to finish in stakes races. Where doping is proved, the horse may be banned from the track for a period of time; the owner may have his entire stable banned from racing for a period of time; and/or the trainer or jockey may lose his license; with the penalty determined by the circumstances.

DORSAL STRIPE.—A continuous black, brown, or dun stripe extending from the line of the neck to the tail, and sometimes continuing down the tail.

DOUBLE BACK.—A term used to describe a horse whose loin muscles rise above his backbone.

DOUBLE-GAITED.—A horse that can both trot and pace with good speed.

DOUBLE OXER.—A hunting term for jumps that have a railing or fence on either side. The word "oxer" comes from ox fence, which refers to a hedge about three feet high protected on one side by a fence.

(Also see JUMPS—Fig. J-5.)

DRAFT HORSES.—Draft horses are 14-2 to 17-2 hands high, weigh 1,400 pounds or more, and are used primarily for pulling loads and other heavy work. They represent the ultimate in power type. Formerly, draft-type horses of quality and style were used on city streets, but these have long since been replaced by trucks. Industry's most glamorous use of draft horses today consists of the six- and eight-horse hitches used for exhibition—a type of advertising. (See Fig. D-10.)

DRAFTY.—Having the characteristics of a draft horse. Heavy and lacking in quality.

DRAG.—Artificial scent made by dragging a bag containing anise seed or litter from a fox's den over the chosen terrain. Later, the hounds are put on the line and follow the scent left by the drag.

DRAG HUNT.—A hunt staged on horseback with hounds following a laid trail, made by dragging a bag containing anise seed or litter from a fox's den.

DRAIN.—A hunting term for an underground drain, pipe, culvert, ditch, or watercourse used as refuge by foxes.

DRAW REIN.—A rein attached to the girth or breastplate and coming to the hand through the snaffle bit rings. A draw rein is a training device used to teach the horse to lower his head and flex at the poll.

DRENCH.—A dose of medicine in liquid form which is put down the throat of a horse.

DRENCHING.—Only the veterinarian or a very experienced horseman should ever drench a horse. The animal can be choked or get foreign-body pneumonia if the head is held too high or if the liquid is released too quickly.

Wine bottles used as follows are suitable for drenching: Insert the long neck in the horse's

Fig. D-10. The magnificent 8-horse hitch of champion Clydesdale horses, exhibited by Anheuser-Busch, Inc. *(Through the courtesy of Anheuser-Busch, Inc., St. Louis, Missouri)*

mouth just ahead of his molars; point the neck of the bottle toward the rear of his mouth; raise his head; and release the drench slowly.

DRESSAGE (AIRS, CLASSICAL).—The guiding of a horse through natural maneuvers without emphasis on the use of reins, hands, and feet.

The term "dressage" comes from the French verb meaning "to train." After the horse has learned to respond to the simple directions of moving forward or backward, turning, changing gait, halting, etc., the horseman who wishes to develop his horse's strength, willingness, and agility as much as possible continues his training by giving him special exercises to develop these traits. This training is called dressage. (Also see AMERICAN DRESSAGE INSTITUTE, THE.)

All of the movements described as dressage or training movements are based on natural movements of the horse while at liberty. Thus, by watching horses (especially young horses) in a corral, one will see them execute with ease changes from one gait to another, sudden halts,

changes of the leading leg at the canter when changing direction, and such intricacies of the Haute École as the Pirouette, the Piaffe, the Passage, and the Pesade. Why, then, must a horse be trained to do these things if he already knows how? There are two reasons: (1) the horse must learn to balance himself under the weight of the rider, and (2) the horse must learn to do these movements when so requested by the rider.

Dressage training is usually divided into three stages:

1. *Light or basic dressage.*—This involves getting the horse obedient at all gaits on straight lines and circles.

2. *Intermediate dressage.*—This takes the horse through the schooling figures, including the *Passage* and the *Flying Charge.*

3. *Heavy dressage.*—This includes the highly collected movements such as the *Piaffe,* as well as off-the-ground movements.

Fig. D-11. Hungarian foal displaying natural maneuvers and aptitude for dressage, at Bitterroot Stock Farm, Hamilton, Montana, owned by Margit Sigray Bessenyey. (Photo by Ernst Peterson, Hamilton, Montana)

Fig. D-12. A Lipizzan stallion shown executing the Levade at the Spanish Riding School in Austria, where dressage in its highest form is featured. (Courtesy, Spanish Riding School, Wels, Austria)

The methods of dressage have varied with the object. The Federation Equestre Internationale's (F.E.I.) definition of the object of Dressage is as follows:

The object of dressage is the harmonious development of the physique and ability of the horse. As a result, it makes the horse calm, supple and keen, thus achieving perfect understanding with its rider.

These qualities are revealed by: the freedom and regularity of the paces; the harmony, lightness and ease of movements; the lightening of the forehand and the engagement of the hindquarters; the horse remaining absolutely straight in any movement along a straight line and bending accordingly when moving on curved lines.

The horse thus gives the impression of doing of his own accord what is required of him.

Confident and attentive, he submits generously to the control of his rider.

His walk is regular, free and unconstrained. His trot is free, supple, regular, sustained, and active. His canter is united, light and cadenced. His quarters are never inactive or sluggish. They respond to the slightest indication of the rider and thereby give life and spirit to the rest of his body.

By virtue of a lively impulsion and the suppleness of his joints, free from the paralyzing effects of resistance, the horse obeys willingly and without hesitation, and responds to the various aids calmly and with precision.

In all his work, even at the halt, the horse must be on the bit. A horse is said to be 'on the bit' when the hocks are correctly placed, the neck is more or less raised according to the extension or collection of the pace, the head remains steadily in position, the contact with the mouth is light and no resistance is offered to the rider.

The object, as stated above, should be borne in mind by everyone interested in dressage, regardless of the method of schooling followed.

In the choice of a method of schooling, it should be remembered that no method is any better than the trainer. All methods of dressage consist of a series of movements and exercises, or a course of horse gymnastics. In the best methods, the sequence of exercises is arranged in such a way that the one is preparatory to the next.

Space limitations do not permit detailing any particular method, but the following two points are of special importance in all methods:

● *Always keep the horse supple and relaxed.* —It is most important always to keep the horse supple and relaxed by overcoming all contractions of his muscles. Each time that the rider feels a contraction in any part of the horse, he should immediately stop the particular exercise, relax the horse's muscles, and then resume the original exercise. The following exercises are recommended for the purpose of relaxing the horse: jumping several times one or two small obstacles and walking over four to six small trestles (see CAVALLETTI) on the longeing rein without rider (the latter should be done daily, at the beginning of each lesson) ; turning on the forehead, the head and neck slightly bent to the side opposite the one to which the hind legs move; applying lateral aids; shoulder-in and shoulder-out and trot on the circle allowing the horse to stretch his head and neck as much forward and downward as possible.

The signs of relaxation are: The horse champs his bit calmly and continuously, preferably with his mouth closed; the horse swings his tail rhythmically from side to side; and practically every muscle is at play and "ripples" when the horse is moving (this being most noticeable on the quarters) .

● *Correct the natural curvature of the horse's spine.*—Another important point is to correct the natural curvature of the horse's spine, i.e., making each hind foot follow exactly the forefoot on the same side, and eventually making the horse equally supple to both sides. In this connection, it is noteworthy that the natural curvature of the spine is characterized by the horse moving at a false, slight half-pass position, usually to the right. The correction in this case consists of practicing frequently a slight shoulder-in position on the right rein and a slight quarter-in position on the left rein, and vice versa if the false half-pass position is to the left.

The attainment of the free and elastic action of the horse and the smooth and supple seat of the rider depend on the development of the muscles of the horse's back. This development should result in the formation of two pronounced "pads" of muscles covering the back, with a groove along the spine.

DRIED SKIMMED MILK.—See SKIMMED MILK, DRIED, ETC.

DRIVE TO THE RIGHT, WHY?—The American custom of driving to the right on the road, instead of to the left as is the practice in some parts of the world, originated among the Conestoga wagon drivers of the 1750s. The drivers of these four- and six-horse teams either sat on the left wheel horse or on the left side of the seat, the better to wield their whip hand (the right hand) over the other horses in the team. Also, when two Conestoga drivers met, they pulled over to the right so that, sitting on the left wheel horse or on the left side of the seat, they could see that the left wheels of their wagons cleared each other. Lighter vehicles naturally followed the tracks of the big Conestoga wagons. Even with the development of highways and automobiles, the American custom of driving to the right persisted.

DRIVING BITS.—See BITS.

DRIVING HAMMER.—See SHOEING—Table S-5.

DRIVING HARNESS.—See HARNESS.

DRIVING HORSES.—At the present time, driving horses are used chiefly for purposes of recreation. According to the specific use made of them, driving horses are classified as heavy harness horses, fine harness horses, roadsters, or ponies.

DROP JUMP.—A jump in which the landing side is lower than the take-off. This is a very dangerous jump for an inexperienced horse.

DROVER.—The word "drover" is reminiscent of one of the most thrilling chapters in American history. Prior to the advent of railroads and improved highways, great herds of cattle, sheep, and hogs were driven over famous trails, often many hundreds of miles long. The crew of "drovers" usually consisted of the boss (often the owner of the herd) , a man to ride along each side, and a fourth man to lead.

The "drovers"--those who did the driving—were rugged, and their lives were filled with adventure. The work was accompanied by an almost ceaseless battle with the elements, clashes with thieves, and no small amount of bloodshed.

DRUGS.—Drugs, or medicinal agents, are substances of mineral, vegetable, or animal origin used in the relief of pain or for the cure of disease. Much superstition cloaks the reasons for the recommended use of many drugs that have been employed for centuries. An example of this is liver wort, which was heralded as a sure cure for liver disorders only because it was shaped like a liver. Unfortunately, there is no known cure-all for a large number of diseases or for the relief of a great number of different parasitisms.

Lacking the knowledge of limitations of drugs and the nature of disease, many horsemen have been sold worthless products. There is a flourishing business in various "cure-alls" that are sold under such names as "tonic," "reconditioner," "worm expeller," "liver medicine," "liver mixture," "mineral and vitamin mix," "regulator," and numerous others. It is poor practice to disregard the advice of reputable veterinarians and experimental workers and to rely on claims made by unscrupulus manufacturers of preparations of questionable or fraudulent nature. Most of these patent drugs are sold for fantastic prices, considering their actual cost, and most of their ingredients are never indicated. To avoid being swindled, purchases should be limited to preparations of reliable firms and then confined to those recommended by the local veterinarian. Fortunately, the Food and Drug Administration has been very vigilant and has been instrumental in the disappearance of many misbranded drugs and remedies from interstate channels.

DRYING UP A MARE.—The following procedure is recommended for drying up a mare: Permanently separate the mare and foal at weaning time; decrease the mare's ration; rub camphorated oil or a mixture of lard and spirits of camphor on the udder, but do not milk it out until 5 to 7 days later—when it's soft and flabby.

(Also see FOAL.)

DUDE.—A tenderfoot, commonly an easterner or newcomer to the West. Also, a guest at a dude ranch.

DUDE RANCH.—A ranch or resort for vacationers offering horseback riding and other activities of Western ranches.

DUMB JOCKEY BITTING RIG.—A contrivance fastened on a young horse to train him to place the head in the desired position. The rigging consists of surcingle, back strap, crupper, side reins, overcheck or sidecheck, standing martingale, and some sort of projection above the top of the surcingle to which reins may be attached.

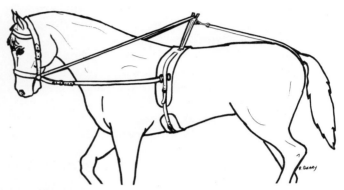

Fig. D-13. Dumb jockey, a bitting contrivance for training a young horse to place his head in the desired position.

DUN (BUCKSKIN).—See COLORS AND MARKINGS OF HORSES.

DUNG.—The excrement of an animal. Manure.

DUNG-EATING.—Eating of dung (manure) or droppings. This vice can be prevented by the use of a muzzle.

DUTCHMAN'S TEAM.—It is customary to hitch the smaller horse of a team on the left side. When a careless horseman hitches his larger horse on the near side, he is said to be driving a "Dutchman's team."

DWELLING.—A noticeable pause in the flight of the foot, as though the stride were completed before the foot reaches the ground; most noticeable in trick-trained horses.

E

EARS.—The size, length, set, carriage, and movements of a horse's ears are most important. The ears should be of medium size and proportionate to the body size, properly set and carried, cleancut and trim in appearance, and with a minimum of long hair on the inside or along the borders. The following types of ears are undesirable: "mulish" ears (long, thick, heavy ears), ears that are set too low down over the eyes or too far back on the poll, and lop-ears.

The movements of the ears are an indication of temperament. Also, a horse expresses himself with his ears much as some people express themselves with their hands.

Until the sixteenth century (and even later in some parts of England) the ears of horses were cut in various ways as a means of identification. For example, a "bitted" ear was bitten (a piece was cut out) from the inner edge. Cropped ears (cut straight across halfway down the ear) were originally used as a means of identification. But the practice became fashionable, much as it is with certain breeds of dogs today, with the result that it persisted into the eighteenth century. This explains why early paintings of horses frequently showed the animals with tiny ears, scarcely two inches long.

(Also see PARTS OF A HORSE—Fig. P-4.)

EAR DOWN.—To restrain an animal by twisting its ear.

EASTERN.—Applied to horses of Arab, Barb, or similar breeding.

EASTERN ENCEPHALITIS.—See ENCEPHALOMYELITIS.

ECLIPSE.—There were two noted Thoroughbred stallions named Eclipse; one was English, and the other American. Eclipse of England was foaled in 1764. He was first raced as a five-year-old; and he was unbeaten throughout his racing career. He was recognized as the horse of his century, and a great breeding horse. The American Eclipse was foaled on Long Island in 1823. He was a grandson of Messenger, and his pedigree traced to the English Eclipse.

EGG BUTT BIT.—A kind of snaffle bit in which the juncture of the mouthpiece and sidepiece somewhat resembles the shape of an egg. The egg butt tends to prevent the ring of a snaffle bit from going into the horse's mouth when the ring on the opposite side is pulled by the rein.

ELBOW (point of the elbow).—The elbow is a true hinged joint formed by the spool-like distal end of the humerus uniting with the proximal ends of the radius and ulna. The point of the elbow projects above and behind the elbow joint.

(Also see PARTS OF A HORSE—Fig. P-4; and SKELETON OF THE HORSE—Fig. S-15.)

EMACIATED.—A severe loss of weight.

ENCEPHALOMYELITIS (SLEEPING SICKNESS).—A virus, epizootic (epidemic) disease that may be carried by birds and mosquitoes. It is caused by four different viruses. The three most common ones are known as the eastern type, the western type, and the Venezuelan type.

SYMPTOMS.—In early stages, animals walk aimlessly about, crashing into objects. Later they may appear sleepy and stand with a lowered head. Grinding of the teeth, inability to swallow, paralysis of the lips, and blindness may be noted. Paralysis may cause animals to fall. If affected animals do not recover, death occurs in 2 to 4 days.

TREATMENT.—Careful nursing is perhaps the most important treatment. Serum treatment is sometimes effective when given very early in the disease. A veterinarian should be consulted about this.

CONTROL.—Control measures include prompt disposal of all infected carcasses; destruc-

Fig. E-1. Western encephalitis (sleeping sickness); showing characteristic sleepy, depressed symptoms. (Courtesy, Veterinary Research Laboratory, Montana State University, Bozeman, Mont.)

tion, if possible, of insect breeding grounds; and as little movement as possible of animals from an epizootic area to a clean one.

PREVENTION.—Vaccinate all animals before May of each year or as soon as the disease makes its appearance in a community.

DISCUSSION.—The disease is widespread. Since 1930, nearly a million horses and mules have been affected in the United States. Some animals make full recovery but other survivors do not. The mortality rate in the western type is about thirty percent; but in the eastern type, it is ninety percent or higher. Birds and wild rodents are natural disease hosts for the western type. Mosquitoes *(Culex tarsalis)* transmit the disease.

(Also see DISEASES AND PARASITES; and VENEZUELAN EQUINE ENCEPHALOMYE-LITIS.)

ENDURANCE.—The ability of a horse to withstand hardship and to perform under adverse conditions. The endurance of an individual horse depends on breeding, conformation, feeding, training, and the horseman. Therefore, there can be no hard-and-fast rule relative to an animal's endurance.

Although type of terrain makes a big differ-

ence, based on tests and long experience, the cavalry concluded that 25 miles a day over long periods of time carrying a full load was about what the average horse could endure and stay in good condition, provided he received proper feed and care.

ENDURANCE TRIALS (RIDES).—Competitive tests designed to test the stamina of horses are known as endurance trials. The riders must take their horses over a prescribed course, which is usually of rugged terrain, and which may require anywhere from one to three days to cover. Regular tests (temperature, pulse, respiration, etc.) are made at intervals.

Eleven 300-mile endurance rides were once held, seven in New England and four in Colorado, but these were discontinued in 1926. Today, there are several well-known 50- to 100-mile competitive trail rides in the United States. The time for the different courses varies according to the topography, elevation, and footing.

One of the best known endurance rides is the Tevis Cup Ride, held at Auburn, California each August. It is 100 miles and over extremely rough terrain. The time limit is 24 hours, and there are three mandatory rest stops of one hour each. During the rest stops, the veterinarians check the pulse, respiration, and temperature of each horse, both at the beginning and the end of the hour, so as to determine whether its rate of re-

Fig. E-2. Minette Rice-Edwards, of England, on the Anglo-Arab horse, Bright Hope, Best Conditioned Horse in the 1973 Tevis Cup 100-miler, shown going over "Cougar Rock," near Auburn, California, at an elevation of 7,400 feet. (Photo by and courtesy of Charles E. Barieau, Auburn, California)

covery is satisfactory. There are two kinds of competition in the Tevis Cup Ride: (1) a race over the 100-mile course, and (2) the best-conditioned horse that completes the ride within the 24-hour period.

Generally over 200 competitors start on the Tevis Cup Ride and about 160 (or 80%) finish. The winning horse makes the ride in approximately 11 hours.

ENEMA.—The injection of a liquid into the intestines by way of the anus to relieve constipation.

ENERGY (POWER).—See AUTOMATION VS. MUSCLE POWER.

ENERGY NEEDS OF THE HORSE.—The energy needs of horses vary with the individuality and size of animals, and the kind, amount, and severity of work performed. In racing, horses may use up to 100 times the energy utilized at rest.

It is common knowledge that a ration must contain proteins, fats, and carbohydrates. Although each of these has specific functions in maintaining a normal body, they can all be used to provide energy for maintenance, for work, or for fattening. From the standpoint of supplying the normal energy needs of horses, however, the carbohydrates are by far the most important, more of them being consumed than any other compound, whereas the fats are next in importance for energy purposes. In comparison with fats, carbohydrates are usually more abundant and cheaper, and they are very easily digested, absorbed, and transformed into body fat. Besides, carbohydrate feeds may be more easily stored in warm weather and for longer periods of time, whereas feeds high in fat content are likely to become rancid, and rancid feed is unpalatable, if not actually injurious in some instances. Also, fats are utilized very poorly by horses.

Generally, increased energy for horses is met by increasing the grain and decreasing the roughage.

A lack of energy may cause slow and stunted growth in foals, and loss of weight, poor condition, and excessive fatigue in mature horses.

Young equines and working (or running) horses must have rations in which a large part of the carbohydrate content of the ration is low in fiber, and in the form of nitrogen-free extract.

ENGLISH HUNTING SEAT.—The traditional hunting seat is back in the saddle with the "feet on the dashboard." The weight of the rider is not as far forward as we are accustomed to seeing in America. But there is a difference in the obstacles. Most of the jumps in America are walls, chicken-coops, post-and-rails, etc. They're high, with the result that the rider gives his horse as much assistance as he can to clear them by riding forward. In English hunts, however, the most common obstacle is a double-oxer, i.e., a low thorn hedge with a ditch, and low rail on both sides. The double-oxer is not high, but the width is formidable. Moreover, when the horse takes off he cannot see the ditch and rail on the far side, which adds to the likelihood of his catching his hind legs in the latter and sprawling on his belly. For this reason, the Englishman prefers to have the horse under him.

ENGLISH SADDLE.—See SADDLES—English Saddle.

ENTERING A STALL.—The horse's natural reaction to sudden fright is to run or kick. If he is in a stall, running is impossible. Most any horse is startled by sudden entrance into his stall, especially if he is dozing on his feet (a situation made possible by the sling type of ligament which encloses the leg joints, thereby allowing the horse to relax and at the same time remain standing). Thus, if startled suddenly, the horse may let fly with his heels before he realizes that you are a friend and not a foe. For this reason, before entering a horse's stall (whether it be a box stall or a tie stall) always speak to him so that he is aware of your presence. Then enter the stall, put your hand on the left side of the horse's croup, and go immediately to his head.

ENTERPRISE ACCOUNTS.—See ACCOUNTS, ENTERPRISE.

ENTIRE.—An ungelded male.

ENTRY *(in a race)*.—An "entry" is the combination of two or more horses entered in a race by a single trainer or owner. The numbers in the program will be the same for these horses but the second horse will have a letter behind it, such as 1 and 1A. The horses will be listed in the program with a bracket before them so that the bet on one or the other includes all horses in that "entry" (there may be more than one entry in a race). Thus, if a bettor picks 1 but 1A wins he will still collect. If either horse should be scratched (removed from the race) his bet still stands on the rest of the "entry."

ENVIRONMENT.—See HEREDITY—Heredity and Environment.

ENVIRONMENTAL CONTROL.—Animals perform better and require less feed if they are raised under ideal conditions of temperature, humidity, and ventilation. Environmental control is of particular importance in horse barn construction because many horses spend most of the time in a stall. The investment in environmental control facilities must be balanced against the expected increased returns because there is a point where further expenditures for environmental control will not increase returns sufficiently to justify added cost.

Before the building is designed, it is necessary to know how much heat and moisture a horse produces. Body heat production varies according to body weight, rate of feeding, environmental conditions, and degree of activity. Under average conditions, a 1,000-pound horse produces about 1,790 British thermal units (Btu.) per hour, and a 1,500-pound horse about 2,450 Btu. per hour. A horse breathes into the air approximately 17.5 pounds, or 2.1 gallons, of moisture per day.

Until more experimental information is available, the following environmental control recommendations, based on confinement systems used for other classes of animals, may be followed.

TEMPERATURE.—A range of 45° to 75° F. is satisfactory, with 55° considered best. Until a newborn foal is dry, it should be warmed to 75° to 80°. This can be done with a heat lamp.

HUMIDITY.—A range of 50 to 75 percent relative humidity is acceptable with 60 percent preferred.

VENTILATION.—The barn should have as little moisture and odor as possible, and it should be free from drafts. In a properly ventilated barn, the ventilation system should provide 60 cubic feet per minute (cfm.) for each 1,000 pounds of horse in winter and 160 cfm. per 1,000 pounds of horse in summer. In summer, satisfactory ventilation usually can be achieved by opening barn doors and by installing hinged walls or panels near the ceiling that swing open.

(Also see BARNS; BUILDINGS; and MOISTURE PRODUCTION BY HORSES.)

ENZOOTIC.—A disease confined to a certain locality.

EOHIPPUS.—This was the first equine ancestor, sometimes referred to as the "dawn horse."

(Also see EVOLUTION OF THE HORSE.)

Fig. E-3. A two-horse barn open to the South. The environmental control accorded horses varies widely; anywhere from a natural windbreak of evergreens to completely enclosed buildings with air circulation, temperature, humidity, and light control. (Courtesy, The Western Horseman)

EQUESTRIAN.—One who rides horseback.

EQUESTRIENNE.—A female equestrian.

EQUINE.—A horse. Correctly speaking, the term includes all the members of the family *Equidae* —horses, zebras, and asses.

EQUINE ABORTION.—See ABORTION, EQUINE.

EQUINE INFECTIOUS ANEMIA (SWAMP FEVER).—An infectious virus disease, found wherever there are horses.

SYMPTOMS.—Symptoms of the disease vary, but usually they include some of the following: high and intermittent fever; depression; stiffness and weakness, especially in the hindquarters; anemia; jaundice; edema and swelling of the lower body and legs; unthriftiness; and loss of condition and weight, even though the appetite is good. Most affected animals die within 2 to 4 weeks.

Fig. E-4. Horse with equine infectious anemia (swamp fever) five days before death. (Courtesy, USDA)

TREATMENT.—No successful treatment is known.

CONTROL.—Segregate infected animals and have them use separate feeding and watering facilities. Kill sick animals and burn or bury their carcasses.

PREVENTION.—Use disposable hypodermic needles when horses are vaccinated against disease, and sterilize all other skin penetrating instruments by boiling them at least fifteen minutes after each use. Practice good sanitation and eliminate or reduce biting insects as much as possible. Watch for sick horses and get a diagnosis by a veterinarian if any are observed. Use separate tack equipment on each horse. Keep stalls, starting gates, and other facilities clean at racetracks and shows. This disease has existed in different sections of the United States for at least fifty years but no preventive vaccination is known.

The "Coggins test" (an immuno-diffusion technique) is the most common method of diagnosis in the United States.

DISCUSSION.—Infected horses may be virus carriers for years and are a danger to susceptible horses.

(Also see DISEASES AND PARASITES; and HEALTH PROGRAM.)

EQUINE INFLUENZA.—An acute, highly contagious, feverish respiratory disease.

SYMPTOMS.—Young animals, except for very young foals that have immunity from the dam's milk, are particularly susceptible. Older animals are usually immune. Symptoms develop 2 to 10 days after exposure. The onset of the disease is marked by a rapidly rising temperature that may reach 106° F. and persist for 2 to 10 days. Other symptoms include loss of appetite, extreme weakness and depression, rapid breathing, a dry cough, and a watery discharge from the eyes and nostrils that is followed by a white to yellow nasal discharge.

TREATMENT.—Treatment should be handled by a veterinarian. Avoid exercising the animals during the period of elevated temperature. The use of antibiotics and/or sulfa drugs may prevent some of the complicated secondary conditions.

CONTROL.—Avoid transmission of the virus on contaminated feed, bedding, water, buckets, brooms, clothing and hands of attendants, and transportation facilities.

PREVENTION.—Vaccinate with a killed virus. Use two doses; follow the manufacturer's directions on the time of the second dose. Also, give each animal an annual booster shot, a booster when animals are exposed, or when an epidemic occurs. Quarantine sick animals, and isolate all new animals to the premises for 3 weeks.

DISCUSSION.—The disease is widespread throughout the world. It frequently appears where a number of horses are assembled, such as racetracks, sales, and shows. The death rate is low but economic loss is high. The disease interrupts training, racing, and showing schedules and it may force the withdrawal of animals from sales. Although horses, swine, and humans are subject to influenza and the symptoms are similar for each, there appears to be no transmission of the disease between any of them.

(Also see DISEASES AND PARASITES; and HEALTH PROGRAM.)

EQUINE PIROPLASMOSIS (BABESIASIS).—Caused by *Babesia caballi* or *B. equi*, protozoan parasites that invade the red blood cells.

SYMPTOMS.—Equine piroplasmosis is similar to equine infectious anemia but a positive diagnosis can be made by determining whether or not protozoa are in the red blood cells. Symptoms include a fever of 103° to 106° F., anemia, jaundice, depression, thirst, a discharge from the eyes, and swelling of the eyelids. Constipation and colic may occur and the urine is a yellow to reddish color. Symptoms appear 1 to 3 weeks after exposure.

TREATMENT.—A number of treatments are used but the choice should be left to a veterinarian. Many states have laws that require reporting the presence of this infection.

PREVENTION AND CONTROL.—Control the ticks that carry the parasites, especially brown dog ticks and tropical horse ticks, both of which are found in the United States.

Practice rigid sanitation in the use of all syringes, needles, and medical instruments. Recovered animals remain carriers for 10 months to 4 years and should be isolated.

DISCUSSION.—This infection is worldwide. In the United States, it was first diagnosed in Florida in 1961. The death rate is from 10 to 15 percent of infected animals.

(Also see DISEASES AND PARASITES; HEALTH PROGRAM; and PARASITES OF HORSES.)

EQUIPMENT DEPRECIATION.—See DEPRECIATION ON HORSE BUILDINGS AND EQUIPMENT; and TAXES, INCOME.

EQUIPMENT, FEED AND WATER.—The design of feed and water equipment should fill the basic need for simple and effective equipment with which to provide hay, concentrates, minerals, and water without waste or hazard to the horse. Whenever possible, for convenience and safety, feed and water equipment should be located so it can be filled without the caretaker entering the stall or corral.

Feed and water equipment may be built-in or detached. Because specialty feed and water equipment is more sanitary, flexible, and suitable, many horsemen favor it over old-style wood mangers and concrete or steel tanks. Bulk-tank feed storage may be used to advantage on large horse establishments to eliminate sacks, lessen rodent and bird problems, and make it possible to obtain feed at lower prices by ordering large amounts.

The kind, size, and location of the most common equipment used to hold concentrates, hay, minerals, and water are as follows:

CONCENTRATES.—Pail, tub, or box.
● A *pail* or *tub* can be made of metal, plastic, or rubber. Usually it has screw eyes and hooks or snaps so it can be suspended. The capacity should be 16 to 20 quarts for horses and 14 to 16 quarts for ponies.

In a stall, the pail or tub should be at the front of the stall. The height should be two-thirds the height of the animal at the withers, or 38 to 42 inches for horses and 28 to 32 inches for ponies.

In a corral, put the tub or pail along a fence line and at the same height as in a stall.

For sanitary reasons, removable concentrate containers are preferable so they can be easily

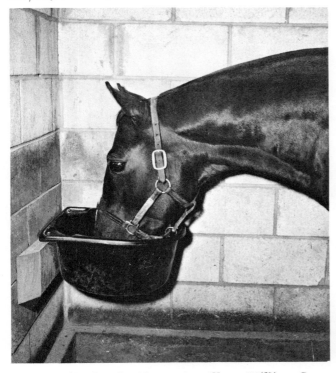

Fig. E-5. Feed tub. (Courtesy, Albers Milling Company)

and frequently cleaned. This is especially important after feeding a wet mash.

● A *wooden box* for horses should be 12 to 16 inches wide, 24 to 30 inches long, and 8 to 10 inches deep. A box for ponies should be 10 to 12 inches wide, 20 to 24 inches long, and 6 to 8 inches deep.

The location and height of a box in a stall are the same as for a pail or tub. Do not use a wooden box in a corral.

If desired, a wedge-shaped metal pan set on a wooden shelf can be mounted in a front corner of the stall and pivoted so it can be pulled out for filling and cleaning and then pushed back into the stall and locked in place.

HAY.—Stall rack, manger, or corral rack.

● A *stall rack* may be made of metal, fiber, or plastic. A rack for horses should hold 25 to 30 pounds of hay, and a rack for ponies 10 to 15 pounds. It should be in a corner of the stall. The bottom of the rack should be the same height as the horse or pony at the withers.

Hayracks lessen hay contamination, parasitic infestation, pawing by horses, and hay waste. Racks should open at the bottom so dirt, chaff,

and trash may be removed or allowed to fall out.

● A *wooden manger* may be used. It should be 30 inches wide and 24 to 30 inches long for horses and 20 inches square for ponies. The height should be 30 to 42 inches for horses and 20 to 24 inches for ponies. Put the manger in the front or in a corner of the stall.

● A *corral rack* is made of wood. It should be large enough to hold a one-day supply of hay

Fig. E-6. Steel hayrack in paddock at Murrieta Stud, Murrieta, Calif. (Courtesy, The Thoroughbred of California)

for the intended number of horses. Put the rack in the fence line of the corral if horses feed from one side only. Put it on high ground if horses feed from both sides.

The top of the rack may be 1 to 2 feet higher than the horses at the withers. Corral hay racks that feed from both sides should be portable.

MINERALS.—Box or self-feeder.

● A *box* may be made of wood and a *self-feeder* may be made of metal or wood. In a stall, the box or self-feeder should be in a corner of the stall and should be the same height as the box or pail used for concentrates.

In a corral, mineral containers should be in a fence corner. The height should be two-thirds the height of the horse at the withers. If a mineral container is in the open, it should be protected from wind and rain. Mineral containers should have two compartments, one for mineral mix and the other for salt.

WATER.—Automatic stall waterer, automatic corral waterer, pail, or tank.

● *Automatic waterers* are made of metal. Waterers should be located in a front corner of a stall or in a fence corner of a corral or pasture.

Watering equipment should be designed to facilitate draining and cleaning. Locate waterers a considerable distance from feed containers if possible. Otherwise, horses will carry feed to the waterer or drip water in the concentrate container. A large 20- by 30-inch automatic waterer will accommodate about 25 horses; a two-cup waterer, about 12.

The daily water requirements for horses are: Mature horse, 12 gallons; foal to two-year-old, and pony, 6 to 8 gallons. In cold areas, waterers should be heated and equipped with thermostatic controls. A satisfactory water temperature range in winter is 40° to 45° F. and in summer 60° to 75°.

Check automatic waterers daily.

Fig. E-7. Automatic waterer, placed at one side of manger. (Courtesy, Sunset Magazine)

● A *water pail* may be made of metal, plastic, or rubber. It should be located in the front of the stall. The height should be two-thirds the height of the horse at the withers, or 38 to 42 inches for horses and 28 to 32 inches for ponies.

● A *water tank* may be concrete or steel. It is used in a corral and should be set in the fence so there are no protruding corners. If it is out in a corral or pasture away from a fence, it should be painted white so the horses can see it at night.

A tank should be 30 to 36 inches high. Allow 1 linear foot of tank space to each 5 horses. A tank should be equipped with a float valve that is protected from the horses.

EQUITATION.—The act or art of riding horseback.

(Also see HORSEMANSHIP.)

EQUITATION CLASSES.—Equitation is the art of riding. Equitation classes are judged solely on the horsemanship of the rider. The American Horse Shows Association specifies the rules for many equitation classes. There are categories according to age, experience, previous show-ring winnings, and type of riding.

EQUUS CABALLUS.—The horse, which is distinguished from the other members of the genus *Equus*—asses and zebras—by the longer hair of the mane and tail, the presence of the "chestnut" on the inside of the hind leg, and other less constant characters such as larger size, larger hoofs, more arched neck, smaller head, and shorter ears.

ERGOT.—The horny growth at the back of the fetlock joint; the spurs of a horse's hoofs. The tuft of hair at the fetlock hides the ergot in most instances. The chestnut is thought to be a vestige of the first toe and the ergot to be a vestige of the second and fifth toes of prehistoric horses.

ESOPHAGUS.—This 50- to 60-inch tube provides passage of feed from the pharynx to the stomach.

ESTATE PLANNING.—Human nature being what it is, most horsemen shy away from suggestions that someone help plan the disposition of their property and other assets. Also, many of them have a long-standing distrust of lawyers, legal terms, and trusts; and, to them, the subject of taxes seldom makes for pleasant conversation.

If no plans are made, estate taxes and settlement costs often run considerably higher than if proper estate planning is done and a will is made to carry out these plans. Today, the horse business is big business; many horsemen have well over $500,000 invested in land, horses, and equipment. Thus, it is not a satisfying thought to one who has worked hard to build and maintain a good horse establishment during his lifetime to feel that his heirs will have to sell the facilities and horses to raise enough cash to pay Federal Estate and Inheritance Taxes. By using a good estate planning service, a horseman can generally save thousands of dollars for his family in estate and inheritance taxes and in estate settlement costs. For assistance, horsemen should go to an estate planning specialist—an individual or company specializing in this work, or to the trust department of a commercial bank.

ESTRUS.—The estrous period is commonly called "heat." Fillies reach puberty at 12 to 15 months of age; each heat period averages 4 to 6 days in duration; and the interval between heat periods averages 21 days.

EVOLUTION OF THE HORSE.—Fossil remains prove that members of the horse family roamed the plains of America (especially what is now the Great Plains area of the U.S.) during most of Tertiary time, beginning about 58 million years ago. Yet, no horses were present on this continent when Columbus discovered America in 1492. Why they perished, only a few thousand years before, is still one of the unexplained mysteries of evolution.

Through fossils, it is possible to reconstruct the evolution of the horse, beginning with the ancient four-toed ancestor, the *Eohippus* (meaning "dawn horse"). This was a small animal, scarcely more than a foot high, with four toes on the front feet and three toes on the hind feet, and with slender legs, a short neck, and even teeth. It was well adapted to traveling in and feeding on the herbage of swamp lands. Gradually, the descendants of *Eohippus* grew in size and changed in form, evolving with a three-toed animal known as *Mesohippus*, which was about 24 inches in height or about the size of a Collie dog. Further changes continued, transforming the animal from a denizen of the swamp to a creature of the prairie. In conformation, the animal grew taller, the teeth grew longer, the cannon bones lengthened, and the middle toe (third toe) grew longer and stronger—forming a hoof. The horse is an excellent example, therefore, of the slow adaptation of animal life to changing conditions in environment, climate, food, and soil.

Fig. E-8. Evolution of the horse, spanning 58 million years. The cannon bone lengthened and the middle toe (third toe) grew longer and stronger—forming a hoof. (Courtesy, American Museum of Natural History)

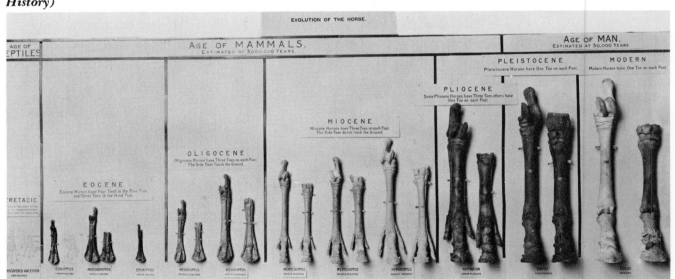

EXACTA, THE.—An exacta bet attempts to pick the first and second horses in the same race. Exacta tickets are sold for $5.00 and $10.00. Payoffs on Exacta wins are usually high.

EXERCISE.—Horses should exercise as much as possible on pasture. They will develop strong, sound feet and legs from outdoor exercise. If no pasture is available, exercise mature animals for an hour or two a day under saddle or in harness.

Horses with bad feet frequently cannot exercise on roads. Those with faulty tendons may not be able to exercise under saddle. Allow these animals to exercise in a large paddock, longeing on a 30- to 40-foot rope, or by leading.

EXMOOR PONY.—A mountain breed of pony found in the British Isles, prized as a mount for children and small adults. It runs wild in the Exmoor forest, in southwest England, partly in Devonshire, but mostly in Somerset, much like the Mustangs in some parts of western United States. They range in height from 12–2 to 12–3 hands; are bay-brown or dun colored; and are further characterized by a very heavy mane, mealy nose, and very prominent, wide-set eyes.

EXPENDITURES.—See COST TO KEEP A HORSE.

EXUDATE.—A fluid oozing from tissue.

EYE.—A large eye is desired. In most breeds, a rich hazel color is preferred. Glass eyes, or wall-eyes, are those in which the iris is of pearly white color, destitute of pigment. Such eyes are functional, but not acceptable in some breeds. Small, narrow, and squinty eyes are known as "pig-eyes," and are undesirable.

(Also see PARTS OF A HORSE—P-4.)

EWE NECK.—A neck like that of a sheep, with a dip between the poll and the withers. Also termed a "turkey neck" and "upside-down neck."

F

FACE.—The area in front of the head below the eyes and above the nose is known as the face. A straight face is usually preferable to a concave profile or a convex one (Roman nose), the former suggesting a timid disposition and the latter strong will-power.

(Also see PARTS OF A HORSE—Fig. P-4.)

FACE FLY.—See FLIES.

FALSE START.—When a horse takes another gait than the one asked of him (by appropriate cue and by use of aids), it is referred to as a false start. When this occurs, the rider should bring him to a walk immediately, then make a fresh start with a more definite signal. In all horse show performance classes in which horses are asked to display different gaits, it is always proper to bring a horse to a walk before asking him to take a new gait. Generally speaking, the judge(s) will ask a class to walk before he asks for a change in gaits. The one exception to this rule is in the five-gaited performance class when horses at the slow gait are usually asked to "rack on"; thereupon, they move from the slow gait directly to a fast rack, without coming to a walk.

FAMILY.—The lineage of an animal as traced through either the males or females, depending upon the breed.

(Also see HEREDITY IN HORSES.)

FARCY.—See GLANDERS (FARCY.)

FARM CHUNKS.—The term "chunks" is descriptive of the farm-chunk type of animals. They are small-sized drafters standing 15 to 16 hands in height and weighing from 1,300 to 1,400 pounds. Currently, farm chunks are of historical interest only.

FARRIER.—A horseshoer.
(Also see SHOEING.)

FAR SIDE.—The right side of a horse.

FAT.—Lipids (fat and fat-like subtances), like carbohydrates, contain three elements: carbon, hydrogen, and oxygen. In horse feeds, fats function much like carbohydrates in that they serve as a source of heat and energy and for the formation of fat. Because of the larger proportion of carbon and hydrogen, however, fats liberate more heat then carbohydrates when digested, furnishing approximately 2.25 times as much heat or energy per pound on oxidation as do carbohydrates. A smaller quantity of fat is required, therefore, to serve the same function.

The physical and chemical properties of fats are quite variable. From a chemical standpoint, a molecule of fat consists of a combination of three molecules of certain fatty acids with one molecule of glycerol. Fats differ in their melting points and other properties depending on the particular fatty acids which they contain.

Some fatty acids are unsaturated, which means that they have the ability to take up oxygen or certain other chemical elements. Chemically, these unsaturated acids contain one or more pairs of double-bond carbon atoms. Thus, because of the high content of unsaturated acids (such as oleic and linoleic) and acids of low molecular weight, corn fat is a liquid at ordinary temperatures; whereas, because of the high content of stearic and palmitic acids, beef fat is solid at ordinary temperatures.

A small amount of fat in the ration is desirable, as fat is the carrier of the fat-soluble vitamins (vitamins A,D,E, and K). There is evidence that some species (humans, swine, rats, and dogs) require certain of the fatty acids. Although the fatty-acid requirements of horses have not been settled, it is thought that ordinary farm rations contain ample quantities of these nutrients.

FATTENING.—See FEED.

FATTY ACIDS.—See FAT; and POLYUNSATURATED FATTY ACIDS.

FAULTS (in hunting and jumping).—When a horse in a hunter or jumper class touches or knocks down an obstacle, disobeys, or falls, it is called a "fault" and penalized according to horse show rules. For faults and scoring see the *Rule Book* of the American Horse Shows Association, which is revised annually.

FAVOR.—To favor one leg; to limp slightly.

FEAR.—See CONTROL OF THE HORSE—Confidence and Fear.

FEATHER IN EYE.—A mark across the eyeball, not touching the pupil; often caused by an injury, it may be a blemish or some other defect.

FEATHERS (on legs).—The long hairs extending from the fetlock joints up the legs, as in the Shire and Clydesdale breeds of draft horses.

FEED.—A feed is any product, whether of natural origin or artificially prepared, which is fed to horses and other animals.

FUNCTIONS OF FEEDS.—The feed consumed by horses is used for a number of different purposes, the exact usage varying somewhat with the class, age, and productivity of the animal. A certain part of the feed is used for the maintenance of bodily functions aside from any useful production. This is known as the maintenance requirement. In addition, feed is used to take care of the functions for which horses are kept. Thus, young growing equines need nutrients suitable for building muscle tissue and bone; horses being readied for show or sale need a surplus of energy feeds for formation of fat; broodmares require feed for the development of their fetuses, and, following parturition, for the production of milk; whereas work (or racing) animals use feed to supply energy for work.

MAINTENANCE.—A horse differs from an engine in that the latter has no fuel requirement when idle; whereas the horse requires fuel every second of the day, whether it is idle or active.

The maintenance requirement may be defined as a ration which is adequate to prevent any loss or gain of tissue in the body when there is no production. Although these requirements are relatively simple, they are essential for life itself. A mature horse must have heat to maintain body temperature, sufficient energy to cover the internal work of the body and the minimum movement of the animal, and a small amount of proteins, vitamins, and minerals for the repair of body tissues.

No matter how quietly a horse may be standing in the stall, it still requires a certain amount of fuel, and the least amount on which it can exist is called its *basal maintenance requirement*. Even under the best of conditions, about one-half of all the feed consumed by horses is used in meeting the maintenance requirements.

GROWTH.—Growth may be defined as the increase in size of the muscles, bones, internal organs, and other parts of the body. Naturally, the growth requirements become increasingly acute when horses are forced for early use, such as the training and racing of a two- or three-year-old.

Growth has been referred to as the foundation of horse production. Breeding animals may have their productive ability seriously impaired if they have been raised improperly. Nor can the most satisfactory performance be expected unless they have been well developed. For example, running horses do not possess the desired speed and endurance if their growth has been stunted or if their skeletons have been injured by inadequate rations during the growth period.

FITTING (FATTENING).—This is the laying on of fat, especially in the tissues of the abdominal cavity and in the connective tissues just under the skin and between the muscles.

Usually, fitting rations contain more energy than do maintenance rations. However, the same formulation may be used for both fitting and maintenance purposes, but with larger quantities being supplied to horses that are being fitted.

In practical fitting rations, higher condition in mature animals is usually obtained through increasing the allowance of feeds high in carbohy-drates and fats—a more liberal allowance of grains. Any surplus of protein may also serve for the production of fat, but usually such feeds are more expensive and are not used for economy reasons. In fitting mature horses, very little more proteins, minerals, and vitamins are required than for maintenance. In fitting young, growing animals, however, it is essential that, in addition to supplying more carbohydrates and fats, ample proteins, minerals, and vitamins be provided to meet their accelerated growth.

REPRODUCTION AND LACTATION.—Regular and normal reproduction is the basis for profit on any horse breeding establishment. Despite this undeniable fact, it has been estimated that only 40 to 60 percent of all mares bred actually produce foals. Certainly, there are many causes of reproductive failure, but most scientists are agreed that inadequate nutrition is a major one.

With all species, most of the growth of the fetus occurs during the last third of pregnancy, thus making the reproductive requirements most critical during this period. The ration of the pregnant mare should supply sufficient amounts of protein, minerals, and vitamins.

The nutritive requirements for moderate to heavy milk production are much more rigorous than the pregnancy requirements. There is special need for a rather liberal protein, mineral, and vitamin allowance.

Fig. F-1. Good pastures provide a highly nutritious feed and stimulate milk production. Hungarian mares and foals on pasture at Bitterroot Stock Farm, Hamilton, Montana, owned by Margit Sigray Bessenyey. (Photo by Ernst Peterson, Hamilton, Mont.)

In the case of young, growing, pregnant females, additional protein, minerals, and vitamins, above the ordinary requirements, must be provided; otherwise, the fetus will not develop properly or milk will be produced at the expense of the tissues of the dam.

It is also known that the ration exerts a powerful effect on sperm production and semen quality. Too fat a condition can even lead to temporary or permanent sterility. Moreover, there is abundant evidence that greater fertility of stallions exists under conditions where a well-balanced ration and plenty of exercise are provided.

WORK (HORSES IN USE).—In many respects, work requirements are similar to the needs for fitting, both functions requiring high-energy feeds.

For mature horses, not in reproduction, work is performed primarily at the expense of the carbohydrates and fats of the ration—energy that can be supplied in the form of additional grain. Theoretically, the protein is not drawn upon so long as the other nutrients are present in adequate amounts. From a practical standpoint, however, it is usually desirable to feed more proteins than the maintenance requirement, merely to insure that the animal can make efficient use of the remainder of the nutrients in the ration. In other words, when a ration too low in protein is fed, more feed is required because the animal is unable to utilize the ration efficiently. For work animals, the mineral and vitamin requirements are practically the same as for comparable idle animals—except for the greater need for salt because of increased perspiration.

SELECTION OF FEEDS.—Individual feeds vary widely in feeding value. Oats and barley, for example, differ in feeding value according to the hull content and weight per bushel, and forages vary according to the stage of maturity at which they are cut and how well they are cured and stored. Also, the feeding value of certain feeds is materially affected by preparation.

Regardless of the feeds selected, they should be of sound quality, and not moldy, spoiled, or dusty. This applies to both hay and grain. This careful selection of feeds is more important for horses than for any other class of livestock.

In general, successful horsemen use well balanced rations, with special consideration given to supplying quality protein, the proper minerals, and the necessary vitamins. Additional attention is given to the laxative or constipating qualities of feeds and the palatability of the ration.

CONCENTRATES (GRAINS).—Unlike ruminants, horses cannot handle very large quantities of roughages. Moreover, horses used for heavy work, for pleasure, or for racing must be even more restricted in their roughage allowance and should receive a higher proportion of concentrates.

Because of less bulk and lower shipping and handling costs, the concentrates used for horse feeding are less likely to be locally grown than the roughages. Even so, the vast majority of grains fed to horses are home grown, thus varying from area to area, according to the grain crops best adapted.

Of all the concentrates, heavy oats most nearly meet the needs of horses; and, because of the uniformly good results obtained from their use, they have always been recognized as the leading grain for horses. Corn is also widely used as a horse feed, particularly in the Central States. Despite occasional prejudice to the contrary, barley is a good horse feed. As proof of the latter fact, it is noteworthy that the Arab—who was a good horseman—fed barley almost exclusively. Also, wheat, wheat bran, and commercial mixed feeds are extensively used. It is to be emphasized, therefore, that careful attention should be given to the prevailing price of feeds available locally, for many feeds are well suited to horses. Often substitutions can be made that will result in a marked saving without affecting the nutritive value of the ration. When corn or other heavy grains are fed, it is important that a little linseed meal or wheat bran be used, in order to regulate the bowels.

(Also see various feed ingredients, such as OATS, CORN, BARLEY, etc., each of which is listed alphabetically.)

HAY.—Through mistaken kindness or carelessness, horses are often fed too much hay or other roughage, with the result that they breathe laboriously and tire quickly. With cattle and sheep, on the other hand, it is usually well to feed considerable roughage. This difference between horses and ruminants is due primarily to the relatively small size of the simple stomach of the horse in comparison with the four-fold stomach of the ruminant.

When limiting the allowance of roughage, it is sometimes necessary to muzzle greedy horses (gluttons) to prevent them from eating the bedding.

Usually, young horses and idle horses can be provided with an unlimited allowance of hay. But one should gradually increase the grain and decrease the hay as work or training begins.

Much good will result from feeding young and idle horses more roughage and less grain.

The hay should be early cut, leafy, green, well-cured, and free from dust and mold. Hay native to the locality is usually fed. However, horsemen everywhere prefer good-quality timothy. With young stock and breeding animals especially, it is desirable that a sweet grass-legume mixture of alfalfa hay be fed. The legume provides a source of high-quality proteins and certain minerals and vitamins.

Horses like variety. Therefore, if at all possible, it is wise to have more than one kind of hay in the stable. For example, timothy may be provided at one feeding and a grass-legume mixed hay at the other feeding. Good horsemen often vary the amount of alfalfa fed, for increased amounts of alfalfa in the ration will increase urination and give a softer consistency to the bowel movements. This means that elimination from kidneys and bowels can be carefully regulated by the amount and frequency of alfalfa feedings. Naturally, such regulation becomes more necessary with irregular use and idleness. On the other hand, in some areas alfalfa is fed as the sole roughage with good results.

(Also see various hays, such as ALFALFA and TIMOTHY, each of which is listed alphabetically.)

HOME-MIXED FEEDS.—A horse feeding guide is given under Rations, in Table R-1. In selecting home-mixed rations, compare them with commercial feeds. If only small quantities are required or little storage space is available, it may be more satisfactory to buy ready-mixed feeds.

When home-mixed feeds are used, feeds of similar nutritive properties can be interchanged in the ration as price relationships warrant. This makes it possible to obtain a balanced ration at lowest cost. Among the feeds that may be interchanged are grains such as oats, corn, barley, wheat, and sorghum; protein supplements such as linseed meal, soybean meal, and cottonseed meal; and hays of many varieties.

More than one kind of hay provides variety and appetite appeal. In season, any good pasture can replace part or all of the hay unless work or training conditions make substitution impractical.

During winter months, add a few sliced carrots to the suggested ration, an occasional bran mash, or a small amount of linseed meal. Also, use bran mash or linseed meal to regulate the bowels.

The proportion of concentrates must be increased and the roughages decreased as energy needs rise with a greater amount of work. A horse that works at a trot needs considerably more feed than one that works at a walk. For this reason, riding horses in medium to light use require somewhat less grain and more hay in proportion to body weight than horses that are racing.

In feeding horses, as with other classes of livestock, it is recognized that nutritional deficiencies (especially deficiencies of certain vitamins and minerals) may not be of sufficient proportions to cause clear-cut deficiency symptoms. Yet, such deficiencies without outward signs may cause great economic losses because they go unnoticed and unrectified. Accordingly, sufficient additives (especially minerals and vitamins) should always be present, but care should be taken to avoid imbalances.

COMMERCIAL FEEDS.—Commercial feeds are feeds mixed by manufacturers who specialize in the feed business. Today, about sixty million tons of commercial feeds are marketed each year in the United States.

Commercial feed manufacturers are able to purchase feed in quantity lots, making possible price advantages and the scientific control of quality. Many horsemen have found that because of the small quantities of feed usually involved, and the complexities of horse rations, they have more reason to rely on good commercial feeds than do owners of other classes of farm animals.

Feed Tag.—Horsemen should be able to study and interpret what's on the feed tag. Table F-1 (front side) and Table F-2 (back side) show a tag taken from a foal ration:

TABLE F-1

FEED TAG (FRONT)

TABLE F-2

FEED TAG (REVERSE SIDE)

(BRAND X)

(Net Weight 50 pounds)

GUARANTEED ANALYSIS

Crude Protein, not less than	21.00%
Crude Fat, not less than	2.00%
Crude Fiber, not more than	9.00%
Ash, not more than	9.00%
Added Mineral, not more than	3.00%
Calcium, not less than	1.00%
Phosphorus, not less than	.75%
Salt, not more than	.50%
Iodine, not less than	.00035%
TDN, not less than	68.00%

Ingredients: Rolled Oats, Dried Whey, Soybean Meal, Cottonseed Meal, Linseed Meal, Dehydrated Alfalfa Meal, Wheat Bran, Wheat Shorts, Wheat Flour, Cane Molasses, Bone Meal, Iodized Salt, Distillers Dried Grains with Solubles, Alfalfa Leaf Meal, Condensed Fish Solubles (Dried), Brewers Dried Yeast, Streptomycin Mycelia Meal, Vitamin A Palmitate with Increased Stability, Fleischman's Irradiated Dry Yeast (Source of Vitamin D-2), d-Alpha-Tocopherol Acetate (Source of Vitamin E), Choline Chloride, Ferrous Carbonate, Niacin, Calcium Pantothenate (Source of d-Pantothenic Acid), Riboflavin Supplement, Copper Oxide, Manganous Oxide, Thiamine, Sulphur, Menadione Sodium Bisulfate (Source of Vitamin K), Calcium Iodate, Folic Acid, Cobalt Carbonate, Vitamin B-12 Supplement, Preserved with Ethoxyquin (1, 2-dihydro-6-ethoxy-2, 2, 4-trimethylquinoline), Anise.

FEEDING DIRECTIONS—SEE OTHER SIDE

Manufactured by

ADAIR MILLING COMPANY

(Address and Phone Number)

(BRAND X

FEEDING DIRECTIONS

Lbs. daily/100

lbs. weight/foal

Before weaning	½ –1
After weaning	1¼ –1½

Plus pasture or hay

An analysis of the tag reveals the following:

- The "brand" or name of the feed.
- The net weight.
- The guaranteed analysis, each stated in percent, in minimum crude protein and crude fat; maximum crude fiber, ash, and mineral; minimum calcium and phosphorus; maximum salt; and minimum iodine and TDN. But guaranteed analysis, within itself, will not suffice. For example, on the basis of chemical composition, soft coal (9.06% crude protein) and coffee grounds (11.23% crude protein) are comparable in protein content to many commonly used grains. Yet, no one would be so foolish as to feed these products to horses.

- The ingredients, (the constituent material making up the feed) listed in descending order of amounts, by weight.
- The name, address, and phone number of the manufacturer.
- The feeding directions, on the reverse side.

Many states differ slightly from the tag just analyzed. Some require both the minimum and maximum percentage of calcium and salt.

By studying this tag, a knowledgeable user can, readily and easily, see what's in the feed and determine if it will meet the requirements of the horse to which it is to be fed.

State Commercial Feed Laws.—Nearly all the states have laws regulating the sale of commercial feeds. These benefit both the horseman and reputable feed manufacturers. In most states, the laws require that each brand of commercial feed sold in the state be licensed, and that the chemical composition be guaranteed.

Samples of each commercial feed are taken each year, and analyzed chemically in the state's laboratory to determine if the manufacturer lived up to his guarantee. Additionally, skilled microscopists examine the sample to ascertain that the ingredients present are the same as those guaranteed. Flagrant violations on the latter point may be prosecuted.

Results of these examinations are generally published, annually, by the state department in charge of such regulatory work. Usually, the publication of the guarantee alongside any "short-changing" is sufficient to cause the manufacturer promptly to rectify the situation, for such public information soon becomes known to both users and competitors.

PROCESSING GRAINS.—If properly done, steam rolling of grains is preferred to grinding for horses, because the ration is lighter and fluffier, and fewer digestive disturbances are encountered. However, there is great variation in steam rolling. Altogether too much steam rolling consists in exposing the grain to steam for 3 to 5 minutes, using a temperature of about 180° F., and adding an unknown amount of moisture. Such processing is little better than dry rolling.

Proper steam rolling of barley and milo is achieved as follows: The grain should be subjected to 20 pounds of steam pressure for 20 minutes, at approximately 205° F.; then at this temperature, and with 18 to 20 percent moisture content, it should be run through large rollers operated at ⅓ to ½ capacity, and rolled to thin flakes. Of course, excess moisture must be removed prior to storage.

Dry rolling, crimping, and grinding can be, and are, used in preparing horse feeds. The important thing is to keep the grain as coarse as possible and to avoid fines.

A very attractive and palatable mixed feed concentrate can be prepared by flaking the grains and pelleting the fines. However, feeds prepared in this manner are very subject to mustiness; hence, it is important that they not contain excess moisture, and that they be stored properly.

Fig. F-2. Milo properly steam rolled into dustless flakes. (Courtesy, Dr. Al Lane, Extension Livestock Specialist, The University of Arizona)

PELLETING.—The preparation of feeds by pelleting may be, and is, applied to (1) concentrates alone, (2) forage alone, and (3) concentrates and roughage combined in a complete ration.

(Also see PELLETS AS A COMPLETE FEED.)

SWEET FEED.—"Sweet Feed" refers to a feed to which has been added one or more ingredients that are sweet. Most commonly, it is considerable molasses (approximately 10%); although brown sugar (about 5%) is sometimes used, and occasionally honey.

The horse has a "sweet tooth"; hence, it's not easy to switch him from a sweet feed to what may be a more nutritious ration. Of course, the manufacturer of the sweet feed would have it that way. Also, it must be remembered that sweet feeds are a way in which a feed manufacturer may make poor quality feed ingredients more appetizing. Remember, too, that most boys and girls would rather eat candy than foods that are more nutritious. But doctors and mothers know what's best!

PALATABILITY OF FEED.—Palatability (liking the feed) is important, for horses must eat their feed if it's to do them any good. But many horses are finicky simply because they're spoiled. For the latter, stepping up the exercise and halving the ration will usually effect a miraculous cure.

Also, it seems possible that well-liked feeds are

digested somewhat better than those which are equally nutritious, but less palatable.

Palatability is particularly important when feeding horses that are being used hard, as in racing or showing. Unless the ration is consumed, such horses will not obtain sufficient nutrients to permit maximum performance. For this reason, lower quality feeds, such as straw or stemmy hay, should be fed to idle horses.

Familiarity and habit are important factors concerned with the palatability of horse feeds. For example, horses have to learn to eat pellets, and very frequently they will back away from feeds with new and unfamiliar odors. For this reason, any change in feeds should be made gradually.

Occasionally, the failure of horses to eat a normal amount of feed is due to a serious nutritive deficiency. For example, if horses are fed a ration made up of palatable feeds, but deficient in one or more required vitamins or minerals, they may eat normal amounts for a time. Then when the body reserves of the lacking nutrient(s) are exhausted, they will usually consume much less feed, due to an impairment of their health and a consequent lack of appetite. If the deficiency is not continued so long that the horses are injured permanently, they will usually recover their appetites if some feed is added which supplies the nutritive lack and makes the ration complete.

PALATABILITY CHECK LIST.—The following check list may be applied where there appears to be a palatability problem with horse feed.

● *Quality of feeds.*—Make very certain on this point. It's almost impossible to detect through a chemical analysis many factors that may lower quality.

● *Mustiness.*—Again, check with care. During warm weather, feeds high in moisture may become musty. If they do, horses will detect it very quickly—much more quickly than a person.

● *Hard pellets.*—If pellets are too hard, horses will spit them out.

● *Flavors.*—In some cases, the addition of a flavoring agent will help in overcoming the lack of palatability due to poor quality feeds, but a flavoring agent will do little to enhance good quality feeds.

● *Premix.*—Check on the "carrier" and premix ingredients which the feed manufacturer is using in his horse feeds. For example, poor qual-ity fish meal in a premix, as a source of unidentified factors, can make for unpalatability.

● *The formulation.*—Of course, some feeds are more palatable to horses than others. Among the well-liked feeds are wheat bran and molasses, both of which are usually incorporated in horse rations.

CHEMICAL ANALYSIS OF FEED.—Feed composition tables ("book values"), or average analyses, should be considered only as guides, because of wide variations in the composition of feeds. For example, the protein and moisture content of milo and hay are quite variable. Wherever possible, especially with large operations, it is best to take a representative sample of each major feed ingredient and have a chemical analysis made of it for the more common constituents—protein, fat, fiber, nitrogen-free extract, and moisture; and often calcium, phosphorus, and carotene. Such ingredients as oil meals and prepared supplements, which must meet specific standards, need not be analyzed so often, except as quality control measures.

Despite the recognized value of a chemical analysis, it is not the total answer. It does not provide information on the availability of nutrients to the animal; it varies from sample to sample, because feeds vary and a representative sample is not always easily obtained; and it does not tell anything about the associated effect of feedstuffs. Nor does a chemical analysis tell anything about taste, palatability, texture, undesirable physiological effects such as digestive disturbances, and laxativeness.

However, a chemical analysis does give a solid foundation on which to start in evaluating feeds. Also, with chemical analysis at hand, and bearing in mind that it's the composition of the total feed (the finished ration) that counts, the person formulating the ration can determine more intelligently the quantity of protein to buy, and the kind and amounts of minerals and vitamins to add.

(Also see SOIL ANALYSIS.)

TERMS USED IN FEED ANALYSES AND GUARANTEES.—Knowledge of the following terms is requisite to understanding feed analyses and guarantees:

● *Dry matter* is found by determining the percentage of water and subtracting the water content from 100 percent.

● *Crude protein* is used to designate the nitrogenous constituents of a feed. The percentage is obtained by multiplying the percentage of total nitrogen by the factor 6.25. The nitrogen is derived chiefly from complex chemical compounds called amino acids.

● *Crude fat* is the material that is extracted from moisture-free feeds by ether. It consists largely of fats and oils with small amounts of waxes, resins, and coloring matter. In calculating the heat and energy value of the feed, the fat is considered 2.25 times that of either nitrogen-free extract or protein.

● *Crude fiber* is the relatively insoluble carbohydrate portion of a feed consisting chiefly of cellulose. It is determined by its insolubility in dilute acids and alkalies.

● *Ash* is the mineral matter of a feed. It is the residue remaining after complete burning of the organic matter.

● *Nitrogen-free extract* consists principally of sugars, starches, pentoses and non-nitrogenous organic acids. The percentage is determined by subtracting the sum of the percentages of moisture, crude protein, crude fat, crude fiber, and ash from 100.

● *Carbohydrates* represent the sum of the crude fiber and nitrogen-free extract.

● *Calcium and phosphorus* are essential mineral elements that are present in feeds in varying quantities. Mineral feeds are usually high in source materials of these elements.

● *TDN.*—The digestible nutrients of any ingredient are obtained by multiplying the percentage of each nutrient by the digestion coefficient. For example, dent corn contains 8.9 percent protein of which 77 percent is digestible. Therefore, the percent of digestible protein is 6.9.

The TDN is the sum of all the digestible organic nutrients—protein, fiber, nitrogen-free extract, and fat (the latter multiplied by 2.25).

FEED ALLOWANCE.—See FEEDING HORSES.

FEED BAG (NOSE BAG).—A bag (usually made of canvas or burlap) which is filled with the desired feed allowance and tied over a horse's head. In some countries, the feed bag is still employed for the noonday feeding of horses used on city streets. In New Delhi, India the author saw a cart horse parked near the monument of Mahatma Gandhi placidly munching his noontime meal from a feed bag.

FEED EQUIPMENT.—See EQUIPMENT, FEED AND WATER.

FEEDING HORSES.—Feeding practices vary from one locality to another—and among horsemen. The size of individual horses, the use to which they are put, the availability of feed, and the size of the enterprise also result in differences.

Fundamentally, the nature of horses remains the same. For this reason, successful feeding in one stable is not much different from successful feeding in another stable.

Skill and good judgment are essential in feeding horses. Horsemen may secure widely different results under similar conditions. Horses may be in the best of condition in one stable and have animation, nerve, speed, and endurance. In another stable, listless animals with dull eyes and rough coats testify to lack of judgment in their feeding and management. The unsatisfactory condition in the latter stable may not mean that the owner tried to economize on feed; horsemen who feed their animals the most economically may have the best horses.

RECOMMENDED PROTEIN AND ENERGY ALLOWANCES.—Unfortunately, little experimental work has been done on the minimum nutritional requirements of horses. However, presently available information indicates that the protein and energy allowances recommended in Table F-3 will meet the minimum requirements for horses and provide a reasonable margin of safety. (For recommended mineral allowances, see MINERALS; for recommended vitamin allowances, see VITAMINS.) A margin of safety is important owing to (1) variations in feed composition because of the soil on which it was grown, stage of maturity when it was harvested, amount of weathering, and losses in processing and storage; and (2) differences in environment and individual animals.

TABLE F-3

RECOMMENDED ALLOWANCES OF PROTEIN, FIBER, AND TOTAL DIGESTIBLE NUTRIENTS (TDN)

Type of Horse	Minimum Crude Protein	Maximum Crude Fiber	Minimum TDN
	(percent)	(percent)	(percent)
Most mature horses used for race, show, or pleasure	12	25	53 to 70[1]
Broodmares	13	25	50 to 60
Stallions	14	25	50 to 68[2]
Young equines:			
Foals, 2 weeks to 10 months old . . .	21	8	68 to 74
Weanlings to 18 months old	14	20	60
18 months to 3 years old	13	25	50 to 60

[1] The heavier the work, the more energy is required.
[2] Increase the energy immediately before and during the breeding season.
(Also see MARE; MINERALS; NUTRITIVE NEEDS; RACEHORSES; STALLION; and VITAMINS.)

Fig. F-3. Well-fed yearlings—curious, contented, and alert. (Courtesy, Theracon, Inc., Topeka, Kansas)

(Also see MARE; MINERALS; NUTRITIVE NEEDS; RACEHORSES; STALLION; and VITAMINS.)

HOW TO FEED.—Feeding horses is both an art and a science. The art is knowing how to feed and how to take care of each horse's individual requirements. The science is meeting the nutritive requirements with the right combination of ingredients.

AMOUNT TO FEED.—Because the horse has a limited digestive capacity, the amount of concentrates must be increased and the roughages decreased when the energy needs rise with more work. The following general guides may be used for the daily ration of horses under usual conditions.

● *Horses at light work* (1 to 3 hours per day of riding or driving).—Allow two-fifths to one-half pound of grain and 1¼ to 1½ pounds of hay per day per 100 pounds of body weight.

● *Horses at medium work* (3 to 5 hours per day of riding or driving).—Allow about three-fourths of a pound of grain and 1 to 1¼ pounds of hay per 100 pounds of body weight.

● *Horses at hard work* (5 to 8 hours per day of riding or driving).—Allow about 1¼ to 1⅓ pounds of grain and 1 to 1¼ pounds of hay per 100 pounds of body weight.

As will be noted from these recommendations, the total allowance of both concentrates and hay should be about 2 to 2½ pounds daily per 100 pounds of body weight.

About 6 to 12 pounds of grain daily is an average grain ration for a light horse at medium or light work. Racehorses in training usually consume 10 to 16 pounds of grain per day; the exact amount varies with the individual requirements and the amount of work. The hay allowance averages about 1 to 1¼ pounds daily per 100 pounds of body weight, but it is restricted as the grain allowance is increased. Light feeders should not be overworked.

The quantities of feeds recommended are intended as guides only. The allowance, especially the concentrates, should be increased when the horse is too thin and decreased when the horse is too fat.

STARTING HORSES ON FEED.—Horses must be accustomed to changes in feed gradually. In general, they may be given as much non-legume roughage as they will consume. But they must be accustomed gradually to high-quality legumes, which may be very laxative. This can be done by slowly replacing the nonlegume roughage with greater quantities of legumes. Also, as the grain ration is increased, the roughage is decreased.

Starting horses on grain requires care and good judgment. Usually it is advisable first to accustom them to a bulky type of ration; a starting ration with considerable rolled oats is excellent for this purpose.

The keenness of the appetite and the consistency of the droppings are an excellent index of a horse's capacity to take more feed. In all instances, scouring should be avoided.

FREQUENCY, REGULARITY, AND ORDER OF FEEDING.—The grain ration usually is divided into three equal feeds given morning, noon, and night. Because a digestive tract distended with hay is a hindrance in hard work, most of the hay should be fed at night. The common practice is to feed one-fourth of the daily hay allowance at each of the morning and noon feedings and the remaining one-half at night when the animals have plenty of time to eat leisurely.

Horses learn to anticipate their feed. Accordingly, they should be fed at the same time each day. During warm weather, they will eat better if the feeding hours are early and late, in the cool of the day.

Usually the grain ration is fed first, then the roughage. This way, the animals can eat the bulky roughages more leisurely.

Sudden changes in diet should be avoided, especially when changing from a less concentrated ration to a more concentrated one. If this rule of feeding is ignored, horses have digestive disturbances and go "off feed." When ingredients are added or omitted, the change should be made gradually. Likewise, caution should be exercised in turning horses to pasture or in transferring them to more lush grazing.

ATTENTION TO DETAILS.—A successful horseman pays great attention to details. In addition to maintaining the health and comfort of his animals, he also considers their individual likes and temperaments. Nervousness and inefficient use of feed are caused by excessive exercise to the point of undue fatigue, and/or stress, rough treatment, noise, and excitement.

GENERAL FEEDING RULES.—Observance of the following rules will help avoid some of the common difficulties that result from poor feeding practices:

● Know the approximate weight and age of each animal.

● Never feed moldy, musty, dusty, or frozen feed.

● Inspect the feed box frequently to see if the horse goes off feed.

● Keep the feed and water containers clean.

● Make certain that the horse's teeth are sound.

● Do not feed concentrates to a hot horse; allow time for his feed to digest before he is worked.

● Feed horses as individuals. Learn the peculiarities and desires of each animal because each one is different.

● See that horses get enough exercise. It improves their appetite, digestion, and overall well-being.

● Do not feed from the hand; this can lead to "nibbling."

Horses fitted for show or sale should be let down in condition gradually. Many horsemen accomplish this difficult task, and yet retain strong vigorous animals, by cutting down gradually on the feed and increasing the exercise.

FEEDING WEANLINGS.—Perhaps the most critical period in the entire life of a horse is that interval from weaning time (about six months of age) until one year of age. Foals suckling their dams and receiving no grain may develop very satisfactorily up to weaning time. However, lack of preparation prior to weaning, and neglect following the separation from the dam, may prevent the animal from gaining proper size and shape. The primary objective in the breeding of horses is the economical production of a well-developed, sound individual at maturity. To achieve this result requires good care and management of weanlings.

As previously indicated, no great setback or disturbances will be encountered at weaning time provided that the foals have developed a certain independence from proper grain feedings during the suckling period. Generally, weanlings should receive 1 to 1½ pounds of grain and 1½ to 2 pounds of hay daily per each 100 pounds of live weight. The amount of feed will vary somewhat with the individuality of the animal, the quality of roughage, available pastures, the price of feeds, and whether the weanling is being developed for show, race, or sale. Naturally, animals being developed for early use or sale should be fed more liberally, although it is equally important to retain clean, sound joints, legs, and feet —a condition which cannot be obtained so easily in heavily fitted animals.

Because of the rapid development of bone and muscle in weanlings, it is important that, in addition to ample quantity of feed, the ration also provide high quality proteins, and adequate minerals and vitamins.

Fig. F-5. Yearling.

pastures may be, they are roughages rather than concentrates.

The winter feeding program for the rising two-year-olds should be such as to produce plenty of bone and muscle rather than fat. From ½ to 1 pound of grain and 1 to 1½ pounds of hay should be fed for each 100 pounds of live weight. The quantity will vary with the quality of the roughage, the individuality of the animal, and the use for which the animal is produced. In producing for sale, more liberal feeding may be economical. Access to salt and to a mineral mixture should be provided at all times; or the minerals should be incorporated in the ration. An abundance of fresh, pure water must be available.

FEEDING TWO- AND THREE-YEAR-OLDS.—Except for the fact that the two- and three-year-olds will be larger, and, therefore, will require more feed, a description of their proper care and management would be merely a repetition of the principles that have already been discussed for the yearling.

With the two-year-old that is to be raced, however, the care and feeding at this time become matters of extreme importance. Once the young horse is placed in training, the ration should be adequate enough to allow for continued development and to provide necessary maintenance and additional energy for work. This means that special attention must be given to providing adequate proteins, minerals, and vitamins in the ration. Overexertion must be avoided; the animal

Fig. F-4. Weanlings. (Courtesy, American Albino Association, Inc., Crabtree, Ore.)

FEEDING YEARLINGS.—If foals have been fed and cared for so that they are well grown and thrifty as yearlings, usually little difficulty will be experienced at any later date.

When on pasture, yearlings that are being grown for show or sale should receive grain in addition to grass. They should be confined to their stalls in the daytime during the hot days and turned out at night (because of not being exposed to sunshine, adequate vitamin D must be provided). This point needs to be emphasized when forced development is desired; for, good as

Fig. F-6. Two-year-olds.

must be properly groomed; and the feet must be cared for properly. In brief, every precaution must be taken if the animal is to remain sound —a most difficult task when animals are raced at an early age, even though the right genetic make-up and the proper environment are present.

FEED MANGER.—See EQUIPMENT, FEED AND WATER—Hay.

FEED, SPACE REQUIREMENTS FOR.—See BUILDINGS—Table B-11.

FEED, WEIGHTS AND MEASURES OF.—See WEIGHTS AND MEASURES OF FEEDS—Table W-2.

FEET *(of horse).*—The value of a horse lies chiefly in his ability to move; therefore, good feet and legs are necessary. The important points in the care of a horse's feet are to keep them clean, prevent them from drying out, trim them so they retain proper shape and length, and shoe them correctly when shoes are needed.

Each day, clean the feet of horses that are shod, stabled, or worked and inspect them for loose shoes and thrush. Thrush is a disease of the foot caused by a fungus and characterized by a pungent odor. It causes a deterioration of tissues in the cleft of the frog or in the junction between the frog and bars. This disease produces lameness and can be serious if not treated. (See Fig. F-7.)

TRIMMING AND SHOEING.—Before trimming or shoeing, a horseman should be able to recognize proper and faulty conformation. Fig. F-8 shows the proper posture of the hoof and incorrect postures caused by hoofs grown too long either in toe or heel. The slope is considered normal when the toe of the hoof and the pastern have the same direction. This angle should be kept in mind and changed only as a corrective measure. If it should become necessary to correct uneven wear of the hoof, correct gradually over a period of several trimmings.

Before the feet are trimmed, the horse should be inspected while standing squarely on a level, hard surface. Then he should be seen at both the walk and the trot. (See Fig. F-8.)

The hoofs should be trimmed every month or 6 weeks whether the animal is shod or not. If shoes are left on too long, the hoofs grow out of proportion. This may throw the horse off balance and put extra stress on the tendons. Always keep the hoofs at proper length and correct posture. Trim the hoofs near the level of the sole; otherwise, they will split off if the horse remains unshod. Trim the frog carefully and remove only ragged edges that allow filth to accumulate in the crevices. Trim the sole very sparingly, if at all, and never rasp the wall of the hoof.

Certain faults of the foot can be corrected by proper trimming and shoeing (see SHOEING—Common Faults and How to Correct Them—Table S-4.)

Horses should be shod when they are used on hard surfaces for any length of time. Also, shoes may be used to change gaits and action, correct faulty hoof structure or growth, protect the hoof from such conditions as corns, contraction, or cracks, and aid in gripping the track. Shoes should be made to fit the foot and not the foot to fit the shoes. Reshoe or reset at four to six week intervals. Do not attempt to shoe a horse without first getting instructions from a farrier.

(Also see FOOT; and SHOEING.)

FEET *(of rider).*—The position of the rider's feet will differ somewhat according to the seat. For example, when riding a three- or five-gaited horse, the rider assumes the show seat in which

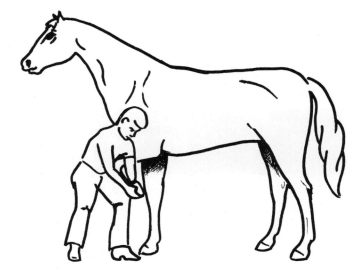

TO PICK UP AND EXAMINE FRONT FOOT

TO PICK UP HIND FOOT

TO EXAMINE HIND FOOT

Fig. F-7. Proper method of examining feet. Foot in-spection should be made daily of horses that are shod, stabled, or worked.

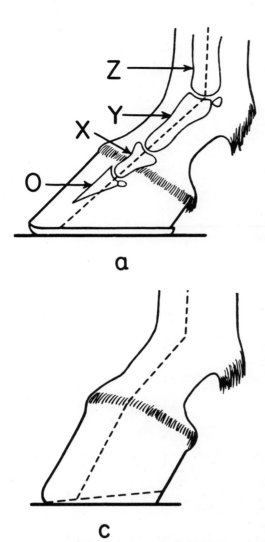

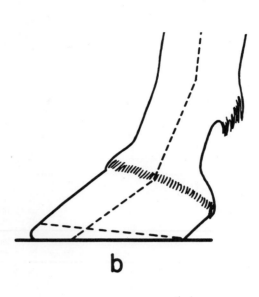

Fig. F-8. (a) Properly trimmed hoof with normal foot axis: O—coffin bone; X—short pastern bone; Y—long pastern bone; Z—cannon bone. (b) Toe too long, which breaks the foot axis backward. Horizontal dotted line shows how hoof should be trimmed to restore normal posture. (c) Heel too long, which breaks the foot axis forward. Horizontal dotted line shows how trimming will restore the correct posture.

the ball of the foot rests directly over the stirrup iron, knees are in, and heels are lower than the toes. When riding Western style, the rider keeps the legs fairly straight or bent slightly forward at the knees and rests the balls of the feet on the stirrup treads with the heels down.

(Also see HORSEMANSHIP.)

FEET ON THE DASHBOARD.—An expression used to indicate riding with the feet too far forward as though bracing them against the dashboard of a vehicle. This position also results in the heels being too far down and the rider being seated too far back in the saddle.

FENCES FOR HORSES.—Good fences (1) maintain boundaries, (2) make horse training and other operations possible, (3) reduce losses to both animals and crops, (4) increase property values, (5) promote better relationships between neighbors, (6) lessen the likelihood of car accidents from animals getting on roads, and (7) add to the attractiveness and distinctiveness of the premises.

Large pastures in which the concentration of horses is not too great may be fenced with woven wire. The mesh of the woven wire fence should be small so horses cannot get their feet through it. Corrals, paddocks, and small pastures require stronger materials. The deficiencies of board and pole fences are: They must be kept painted; they splinter, break, and rot; and they are chewed by horses.

Until recently, conventional metal fences of steel, aluminum, wrought iron, chain link, or cable had one or more deficiencies. But metal fences have greatly improved in recent years.

Table F-4 lists the materials and specifications commonly used for horse fences.

TABLE F-4

HORSE FENCES

Post and Fencing Material	Post Length and Diameter	Size of Rails, Boards, or Poles, and Gage of Wire	Fence Height	Number of Rails, Boards, or Poles, and Mesh of Wire	Distance Between Posts On Centers
			(inches)		(feet)
Steel or aluminum posts and rails.[1]	7½ ft.	10 or 20 ft. long	60	3 rails	10
	7½ ft.	10 or 20 ft. long	60	4 rails	10
	8½ ft.	10 or 20 ft. long	72	4 rails	10
Wooden posts and boards.	7½ ft.; 4 to 8 in.	2 x 6 or 2 x 8 in. boards	60	4 boards	8
	8½ ft.; 4 to 8 in.	2 x 6 or 2 x 8 in. boards	72	5 boards	8
Wooden posts and poles.	7½ ft.; 4 to 8 in.	4 to 6 in. diameter	60	4 poles	8
	8½ ft.; 4 to 8 in.	4 to 6 in. diameter	72	5 poles	8
Wooden posts and woven wire.[2]	7½ ft.; 4 to 8 in.	9 or 11 gage staywire	55 to 58	12-in. mesh	12

[1] Because of the strength of most metal, fewer rails and posts are necessary than when wood is used.
[2] Use 1 or 2 strands of barbed wire—with barbs 3 to 4 inches apart—on top of the fence.

Fig. F-9. An attractive board fence.

Fig. F-10. Pasture paddock at Gem State Stables, enclosed with a well-built metal fence. (Courtesy, Velma V. Morrison, owner, Tipton, Calif.)

DIVISION FENCE.—Where the partition fence extends north and south, custom decrees that the owner whose land is east of the fence builds the north half, and the owner whose land lies on the west side of the fence builds the south half. Where the partition fence extends east and west, the owner whose land lies north of the fence builds the west half and the owner whose land lies south of the fence builds the east half. A simple customary rule regarding the apportionment of a division fence is one which gives a responsibility to the landowner for that portion of the fence which is on his right as he stands on his own property and faces the fence. Where landowners agree to some other division, the agreement should be put in writing, acknowledged before a Notary Public, and recorded by the County Recorder.

(Also see LAW AND HORSES—Fencing, Legal Aspects.)

FENDER.—An oblong or triangular shield of leather attached to the stirrup leather of a Western saddle to protect a rider's legs. Fenders are not commonly used on English saddles.

(Also see SADDLES—Fig. S-3.)

FERAL.—A wild horse. One that has escaped from domestication and has become wild, as contrasted to one originating in the wild.

FERTILITY.—Reproductive ability as indicated by offspring.

(Also see MARE; and STALLION.)

FERTILIZATION.—See BREEDING HORSES.

FERTILIZING HORSE PASTURES.—If used properly, inorganic fertilizers will produce more pasture growth and make for sounder horses. Of course, improper fertilization of horse pastures can result in an imbalance of the mineral content of the forage, which, in turn, will affect the animal. But when soil samples are properly taken and analyzed, then used as a guide for fertilizer application, the mineral content of the grass will be improved.

It's the total mineral intake of the horse that's important. This calls for (1) soil testing, with fertilizer application based thereon, (2) grass testing, and (3) ration testing; with the mineral supplement balancing out the needs of the horse.

FETLOCK JOINT.—The connection between the cannon and the pastern bones.

(Also see PARTS OF A HORSE—Fig. P-4.)

FETUS.—The unborn animal as it develops in the uterus.

FEVER.—Normal rectal temperature for the horse is 100.5° F., with a range of 99 to 100.8° F. If the temperature runs above 100.8° F., the horse should be watched carefully. If the fever persists or gets much higher, a veterinarian should be called.

FIADOR.—A cord fastened to a hackamore and acting as a throatlatch.

FIBULA, FRACTURED.—Most cases of acute or chronic lameness due to fibula fractures are found on the racetrack.

The fibula is a small, long bone extending along the back side of the tibia from the stifle downward. The upper end articulates with the end of the tibia and the lower end eventually becomes fused with this same bone. In young horses, only the upper third is visible on X-ray plates, because the long, thin shaft has not changed from cartilage to bone. In older horses, the entire length is easily seen on X-ray plates.

The fracture of the fibula causes lameness of the stifle, hip, and back. Horses in training are able to negotiate turns well, but they tend to turn sideways (away from the injured leg) on the straight. An X-ray examination is the only conclusive way to arrive at a diagnosis.

Fibula fracture is caused by undue stress, a strain, or a blow. It may result from (1) a sudden start from an off-balanced position at the starting gate, (2) a bad racetrack, (3) a sudden stop, (4) a sudden shifting of the weight in rearing and shying, (5) a kick, or (6) being cast in a stall. Also, faulty nutrition may be a causative factor in some cases.

Rest is the only effective treatment at the present time. Counter-irritant injections and blisters, anti-inflammatory drugs (corticosteroids) and drugs which tend to relieve muscle spasms, and improved nutrition may be used along with rest.

FIELD HORSES.—There is a maximum of twelve betting units on the Totalisator Board. If there are more than twelve horses entered, all those over eleven are coupled together in the wagerings as "field horses," under the number 12. A bet on one field horse is a bet on all field horses.

FIELD MASTER.—The person in charge of the field (all riders who are not officials) of a fox hunt. The Field Master is responsible for the conduct of the field. It is his responsibility to see that all members of the field are courteous, informed, do not interfere with the hounds, and do not cause trouble in other ways.

FIGHTING THE BIT.—Fighting the bit is evidenced by a horse throwing his nose up, depressing his head, shaking his head, and/or refusing to go against a light tension on the bit.

FIGURE EIGHT.—This is an equitation exercise in which the course is a figure eight. It is designed to make the horse flexible and obedient and able to change leads. In certain performance classes, this particular exercise is used to test the horse's ability.

FILLED LEGS (SWOLLEN LEGS; "STOCKED UP").—Swollen limbs, which may become tender and stiff. This condition is usually caused by overfeeding and/or lack of exercise.
(Also see SWOLLEN LEGS.)

FILLY.—A young female horse under three years of age; in Thoroughbreds, it includes four-year-olds.

FILM PATROL.—The practice of recording a race on film.

FILTERABLE VIRUS.—An organism so small that is is capable of passing through filters which will retain the ordinary bacteria.

FINE HARNESS HORSES.—A fine harness horse is exactly what the name implies—a fine horse presented in fine harness. The entire ensemble is elegant and represents the ultimate in grace and charm.
In the show-ring, fine harness horses are, according to the rules of the American Horse Shows Association, limited to the American Saddle Horse breed. In some shows, however, other breeds are exhibited in fine harness classes. Fashion decrees that fine harness horses shall be shown wearing long mane and tail and drawing a four-wheeled road show wagon without top, or with top drawn. Light harness with a snaffle bit is required. Fine harness horses are shown at an animated park trot and at an animated walk.
(Also see SADDLE HORSES, THREE- AND FIVE-GAITED.)

FIRING (PIN-FIRING, OR POINT-FIRING).—The application of pointed irons or needles, which are subjected to great heat, to the affected tissue being treated. The treatment may be graduated from a mere puncturing of the skin to a penetration as deep as the bone. Firing is designed to stimulate the growth of tissue.

FIRST AID FOR HORSES.—First Aid for horses, as for humans, refers to the immediate and temporary care given in the case of accident or sudden illness before the veterinarian arrives. Its purposes: (1) to prevent accidents, (2) to avoid further injury and unnecessary suffering in case of injury, (3) to recognize serious trouble if and when it strikes, (4) to assist the veterinarian in carrying out the prescribed treatment, and (5) to teach simple remedies and treatments which may be used safely if it is not possible to get a practitioner.
First Aid does not alleviate the need for professional assistance; rather, a well thought out plan in advance of a possible emergency may save the horse's life and usefulness. To this end, the horseman needs to be knowledgeable relative to the following.

WOUNDS.—Lacerations may or may not require suturing. Minor wounds, not of sufficient severity to require the services of a veterinarian, may be treated by (1) controlling bleeding, (2) clipping the hair from around the edges of the wound, (3) removing any dirt with a physiologic saline solution, (4) clipping away any jagged or damaged tissue, (5) applying a mild antiseptic, but no greasy ointments (as the latter delays healing), (6) bandaging for two or more days if necessary, then removing the bandage and applying a healing powder as required, (7) treating for screwworms in screwworm-infested areas, and (8) administering tetanus antitoxin or a tetanus booster.
Where the wound needs suturing, call the veterinarian. Then, while awaiting his arrival, control bleeding and keep the wound moistened with physiologic saline solution.
Severe bleeding accompanying wounds can be fatal. Arteries bleed with intermittent spurts, whereas veins flow steadily. A pressure pack is usually applied to body wounds, while a tourniquet can be used on limbs. The latter may be

made from rubber tubing, bound tightly above the laceration. The pressure of a tourniquet should be released every 15 to 20 minutes to prevent gangrene.

Nail and rock puncture wounds of the hoof are rather common. Where severe, and especially when the horseman is inexperienced, it is best to call a veterinarian. If the veterinarian is not readily available, or if the horseman is experienced, proceed to (1) remove dirt and debris with a hoof pick, (2) wash the hoof with warm water and soap, (3) remove the foreign body and immediately (before you lose track of the location of the hole) enlarge the puncture to assure drainage, (4) poultice the wound for several days with a cotton pack saturated with disinfectant solution, (5) protect with a pad or other means until healing is complete, and (6) treat the horse with tetanus antitoxin or tetanus booster.

Following any wound treatment, the horse should be placed in a clean place and watched to make certain that he does not mutilate the injured area.

BRUISES AND SWELLINGS.—Blows may produce hemorrhages in the tissues under the skin. First Aid for such injuries consists of (1) measures to stop the hemorrhage—cold applications together with firm, even pressure, (2) cold water showers and cold water bandages until the swelling stops, and (3) heat or linament applied after the swelling has stopped.

FRACTURE.—In all cases of fracture, professional assistance should be secured as quickly as possible. Until help arrives, keep the horse as quiet as possible. With leg fractures, it may be necessary to splint the affected limb with wood or pipe to hold the break in place; then wrap it with towels or other padding.

COLIC.—When colicky symptoms appear, keep the animal on its feet; walk slowly and quietly, by leading; and apply heat to the abdomen.

AZOTURIA.—When the characteristic wine-colored urine, sweating distress, and stiffness are noted, (1) stop all exercise, (2) rub the horse dry and blanket him, (3) apply hot water bottles or heated blankets or cloths to the swollen and hardened muscles, and (4) secure professional help as quickly as possible.

FOUNDER (LAMINITIS).—Pending the arrival of the veterinarian, pull the shoes if the horse is shod, and stand the animal in a cold water bath or apply cold bran poultices (preferably using ice water in either treatment).

BLEEDERS.—Hemorrhage in the nasal cavity occurs in certain families of race-horses. When observed, cease exercise, apply ice packs to the muzzle to help clot the blood, and call the veterinarian.

MERCURY POISONING.—Mercury poisoning from consuming grains treated with fungicides is not uncommon. While professional help is on the way, drench the horse with an antidote of a dozen egg whites.

FIRST AID SUPPLIES.—First Aid supplies should be conveniently available, but stored where neither children nor horses have access to them. The following items are rather basic; but the horseman is admonished to seek the counsel and advice of his local veterinarian relative to these and additional supplies:

Adhesive tape	Metal syringe
Bandages	Physiologic saline
Blanket	(sterile solution)
Boric Acid	Plastic ice bag
Bucket	Potassium Iodide
Clippers	Scalpel
Disinfectants	Scissors
Epsom salts	Screwworm preparation
Eyedropper	Splints
Germicidal soap	Sterile absorbent cotton
Hoof knife	Stomach tube
Hot water bottle	Thermometer
Linament	Tourniquet

Common sense should always prevail when administering first aid; and the horseman should realize his limitations and consult a professional when he is unsure of himself or his ability.

FIRST LOCK.—The first lock of the mane on or in back of the poll (when the poll is clipped).

The first lock is sometimes braided with a ribbon, as is the foretop.

FISTULOUS WITHERS.—Fistulous withers is an inflamed condition in the region of the withers, commonly thought to be caused by bruising. Fistula and poll evil are very similar except for location. As in poll evil, therefore, treatment for fistulous withers, which should be handled by a veterinarian, consists of establishing proper drainage and removing all dead tissue. Caustic applications to destroy the diseased tissues should be used only on the advice of a veterinarian.

(Also see UNSOUNDNESSES.)

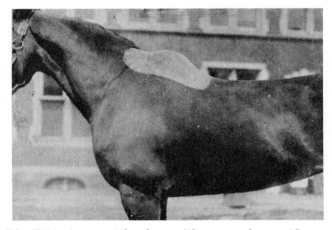

Fig. F-11. A case of fistulous withers on a horse. (Courtesy, University of Pennsylvania, and Pitman-Moore, Indianapolis, Ind.)

FITTING.—See FEED—Fitting (Fattening).

FIVE-GAITED SADDLE HORSES.—See SADDLE HORSES, THREE- AND FIVE-GAITED.

FLANKS *(fore flank; hind flank)*.—Horses should be deep in both the fore flank and the hind flank. Deep flanks contribute to symmetry and balance. Racehorses in training may show much less depth in the rear flank than other types of horses. Even with racehorses, however, the extremely high-cut, "wasp-waisted" ones will not endure heavy racing. Moreover, racehorses usually deepen materially in the rear flank with age or higher condition.

(Also see PARTS OF A HORSE—Fig. P-4.)

FLAT BONE.—See BONE.

FLAT FOOT.—A foot the angle of which is less than 45°, or one in which the sole is not concave, or one with a low, weak heel.

FLAT RACE.—A race on a level course without hurdles or other obstacles, and under saddle.

(Also see, RACING; and RUNNING RACEHORSES.)

FLAT-SIDED (FLAT-RIBBED, SLAT-SIDED, or SLAB-SIDED).—A horse is said to be flat-sided when its ribs are not rounded or well-sprung.

FLAXEN.—A light-colored mane or tail.

FLEA-BITTEN.—Describes a white horse covered with small, brown marks, or any mangy-looking animal.

FLEXING *(the hocks)*.—A term usually applied to Hackney action, as they, more than other breeds, bend their hocks and get their legs further under the belly.

FLEXING *(the jaw)*.—A horse is said to be flexed when he yields his jaw to the pressure of the bit, with his head bent at the poll. When a good trainer has "developed the horse's mouth" —when the horse understands what pressure on the bit means—there is no need to worry about the horse's head set; it will be set.

FLIES.—Flies are probably the most important insect pests of horses. Biting stable flies, many species of horse flies and deer flies, and horn flies are, without doubt, the most annoying species affecting horses. Nonbiting house flies (*Musca domestica L.*) and the face fly (*Musca autumnalis de Geer*) are great nuisances. Because of their varying habits, different materials and methods are required for the control of different species of flies.

Fig. F-12. Horsefly (Tabanus atratus). *It is a biting insect, whose bites are painful. (Courtesy, USDA)*

(In addition to the discussion which follows pertaining to each fly, see DISEASES AND PARASITES; HEALTH PROGRAM; and PARASITES OF HORSES. Also, always follow the manufacturer's directions.)

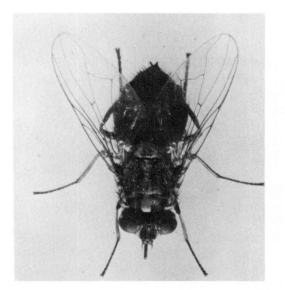

Fig. F-13. Stablefly (Stomaxys calcitrans). *(Courtesy, USDA)*

BLOWFLY.—The blowfly group consists of several species of flies that breed in animal flesh.

SYMPTOMS.—The maggots of blowflies infest wounds and spread over the body, feeding on the skin surface, producing severe irritation, and destroying the ability of the skin to function. In-

fested animals rapidly become weak, fevered, and unthrifty.

TREATMENT.—A 0.25% Coumaphos (Co-Ral) spray is effective for controlling blowfly larvae infesting soiled hair and wounds.

PREVENTION AND CONTROL.—To control the blowfly, destroy dead animals by burning or deep burial and by using traps, poisoned baits, electrified screens, and repellents.

DISCUSSION.—Blowfly attacks are widespread but they present the greatest problem in the Pacific Northwest, the South, and the Southwest. Death losses are not large but work efficiency is lowered.

FACE FLY.—Face flies gather in large numbers on the faces of horses, especially around the eyes and nose.

TREATMENT.—Use a 0.3 percent Ciodrin® spray or brush the forehead lightly with a sirup bait containing 0.5 percent dichlorvos (Vapona). These two treatments are effective for only a short time and may have to be applied almost daily.

PREVENTION AND CONTROL.—Shelters for horses on pastures give some protection.

HORN FLY.—Horn flies are primarily pests of cattle but they sometimes seriously annoy horses.

TREATMENT.—Treat infested animals with any of the insecticides recommended for horn flies in the treatment section under "House Fly and Stable Fly."

HORSEFLY, DEERFLY, AND MOSQUITO.—All of these are biting insects. Bites of horseflies and deerflies are painful.

TREATMENT.—Use repellent sprays containing 0.05 to 0.1 percent pyrethrins, with or without 0.5 to 0.1 percent synergist. Mists or wet sprays of such formulations will lessen the attacks of biting insects for several hours to a full day. Sprays containing 0.3 percent Ciodrin® will provide short-time protection from biting flies and mosquitoes, but do not apply more often than every seven days.

PREVENTION AND CONTROL.—The best method of controlling mosquitoes is to provide drainage or landfill in breeding areas.

DISCUSSION.—Mosquitoes transmit equine encephalomyelitis.

HOUSE FLY AND STABLE FLY.—House flies are nonbiting, nuisance insects. Stable flies are biting insects that bite principally on the legs.

SYMPTOMS.—Flies annoy horses, causing them to fight. Horses may strike the ground with their feet, toss their heads, switch their tails, and run.

TREATMENT.—Treat animals infested with house and stable flies with any of the following insecticides, using the dosages given. Indication is shown if the treatment is also effective against horn flies.

● Carbaryl spray, 0.5 percent, 1 quart, not more often than every 4 days. (Also for horn flies.)

● Ciodrin spray, 0.15 to 0.3 percent, 1 quart per horse, not more often than every 7 days. (Also for horn flies.)

● Ciodrin mist spray, 2 percent in oil, 1 to 2 ounces. (Mist spray is composed of very fine, or minute, droplets.)

● Coumaphos spray, 0.06 to 0.25 percent, 1 to 2 quarts per horse, to backs of animals every 3 weeks or as needed. (Also for horn flies.)

● Dioxathion spray, 0.15 percent, 1 to 2 quarts per horse, not more often than once every 2 weeks. (Also for horn flies.)

● Dichlorvos mist spray, 1 percent in oil, 1 to 2 ounces. (Also for horn flies.)

● Malathion spray, 0.5 percent, 2 quarts per horse, to backs every 3 weeks or as needed. (Also for horn flies.)

● Methoxychlor spray, 0.5 percent, 1 to 2 quarts per horse, to backs every 3 weeks or as needed. (Also for horn flies.)

● Ronnel spray, 0.25 to 0.5 percent, 1 to 2 quarts per horse, to backs every 3 weeks or as needed. (Also for horn flies.)

● Pyrethrins and synergist, 1 to 2 quarts, when used as a wet spray, or 1 to 2 ounces as a mist spray; repeat every 2 to 3 days as needed.
Spray should be applied liberally under pressure to wet the haircoat to the skin.

The following are effective against house flies but not stable flies: (1) baits consisting of a 0.5 to 2 percent organophosphate toxicant such as dichlorvos, diazinon, malathion, naled, or trichlorfon mixed with a food attractant such as sugar or syrup; or (2) treated cotton cord impregnated with 10 percent parathion or 25 percent diazinon and suspended from the ceiling.

PREVENTION AND CONTROL.—Practice good sanitation, including proper disposal of all fly breeding media such as manure and waste feed. Use screens when practical.

DISCUSSION.—*Habronema spp.,* a roundworm, is transmitted by house flies. Stable flies can carry anthrax, infectious anemia, and surra. (Surra is an Old World febrile and hemorrhagic disease characterized by edema and anemia, caused by a protozoan and transmitted by biting insects. It is commonly fatal to horses and mules.)

FLOATING.—Filing off the sharp edges of a horse's teeth.

FLUORINE POISONING (FLUOROSIS).—

CAUSE.—Ingesting excessive quantities of fluorine through either the feed or water.

SYMPTOMS.—Abnormal teeth (especially mottled enamel) and bones, stiffness of joints, loss of appetite, emaciation, reduction in milk flow, diarrhea, and salt hunger.

DISTRIBUTION AND LOSSES.—The water in parts of Arkansas, California, South Carolina, and Texas has been reported to contain excess fluorine. Occasionally throughout the U.S. high fluorine phosphates are used in mineral mixtures.

TREATMENT.—Any damage may be permanent, but animals which have not developed severe symptoms may be helped to some extent if the sources of excess fluorine are eliminated.

CONTROL AND ERADICATION.—Discontinue the use of feeds, water, or mineral supplements containing excessive fluorine.

PREVENTION.—Avoid the use of feeds, water, or mineral supplements containing excessive fluorine. Not more than 65 to 100 ppm fluorine should be present in dry matter of rations when rock phosphate is fed. Phosphorus sources should not contain more than 0.1% F.

FLYING CHANGE.—When a horse changes from one lead to another at the gallop without coming to a half-halt or reducing the gait, it is known as a "flying change." A well-trained horse will do a flying change with the proper aids; a slight increase of pressure on the rein on the side with which the horse is leading and a light pressure on the leg on the same side just behind the stirrup leather.

FOAL.—By definition, a foal is a young, unweaned horse of either sex.

THE NEWBORN FOAL.—After the newborn foal starts breathing and has been rubbed dry, put it in one corner of the stall on clean, fresh straw. The mare usually will be less restless if this corner is in the direction of her head.

Protect the eyes of a newborn foal from bright lights.

Fig. F-14. Newborn Hungarian foal taking its first faltering steps at Bitterroot Stock Farm, Hamilton, Montana, owned by Margit Sigray Bessenyey. (Photo by Ernst Peterson, Hamilton, Mont.)

TREATMENT OF THE NAVEL CORD.—If left alone, the navel cord of the newborn foal usually breaks within 2 to 4 inches of the belly. If it does not break, cut it about 2 inches from the belly with clean, dull shears or scrape it in two with a knife. A torn or broken blood vessel will bleed very little, but one cut directly across may bleed excessively. Treat the severed cord immediately with tincture of iodine, or other reliable antiseptic; then leave the mare and foal alone so they can rest and gain strength.

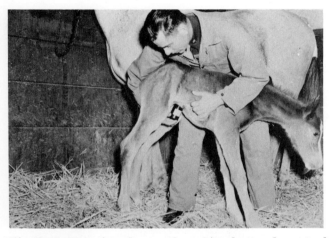

Fig. F-15. Treating the navel cord of the newborn foal with iodine. This is done by placing the end of the cord in a wide-mouthed bottle nearly full of tincture of iodine while pressing the bottle firmly against the abdomen. (Courtesy, California Thoroughbred Breeders' Association, Arcadia, Calif.)

VALUE OF COLOSTRUM.—Colostrum is milk secreted by the dam for the first few days after parturition. It differs from ordinary milk in that it is more concentrated; is higher in protein content, especially in globulin; is richer in vitamin A; contains antibodies that protect the foal temporarily against certain infections; and is a natural purgative that removes fecal matter accumulated in the digestive tract.

Do not dissipate the benefits of colostrum by "milking out" a mare shortly before foaling time.

THE FIRST NURSING.—A strong, healthy foal will be on its feet and ready to nurse within ½ to 2 hours after birth. Before allowing the foal to nurse for the first time, wash the mare's udder with a mild disinfectant and rinse thoroughly with clean, warm water.

A big, awkward foal occasionally needs assistance and guidance when it nurses the first time. If the foal is stubborn, forced feeding will be useless. Back the mare onto additional bedding in one corner of the stall and coax the foal to the teats with a bottle and nipple. An attendant may hold the bottle while standing on the op-

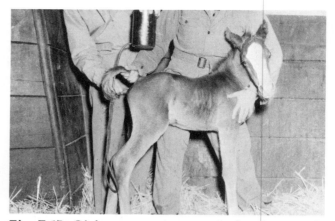

Fig. F-17. Giving an enema to a foal, using a tube and can. (Courtesy, USDA)

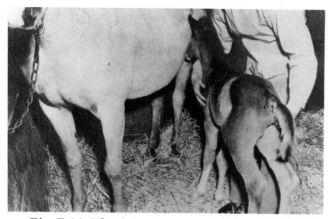

Fig. F-16. The first nursing. (Courtesy, USDA)

posite side of the mare from the foal.

A very weak foal should be given the mare's first milk even if it is necessary to draw this milk into a bottle and feed the foal one or two times by nipple. An attendant sometimes must steady a foal before it will nurse.

BOWEL MOVEMENT.—Regulation of the bowel movement of the foal is very important. Constipation and diarrhea (scours) are common ailments.

Excrement impacted in the bowels during prenatal development—material called meconium—may kill the foal if it is not eliminated promptly. A good feed of colostrum usually will cause natural elimination. This is not always the case, however, especially when foals are from stall-fed mares.

Observe the foal's bowel movement 4 to 12 hours after birth. If there has been no fecal discharge by this time, and the foal seems sluggish and fails to nurse, give it an enema. Use 1 to 2 quarts of water at body heat (101° F.) mixed with a little glycerin, or use 1 to 2 quarts of warm, soapy water. Inject the solution with a baby syringe that has about a 3-inch nipple, or use a tube and can. Repeat the treatment until

normal yellow feces appear.

If the foal is scouring, reduce the mare's feed and take away part of her milk from the foal at intervals by milking her out.

Diarrhea or scours in foals may result from infectious diseases or dirty surroundings. It is caused by an irritant in the digestive tract that should be removed. Give an astringent only in exceptional cases and on the advice of a veterinarian.

Conditions that may cause diarrhea are contaminated udder or teats, nonremoval of fecal matter from the digestive tract, fretfulness or temperature above normal in the mare, too much feed affecting the quality of the mare's milk, a cold damp bed, or continued exposure to cold rains.

CARE OF THE SUCKLING FOAL.—Weather conditions permitting, there is no better place for a mare and foal than on pasture. When the foal is from 10 days to 3 weeks old, it will begin to nibble on a little grain and hay. To promote thrift and early development, and to avoid any setback at weaning time, encourage the foal to eat supplementary feed as early as possible (Fig. F-18). The foal should be provided with a low-built grain box especially for this purpose, or, if on pasture, the foal may be creep fed.

Rolled oats and wheat bran, to which a little brown sugar has been added, is especially palatable as a starting ration. Crushed or ground oats, cracked or ground corn, wheat bran, and a little linseed meal may be provided later with good results. Or a good commercial ration may be fed

Fig. F-18. Feeding the foal. (Courtesy, Gem State Stables, Tipton, Calif.)

if desired and available.

Give the foal good hay, preferably a legume, or pasture in addition to its grain ration. A normal healthy foal should be eating one-half pound of grain daily per 100 pounds of body weight at 4 to 5 weeks of age. This ration should be increased by weaning time to about three-fourths of a pound or more per 100 pounds of body weight. The exact amount of the ration varies with the individual, the type of feed, and the development desired.

Foals normally reach one-half of their mature weight during the first year under such a system. Most breeders of Thoroughbreds and Standardbreds plan to have their 2-year-old animals at full height. Such results require liberal feeding from the beginning. A foal stunted in the first year by insufficient feeding cannot be developed properly later in life. It is well recognized that forced development must be done expertly if the animals are to remain durable and sound.

TRAINING THE FOAL.—See TRAINING.

WEANING.—Foals usually are weaned at 4 to 6 months of age. Thorough preparation facilitates weaning.

It may be advisable to wean the foal at a comparatively early age if either the foal or mare is not doing well, if the mare is being given heavy work, or if the mare was rebred on the ninth day after foaling.

If by using a creep or a separate grain box the foal has become accustomed to eating a considerable amount of hay and about three-fourths of a pound of grain daily per 100 pounds of body weight, weaning will cause only a slight disturbance or setback. If the ration of the dam is cut in half a few days before the separation, her udder usually will dry up without difficulty.

Move the mare to new quarters from the stall she shares with the foal. Remove anything in the stall on which the foal might hurt itself during the first unhappy days that it lives alone. Make the separation of the foal from the mare complete and final. If the foal sees, hears, or smells its dam again, the separation process must be started all over again.

Decrease the mare's ration before and during weaning. Rub camphorated oil or a mixture of lard and spirits of camphor on the udder, but do not milk out the udder until 5 to 7 days later when it is soft and flabby.

Turn the foal out on pasture after a day or two. If there are several weanlings together, some of them might get hurt while running and frolicking in the pasture. Guard against this by first turning out two or three less valuable individuals and letting them tire themselves; then turn out the rest.

At this stage, if numerous weanlings are involved, separate them by sexes. Put the more timid ones by themselves. Do not run weanlings with older horses.

CASTRATION.—Geldings, or castrated males, are safer and easier to handle than stallions. Therefore, a colt should be castrated unless he is to be saved for breeding purposes. Have a veterinarian perform this operation. A colt may be castrated when only a few days old, but most horsemen prefer to delay the operation until the animal is about a year old. While there is less real danger to the animal and much less setback with early altering, it results in imperfect development of the foreparts. Delaying castration for a time results in more muscular, bolder features and better carriage of the foreparts.

Weather and management conditions permitting, the time of altering should be determined by the development of the individual. Underdeveloped colts may be left uncastrated six months or even a year longer than overdeveloped ones.

Breeders of Thoroughbred horses usually prefer to race them first as uncastrated animals.

There is less danger of infection if colts are castrated in the spring soon after they are turned out on clean pasture and before hot weather and "fly time" arrive. This is extremely important in the southern states because of the danger of screwworm infestation.

BREAKING.—A foal will not need breaking if it has been trained properly. When a young horse can be saddled or harnessed with satisfactory ease, it is because the suggested training program has been followed. Saddling and harnessing are just additional steps. A good time to harness and work the horse for the first time is during the winter as a rising two-year-old.

(Also see TRAINING.)

RAISING THE ORPHAN FOAL.—Occasionally, a mare dies during or immediately after parturition, leaving an orphan foal to be raised. At other times, a mare may fail to give sufficient milk, or she may have twins. In such cases, the foal may be (1) shifted to another mare, known as a foster mother or nurse mare, or (2) placed on mare's milk replacer, or synthetic milk, that is mixed and fed according to the manufacturer's directions.

It is important, however, that the orphan foal receive colostrum, preferably for about the first four days of life. For this purpose, colostrum from a mare that produces excess milk or one that has lost her foal should be collected and frozen from time to time; then, as needed, it may be thawed and warmed to 100° to 105° F. and fed.

For the first few days, the orphan foal should be fed with a bottle and rubber nipple. Within about two weeks, it may be taught to drink from a pail. All receptacles must be kept sanitary (clean and scald each time they are used) and feeding must be at regular intervals. Dry feeding should be started at the earliest possible time with the orphan foal.

The following formula may be used for feeding the orphan foal if a substitute milk must be used:

    1 pint of low fat cow's milk (3% fat).
    4 ounces of lime water.
    1 teaspoon of sugar.

Two teaspoons of lactose or corn syrup may be used to replace the sugar and one large can

of evaporated cow's milk can be used with one can of water to replace the fresh milk. The foal should be fed about one-half pint every hour. Give large foals slightly more than a pint. After 4 or 5 days increase the interval to 2 hours. After a week, feed every 4 hours and increase the quantity accordingly.

CARE OF THE FOAL'S FEET.—Foals may damage their limbs when the weight is not equally distributed because of unshapely hoofs. On the other hand, faulty limbs may be helped or even corrected if the hoofs are trimmed regularly. Also, trimming helps educate the foal and makes shoeing easier at maturity. If the foal is run on pasture, trimming the feet may be necessary long before weaning time. A good practice is to check the feet every month or six weeks and, if necessary, trim a small amount each time rather than a large amount at one time. Tendons should not become strained because of incorrectly trimmed feet. Usually, only the bottom rim of the hoof should be trimmed, although sometimes the heel, frog, or toe of the hoof may need trimming. The

Fig. F-19. Care of the foal's feet.

hoofs are trimmed with a rasp, farrier's knife, and nippers. A rasp is used more than the other tools.

Before the feet are trimmed, the foal should first be inspected while standing squarely on a hard surface and then inspected at the walk and the trot.

FOAL-HEAT.—The first heat after foaling, which generally occurs between the 9th and 13th days after parturition.

FOALING, SIGNS OF.—See PARTURITION, SIGNS OF.

FOLLICLE.—A bubblelike structure on the ovary which contains an egg.

FOOD USE.—See USES OF HORSES.

FOOT.—When it is realized that the horse has been transplanted from his natural roving environment and soft, mother-earth footing to be used in carrying and drawing loads over hard, dry-surfaced topography by day and then stabled on hard, dry floors at night, it is not surprising that foot troubles are commonplace. Nor are these troubles new. The Greeks alluded to them in the age-old axiom, "No foot, no horse."

In order to lessen foot troubles, and to permit intelligent shoeing, knowledge of the anatomy of a horse's foot, pasterns, and legs is necessary.

(Also see FEET; LEGS; and SKELETON OF THE HORSE.)

PARTS OF THE FOOT.—Fig. F-20 shows the parts of the foot, and Table F-5 gives the pertinent facts about each part. (Also see PARTS OF A HORSE—Fig. P-4.)

HOW THE HOOF GROWS.—The hoof grows downward and forward. A complex system of arteries, veins, and nerves inside the outer structure provides for its growth. The average rate of growth of the horny portions of the hoof (wall, sole, and frog) is 1/8 to 1/4 inch per month.

DRY HOOF.—See HOOFS, DRY.

FOOT BOARD.—The small platform at the rear of a carriage, for the footman. Also, it refers to the board on which the coachman's feet rest in a coach.

FOOT-LOCK OR FEATHER.—Long hair which grows back of the fetlock.

FORAGE.—Vegetable material in a fresh, dried, or ensiled state which is fed to horses and other animals (pasture, hay, silage).

FOREARM.—The area below the arm. Since little or no fat can be deposited in the forearm and gaskin, these areas are a good indication of the muscular development of the entire animal, even when horses are in high condition.

(Also see PARTS OF A HORSE—Fig. P-4.)

FOREFOOTED.—The roping of a horse by the forefeet is known as forefooted. The practice is practically obsolete today. When the West was young and horses were needed for ranch work, it was not uncommon to herd them into a corral, where they were caught, saddled, and bridled for the day's work. As they rounded the corral, a deft roper caught each horse by the two forefeet, pulled these feet from under him, and sent him sprawling to the ground. Two or three treatments of this kind usually made a horse extremely respectful of a rope.

FOREHAND.—The "front" of the horse, including head, neck, shoulders, and forelegs—in other words, that portion of the horse in front of the center of gravity.

FOREHEAD.—The front part of the head from the eyes to the poll. A broad, full forehead with great width between the eyes indicates intelligence.

(Also see PARTS OF A HORSE—Fig. P-4.)

FORETOP, FORELOCK.—The lock of hair falling forward over the face.

FORGE.—See SHOEING—Table S-5.

FORGING (CLICKING).—Striking forefoot with toe of hindfoot. This defect can be rectified by corrective shoeing. The usual method of correcting the fault consists in (1) shortening the toes of the front feet and raising the heels slight-

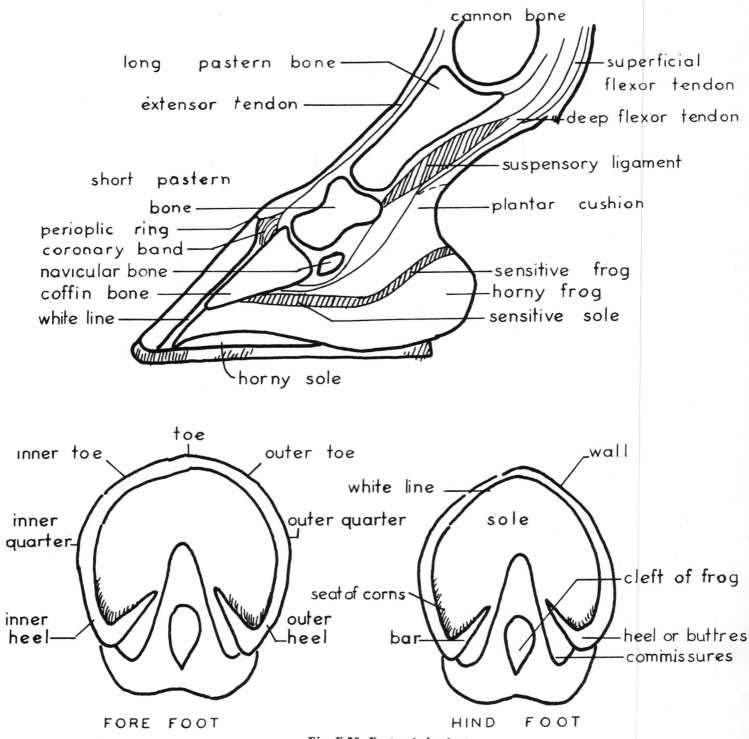

Fig. F-20. Parts of the foot.

TABLE F-5

PARTS OF THE HOOF

The Parts	Description	Functions	Comments
The Four Major Parts: The bones	They are: Long pastern bone Short pastern bone Coffin bone Navicular bone	Provide framework of the foot and facilitate locomotion.	Long pastern bone lies entirely above the hoof. Only lower end of short pastern bone is within hoof.
The elastic structure	Consists of: Lateral cartilages Planter cushion	Overcomes concussion or jar when the foot strikes the ground.	Normally, heel expands about 1/16 in. on each side of foot.
The sensitive structure, called the corium or pododerm	Consists of: Coronary band Perioplic ring Sensitive laminae Sensitive sole Sensitive frog	Furnishes nutrition to corresponding part of the hoof.	All five parts are highly sensitive and vascular.
The horny wall	The outer horny covering	Encloses and protects the sensitive parts beneath.	
The Exterior of the Hoof: The horny wall	The basic shell and wearing surface of the foot.	Protects; there is no feeling in the wall of the foot until the area of the coronary band is reached.	The horny wall extends vertically from the edge of the hair around the front and sides of the foot, then turns in upon itself at the heel, forming the bar which extends forward·toward the center.
The perioplic ring	The seat where periople is produced.	Produces periople, the varnish-like substance that covers the outer surface of the wall and seals it from excess drying	The wall of a normal foot consists of about one-fourth water, by weight.
The white line	The juncture of the wall and horny sole. It is about 1/8 in. wide.	Serves as the horseman's "red light," beyond (toward the inside of the foot) which nails should not go.	A nail past the white line may either enter the sensitive structure or produce pressure, with resulting lameness.
The horny frog	The V-shaped pad in the middle of the sole.	Compresses under weight, and transmits pressure to the elastic structures. Aids blood circulation, absorbs concussion, and prevents slippage.	Without this normal pressure, the hoof has a tendency to shrink and become dormant, with contracted feet and unsoundness resulting.
The commissures	The deep grooves on both sides of the frog.	Give elasticity.	Thrush is often found in the commissures.
The horny sole	The bottom of the foot. It is a thick (about 3/8 in.) plate or horn which grows out from the fleshy sole.	Protects the foot from the bottom. Nature didn't intend that the horny sole should carry weight, for it is convex in shape so that most of the weight rests on the wall and frog area.	The sensitive sole is directly under the horny sole. Pressure on the horny sole area will usually produce lameness.
The bars	The horny protrusions that lie along the frog between the commissures and the sole.	Help support the foot and keep it open at the heels.	
The Perimeter Sections: Inside and outside toe The quarters The heel		*(See above)*	

ly, to help the horse pick his front feet off the ground more quickly and get them out of the way of the hind ones; (2) using front shoes that are light, rolled at the toe, and no longer and no wider than the hoof; and (3) sparing (leaving them long) the toes of the hind feet and lowering the heels, to slow down the break-over behind.

FORM.—The past performance of a racehorse; often a table giving details relating to a horse's past performance.

FORWARD SEAT.—In riding hunters (including cross country riding) and jumpers, the stirrups are shortened; the foot is shot home farther than when working at slower gaits (but with some portion of the ball of the foot still resting on the stirrup, and with the heel slightly down); and the upper part of the rider's body is thrust forward, giving the "forward seat." The higher the jumps, the shorter the stirrups should be and the more pronounced the forward inclination of the body.

FOUNDER (OR LAMINITIS).—

CAUSE.—Overeating (either (1) grain or (2) lush legume or grass—the latter is known as "grass founder"), overdrinking, or from inflammation of the uterus following parturition. Also intestinal inflammation.

Fig. F-21. The feet of a foundered pony. Note extensive overgrowth of the feet and rings on hoof wall. (Reproduced with the permission of Haileybury Farm and Tampa Tracing, The Wickes, Newville, Pa.)

SYMPTOMS.—Extreme pain, fever (103° to 106° F.) and reluctance to move. If neglected, chronic laminitis will develop, resulting in a dropping of the hoof soles and a turning up of the toe walls.

DISTRIBUTION AND LOSSES.—Worldwide. Actual death losses from founder are not very great.

TREATMENT.—Pending arrival of the veterinarian, the attendant should stand the animal's feet in a cold-water bath.

CONTROL AND ERADICATION.—Control the causes; namely, (1) overeating, (2) overdrinking, and/or (3) inflammation of the uterus following parturition.

PREVENTION.—Prevent the horse from overeating and overdrinking (especially when hot). Avoid retained afterbirth. After foaling, the afterbirth should pass out within twelve hours; otherwise call a veterinarian.

REMARKS.—Unless foundered animals are quite valuable, it is usually desirable to dispose of them following a case of severe founder. (Also see FIRST AID FOR HORSES; and UNSOUNDNESSES.)

4-H CLUB HORSE PROJECTS.—The H's of the four-leaf clover stand for Head, Heart, Hands, and Health. Back in the 1890s and the early 1900s, many forces focused attention on farm boys and girls; among them (1) concern over the needs of adolescents, and (2) concern over drift of farm youth to the city.

In 1966, for the first time, the number of 4-H Club horse and pony projects, nationally, moved ahead of beef cattle projects; and the gap between the two has been widened each year since. A comparison of 4-H Club beef cattle and horse and pony projects for the years 1966 and 1972 follows:

	Number of Projects	
	Year 1966	Year 1974
Beef Cattle	157,949	160,846
Horse and Pony	165,510	320,767

As shown, there are twice as many 4-H Club horse and pony projects as beef cattle projects.

FOUR-IN-HAND.—A hitch of four horses, consisting of two pairs, with one pair in front of the other.

FOX HUNT.—A hunt with hounds, staged on horseback, after a live fox. The fox may have been released from captivity or tracked and flushed out of hiding by the hounds. It originated in England, where it is still a popular event.

FOX TROT.—The fox trot is a slow, short, broken type of trot in which the head usually nods. In executing the fox trot, the horse brings each hind foot to the ground an instant before the diagonal forefoot. This gait is accepted as a slow gait, but it is not as popular as the stepping pace.

FRACTURE.—See FIRST AID FOR HORSES.

FRACTURED FIBULA.—See FIBULA, FRACTURED.

FREDERIKSBORG.—A very old breed of horses found in Denmark where it is used for both agricultural work and riding purposes.

FRESH (in horses).—A term descriptive of a horse that is alert and gay, somewhat excitable, and probably short of exercise. Horses are more prone to be fresh in cold weather than in warm weather.

If a fresh horse is to be ridden by a beginner, he should first be calmed down. This may be accomplished either by (1) saddling and bridling him (put the reins over the saddle seat, and the stirrups over the reins), then turning him loose in a small paddock or indoor ring; (2) working him on a longe line; or (3) having him accompanied by a lead pony for 20 to 30 minutes.

FROG.—A triangular-shaped, elasticlike formation in the sole of the horse's foot. (See Fig. F-20. Parts of the foot.)

FRONT.—To horsemen, the word "front" usually refers to the front end—the head, neck, and shoulders—of a horse. The head should be well proportioned to the rest of the body, refined and clean-cut, with a chiseled appearance. The forehead should be broad and full. A straight face is usually preferable to a concave profile or a convex one (Roman nose), the former suggesting a timid disposition and the latter strong will-power. The jaw should be broad and strongly muscled. There should be great width between large, clear eyes; and the ears should be of medium size, well carried and active. The neck should be fairly long. It should be carried high, slightly arched, lean and muscular, and clean-cut about the throatlatch, with the head well set on. Also, the neck should join neatly to long, oblique, smooth shoulders. The head and neck of the animal should show sex character—boldness and masculinity in the stallion and refinement and femininity in the broodmare.

FULL BROTHERS (or SISTERS).—Horses having the same sire and the same dam.

FULL MOUTH.—A horse at five years of age.

FUNERAL PROCESSION HORSE (S).—About the only remaining function of horses in the U.S. Armed Services is for use in parades or in funeral processions. In the latter capacity, either a team may draw a caisson or there may be a riderless horse.

A riderless horse, decked out with the ornamental trappings, accompanies the bodies of general officers and former cavalry officers. Also, this consideration may be accorded a current (or former) U.S. President, as Commander-in-Chief. The practice of having the caparisoned (or decked out) charger of the deceased military officer led in the funeral procession stems from an ancient custom surrounding the burial of warriors. The horse bore a saddle with the stirrups inverted and a sword through them to symbolize that the warrior had fallen and would ride no more. Also, the horse was sacrificed at the time, because it was believed that the equine spirit would find his master in the hereafter; otherwise, the departed warrior would have to walk. Horses are no longer sacrificed. But a riderless horse, with boots and spurs reversed, is still led in the funeral procession to symbolize that the warrior has fallen.

Fig. F-22. A horse-drawn caisson shown taking the body of former President Lyndon B. Johnson to the Capitol on January 25, 1973. (Wide World Photos)

FUNGI.—Certain vegetable organisms such as molds, mushrooms, and toadstools.

FURLONG.—A racing distance of ⅛th mile, or 40 rods, or 220 yards, or 201.17 meters.

FUTURE OF U.S. HORSE INDUSTRY.—See NUMBER OF HORSES — *FUTURE OF U.S. HORSE INDUSTRY.*

FUTURITY RACE.—When a breeder enrolls his unborn foal in a race two years away, it is called a "futurity race." As in any other stake race, a fee must accompany the entry of the mare's unborn produce, and further payments must be made to keep the youngster eligible. All these fees go into the winner's kitty.

G

GAG BIT.—Gag bits are of two kinds: (1) those used alone, and (2) those used in a double bridle where they give a greater upward action than a normal bridoon.

The term "gag" denotes any bit used with a rounded leather cheek-piece passing through holes in the bit ring or through rollers, pulleys, etc. There are numerous designs. Where a gag is used in place of a bridoon on a double bridle, they are the Duncan and Shrewsbury patterns.

The basic function of the gag is to raise the head. It is also frequently used in conjunction with a standing martingale as a method of control on very strong, impetuous animals.

GAG REIN.—A rein that is fastened to the top of the horse's bridle and run through snaffle bit rings and thence to the rider's hand is known as a gag rein. The gag rein is designed to make the bit pressure operate upward on the corners of the horse's mouth rather than downward on his bars. Its greatest use is on the racetrack, although trainers of barrel horses are now recommending the use of the gag rein in training. The novice should not use the gag rein unless he does so under the supervision of an expert.

GAITED HORSE.—The term "gaited horse" refers to a five-gaited horse that is schooled to artificial as well as natural gaits. Usually gaited horses are of the American Saddle Horse breed. In addition to the three natural gaits (walk, trot, and canter), gaited horses are trained to slow gait and rack. The slow gait may be either the running walk, fox-trot, or slow pace.

(Also see AIDS.)

GAITS.—A gait is a particular way of going, either natural or acquired, that is characterized by a distinctive rhythmic movement of the feet and legs.

In the wild state, the horse executed four natural gaits—the walk, trot, pace, and gallop or run. Under domestication, these gaits have been variously modified, and additions have been made through (1) type, (2) breeding and selection, and (3) schooling.

After the rider has mastered the art of starting, stopping, and turning the mount, attention may be given to the gaits. But, knowledge of the different gaits should be mastered before one attempts to execute them.

(Also see the alphabetical listing of each of the gaits: CANTER, FOX TROT, GALLOP, LOPE, PACE, RACK, RUNNING WALK, SLOW PACE, STEPPING PACE, TRAVERSE OR SIDE-STEP, TROT, and WALK.)

GALICENO.—see BREED (S).

GALICENO HORSE BREEDERS' ASSN., INC., THE.—111 E. Elm St., Tyler, Tex. 75701. (See Appendix for complete breed registry association list.)

GALLOP DEPART.—Gallop depart is the term for the start of the gallop. In show riding the gallop depart is started from the walk; in dressage work it is frequently started from the halt; and in military riding (in the cavalry) it is usually started from the trot.

GALLOP OR RUN.—A fast, four-beat gait in which the feet strike the ground separately—first one hind foot, then the other hind foot, then the front foot on the same side as the first hind foot, and then the other front foot, which decides the lead. There is a brief interval when all four feet are off the ground. The gallop is the fast natural gait of both wild horses and Thoroughbred racehorses. (See Fig. G-1.)

GALLOWAY.—A riding breed of pony, standing about 14 hands high, that was developed in Galloway, Scotland.

GALLS.—Sores on the hide caused by the rubbing of harness or saddle. Treatment: see that the tack fits properly, let the horse rest, wash and dry the sores daily, and apply Veterinary Healing Oil.

"GALTON'S LAW".—The theory of inheritance expounded by Sir Francis Galton (1822–1911). According to this genetic theory, the individual's inheritance is determined as follows: $\frac{1}{4}$ by its sire and $\frac{1}{4}$ by its dam, $\frac{1}{16}$ by each of the four grandparents, $\frac{1}{64}$ by each of the 8 great grandparents, and on and on, with each ancestor contributing just $\frac{1}{4}$ as much to the total inheritance as did the one a generation nearer to the individual. "Galton's law" is correct in the sense that the relationship between ancestor and descendant is halved with each additional generation which intervenes between them. It is not correct in the sense that the individual's heredity is completely determined by the heredity of its ancestors. Rather, in a random-bred population, the individual is $\frac{1}{4}$ determined by each parent and $\frac{1}{2}$ determined by chance in Mendelian segregation. Determination by more remote ancestors is included in the determination by the parent.

Galton's law is often used as a stamina index by Thoroughbred breeders.

GAMES.—See GYMKHANA.

GAMETE.—A mature sex cell (sperm or egg).

GASKIN.—A distinctive muscular development which lies outside and above the point of the hocks and joins the buttocks. It should equal the forearm in length and be heavily muscled.

(Also see PARTS OF A HORSE—Fig. P-4.)

GAUCHO.—The South American cowboy. In particular, the term is used in the Pampas area of Argentina. The gaucho is considered by many to be the world's finest rough-rider.

GEAR.—1. A type of duffle bag used by cowboys to carry their personal belongings when traveling on horseback. It is usually tied behind the saddle.

2. The equipment and accessories used in har-

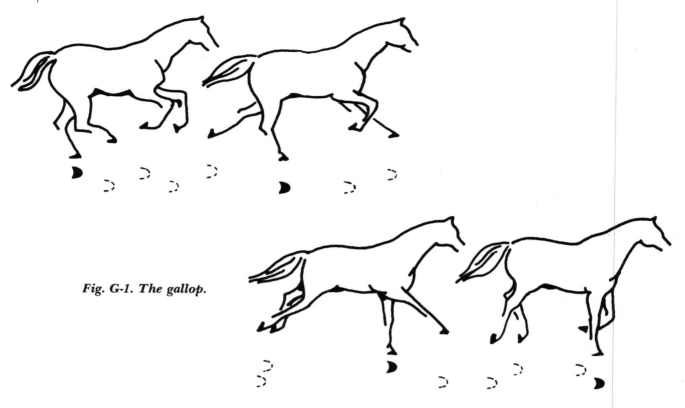

Fig. G-1. The gallop.

ness driving (except the vehicle) and in polo playing (except the bridles and saddles).
(Also see TACK.)

GEE.—The teamster's term signaling a turn to the right.

GELD.—To cut or castrate a male horse.

GELDING.—A male horse that was castrated before reaching maturity.

GENES.—The gene is the unit of heredity. In the body cells of horses, there are pairs of bundles, called chromosomes. In turn, the chromosomes carry pairs of minute particles, called genes, which are the basic hereditary material. The nucleus of each body cell of horses contains 32 pairs of chromosomes, or a total of 64; whereas there are thousands of pairs of genes. When a sex cell (a sperm or an egg) is formed, only one chromosome and one gene of each pair goes into it. Then when mating and fertilization oc-

cur the single chromosomes and genes are again present in duplicate in the body cells of the embryo. Thus, with all possible combinations of 32 pairs of chromosomes (the specie number in horses) and the genes that they bear, it is not strange that full sisters (except identical twins from a single egg split after fertilization) are so different. Actually, we can marvel that they bear as much resemblance to each other as they do.

Because of this situation, the mating of a mare with a fine track record to a stallion that on the average transmits relatively good performance will not always produce a foal of a merit equal to its parents. The foal could be markedly poorer than the parents or, happily, it could in some cases be better than either parent.
(Also see HEREDITY IN HORSES.)

GENETICS.—See HEREDITY IN HORSES.

GENOTYPE SELECTION.—Selection of breeding stock not necessarily from the best looking but from the best breeding animals, according to genetic make-up.

GERM PLASM.—Germ cells and their precursors, bearers of hereditary characters.

GESTATION.—The period of pregnancy, from conception to foaling. The normal period for the mare is 336 days.

GET.—Progeny or offspring.

GET-UP.—The command to go; proceed; move forward. When repeated, it means to increase speed. "Giddap," slang.

GIG.—1. A light carriage that has two wheels and is drawn by one horse.

2. In western United States, the word "gig" also means to spur.

GIMPY.—A horse with a slight limp. Sometimes the lameness is so slight, or the horse has been so treated, that lameness is difficult to detect. The experienced horseman refers to such an animal as "gimpy."

GIRTH.—1. The strap or webbing that holds the saddle or backband in place. The most common type is the folded leather girth with two buckles on each end. Web girths with one or two buckles are also common.

Girths are used on English saddles. Western saddles are held in place by cinches (from the Spanish *cincha*). They have iron rings instead of buckles and fasten by means of straps attached to the saddle.

The girth should not be so tight that it pinches the horse. Neither should it be so loose that there is danger of the saddle turning. The exact adjustment will depend upon the conformation of the animal. If the horse has high withers, and the saddle fits him well, the girth need not be too tight. However, if the horse has low, flat withers (mutton withers), the girth will have to be tight.

2. The circumference of the chest behind the withers and in front of the back.

(Also see SADDLING THE MOUNT.)

GIRTH-PLACE.—The place for the girth, as the name implies; it is marked by a depression in the underline just in back of the front legs.

GLANDERS (FARCY).—An acute or chronic infectious disease caused by *Malleomyces mallei*, a bacterium.

SYMPTOMS.—The chronic form most often attacks horses, affecting the lungs, skin, or nasal passages. There may be a nasal discharge that later becomes pus, and nodules and ulcers may appear in the skin. With the lung type, there generally is loss in condition, lack of endurance, bleeding and a mucous discharge from the nose, and coughing. The skin of the extremities may develop ulcers that exude a honeylike tenacious discharge.

The acute form more often attacks mules and donkeys. The symptoms are similar to the chronic form, but more severe. Death usually occurs in a week.

TREATMENT.—No cure is known.

CONTROL.—Use the mallein test to detect infected animals or animals suspected of having the disease. Destroy infected animals and clean and disinfect contaminated equipment and premises.

PREVENTION.—Avoid inhalation or ingestion of the causative organism. Do not use public watering places.

DISCUSSION.—Glanders is prevalent in areas where horses still are used for transportation and work. The disease has largely disappeared from the mechanized areas of the world, including the United States, but it is not eradicated. Through the transport of animals, glanders can make its appearance anytime in any area.

(Also see DISEASES AND PARASITES; and HEALTH PROGRAM.)

GLASS-EYED.—Term applied to an eye, the iris of which is devoid of pigment.

GLOVES.—Leather or string gloves are the only kinds which are practical for riding. String gloves are particularly good during wet weather because they do not slip on reins. Unlined pigskin gloves are good for cold weather. For Western riding in brush country, horsehide gloves are recommended.

GODOLPHIN ARABIAN.—This was one of the three foundation sires of the Thoroughbred breed. He was Arabian and was imported by King Charles II into England from Paris in 1724. The Matchem line of Thoroughbreds traces to the Godolphin Arabian.

GONE AWAY.—The exclamation given by riders to hounds when the fox has started to run, and the hounds are in pursuit.

GOOD HANDS.—A rider is said to have good hands when he keeps a light contact with his horse's mouth.
  (Also see HORSEMANSHIP—Holding The Reins.)

GOOD MOUTH.—Said of an animal 6 to 10 years of age.

GOOSE-RUMPED.—An animal having a short, steep croup that narrows at the point of the buttocks.

GOTLAND HORSE.—See BREED (S).

GOVERNESS CART (TUB-CART).—A light two-wheeled cart which is entered from the rear. It generally has seats for four persons.

GRADE.—An animal of unknown ancestry. If it shows some specific breed characteristics, it may be suffixed with the name of that breed; e.g., grade Shetland.

GRADING UP.—Breeding a purebred sire of a given breed to a native, or grade, female is known as grading up.

(Also see BREEDING HORSES—Systems of Breeding.)

GRAIN.—Harvested cereals or other edible seeds, including oats, corn, milo, barley, etc.
  (Also see FEEDING.)

GRAND NATIONAL, THE.—A steeplechase course at Aintree, in Lancashire, England. It is 4 miles, 856 yards in length and has 30 fences; the "water" is 15 feet wide. The race was first started in 1837, but it did not acquire its present name until 1847.

GRASS.—See PASTURES.

GRAVEL.—Gravel is usually caused by penetration of the protective covering of the hoof by small bits of gravel or dirt. Access to the sensitive tissue is usually gained at the "white line" or junction of the sole and wall, where the horn is somewhat softer. Once in the soft tissue inside the wall or sole, bacterial infection carried by the foreign material develops rapidly, producing pus and gas that create pressure and intense pain in the foot. In untreated cases, it breaks out at the top of the coronary band and the pus and gas are forced out through this opening.

TREATMENT.— (1) Open the pathway used by the gravel or dirt going into the foot, thus draining the pus at the bottom and relieving the pressure, (2) administer antitoxin, and (3) protect the opening from further infection.

GRAY.—See COLORS AND MARKINGS OF HORSES.

GREASE HEEL.—See SCRATCHES.

GREEN BROKE.—A term applied to a horse that has been ridden or hitched only one or two times.

GREEN HORSE.—1. A horse that has had very little training.

2. Horse dealers sometimes use the term "green horse" to indicate an animal that has been shipped in from the area where he was raised and has not been handled much.

GRINDERS.—See AGE (Table A-1).

GROOM.—A person who cares for horses; an attendant, horseman, hostler, swipe (swipe is not preferred).

GROOMING A HORSE.—Proper grooming is necessary to keep a horse attractive and help maintain his good health and condition. Grooming cleans the hair, helps keep the skin functioning naturally, lessens skin diseases and parasites, and improves the condition and fitness of the muscles.

Grooming should be rapid and thorough but not so severe that it makes the horse nervous or irritates his skin. Horses that are kept in stables or small corrals should be groomed thoroughly at least once a day. When horses are worked or exercised, they should be groomed both before and after the work or exercise.

Wet or sweating animals should be handled as follows:

1. Remove the tack as fast as possible, wipe it off, and put it away.

2. Remove excess water from the horse with a sweat scraper and then rub him briskly with a grooming or drying cloth to dry his coat partial-

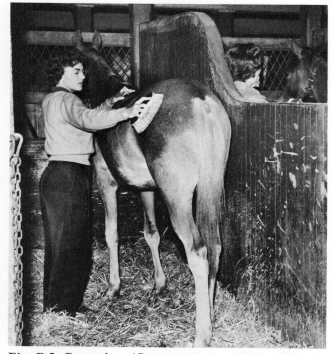

Fig. G-2. Grooming. (Courtesy, Byron H. Good, Michigan State University)

ly.

3. Cover the horse with a blanket and walk him until he is cool.

4. Allow the horse to drink two or three swallows of water every few minutes while he is cooling and drying.

GROOMING EQUIPMENT; HOW TO GROOM.—For proper grooming, certain articles of grooming equipment are necessary and must be used properly. Also, to assure that the horse

TABLE G-1

GROOMING EQUIPMENT AND HOW TO USE IT

Article	What It Is; How To Use It	Used For	Grooming Procedure: How To Do It
Hoof Pick	A hooked implement used to remove foreign objects from a hoof.	To clean out the feet.	To assure that the horse will be groomed thoroughly and that no body parts will be missed, follow a definite order. This may differ according to individual preference, but the following procedure is most common: 1. **Clean out feet**—Use the hoof pick. Work from heel toward toe. Clean thoroughly the depressions between the frog and the bars. Inspect for thrush and loose shoes.

(Continued)

Article	What It Is; How To Use It	Used For	Grooming Procedure: How To Do It
Curry Comb (Rubber or Metal)	Use gently and in small circles, rather than with pressure and in long strokes. Do not use the metal curry comb below the knees or hocks, about the head, or over body prominences. Nor should it be used on horses that have been clipped recently, or that have a thin coat of hair.	To groom horses that have long, thick coats. To remove caked mud. To loosen matted scurf and dirt in the hair. To clean the brush.	2. **Groom the body**—Hold curry comb in right hand and brush in left hand, and proceed as follows: a. Start with left side. b. Follow this order: Neck, breast, withers, shoulders, foreleg down to knee, back, side, belly, croup, and hind legs down to hock. Then brush from knee and hock down toward hoofs. At frequent intervals, clean the dust and hair from the brush with the curry comb, and knock the curry comb against your heel or the back of the brush to free it from dirt. Curry gently, but brush vigorously. Brush hair in direction of its natural lay. Brush with care in regions of flanks, between fore and hind legs, at the point of elbows, and in fetlocks. After grooming left side, transfer brush to right hand and curry comb to left hand; then groom the right side in same order as described above.
Body Brush	The body brush is the principal tool used for grooming.	To brush the entire body.	
Dandy Brush	The dandy brush is made of stiff fiber, usually about two inches in length.	To remove light dirt from the skin. To brush the mane and tail.	3. **Brush the head; comb and brush the mane and tail**—Use the body brush on the head. Groom the mane and tail as follows: a. Brush downward, using either the body brush or the dandy brush. b. Clean the tail by— (1) Brushing upward, a few strands of hair at a time; or by (2) Picking or separating out a few hairs at a time by hand. (3) Occasionally washing with warm water and soap.
Mane and Tail Comb	Use as directed in last column.	To comb out matted mane and tail.	
Sweat Scraper		To remove excess perspiration from heated, wet, and sweating animals.	
Grooming Cloth	The grooming cloth can be made from old toweling or blankets. It should be about 18 to 24 inches square.	To remove dirt and dust from the coat. To wipe out the eyes, ears, lips, nostrils, and dock. To give the coat a final sheen or polish. To dry or ruffle the coat before brushing.	4. **Wipe with grooming cloth**—Use the grooming cloth to— a. Wipe about the ears, face, eyes, nostrils, lips, sheath, and dock, and b. Give a final polish to the coat. 5. **Check the grooming**—Pass the fingertips against natural lay of hair. If coat and skin are not clean, fingers will be dirtied and gray lines will show on coat where fingers passed. Also inspect ears, face, eyes, lips, nostrils, sheath, and dock. 6. **Wash and disinfect grooming equipment**—Wash with soap and warm water often enough to keep clean. Disinfect as necessary as precaution against spread of disease.

is groomed properly and no body parts are missed, a definite order of grooming should be followed. Table G-1 lists grooming equipment and tells how to use it.

CLIPPING AND SHEARING.—Besides routine grooming, horses should be clipped as often as needed. Clip the long hairs from the head, the

inside of the ears, on the jaw, and around the fetlocks. A wad of cotton may be put in the horse's ears to cut down on noise from the clippers and to prevent hair from falling in his ears.

According to custom, certain breeds are clipped and sheared in different hair cuts and hair styles. These are illustrated in Fig. G-3.

Fig. G-3. "Hair cuts" and "hair do's" common to breeds and uses of horses. (Drawings by Dennis Gadberry)

The natural appearing mane and tail of the Arabian.

The clipped or roached mane and the cut, set, and shaved tail of the 3-gaited American Saddle Horse.

The shortened, pulled mane and the tightly braided tail of the polo pony. This type of mane treatment is also often seen on Quarter Horses.

The usual mane and tail treatment of the Quarter Horse. The mane is clipped with the foretop and a tuft of hair at the withers left. The tail is shortened and shaped by pulling.

Typical mane and tail treatment of the Tennessee Walking Horse.

The braided mane and the thinned tail and braided dock of the hunter.

(CONTINUED)

The tightly braided mane and the docked and set tail of the Hackney.

The full mane with braided foretop and first lock and the full waterfall tail of the 5-gaited American Saddle Horse.

GROWTH.—See FEED.

GRUB STAKED.—Prospectors (miners) are sometimes "grub staked," which means they are provided with food in turn for a share of the minerals should they be lucky enough to locate a mine. Cattle herders or owners are sometimes "grub staked" until such time as they may cash in on their animals.

GUMMY-LEGGED.—Having legs in which the tendons lack definition and do not stand out clearly.

GYMKHANA.—A horseback riding meet featuring games and novelty contests (such as spearing rings, musical chairs, potato spearing, bareback jumping, etc.) .

The Gymkhana originated in India, where its original purpose was to relieve the boredom of life in a British military post. Since horses of show caliber were scarce, they developed all sorts of ingenious mounted contests. Gymkhanas are fun events, and excellent for children.

Fig. G-4. Child spearing rings in a Gymkhana. (Courtesy, Horse Association of America)

HABIT, RIDING.—The term "riding habit" is usually applied to women's riding apparel.
(Also see CLOTHES FOR RIDERS.)

HACK.—A horse used for ordinary pleasure riding over roads or trails as distinguished from racing, hunting, or showing.

HACKAMORES (HACKAMORE BIT).—The bosal hackamore and the hackamore bit-bridle are used on horses with tender mouths and as training devices for Western horses.

The bosal hackamore has a pair of reins and an ordinary headstall that holds in place a braided rawhide or rope noseband knotted under the horse's jaw. It is an excellent device for controlling a young horse without injuring his mouth and is used extensively in training polo and cow ponies.

When properly adjusted, the hackamore should rest on the horse's nose about 4 inches from the top of the nostrils, or at the base of the cheek bones. It should also permit the passage of two fingers held edgeways between it and the jaw.

The hackamore bit-bridle is a "fake" bridle;

HACKAMORES

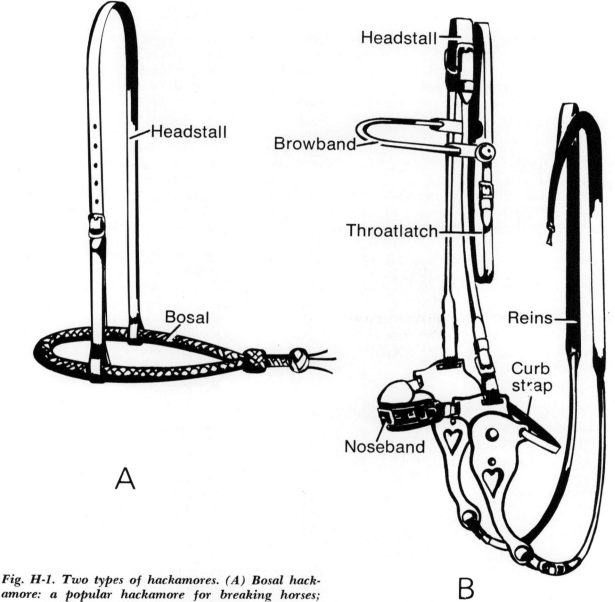

Headstall

Bosal

A

Headstall

Browband

Throatlatch

Reins

Curb strap

Noseband

B

Fig. H-1. Two types of hackamores. (A) Bosal hackamore: a popular hackamore for breaking horses; (B) Hackamore bit-bridle: a hackamore with a removable mouthpiece that is used on Western cow ponies and on young horses when they are being broken because it eliminates the possibility of injuring the mouth.

it has the shanks on each side but no mouthpiece.

The kind of hackamore used will depend on the horse's training and intended use. Fig. H-1 shows the most common types of hackamores.

HACKNEY.—See BREED (S).

HAFLING (HAFLINGER, OR HAFFLINGER).—This is a breed of mountain pony found in Austria and Italy. The village of Haffling is said to be its original home. Haflings are rather thick set, heavy-boned ponies, with great strength and sure-footedness.

HAIR, FUNCTIONS OF.—The hair of the horse performs a thermoregulatory function, to protect the animal from cold or heat. It becomes long and shaggy during the winter months in cold areas, especially if the horse is left outside. Then, during the warm season, or when the animal is blanketed, the horse sheds and the coat becomes short.

HALF-BRED ARABIAN.—These are half Arabians. They may be registered in the International Arabian Horse Association, 224 E. Olive Avenue, Burbank, California 91503.

HALF-BRED THOROUGHBRED.—Foals by registered Thoroughbred stallions and out of mares not registered in The American Stud Book (Jockey Club). They may be registered in the American Remount Association, P. O. Box 1066, Perris, California 92370.

HALF-BROTHERS.—Horses out of the same dam but by a different sire.

HALF HALT.—The moment of hesitation which some horses require for change of leads when executing the figure eight. The change of leads comes in the middle of the figure, when the horse is starting to change directions in the ring —where the lines of the figure eight cross. As the horse completes the first circle, he is collected on his canter slightly, there is an instant of suspension, or half halt, as the collection is increased and the signals for the change of lead given. Thereupon, he shifts his balance and changes his lead as he steps out on the second circle. The horse must not be held at the half halt for more than an instant; otherwise he will lose animation and come to a complete halt.

HALF TURN.—This is an equitation exercise, used by some instructors. When a group of riders is moving in single file next to the fence or wall of the arena and the command "Half turn" is given, they respond as follows: Without changing gait or speed, each individual horse turns toward the center of the ring and proceeds to the opposite side of the ring, thence goes in the reverse direction from which he started. Of course, if the horse is at the canter or gallop when the command to half turn is given, when he reaches the other side of the ring and changes directions he should change leads.

HALT.—To bring a horse to a stop. This is done by applying light pressure with the legs and reins. If a horse is on a trot or canter, he should be brought to the walk before being halted. In halting, the rider should cease posting, sit down in the saddle, apply a slight grip with his legs, and apply light pressure with the reins—bringing the horse's chin in and causing him to flex at the poll and relax the jaw. As soon as the horse has obeyed and come to a halt, the pressure should be discontinued and the rider's legs should be relaxed.

HALTER (HEAD COLLAR).—A halter is used for leading a horse or tying him. There are many types of halters made from a number of different materials. The Johnson rope halter (formerly made of cotton, now made of nylon) is very strong and inexpensive. It will outlast most leather halters, and it is easy to put on and take off. But care must be taken to fit it loosely, otherwise it will rub the cheek bones.

Leather halters are also widely used. The better ones are mounted with brass. Show halters are of finer, lighter leather than the ordinary stable halter, and usually they have brow bands.

Sometimes the novice has difficulty in figuring out how to put a halter on. The following procedure will alleviate this problem: Take the buckle in the left hand and the strap in the right hand, making sure that the three short parallel straps are on the bottom; slip the horse's nose through the noseband; swing the strap over from the far side, place it behind the ears, catch it with the left hand, bring the right hand back and buckle the strap snugly enough to prevent the horse from getting it over his head.

Never leave a halter on a horse in the pasture. Although a haltered horse may be easier to catch, there is risk of the halter getting caught on some object and the animal not being able to free himself.

HALTER BREAKING.—The foal should become acquainted with the halter early in life, at which time the procedure is more properly training rather than breaking.

(Also see TRAINING.)

HALTER-CLASS.—A term used in the U.S. and elsewhere, which has the same meaning as "in-hand class." The horses are shown by being led rather than ridden and without a saddle.

HALTER PULLING.—Halter pulling refers to the act of pulling back on the halter rope when tied to an object.

(Also see VICES—Halter Pulling.)

HALTER SHANK (TIE ROPE).—The halter shank may be made of rope, leather, or part leather and part chain (18 to 24 inches of chain). It attaches to the halter by means of a two-inch snap and is used to lead or tie the horse. Halter shanks are usually five to six feet long.

HALTING (a group of riders).—Prior to going on a group ride, the leader should inform everyone as to the warning signal that will be used if it is desirable or necessary to stop. Otherwise, the riders will pile up on each other, with the result that someone may get kicked. The most common signal is the raised hand; with the leader raising his hand, then every rider in turn raising his

hand. Each rider should stop four feet from the horse in front of him. If a horse is restless and tries to back or move forward, he should be turned at a right angle to the rest of the group, with his rear end away from the trail. If the terrain permits, he may be ridden out of line and turned in a small circle. When a group is halted on a narrow trail a restive horse may have to be calmed by the rider dismounting (if there is room) or stroking him on the neck and restraining him by light pressure on the reins. If the leader's horse is restless, he should be turned to face the other horses. Above all, the leader of a group should have a well-mannered horse.

HAMBLETONIAN 10 (ALSO KNOWN AS RYSDYK'S HAMBLETONIAN).—Great pillar of the Standardbred breed, and descendant of Messenger. William Rysdyk, a poor farm hand, purchased him as a suckling colt, along with his dam, for $125. Hambletonian 10 never raced. He began his stud career at two and lived to the age of twenty-seven, during which time he earned approximately $500,000 for his owner. Today, it is estimated that 99 percent of the trotters and pacers in America trace to this great sire.

Fig. H-2. The immortal Hambletonian 10 (also known as Rysdyk's Hambletonian). (Courtesy, United States Trotting Association)

HAMMER.—See SHOEING—Table S-5.

HAMMER, DRIVING.—See SHOEING—Table S-5.

HAMMER-HEAD.—A coarse-headed animal.

HAMSTRING.—This is the large tendon which runs upward from the point of the horse's hock, technically known as the tendon of Achilles. Its counterpart in the human leg is the big tendon which extends upward from the back of the heel.

HAMSTRUNG.—Disabled by an injury to the tendon above the hock.

HAND.—A hand is a four-inch unit of measure used in expressing the height of a horse from the highest point of the withers to the ground. Thus, a horse measuring 62 inches is said to be 15-2 hands (15 hands and 2 inches) high. (Also see MEASURING HORSES.)
BREED (S)—Table B-2.

HAND BREEDING.—See BREEDING HORSES.

HAND-CANTER.—A semiextended canter, midway between a promenade, canter, and a gallop.

HAND HOLDS.—See HARNESS—Fig. H-5.

HANDICAP JUMPING.—In handicap jumping the height of the jump is varied according to the size of the horse or pony and the ability of the rider. This procedure is sometimes resorted to in informal shows where there is a shortage of jumpers of similar size and experience. Thus, the jumps may be as low as 1½ to 2 feet for Shetlands and as high as 3½ feet for experienced riders on horses.

HANDICAPPING.—Unlike games of chance such as roulette or craps, which depend on the spin of a wheel or the roll of the dice, picking racehorses can become a matter of skill and judgment. A player can at least gauge the probable outcome of a race, even though he cannot control it.

Only a small percentage of the thousands of persons who attend a race make studied and objective efforts to pick winners. The rest go by the opinions of professional handicappers, whose selections appear in the newspapers or other turf publications, or they bet on tips they pick up at the track, or they play hunches.

Remember that out of all the money wagered on a race, about 88 percent is returned in the form of winnings, with the take-out prescribed by law for each state and varying slightly from state to state. Therefore, a bettor is competing with his fellow bettors for the major share of the pot, as if he were playing poker with friends.

There are really no simple methods of handicapping. The most common method utilizes the Daily Racing Form, which mainly gives information on past performances. Other methods depend on the advice supplied by professional handicappers.

Actually there are hundreds of books and thousands of systems devoted to handicapping, because there are probably more serious students of Thoroughbred racing and handicapping than any other sport or form of wagering.

As in any sport, the more a spectator knows about the participants and the "game," the more he will enjoy it. If a spectator has a couple of dollars riding on a horse that is charging down the stretch, he will get as big a thrill as watching his team score a touchdown or a home run. But a word of warning: "Bet what you can afford to lose, not what you hope to win."

HANDICAP RACES.—Races in which the horses (usually older horses) run at weights assigned to them by the handicapper. The handicapper's objective is to assign weights to horses that will even out the entire field of entrants and result in a 100 percent dead heat. Hence, heaviest weights are given to the best horses. Added weight is in the form of lead.

HANDS (position in riding).—According to the Rule Book of the American Horse Shows Association, the correct position of the hands is as follows:

● Saddle Seat Equitation Section.—Hands should be held in an easy position, neither perpendicular nor horizontal to the saddle, and should show sympathy, adaptability, and control. The height the hands are held above the horse's withers is a matter of how and where the horse carries his head. The method of holding the reins is optional, except that both hands shall be used and all reins must be picked up at one time. Bight of rein should be on the off side.

● *Stock Seat Equitation Section.*—In repose, arms are in a straight line with body, the one holding reins bent at elbow. Only one hand is to be used for reining and hands shall not be changed. Hand to be around reins. When ends of split reins fall on near side, one finger between reins is permitted. When using romal or when ends of split reins are held in hand not used for reining, no finger between reins is allowed. The position of the hand not being used for reining is optional but it should be kept free of the horse and equipment and held in a relaxed manner with the rider's body straight at all times. Rider may hold romal or end of split reins to keep from swinging and to adjust the position of the reins provided it is held at least 16 inches from the reining hand. Hands to be above horn and as near to it as possible. Bracing against horn or coiled reata will be penalized. *Except in Medal Classes, show committee may, according to local conditions, designate whether a romal or split reins are to be used, provided it is so stipulated in the prize list.*

The important thing is that the rider both receive and give communication through the reins. To this end, there should be as much flexibility as possible in the wrist, arm, and hands of the rider. Except in show classes where the rider is being judged, experienced riders vary the position of their hands according to what is being done. For example, to obtain speed, action, or balance on the hind quarters, one rider may carry his hands very high. Another rider in the same class may carry his hands relatively low. Yet, the end result secured by each rider may be the same.

(Also see HORSEMANSHIP—Holding the Reins.)

HANDY HUNTER.—A handy hunter is a hunter that is suitable for hunting trappy country. This implies difficult jumps—jumps in which there is not much takeoff, jumps that are not on level ground, jumps in which the landing is lower than the takeoff, and an in-and-out jump with the two obstacles 24 to 26 feet apart.

The American Horse Shows Association *Rule Book* gives the following specifications for the handy hunter course:

In handy classes fences shall simulate those found in trappy hunting country; the course must have at least two changes of direction and at least one combination; horses are required to trot over one fence toward the end of the course and may be asked to lead over one fence. A chicken coop hinged at the top and free at the bottom and jumps such as triple bar and hogs back and any spread over 4' are prohibited.

The suggested distance for an in-and-out when used in a ring is 24 to 26 feet and on an outside course 26 to 28 feet.

HANOVERIAN.—A breed of German horses, which descended from the Great Horse of the Middle Ages.

HARD-MOUTHED.—Term used when the membrane of the bars of the mouth where the bit rests have become toughened and the nerves deadened because of the continued pressure of the bit.

HARDY.—See SHOEING—Table S-5.

HARNESS.—It is not within the scope of this book to cover all types and parts of harness. But some conception of the subject may be obtained by studying Figs. H-3, H-4, and H-5.

HARNESS (*care of*).—See TACK.

HARNESS CLASSES.—Harness classes in shows are divided into three classes: fine harness, heavy harness, and roadster.

(Also see FINE HARNESS HORSES; HEAVY HARNESS HORSES; and ROADSTERS.)

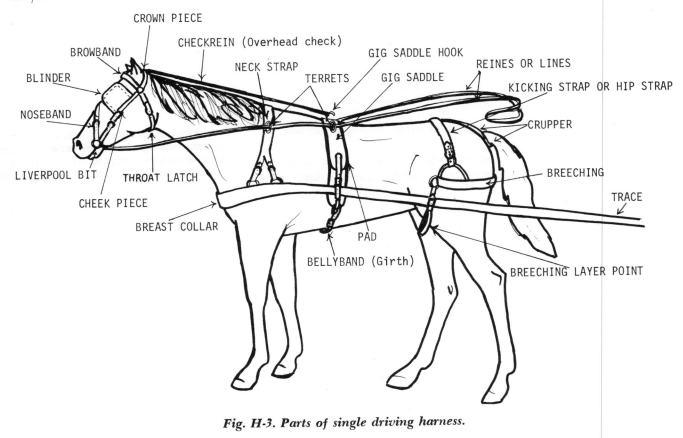

Fig. H-3. Parts of single driving harness.

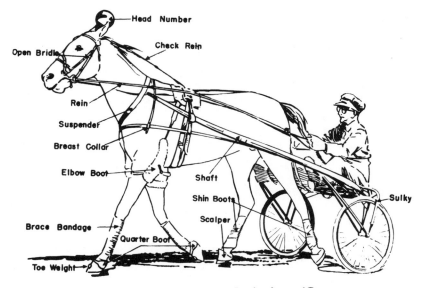

Fig. H-4. Trotter's harness and rigging. (Courtesy, The United States Trotting Association)

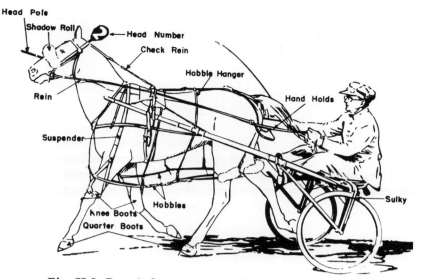

Head Pole
Shadow Roll
Head Number
Check Rein
Hobble Hanger
Rein
Hand Holds
Suspender
Sulky
Hobbles
Knee Boots
Quarter Boots

Fig. H-5. Pacer's harness and rigging. (Courtesy, The United States Trotting Association)

HARNESS HORSES, FINE.—See FINE HARNESS HORSES.

HARNESS HORSES, HEAVY.—See HEAVY HARNESS HORSES.

HARNESS RACEHORSES (TROTTERS AND PACERS).—Prior to the advent of improved roads and the automobile, but following the invention of the buggy, there was need for a fast, light-harness type of horse. This horse was used to draw vehicles varying in type from the light roadster of the young gallant to the dignified family carriage. In the process of meeting this need, two truly American breeds of horses evolved: the Morgan and the Standardbred. The first breed traces to the foundation sire, Justin Morgan; and the latter to Hambletonian 10, an animal which was linebred to imported Messenger.

As horse and buggy travel passed into permanent oblivion, except for recreation and sport, the Standardbred breeders wisely placed greater emphasis upon the sport of racing; whereas the Morgan enthusiasts directed their breeding programs toward transforming their animals into a saddle breed.

The early descendants of Messenger were sent over the track, trotting (not galloping) under the saddle; but eventually the jockey races in this country came to be restricted to a running type of race in which the Thoroughbred was used. With this shift, beginning in 1879, qualifying standards—a mile in 2:30 at the trot and 2:25 at the pace when hitched to the sulky—were set up for light harness races; and those animals so qualifying were registered. On January 1, 1933, registration on performance alone was no longer granted, and registration of both sire and dam was required.

The pneumatic-tire racing vehicles, known as sulkies, were first introduced in 1892. With their use that year, the time was reduced nearly four seconds below the record of the previous year. Thus, were developed harness racing and the Standardbred breed of horses, which today is the exclusive breed used for this purpose.

Trotters and pacers are of similar breeding and type, the particular gaits being largely a matter of training. In fact, many individuals show speed at both the trot and the pace. It is generally recognized, however, that pacers are handicapped in the mud, in the sand, or over a rough surface.

In the beginning, horses of this type found their principal use in harness races at county and state fairs. However, in recent years pari-mutuel harness racing has been established at a number of tracks. Today, harness racehorses are almost exclusively of the Standardbred breed.

HAT GUARD.—The cord worn, especially in the hunt field, to prevent the hat from being blown or knocked off. It usually runs from the brim of the hard hunting derby or silk hat to a ring inside the collar of the coat.

HAT-RACK.—An emaciated animal.

HAUTE ÉCOLE.—"High school," the highest form of specialized training of the riding horse.
(Also see DRESSAGE; and SCHOOLING.)

HAW.—The teamster's term signaling a turn to the left.

HAY.—Dried forage of different grasses and legumes used as horse feed.
(Also see FEED.)

HAY QUALITY.—The easily recognizable characteristics of hay of high quality are:
● It is made from plants cut at an early stage of maturity, thus assuring the maximum content of protein, minerals, and vitamins, and the highest digestibility.
● It is leafy, thus giving assurance of high protein content.
● It is bright green in color, thus indicating proper curing, a high carotene or provitamin A content (provided it is not over a year old), and palatability.
● It is free from foreign material, such as weeds, stubble, etc.
● It is free from must or mold and dust.
● It is fine-stemmed and pliable—not coarse, stiff, and woody.
● It has a pleasing, fragrant aroma; it "smells good enough to eat."

HAY BELLY.—Having a distended barrel due to the excessive feeding of bulky rations, such as hay, straw, or grass. Also called "grass belly."

HAY-NET.—A thick, corded net into which hay is put, and which is suspended in the stall or trailer. It prevents hay from being wasted and thrown to the stall floor.

HAZER.—In rodeos, the assistant to the bulldogger who attempts to keep the animal running in a straight line and endeavors to protect the bulldogger from being gored.

HEAD.—The head should be well proportioned to the rest of the body, refined and clean-cut, with a chiseled appearance. A broad, full forehead with great width between the eyes indicates intelligence. A straight face is usually preferable to a concave profile or a convex one (Roman nose), the former suggesting a timid disposition and the latter strong will power. The jaw should be broad and strongly muscled. There should be great width between large, clear eyes; and the ears should be of medium size, well carried and active. The head and neck of the animal should show sex character—boldness and masculinity in the stallion and refinement and femininity in the broodmare.

HEADLESS HORSEMAN OF SLEEPY HOLLOW.—This refers to the famous character of Washington Irving, who scared the wits out of the gangling schoolmaster, Ichabod Crane. The story is found in *The Sketch Book,* written in 1819. The Headless Horseman of Sleepy Hollow is well suited to a costume class. It consists of a sheet thrown over the rider's head, with holes cut to see through, and with a pumpkin under one arm.

HEAD NUMBER.—See HARNESS—Figs. H-4 and H-5.

HEAD POLE.—See HARNESS—Fig. H-5.

HEAD SET.—"Head set" refers to flexing the neck just behind the head and to holding the head high enough to conform to current show standards for the particular breed and type. A bitting rig (see BITTING RIG) is frequently used for this purpose, primarily because several horses can be worked on bitting rigs at the same time. It is to be emphasized, however, that a bitting rig may ruin the mouth and disposition of a horse. Moreover, after a horse has learned to respond to the reins, he will set his own head; and it will be far more beautiful than that of any animal who has had his head set for him.

Fashion decrees different head sets for different classes. Thus, the head of a three-gaited American Saddler is carried higher, and the neck is more flexed than in Western classes.

HEALTH PROGRAM.—A strict program of sanitation, disease prevention, and parasite control is necessary to protect the health of horses. Although the exact program will vary from farm to farm, the basic principles are the same. A horseman may compare the following general program with his existing program and use it to develop similar and more specific programs.

● Avoid public feeding and watering facilities.

● Read the sections in this book that discuss the diseases and parasites of horses; become familiar with symptoms and treatments.

● When signs of infectious disease appear, isolate affected animals promptly, provide them with separate water and feed containers, and follow the instructions and prescribed treatment of a veterinarian.

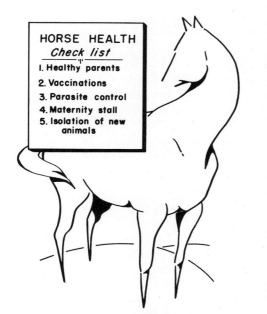

Fig. H-6. Horse health program.

● Prevent or control parasites by adhering to the following program:
　• Provide good sanitation and a high level of nutrition.
　• Have adequate acreage. Use a maximum of temporary seeded pasture rather than permanent pasture, and practice rotation grazing.
　• Pasture young animals on clean pastures. Never allow them to graze on an infested area unless the area has been either plowed or left idle for a year.
　• Do not spread fresh horse manure on pastures grazed by horses. Either store the manure in a suitable pit for at least 2 weeks or spread it on fields that are to be plowed and cropped.
　• When small pastures or paddocks must be used, pick up droppings at frequent intervals.
　• Keep pastures mowed and harrowed. Use a chain harrow.
　• Prevent fecal contamination of feed and water.
　• Administer suitable vermifuges when internal parasites are present. The choice of vermifuges and administration of them should be by a veterinarian. Later move horses to a clean area.
　• Apply the proper insecticide when external parasites are present.
　• If cattle are on the farm, alternate the use of pastures between cattle and horses because horse parasites die in cattle.
　• Avoid overgrazing because more parasites are present on the bottom inch of grass.

● As a disease preventive measure, arrange a scheduled yearly vaccination program with your veterinarian.

(Also see DISEASES AND PARASITES; and PARASITES OF HORSES.)

HEALTH PROGRAM FOR NEW HORSES AND VISITING MARES.—

● Isolate new animals for three weeks before adding them to the herd. During this period, a veterinarian may administer sleeping sickness vaccine in season and tetanus toxoid, make a thorough general and parasitic examination, make a genital examination of breeding animals, and treat animals when necessary.

● Make sure that mares brought in for breeding are accompanied by a health certificate issued by a veterinarian. Closely watch mares that have had trouble foaling or have lost foals.

● If possible, saddle, bridle, or harness visiting mares near their own isolation quarters and use tack and equipment that is not used by mares kept on the establishment.

HORSE HEALTH SIGNS.—"Bright-eyed and bushy-tailed" is a common expression, indicative of health and well-being.

Fig. H-7. Bright-eyed and busy-tailed! (Photo by Dave Smith, Mesa, Ariz.)

In order that horsemen may recognize when disease strikes, they must first know the signs of equine health; any departure from which constitutes a warning of trouble. Some of the signs of good health are:

● *Contentment.*—Healthy horses appear contented. They look completely unworried when resting, and they roll and shake themselves with vigor.

● *Alertness.*—Healthy horses are alert; they prick up their ears at the slightest provocation.

● *Eating with relish.*—The appetite is good and feed is consumed with relish, as indicated by nickering and eagerness to get to it.

Fig. H-8. Contentment. Hungarian foal at Bitterroot Stock Farm, Hamilton, Montana, owned by Margit Sigray Bessenyey. (Photo by Ernst Peterson, Hamilton, Mont.)

● *Sleek coat and pliable, elastic skin.*—A sleek, oily coat and a pliable and elastic skin characterize healthy animals. When the hair coat loses its luster and the skin becomes dry, scurfy and hide-bound, there is usually trouble.

● *Bright eyes and pink eye membranes.*—In healthy animals, the eyes are bright and the membranes—which can be seen when the lower lid is pulled down—are pink in color and moist.

● *Normal feces and urine.*—The consistency of the feces varies with the diet; for example, horses are somewhat loose when on lush pasture or on an all-pelleted ration. Above all, the feces should not be too dry. And there should not be large quantities of undigested feed. The urine should be clear. Both the feces and urine should be passed without effort, and should be free from blood, mucus, or pus.

● *Normal temperature, pulse rate, and breathing rate.*—For the healthy horse, these are:

Normal rectal temperature: Average = 100.5° F., Range = 99.0–100.8° F.

Normal pulse rate: 32–44 per minute.

Normal breathing rate: 8–16 per minute.

In general, any marked and persistent deviations from these normals should be looked upon as a sign of ill health.

Every horseman should provide himself with an animal thermometer, which is heavier and more rugged than the ordinary human thermometer. The temperature is measured by inserting the thermometer full length in the rectum, where it should be left a minimum of three minutes. Prior to inserting the thermometer, a long string should be tied to the end.

In general, infectious diseases are ushered in with a rise in body temperature, but it must be remembered that body temperature is affected by stable or outside temperature, exercise, excitement, age, feed, etc. It is lower in cold weather, in older animals, and at night.

The pulse rate indicates the rapidity of the heart action. It may be taken either at the margin of the jaw where an artery winds around from the inner side, at the inside of the elbow, or under the tail. It should be remembered that the younger, the smaller, and the more nervous the animal, the higher the pulse rate. Also, the pulse rate increases with exercise, excitement, digestion, and high outside temperature.

The breathing rate can be determined by placing the hand on the flank, by observing the rise and fall of the flanks, or, in the winter, by watching the breath condensate in coming from the nostrils. Rapid breathing due to recent exercise, excitement, hot weather, or stuffy buildings should not be confused with disease. Respiration is accelerated in pain and in febrile (feverish) conditions.

HEART GIRTH.
—The circumference of the chest behind the withers and in front of the back. A large heart girth is desired because it indicates ample space for such vital organs as the heart and lungs.

(Also see PARTS OF A HORSE—Fig. P-4.)

HEAT *(in racing).*
—One trip in a race that will be decided by winning two or more trials. Present-day harness races are heat races, generally three heats of one mile each. They are called heat races because the heated animals must be cooled between races.

HEAT PERIOD (ESTRUS).
—The estrous period. Fillies come in heat at 12 to 15 months of age. Each heat period averages 4 to 6 days in duration, and the interval between heat periods averages 21 days.

HEAT PRODUCTION BY HORSES.
—The heat produced by horses varies according to body weight, rate of feeding, environmental conditions, and degree of activity. Under average conditions, a 1,000-pound horse gives off about 1,790 Btu's per hour; and a 1,500-pound horse, 2,450 Btu's per hour.

HEAVES.
—A respiratory disease of horses characterized by difficulty in forcing air out of the lungs, chronic cough, unthriftiness, and lack of stamina.

CAUSE.—Exact cause unknown, but it is known that the condition is often associated with the feeding of damaged, dusty, or moldy hay. It often follows severe respiratory infection such as strangles.

SYMPTOMS.—Difficulty in forcing air out of the lungs, resulting in a jerking of flanks (double flank action) and coughing. The nostrils are often slightly dilated and there is a nasal discharge.

DISTRIBUTION AND LOSSES.—Worldwide. Losses are negligible.

TREATMENT.—Affected animals are less bothered if turned to pasture, if used only at light work, if fed an all-pelleted ration, or if the hay is sprinkled lightly with water at feeding. Antihistamine granules can be administered in feed to control coughing due to lung congestion.

CONTROL.— (See Prevention.)

PREVENTION.—Avoid the use of damaged feeds. Feed an all-pelleted ration, thereby alleviating dust. Keep dust down in stables and corrals.

HEAVY HANDS.
—A rider whose hands are like dead weight on the reins is said to have "heavy hands." It is the opposite of the desired light hands. A rider with heavy hands cannot communicate effectively with his horse.

The heavy-handed rider must first perfect his seat before he can expect to lighten his hands. The best way in which to accomplish this is to ride at all gaits with and without a saddle, and with the arms folded or the hands placed on the hips, reins dangling. After becoming independent of the reins to maintain his balance, as his hands become lighter and his seat more secure, he may proceed, step by step, from a gentle snaffle-bitted mount to high-spirited horse with full bridle or pelham.

HEAVY HARNESS HORSES.—These are also known as carriage horses. At the present time, this type of horse has very little place in the utility field, its use being largely confined to the show-ring. As the name implies, the heavy harness horse of the show-ring wears heavier leather than the fine harness horse or the roadster, though it in no way approaches draft harness. The heavy leather used on these animals was first decreed by fashion in England, the idea being that to drive handsomely one must drive heavily. The vehicles drawn were of heavy construction and elegant design and logically and artistically the harness had to be in proportion thereto.

Fig. H-9. The Heavy Harness Horse, Cassilis Soverein, shown hitched to a gig and driven by Mrs. J. Macy Willets, breeder and owner, Cassilis Farm, Great Barrington, Mass. (Courtesy, Mrs. Willets)

Heavy harness horses were especially popular during the Victorian era, and the ownership of a handsome pair was an indication of social prestige. In this country during the gay nineties, bob-tailed hackneys attached to high-seated rigs made a dashing picture as they pranced down the avenue.

At one time, there were several heavy harness breeds, but at present all except the Hackney have practically ceased to exist in America. In this country, therefore, the Hackney is now the heavy harness breed; and the American Horse Shows Association officially refers to show classifications as Hackneys rather than as Heavy Harness Horses.

The heavy harness horse should possess the following distinguishing characteristics:

● *Beauty.*—Beauty is obtained through graceful, curved lines; full-made form; and high carriage. Show-ring style decrees that heavy harness horses be docked and have their manes pulled.

● *High action.*—Animals of this type are bred for high hock and knee action; but skilled training, bitting, and shoeing are necessary for their development. In the show-ring, heavy harness horses must be able to fold their knees, flex their hocks, and set their chins. "Wooden-legged" horses cannot take competition.

● *Manners and temperament.*—Perfection in the manners and disposition of pleasure horses of this type is a requisite of first rank.

● *Color.*—Seal brown, brown, bay, and black colors are preferred in heavy harness horses. White stockings are desired for the purpose of accentuating high action.

● *Height.*—For horse show purposes, the maximum height of Hackney ponies shall be 14-2 hands.

HEAVY HORSE.—Any one of the draft breeds.

HEDGE JUMP (BRUSH JUMPS).—In hunt and race courses, the hedge jump is usually made of evergreens. The horse is allowed to brush the tops of such jumps.

HEEL *(Hounds).*—A hunting term. When the huntsman rides (hacks) to the meet, the hounds are required "to heel," or to stay in a group at the heels of his horse. The discipline is maintained by men called whips, who ride behind and on either side of the hounds.

HEEL, HEELER, HEALING *(in roping event).*—In steer roping or team tying, the heeler ropes the bovine's feet and the header ropes the head.

HEELS *(of rider)*.—The heels of a mounted rider are used as aids. They should be carried well below the toes and at least an inch away from the horse's sides. When the heels are carried in this position, the rider can wear long, sharp, rowelled spurs without touching his horse with them unless he desires to do so. The importance of heels becomes clear when it is realized that the position of the heels, ankles, and feet determine the position of the rider's thighs and the security of his seat.

HEIGHT.—See MEASURING HORSES.

HELMINTHS (OR WORM PARASITES).—Helminths are many-celled worm parasites varying greatly in size, shape, structure, and physiology. With few exceptions, the eggs or larvae must leave the host animal in which they originate to undergo further development on the ground, elsewhere in the open, or in intermediate hosts. For purposes of description they are classified here as (1) flukes (or trematodes), (2) tapeworms (or cestodes), (3) roundworms (or nematodes), and (4) thorny-headed worms (or acanthocephala).

HEREDITY IN HORSES.—Heredity refers to characteristics which are transmitted to offspring from parents and other ancestors.

The gene is the unit that determines heredity. In the body cells of horses there are many chromosomes. In turn, the chromosomes carry pairs of minute particles, called genes, which are the basic hereditary material (Fig. H-10). The nucleus of each body cell of horses contains 32 pairs of chromosomes, or a total of 64; whereas there are thousands of pairs of genes.

When a sex cell (a sperm or an egg) is formed, only one chromosome and one gene of each pair goes into it. Then, when mating and fertilization occur, the 32 single chromosomes from the germ cell of each parent unite to form new pairs, and the chromosomes with their genes are again present in duplicate, in the body cells of the embryo. Thus, with all possible combinations of 32 pairs of chromosomes and the genes that they bear, it is not strange that full sisters (except identical twins from a single egg split after fertilization) are so different. Actually we can marvel that they bear as much resemblance

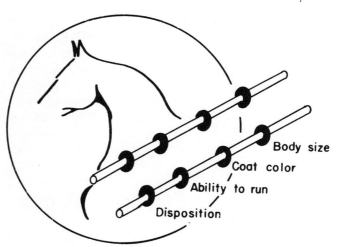

Fig. H-10. A pair of bundles, called chromosomes, carrying minute particles called genes. The genes determine all the hereditary characteristics of living animals, from length of leg to body size. (Drawing by R. F. Johnson)

to each other as they do.

Because of this situation, the mating of a mare with a fine track record to a stallion that transmits good performance characteristics will not always produce a foal of a merit equal to its parents. The foal could be markedly poorer than the parents or, in some cases, it could be better than either parent.

Simple and multiple gene inheritance occurs in horses, as in all animals. In simple gene inheritance, only one pair of genes is involved; thus, a pair of genes may be responsible for some one specific trait in horses. However, most characteristics, such as speed, are due to many genes; hence, they are called multiple-gene characteristics.

For most characteristics, many pairs of genes are involved. For example, growth rate in foals is affected by (1) appetite and feed consumption, (2) the proportion of the feed eaten that is absorbed, and (3) the use to which the nutrients are put—whether they are used for growth or fattening, and each in turn is probably affected by different genes. Because multiple characteristics show all manner of gradation from high to low performance, they are sometimes referred to as quantitative traits. Thus, quantitative inheritance refers to the degree to which a characteristic is inherited. For example, all racehorses can run and all inherit some ability to run, but it is the degree to which they inherit the ability that is important.

Dominant and recessive factors exist in horses. Some genes have the ability to prevent or mask the expression of others, with the result that the genetic makeup of such animals cannot be recognized with accuracy. This is called dominance. The gene that is masked is recessive. Because black is dominant to chestnut, all of the offspring will be black when a pure black stallion is crossed with a chestnut mare.

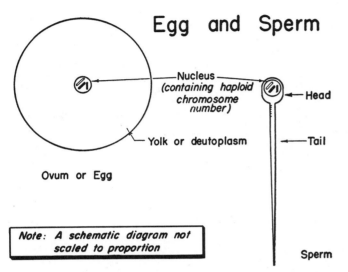

Egg and Sperm

Note: A schematic diagram not scaled to proportion

Fig. H-11. Egg and sperm. *The parent germ cells, the egg from the female and the sperm from the male, unite and transmit to the offspring all the characters that it will inherit. (Drawing by R. F. Johnson)*

The resulting black offspring are not genotypically pure; they are Bb, where B stands for the dominant black and b for the recessive chestnut. These black, or F_1 (first cross) animals will produce germ cells carrying black and chestnut genes in equal proportion (Fig. H-12). Then if an F_1 stallion is crossed with F_1 mares, the F_2 (second cross) population will, on the average, consist of three blacks to one chestnut.

The chestnut in the F_2 population, being a recessive, will be pure for color. That is, the mating of any two chestnut horses will produce, according to the most authoritative work, chestnut offspring; this is the situation in the Suffolk breed of draft horses where all animals of the breed are chestnuts. Of the three blacks in the F_2, however, only one is pure for black with the genetic constitution BB. The other two will be Bb in genetic constitution and will produce germ cells carrying B and b in equal proportion.

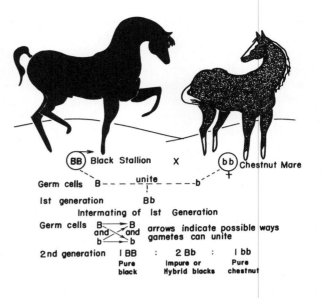

Fig. H-12. *An example of gene inheritance in horses. Note—*

1. That each horse has at least a pair of genes for color, conveniently represented by symbols.

2. That each reproductive cell (egg or sperm) contains but one of each pair.

3. That the Bb genotypes, in the 1st (F_1) generation, can vary in the degree of blackness thus tending to resemble the one black parent.

4. That the 2nd (F_2) generation has the ratio of three blacks to one chestnut (phenotypically). The Bb's may be black or shading into brown.

5. That the pure blacks and certain hybrid blacks may not be distinguished on the basis of appearance, because the B gene obscures the b gene in varying degrees.

6. That the chestnut (bb) is quite likely the only pure color, in this example, that can be detected on sight.

Dominance often makes it difficult to identify and discard all animals carrying an undesirable recessive factor. In some cases, dominance is neither complete nor absent, but incomplete, or partial, and expressed in a variety of ways. The best known case of partial dominance in horses is the palomino coloring.

Heredity and environment in quantitative traits function in horses just as they do in all animals. Therefore, maximum development of characteristics of economic importance such as growth, body form, or speed cannot be achieved unless horses receive proper training, nutrition, and management.

The problem of the horse breeder is to select the best animals available genetically to be parents of the next generation. Because only 15 to 30 percent of the observed variation among animals may be due to heredity, and because environmental differences can produce misleading variations, mistakes in the selection of breeding animals are inevitable.

Both the stallion and the mare are equally important to any one offspring. But a stallion generally can have many more offspring than a mare can and, from a hereditary standpoint, is more important to the herd or breed.

Prepotency is the ability of an animal to stamp its characteristics on its offspring so the offspring resemble that parent or they resemble each other more than usual.

Nicking results when the right combination of genes for good characteristics is contributed by each parent. Thus, animals nick well when their respective combinations of good genes complement each other.

Family names of horses have genetic significance only if (1) they are based on a linebreeding program that keeps the family closely related to the admired stallion or mare carrying the particular name, and (2) members of the family have been rigidly culled. Family names, therefore, lend themselves to speculation, and often have no more significance than human family names.

HEREDITY AND ENVIRONMENT.—A racehorse or show horse is the result of two forces—heredity and environment. Heredity may be thought of as the foundation, and environment as the structure. Heredity has already made its contribution at the time of fertilization, but environment works ceaselessly away until death.

Generally, horse trainers believe that heredity is most important, whereas horse owners believe that environment, particularly training, is most important—especially if they lose a race. Actually, maximum development of characters of economic importance—growth, body form, speed, etc.—cannot be achieved unless there are optimum conditions of nutrition and management.

The problem of the horse breeder is that of selecting the very best animals available genetically—these to be parents of the next generation. The fact that only 15 to 30 percent of the observed variation may be due to heredity, and that environmental differences can produce misleading variations, makes mistakes in the selection of breeding animals inevitable.

HERNIA (OR RUPTURE).—Hernia (or rupture) refers to the protrusion of any internal organ through the wall of its containing cavity, but it usually means the passage of a portion of the intestine through an opening in the abdominal muscle. Umbilical, scrotal, and inguinal hernias are fairly common in young foals.

An umbilical hernia may be present at birth or may develop soon thereafter. In the majority of cases, the condition corrects itself. If surgery becomes necessary, it is usually postponed until after weaning.

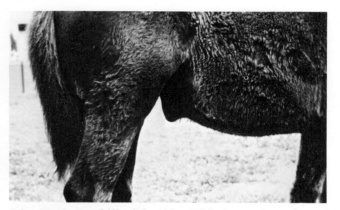

Fig. H-13. Umbilical hernia. This is a separation of the abdominal muscles where the umbilical cord was attached; the contents of the abdomen pushed through the gap in the muscles and pushed the skin outward. This one had to be repaired surgically. (Reproduced with permission of Haileybury Farm and Tampa Tracings, 1971; Courtesy, the Wickes, Newville, Pa.)

A scrotal hernia, which may be noticed at birth or shortly thereafter, will usually correct itself also, although such natural correction may require several weeks' time. Nevertheless, it is well to advise the veterinarian of the trouble.

HERRING-GUTTED.—Lacking depth of flank, which is also termed "single-gutted."

HETEROZYGOUS.—Having unlike genes which can be present for any of the characteristics such as coat color, size, etc.

HIDEBOUND.—Having the hide tight over the body. Horses that are hidebound usually are out of condition, have a rough hair coat, and show signs of malnutrition. The condition is usually caused by parasites and/or poor feeding. Treatment consists in discovering the cause, then rectifying the situation.

HIGH BLOWING ("CRACKING" THE NOSTRILS).—A very distinct sound made by some horses at the gallop. Often an amateur suspicions defective wind, or a respiratory disorder. However, it is nothing more than excess flapping of the false nostrils due to fast movement. It disappears as speed is increased.

HIGHLAND PONY.—This is the largest and strongest of the mountain and moorland breeds of ponies. It is found in the Highlands of Scotland and certain islands adjacent thereto.

HIGH SCHOOL.—The highest form of specialized training of riding horses.

HINNY.—The offspring of a stallion mated to a jennet is known as a hinny. The hinny and the mule are indistinguishable; and, with rare exceptions, both are infertile.

HIP.—The hip is a ball-and-socket joint.
(Also see PARTS OF A HORSE—Fig. P-4.)

HIPPOLOGY.—The study of the horse.

HISTORY OF HORSES (early and domestication).—See DOMESTICATION AND EARLY USE OF THE HORSE.

HISTORY OF HORSES IN U.S.—It has been established that most of the evolution of the horse took place in the Americas, but this animal was extinct in the Western World at the time of Columbus' discovery, and apparently extinct even before the arrival of the Red Man some thousands of years earlier.

Columbus first brought horses to the West Indies on his second voyage in 1493. Cortez brought

Spanish horses with him to the New World in 1519 when he landed in Mexico (16 animals were in the initial contingent, but approximately 1,000 head more were subsequently imported during the two-year conquest of Mexico). Horses were first brought directly to what is now the United States by DeSoto in the year 1539. Upon his vessels, he had 237 horses. These animals traveled with the army of the explorer in the hazardous journey from the Everglades of Florida to the Ozarks of Missouri. Following DeSoto's death and burial in the upper Mississippi three years later, his followers returned by boats down the Mississippi, abandoning many of their horses.

Fig. H-14. DeSoto discovers the Mississippi. The energetic Spanish explorer brought the first horses to the United States in 1539. (Courtesy, The Bettman Archive)

Fig. H-15. A covered wagon, drawn by horses. This was a common method of transportation in this country prior to the advent of the railroad and the motor vehicle. (Photo by Ewing Galloway, New York)

One year following DeSoto's landing in what is now Florida, in 1540, another Spanish explorer, Coronado, started an expedition with an armed band of horsemen from Mexico, penetrating to a point near the boundary of Kansas and Nebraska.

Beginning about 1600, the Spaniards established a chain of Christian missions among the Indians in the New World. The chain of missions extended from the eastern coast of Mexico up the Rio Grande, thence across the mountains to the Pacific Coast. Each mission brought animals, including horses, from the mother country.

There are two schools of thought relative to the source of the foundation stock of the first horses of the American Indians, and the hardy bands of Mustangs—the feral horses of the Great Plains. Most historians agree that both groups were descended from animals of Spanish (Arabian) extraction. However, some contend that their foundation stock came from the abandoned and stray horses of the expeditions of DeSoto and Coronado, whereas others claim that they were obtained chiefly from Sante Fe, ancient Spanish mission founded in 1606. It is noteworthy that Santa Fe and other early Spanish missions were the source of Spanish Longhorn cattle, thus lending credence to the theory that the missions were the source of foundation horses for the Indian and the wild bands of Mustangs.

Much romance and adventure is connected with the Mustang, and each band of wild horses was credited with leadership by the most wonderful stallion ever beheld by man. Many were captured, but the real leaders were always alleged to have escaped by reason of speed, such as not possessed by a domesticated horse. The Mustang multiplied at a prodigious rate. In one high luxuriant bunch grass region in the state of Washington, wild horses thrived so well that the region became known as "Horse Heaven," a name it bears even today.

The coming of the horse among the Indians increased the strife and wars between tribes. Following the buffalo on horseback led to greater infringement upon each other's hunting grounds, which had ever been a cause for war. From the time the Indians came into possession of horses until the country was taken over by the white man, there was no peace among the tribes.

Later, animals of both light- and draft-horse breeding were introduced from Europe by the colonists. For many years, however, sturdy oxen continued to draw the plows for turning the sod on many a rugged New England hillside. Horses were largely used as pack animals, for riding, and later for pulling wagons and stagecoaches. It was not until about 1840 that the buggy first made its appearance.

Six mares and two stallions were brought to Jamestown in 1609, these being the first European importations. Some of these animals may have been eaten during the period of near starvation at Jamestown, but importations continued; and it was reported in 1611 that a total of seventeen horses had been brought to this colony.

The horse seems to have been much neglected in early New England, as compared with cattle and sheep. This is not surprising, inasmuch as oxen were universally used for draft purposes. Roads were few in number; speed was not essential; and the horse had no meat value like that of cattle. Because of the great difficulty in herding horses on the commons, they were usually hobbled. Despite the limited early-day use of the horse, the colonists must have loved them, because, very early, the indiscriminate running of stallions among the mares upon the commons was recognized as undesirable. Massachusetts, before 1700, excluded from town commons all stallions "under fourteen hands high and not of comely proportion."

Even before horses found much use in New England, they became valuable for export purposes to the West Indies for work in the sugar mills. In fact, this business became so lucrative that horse stealing became a common offense in New England in the eighteenth century. Confiscation of property, public whippings, and banishment from the colony constituted the common punishments for a horse thief.

As plantations materialized in Virginia, the need for easy-riding saddle horses developed, so that the owners might survey their broad estates. Racing also became a popular sport among the cavaliers in Virginia, Maryland, and the Carolinas—with the heat races up to four miles being common events. The plantation owners took considerable pride in having animals worthy of wearing their colors. So great was the desire to win that by 1730 the importation of English racehorses began.

George Washington maintained an extensive horse- and mule-breeding establishment at Mount Vernon. The President was also an ardent race fan, and riding to hounds was a favorite sport with him. As soon as Washington's views on the subject of mules became known abroad, he received some valuable breeding stock through gifts. In 1787, the Marquis de Lafayette presented him with a jack and some jennets of the Maltese breed. The jack, named Knight of Malta, was described as a superb animal, of a black color, with the form of a stag and the ferocity of a tiger. In 1795, the King of Spain gave Washington a jack and two jennets that were selected from the royal stud at Madrid. The Spanish jack, known as Royal Gift, was 16 hands high, of a gray color, heavily made, and of a sluggish disposition. It was said that Washington was able to combine the best qualities of the two gift jacks, especially through one of the descendants named Compound. General Washington was the first to produce mules of quality in this country, and soon the fame of these hardy hybrids spread throughout the South.

Fig. H-16. Conestoga freight wagon drawn by six Conestoga horses, in front of a country inn. These improved horses and large wagons were both given the name Conestoga, after the Conestoga Valley, a German settlement in Pennsylvania. The advent of the railroads drove the Conestoga horses into oblivion, and the Conestoga wagon was succeeded by the prairie schooner. (Courtesy, The Bettmann Archive)

The Dutch, Puritan, and Quaker colonists to the north adhered strictly to agricultural pursuits, frowning upon horse races. They imported heavier types of horses. In Pennsylvania, under the guidance of William Penn, the farmers prospered. Soon their horses began to improve, even as the appearance and fertility of their farms had done.

Eventually, their large horses were hitched to enormous wagons and used to transport freight overland to and from river flatboats and barges along the Ohio, Cumberland, Tennessee, and Mississippi rivers. Both horses and wagons were given the name Conestoga, after the Conestoga Valley, a German settlement in Pennsylvania. The Conestoga wagon was the forerunner of the prairie schooner, and before the advent of the railroad it was the freight vehicle of the time. It was usually drawn by a team of six magnificent Conestoga horses, which were well groomed and expensively harnessed. At one time, the Conestoga horses bid to become a new breed—a truly American creation. However, the railroads replaced them, eventually driving them into permanent oblivion. Other breeds were developed later, but this is another story.

HITCH.—1. To fasten a horse; e.g., when hitched to a rail.

2. A connection between a vehicle and a horse.

3. A defect in gait noted in the hind legs, which seem to skip at the trot.

HITCHING POST.—A fixed, and often elaborate, standard to which a horse or team can be tied to prevent straying.

HOBBLE HANGER.—See HARNESS—Fig. H-5.

HOBBLES.—Leather straps which encircle the pasterns or fetlock joints on the front legs of the horse and are connected with a short strap or chain, to prevent it from roaming too far when turned out to graze. Another type of hobble is used on the hind legs (often around the hocks) of a mare in breeding, to prevent her from kicking the stallion.

(Also see HARNESS—Fig. H-5.)

HOBBYHORSE.—A figure designed to resemble a horse and used as a child's plaything.

HOBBY VS. BUSINESS.—See TAXES, INCOME.

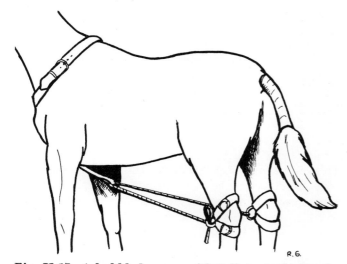

Fig. H-17. A hobbled mare, with tail properly bandaged, ready for service. The hobbles are used to protect the stallion as he approaches and dismounts, and not in any way to force the mare into submission to service when not ready.

HOCK (POINT OF HOCK).—The hock, which lies between the gaskin and the hind cannon, corresponds to the human ankle. It is the most important single joint in the horse's body, and the most ingeniously constructed. A horse "jumps from his hocks," i.e., he receives the necessary spring and propulsion from this joint. Thus, if the hock is weak the horse will not make a satisfactory hunter or jumper.

The hock should be wide, deep, flat, clean, hard, strong, well supported, and correctly set with prominent points.

The hock is the seat of more serious unsoundnesses than any other part of the body—among them blood spavin, bog spavin, bone spavin or jack, capped hock, curb, and thoroughpin.

(Also see PARTS OF A HORSE—Fig. P-4.)

HOGGED.—A mane that is clipped—entirely removed.

HOLSTEIN.—A German breed of horses, dating back to the 13th century. They are used for riding, driving, hunting, and steeplechasing.

HOMOZYGOUS.—Having like genes which can be present for any of the characteristics of the animal such as coat color, size, etc.

HOMOZYGOUS DOMINANT.—A dominant character that produces only one kind of gamete.

HOMOZYGOUS RECESSIVE.—A recessive character that produces two kinds of gametes; one carries the dominant gene, while the other carries the recessive gene.

HONDA.—A ring of rope, rawhide, or metal on a lasso through which the loop slides.

HONEY.—See SUGAR AND HONEY.

HOOD.—A covering, made from various kinds of materials, for the head, ears, and neck, commonly used when horses are being transported.

HOOF.—The insensitive cornified layer of epidermis covering the distal end of each leg. White hooves are found where the hair at the upper margin of the hoof is also white, and dark hooves are associated with dark hairs in this area.

The insensitive structures of the hoof include the periople, wall, bars, laminae, sole, and frog. Each is produced by a corresponding sensitive structure consisting of the germinating layer of epidermis closely applied to the underlying corium of the same name, which is well supplied with vessels and nerves.

The hoofs should be large, dense, and wide at the heels.

(Also see FEET; FOOT; and SHOEING.)

HOOFS, DRY.—Hoofs may become dry and brittle; sometimes they split and cause lameness. The frogs lose their elasticity and are no longer effective shock absorbers. If the dryness is prolonged, the frogs shrink and the heels contract.

Dry hoofs usually can be prevented by packing them with a specially prepared formulation, applying a good hoof dressing, keeping the ground wet around the watering tank, and/or attaching wet burlap sacks around them.

HOPPLES.—The term applied to hobbles (leather or plastic straps with semicircular loops) used in harness racing, which are placed on the gaskin and forearm, connecting the fore and hind legs of the same side in pacers, and running diagonally in trotters, connecting the diagonal fore and hind legs. Such hopples, which were invented by a railroad conductor named John Browning in 1885, are used to keep a horse on gait; i.e., to prevent trotters from pacing and pacers from trotting.

(Also see HARNESS—Fig. H-5.)

HORMONE.—A body-regulating chemical secreted by an endocrine gland into the bloodstream. The endocrine glands include the pituitary, parathyroid, thyroid, adrenal, pancreas, and the gonads or sex organs.

HORN FLY.—See FLIES.

HORSE.—1. The name "horse" is derived from the Anglo-Saxon *hors,* meaning swiftness—a characterization which evolved because the very survival of wild horses was dependent upon their swiftness to provide escape from both beast and man.

2 In the restricted sense this applies to an entire, not a gelding or mare.

HORSE BALLET.—The horse ballet is an equine dance to music. It requires intense concentration of both horse and rider, since the prescribed figures must be executed with absolute precision. For anyone who sees these exacting exercises performed to the strains of classical music, with effortless ease at the Spanish Riding School, the past seems to come alive again and history lingers on long after the white stallions have filed out of the ring.

HORSE (S), CLASSIFICATION OF.—Horses may be classified as light horses, ponies, or draft horses, according to size, build, and use.

(Also see DRAFT HORSES; LIGHT HORSES; and PONIES.)

HORSE DEALER.—One who is engaged in buying and selling horses.

HORSE DEPRECIATION.—See TAXES, INCOME.

HORSEFLY.—See FLIES.

HORSE INDUSTRY, SIZE OF.—See MAGNITUDE OF HORSE INDUSTRY.

HORSEMANSHIP.—By definition, horsemanship is the art of riding horseback. For greatest enjoyment, one should learn to ride correctly.

For the beginner, the author favors the following simple approach: (1) become familiar with the horse and equipment, and (2) learn to use that equipment properly. Knowledge of correct grooming and care of the horse, care of equipment, saddling, bridling, and leading are essential, also.

MOUNTING AND DISMOUNTING, ENGLISH.—Before mounting, two precautions should be taken: always check the saddle girth for tightness and the stirrup straps or leathers for length. A loose girth may let the saddle slip down on the horse's side or belly, especially when one is mounting and dismounting. When the girth is adjusted properly, one should be able to get only the first half of the fingers under it without considerable forcing.

Fig. H-18. "Ballet of the White Stallions," at famed Spanish Riding School, in Austria. (Courtesy, Spanish Riding School, Wels, Austria)

Fig. H-19. Good horsemanship demonstrated by Miss Gloria Rawcliffe, Clovis, Calif. (Photo by A. H. Ensminger)

When all precautions have been taken, the steps in mounting and dismounting a horse are as shown in Fig. H-20.

From the accompanying figures the novice should not gain the impression that in mounting and dismounting each step is so distinct and different as to be marked by intermittent pauses. Rather, when properly executed, mounting or dismounting is a series of rhythmic movements, and the entire operation is done so smoothly and gracefully that it is difficult to discern where one stage ends and the next one begins.

Dismounting is just the reverse of mounting. In succession, the rider should carefully gather the reins in the left hand, place the left hand on the horse's withers and the right hand on the pommel of the saddle, stand up in the stirrups, kick the right foot free from the stirrup, transfer the weight to the left foot as the right leg is swung backward across the horse's back and croup, shift the right hand to the cantle of the saddle, descend to the ground, and remove the left foot from the stirrup.

Another accepted way of dismounting from the English saddle consists in removing the left foot from the stirrup and sliding down with relaxed knees. The rider will never get hung in the stirrups when dismounting in this manner and small children can get off a horse easily and without assistance.

Fig. H-20. Pictures showing the steps in mounting a horse. Photos made for the author of this book by Fern P. Bittner, Instructor in Horsemanship, Lindenwood College, St. Charles, Mo.

Mount from left or "near" side, gather reins in left hand, and place left hand on or just in front of withers.

Turn stirrup iron one-quarter turn, steady stirrup with right hand and shove left foot into it.

(Continued)

Hop off the right foot, swing around to face the horse, grasp the cantle with right hand, and spring upward until standing position is reached. Lean on left arm, shift right hand from cantle to pommel (usually right-hand side of pommel) of saddle; then swing extended right leg over horse's back and croup.

Ease down into the saddle; then shove right foot into right stirrup without looking down.

Sit easily, be alert and keep head up, and allow legs to hang comfortably with heels well down and toes turned out slightly.

MOUNTING AND DISMOUNTING, WESTERN.—The steps in mounting a horse in Western riding are: take the reins in the left hand and place the left hand on the horse's neck in front of the withers. Keep the romal or end of the reins on the near side. Grasp the stirrup with the right hand, place the left foot in the stirrup with the ball of the foot resting securely on the tread. Brace the left knee against the horse, grasp the saddle horn with the right hand, and spring upward and over. Settle into the saddle and slip the right foot into the off stirrup.

HOLDING THE REINS.—The rider may hold the reins either in the left hand alone or in both hands. In Western riding, only one hand, usually the left, holds the reins.

Fig. H-21. Mounting in western riding.

fall to the left side of the horse's neck and the right hand should be dropped loosely down the side or placed comfortably on the thigh of the right leg. The free hand should never be placed on the pommel of an English saddle or on the pommel or horn of a Western saddle.

Figs. H-22 and H-23 illustrate better than words the correct method of holding the reins.

In no case should the rein pressure be more vigorous than absolutely necessary, nor should the reins be used as a means of staying on the horse. A horse's mouth is tender, but it can be toughened by unnecessary roughness. Good hands appear to be in proper rhythm with the head of the horse. Beginners are likely to let the hands bob too much, thus jerking the horse's mouth unnecessarily and using the reins as a means of hanging on the horse. The desired light hands exist when a light feeling extends to the horse's mouth via the reins.

When holding the reins with both hands—as is usual in show-ring riding and training—toss the "bight" (ends) of the reins to the right (off) side of the horse's neck; in hunting and jumping, toss the bight to the left.

When holding the reins in one hand, the left for example—as in English style, cross country riding, or in Western riding—the bight should

Fig. H-22. Holding the reins Western style: (A) Only one hand can be used and hands cannot be changed; (B) the hand must be around the reins with no fingers between reins unless split reins are used; (C) when using split reins, one finger between reins is permitted.

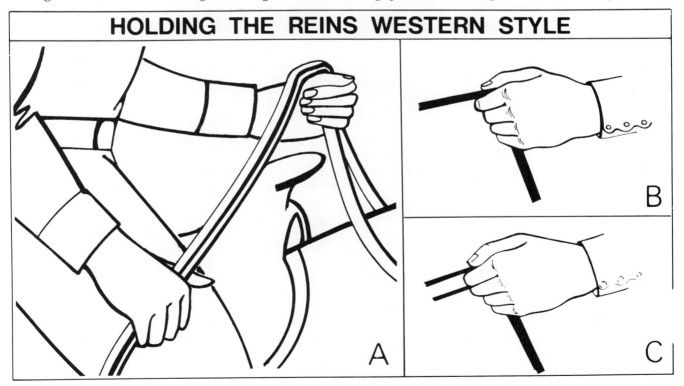

HOLDING THE REINS WESTERN STYLE

A

B

C

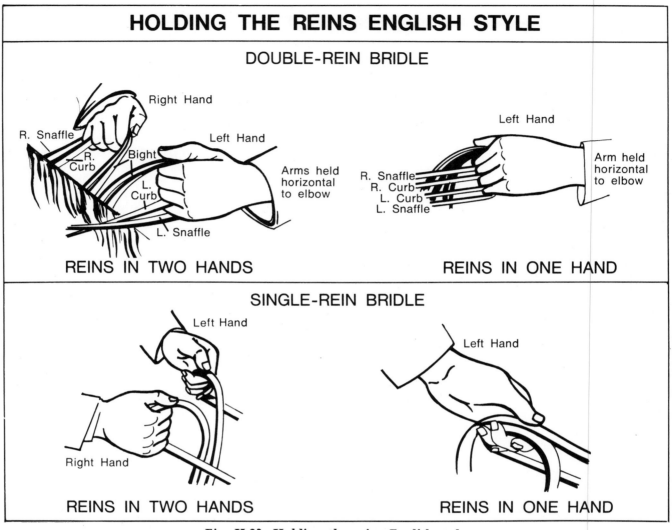

HOLDING THE REINS ENGLISH STYLE

DOUBLE-REIN BRIDLE

Right Hand

R. Snaffle

R. Curb

Bight

Left Hand

L. Curb

Arms held horizontal to elbow

L. Snaffle

REINS IN TWO HANDS

Left Hand

R. Snaffle
R. Curb
L. Curb
L. Snaffle

Arm held horizontal to elbow

REINS IN ONE HAND

SINGLE-REIN BRIDLE

Left Hand

Right Hand

REINS IN TWO HANDS

Left Hand

REINS IN ONE HAND

Fig. H-23. Holding the reins English style.

SEAT, THE.—As in any type of sport, correct riding must include rhythm and balance. The rider's movements must be in complete harmony with the horse's movements, for this assures greater security of the rider and freedom of action by the horse.

Figs. H-24 through H-28 show the correct riding seat for a three-gaited horse, a five-gaited horse, a plantation walking horse, a Western horse, and a hunter and jumper.

The balanced seat may be defined as that position of the mounted rider that requires the minimum of muscular effort to remain in the saddle and which interferes least with the horse's movements and equilibrium. In essence, it means that the rider must be "with the horse," rather than ahead of or behind him. When a balanced seat is maintained, the center of gravity of the rider is directly over the center of gravity of the horse. With the proper seat, the minimum use of aids will be necessary to get immediate and correct response from the horse at any gait.

The balanced seat is obtained largely through shifting the point of balance of the upper body from the hips up; the knees, legs, ankles, and to a great extent the thighs remain in fixed position. Thus, the degree of forward inclination of the upper body will vary according to the speed and gait of the horse; but always the rider should remain in balance over his base of support. The eyes, chin, and chest are lifted, thus

Fig. H-24. Correct saddle seat and riding attire for a three-gaited horse.

Fig. H-25. Correct saddle seat and riding attire for a five-gaited horse.

Fig. H-26. Correct seat and riding attire at the running walk.

Fig. H-27. Correct Western seat and riding attire.

Fig. H-28. Correct hunter seat. The eyes should be up and the shoulders back. The toes should be out at an angle best suited to the rider's conformation; ankles flexed in, heels down, calf of leg in contact with horse and slightly behind girth. Iron may be either on toe, ball of foot, or "home."

At the walk and slow trot, the body should be vertical; at the posting trot, it should incline forward; at the canter, it should be half way between the posting trot and the walk; when galloping and jumping, it should have the same inclination as the posting trot.

permitting clear vision ahead and normal posture of the back. It must also be remembered that the greater the speed and the inclination of the body forward, the shorter the stirrups. The jockey, therefore, rides his mount with very short stirrups and reins and a pronounced forward position. He rises out of his saddle and supports himself almost entirely with the stirrups, knees, and legs. In steeplechasing, the position of the rider is less extreme than in flat racing, for in this type of riding it is necessary to combine speed with security.

From what has been said, it can be readily understood that there are different seats or positions for different styles of riding. Fashion, particularly in the show-ring, also decrees that certain form be followed.

Each style of riding differs in appearance, but the end result is the same—balanced riding. An accomplished rider can and does change the seat to meet the style of riding.

(Also see SADDLE SEAT; WALKING HORSE SEAT; and WESTERN SEAT.)

RULES OF GOOD HORSEMANSHIP.—
Horsemen should always practice safety and show consideration for other riders. The following are some of the rules of good horsemanship:

● Approach a horse on his left. Never walk or stand behind a horse unannounced; let him know you are there by speaking to him and placing your hand on him. Otherwise, you may get kicked.

● Pet a horse by first placing your hand on his shoulder or neck. Do not dab at the end of his nose.

● When leading a horse, grasp the reins close to the bit on his left side.

● Walk a horse to and from the stable; this prevents him from running to the stable and from refusing to leave the stable.

● Make sure the saddle blanket or pad is clean and free of any rough places to prevent a sore back.

Fig. H-29. Good horsemen know and follow the rules of good horsemanship. (Courtesy, Prof. Byron H. Good, Michigan State College)

● Check the saddle and bridle, or hackamore, before mounting. The saddle should fit just back of the withers; it should not bear down on or rub the withers, but also it should not be placed too far back. The girth should be fastened snugly and should not be too close to the forelegs. Be sure that the bridle, or hackamore, fits comfortably and that the curb chain, or strap, is flat in the chin groove and fastened correctly.

● Mount and dismount from the left side. The horse must be made to stand still until the rider is properly seated in the saddle or has dismounted.

● Sit in the correct position for the style of riding.

● Keep the proper tension on the reins; avoid

either tight or dangling reins.

● Keep the hands and voice quiet when handling a horse. Never scream, laugh loudly, or make other noises that will upset the horse. Do not slap a horse with the ends of the reins when he is excited.

● Warm up a horse gradually; walk him first and then jog him slowly.

● Keep to the right side of the road except when passing. Yield the right-of-way courteously.

● Walk a horse across bridges, through underpasses, on pavements and slippery roads, and when going up or down hill. Do not race a horse; he will form bad habits and may get out of control.

● Slow down when making a sharp turn.

● Keep a horse moving when a car passes. If he stops, he may back into the passing vehicle.

● Anticipate such distractions as cars, stones, paper, trees, bridges, noises, dogs, and children.

● Vary the gaits; do not force a horse to take a rapid gait such as a canter, rack, or trot for more than a half mile without allowing a breathing spell.

● Keep a horse under control at all times if possible. Try to stop a runaway horse by sawing the bit back and forth to break his stride and his hold on the bit; in an open space, pull one rein hard enough to force the horse to circle.

● Be firm with a horse and make him obey. At the same time, love and understand him and he will be a good friend.

● Never become angry and jerk a horse; a bad-tempered person can make a bad-tempered horse.

● Lean forward and loosen the reins if a horse rears. Do not lean back and pull because the horse might fall over backwards.

● Pull up the reins of a bucking horse and keep his head up.

● Loosen the reins and urge a horse forward with your legs if he starts backing. Do not hold the reins too tightly when a horse is standing still.

● Walk a horse at the end of a ride to let him get cool.

● Do not allow a horse to gorge on water when he is hot; allow a warm horse to drink only a few swallows at a time.

● Do not turn a horse loose at the stall entrance. Walk into the stall with him and turn him around so that he is facing the door. In a tie stall, make certain that the horse is tied securely with a proper length rope.

● Groom a horse thoroughly after each ride.

● Wash the bit thoroughly before it is hung in the tack room. Remove hair and sweat from the saddle and girth before putting them on the rack.

● When riding in a group, keep about 5 feet apart when abreast or a full horse's length behind other mounts when in line, to prevent kicking.

● Never rush past other riders; this may startle the horses and riders and cause an accident. Instead, approach slowly and pass cautiously on the left side.

● Never dash up to another horse or group of horses at a gallop; this can injure riders or horses.

● Wait quietly when a rider must dismount. Do not start moving again until he has remounted and is ready to go.

● Never chase a mounted runaway horse because this will only make him run faster; if possible, another rider should circle and come up in front of him. In case a rider is thrown, stop the other horses and keep quiet; generally the loose horse will return to the group where he can be caught.

● Do not trespass on private property.

● Leave gates closed; otherwise, livestock may get out.

HORSE MEAT.—In France and Belgium, and other parts of the world, horse meat is considered a delicacy for human consumption. In this country, many horses that have outlived their usefulness or that are less valuable for other purposes are processed in modern, sanitary slaughtering plants for pet food. Once, a considerable number of feral (wild) horses were rounded up for this purpose, but few such herds remain and laws are restrictive.

HORSE NUMBERS.—See NUMBER OF HORSES.

HORSEPOWER.—The historical importance of horses is attested to by the continued use of the term "horsepower." Originally, it was a measure of the power that a horse exerts in pulling. Technically speaking, a horsepower, or English gravitational unit, is the rate at which work is accomplished when a resistance (weight) of 33,000 pounds is moved 1 foot in 1 minute, or 550 pounds is moved 1 foot in 1 second. Despite their sophistication, modern motors are rated in horsepower, based on tests made on a machine known as the dynamometer.

HORSESHOE.—A shoe for a horse, usually consisting of a narrow plate of iron conformed to the rim of the horse's hoof. Running horses, which race under saddle, wear aluminum shoes. The latter are manufactured, light, and not very durable.

Horseshoes are used to protect the hoof against hard surfaces, and to change gaits and action, correct faulty hoof structure on growth, and protect the hoof from such conditions as corns, contraction, or cracks. Also, on race horses, shoes aid in gripping the track.

Handmade (hot) shoes, made by an expert farrier are best, but they are costly. Therefore, manufactured or "keg" shoes are worn by most horses. For show horses and harness racehorses, many of which are worth thousands of dollars, only handmade shoes should be used.

(Also see SHOEING—Kinds of Shoes.)

HORSESHOEING.—See SHOEING.

HORSE-SHOW CLASSES.—There are hundreds of horse-show classes; hence, it is impractical to cover all of them in this book. Instead, any horseman intending to compete in a horse show should apply for membership in the American Horse Shows Association (AHSA), and familiarize himself with the AHSA *Rule Book,* which is updated annually.

Horse-show classes may be divided into three general categories: (1) in hand, (2) in harness, and (3) under saddle.

(Also see SHOWS, HORSE.)

HORSE-SHOW JUDGES.—According to the American Horse Shows Association *Rule Book,* judges shall be of four classes: Registered, Recorded, Special, and Guest. Only Recognized Judges in good standing may officiate at Recognized Shows in those divisions covered by the rules and specifications of the current *Rule Book.*

The essential qualifications that a good horse judge must possess, and the recommended procedure to follow in the judging assignment, are as follows:

● *Knowledge of the parts of a horse.*—This consists of mastering the language that describes and locates the different parts of a horse (see PARTS OF A HORSE—Fig. P-4). In addition, it is necessary to know which of these parts are of major importance; that is, what comparative evaluation to give to the different parts.

● *A clearly defined ideal or standard of perfection.*—The successful horse judge must know for what he is looking. That is, he must have in mind an ideal or standard of perfection.

● *Keen observation and sound judgment.*—The good horse judge possesses the ability to observe both good conformation and performance, and defects, and to weigh and evaluate the relative importance of the various good and bad features.

● *Honesty and courage.*—The good horse judge must possess honesty and courage, whether it be in making a show-ring placing or in conducting a breeding and selling program. For example, it often requires considerable courage to place a class of animals without regard to (a) winnings in previous shows, (b) ownership, and (c) public applause. It may take even greater courage and honesty within oneself to discard a costly stallion or mare whose progeny have failed to measure up.

● *Logical procedure in examining.*—There is always great danger of the beginner making too close an inspection; he often gets "so close to the trees that he fails to see the forest."

Good judging procedure consists of the following three steps:

1. Observing at a distance and securing a panoramic view where several horses are involved.

2. Seeing the animals in action.

3. Inspecting close up.

Also, it is important that a logical method be used in viewing an animal from all directions (front view, rear view, and side view), and in judging its action and soundness—thus avoiding overlooking anything and making it easier to retain the observations that are made.

● *Tact.*—In discussing either (1) a show-ring class or (2) horses on a farm or ranch, it is important that the judge be tactful. The owner is likely to resent any remarks which indicate that his animal is inferior.

HORSE SHOWS.—See SHOWS, HORSE.

HORSE TRIALS.—See THREE-DAY-EVENT.

HOT-BLOODED (WARM BLOODED).—Of Eastern or Oriental blood, especially Arabian.

HOT-WALKER.—One employed to cool out horses.

HOUNDS, THE (FOXHOUNDS).—Foxhounds are not called dogs.

The desirable characteristics of a good Foxhound are: A good nose (ability to pick up a scent), speed, stamina, endurance, obedience to the huntsman's horn and voice, and willingness to hunt with the pack.

The American Foxhound descends from the English Foxhound. He is America's oldest sporting dog. Representatives of the breed are medium-sized (weigh about 60 pounds), short-coated, have long pendant ears and a saber-shaped tail,

Fig. H-30. Hunters and Foxhounds at Southern Acres Farm, Shelburne, Vermont. The sport is traditional in England, and each year it is sharing its glamor with greater numbers in the United States. (Courtesy, J. Watson Webb, owner, Southern Acres Farm)

are of various colors, and have a close, hard coat of medium length.

The English Foxhound is a very old breed. The stud books of the Masters of Foxhounds Association date back prior to 1800. But the foxhound existed in England long before that time. The English Foxhound is stouter appearing than his American cousin. He is a medium-sized (about 70 pounds), well-proportioned hound with pendant ears, gaily-carried tail, and a smooth coat of various hound colors.

HOUSE FLY.—See FLIES.

HUMANE SOCIETY OF THE UNITED STATES.—The Humane Society of the United States (HSUS) is a voluntary, nonprofit organization working to prevent cruelty to all animals, from household pets to exotic wildlife. The Humane Society and the ASPCA are two separate organizations.

ADDRESS.—The Humane society of the United States, 1604 K Street N.W., Washington, D.C. 20006.

(Also see AMERICAN SOCIETY FOR THE PREVENTION OF CRUELTY TO ANIMALS —THE A.S.P.C.A.)

HUNGARIAN HALF-BRED.—To the uninformed, the connotation "Hungarian Half-Bred" would imply a non-purebred of fifty percent Hungarian breeding. Instead, they're a distinct breed in Hungary, as old as antiquity, going back to the conquering Magyars, who came to Hungary at the close of the ninth century, bringing with them horses of Asiatic origin, improved with Persian blood. In the year 897, Arpad, the leader of the conquering Magyars, charged Csepel, one of his lieutenants, with collecting together for breeding purposes the best of Hungary's horses of the time. These were assembled at Csepel Island, named after the lieutenant, and now a part of greater Budapest. This was the first Hungarian Stud of which there is written record, and the first Stud Farm of any breed.

Through this breeding program evolved the famous cavalry horse of Hungary—one of the gamest, hardiest, fleetest, and most durable cavalry horses that the world has ever known. Today, Hungary continues to infuse the blood of Thoroughbreds and Arabians, usually not more than one cross of either before returning to straight Hungarian breeding; yet, there is no upper limit —a registered Hungarian Half-Bred may carry in his veins up to ninety percent Thoroughbred and/or Arabian breeding, and still be registered as a purebred. Of course, in Hungary, all registered animals must first pass a rigid inspection, made by government inspectors; and, too, the breed registry is operated by the State.

So, the Hungarian Half-Bred is a distinct, registered breed of horses both in Hungary and in the United States, and they're considered purebreds—as much so as Thoroughbreds and Arabians.

Hungarian Half-Breds have the ruggedness of Standardbreds and Morgans, with the quality of Arabians.

(Also see BREED (S) .)

HUNGARIAN HORSE.—See BREED (S) .

HUNGARIAN HORSE ASSOCIATION.—Bitterroot Stock Farm, Hamilton, Montana 59840. (See Appendix for complete list of breed registry associations.)

HUNT.—Pursuit of game. As used by horsemen, the term usually implies a hunt on horseback with hounds.

HUNTER (S) .—The hunter is that type of horse used in following the hounds in fox hunting. The sport is traditional in England, and each year it is sharing its glamour with greater numbers in the United States.

Again, the hunter is not necessarily of any particular breeding, but Thoroughbred blood predominates. The infusion of some cold blood (draft breeding) is often relied upon in order to secure greater size and a more tractable disposition.

Hunters are classified as small (those under 15–2½ hands in height) ; lightweight (those expected to carry a rider weighing under 165 pounds) ; middleweight (those expected to carry weights ranging from 165 to 185 pounds) ; and

heavyweight (those expected to carry over 185 pounds but under 205 pounds) . As many folks who ride to hounds do so in order to keep down their weight, their need for a sizeable mount can be fully appreciated. It must also be realized that a 5-foot object is 4 inches lower for a 16-hand horse than for one only 15 hands in height. Hunters are further classified as "green" or "qualified," the latter having hunted one season with a pack recognized by the United Hunts and Steeple Chase Association.

Fig. H-31. A hunter in action, and well ridden. (Courtesy, A. Mackay-Smith, Editor, **The Chronicle)**

In addition to being of ample size and height, the hunter must possess the necessary stamina and conformation to keep up with the pack. He must be able to hurdle with safety such common field obstacles as fences and ditches. The good hunter, therefore, is rugged, short coupled, and heavily muscled throughout.

All hunters are jumpers to some degree, but a high jumper is not necessarily a good hunter. To qualify as a hunter, the horse must do more. He must execute many and varied jumps over a long period of time.

HUNTER CLASSES.—The numerous horse show hunter classes are detailed in the American Horse Shows Association *Rule Book.* Thus, anyone planning to exhibit hunters should obtain a copy of same.

HUNTER TRIALS.—These are competitive events for hunters over an outside course which, as nearly as possible, simulates actual hunting conditions—including natural obstacles such as would be encountered within the hunt field. Horses are judged on manners, performance, way of going, and sometimes conformation. There are usually competitions for hunt teams and pairs of hunters. The classes are generally limited to amateurs, and the prizes are trophies rather than cash.

HUNTING CALLS.—The hunting horn used in England and America will produce one note only. Yet, by distinctive rhythms and tonal variations, the huntsman communicates much information to his hounds and his field (the members of his hunt club). Also, the huntsman's voice is as important as his horn. Although it is rarely possible to understand what he is saying, the tones will tell the listener how the hunt is going.

HUNTING CAP.—A specially designed velvet cap, reinforced with cork to make it hard, and decorated with grosgrain bows at the back and a high button on top, worn by children under eighteen, farmers, and the official hunt staff consisting of the Master, Huntsman, Whips, and Field Master. The hunting cap originated in the days when there was a "hat tax" or "capping fee." In passing his cap to collect the fees the Hunt Secretary could tell exactly who owed and who didn't—all those wearing a hunting cap were exempt. Farmers were exempt from the hat tax, and were privileged to wear the hunting cap, since it was due to their courtesy that the hounds were permitted to hunt on their own or their neighbors' lands.

HUNTING COUNTRY.—The type of country to be hunted governs the method of hunting the fox, the type of horse used, and the type of hound. Those who have hunted extensively in many countries are generally agreed that England and Ireland are best suited to the sport. Yet, very satisfactory hunting country exists in most countries, including the United States. New England hunts are characterized by rocky fields and stone walls; Pennsylvania and Maryland hunts are in open rolling country; and Ohio hunts involve wire fences that can be jumped safely only over chicken coops (paneling). Each area provides its own special challenges and enjoyments.

HUNTING HORN.—Hunting calls are made by means of a hunting horn. Horns were originally made of the horns of animals—generally oxen, embellished with silverwork or engravings. Later they were made of copper and/or silver. The hunting horn is carried by either the Master or the Huntsman, in a leather case attached to the front of the saddle or tucked in the vest.

HUNTING THONG.—A long, braided, leather lash attached to the hunting crop. It is used to discipline hounds. The professional rides with his thong hanging along his horse's shoulder; the amateur keeps his coiled in his hand.

HUNTSMAN.—The Huntsman is the most important member of the hunt staff. Many Masters hunt their own hounds, thus holding both positions. But frequently the Master prefers to hire a professional Huntsman. The Huntsman's sole obligation in the field is to his hounds. He decides on the strategy of the hunt, who governs the actions of hounds, whips, and field. The Huntsman must accept the blame or credit, as the case may be, for the performance of hounds.

Hounds are taught to come to the Huntsman for protection and affection. For this reason he rarely disciplines his hounds; he leaves that to his whippers-in.

In the field, the Huntsman rides first, keeping in close contact with the hounds, cheering them on.

Matters of discipline of members are the responsibility of the Field Master.

HURDLE RACING.—See STEEPLECHASING.

HURDLES.—Obstacles used in jumping or hunter classes in horse shows, steeplechases, and races.

HYBRIDS WITH THE HORSE AS ONE PARENT.—The mule, representing a cross between the jack (male of the ass family) on the mare (female of the horse family), is the best known hybrid in the United States. The resulting offspring of the reciprocal cross of the stallion mated to a jennet is known as a hinny.

Fig. H-32. Old Beck, a mare mule, and her horse-like foal born September 26, 1923. Owned by Texas A & M University. (Courtesy, Texas A & M University)

Rarely have mules proved fertile; only five authentic cases of mare mules producing foals have been reported in the United States. This infertility of the mule is probably due to the fact that the chromosomes will not pair and divide equally in the reduction division.

The offspring of fertile mules are generally horse-like in appearance, showing none of the characteristics of the mule's sire (or ass). For the most part, therefore, the eggs (ova) which produce them do not carry chromosomes from the ass; they are pure horse eggs without any inheritance from their maternal grandfathers. This indicates that in the production of eggs in mare mules the reduction division is such that all of the horse chromosomes go to the egg and none to the polar bodies.

The zebroid—a zebra x horse hybrid—is rather popular in certain areas of the tropics because of its docility and resistance to disease and heat.

HYDROPHOBIA (RABIES, OR MADNESS).—A virus-caused disease, usually transmitted by dogs, skunks, foxes, or bats. Rabies is best controlled by vaccinating all dogs. When horses are bitten by or exposed to a rabid animal, see your veterinarian immediately.

HYDROPONICS.—Hydroponics (or sprouting grain) is the growing of plants with their roots immersed in an aqueous solution containing the essential mineral nutrient salts, instead of in soil. In plain, simple terms, then, sprouted grain for feed is produced with water and chemicals, and without dirt. It is not new; it dates back over 400 years.

Without doubt, sprouted grains will give an assist when added to poor rations—and the poorer the ration, the bigger the boost. However, with our present knowledge of nutrition, efficient and balanced rations can be had without the added labor and expense of sprouting grain.

In a study of sprouted oats as a feed for dairy cows, the Michigan Agricultural Experiment Station obtained the following results (Report from Quarterly Bulletin, Michigan State University, East Lansing, Vol. 44, No. 4, May, 1962, pages 654–665.):

● *Increase in feed weight.*—The sprouted grain weighed from 4.2 to 7.5 times more than the dry oats, but this increase was mostly water.

● *Comparative analysis.*—In comparison with the dry oats, the sprouted grain showed 61% increase in fiber, 17% increase in crude protein, 15% decrease in nitrogen free extract, and 8 to 23% less dry matter.

● *Digestibility.*—The dry matter, energy, protein, and TDN in the sprouted oats were less digestible than that in the dry oats.

● *Yield of milk and butterfat.*—No statistically significant differences in milk yield or butterfat production were obtained when sprouted oats were compared with oats in a dairy trial.

● *Low energy dairy ration.*—When sprouted oats was added to a low energy dairy ration (one in which cows were fed only 1 lb. of grain for every 5.0 lbs. of milk produced; instead of the usual 1: 2½ to 3.0), a small increase in milk production resulted. But, on this point, the Michigan State scientists reasoned—"Any form of additional energy would have produced a similar result. . . . This could explain some of the results observed on farms."

● *Cost.*—The sprouted oats cost over four times more than plain oats, or similar grains.

● *Conclusion.*—As a result of this experiment, the Michigan scientists concluded:

> The cost of sprouted oats was over four times that of the original oats or similar grains. This high cost plus (1) loss in nutrients during sprouting, (2) the decreased digestibility of sprouted oats, and (3) no observed increase in milk production when sprouted oats was added to an adequate ration indicate that this feed has no justification for being included in any modern dairy ration.

Without doubt, the findings of the Michigan study are applicable to horses, or to any other class of livestock.

HYPERION.—A Thoroughbred horse bred and owned by Lord Derby. Hyperion was winner of the Derby and the St. Leger in 1933. Also, he made a phenomenal record as a sire. Hyperion died in 1960.

HYPERSENSITIVITY.—A state in which the body reacts to a foreign agent more strongly than normal.

I

ICELAND PONY.—This is the leading pony breed of Iceland, from which it takes its name. There are two types of Iceland Ponies; one used for riding, and the other for draft purposes. Representatives of the breed are short and stocky, and have a large head, intelligent eyes, a short neck, and a heavy mane and forelock. They stand 12 to 13 hands high.

IDENTIFICATION.—Horses are identified by methods much like the human system of fingerprinting used by the FBI and by police departments throughout the world.

With registered horses, marking is a means of ascertaining ancestry or pedigree. In racehorses, an infallible means of identification is necessary to prevent a "ringer"; the name once given to a

Fig. I-1. Close-up view of a lip tattoo under the upper lip of a horse. The prefix letter denotes the age of the horse, and the numbers denote The Jockey Club registry number. Any attempts to tamper with or remove the tattoo would be immediately revealed by scars on an otherwise smooth lip.

horse that was falsely identified, with the idea of entering him in a race with slower horses where he was almost certain to win. In the early 1920's, the most common camouflage for a ringer was a coat of paint—hence the terms "dark horse" and "horse of another color." Formerly, the ringer's nemesis was rain; today it is the lip tattoo system or the photographs of his chestnuts. Through these the public is guaranteed the identity of each and every horse running in major races. The lip tattoo consists of branding, with forgery-proof dye, the registry number under the upper lip of the horse, with a prefix number added to denote age. The process is both simple and painless.

Pinkerton's and others have "fingerprinted" the horse's chestnuts or night-eyes—the horny growth on the inside of each of the four legs. Studies have revealed that the chestnuts of no two horses are alike, and that, from the yearling stage on, these protrusions retain their distinctive sizes and shapes. The chestnuts are photographed, and then classified according to size and distinctive pattern.

Cold branding is a new method of horse identification. It makes use of a super-chilled (by dry ice or liquid nitrogen) copper branding "iron" which is applied to a closely-clipped surface, to produce either (1) no hair or "bald brands" on

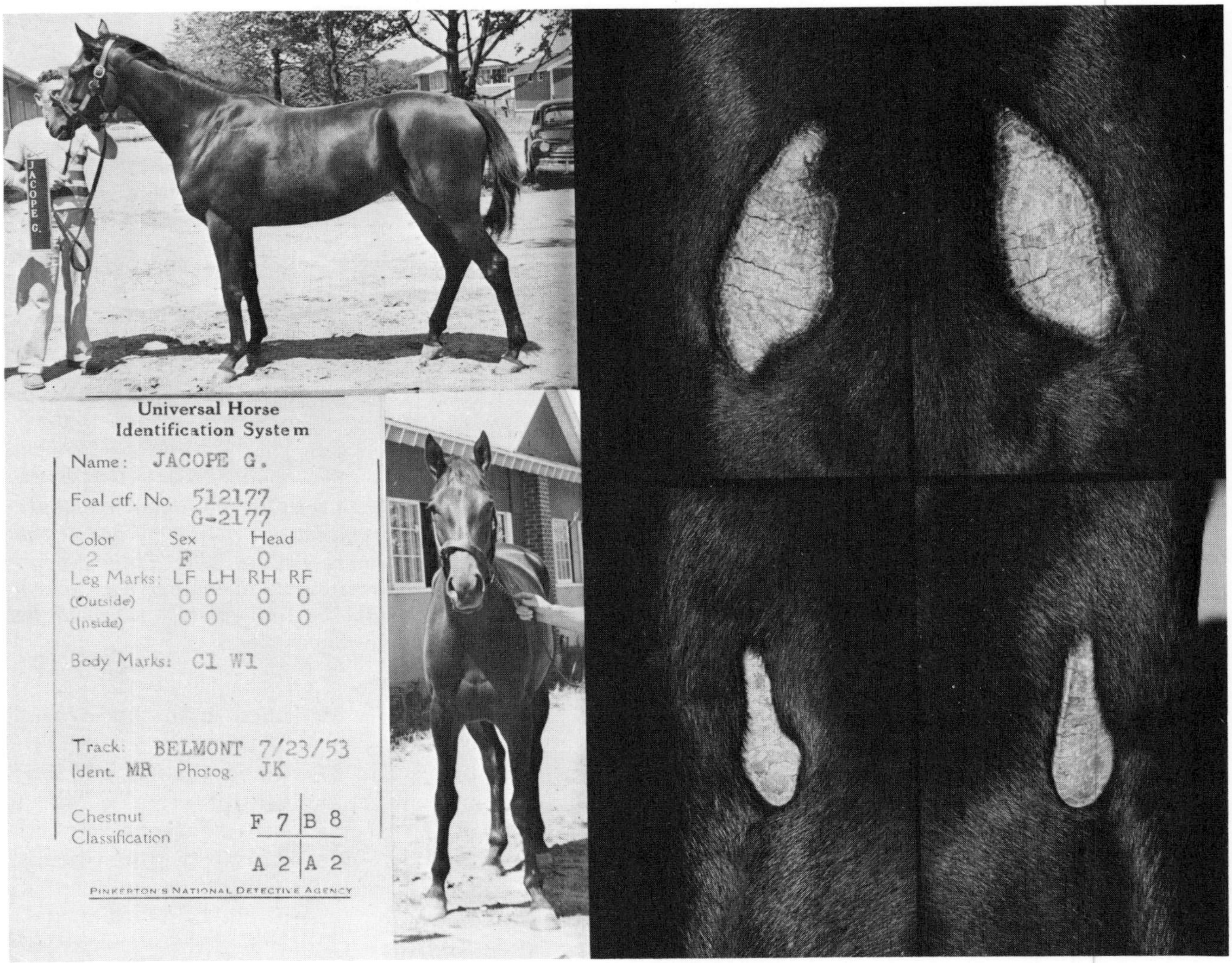

Fig. I-2. *Universal Horse Identification System, showing (1) code card, and (2) horse "chestnut." (Courtesy, Pinkerton's National Detective Agency, Inc.)*

white areas or on white animals, or (2) white hair brands on colored animals. Horses may be cold branded under the mane, with brands one to two inches high. Horsemen who have need for some method of individually marking or identifying horses would do well to try cold branding.

(Also see BRAND.)

IMMUNITY.—When an animal is immune to a certain disease, it simply means that it is not susceptible to that disease.

The animal body is remarkably equipped to fight disease. Chief among this equipment are large white blood cells, called phagocytes, which are able to overcome many invading organisms.

The body also has the ability, when properly stimulated by a given organism or toxin, to produce antibodies and/or antitoxins. When an animal has enough antibodies for overcoming particular (disease-producing) organisms, it is said to be immune to that disease.

When immunity to a disease is inherited, it is referred to as a natural immunity.

Acquired immunity or resistance is either active or passive. When the animal is stimulated in such manner as to cause it to produce antibodies, it is said to have acquired active immunity. On the other hand, if an animal is injected with the antibodies (or immune bodies) produced by an actively immunized animal, it is referred to as an acquired passive immunity. Such immunity is usually conferred by the injection of blood serum from immunized animals, the serum carrying with it the substances by which the protection is conferred. Passive immunization confers immunity upon its injection, but the immunity disappears within three to six weeks.

In active immunity, resistance is not developed until after one or two weeks; but it is far more lasting, for the animal apparently keeps on manufacturing antibodies. It can be said, therefore, that active immunity has a great advantage.

It is noteworthy that young suckling mammals secure a passive immunity from the colostrum that they obtain from the mother for the first few days following birth.

IMPORT.—To bring horses from another country.

IMPORTED HORSES, DESIGNATION OF.—In registering horses from another country in the registry's stud book of their breeds, the certificates of registration issued bear the abbreviation Imp. and the country of export; e.g., Imp. Hydroplane (Eng.). When a name, such as Hydroplane has been previously granted to a horse foaled (born) in this country, a symbol is added; e.g., Imp. Hydroplane II (Eng.). Imported is also denoted by an asterisk in front of the name; e.g., *Hydroplane II (Eng.).

INBREEDING.—See BREEDING HORSES.

INCENTIVE BASIS FOR THE HELP.—Big horse establishments must rely on hired labor, all or in part. Good help—the kind that everyone wants—is hard to find; it's scarce, in strong demand, and difficult to keep. And the horse enterprise manpower situation is going to become more difficult in the years ahead. There is need, therefore, for some system that will (1) give a big assist in getting and holding top-flight help, and (2) cut costs and boost profits. An incentive basis that makes hired help partners in profit is the answer.

On a horse establishment, the author recommends that profits beyond the break-even point (after deducting all expenses, including the sal-

ary of the owner) be split on an 80:20 basis. This means that every dollar made above a certain level is split, with the owner taking 80 cents and the employees getting 20 cents. Also, there is merit in an escalator arrangement; with the split changed to 70:30, for example, when a certain plateau of efficiency is reached. Moreover, that which goes to the employees should be divided on the basis of their respective contributions, all the way down the line; for example, 25 percent of it might go to the manager, 25 percent might be divided among the foremen, and 50 percent of it divided among the rest of the help; or that which goes to the employees may be divided on a prorata of salary basis.

INCENTIVE BASIS FOR THE BREEDING ESTABLISHMENTS.—On horse breeding establishments there is need for some system which will encourage caretakers to (1) get a high conception rate; (2) be good nursemaids to newborn foals, though it may mean the loss of sleep; and (3) develop and sell surplus animals advantageously.

From the standpoint of the owner of a horse breeding establishment, production expenses remain practically unchanged regardless of the efficiency of the operation. Thus, the investment in land, buildings and equipment, stallion and broodmares, feed, and labor differs very little with a change (up or down) in the percent foal crop; and income above the break-even point is largely net profit. Yet, it must be remembered that owners take all the risks; hence, they should benefit most from profits.

Gross income in horse breeding operations is determined primarily by (1) percent conception on mares bred, (2) percent foal crop, and (3) prices on horses sold. The first two factors can easily be determined. Usually, enough horses are sold to establish prices or values; otherwise, the going price can be used.

INCENTIVE BASIS FOR A RIDING STABLE.—An incentive basis for riding stable help is needed for motivation purposes, just as it is in breeding horses. It is the most effective way in which to lessen absenteeism; make for superior training, teaching, and public relations; and improve housekeeping.

For an incentive basis in a riding stable to work at its best, the organization should have each Instructor-Trainer under the supervision of the Director of Riding Stable, and responsible for a specific unit of 40 to 80 horses. This includes serving as a working foreman in their care, and handling all the instruction and training therewith.

This unit-responsibility-and-care arrangement is patterned after Grosbois in France, and Newmarket in England, where it has been highly successful for many years. It will require that the facilities be developed with the unit type of operation in mind. But it has the very great virtue of making each Instructor-Trainer responsible for the success of his (or her) division—horses, facilities, keep of premises, and instruction—thereby minimizing supervision and avoiding "passing the buck." In addition, each Instructor-Trainer is responsible for such assignments as delegated by the Director, including record keeping.

In the operation of a riding stable, where teaching equitation and training horses are the two primary sources of income, there is need for Instructor-Trainers who are able to (1) keep their stables filled with horses in training, and (2) keep their classes filled with students; for, here again, the overhead cost is little different between well-filled and empty classrooms and stables. The incentive basis will accomplish these objectives.

INCISORS *(teeth)*.—The 12 front teeth of a horse. The 2 central incisors are known as middle incisors, centrals, pinchers, or nippers; the next 2—one on each side of the nippers—are called intermediates; and the last, or outer pair, the corners.

(Also see AGE.)

INCOME TAX.—See TAXES, INCOME.

INDIAN BROKE.—Horses trained to allow mounting from the off side.

INDIAN PONY.—An unimproved, small, hardy, vigorous Western horse descended from stock introduced by the Spaniards and redomesticated by the Indians.

INDIRECT REIN *(neck reining)*.—An opposite or bearing rein, the action of which is to press against the horse's neck on the side opposite to the direction in which the horse is required to move. In all dressage work, the indirect rein plays an important part. When used on Western horses, it is called neck reining.

INDOOR RINGS.—See RINGS (indoor and outdoor.)

INDUSTRY, MAGNITUDE OF HORSE.—See MAGNITUDE OF HORSE INDUSTRY.

INFLUENZA, EQUINE.—See EQUINE INFLUENZA.

INGESTION.—The taking in of food and drink.

IN-HAND.—Refers to horses shown in breeding classes or halter classes.

(Also see SHOW—In hand.)

INHERITANCE.—See HEREDITY IN HORSES.

INHERITANCE.—The gift and estate tax systems were completely changed by the Tax Reform Act of 1976. In the past, there were 2 separate tax systems: (1) a gift tax with its own rate schedule and its own $30,000 lifetime exemption for every donor (and also a $3,000 annual exclusion per donee not changed by the '76 Act); and (2) an estate tax with its own schedule of rates and with its own $60,000 exemption. To get maximum benefits, family estate planning often had to be based on the best combination of lifetime gifts and estate bequests. The '76 Tax Reform Act changed all this. In place of the $30,000 lifetime gift exemption and the $60,000 estate exemption, there is a single "unified" credit against both estate and gift taxes and a single "unified" gift and estate tax rate schedule. The result is that gifts made during life are taxed at the same rate as transfers made after death by will, joint tenancy or otherwise. The amount of tentative tax in either case is figured from the unified gift and estate tax schedule and the credit subtracted to find the tax payable. The credit can be used against gift tax, entirely or in part, or it may be used against estate taxes. But whatever amount is used against gift tax is not available for use against estate tax. The credit is phased in over a 5 year period; $30,000 in 1977, $34,000 in 1978, $38,000 in 1979, $42,500 in 1980, and $47,000 in 1981 and thereafter. The unified gift and estate tax schedule follows:

If Tentative Tax Base is More Than——	But Not Over——	Tentative Tax is——	Of Excess Over——
($)	($)	($ + %)	($)
0	10,000	18% of such amount	
10,000	20,000	1,800 + 20%	10,000
100,000	150,000	23,800 + 30%	100,000
500,000	750,000	155,800 + 37%	500,000
1,000,000	1,250,000	345,800 + 41%	1,000,000
5,000,000	——	2,550,800 + 70%	5,000,000

INSIDE ROLL.—The inside roll, which is becoming a conventional part of Western competitions, is performed as follows:

1. *First, perfect the rollback.*—The rollback is a turnaround in place in which the horse pivots on his rear feet to reverse his direction. It's like the military drill, "To the rear—march." Perfecting the rollback may take days, weeks, or months, depending upon the temperament of horse and rider.

2. *Second, do the inside roll.*—Take your horse to the arena; walk him until he is moving freely and calmly; gallop him counter-clockwise (to the left) around the ring, which, of course, calls for a left lead; when midway down one side of the ring, turn your horse toward the center of the ring, or to the left; when he has taken 5 to 10 strides toward the center, turn him again to the left, head straight back toward the arena fence (or edge) that you just left; as he reaches the fence, without slackening speed, turn him to the right, and proceed on a right lead.

INSURANCE, HORSE.—The ownership of a fine horse constitutes a risk, which means that there is a chance of financial loss. Unless the owner is in such strong financial position that he alone can assume this risk, the animal should be insured.

Several good companies write horse insurance; and, in general, the policies and rates do not differ greatly. The provisions and rates quoted in Table I-1 approximate those used by most underwriters.

It is noteworthy that the two major causes of death to horses (other than old age) are fire and colic. Fire claims more lives, but the value of horses dying from colic is greater. This is because valuable horses are more often stabled in fireproof buildings.

In order to obtain insurance, the following information is generally required: identification (markings and/or tattoo) of animal, age, individual valuation, and a statement of health from the local veterinarian.

It is recommended that the person desiring or having insurance confer with a broker who makes a specialty of horse insurance, read the policy with care, and change the provisions of the policy at such intervals as required or when special circumstances arise.

(Also see LAW AND HORSES.)

INTELLIGENCE OF HORSES.—Psychologists judge the intelligence of an animal (1) by the size of its brain in relation to body size, and (2) by its ability to learn to find food. Based on these criteria, the horse stands very low on the totem pole of animals. The brain is small in relation to body size, and the dog, pig, and rat are far more adept at solving a maze in order to get food. However, it is the author's contention that the horse is far more intelligent than these two measures would indicate. For one thing, solving a maze in order to find food favors the scavengers. The dog, the pig, and the rat are all scavengers; hence they have connived for their food since the beginning of time. But the horse, whose natural food was the grass that lay all around him, never had to develop this kind of intelligence. Indeed, had equines not been smart, they would not have made it through fifty-eight million years. Were it not for his mental faculties rather than muscular force, man might find himself under the saddle or between the shafts.

A well-mannered horse may be said to be the

TABLE I-1

HORSE INSURANCE; COVERAGE AND RATES

Type of Coverage	Annual Rate	Comments
	%	
Full mortality. This pays the policy holder the insured value of the horse upon death from any cause or when an injury is so severe as to justify death to relieve pain and suffering. a. For broodmare or stallion . . . . b. For show horse or hunter . . . . c. For flat racing: (1) Mare or stallion . . . . (2) Gelding . . . . d. For steeplechase horse	 4½ 5½ 7¾ 8½ 9	Value usually set by purchase price. But, value may be reappraised on basis of horse's accomplishments. Rates given to the left apply to age 12. From 13 on, insured value of animal decreases 20%/year and premium rate increases 1%/year. Rate decreases as value increases.
Limited mortality. It does not pay for death attributable to disease, but covers death losses due to other causes.	3	Not a popular insurance. Sometimes used where animals are exposed to such hazards as heavy traffic or game hunters.
Loss of use. Available for show horses (not race horses). Covers inability to perform, due to injury or disease, that does not result in death.	2½	Animals must first have full coverage; hence, the rate is added thereto. With loss of use, owner collects 60% of insured value and keeps the horse.
Fire, lightning, and transportation.	1½	Public carriers are insured, but only up to $200 per horse.
Stallion fertility. Pays if stallion is unable to breed because of infertility or physical injury.	2½	Available to owner or syndicate members.
Unborn foal. Covers from time pregnancy examination shows mare in foal until 30 days after birth.	17	Value of foal is calculated at 3 times stud fee if stud fee is under $10,000; or 2½ times if stud fee is over $10,000.

combined result of desirable heredity, skillful training, and vigilant control. Once conception has taken place, it is too late to change the genetic makeup—the native intelligence—of the animal. However, the eventual training and control of the horse are dependent upon how well the trainer understands equine mental faculties as well as methods of utilizing these faculties so that the desired performance may be obtained.

The following points are submitted in support of the intelligence of the horse:

● *The horse has primeval instincts and a highly developed, but very specialized, degree of intelligence.*—The horse learned to be ever alert —to interpret the slightest rustle of a leaf and the faintest whiff of an unknown scent. He remembered the best grazing areas, the freshest water holes, and the most protected areas; these he returned to with the seasons. He learned to

Fig. I-3. Foals are intelligent—and curious, too. (Photo by Ernst Peterson, Hamilton, Montana; courtesy, Margit Sigray Bessenyey)

free himself when trapped in boggy or craggy country. He learned to communicate warning concerning danger and movement, so that the herd could stick together in its flight and fight.

● *Horses can find and communicate with each other.*—Without doubt, this trait accounts, in part at least, for the foundation stock for the American Indians and the hardy bands of Mustangs—the feral horses of the Great Plains. In some mysterious manner, the abandoned and stray horses of the expeditions of De Soto and Coronado found and communicated with each other; otherwise they could not have reproduced.

Fig. I-4. Horses do find and communicate with each other. (Photo by Dave Smith, Mesa, Ariz.)

● *The horse has a homing instinct.*—Through sound, scent, or some sense of which we do not know, the horse is able to find his way back to his own stable over many miles of unknown and previously untraveled territory.

● *The horse will protect and defend himself, but he is not an animal of aggression.*—Each stallion leader is very good at protecting his harem.

When frightened or facing danger, the stallion warns his band with snorting and restless movements and takes his place at the head of the herd, ready for battle if necessary. The members of his group immediately fall behind him, the foals and the pregnant mares in the middle and the barren mares bringing up the rear. Then, led by the stallion, the whole band gallops away.

Except for a stallion that challenges another because he wants to take over his mares, the horse does not attack—he only defends.

● *The horse has the intelligence to untie knots and open latches.*—Horses will figure out how to undo knots and latches of the most intricate kinds.

● *The horse has an excellent memory.*—To a very considerable degree the horse's aptitude for training is due to his memory, for he remembers or recognizes the indications given him, the manner in which he responded, and the rewards or punishments that followed his actions.

Many examples substantiating the excellent memory of horses could be cited, but only one will be related. Legend has it that the Arabs selected their mounts for memory and discipline by shutting them in a corral without water until they were extremely thirsty. Then they would turn them out so that they could go drink from a nearby stream. But before they reached the water, they would call them by blowing a bugle. The ones who remembered—who responded to the bugle and returned to the corral, rather than quench their thirst—were retained; the ones who forgot—who ignored the call and went for water —were culled.

(Also see BEHAVIOR OF HORSES; and MOHAMMED'S TEN HORSES.)

INTERFERING.—The striking of the fetlock or cannon by the opposite foot that is in motion is known as interfering. This condition is predisposed in horses with base-narrow, toe-wide, or splay-footed standing positions.

If a faulty position of the limbs is the cause, corrective shoeing involves the following: Ascertain the exact part of the hoof that does the striking, diminish the size of the hoof at that point, regulate the entire plantar surface of the hoof, make the shoe straight along the region that strikes—that is, without curve, and so fit the shoe to the foot that one-third the thickness of the wall will extend beyond the shoe. Where interfering is so pronounced as to produce serious injuries, use a shoe with no nails in the inner branch.

INTERNATIONAL ARABIAN HORSE ASSOCIATION.—224 E. Olive Ave., Burbank, Calif. 91503 (See Appendix for complete breed registry association list.)

INTERNATIONAL BUCKSKIN HORSE ASSOCIATION, INC.—P. O. Box 357, St. John, Indiana 46373. (See Appendix for complete breed registry association list.)

INTESTINAL THREADWORMS.—See THREADWORMS.

INTESTINE (LARGE AND SMALL).—

LARGE INTESTINE.—The large intestine of the horse is divided into the cecum (4 feet long and 1 foot in diameter; contents fluid), great colon (12 feet long and 10 inches in diameter; contents fluid to semi-fluid), small colon (10 feet long and 4 inches in diameter; contents solid), and rectum.

In the cecum, sometimes called the water gut, digestion (fermentation) continues, limited vitamin synthesis occurs, and nutrients are absorbed.

The great colon is usually distended with feed. In it, there is a continuation of the digestion of feed by digestive juices, bacterial action, and absorption of nutrients.

In the small colon, the contents of the digestive tract become solid and balls of dung are formed.

SMALL INTESTINE.—The small intestine is the tube that connects the stomach with the large intestine. The average is about 7 feet long, and 3 to 4 inches thick when distended, with a capacity of about 12 gallons.

The small intestines of the horse and the cow have about the same total capacity, although the organ of the cow is nearly twice as long and half as thick.

In the horse, as in the ruminant, the enzymes of the pancreas and liver assist in further breaking down the protein, fats, and sugars which escape breakdown by the gastric juices of the stomach.

IN THE MONEY.—A racehorse, show horse, or jumper that wins and receives prize money is said to have been "in the money."

INTRADERMAL.—Into, or between, the layers of the skin.

INTRAMUSCULAR.—Within the substance of a muscle.

INTRAPERITONEAL.—Within the peritoneal (abdominal) cavity.

INTRAUTERINE.—Within the uterus.

INTRAVENOUS.—Within the vein or veins.

INTRODUCTION OF HORSES TO U.S.—See HISTORY OF HORSES IN U.S.

IN VITRO.—Occurring in a test tube.

IN VIVO.—Occurring in the living body.

IODINE.—See MINERALS.

IODINE DEFICIENCY (GOITER).—A deficiency of iodine. Iodine deficiency in the pregnant mare may result in the birth of goitrous (enlargement of the thyroid gland) foals, and/or foals that are weak at birth—that may be unable to suckle and may die.

CAUSE.—A failure of the body to obtain sufficient iodine from which the thyroid gland can form thyroxine (an iodine-containing compound).

SYMPTOMS.—Foals may be goitrous and/or weak.

Fig. I-5. Newborn weak colt affected with simple goiter due to deficiency of iodine during prenatal period. (Courtesy, Western Washington Agricultural Experiment Station)

DISTRIBUTION AND LOSSES CAUSED BY.—Northwestern U.S. and the Great Lakes region.

TREATMENT.—Once the iodine-deficiency symptoms appear in foals, no treatment is very effective.

CONTROL.—At the first signs of iodine deficiency, an iodized salt should be fed to all horses.

PREVENTION.—In iodine-deficient areas, feed iodized salt to all horses throughout the year. Salt containing 0.01 percent potassium iodide is recommended.

REMARKS.—The enlarged thyroid gland (goiter) is nature's way of attempting to make sufficient thyroxine under conditions where a deficiency exists.

IRISH HUNTERS.—The Irish Hunter originated from crossing Thoroughbreds on Irish Draft Horses. It is characterized by its very considerable size and ruggedness, with a heart to match.

IRON.—See MINERALS.

ISOLATION.—See QUARANTINE.

J

JACK.—1. *Equus asinus.* A male ass or donkey. (Also see BREED (S) .)
2. A bone spavin. (Also see UNSOUNDNESSES.)

Fig. J-1. American Jack. Note his heavy bone, well set legs, and good head and ears.

JACKASS.—See ASS.

JACK SPAVIN.—See BONE SPAVIN.

JAW.—As commonly used by horsemen, the word "jaw" refers to the lower part of the head from the throatlatch to the lower lip. The jaw should be broad and strongly muscled.
(Also see PARTS OF A HORSE—Fig. P-4.)

JENNET (A JENNY).—1. *Equus asinus.* A female ass or donkey. (Also see BREED (S).)
2. A small Spanish horse, popular in the twelfth century and valued for its easy gaits, called a Jennet or Genet. It is probable that most easy-gaited horses—including the Narragansett Pacer, the American Saddle Horse, the Tennessee Walking Horse, and the Paso Fino—carry blood of the Jennet of Spain.

JERK LINE.—A single rein, originally used in Western U.S. It was fastened to the brake handle and ran through the driver's hand to the bit of the lead animal.

JEWELRY.—Excess jewelry in horse shows is frowned upon. Hence, jewelry should be appropriate and worn with discretion.
(Also see CLOTHES FOR RIDERS.)

JIGGING.—The action of a horse which refuses to walk and substitutes a short-paced uneasy trot. It is a most annoying habit. Such a horse has not been properly trained. Hence, a fresh start should be made in schooling. The animal should be longed and ridden many hours at the walk.

JOB DESCRIPTION.—See MANAGEMENT.

JOCKEY.—A rider of either sex, whether professional or amateur, who rides racehorses.
Jockeys are both born and made. They were born to be small people; and they are made as jockeys if they possess courage and intelligence. A famous observation, which the author once overheard in a jockeys' room before a race, was: "What would we all be if it weren't for racing? We'd all be bell-hops." But, the jockey might well have added that they would be bell-hops anyway if they didn't have the "guts" to ride hell-bent down a track at 40 miles an hour, delicately balanced in a pair of short stirrups, amid forty-eight flying steel plates and six thundering tons of horseflesh—calmly, but with split-second timing, planning every move as they ride.
Jockeys weigh anywhere from 94 to 116 pounds, with an average of about 105 pounds. The author's friend, Johnny Longden, one of the all-time greats, weighed 113 pounds.

JOCKEY CLUB.—Probably the most exclusive club in America, with only 78 members. The Jockey Club is custodian of the American Stud Book, registry of Thoroughbred horses. It was started in 1893, and was patterned after The Jockey Club of England, which was formed in 1752. (See Appendix for complete breed registry association list.)

ADDRESS.—300 Park Avenue, New York City, New York 10022.
The Jockey Club of England is headquartered at Newmarket.

JOCKEY SEAT.—The seat used by jockeys in flat racing. They use incredibly short straps so that they may keep all of the weight out of the saddle.

JOCKEY STICK.—A device to prevent crowding when driving with a single rein. It consists of a stick fastened to the hame of the near horse and the bit of the off horse.

JODHPUR BOOTS.—A type of boot worn under jodhpur breeches, with elastic sides or buckle over the front so as to protect the instep from undue pressure of the stirrup iron.

JODHPUR BREECHES.—A popular type of breeches named after the state of Jodhpur, in India, where they are still worn. The legs of Jodhpur breeches extend down to the ankle, thereby rendering unnecessary high boots or leggings.

JOG CART.—A cart longer and heavier than a racing sulky, used in warm-up miles because it's more comfortable for the driver than a sulky.

JOGGING.—A slow warm-up exercise of several miles with the horse going the wrong way of the track.

JOG TROT.—A slow, smooth trot required in some Western classes.

JOINT ILL.—See NAVEL INFECTION.

JUDGES.—See HORSE-SHOW JUDGES.

JUDGING HORSES.—The word judging implies the comparative appraisal or placing of several animals in which they are measured against a standard or ideal.

Judging horses, like all livestock judging, is an art, the rudiments of which must be obtained through patient study and long practice. Successful horsemen are usually competent judges. Likewise, shrewd traders are usually masters of the art, even to the point of deception.

Fig. J-2. Prof. Richard Johnson, Head, Department of Animal Science, California Polytechnic State College, San Luis Obispo, officiating at Poly Royal. (Courtesy, California Polytechnic State College)

Accomplished stockmen generally agree that horses are the most difficult to judge of all classes of farm animals. In addition to considering conformation—which is the main criterion in judging other farm animals—action and numerous unsoundnesses are of paramount importance.

To become a good horse judge, study and know (1) the parts of a horse (see PARTS OF A HORSE), (2) the proper weight or value of each part—a score card may be used for this purpose (see SCORE CARD), (3) blemishes and unsoundnesses (see UNSOUNDNESSES), (4) how to determine age (see AGE), (5) the gaits (see GAITS), and (6) colors and markings (see COLORS AND MARKINGS OF HORSES).

(Also see CONFORMATION; and SELECTING AND JUDGING HORSES.)

WHAT TO LOOK FOR IN HALTER CLASS.—A horse must first conform to the specific type which fits him for the function he is to perform. Secondly, he should be true to the characteristics of the breed that he represents. Regardless of type or breed, however, Table J-1 is a handy judging guide.

JUDGING PROCEDURE FOR PERFORMANCE CLASSES.—Custom decrees somewhat different show-ring procedure in judging different classes. Halter classes are first examined while lined up side by side, or while being led in a circle and later inspected while moved one at a time; whereas performance classes are first examined with the entire class in action, and later lined up for close inspection. In judging performance classes, the officials should be thoroughly familiar with, and follow, the show rules; either local or the American Horse Shows Association, Inc., whichever applies. If the judge is in doubt as to what is expected of a performance class, he should seek the advice of the steward.

After a judge has inspected a light horse performance class, both in action and when lined up, it is considered entirely proper to request that certain animals be pulled out and again put through their gaits. Fig. J-3 shows the common method of examining a three-gaited Saddle Horse performance class.

TABLE J-1

HANDY JUDGING GUIDE FOR LIGHT HORSES

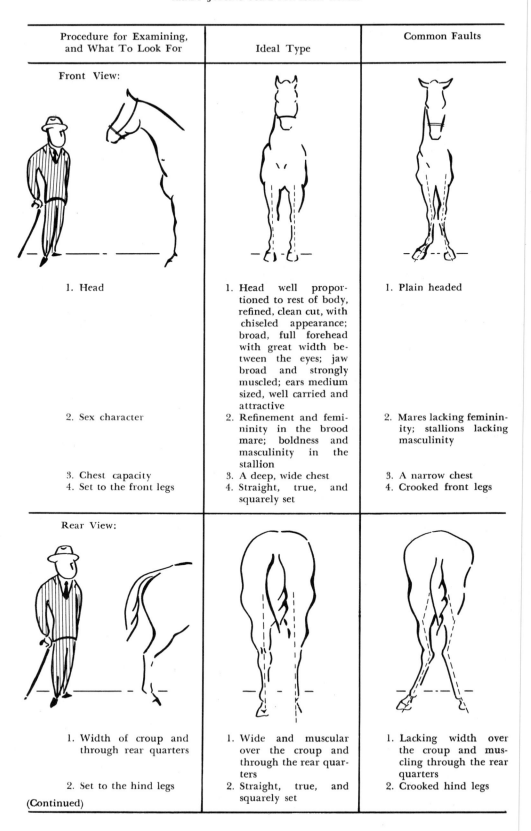

Procedure for Examining, and What To Look For	Ideal Type	Common Faults
Front View:		
1. Head	1. Head well proportioned to rest of body, refined, clean cut, with chiseled appearance; broad, full forehead with great width between the eyes; jaw broad and strongly muscled; ears medium sized, well carried and attractive	1. Plain headed
2. Sex character	2. Refinement and femininity in the brood mare; boldness and masculinity in the stallion	2. Mares lacking femininity; stallions lacking masculinity
3. Chest capacity	3. A deep, wide chest	3. A narrow chest
4. Set to the front legs	4. Straight, true, and squarely set	4. Crooked front legs
Rear View:		
1. Width of croup and through rear quarters	1. Wide and muscular over the croup and through the rear quarters	1. Lacking width over the croup and muscling through the rear quarters
2. Set to the hind legs	2. Straight, true, and squarely set	2. Crooked hind legs

(Continued)

Procedure for Examining, and What To Look For	Ideal Type	Common Faults
Side View: 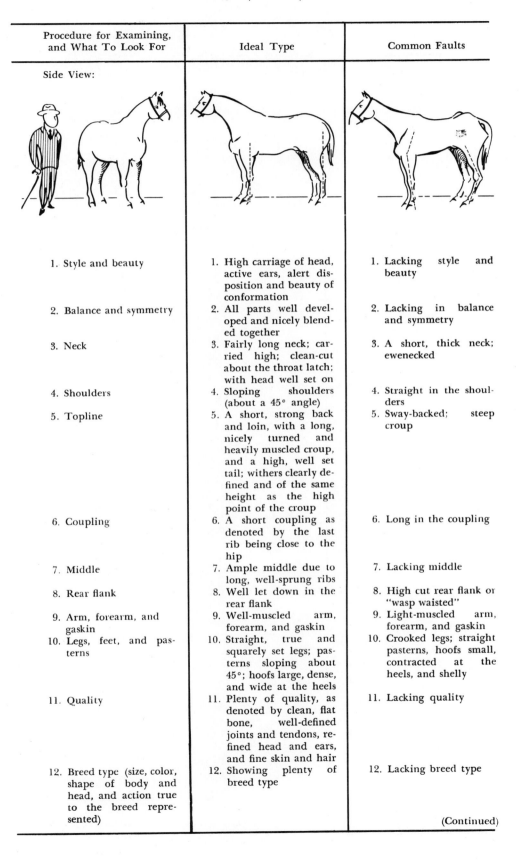		
1. Style and beauty	1. High carriage of head, active ears, alert disposition and beauty of conformation	1. Lacking style and beauty
2. Balance and symmetry	2. All parts well developed and nicely blended together	2. Lacking in balance and symmetry
3. Neck	3. Fairly long neck; carried high; clean-cut about the throat latch; with head well set on	3. A short, thick neck; ewenecked
4. Shoulders	4. Sloping shoulders (about a 45° angle)	4. Straight in the shoulders
5. Topline	5. A short, strong back and loin, with a long, nicely turned and heavily muscled croup, and a high, well set tail; withers clearly defined and of the same height as the high point of the croup	5. Sway-backed; steep croup
6. Coupling	6. A short coupling as denoted by the last rib being close to the hip	6. Long in the coupling
7. Middle	7. Ample middle due to long, well-sprung ribs	7. Lacking middle
8. Rear flank	8. Well let down in the rear flank	8. High cut rear flank or "wasp waisted"
9. Arm, forearm, and gaskin	9. Well-muscled arm, forearm, and gaskin	9. Light-muscled arm, forearm, and gaskin
10. Legs, feet, and pasterns	10. Straight, true and squarely set legs; pasterns sloping about 45°; hoofs large, dense, and wide at the heels	10. Crooked legs; straight pasterns, hoofs small, contracted at the heels, and shelly
11. Quality	11. Plenty of quality, as denoted by clean, flat bone, well-defined joints and tendons, refined head and ears, and fine skin and hair	11. Lacking quality
12. Breed type (size, color, shape of body and head, and action true to the breed represented)	12. Showing plenty of breed type	12. Lacking breed type

(Continued)

Procedure for Examining, and What To Look For	Ideal Type	Common Faults
Soundness:		
1. Soundness, and freedom from defects in conformation that may predispose unsoundness	1. Sound, and free from blemishes	1. Unsound; blemished (wire cuts, capped hocks, etc.)
Action:[1]		
1. At the walk	1. Easy, prompt, balanced; a long step, with each foot carried forward in a straight line; feet lifted clear of the ground	1. A short step, with feet not lifted clear of the ground
2. At the trot	2. Rapid, straight, elastic trot, with the joints well flexed	2. Winging, forging, and interfering
3. At the canter	3. Slow collected canter, which is readily executed on either lead	3. Fast and extended canter

[1] The three most common gaits are given here. Five-gaited horses must perform two additional gaits. In selecting for gait (1) observe horse at each intended gait, and (2) examine trained horses while performing at use for which they are intended.

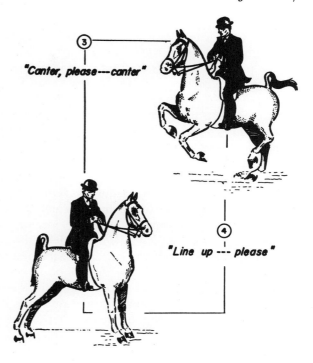

"Walk your horses"

"Trot your horses"

"Canter, please---canter"

"Line up --- please"

Fig. J-3. Diagram showing the customary procedure in examining a three-gaited Saddle Horse in the show-ring. The animal herein shown (1) walking, (2) trotting, (3) cantering, and (4) lined up. Traditionally, the judge or judges work from the center of the ring while the ringmaster requests the riders to execute the different gaits. Three-gaited horses are expected to walk, trot, and canter. Five-gaited horses must perform two additional gaits; namely, (a) slow gait (which is the stepping pace in the show-ring), and (b) the rack. In addition to performing the gaits with perfection, both three- and five-gaited horses should possess desirable conformation, perfect manners, and superior style and animation. (Drawings by R. F. Johnson)

JUGHEAD.—1. A stupid horse.

  2. Also one with a large, ugly head.

JUMPER.—A jumper may be of any breed or conformation. The only requisite is that he be able to jump. Only actual faults over the jumps are scored against him.

JUMPING (*Learning to Jump*).—Before attempting to jump, the rider and mount should master the following prerequisites: walk, trot,

Fig. J-4. Mrs. George R. Draper up on Lavoye, champion jumper in the Fort Leavenworth Show. (Courtesy, Horse Association of America)

and canter; turns and half turns; to ride without stirrups and reins at all gaits; to take the forward seat at the gallop; and to do circles and such exercises as weaving in and out of posts at the gallop, keeping the forward position.

Different riding school instructors use different procedures in teaching jumping, but, with an able instructor and an apt student, the end result is always the same—a competent jumper. With slight variations, the following procedure is used by most instructors in teaching jumping:

● *Step 1, learning balance and movement with the horse's rhythm.*—The first phase, which will take about a month, may be given in a jumping lane. The horse is taught to take the jumps without any help from the rider. The bar is set at one foot. A belt, stirrup leather, or other wide strap, is placed around the horse's neck just in front of the withers. The rider is required to hold on to this strap until he has learned to balance himself properly and to take the jolt of the horse landing with his knees. The student should go through the lane several times at each lesson. When he can balance well, he should be asked to take the same jumps without stirrups, followed by letting go of both the strap and reins (tie up the reins) and extending his arms as the horse jumps.

Next, the rider may dispense with the strap about the horse's neck and hold the reins in the usual manner—with the hands well separated, down, and maintaining constant, but light, pressure on the reins, by going with the mouth. As the rider progresses in skill, the jumps may be raised as high as three feet, but no more.

● *Step 2, learning to steer and control the horse while keeping a jumping position.*—Bars are laid all around the ring. The rider is required to gallop his horse over them, not necessarily in succession, but in and out among them as directed by the instructor.

● *Step 3, learning to negotiate higher jumps.*—After acquiring good control (through Step No. 2), the jumps may be raised, but no wings should be used. Jumps should not be raised until the previous height has been negotiated successfully and in good form; and no more than 10 to 12 jumps should be attempted in one lesson.

● *Step 4, change courses.*—Jump cross-country or in an outside course, with emphasis on control of the gait of the horse.

● *Step 5, change mounts.*—Jump with a variety of horses. Learn to urge the slow horse and to hold back the fast, excitable one.

● *Step 6, jump difficult obstacles.*—Learn to jump the horse over difficult, but not necessarily high, obstacles, such as two chairs placed seat to seat, a saw-horse, a wheelbarrow, a bathtub, etc.

● *Step 7, be a competent jumper.*—When a jumper can clear a half-dozen cots with a man lying on top of one of them, a table with four men sitting around it, a small automobile, and/or a man held in a horizontal position by two other men, he is a competent jumper.

JUMPING COMPETITIONS.—For use in riding schools and small shows, any number of competitive jumps may be devised in addition to the orthodox jumping competitions seen in major shows. The difficulty and nature of the jumps should be determined by the degree of excellence of the competitors. Among the unusual jumping competitions are the following:

● *Mental hazard jumps.*—This type of jumping competition tests the training of the horse. The jumps are not high, but they are unusual. Among them may be a wheelbarrow, a pair of chairs placed seat to seat, a bathtub filled with water, a row of pails hung on a rod which are rattled as the horse approaches, etc.

● *Maze jumps.*—This usually consists of at least 10 jumps, of various types, scattered about the ring, each marked by a red flag. The competitor, who does not see the course until he enters the ring, must take each obstacle at least once, always with the flag on his right. Each rider is timed, and the one who completes the course in the least amount of time is declared the winner. Such a competition demands quick thinking and complete control.

● *Other jumps.*—Among other crowd pleasers are (1) jumping with a glass of water in one hand; (2) taking off a coat while jumping; and (3) jumping in pairs, with the first two jumps taken abreast, followed by the riders separating and coming back over the jumps from opposite directions.

JUMPING FAULTS.—When a jumper touches or knocks down an obstacle, disobeys, or falls, it is called a "fault" and penalized according to horse show rules. For faults and scoring, see the *Rule Book* of the American Horse Shows Association, which is revised annually.

JUMPS *(types).*—There are numerous types of jumps; some are upright, others are spread. Fig. J-5 shows some of the more common types.

LIVERPOOL

DOUBLE OXER

CHICKEN COOP

POST-AND-RAIL

HOG'S BACK

SNAKE FENCE

PEN JUMP

Fig. J-5. Some common types of jumps.

JUSTIN MORGAN.—He was the progenitor of the first famous breed of horses developed in America.

The origin of the Morgan breed was a mere happenstance, and not the result of planned effort on the part of breeders to produce a particular breed of horse which would be adapted to local conditions. Whatever may be said of the greatness of Justin Morgan, he was the result of a chance mating—one of nature's secrets for which there is no breeding formula. In fact, it may be said that had a British general downed his liquor in his own parlor and had a Springfield, Massachusetts farmer been able to pay his debts, the first family of American horses might never have existed. Legend has it that, one evening during the Revolutionary War, Colonel De Lancey, commander of a Tory mounted regiment, rode up to an inn at King's Bridge and after hitching his famous stallion, True Briton, to the rail, went into the inn for some liquid refreshments, as was his custom. While the Colonel was celebrating with liquor and song, the Yankees stole his horse, later selling the animal to a farmer near Hartford, Connecticut. The whimsical story goes on to say that True Briton later sired the fuzzy-haired colt that was to be christened after his second owner, Justin Morgan.

According to the best authorities, Mr. Morgan, who first lived for many years near Springfield, Massachusetts, moved his family to Randolph, Vermont, in 1788. A few years later, he returned to Springfield to collect a debt. But instead of getting the money, he bartered for a three-year-old gelding and a two-year-old colt of Thoroughbred and Arabian extraction. The stud colt, later named after the new owner as was often the custom of the day, became the noted horse, Justin Morgan, the progenitor of the first famous breed of horses developed in America.

Justin Morgan was a dark bay with black legs, mane, and tail. His high head was shapely; his dark eyes were prominent, lively, and pleasant; his wide-set ears were small, pointed, and erect; his round body was short-backed, close-ribbed, and deep; his thin legs were set wide and straight, and the pasterns and shoulders were sloping; his action was straight, bold, and vigorous; and his style was proud, nervous, and imposing. Justin Morgan was a beautifully symmetrical, stylish, vibrant animal—renowned for looks, manners, and substance. It was claimed of him that he could outrun for short distances any horse against which he was matched. He was a fast trot-

ter, a great horse on parade under saddle, and he could outpull most horses weighing several hundred pounds more.

Justin Morgan lived his thirty-two years (1789–1821) in an era of horses rather than in an era of power machinery.

K

KAFIR—See SORGHUMS, GRAIN.

KENTUCKY DERBY.—One of the three Classic Races in America. It was founded in 1875. In 1896, its distance was lowered from 1½ miles to 1¼ miles. The race is for three-year-olds, and it is run at Churchill Downs, Kentucky, on the first Saturday of May.

KICK.—Movement by a horse of the back or front leg, or legs, with intent to hit a person or other object.

KICKING.—See VICES—Kicking.

KICKING STRAP.—A device which should be used on every horse the first time he is put in harness. The kicking strap, which is made of heavy trace leather, passes through the loop

Fig. J-6. Memorial to Justin Morgan, foundation sire of the Morgan breed, located on the former U.S. Morgan Horse Farm (now operated by the University of Vermont), Middlebury, Vermont. The inscription reads as follows: "1921. Given by the Morgan Horse Club to the U.S. Department of Agriculture in memory of Justin Morgan who died in 1821." (Photo by M. E. Ensminger)

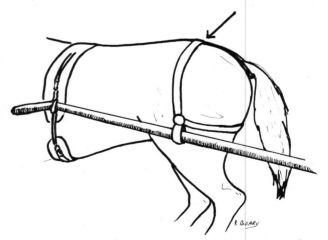

Fig. K-1. Kicking strap, a device for keeping a horse in harness from kicking.

above the crupper, and each end is buckled to a shaft. When properly made and used, a kicking strap will prevent a kicker from (1) raising his croup high enough to damage with his heels, and (2) breaking loose from the vehicle to which he has been hitched.

KNEE.—The joint located at the top of the cannon bone on the front leg. The knee joint in the horse is the counterpart of the wrist joint in man. It should be deep from front to rear, wide when viewed from the front, straight, and taper gradually into the leg. Since the knee and hock joints of the horse are the seat of many unsoundnesses, they should receive every attention.

(Also see PARTS OF A HORSE—Fig. P-4.)

KNEE-SPRUNG (OVER AT THE KNEES; *knee-sprung*).—A condition of over in the knees, or with the knees protruding too far forward. is known as knee-sprung or buck-kneed.

(Also see UNSOUNDNESSES.)

KNIFE.—See SHOEING—Table S-5.

L

LAMENESS.—A defect characterized by the animal favoring the affected foot when standing. The load on the ailing foot in action is eased and a characteristic bobbing of the head occurs as the affected foot strikes the ground. Lameness is a symptom of an ailment or affliction, and not within itself a disease. It is the manifestation of a structural or functional disorder of some part of the locomotory apparatus, evidenced by a limping or halting gait. Any body condition, therefore, that causes pain which is increased by the bearing of weight upon the affected member or by the moving of such distressed part, or which mechanically interferes with the movement of any part, results in an irregularity of locomotion known as lameness. The degree of lameness, though variable in different instances, is in most

Fig. L-1. A lame horse shown favoring the ailing foot—the left front foot.

cases proportionate to the amount of pain caused by movement. This fact serves as a helpful indicator in the matter of establishing a diagnosis and giving the prognosis. This is especially true in cases that are somewhat unusual in character.

TYPES OF LAMENESS.—The following three types of lameness are recognized:

● *Supporting-leg lameness,* which is the most common. The greatest pain is evidenced as the full weight is borne, either in motion or at rest. Diseases of the foot, the lower joints and their ligaments, and the supporting structures of the leg are indicated by this type of lameness.

● *Swinging-leg lameness* in which the movement of the limb in its extension or flexion causes the great pain. Diseases of the shoulder, elbow joints, or the muscles of extension and flexion are indicated by this type of lameness.

● *Mixed lameness,* which is manifested by the symptoms of both of the other types of lameness. This is generally indicative of true joint lameness.

MANIFESTATION OF LAMENESS.—The manifestation of lameness differs according to location; that is, whether it is in the foreleg or hind leg.

● *Lameness in a foreleg.*—In the case of a supporting-leg lameness of the left foreleg, for example, the contact with the ground is lighter and of shorter duration than that of the unimpaired right, and the beat or sound of contact of the diseased member is less distinct. At the moment of contact of the left foot, the head is approaching the summit of an upward gesture or movement of the head and neck, which was begun while the diseased member was in flight. This gesture, by force of inertia, decreases somewhat the weight and concussion borne by the diseased left leg. The head is lowered as the sound right foot contacts the ground and the horse seems to nod. Note that the head is in its lowest position as the sound foot is in contact. The diseased left foot is carried well forward in flight and planted well in advance of the point of contact of the right foot, but the right foot is planted soon after passing the point of contact of the left. In other words the length of the step (distance the foot is advanced beyond the point of contact of the opposite foot) of the diseased leg is lengthened and that of the sound leg is shortened.

In the case of a swinging-leg lameness of the left foreleg, the manifestations would be almost the exact opposite of those outlined above and practically the same as those of a supporting-leg lameness of the right foreleg.

● *Lameness in hind leg.*—In the case of a supporting-leg lameness of the left hind leg, for example, the manifestations are the same as in the case of a similar lameness in the left fore, except that in the head gesture the head is approaching its *lowest* position at the moment the left hind foot strikes the ground, and at the same time the croup is being elevated. The croup is lowered as the sound right hind foot strikes the ground. As in the case of lameness in the foreleg, the gesture or movement of the head and neck is used to lighten the contact on the diseased member. In the case of a swinging-leg lameness of the left hind leg, the manifestations would be the opposite of those just stated.

DIAGNOSIS OF THE CAUSE OF LAMENESS.—Obviously, it is very necessary to locate the cause of lameness before any rational treatment can be instituted. In fact, the diagnosis is often far more difficult than the treatment. In many cases the cause is perfectly obvious, such as an acute tendinitis or a bad quarter crack that is bleeding. In a large percentage of cases it re-

quires, however, a careful and painstaking examination, coupled with a most thorough knowledge of the parts. A routine examination should proceed as follows:

● *Step 1.*—Obtain a complete history of the case.

● *Step 2.*—Stand off and watch the animal at rest. Note the posture, the shoeing, and the evidence of pain, and look for wounds or swelling.

● *Step 3.*—Have the animal walked and trotted up and down grade on both soft and hard footing. Observe the motion of the head, neck, and each hip. Note the length of the steps, the manner in which the legs are moved when extended and flexed, and the length of time each foot is on the ground. This examination should lead to a determination of the lame leg, the type of lameness, and its degree of severity.

● *Step 4.*—Make a detailed examination of the leg starting at the foot and working up. The forelegs are far more frequently the seat of lameness than are the hind legs. Fully 60 percent of all lameness in front is caused by injury or disease of the foot; in 95 percent of all cases the cause is found from the knee down. Shoulder lameness is rare. The cause of a large percentage of lameness in the hind leg is found in the hock joint; other causes are located largely in the foot, pastern, and fetlock. The possibility of each region is eliminated as one works up from the foot. If still in doubt, the foot is examined again. The examination must not be started with a preconceived prejudice towards finding the cause at some particular place, but must be approached with an open mind. The diagnosis of lameness is one of the most difficult tasks and requires a most thorough knowledge of anatomy, physiology, and gaits, as well as a sound and logical manner of procedure.

TREATMENT OF LAMENESS.—The treatment of lameness should be left in the hands of a veterinarian. In certain types of lameness, a farrier can rectify the situation with proper shoeing.

LAMINITIS.—See FOUNDER.

LANDAU.—A vehicle named after Landau, Germany, where it was first manufactured about

1790. It is a four-wheeled covered carriage with the top divided into two sections. The back section can be let down or thrown back while the front section can be removed or left stationary. This vehicle was very popular in England from Mid-Victorian times onward.

Fig. L-2. The Landau, the convertible of great grandfather's time. It was like a coach in shape, except that it was made to open in the center of the roof. Landaus held four people and were usually drawn by two horses.

LANDING.—The contact made by a hunter or jumper with the ground on the far side of an obstacle.

LARGE INTESTINE.—See INTESTINE.

LARGE ROUNDWORMS.—See ASCARIDS.

LARIAT.—A long, light, but strong rope usually made of hemp or strips of hide, used with a running noose for catching livestock.

LASH.—The flexible part of a whip—the end of the whip.

LATCHES (for doors and gates).—Latches used on stable doors and on gates should be designed so that horses cannot open them, and will not be injured by them.

LATIGOS.—The straps used to tighten and fasten the cinch of the stock saddle.

LAW AND HORSES.—In these days of high judgments and high lawyer fees, every horse owner should have a working knowledge of the legal aspects of the horse business. He should know both his rights and his liabilities. To this end, some pertinent points pertaining to law and horses follow:

● AGISTERS.—The term agister is taken from English law. *It refers to a person who feeds, pastures, or cares for horses or other livestock, on a charge basis.*

Most states possess lien laws in favor of agisters; that is, the right to charge against the property of another until a debt is settled. Such laws generally provide that agisters shall have a claim against the horse(s) for agreed or reasonable charges, and that such claim may be enforced by retention and sale of the horse(s) to satisfy it. Unless the law so states, it is usually assumed that the lien expires when possession of the horse(s) terminates.

In order to be entitled to lien consideration, the agister must keep his premises properly fenced, take reasonable precautions against injury to the horse(s), and provide suitable feed, water, and shelter. Also, in case of death or injury loss due to neglect, such as from feeding poisoned grain, the agister is liable if he knows or should have known of the circumstances.

Although interpretations have varied, generally the courts have established that the following rules shall prevail:
  • *That the agister must have the horse(s) in his possession.*—To be entitled to a statutory lien, the person claiming it must have the horse(s) in his charge and under his control. Thus, commercial feed companies are not entitled to a lien on the basis that they supply feed on credit.
  • *That there must be a signed or implied agreement.*—To be entitled to a lien, there must have been an agreement (such as a boarding agreement), either signed or implied, covering the feed, pasture, and/or care of the horse(s).
  • *That a chattel mortgage shall take precedence.*—A chattel mortgage (a mortgage on personal property) takes precedence over an agister's lien unless—
    1. the mortgagee consents to an agreement whereby persons other than the mort-

gagor shall feed and care for the horse (s) , or

2. the mortgage is executed while the horse (s) is under agistment.

• *That the agister must give the owner written notice of sale and publicize same.* —After unsuccessfully requesting reasonable compensation and while still in possession of the horse (s), the agister must give the owner written notice of the time and place of sale as required by the particular lien statute. Also, there must be due publication of notice. The horse (s) may then be sold, with the agister retaining the amount which he claims and paying the balance, if any, to the owner.

● HORSES ON HIGHWAYS.—Sometimes horses get out on highways. If, under these circumstances, a user of the highway runs into a loose horse and is injured and/or has his vehicle damaged, he frequently tries to collect damage from the owner of the horse. Although state, county, and/or township laws vary, and it is not possible to predict with accuracy what damages, if any, may be recovered in particular instances, the following general rules apply:

• If a horse owner is negligent in maintaining his fences and allows his horse (s) to get on the road, he can be held liable for damage resulting to persons using the highway.

• If a horse owner has good fences that are well maintained, but has one or more horses which he knows are in the habit of breaking out, he may be held liable for damages caused by such horse (s) .

• If a horse (s) gets onto the highway, despite the facts that there are both good fences and the horse (s) is not known habitually to get out, the owner may be held liable for any damage inflicted provided he knew that the horse (s) was out and made no reasonable effort to get him in.

• If the horse owner is not negligent in any way, he may or may not be judged liable for the damage inflicted by his horse (s) , depending on the state law and other circumstances.

• If a horseman is driving a horse (s) along or across a highway, he is not likely to suffer liability for any damages unless it can be proved that he was negligent. Stock-crossing signs usually increase the caution exercised by motorists, but do not excuse a horse owner from exercising due care.

• In some states, laws provide that a horse owner may, under the supervision of and with varying amounts of assistance from highway authorities, construct an underpass for his horse (s) and for general farm use.

● BRANDS AND BRAND INSPECTION.—In the range country, brands are used as a means of determining the ownership of horses, and other animals, and of lessening theft. To meet these needs, each of the western states has laws governing the recording and inspection of brands and the transfer of branded animals. These laws generally contain the following provisions:

• *Recorded brands.*—Western horsemen are required to register any brand they use, and, after its approval by the Registrar of Brands of the state agency in charge, to use that specific brand on their horses.

• *Bill of sale.*—When a branded horse (s) is sold, a bill of sale or other written evidence of transfer must be signed by the seller and given to the purchaser.

• *Brand inspectors.*—Brand inspectors, usually under the supervision of the state department or commissioner of agriculture, inspect all horses leaving their state to determine if any are being sold by a person other than the rightful owner. Hence, any branded horse transported across state lines must be accompanied by a brand certificate, issued at the point of origin.

• *Penalties.*—Violations, especially theft and effacing or changing of brands, are subject to severe penalties.

Horsemen operating in those states which have brand laws should become thoroughly familiar with the provisions thereof, and should recognize that law enforcement against rustlers and thieves can only be as good as the existing brands and brand inspection program. In case of suspected theft, the first question that the sheriff is prone to ask is: "What brand did the lost horse have?" Unbranded range horses are an open invitation to thieves, and in the case of loss, make for a cold reception from law enforcement officials, for they can be of little help unless there is positive animal identification.

● ESTRAY (STRAY) HORSES.—*An estray is a domestic animal of unknown ownership running at large, commonly called a stray.*

Although there is no uniformity in the state laws governing the handling of stray horses, some of the more common provisions are:

• That either (1) landowners or (2) local authorities may confine such a stray horse (s) and care for him.

• That following confinement of a stray, a reasonable attempt must be made to locate the owner. Some laws specify public posting and the giving of notice in local papers.

• That the taker-up is entitled to make reasonable use of a stray while he is in his custody; for example, work the horse.

• That upon coming for a stray, the owner must satisfy the claims of the taker-up for feed, housing, care, and other costs.

• That if the owner does not claim his horse (s), he either (1) becomes the property of the taker-up, or (2) must be sold at public auction, with reimbursement made to the taker-up for expenses incurred and with the balance turned in as county funds.

● TRESPASS BY ANIMALS.—Horse owners who do not use reasonable care in restraining a horse (s) may be held liable for damages caused by his trespassing. Among the kinds of damages for which the courts have held that the owner may be responsible are:

• The destruction of growing crops.

• The transmitting of disease.

• The breeding of a mare (s) by a trespassing stallion. The amount of damages in such cases is based on the difference in value to the owner between the actual progeny and intended progeny. Damage may be considered where the mare is a registered purebred and the culprit is a scrub.

Generally state laws stipulate that the owner of land on which a horse (s) is trespassing may do anything reasonable to terminate the trespass, including the following:

• Drive him back to the place from whence he came.

• Call the owner and ask him to get him.

• Confine, feed, and care for the horse (s) until the owner comes and takes him; collect costs for same.

● FENCING, LEGAL ASPECTS OF.—Most states have laws pertaining to boundary fences. In some states, however, the fencing regulations are left largely to the counties and townships. Although these laws vary greatly from state to state and are subject to frequent change, the following conditions usually prevail:

• *Boundary fences.*—Usually state laws require every landowner to enclose his land with a fence tight enough and strong enough to turn a horse (s).

Some states deny the landowner any damages for trespass of a horse (s) even if he does have his land properly fenced; whereas other states permit collection of damages for trespass by a horse (s) though the landowner suffering the damages does not have his own land fenced.

Also, it is a rather common point of law that the condition of the fence at the point where the horse (s) passes over or through in trespassing determines whether it is a suitable fence. The fact that it is not high enough at some other point, or that someone left a gate open on the other side of the farm, has nothing to do with the case. Thus, the argument is settled solely by the condition of the fence at the place where the horse (s) went through, and not by its condition at any other place.

Although state laws vary rather widely, the predominant decisions of state courts on various situations involving horses and fences are as follows:

1. When the horse owner has good fences, is not aware that his horse (s) habitually breaks out, has not been negligent, and makes an immediate attempt to get him back when he does break out, he is not liable for damage caused by him.

2. When a horse (s) breaks through an adjoining owner's part of a division fence, and such fence is not good, the owner of the horse (s) cannot be held liable for damages inflicted by his trespass.

3. The owner of a horse (s) may be held liable for damages inflicted by his trespass provided—

a. His horse (s) is known to be in the habit of breaking out, regardless of how good the fences may be.

b. His fences are not good.

c. He has caused their trespass through negligence, such as by leaving a gate open, or by stampeding a horse (s) until he breaks out.

● *Misdemeanor.*—In some states, if anyone willfully or negligently (1) leaves open or tears down a gate provided for the convenience of the public, (2) tears down a fence on another person's property, or (3) allows a horse (s) to run at large, the act is classed as a misdemeanor. Upon conviction, such person is subject to fine or imprisonment or both.

● LICENSED LIVESTOCK OPERATIONS.—Although state laws vary, the following horse and related livestock operations are generally subject to license and regulation:

    Auction sale ring operations
    Auctioneers
    Commission merchants handling horses and horse products
    Dead animal disposal
    Dealers of horses
    Feed dealers
    Horseshoers
    Public carriers of horses and other livestock
    Racetrack operators
    Rendering plant operation
    Stallions for public service
    Traders (itinerant) of horses
    Veterinarians

● ZONING.—In recent years, there has been much concern over the problem of pollution of the environment (air, water, and soil) and its effect on human health. Some of this concern stems from horses kept in the suburbs, with some environmentalists protesting on the basis that they make for more flies, dust, and odors. This has resulted in zoning.

Thus, the horse owner who desires to keep a horse in his back yard, on a plot of land within corporate limits of a municipality or within an urban area, should first consult the zoning ordinance to determine if there are any restrictions against keeping a horse (s) .

Most zoning regulations are local ordinances, covering a municipality, a county, or certain zoning districts. Also, there are rapid and basic changes in zoning ordinances; many cities and counties are rewriting and making changes in them. Thus, a prospective horse owner should check with local zoning authorities before purchasing a horse to be kept at home.

● LIABILITY.—Most horse owners are in such financial position that they are vulnerable to damage suits. Moreover, the number of damage suits arising each year is increasing at an almost alarming rate, and astronomical damages are being claimed. Studies reveal that about 95 percent of the court cases involving injury result in damages being awarded.

The owner of a horse (s) may be held liable for personal injuries caused by the horse (s) under the following circumstances:

● When he negligently allows or causes the horse (s) to commit the injury.

● When he is aware that he owns a vicious horse (s) , and when such a horse (s) inflicts injury upon someone who was not acting negligently.

● When his horse (s) gets loose at a show and injures a spectator.

● When his horse (s) jumps out of his corral or pasture and is hit by a car, causing damage to the car or injury to its passengers.

Several types of liability insurance offer horses (s) owners a safeguard against liability suits brought as a result of alleged injuries suffered by other persons or damage to their property caused by a horse (s) .

Comprehensive personal liability insurance protects a farm operator who is sued for alleged damages suffered from an accident involving his property or family. The kinds of situations from which a claim might arise are quite broad, including suits for injuries caused by horses, equipment, or personal acts.

Both employer's liability insurance and workmen's compensation insurance protect horse owners against claims or court awards resulting from injury to hired help. Workmen's compensation usually costs slightly more than straight employer's liability insurance, but it carries more benefits to the worker. An injured employee must prove negligence by his employer before the company will pay a claim under employer's liability insurance, whereas workmen's compensation benefits are established by state law, and settlements are made without regard to who was negligent in causing the injury. Comditions governing participation in workmen's compensation insurance vary among the states.

● LIABILITY INSURANCE.—Private insurance companies have available, at nominal premiums, general farm liability policies that give horse owners complete coverage, including all the farm, home, automobile, and personal liability insurance. For information relative to such policies, one should check with his local insurance agent.

In these times of high court judgments, some of which exceed $100,000, it is imperative that the horseman have adequate insurance protection. Without such protection, or without substantial wealth, he is at the mercy of the claims-conscious public. A simple judgment of $50,000 to $100,000, or even less, could put him out of business unless he had adequate insurance to cover the judgment.

Most horsemen strive to keep their fences in proper repair, their equipment in satisfactory order, their employees properly educated about the hazards of the occupation in which they are engaged, and to handle their entire operation in a safe and sane manner. Yet, accidents do happen, and, when that time comes, an insurance policy is the answer to the financial part of the problem.

Recently, the insurance industry developed liability policies designed specifically for the farmer and stockman. These policies are blanket-type liability policies designed to cover the farmer's legal liability arising out of his operation of the farm or ranch. Some of the general provisions covered by such policies are:

• Liability for bodily injury or property damage to employees or guests.

• Medical aid where the policyholder is liable.

• Property damage as a result of breachy animals.

• Liability for accidents on highways and public roads caused by animals.

• Bodily injury and property damage liability for personal acts of the horseman and his family.

Such policies, being tailored for the actual needs of farmers and ranchers, are quite flexible and can be written to suit each individual's particular needs.

The important thing is that the horseman should take advantage of adequate liability coverage, which can be obtained at little added cost, for the time is past when one can have a secure feeling with a $10,000 policy. The high cost of claim settlement and the increased amount of jury verdicts makes it desirable that limits of liability be increased to at least $100,000, and there are times when that limit of liability is not adequate. There should be adequate coverage to assure the horseman protection when and if needed and to keep him in business.

● WORKMEN'S COMPENSATION ACTS.—The workmen's compensation acts are laws making industrial employers responsible for injuries to their employees and laying down certain conditions with respect to liability insurance. Under certain conditions, the courts have ruled that those laws also apply to farm workers, including horse farm workers.

Horse owners who employ three or more workers, even if only part time, and do not carry workmen's compensation insurance, may be liable for judgment for damages if an accident injures a workman.

Workmen's compensation insurance, available to farmers at moderate cost, protects the employer against all claims for damages arising from injuries to an employee. Horse owners can obtain full information on this insurance, as well as help in preparing the application, from the local county agricultural agent.

● GUIDES TO KEEPING OUT OF LEGAL DIFFICULTIES.—Herewith are some handy guides to keeping out of legal difficulties:

• *Use written contracts.*—Use written contracts instead of verbal contracts whenever possible, because there is less opportunity for dispute later.

• *Pay for an option.*—An option or promise to leave an offer open should always be secured by a small payment; otherwise the agreement may be revoked at pleasure.

• *Require surrender of a note.*—Upon paying a note, require its surrender. Otherwise it may be sold and you may be required to pay it again.

• *Give adequate warning when lending a treacherous horse.*—If a treacherous horse is lent to a neighbor or friend, he should be warned in writing of these traits; otherwise the owner may be held liable for any harm or damage that the horse may inflict.

• *Consider trees on boundary lines as joint property.*—Trees standing on boundary lines are the property of both owners, and their disposal must be by mutual agreement. Also, one cannot legally claim fruit from a tree standing upon another man's property even though the branches extend over the boundary.

• *Be aware of auto passenger responsibility.*—If the owner of an auto offers a pedestrian (or hitchhiker) a ride, he may be liable for any injury to him because of careless driving, defective equipment, or any action whereby an accident results.

• *Pay money only to an authorized agent.*—Never pay money to an agent unless you know he is authorized to make collections. When payment is made, be certain to secure a signed receipt.

• *Pay by check.*—Pay debts and bills by check; then there is written proof of payment.

• *Have a will made.*—Most important of all, the horseman should have a will that covers his property and disposes of it in keeping with his wishes. A properly drawn will may be as important as a deed to a farm or ranch; can help the survivors avoid many problems; and may save a considerable amount of expense in that it usually simplifies the probating of an estate. The latter point is increasingly important in these times of high state and federal taxes on estates.

With the advent of increased use and speed of automobiles, and of increased air travel, the will not only should cover the possibility of the husband and wife passing away at about the same time, but also should stipulate who is to be the guardian and trustee of any minor children, should both parents be killed.

For information relative to estate planning, the horseman should see his local attorney or the trust department of his local bank or trust company.

(Also see TAXES, INCOME.)

LAXATIVE.—A feed or drug that will produce bowel movements and relieve constipation. Linseed meal and bran mashes are laxative feeds. Common drug laxatives used by horsemen include epsom salts, Glauber's salts, and linseed oil.

LEAD.—The leading foot (leg) of a horse under saddle. When cantering circularly, the foot to the inner arc of the circle—clockwise, a right foot lead; and counter-clockwise, a left foot lead.

LEADERS.—The head team in a four-, six-, or eight-horse hitch.

LEADING THE HORSE.—Always lead the horse from the left side. Reduce the length of the lead strap or rope by a series of "figure 8" folds or by coils held in the left hand. Hold the upper part of the lead strap or rope in the right hand. If the horse is well-mannered, give him 2 to 3 feet of lead so that he can keep his head, neck, and body in a straight line as he moves forward. But keep the lead taut so the horse is always under control. Do not look back.

Horses wearing a bridle are led the same way as indicated above, with the reins grasped in the same manner as a lead strap or rope.

• *Leading a foal.*—A well-fitted halter should be put on the foal when it is 10 to 14 days of age. After it has become accustomed to the halter, in a day or two, tie the foal securely in the stall beside its mother, 30 to 60 minutes daily for 2 or 3 days. Then lead it around with the mare for a few days, and then by itself.

• *Leading a balky horse.*—Never try to pull a balky horse, nor should you whip him. If the horse refuses to go forward, turn him to one side and then to the other; and, before he realizes what's happening, start him out in the desired direction. If this does not work, turn him around several times, then move forward in the desired direction.

• *Leading by the foretop.*—This is not a recommended method of leading. However, on occasion a gentle horse may be led in the following manner: Grasp the foretop in the right hand, put your left hand on the horse's nose above the nostrils, turn the horse slightly to one side, then

Fig. L-3. Proper lead at the canter is important. When going clockwise of the ring, the right foot leads (see top picture). Counter-clockwise, the left foot leads (see bottom picture).

lead off in the desired direction.

• *Leading with a rope or strap.*—If the horse has no halter, bridle, or foretop, take a short length of rope or a strap, slide it over the crest behind the ears, in the right hand grasp the two ends close to and under the throat, put your left hand on his nose above the nostrils, then lead off. The writer has seen Thoroughbred stallions handled in this manner when being shown in their corrals.

• *Leading through a narrow passage.*—Face the horse, take the bridle reins in each hand, raise the hands to about the height of the bit, then walk backward steering and calming the horse so that he does not hit his hips or plunge forward.

• *Leading a horse over rough terrain.*—A rider is much safer on a horse's back than in front of him over rough terrain. When the horse is excessively fatigued or exhausted, or when for other reasons it is desired to dismount and lead him over rough terrain, proceed as follows: Pull the reins over the horse's head, give plenty of slack, keep far enough ahead of the horse so that he doesn't tread on your feet, and hold the eager horse back at intervals by standing directly on the trail and putting both arms straight out. No rider should attempt to take a horse over extremely rough terrain until he has developed considerable skill in horsemanship.

LEAD LINE.—A chain, rope, or strap, or combination thereof, used for leading a horse.

LEAD REIN.—Sometimes a lead rein is used when teaching children to ride. When a beginner is on a lead and riding alongside an instructor or experienced rider, it is usually indicative (1) that the horse is too large or too spirited, or (2) that the beginner suddenly joined a more advanced group of riders. Sometimes the latter is understandable. Generally speaking, a more desirable way is to mount the beginner on a gentle animal of the right size, and let him be responsible for handling his own horse or pony from the start. By so doing, the rider builds confidence, and does not form the habit of wanting the lead rein as a crutch.

LEATHER *(selection and care of).*—Leather tack of superior quality is expensive, but it is usually cheaper in the long run. Good tack should have good care. If properly cared for, it will last for years.
(Also see TACK.)

LEATHER *(to pull, reach for, or grab).*—In the old West, the rider who "pulled leather" (or "reached for leather" or "grabbed leather"—meaning that he took hold of the saddle horn to keep from being thrown) was ostracized by the cowboys. In rodeos, even today a rule in the saddle bronc events is that the rider must never touch the saddle with his hand. He must keep his right hand high in the air and his left hand on the braid of rope attached to the horse's halter.

Among English riders, there is also strong prejudice against holding on to the saddle to help maintain balance. The author is in agreement. However, when a beginner's options are (1) pulling the reins, (2) tumbling off, or (3) holding on to the saddle, good judgment dictates the last choice.

LEFT LEAD.—Left front foot and left rear foot lead on the canter.

LEGAL.—See LAW AND HORSES.

LEGS *(of horse).*—There has long been a saying "no foot, no horse." After all, the value of a horse lies chiefly in his ability to move, hence the necessity of good underpinning. The legs should be straight, true, and squarely set; the bone should be well placed and clearly defined. The pasterns should be sloping; the feet large and wide at the heels and tough in conformation.

The hock should be large, clean, wide from front to back, deep, clean-cut, and correctly set. The knee should be deep from front to rear, should be wide when viewed from the front, should be straight, and should taper gradually into the leg. Since the hock and knee joints of the horse are subject to great wear and are the seat of many unsoundnesses, they should receive every attention.
(See Fig. L-4 and Fig. L-5.)

LEGS *(of rider).*—When mounted, the legs of the rider should hang comfortably with the heels well down and the toes turned out slightly. This position permits proper leg contact with the horse and makes for a more secure seat. The rider's legs are used primarily for the purpose of producing forward movement and increasing the gait. These results are obtained by simple pressure on the horse by the inner calf muscles of the rider. One of the rider's legs may be used with greater force than the other, thereby displacing the horse's hindquarters laterally to prevent him from side stepping, to straighten him, or to change direction in a cramped space.

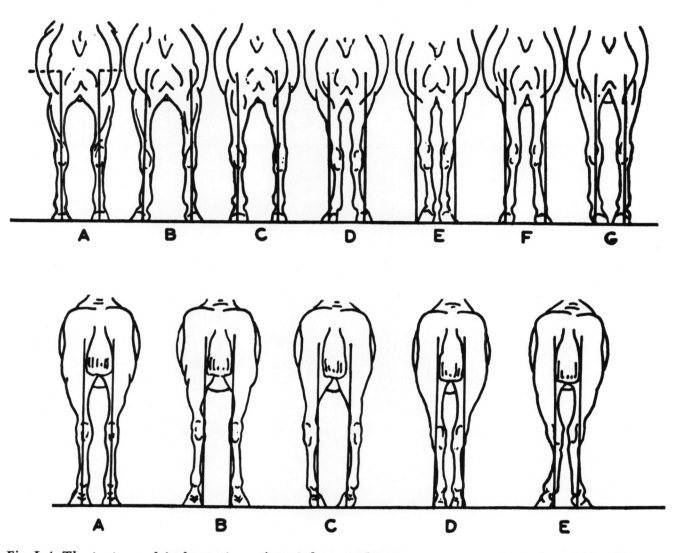

Fig. L-4. The proper and faulty conformation of the forelegs when viewed from the front, and the hind legs when viewed from the rear. The forelegs: A, represents correct conformation; B, splay-footed or base-narrow forefeet, toes cut out, heels in; C, bowed legs; D, knock-kneed, knees set close together with the toes pointing outward; E, conformation predisposing to interfering; F, knees set close together; G, pigeon-toed or toe narrow—a conformation which will cause the animal to wing or throw out the feet as they are elevated. The hind legs: A, represents correct conformation; B, hind legs set too far apart; C, bandy-legged—wide at the hocks and hind feet toe in; D, hind legs set too close together; E, cow-hocked. The direction of the leg and the form of the foot are very important in the horse. (Courtesy, USDA)

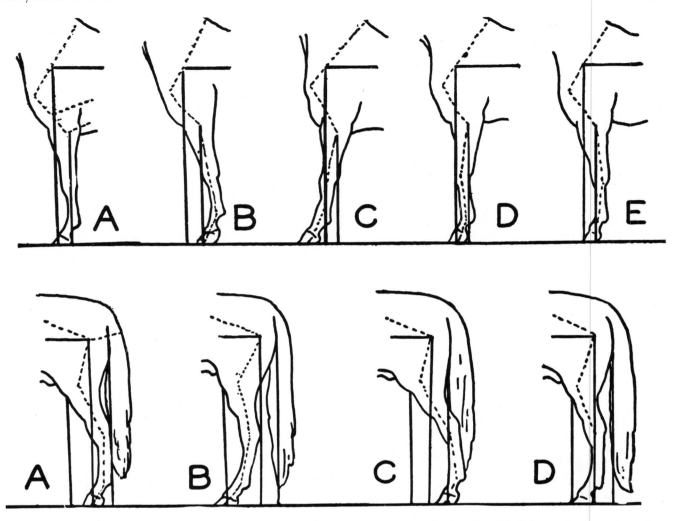

Fig. L-5. The proper and faulty conformation of the forelegs when viewed from the side, and hind legs when viewed from the side. The forelegs; A, correct conformation; B, forelegs too far under the body; C, forelegs too far advanced; D, knee-sprung or buck-kneed—over in the knees; E, calf-kneed—standing with knees too far back. The hind legs; A, correct conformation; B, sickle-hocked—hind legs too far under the body; C, legs set too far back; D, hock joint is too straight. The direction of the legs and the form of the foot are very important in the horse. (Courtesy, USDA)

LEGS OUT OF THE SAME HOLE.—Very narrow-fronted. Such horses usually stand basewide; i.e., the feet stand wider apart than the distance across the legs at the chest.

LEGUMES.—The legumes are soil-building plants. As they grow, the symbiotic bacteria responsible for the formation of the nodules on the roots are able to use the nitrogen in the air and to multiply in the nodules. In turn, the nitrogen becomes available to the legume plant and aids in its nourishment and growth.

The most common legume hays fed to horses are: alfalfa, red clover, alsike clover, crimson clover, and ladino clover. In comparison with grasses, legumes are (1) higher in protein, vitamins, and minerals; (2) higher yielding; and (3) nitrogen-fixing when inoculated. However, a mixture of grasses and legumes is often preferred for reasons of palatability, ease of curing, and erosion control.

LEG UP.—When a rider is assisted into the saddle by someone standing nearby, he is said to be given a "leg up." The person helping should stand to the left and somewhat behind the rider, and should grasp the rider's left leg above the ankle with the right hand. As the rider springs upward, the assistant should lift the leg firmly and somewhat sharply, enabling the rider to clear the saddle with his right leg and then sink into it.

LEPPER.—This is the Irish term for a good jumper.

LETHALS IN HORSES.—Traits that cause death of the animal—either embryonically, at birth, or shortly after birth—are known as lethals. Those that cause death later in life are called sublethals. Many of these conditions are caused by undesirable genes. Any stallion or mare that possesses and transmits a lethal is a detriment to the species.

Most lethal genes are recessive and perpetuated in a population by heterozygous, or carrier, individuals. Fortunately, the frequency of carriers of lethal genes in a population is usually low as a result of natural selection. That is, the individual possessing the lethal trait does not survive to reproduce, with the result that the gene is constantly removed from the population and its frequency is automatically lowered.

Occasionally, breeders unknowingly select and use the carrier of an undesirable gene. A prominent stallion mated to many mares could be involved in such circumstances. A "chance" of this kind could materially increase the frequency of an undesirable gene in a given population.

The author does not wish to imply that lethals are a major threat to the horse industry. It is important, however, that breeders recognize lethals when they occur, and that they take immediate steps to curtail them. Horse populations will always have some undesirable genes. The important thing is that the frequency of such genes remains low.

Among the lethals or sublethals occurring in horses are the following:

• *Bleeding.*—This condition is characterized by fragile blood vessels of the nasal mucosa. It is observed in Thoroughbred horses, and it is thought to be a recessive sublethal.

• *Abnormal sex ratio.*—This is a recessive condition caused by a sex-linked gene, which was first reported in the Oldenburger breed of horses. Ratios of 55 males to 90 females have been reported. About one-half of the males die before birth or during the early stages of postnatal development.

• *Atresia coli.*—This is a recessive condition characterized by closure of the ascending colon. Affected foals stand with difficulty, soon develop colic, and die. Surgery is unsuccessful.

• *Lethal white.*—This low fertility was first reported as occurring in the white horses of the Frederiksborg stud. Some have assumed that factors destroying either gametes or zygotes are responsible.

• *Stiff forelegs.*—This factor, probably a recessive, results in foals being born with stiff forelegs.

• *Epithelio-genesis imperfecti.*—This condition is characterized by skin imperfectly formed on some body areas. Death occurs a few days following birth. It's a recessive.

• *Abracia.*—This lethal, which results in the absence of forelegs, is recessive.

• *Hereditary foal ataxia.*—This is a periodic failure of muscular coordination, with final collapse and death within two weeks.

LEVADE.—An exercise of the *haute école,* especially as performed in the Spanish Riding School in Vienna. In the Levade the horse is in a half-rearing position, with the forelegs well bent and the hind legs in a crouching position. (See Fig. L-6.)

LEVEL, HOOF.—See SHOEING—Table S-5.

LIABILITY.—See LAW AND HORSES.

LICE.—These are small, flattened, wingless insect parasites. Horses are commonly infested by two species of lice; they are the common horse biting louse *Damalinia equi,* and the horse sucking louse, *Haematopinas asini.*

SYMPTOMS.—Symptoms include intense irritation, restlessness, and loss of condition. There may be severe itching and the animal may be seen scratching, rubbing, and gnawing the skin;

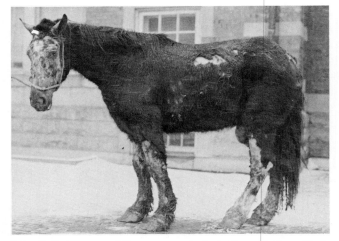

Fig. L-7. Horse with a severe infestation of lice. Note the rough coat and loss of hair caused by gnawing and rubbing. (Courtesy, Department of Veterinary Pathology and Hygiene, College of Veterinary Medicine, University of Illinois)

Fig. L-6. Lipizzan stallion at the Spanish Riding School in Austria doing the Levade between the Pillares. (Courtesy, Spanish Riding School, Wels, Austria)

scabs may be evident and the hair may be rough, thin, and without luster. Lice are likely to be most plentiful around the root of the tail, on the inside of the thighs, over the fetlock region, and along the neck and shoulders.

TREATMENT.—Treat infested animals with any of the following insecticides: Spray with 0.5 percent carbaryl but do not treat more often than every 4 days; spray with 0.3 percent Ciodrin but do not treat more often than every 7 days; spray with 0.125 percent Coumaphos (Co-Ral); spray with 0.15 percent dioxathion (Delnav), but only at 2-week intervals and do not treat foals; or spray with 0.5 percent malathion but do not treat foals under one month old. A second application after an interval of 12 to 14 days may be required. Repeated treatments are rarely necessary to control lice.

PREVENTION AND CONTROL.—Because of the close contact of horses during the winter, it is practically impossible to keep them from becoming infested with lice. For effective control, all horses should be treated with insecticides simultaneously at intervals as needed, especially in the fall about the time they are placed in winter quarters.

DISCUSSION.—Lice are widespread. They retard growth, lower work efficiency, and produce unthriftiness. They show up most commonly on neglected animals in winter.

(Also see DISEASES AND PARASITES; HEALTH PROGRAM; and PARASITES OF HORSES.)

LIGHT DRESSAGE.—The first level of dressage. This involves getting the horse obedient at all gaits on straight lines and circles.

(Also see DRESSAGE.)

LIGHT HANDS.—The desired "light hands" exist when a light feeling extends to the horse's mouth via the reins. In no case should the rein pressure be more vigorous than absolutely necessary, nor should the reins be used as a means of staying on the horse. A horse's mouth is tender, but it can be toughened by unnecessary roughness. Good hands appear to be in proper rhythm with the head of the horse. Beginners are likely to let the hands bob too much, thus jerking the horse's mouth unnecessarily and using the reins as a means of "hanging on" the horse.

LIGHT HORSES.—Light horses are 14-2 to 17 hands high measured at the withers, and they weigh 900 to 1,400 pounds. A hand is 4 inches; thus 14-2 hands is 58 inches, or 14 hands, 2 inches.

LIGHTING (*in the stable*).—Barns and stables should be well lighted, both natural and artificial. All lights, of whatever kind, should be placed above the eye level of the horse. Bulbs in stalls should be protected (recessed or covered with strong metal material) to prevent injury to a horse should he rear and strike them. Artificial lighting should be properly installed and checked at intervals so as to alleviate any fire hazard.

LIMIT CLASS.—According to the *Rule Book* of the American Horse Shows Association, "Limit class is open to horses which have not won six first ribbons at Regular Member Shows of this Association or the Canadian Horse Shows Association in the particular performance division in which they are shown. This rule does not apply to winning at Regular and local Member Shows."

LINEBACK.—An animal having a stripe of distinctive color along the spine.

LINES, REINS.—A leather strap, webbing, or rope attached to the bit or bits for control and direction. In driving, lines are sometimes called reins. In riding, reins are never called lines.

LINIMENT FOR THE HORSE.—A good liniment, properly used, will hasten and assist nature in returning an injured part to normal and relieve fatigue, overexertion, and soreness.

Exercise and work cause greatly increased need for oxygen, carbohydrates, and other nutrients of muscular tissues. When a muscle contracts, certain mechanical, electrical, chemical, and thermal changes take place. It has been shown that during prolonged hard work the expenditure of energy may be eight times greater than during rest; and during very intense muscular use, such as racing, horses may expend one-hundred times more energy than at rest. Such activity cannot be long maintained because of the onset of fatigue.

Fatigue is produced when wastes accumulate faster than they can be removed by the circulation; and, unless the condition is rectified, aches, pains, and soreness follow. Thus, it is imperative that the circulation of the blood be increased in proportion to the demands of the muscle for energy, food, and removal of waste materials. The application of massage, heat, and counter-irritants are methods of providing muscles (and tendons, ligaments, and skin) with better blood circulation.

Liniment is an astringent. Its use, along with massage, stimulates circulation, assists the body in removing waste products of muscle metabolism, and hastens nature in returning an injured part to normal.

The use of liniment is recommended for the following conditions: lameness, stiffness, soreness, strained tendons, sore shins, certain types of arthritis, and swellings, bumps, and bruises. It hastens recovery time and helps to prevent everyday injuries from turning into serious problems.

Also, liniment may be used as a body wash or brace after strenuous workouts or transportation, especially on the horse's legs, to relieve fatigue and overexertion and prevent soreness.

Liniment should be applied (pour-on or dab) to the affected area at full strength, except when used as a body wash and brace. Then, the tissue should be massaged vigorously for 3 to 5 minutes to stimulate circulation, and the animal should be allowed to rest. Repeat treatment every 3 to 4 hours until relief is obtained, and as necessary thereafter.

Where the shoulder, back, and loin areas are involved, best results will be obtained by (1) first applying hot (but do not scald), steaming towels to the affected area, so as to stimulate natural circulation; and (2) then following with an application of liniment, rubbed until dry.

Where a "body wash and brace" is desired, use the liniment according to the manufacturer's directions. Such a brace may be used as a leg and body wash after workouts, to relieve fatigue and overexertion and prevent soreness. Sponge generously over the horse's body and legs.

LINSEED (FLAXSEED).—Linseed or flaxseed is obtained from flax, a fiber plant which antedates recorded history. In this country, most of the flax is produced as a cash crop for oil from the seed and the resulting by-product, linseed meal. Practically none of the U.S. flax crop is grown for fiber, for it is more economical to import it from those countries where cheaper labor is available.

Most of the nation's flax is produced in North Dakota, South Dakota, Minnesota, Montana, Arizona, and California. Normally, an additional quantity of seed is imported and processed in U.S. plants.

LINSEED MEAL.—Linseed meal is a by-product of flaxseed following oil extraction. The oil is extracted by either of two processes: (1) the mechanical process (or what is known as the "old process"), or (2) the solvent process (or "new process"). If solvent extracted, it must be so designated. Horsemen prefer the mechanical process, for the remaining meal is more palatable, has a higher fat content, and imparts more gloss to the haircoat.

Linseed meal averages about thirty-five percent protein content. For horses, the proteins of linseed meal do not effectively make good the deficiencies of the cereal grains; linseed meal being low in the amino acids, lysine and tryptophan. Also, linseed meal is lacking in carotene and vitamin D, and is only fair in calcium and the B vitamins. Because of its deficiencies, linseed meal should not be fed to horses as the sole protein supplement.

Because of its laxative nature, linseed meal in limited quantities is a valuable addition to the ration of horses. Also, it imparts a desirable "bloom" to the hair of show and sale animals.

LIPIZZAN.—See BREED (S).

LIPS.—The lips should be firm but flexible, and carried closed. A drooping lower lip is unsightly and is supposed to be a sign of old age or a lack of courage.

LIP STRAP.—The strap running through the pendant ring on the curb chain and fastening into eyelets on the lower cheekpieces of the bit. It functions in two ways: (1) It helps to regulate and maintain the position of the curb chain with reference to the lower jaw, and (2) it prevents a horse from grabbing the lower cheekpieces of the bit with his lips.

LITERATURE, HORSES IN.—Through the ages, the contribution of horses has extended far beyond their utility value. They have been accorded a conspicuous place in the literature of the day.

By Shakespeare's time (1564–1616), the beautiful Arabian had been imported into Britain; and all over Continental Europe the nobility were establishing magnificent riding stables, staffed by talented riding masters who taught haute école. High-stepping horses prancing down the avenue were a mark of social prestige. Thus, Shakespeare in his first major work, *Venus and Adonis*, describes the stallion as follows:

Sometimes he trots, as if he told the steps,
With gentle majesty and modest pride;
Anon he rears upright, curvets and leaps,
As who should say, 'Lo, thus my strength is tried . . .

Round-hooft, short-jointed, fetlocks shag and long,
Broad breast, full eye, small head, and nostril wide,
High crest, short ears, straight legs and passing strong,
Thin mane, thick tail, broad buttock, tender hide . . .[1]

Few books are destined for the immortality of Anna Sewell's *Black Beauty*, first published in 1877. It's a favorite children's story in which the main character is a horse, *Black Beauty*. It is beautifully written, has great feeling, and is full of practical knowledge. Also, the book has been instrumental in getting people to accord more humane treatment to their horses.

Today, there is an almost limitless output of horse books. The relentless wheels of progress have lifted from the horse—that faithful beast of burden—his role in both agriculture and war. Again the horse is rising, as in Shakespeare's time, to a happy position in recreation and sport. Without doubt, in this role, man's good friend and stout companion will inspire more literature.

---

1. William Shakespeare, *Venus and Adonis* (Stratford-on-Avon: The Shakespeare Head Press, 1905), pp. 12–13.

LIVERY STABLE.—A stable where horses and vehicles were kept for hire, and where stabling was provided. Until the advent of the automobile, the town livery stable, watering trough, and hitching post were trademarks of every town and village. The livery stable was the "rent-a-car" agency of its day. It provided transportation for the country doctor, and for traveling men who arrived by train. Then, in 1908, Henry Ford, produced a car to sell at $825. Improved highways followed closely in period of time. Old dobbin didn't know it at the time, but his days were numbered. Today, the livery stable is of historic interest only.

LOIN.—The loin is that portion of the top from the last ribs to the hips. It should be short, heavily muscled, and strong.

(Also see PARTS OF A HORSE—Fig. P-4.)

LONG-COUPLED.—Too much space between the last rib and the point of the hip.

LONGE (LUNGE).—The longe is a strong light strap (usually made of webbing or leather) about 30 feet long, one end of which is attached by a swivelled snap to the noseband of the cavesson. The young horse can begin training at an early age by means of the longe line. He can be circled to the left and to the right; made to walk, trot, canter, and halt; and to get used to and obey words of command. The longe is especially useful for urban-raised foals, who are limited in space for exercising on natural footing.

Although a young horse can do all kinds of gymnastics without injury when running loose in a corral or pasture, he can be injured by improper use of the longe line. If his head is pulled at the wrong time, or too quickly or too severely, his balance will be destroyed and he may injure a foreleg or foot, throw a curb, or be stifled. (See Fig. L-8.)

LONGEING WHIP.—A typical longeing whip has a stock about four feet long and a lash six to eight feet long. It is used when exercising and disciplining the horse in longeing.

Fig. L-8. Correct method of longeing a horse, with a longeing cavesson and long web tape longe line in use. (Drawing by R. F. Johnson)

LONGELINE (LONGE REINING).—To longeline a young horse, the trainer walks behind it and drives it by a pair of lines long enough for him to stay out of the range of the horse's heels. Basic training can be given by this method without the horse having to bear the weight of a rider. Some trainers believe that such driving of a young horse by the trainer on foot produces more finesse in early training than can be achieved by longeing, though there is not agreement on this point.

LONG HAY.—Uncut hay. It may be in bales or loose.

LOOSE REIN.—"Riding with a loose rein" connotes different things to the Eastern rider and the Western rider.

To the Eastern rider, it means a rein which hangs loosely, without contact between the horse's mouth and the horseman's hand. It is a way of resting a horse. After all, keeping a horse in a high state of collection over a long period of time is rather tiring. Such loose reining should be done at the proper place. It should never be done when riding over rough terrain or when going up and down hill. Also, when on the loose rein the rider should be on constant alert for anything that might frighten the horse and cause him to shy or jump.

To the Western rider, riding with a loose rein means that the reins are held with no tension. The well-trained Western horse is just as aware of movements on the loose rein (a rein with some slack in it) as the Eastern horse is aware of movements of the rein that continually has pressure on it.

In certain horse show classes—notably road hack, hunter hack, and Western pleasure classes—the horses are required to work on a loose rein, to prove that they are not excitable.

LOPE.—The Western adaptation of a very slow canter. It is a smooth, slow gait in which the head is carried low.

(Also see CANTER.)

LOP EARS.—Ears which tend to flop forward and downward, or toward each side.

LOP-NECK, FALLEN-NECK, or BROKEN-CREST.—A heavy neck that breaks over or falls to one side.

LUGGER.—A horse that pulls at the bit.

LUGGING AND PULLING.—Some horses pull on the reins, "lug" on one rein, or bear out or in with the driver, making it hard to drive them and to rate the mile at an even clip.

LUNGE.—See LONGE.

LUNGWORMS (*Dictyocaulus arnfieldi*).—The equine lungworm is very rare in the United States.

SYMPTOMS.—Donkeys seem to be able to carry large numbers of lungworms without showing any symptoms. They develop a tolerance. However, infected foals may become unthrifty and develop a cough. There is a rise in temperature with lungworm infection.

PREVENTION AND CONTROL.—Where

lungworm infection is suspected, a fecal examination should be made. Infected burros should be kept away from foals.

DISCUSSION.—Lungworms may be found in the air passages of the horse and other equines. The male worm reaches a length of about 1 inch, and the female may be about 2 inches long. The eggs are laid in the lungs and pass out of the horse's body through the intestine. They hatch into first-stage larvae that develop eventually into the third, or infective, stage. The infective larvae enter the body through the mouth, travel in the lymph vessels into the thoracic duct, then to the heart, and eventually to the lungs.

(Also see DISEASES AND PARASITES; HEALTH PROGRAM; and PARASITES OF HORSES.)

MADNESS.—See HYDROPHOBIA.

MAGAZINES, HORSE.—The horse magazines publish news items and informative articles of special interest to horsemen. Also, many of them employ field representatives whose chief duty is to assist in the buying and selling of animals.

In the compilation of the list presented (see Appendix II), no attempt was made to list the general livestock magazines of which there are numerous outstanding ones. Only those magazines which are chiefly devoted to horses are included.

MAGNESIUM.—See MINERALS.

MAGNITUDE OF HORSE INDUSTRY.—The following figures show the size of the industry:
- *Number of horses.*—An estimated 8 million.
- *Total investment.*—$13 billion.
- *4-H Club members with horses and ponies.*—320,767 in 1974, double the number that had beef cattle projects.
- *Annual expenditures for horse feed, drugs, tack, and equipment.*—$1,000 per horse, for a total of $8.0 billion.
- *Annual wages paid in the horse industry.*—

Over $1 billion.

• *Annual pari-mutuel taxes paid to the various states.*—Approximately $500 million.

• *Race spectators.*—79 million in 1974, which was 31 million more than went to automobile racing, the second ranking spectator sport.

MAIDEN.—1. A mare that has never been bred.

2. On the racetrack, it refers to a horse (stallion, mare, or gelding) that has not won a race on a recognized track.

3. In the show-ring, it refers to a horse that has not won a first ribbon in a recognized show in the division in which it is showing.

MAINTENANCE.—See FEED.

MAKING A CAST.—This is a hunting term meaning that the Huntsman is having his hounds search a given territory in order to pick up the scent of a fox. If the line (scent) has been lost, the Huntsman may "lift" his hounds and make a cast in a place where he thinks the scent is better or where the fox may have crossed. Or if he feels that the original fox is beyond reach, he may make an entirely new cast in an effort to find a new fox.

MALLENDER *(Chestnut).*—See CHESTNUTS.

MANAGEMENT.—Management is the act, art, or manner of managing, or handling, controlling, directing, etc.

Management gives point and purpose to everything else. The skill of the manager materially affects how well horses are bought and sold, the health of the animals, the results of the rations, the stresses of the horses, the growth rate of the young stock, the performance of labor, the public relations of the establishment, and even the expression of the genetic potential of the horses. Indeed, a manager must wear many hats—and he must wear each of them well.

The bigger and the more complicated the horse operation, the more competent the management required.

Fig. M-1. Good management and good horses make for success in the horse business. (Courtesy, Margit Sigray Bessenyey. Photo by Ernst Peterson)

TRAITS OF A GOOD MANAGER.—There are established bases for evaluating many articles of trade, including hay and grain. They are graded according to well-defined standards. Additionally, we chemically analyze feeds and conduct feeding trials. But no such standard or system of evaluation has evolved for managers, despite their acknowledged importance.

The author has prepared the Manager Check List given in Table M-1, which (1) employers may find useful when selecting or evaluating a manager, and (2) managers may apply to themselves for self-improvement purposes. No attempt has been made to assign a percentage score to each trait, because this will vary among horse establishments. Rather, it is hoped that this check list will serve as a useful guide (1) to the traits of a good manager, and (2) to what the boss wants.

ORGANIZATION CHART AND JOB DESCRIPTION.—It is important that every worker know to whom he is responsible and for what he is responsible; and the bigger and the more complex the operation, the more important this becomes. This should be written down in an organization chart and a job description. (See Tables M-2 and M-3.)

TABLE M-1
MANAGER CHECK LIST

☐ **CHARACTER**
Has absolute sincerity, honesty, integrity, and loyalty; is ethical.

☐ **INDUSTRY**
Has enthusiasm, initiative, and aggressiveness; is willing to work, work, work.

☐ **ABILITY**
Has horse know-how and experience, business acumen—including ability systematically to arrive at the financial aspects and convert this information into sound and timely management decisions, knowledge of how to automate and cut costs, common sense, and growth potential; is organized.

☐ **PLANS**
Sets goals; prepares organization chart and job description; plans work and works plans.

☐ **ANALYZES**
Identifies the problem, determines pros and cons, then comes to a decision.

☐ **COURAGE**
Has the courage to accept responsibility, to innovate, and to keep on keeping on.

☐ **PROMPTNESS AND DEPENDABILITY**
Is a self-starter; has "T.N.T.," which means that he does it "today, not tomorrow."

☐ **LEADERSHIP**
Stimulates subordinates and delegates responsibility.

☐ **PERSONALITY**
Is cheerful; not a complainer.

TABLE M-2

ORGANIZATION CHART FOR _____
(name of horse establishment)

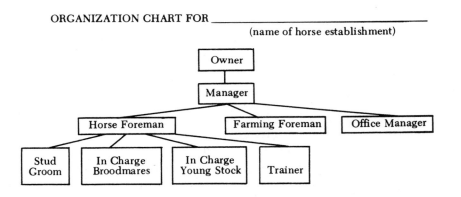

TABLE M-3

JOB DESCRIPTIONS ON _____
(name of horse establishment)

| Owner |
Responsible for:
1. Making policy decisions.
2. Borrowing capital.
(List other.)

| Manager |
Responsible for:
1. Supervising all staff.
2. Preparing proposed long-time plan.
3. Budgets.

| Horse Foreman |
Responsible for:
1. All horse operations.
2. Directing his staff.

| Stud Groom |
Responsible for:
1. Care of stallions.
2. Teasing and breeding mares.
3. Breeding records.

| In Charge Broodmares |
Responsible for:
1. Care of broodmares.
2. Foaling.

| In Charge Young Stock |
Responsible for:
1. Care of young stock, including—
   a. Feeding.
   b. Trimming feet.
   c. Gentling and green breaking.
2. Sale of young stock.

| Trainer |
Responsible for:
1. Preparation of horses for the track.
2. Care and training of horses on the track.

| Farming Foreman |
Responsible for:
1. Crop operations.
2. Maintenance.

| Office Manager |
Responsible for:
1. Records.
2. Budgets.

MANE.—Long hair on the top of the neck.

(See GROOMING A HORSE—Fig. G-3, for styles.)

MANGANESE.—See MINERALS.

MANGE (MITES).—See MITES.

MANGER.—A feed container for horses. It should be placed in the front or in a corner of the stall. Most mangers are made of wood, although many different kinds of materials can be and are used. Also, there are many designs of mangers.

Wooden mangers are usually 30 inches wide and 24 to 30 inches long for horses and 20 inches square for ponies. The height should be 30 to 42 inches for horses and 20 to 24 inches for ponies.

(Also see EQUIPMENT—Feed and Water.)

MANNERS.—A way of behaving. The manners of a horse are very important. They make for pleasurable everyday use, and they count heavily in many horse show classes.

A well-mannered horse responds generously and willingly. He is quiet in the stall; he follows easily when led by the halter shank or bridle; he performs well; and he never kicks, bites, rears, bucks, or balks.

MAN O'WAR.—Ask the person on the street—one who may never have gone to a race—to name the greatest horse of all time and chances are that he'll say, Man O'War. Indeed, if there is any absolute against which greatness in a horse may be measured, it is the legendary Man O'War. "Big Red," as he was known, seemed to have limitless speed. Only once in his 21 starts did his machine-like power fail to propel him first across the finish line; that was when he was beaten by the aptly named, "Upset," at Saratoga on August 13, 1919, after an unfortunate start. As if to redress that wrong, Man O'War trounced Upset with authority the next three times they met. In 8 times of his 11 starts as a three-year-old, he broke either a track or world's record.

Man O'War was born in 1917. Samuel D. Riddle bought him as a yearling at the Saratoga sale, on August 17, 1918, for $5,000.

During his career, talented writers and eloquent speakers extolled him with such superlatives as "look of eagles" and "living flame." But it fell to his groom, Will Harbut, who had quite a way with words as well as with horses, to devise the most fitting description of all. "Man O'War," as Will never tired of telling the thousands who came to see him, "was de mostest hoss dat ever was." During his lifetime, more visitors went to see Man O'War than Mammoth Cave.

Fig. M-2. Man O'War and his groom, Will Harbut. (*Courtesy,* **The Thoroughbred Record.**)

Physically, Man O'War was a glowing chestnut, almost red, standing 16 hands 1⅝ inches. He measured 71¾ inches at the girth and weighed 1,100 pounds in training. As a stallion, his weight reached 1,370 pounds. He was unusually long bodied and powerfully muscled in the gaskins. Estimates of his stride varied anywhere from 25 to 28 feet, although, oddly enough, it was never officially measured.

When training, Big Red's morning came early. He was given his first meal at 3:30 a.m. At 7:30 a.m., he was brushed and massaged; the bandages that he wore at all times except when in action were removed, and his legs were washed; his face, eyes, and nostrils were sponged; and he was given a rubdown with a soft cloth. After work on warm days, he was washed; then he was rubbed thoroughly, his feet were cleaned and dressed, and he was left to rest in his stall. He was fond of his caretaker; he liked to snatch his hat and carry it around as he showed off for visitors.

Most Thoroughbred horses share a universal birthday—January 1. But Big Red was different! At Faraway Farm, near Lexington, where he spent most of his life, his actual foaling date, March 29, was duly observed as a special occasion. He received telegrams, carrots, and other tokens of recognition from all over the country.

The great horse, who was the first to command a $5,000 service fee, was maintained largely for private use. He sired over 300 offspring who won over 1,200 races and earned more than $3½ million.

Big Red died in 1947, at the age of thirty. The author's good friend, the late Ira Drymon, as the Thoroughbred Club's representative, delivered the eulogy before the 2,000 people assembled and over a nationwide radio hookup. As taps were sounded and the mammoth coffin of polished oak containing the body of Man O'War was lowered into his final resting place, men, women, and children wept unashamedly. Today, above the grave stands a life-size-and-a-half statue of the great champion.

The Man O'War legend keeps on keeping on, for he lived and died and won a lasting name and fame—a rare achievement by any beast, or man.

MANURE.—The term manure refers to a mixture of animal excrements (consisting of undigested feeds plus certain body wastes) and bedding.

The rise in light horse numbers, along with the shift of much of the horse population from the nation's farms and ranches to stables and small enclosures in suburban areas, has made for manure disposal problems.

From the standpoint of soils and crops, barnyard manure contains the following valuable ingredients:

● *Organic matter.*—It supplies valuable organic matter which cannot be secured in chemical fertilizers. Organic matter—which constitutes 3 to 6 percent, by weight, of most soils—improves soil tilth, increases water-holding capacity, lessens water and wind erosion, improves aeration, and has a beneficial effect on soil microorganisms and plants. It is the "lifeblood" of the land.

● *Plant food.*—It supplies plant food or fertility—especially nitrogen, phosphorus, and potassium. In addition to these three nutrients, manure contains organic matter, calcium, and trace elements such as boron, manganese, copper, and zinc. A ton of well-preserved horse manure, free of bedding, contains plant food nutrients equal to about 100 pounds of 13–2–12 fertilizer (see Table M-4). Thus, spreading manure at the rate of 8 tons per acre supplies the same amounts of nutrients as 800 pounds of a 13–2–12 commercial fertilizer.

AMOUNT, COMPOSITION, AND VALUE OF MANURE PRODUCED.—The quantity, composition, and value of manure produced vary according to species, weight, kind and amount of feed, and kind and amount of bedding. The author's computations are on a fresh manure (exclusive of bedding) basis. Table M-4 presents data for horses per 1,000 pounds live weight.

The data in Table M-4 are based on animals confined to stalls the year around. Actually, the manure recovered and available to spread where desired is considerably less than indicated because (1) animals are kept on pasture and along roads and lanes much of the year, where the manure is dropped, and (2) losses in weight often run as high as 60% when manure is exposed to the weather for a considerable time.

About 75% of the nitrogen, 80% of the phosphorus, and 85% of the potassium contained in horse feeds are returned as manure. In addition, about 40% of the organic matter in feeds is excreted as manure. As a rule of thumb, it is commonly estimated that 80% of the total nutrients in feeds are excreted by animals as manure.

The urine makes up 20% of the total weight of the excrement of horses. Yet the urine, or liquid manure, contains nearly 50% of the nitrogen, 6% of the phosphorus, and 60% of the potassium of average manure; roughly one-half of the total plant food of manure. Also, it is noteworthy that the nutrients in liquid manure are more readily available to plants than the nutrients in the solid excrement. These are the reasons why it is important to conserve the urine.

TABLE M-4

QUANTITY, COMPOSITION, AND VALUE OF FRESH HORSE MANURE

(FREE OF BEDDING) EXCRETED PER 1,000 POUNDS LIVE WEIGHT

Tons Excreted/ year/1000 Lbs. Live Weight[1]	Composition and Value of Manure on a Tonnage Basis[2]						
	Excrement	Lbs./ Ton[3]	Water	N	P[4]	K[4]	Value/ Ton[5]
			(%)	(lbs.)	(lbs.)	(lbs.)	($)
8	Liquid	400					
	Solid	1600					
	Total	2000	60	13.8	2.0	12.0	4.20

[1] *Manure Is Worth Money—It Deserves Good Care.* University of Illinois Circ. 595, 1953, p. 4.

[2] Last 5 columns on the right from: *Farm Manures,* University of Kentucky Circ. 593, 1964, p. 5. Table 2.

[3] From: Reference Material for 1951 Saddle and Sirloin Essay Contest, p. 43, compiled by M. E. Ensminger, data from *Fertilizers and Crop Production,* by Van Slyke, published by Orange Judd Publishing Co.

[4] Phosphorus (P) can be converted to P_2O_5 by multiplying the figure given above by 2.29, and potassium (K) can be converted to K_2O by multiplying by 1.2.

[5] Calculated on the assumption that nitrogen (N) retails at 20¢, phosphorus (P) at 24¢, and potassium (K) at 8¢ per pound in commercial fertilizers.

Horsemen sometimes fail to recognize the value of this barnyard crop because (1) it is produced whether or not it is wanted, and (2) it is available without cost.

WAYS OF HANDLING HORSE MANURE. —Clay floors cannot be cleaned by flushing with water, and hard stable floors of concrete, asphalt, or wood require considerable bedding to provide softness and comfort. These conditions make it impractical to handle horse manure as a liquid. But horse manure is relatively dry and well adapted to handling as a solid.

In large horse establishments, the use of automatic gutter cleaners can eliminate much of the hand labor in handling manure as a solid. Automatic gutter cleaners may be (1) located in the alleyway or immediately outside the barn, (2) covered except for trapdoors, and (3) designed to carry the manure from the gutter directly into a spreader.

Some large establishments fork the manure from the stalls into the alley and then load it by means of a scraper or power loader. But this method is more messy and less convenient than an automatic gutter cleaner.

Both small and large horse establishments face the problem of what to do with horse manure after it is removed from the stable. Because the feces of horses are the primary source of infection by internal parasites, fresh horse manure should never be spread on pastures grazed by horses. The alternatives for the disposal of horse manure are as follows:

• Spread fresh manure on fields that will be plowed and cropped if there is sufficient land and this is feasible.

• Contract with a nearby vegetable grower to remove the manure.

• Store the manure in a tightly constructed pit for at least 2 weeks before spreading it; this allows the spontaneously generated heat to destroy the parasites.

• Compost the manure in an area where it will neither pollute a stream nor offend the neighbors; then spread it on the land.

OBJECTIONABLE FEATURES OF MANURE. —Despite the recognized value of horse manure, it does possess the following objectionable features:

• It may propagate insects.

• It may spread diseases and parasites.
• It may produce undesirable odors.
• It may scatter weed seeds.

MARE.—By definition, a mare is a mature female, four years or older; in Thoroughbreds, five years or older.

Fig. M-3. Hungarian mare and foal. Owned by Margit Sigray Bessenyey, Hamilton, Mont. Photo by Ernst Peterson, Hamilton, Mont. (Courtesy, Mrs. Bessenyey)

Characteristics found in the mare are likely to be reflected in the offspring. It is fundamental that "like tends to produce like." The broodmare should possess an abundance of femininity in addition to being sound and of good type. She should be of good ancestry, whether purebred or grade.

REPRODUCTIVE ORGANS OF THE MARE. —The mare's functions in reproduction are to (1) produce the female reproductive cells, the eggs or ova; (2) develop the new individual, the embryo, in the uterus; (3) expel the fully developed young at the time of birth, or parturition; and (4) produce milk for the nourishment of the young.

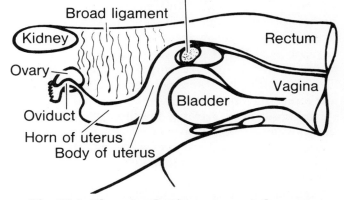

Fig. M-4. The reproductive organs of the mare.

The part played by the mare in the generative process is much more complicated than that of the stallion. It is imperative, therefore, that the modern horseman have a full understanding of the anatomy of the reproductive organs of the mare and the functions of each part. Fig. M-4 shows the reproductive organs of the mare.

The two ovaries are the primary sex organs of the mare. They are somewhat bean-shaped organs 2 to 3 inches long. The ovaries produce eggs. Each egg is contained in a bubble-like sac on the ovary, called a follicle. There are hundreds of follicles on each ovary. Generally, the follicles remain unchanged until puberty when one of them begins to grow because of an increase in the follicular liquid in it; the others remain small. The egg is suspended in the follicular fluid.

When the growing follicle is about an inch in diameter, a hormone causes it to rupture and discharge the egg. This is known as ovulation and is the time when mating should take place. The egg is trapped in a funnel-shaped membrane, called the infundibulum, that surrounds the ovary. The infundibulum narrows into a tube called the oviduct. The oviduct then carries the egg to the uterus, or womb, the largest of the female reproductive organs, where the unborn young, or fetus, will develop.

The lining of the uterus is soft and spongy. It contains a vast network of blood vessels that provide a "bed" for the fertilized egg to settle into and develop. At birth, the heavy layers of muscles of the uterus wall contract with great pressure to force the new animal out through the cervix and vagina.

EXAMINATION OF THE MARE.—Before accepting an outside mare for service, the stallion owner should check every possible condition with care. The stallioner should examine the mare closely and question the owner concerning her health, last foaling date, breeding record, and similar matters. It is wise to require that barren mares be accompanied by a health certificate signed by a veterinarian.

The following types of mares should be rejected:

• Mares showing the slightest symptoms of venereal disease.

• Mares that have an abnormal discharge (such as blood or pus) from the vagina, commonly known as the "Whites."

• Mares affected with skin diseases and parasites.

• Mares suffering from high fevers, which accompany colds, strangles, influenza, shipping fever, and pneumonia.

• Mares that have recently given birth to foals affected with navel-ill.

• Mares that have recently suffered from retained afterbirth.

• Mares that have suffered lacerations in foaling.

• Mares that do not show definite signs of heat.

• Mares under three years of age unless mature and well developed.

• Mares that have a very narrow or deformed pelvis.

• Mares that stay in heat incessantly (nymphomaniacs).

• Mares that are extremely thin or emaciated.

• Mares that have severe unsoundnesses which may be hereditary.

When mares have been barren over an extended period or when there is the slightest suspicion of infection, it is good protection to require a veterinarian's certificate to the effect that the mare is in a healthy breeding condition.

BREEDING HABITS AND CARE OF THE MARE.—A knowledge of the mare's normal breeding habits will help to improve the fertility rate. However, not all mares that conceive give birth to live foals. So, improved care and management of the pregnant mare are important, also. The age of puberty for mares is 12 to 15 months; the duration of heat ranges from 1 to

37 days, and averages 4 to 6 days; the interval between heat periods ranges from 10 to 37 days, and averages 21; and the gestation period ranges from 310 to 370 days, and averages 336.

The following points are pertinent to the care and management of the mare:

● *Age to breed.*—Well-grown fillies may be bred as 2-year-olds, but most fillies are not bred until they are 3 years old.

● *Normal breeding season and time of foaling.*—Spring is the ideal season for both breeding and foaling. Persons who race or show horses want foals to be born as soon as possible after January 1.

Fig. M-5. Foals arriving in the spring have a good start in life. (Courtesy, Margit Bessenyey. Photo by Ernst Peterson)

● *Conditioning for breeding.*—Mares are conditioned by proper feeding and adequate exercise.

SIGNS OF HEAT.—In season, mares generally exhibit (1) relaxation of the external genitals, (2) more frequent urination, (3) teasing of the other mares, (4) apparent desire for company, and (5) slight mucous discharge from the vagina.

THE BREEDING OPERATION.—No phase

of horse production has become more unnatural or more complicated with domestication than the actual breeding operation. This is so because breeders try to get mares bred in about 4 months instead of 12 and have arbitrarily limited the breeding season to late winter and early spring. The following facts and pointers are pertinent to the breeding operation:

● *Hand mate.*—Hand mating, in which the animals are coupled under supervision, is the most common method of breeding. It guards against injury to both the stallion and the mare. However, corral or pasture breeding may be preferable under certain conditions. For example, corral breeding may be resorted to when only one person is handling the breeding operation, and pasture breeding is sometimes followed on the ranges of the West. In corral breeding, the stallion and the mare are turned together in a corral; in pasture breeding, the stallion is turned to pasture with a band of mares.

● *Breed only healthy mares to a healthy stallion.*—Require that all mares from the outside be accompanied by a health certificate signed by a veterinarian.

● *Tease.*—Teasing is the best way in which to make certain that a mare is in season.

● *Wash reproductive organs; bandage mare's tail.*—After making certain that the mare is in season, wash the reproductive organs of the stallion and the external parts of the mare that are likely to come in contact with the reproductive organs of the stallion; bandage the upper 6 to 8 inches of the mare's tail. Place a twitch and hobbles on the mare and allow the sexual act to be completed. Return the mare for retrial approximately 21 days later.

● *Serve.*—It is recommended that the mare be served daily or every other day during the heat period, beginning with the third day.

SIGNS AND TESTS OF PREGNANCY.—The signs of pregnancy are (1) cessation of the heat period, and (2) observed movement of the fetus through the abdominal walls. A veterinarian or an experienced horseman can determine pregnancy by making a rectal examination 40 to 60 days after the last service. Also, tests can be made by a laboratory.

(Also see PREGNANCY SIGNS AND TESTS.)

QUARTERS FOR THE PREGNANT MARE.—Pregnant, idle mares should be turned to pasture. Pregnant mares that are used under saddle or in harness may be given quarters like those of other horses used similarly.

FEEDING THE BROODMARE.—Regular and normal reproduction is the basis for profit on any horse breeding establishment. However, only 40 to 60 percent of mares bred produce foals. There are many causes of reproductive failure, but inadequate nutrition is a major one. The following pointers are pertinent to feeding a broodmare properly:

• Condition the mare for breeding by providing adequate and proper feed and the right amount of exercise prior to the breeding season.

• See that adequate proteins, minerals, and vitamins are available during the last third of pregnancy when the fetus grows most rapidly.

• Lessen and lighten the ration at and after foaling; give less feed and add some wheat bran to the feed. During cool weather, it is important to take the chill off water at foaling time.

• Provide adequate nutrition during lactation, because the requirements during this period are more rigorous than the requirements during pregnancy.

• Make sure that young growing mares receive adequate nutrients; otherwise, the fetus will not develop properly or the dam will not produce milk except at the expense of her body tissues.

EXERCISE.—Mares that have the run of a large pasture will usually get sufficient exercise. Stabled mares should be exercised moderately for an hour daily under saddle or hitched to a cart. Continue this routine to within a day or two of foaling. During the last couple of days, mares may be led.

SIGNS OF APPROACHING PARTURITION.—These signs are a distended udder, which may be observed 2 to 6 weeks before foaling; a shrinkage or falling away of the buttocks muscles near the tailhead and a falling of the abdomen 7 to 10 days before foaling; filling out of the teats 4 to 6 days before foaling; and the appearance of wax on the ends of the nipples 4 to 6 days before foaling. As foaling time draws nearer, the vulva becomes full and loose; milk drops from the teats; and the mare becomes restless, may break into a sweat, urinates frequently, and

lies down and gets up. But there are times when all signs fail, so be prepared 30 days in advance of the expected time.

FOALING PLACE.—When the weather is warm and it can be arranged, allow the mare to foal in a clean pasture away from other livestock. During bad weather, use a box stall which has been cleaned and disinfected with 13 ounces of lye in 10 gallons of water; use one-half strength solution in scrubbing mangers and grain boxes. Sprinkle the floor and walls lightly with quick lime or burnt lime. Provide plenty of bedding for the occasion.

Fig. M-6. Foaling on clean pasture.

Fig. M-7. A few hours old.

FOALING TIME.—The following information and procedure may be helpful during foaling:

● The feed should be decreased and wheat bran should be added.

● An attendant should be near but not in sight.

● Normal presentation consists of the front feet coming first with the heels down (Fig. M-8.). If there is any other presentation, a veterinarian should be summoned at once.

● Make certain that the newborn foal is breathing and that the membrane has been removed from its mouth and nostrils. Then rub and dry the foal with towels, treat the navel cord with tincture of iodine, and let the mare and foal rest for a time. Remove the expelled afterbirth from the stall and burn or bury it; it is usually expelled within 1 to 6 hours after foaling. Clean and rebed the stall after the mare and foal are up. Give the mare small quantities of lukewarm water at intervals and feed considera-

Fig. M-8. Normal presentation. The back of the fetus is directly toward that of the mother, the forelegs are extended toward the vulva with the heels down, and the nose rests between the forelegs (of course, the mare will usually foal lying down, flat on the side with all four legs stretched out).

ble wheat bran for the first few days after foaling; take 7 to 10 days to get the mare on full feed. Be observant; if the mare has much tem-

perature, call a veterinarian. The normal temperature is 100.5°F.

BREEDING AFTER FOALING.—Some horsemen rebreed mares during the first heat after foaling, usually on the eighth or ninth day, providing the birth was normal and the mare suffered no injury or infection. Other horsemen prefer to rebreed mares during the heat period that follows the foal heat (25 to 30 days from foaling), provided there is no discharge or evidence of infection.

WEANING.—See FOAL.

STERILITY OR BARRENNESS IN MARES. —Sterility is a condition of infertility. Whatever the cause, there are no cure-alls for the condition. Rather, each individual case requires careful diagnosis and specific treatment for what is wrong. It should be recognized also that there are two types of sterility—temporary and permanent—although no sharp line can be drawn between them.

Regardless of the cause of sterility, it is well to give a word of caution against the so-called "opening up" of mares, which is the practice of inserting the hand and arm into the genital organs for the purpose of rearranging the organs in order to insure conception. Few laymen, no matter how expert they may classify themselves, have either sufficient knowledge of the anatomy of the mare or appreciation of the absolutely sterile methods necessary in such procedure to be probing about. Moreover, it is only rarely that the reproductive organs are out of place. Unless the "opening up" is recommended and conducted by a veterinarian, it should not be permitted. When performed by an amateur, or even most would-be experts, it is a dangerous practice that is to be condemned.

TEMPORARY STERILITY.—Some common causes of temporary sterility are:

● Lack of exercise, irregular work, and overfeeding accompanied by extremely high condition.

● Overwork, underfeeding, and an extremely thin and rundown condition.

● Nutritional deficiencies.

● Infections of various kinds.

● Some types of physiological imbalances characterized by such things as cystic ovaries or failure to ovulate at the proper time.

• Retained afterbirth or other difficulties encountered in foaling. These may cause inflammation and infection that will prevent conception as long as the condition exists. There is real danger of spreading the infection if the mare is bred while in such a condition.

Temporary sterility can be reduced by removing the cause and correcting the difficulty, whatever it may be.

PERMANENT STERILITY.—Naturally, permanent sterility is much more serious to the horse breeder. Perhaps the most common causes of permanent sterility are:

• Old age, which is usually accompanied by irregular breeding and eventual total sterility.

• Infections in the reproductive tract, usually in the cervix, uterus, or fallopian tubes.

• Some types of physiological imbalances characterized by such things as cystic ovaries or failure to ovulate at the proper time.

• Closure of the female genital organs.

Sometimes a veterinarian is able to correct the latter two conditions; and, on an extremely valuable breeding mare, it may be worthwhile to obtain such professional service in an effort to bring about conception.

MARENGEO.—The favorite mount of Napoleon.

MARK A FOX (to ground).—A hunting term. When hounds bay outside the den of a hunted fox, they are said to "mark the fox to ground."

MARKING.—See IDENTIFICATION.

MARKINGS.—See COLORS AND MARKINGS OF HORSES—Figs. C-9 and C-10.

MARTINGALES.—Martingales are of two types: standing (or sometimes called a tie-down) and running (or ring). The standing martingale consists of a strap which extends from around the girth, between the forelegs, to the noseband and a light neck strap to keep the martingale from getting under the horse's feet when the head is lowered. When properly adjusted, it has the effect of preventing the elevation of the head beyond a certain level without cramping the horse. The standing martingale is most generally employed on saddle horses that rear and on polo ponies and stock horses that endanger their riders by throwing their heads up in response to a severe curb when pulled up sharply. On the other hand, some competent horsemen prefer to use the running martingale on horses that habitually rear. Such horsemen feel that the standing martingale sets the head too high.

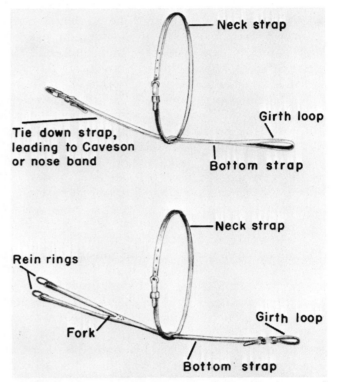

Fig. M-9. The two types of martingales: Upper, standing martingale, sometimes called a tie-down. It is sometimes used on saddle horses that rear and on polo ponies and stock horses that endanger their riders by throwing their heads up in response to a severe curb when pulled up sharply. Lower, a running martingale. It is used for the same purposes as the standing martingale, but permits more freedom of movement; thus it may be used on jumpers. (Drawings by Steve Allured)

The running martingale is not attached to the horse's head but terminates in two rings through which the reins pass. It is used for the same purpose as the standing martingale but permits more freedom of movement. Thus, it is better adapted to and more frequently used for jumping than the standing martingale.

Proper adjustment of the running martingale is obtained when, with the horse's head in a normal position, the snaffle reins stretched from the pommel forms a straight line from bit to pommel.

MASCOT.—A companion for a nervous, high-strung horse that does not like to be alone is known as a mascot. The most common mascots are: ponies, goats, dogs, cats, and chickens. The great Stymie, Thoroughbred winner of $918,485, became attached to a hen of nondescript breeding who came to dinner one day and never left.

Probably the most publicized mascot of all time was the pony, Peanuts, constant companion to the Thoroughbred racehorse Exterminator. Peanuts died three years ahead of the great old gelding. When his pony-pal failed to appear in the stall the next morning, Exterminator stopped eating. He would likely have died of a broken heart had his handlers not acted wisely. They left the remains of Peanuts in the Thoroughbred's stall one night, to demonstrate to him that his mate was dead. All night long, Exterminator lay with his head over the pony's body. By morning he was resigned to the situation. A new pony was brought to him, and the old warrior carried on.

The expression "to get his goat" was born of the common custom of having goats for mascots. Back in the days when skulduggery was as important as form in winning races, the men of one stable sometimes plotted to kidnap the goat-mascot of a rival's horse. By "getting the goat" of a favorite, they cleaned up by betting against a horse that was odds-on to win, but too upset to run at his best.

MASHES.—Mashes are usually made from bran, to which hot water has been added. A hot bran mash is made by putting bran in a pail, then pouring boiling water over it. Cover and allow to steam until cool enough to feed. Sometimes horsemen add a bit of salt or a few carrots to the mixture. Hot bran mashes are excellent for horses if given once a week before a day of rest.

MASSAGE.—The manipulation of tissues by rubbing or stroking with the hand. A hand massage is particularly valuable for certain leg conditions and injuries. It stimulates the circulation and promotes healing of the tissues.

Sometimes massaging is done with a bandage. The horse's flexed lower leg is held across the worker's knee. Then, a straight bandage is put around the cannon once. By holding the ends of the bandage, the worker can seesaw back and forth, thereby creating friction.

MASTER OF FOXHOUNDS (MFH).—The "Master" is the ruler. Where his pack is concerned, his word is law.

MASTER OF FOXHOUNDS ASSOCIATION OF AMERICA.—The Master of Foxhounds Association of America was formed in 1907. Among its functions are (1) the assignment of territories to the various hunts, (2) the designation of "recognized" hunts, and (3) qualifying hunters. Recognized hunts are eligible to compete in horse show classes so designated by the American Horse Shows Association. To qualify, a hunter must have hunted regularly with a Recognized Hunt.

ADDRESS.—Master of Fox Hounds Association, 1044 Exchange Building, Boston, Massachusetts 02109.

MASTICATE.—The act of grinding or crushing feed with the teeth in preparation for swallowing and digestion.

MASTURBATION.—Orgasm (ejaculation) without sexual intercourse.
(Also see STALLION.)

MATRON.—A mare that has produced a foal.

MAVERICK.—A maverick, by definition, refers to any unbranded "critter." The word "Maverick" originated with Texas lawyer-cattleman, Samuel A. Maverick (1803–1870). He once accepted 600 head of cattle as an attorney's fee, and turned them out without branding his young stock. As a result, year after year, his unbranded yearlings fell into the hands of other cattlemen who promptly placed their brands on them. After ten discouraging years of such operation, Maverick sold his depleted herd for the amount of the original fee.

McCLELLAN SADDLE.—This was an old-time U.S. Army saddle, designed by a Union Cavalry officer whose name it bears. It had a split tree and a high pommel and cantle, and it was light. It was very easy on the horse and practical for carrying field equipment. But it was not suitable for equitation, jumping, polo, etc. It is now obsolete.

MEASURING HORSES.—The normal measurements pertinent to a horse are his (1) height, (2) weight, (3) girth, and (4) bone.

HEIGHT.—The height of a horse is determined by standing him squarely on a level area and measuring the vertical distance from the highest point of his withers to the ground. The unit of measurement used in expressing height is the "hand," each hand being 4 inches. Thus, a horse measuring 62 inches is said to be 15–2 hands (15 hands and 2 inches) high. Animals standing less than 14–2 (meaning 14 hands and 2 inches) are classed as ponies.

Instead of actually measuring by calipers or tape, the experienced horseman deftly estimates the height of a horse in relation to his own stature. Thus, by knowing the exact height from the ground to the level of his eyes, the horseman can stand opposite the front limbs of the horse, look to the highest point of the withers, and estimate the height very quickly and accurately.

WEIGHT.—The weight of a horse is best determined by placing the animal on a properly balanced scale. The weight is recorded in pounds in the U.S., and in kilograms in those countries on the metric system.

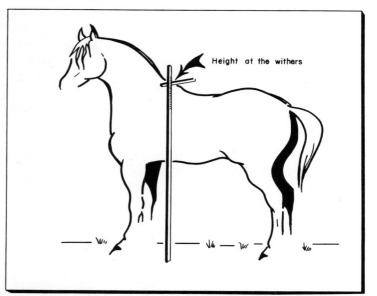

Fig. M-10. The height of a horse is measured from the highest point of the withers to the ground. The experienced horseman deftly estimates the height of a horse in relation to his own stature, and does not use any measuring device. (Drawing by R. F. Johnson)

GIRTH.—The girth is a measure of the circumference of the chest behind the withers and in front of the back. A large girth is desired because it indicates ample space for such vital organs as the heart and lungs.

BONE.—The size of the bone is usually determined by placing a tape measure around the cannon bone halfway between the knee and fetlock joints. The reading is recorded in inches.

MEASURING STICK.—A straight shaft of wood with inches and hands marked on it, and with a sliding right-angle arm which is placed over the withers. By raising or lowering the arm on the upright, the height of the horse can be measured directly on the shaft. Sometimes a similar device is built into an umbrella or cane, by means of a hollow shaft.

MEGRIMS.—See BLIND STAGGERS.

MELONS.—See PUMPKINS, SQUASHES, AND MELONS.

MELTON.—A heavy coating material, usually made of wool, originally produced in Melton, England, from which town it takes its name. This material is often used in hunting coats.

MEMORY.—See CONTROL OF THE HORSE.

MENDEL.—Modern genetics was really founded by Gregor Johann Mendel, a cigar-smoking Austrian monk, who conducted breeding experiments with garden peas from 1857 to 1865, during the time of the Civil War in the United States. In his monastery at Brunn (now Brno, in Czechoslovakia), Mendel applied a powerful curiosity and a clear mind to reveal some of the basic principles of hereditary transmission. In 1866, he published in the proceedings of a local scientific society a report covering eight years of his studies, but for 34 years his findings went unheralded and ignored. Finally, in 1900, 16 years after Mendel's death, three European biologists independently duplicated his findings, and this led to the dusting off of the original paper published by the monk 34 years earlier.

The essence of Mendelism is that inheritance is by particles or units (called genes), that these genes are present in pairs—one member of each pair having come from each parent—and that each gene maintains its identity generation after generation. Thus, Mendel's work with peas laid the basis for the two basic laws of inheritance: (1) the law of segregation, and (2) the independent assortment of genes. Later, other genetic principles were added; but all the phenomena of inheritance, based upon the reactions of genes, are generally known under the collective term, Mendelism.

Thus, modern genetics is really unique in that it was founded by an amateur who was not trained as a geneticist and who did his work merely as a hobby. During the years since the rediscovery of Mendel's principles (in 1900), many additional genetic principles have been added, but the fundamentals as set forth by Mendel have been proved correct in every detail. It can be said, therefore, that inheritance in both plants and animals follows the biological laws formulated by Mendel.

Fig. M-11. Gregor Johann Mendel (1822–1884), a cigar-smoking Austrian monk, whose breeding experiments with garden peas founded modern genetics. (Courtesy, The Bettmann Archive)

MENTAL HAZARD JUMPING.—Mental hazard jumps are formidable due to their peculiarity, rather than because of their height or width. Each jump is made of something that normally frightens a horse, whether by sight, sound, or smell. Jumps may include such things as a row of pails hung on a rod, which are rattled as the horse approaches; a wheelbarrow; and a bathtub filled with water. Mental hazard jumping is a test of the training and sensibleness of a horse.

MERCURY POISONING.—See FIRST AID FOR HORSES.

MESOHIPPUS.—An equine ancestor, with three toes on each foot. This animal was about 24 inches in height, or about the size of a dog.

MESSENGER.—A gray Thoroughbred stallion

imported from England to Philadelphia in 1788, at the age of eight. Messenger was the foundation sire for all trotting, pacing, and gaited horses in America. There has been much speculation as to why Messenger, a running horse, should have served as the progenitor of trotting and pacing horses.

METABOLIC.—Pertaining to the nature of metabolism.

METABOLISM.—Refers to all the changes which take place in the nutrients after they are absorbed from the digestive tract including (1) the building-up processes in which the absorbed nutrients are used in the formation or repair of body tissues, and (2) the breaking-down processes in which nutrients are oxidized for the production of heat and work.

METRIC SYSTEM.—From time to time, horsemen have need to convert avoirdupois weights and measures into the metric system, and vice versa. The following table may be used for this purpose.

TABLE M-5

U. S. WEIGHTS AND MEASURES AND METRIC EQUIVALENTS

U. S.	METRIC
Length	
1 inch	= 2.54 centimeters
1 foot	= 30.48 centimeters
	= 0.3048 meter
1 yard	= 0.9144 meter
1 mile	= 1609.34 meters
	= 1.609 kilometers
Area	
1 square inch	= 6.452 square centimeters
1 square foot	= 0.0929 square meter
1 square yard	= 0.8361 square meter
1 acre	= 0.4047 hectare
1 square mile	= 259.0 hectares
Capacity or volume	
1 cubic inch	= 16.387 cubic centimeters
1 cubic foot	= 0.0283 cubic meter
1 cubic yard	= 0.7646 cubic meter
1 fluid ounce (U.S.)	= 29.573 milliliters
1 liquid pint (U.S.)	= 0.4732 liter
1 liquid quart (U.S.)	= 0.9463 liter
1 gallon (U.S.)	= 3.7853 liters
Weight	
1 ounce (avdp.)	= 28.50 grams
1 pound (avdp.)	= 453.592 grams
	= 0.4536 kilogram
1 ton (short)	= 0.907 ton (metric)
1 ton (long)	= 1.016 ton (metric)
	= 1016.05 kilograms
Volume per unit area	
1 gallon (U.S.)/acre	= 9.354 liters/hectare
Weight per unit area	
1 pound (avdp.)/square inch	= 0.0703 kilogram/square centimeter
1 pound (avdp.)/acre	= 1.121 kilograms/hectare
Area per unit weight	
1 square inch/pound (avdp.)	= 14.22 square centimeters/kilogram

(Continued)

Length
1 millimeter	=	0.03937 inch
1 centimeter	=	0.3937 inch
1 meter	=	39.37 inches
	=	3.281 feet
	=	1.094 yards
1 kilometer	=	0.6214 mile

Area
1 square centimeter	=	0.155 square inch
1 square meter	=	1.196 square yards
	=	10.764 square feet
1 hectare (10,000 m2.)	=	2.471 acres
1 square kilometer	=	0.386 square mile
	=	247.1 acres

Capacity or Volume
1 cubic centimeter	=	0.061 cubic inch
1 cubic meter	=	35.315 cubic feet
	=	1.308 cubic yards
1 milliliter	=	0.0338 fluid ounce (U.S.)
1 liter	=	33.81 fluid ounces (U.S.)
	=	2.1134 pints (U.S.)
	=	1.057 quarts (U.S.)
	=	0.2642 gallon (U.S.)
1 kiloliter	=	264.18 gallons (U.S.)

Weight
1 gram	=	0.03527 ounce (avdp.)
1 kilogram	=	35.274 ounces (avdp.)
	=	**2.205 pounds (avdp.)**
1 metric ton (1,000 kg.)	=	0.984 ton (long)
	=	1.102 tons (short)
	=	2204.6 pounds (avdp.)

Volume per unit area
1 liter/hectare	=	0.107 gallon (U.S.)/acre

Weight per unit area
1 kilogram/square centimeter	=	14.22 pounds (avdp.)/square inch
1 kilogram/hectare	=	0.892 pound (avdp.)/acre

Area per unit weight
1 square centimeter/kilogram	=	0.0703 square inch/pound (avdp.)

Temperature conversion formulas
Centigrade (Celsius)	=	5/9 (Fahrenheit — 32)
Fahrenheit	=	9/5 centigrade (Celsius) + 32

Illumination
1 foot-candle	=	10.764 lux
1 lux	=	0.0929 foot-candle

When conversions are made the results should be rounded to a meaningful number of digits, relative to the accuracy of original measurements. Values for weights and volumes are based on pure water at 4° C. under 760 mm. of atmospheric pressure.

For additional conversion factors, or for greater accuracy, refer to National Bureau of Standards Misc. Pub. 233 or to the Handbook of Chemistry and Physics.

MICROORGANISM.—Any organism of microscopic size, applied especially to bacteria and protozoa.

MIDDLE.—The central portion of a horse, bounded by the chest in front and the coupling and rear flank at the back. Ample middle, due to well-sprung ribs, is desired. A good middle provides needed space for the vital organs and indicates good feeding qualities.

All horses should be fairly well let-down in the hind flank, though racehorses in training may show much less depth at this point than other types of horses. Even with racehorses, however, the extremely high-cut, so-called "wasp-waisted" ones will not endure heavy racing. Moreover, racehorses usually deepen in the rear flank with age and higher condition.

MIDDLEWEIGHT (HUNTERS).—Hunters capable of carrying a rider weighing up to 185 pounds. There are two other weight divisions of hunters; lightweight hunters capable of carrying up to 165 pounds, and heavyweight hunters capable of carrying up to 205 pounds. By implication, hunters weighing over 205 pounds are not supposed to ride to hounds—but they do.

MILITARY HORSES.—See WARFARE, HORSES IN.

MILITARY USE.—See USE OF HORSES.

MILK.—The natural, whitish or cream-colored secretion from the mammary glands of all mammals (warm-blooded, hairy animals that produce their young alive and suckle them for a variable period).

MILK, MARE'S.—A comparison of cow's and mare's milk is given in Table M-6.

As can be observed, mare's milk is higher in percentage of water and sugar than cow's milk and is lower in other components.

MILK REPLACER.—As indicated by the name, a milk replacer is a replacement for milk. Such replacers generally contain the following composi-

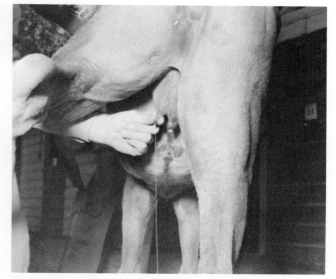

Fig. M-12. A 1,000-pound mare will provide her foal with about 30 pints, or nearly 4 gallons, of milk per day.

tion: Animal or vegetable fat, 17–20%; crude soybean lecithin, 1–2%; skimmed milk solids, 78–82% (10–15% dried whey powder can be included in place of an equivalent amount of skimmed milk solids); plus fortification with minerals and vitamins.

Foals suckling their dams generally develop very satisfactorily up to weaning time. But the most critical period in the entire life of a horse is that space from weaning time (about six months of age) until one year of age. This is especially so in the case of young horses being fitted for shows or sales, where condition is so important. Thus, where valuable weanlings or yearlings are to be shown or sold, the use of a milk replacer may be practical.

TABLE M-6

COMPOSITION OF MILK FROM COWS AND MARES [1]

Source	Water	Protein	Fat	Sugar	Ash
	%	%	%	%	%
Cow	87.17	3.55	3.69	4.88	0.75
Mare	90.78	1.99	1.21	5.67	0.35

[1] USDA Farmer's Bulletin No. 803.

MILK BY-PRODUCTS.—The superior nutritive values of milk by-products are due to their high quality proteins, vitamins, a good mineral balance, and the beneficial effect of the milk sugar, lactose. In addition, these products are palatable and highly digestible. They are an ideal feed for young equines and for balancing out the deficiencies of the cereal grains. Most foal rations contain one or more milk by-products, primarily dried skim milk, with some dried whey and dried buttermilk included at times. The chief limitation to their wider use is price.

(Also see SKIMMED MILK; and WHEY.)

MILO.—See SORGHUMS, GRAIN.

MINERALS.—When we think of minerals for the horse, we instinctively think of bones and unsoundness. This is so because (1) a horse's skeleton is very large, weighing 100 pounds or more in a full-grown horse, of which more than half consists of organic matter or minerals, and (2) experienced trainers estimate that one-third of the horses in training require treatments for unsoundness, in one form or another. But in addition to furnishing structural material, minerals regulate many of the life processes.

The classical horse ration of grass, grass hay, and farm grains is usually deficient in calcium, but adequate in phosphorus. Also, salt is almost always deficient; and many horse rations do not contain sufficient iodine. Thus, horses usually need special mineral supplements. But do not feed them either more or less minerals than needed.

On the average, a horse will consume about 3 ounces of salt daily or 1⅓ pounds per week, although the salt requirements vary with work and temperature.

The salt requirements, and any calcium or phosphorus requirements not met by feeds, can best be supplied by allowing free access to a two-compartment box containing minerals. One compartment should have iodized salt and the other should contain a suitable mineral mixture.

It is important to have slightly more calcium than phosphorus in horse rations. Although the correct calcium to phosphorus ratio is not known, it is suggested that it be kept at between one to two parts calcium to one part phosphorus. A ration low in calcium and high in phosphorus may

cause osteomalacia in mature horses. This condition may develop when rations with a Ca:P ratio of 0.8 to 1 are fed 6 to 12 months, and it will progress rapidly when the ratio is 0.6 to 1. Either a home-mixed or a commercial mineral may be used.

MINERAL IMBALANCES AND ALLOWANCES.—It has become increasingly evident that there is a delicate relationship between certain mineral elements. Thus, the requirements of any mineral may be modified by another mineral which enhances or interferes with its utilization. For this reason, excess fortification of the horse's diet with trace elements may prove more detrimental than helpful. It is important, therefore, to provide minerals on the basis of recommended allowances.

In recommended allowances, reasonable margins of safety are provided to allow for variations in feed composition (due to soils on which grown, stage of maturity, weathering, processing, and storage), environment, stress, and individuality. Also, when fortifying with minerals, consideration should be given to the minerals provided by the ingredients of the normal ration, for it is the total composition of the feed that counts.

Table M-7 gives the recommended allowances of minerals.

SALT (SODIUM CHLORIDE).—Salt, which serves as both a condiment and a nutrient, is needed by all classes of animals, but more especially by herbivora (grass-eating animals). It may be provided in the form of granulated, rock, or block salt. In general, the form selected is determined by price and availability. It is to be pointed out, however, that it is difficult for horses to eat very hard block and rock salt. This often results in sore tongues and inadequate consumption. Also, if there is much competition for the salt block, the more timid animals may not get their requirements.

Both sodium and chlorine are essential for animal life. They are necessary in maintaining the osmotic pressure of body cells (thereby assisting in the transfer of nutrients to the cells and the removal of waste materials). Also, sodium is important as one of the main body buffers and in making bile, which aids in the digestion of fats and carbohydrates. Chlorine is required for the formation of the hydrochloric acid in the gastric juice so vital to protein digestion. The blood

TABLE M-7

RECOMMENDED ALLOWANCES OF MINERALS

Kind of Mineral	Daily Allowance per 1,000-Pound Horse[1]	Allowance per Ton of Finished Feed (hay and grain combined) [2]
Salt	2 oz	10 lb
Calcium	70.0 gm	12.33 lb
Phosphorus	60.0 gm	10.57 lb
Potassium	68.1 gm	12.0 lb
Magnesium	6.4 gm	1.8 lb
Iron	640 mg	51.2 gm
Zinc	400 mg	32.0 gm
Manganese.	340 mg	27.2 gm
Copper	90 mg	7.2 gm
Iodine	2.6 mg	.21 gm
Cobalt	1.5 mg	.12 gm

[1] This is based on an allowance of 25 pounds of feed per 1,000-pound horse per day, or 2.5 pounds of feed per 100 pounds of body weight.

[2] Where hay is fed separately, double this amount should be added to the concentrate.

contains 0.25% chlorine, 0.22% sodium, and 0.02 to 0.22% potassium; thus, the chlorine content is higher than that of any other mineral in the blood. The salt requirement is greatly increased under conditions which cause heavy sweating, thereby resulting in large losses of this mineral from the body. Unless it is replaced, fatigue will result. For this reason, when engaged in hard work and perspiring profusely, horses should receive liberal allowances of salt.

Salt can be fed free-choice to horses, provided they have not been salt-starved. That is, if the animals have not previously been fed salt for a considerable length of time, they may overeat, resulting in digestive disturbances and even death. Salt-starved animals should first be hand-fed salt, and the daily allowance should be increased gradually until they start leaving a little in the mineral box. When this point is reached, self-feeding may be followed. The Indians and the pioneers of this country handed down many legendary stories about the large numbers of buffalo and deer that killed themselves simply by gorging at a newly found "salt-lick" after having been salt-starved for long periods of time.

When added to the concentrate ration, salt should be added at a level of 0.5 to 1.0%.

CALCIUM AND PHOSPHORUS.—Horses are more apt to suffer from a lack of phosphorus and of calcium than from any of the other minerals except salt. These two minerals comprise about three-fourths the ash of the skeleton and from one-third to one-half of the minerals of milk.

The following general characteristics of feeds in regard to calcium and phosphorus are important in rationing horses:

• The cereal grains and their by-products and straws, dried mature grasses, and protein supplements of plant origin are low in calcium.

• The protein supplements of animal origin and legume forage are rich in calcium.

• The cereal grains and their by-products are fairly high or even rich in phosphorus, but a large portion of the phosphorus is not readily available.

• Almost all protein-rich supplements are high in phosphorus. But, here again, plant sources of phosphorus contain much of this element in a bound form.

• Beet by-products and dried, mature nonleguminous forages (such as grass hays and fodders) are likely to be low in phosphorus.

• The calcium and phosphorus content of plants can be increased through fertilizing the soil upon which they are grown.

In considering the calcium and phosphorus requirements of horses, it is important to realize that the proper utilization of these minerals by the body is dependent upon three factors: (1) an adequate supply of calcium and phosphorus in an available form (growing horses should be provided calcium at a level of approximately 0.6 to 0.7% of the diet, and phosphorus at a level of about 0.5%), (2) a suitable ratio between them (somewhere within the range 1.1 to 1.4:1. Although the exact calcium to phosphorus ratio is not known, and although it appears to differ according to age, older horses can have a calcium to phosphorus ratio of 2.0 to 1.0—it is important to have slightly more calcium than phosphorus.), and (3) sufficient vitamin D to make possible the assimilation and utilization of the calcium and phosphorus. Many "cure-alls" and commercial mineral mixtures fail to take these factors into consideration.

If plenty of vitamin D is present (as provided either by sunlight or through the ration), the ratio of calcium to phosphorus becomes less important. Also, less vitamin D is needed when there is a desirable calcium-phosphorus ratio.

Table M-8 gives several sources of calcium and phosphorus and the approximate percentages of the two elements in various mineral supplements.

Where both calcium and phosphorus are needed, the author favors the use of high-quality steamed bone meal for horses, because bone meal contains many ingredients in addition to calcium and phosphorus. It is a good source of iron, man-

TABLE M-8

COMPOSITION OF CALCIUM AND PHOSPHORUS SUPPLEMENTS [1]

Mineral Supplement	Calcium		Phosphorus	
	(percent)	(grams per pound)	(percent)	(grams per pound)
Oyster shells, ground	38.05	172	. . . .	. . .
Limestone, ground	33.84	154	. . .	. . .
Bone black, spent	22.00	100	13.10	60
Bone meal, raw feeding . . .	22.70	103	10.10	46
Bone meal, steamed	30.00	136	13.90	63
Dicalcium phosphate	26.50	120	20.50	93
Tricalcium phosphate	32.00	145	18.00	82
Defluorinated phosphate . . .	33.00	150	18.00	82
Monosodium phosphate . . .	. . . .	. . .	22.40	102
Defluorinated phosphate . . .	. . . .	. . .	23.00	104

[1] From Table 4, *Nutrient Requirements of Domestic Animals,* Number 3, pub. 1349, 3rd. Ed., NRC, National Academy of Sciences.

ganese, and zinc, and it contains such trace minerals as copper and cobalt; but it is felt that the content of the latter is too low to be of much value as a supplement for them. However, it is recognized that it is increasingly difficult to get good bone meal. Some of the imported products are high in fat, rancid, and/or odorous and unpalatable. Where good bone meal is not available, dicalcium phosphate is generally recommended.

When calcium alone is needed, ground limestone or oyster shell flour are commonly used, either free-choice or added to the ration in keeping with nutrient requirements.

Where phosphorus alone is needed, monosodium phosphate or defluorinated phosphate are minerals of choice.

Earlier experiments cast considerable doubt on the availability of phosphorus when the phosphorus was largely in the form of phytin. Although wheat bran is very high in phosphorus, containing 1.32%, there was some question as to its availability due to the high phytin content of this product. More recent studies, however, indicate that cattle, and perhaps mature swine, can

partially utilize phytin phosphorus. Cattle can utilize about 60% of the total phosphorus from most plant sources, whereas swine can utilize only about 50%. The situation relative to horses is unknown. It must be emphasized, however, that phosphorus availability depends to a large extent on phosphorus sources, dietary supplies of calcium, and adequate vitamin D.

Likewise, for humans, the availability of the calcium of certain leafy materials is impaired by the presence of oxalic acid—the acid precipitating the calcium and preventing its absorption. On the other hand, the deleterious effects of oxalic acid are reduced in the ruminant because of the ruminant's apparent ability to metabolize oxalic acid in the body. The situation relative to horses is unknown.

During World War II, the shortage of phosphorus feed supplements led to the development of defluorinated phosphates for feeding purposes. Raw, unprocessed rock phosphate usually contains from 3.25 to 4.0% fluorine, whereas feeding steamed bone meal normally contains only 0.05 to 0.10%. Fortunately, through heating at high temperatures under conditions suitable for elimination of fluorine, the excess fluorine of raw rock phosphate can be removed. Such a product is known as defluorinated phosphate.

Under the definition of the Association of American Feed Control Officials, to qualify as a defluorinated phosphate, rock phosphate cannot contain more than one part of fluorine to 100 parts of phosphate.

Excess fluorine results in abnormal development of bones; softening, mottling, and irregular wear of the teeth; roughened haircoat; delayed maturity; and less efficient utilization of feed.

TRACE MINERALS.—A capsuled discussion of each of the trace minerals follows.

● MAGNESIUM.—It appears that the magnesium requirement of farm animals for growth is of the order of 0.06% of the dry ration, assuming that the calcium and phosphorus intakes are adequate but not excessive. On this basis, a 1,000-pound horse consuming 25 pounds of feed per day would require 6,810 mg of magnesium per day.

Horse rations containing 50% forage will likely contain sufficient magnesium for unstressed horses. But remember that horses at hard work (as in racing and showing) consume more grain (which is low in magnesium) and less forage. Remember, too, that horses being raced or shown, or otherwise stressed, are frequently keyed up, high strung, and jumpy; similar to the nervousness that characterizes animals and humans known to be suffering from a magnesium deficiency.

In view of the above, it would appear prudent that one-half to two-thirds of the recommended daily magnesium allowance of the horse be added to the ration; or about 6.4 gm daily/1,000-pound horse.

● IRON.—The National Research Council (NRC) estimates the iron requirement of the horse at 40 ppm. However, it has been reported that horses which are subjected to pressure from racing, showing, or other heavy use, require 80 to 100 ppm of iron in their daily ration; which calls for 907 to 1,134 mg of iron in the ration of a 1,000-pound horse consuming 25 pounds of feed per day. To be on the safe side, approximately one-half of the iron requirement of the horse should be added to the ration; and it should be in a biologically available form (iron oxide should not be used as a source of iron for horses because it is poorly absorbed).

● ZINC.—Swine require 50 ppm zinc on diets properly balanced with calcium. But if excessive levels of calcium are fed (1.0% or more), then the requirement is increased to about 100 ppm. Research with cattle has shown that supplementing the ration with 50 to 100 ppm of zinc will improve the haircoat. Obviously, zinc is necessary for the maintenance and development of skin and hair.

Since beautiful haircoats are important in horses, fortifying the daily ration with about 266 mg of zinc per day will prevent any possibility of a zinc deficiency; and if the zinc in the feed is on the low side, the added zinc should improve the haircoat.

● MANGANESE.—Based on research with other species, it is reasonable to assume that horses should meet their daily requirements on feeds containing 20 ppm and no more than 40 ppm of manganese.

Thirty ppm calls for 340 mg of manganese in the ration of a 1,000 pound horse consuming 25 pounds of feed per day. But since most natural feedstuffs are rich in manganese, it can be assumed that part of the requirement for this element will be met by the normal ration.

● COPPER.—A copper deficiency has been reported in horses in Australia grazing on pastures low in copper. Also, mare's milk (along with milk from all species) is low in copper.

Copper is of special interest to horsemen because, in addition to its effect on iron metabolism, it is closely associated with normal bone development in young growing animals. In copper-deficient dogs and swine, there is a marked failure of deposition of bone in the cartilage matrix and deformed bones. Cattle and sheep grazing copper-deficient areas develop brittle bones which fracture easily. Abnormal bone development has been reported in foals on low copper diets.

The recommended copper allowance for a 1,000-pound horse is 90 mg per day, about half of which should be added to the ration.

● IODINE.—Pregnant mares are very susceptible to iodine deficiency. Where such a deficiency exists, the foals are usually stillborn or so weak that they cannot stand and suck. There is also some evidence to indicate that navel-ill in foals may be lessened by feeding iodine to broodmares.

The addition to the daily ration of 2.6 gms of iodine will be ample.

● COBALT.—Cobalt is required for the synthesis of vitamin B_{12} in the intestinal tract of the horse. A lack of cobalt and/or B_{12} will result in anemia. Since the feeds normally used by horses are deficient in vitamin B_{12}, it is advisable to supply a low level of cobalt in the ration of horses. The addition to the ration of 1.5 mg. of cobalt per day will be adequate.

CHELATED TRACE MINERALS.—The word chelate is derived from the Greek "chelae," meaning a claw or pincer-like organ. Those selling chelated minerals generally recommend a smaller quantity of them (but at a higher price per pound) and extoll their "fenced-in" properties.

When it comes to synthetic chelating agents, much needs to be learned about their selectivity toward minerals, the kind and quantity most effective, their mode of action, and their behavior with different species of animals and with varying rations. It is possible that their use may actually create a mineral imbalance. These answers, and more, must be forthcoming through carefully controlled experiments before they can be recommended for valuable horses.

MINERAL BOX OR SELF-FEEDER.—A box may be made of wood and a self-feeder may be made of metal or wood. In a stall, the box or self-feeder should be in a corner of the stall and should be the same height as the box or pail used for concentrates.

In a corral, mineral containers should be in a fence corner. The height should be two-thirds the height of the horse at the withers. If a mineral container is in the open, it should be protected from wind and rain. Mineral containers should have two compartments, one for mineral mix and the other for salt.

MINIATURE DONKEY REGISTRY OF THE UNITED STATES, INC.—1108 Jackson St.,
Omaha, Neb. 68102. (See Appendix for complete breed registry association list.)

MISREPRESENTATION.—This usually refers to falsification of age, soundness, vices, and the training and working ability of the horse. The inexperienced person may encounter such misrepresentations. Knowing the seller as well as the horse is the best preventative of this sort of thing.

MISSOURI FOX TROTTING HORSE.—See BREED (S).

MISSOURI FOX TROTTING HORSE BREED ASSOCIATION.—P. O. Box 637, Ava, Missouri 65608. (See Appendix for complete breed registry association list.)

MITES (MANGE).—These are very small parasites that cause mange (scabies, scab, and itch). The two chief forms of mange are sarcoptic mange caused by burrowing mites and psoroptic mange caused by mites that bite the skin and suck the serum and lymph but do not burrow. Mites also may cause chorioptic mange.

SYMPTOMS.—Symptoms are irritation, itching, and scratching. The skin crusts over and becomes thick, tough, and wrinkled. Mange appears to spread most rapidly during the winter months.

Fig. M-13. Horse with severe infestation of sarcoptic mites, producing a condition commonly known as mange (or scabies, scab, or itch). (Courtesy, USDA)

TREATMENT.—Treat animals with sprays containing (1) 0.25% coumaphos, (2) 0.1 to 0.3% Ciodrin®, or (3) 0.5% malathion; give two treatments 10 to 14 days apart. Lime-sulfur and nicotine sprays are effective but they are little used on horses today.

PREVENTION AND CONTROL.—Keep healthy horses away from diseased animals or infested premises. Spray infested animals with insecticides and quarantine affected herds.

DISCUSSION.—Mites are widespread. They retard growth, lower work efficiency, and produce unthriftiness. When sarcoptic and psoroptic mange appear, they must be reported to State or Federal animal health agencies. Also, in many states, chorioptic mange must be reported.

(Also see DISEASES AND PARASITES; HEALTH PROGRAM; and PARASITES OF HORSES.)

MIX-GAITED.—Said of a horse that will not adhere to any one true gait at a time.

MOHAMMED'S TEN HORSES.—It is easy to understand how the environmental conditions in Arabia could and did give rise to myth and exaggerated statements relative to horses. At one moment, the Arab was cruel to his mount; then again he would shower him with kindness.

In the days of Mohammed, intelligence and obedience were the main requisites of the Arab's horse. For war purposes, only the most obedient horses were used, and they were trained to follow the bugle.

Legend has it that the Prophet himself had need for some very obedient horses, so he inspected a certain herd to make personal selections.

The horses from which he wished to make selections were pastured in a large area bordering on a river. The Prophet gave orders that the animals should be fenced off from the river until their thirst became very great.

He then ordered the fence removed, and the horses rushed for the water. When they were just about to dash into the river to quench their thirst, a bugle was sounded.

All but ten of the horses ignored the call of the bugle. The obedient ten turned and answered the call of duty, despite their great thirst. The whimsical story goes on to say that these ten head constituted the foundation of the "Prophet Strain."

MOISTURE PRODUCTION BY HORSES *(by breathing).*—Most building designers are inclined to govern the amount of air change by the need for moisture removal. A horse breathes into the air approximately 17.5 pounds, or about 2.1 gallons, of moisture per day. For 40 horses, there would be given off 700 pounds, or about 84 gallons, of water per day. The removal of such a large quantity of moisture, especially in the winter when the barn is closed, is a difficult problem for the designer to solve.

(Also see ENVIRONMENTAL CONTROL.)

MOLARS (or GRINDERS).—The large grinding teeth to the back of a horse's mouth. The mature horse has 24 molars; 12 in the upper jaw, and 12 in the lower jaw. The molars do not always wear evenly, primarily because the upper jaw is wider than the lower jaw. As a result, sharp points may develop, which may lacerate the cheeks and tongue and prevent proper mastication of feed. When this happens, the horse should have his teeth "floated" (the sharp edges filed off).

(Also see AGE.)

MOLASSES (CANE or BEET).—Molasses is a by-product of sugar factories, with cane molasses coming from sugarcane and beet molasses coming from sugar beets. Cane molasses is slightly preferred to beet molasses for horses, although either is satisfactory.

For horses, molasses is 80 to 95% as valuable as oats, pound for pound. However, molasses is used primarily as an appetizer.

In hot, humid areas, molasses should be limited to 5% of the ration; otherwise, mold may develop. Where mustiness is a problem, add calcium propionate to the feed according to the manufacturer's directions.

MOON BLINDNESS (PERIODIC OPHTHALMIA).—An inflammatory disease of the eyes of horses and mules characterized by sudden onset of acute clinical signs which subside, but recur following quiescent periods of varying length.

CAUSE.—(1) Leptospirosis, (2) parasites—*Flaria equina* in the eye, or systemic parasitism, (3) eye reaction to repeated streptococcal infections, or (4) lack of riboflavin.

SYMPTOMS.—Periods of cloudy vision, in one or both eyes, which may last for a few days to a week or two and then clear up; but it recurs at intervals, eventually culminating in blindness in one or both eyes.

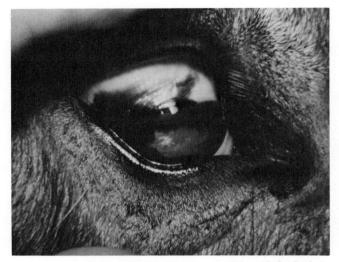

Fig. M-14. Moon blindness (periodic ophthalmia); showing the cloudy condition of the eye. (Courtesy, Dr. K. N. Gelatt, DVM, College of Veterinary Medicine, University of Minnesota, St. Paul, Minn.)

DISTRIBUTION AND LOSSES.—In many parts of the world. In the U.S., it occurs most frequently in the states east of the Missouri River.

TREATMENT.—Antibiotics administered promptly are helpful in some cases.

CONTROL.—If symptoms of moon blindness are observed, immediately (1) change to greener hay or grass, or (2) add riboflavin to the ration at the rate of 40 mg per horse per day.

PREVENTION.—Feed high-riboflavin green grass or well-cured green leafy hays; or add riboflavin to the ration at the rate of 20 mg per horse per day. Control parasites.

REMARKS.—This disease has been known to exist for at least 2,000 years.
(Also see UNSOUNDNESSES.)

MORAB.—The Morab Horse Registry was formed in 1973. The Morab is predominantly Morgan and Arabian, although it may be part Thoroughbred. They are used for show, pleasure riding, endurance rides, and ranch work.

MORAB HORSE REGISTRY OF AMERICA.—P. O. Box 143, Clovis, California 93612. (See Appendix for complete breed registry association list.)

MORBIDITY.—Sick rate.

MORGAN.—See BREED (S).

MORNING GLORY.—A horse that works out in record time in the morning but that does not live up to its promise in an actual race.

MOROCCO SPOTTED HORSE.—See BREED (S).

MOROCCO SPOTTED HORSE COOP. ASSOC. OF AMERICA, INC.—Rt. 1, Ridott, Illinois 61067. (See Appendix for complete breed registry association list.)

MORRAL (FEED BAG; NOSE BAG).—A fiber bag used as a feed bag for horses.
(Also see FEED BAG; and NOSE BAG.)

MORTALITY.—Death rate.

MOSQUITO.—See FLIES.

MOTION PICTURE HORSES.—Horses became film stars right from the start of silent movies; and their use in sound movies (including color) and television has continued unabated. The wild horse and the cowboy are part of Western history and folklore. A western film without horses is inconceivable.
Film horses are cast in one of four classes: (1) starring horses playing leading roles or significant parts, selected for their beauty, intelligence, and above all their adaptability; (2) horses used by leading actors, selected for their handsome bearing; (3) stunt horses; and (4) cast horses, which

Fig. M-15. Roy Rogers and Trigger, who starred and shared billing together. Without doubt, Trigger was the best known and most extensively trained of all movie horses. (Courtesy, Roy Rogers)

Fig. M-16. John Wayne—the "Duke," star of Western movies, and horse. (Courtesy, The American Humane Association, Denver, Colo.)

are docile animals used for atmosphere, town scenes, posses, or pulling stage coaches or wagons.

For big film parts, a horse may have a double. In fact, there may be several doubles, each good at a different thing; and they may be changed according to action.

All breeds are used. Palomino and snow white colors are especially popular.

Three major stables supply most of the trained and cast horses to the American film industry. Generally they rent tack and vehicles to match any desired historical period.

Although each trainer of a movie horse has his particular training technique, virtually all of them start by whip breaking. Standard film repertoire usually includes coming to the trainer when signaled; stopping immediately when cued; and standing still, turning right and left, backing up, lying down, limping, pretending pain (usually by nuzzling a sore leg), and rearing.

All of the basic actions are performed on silent cue (silent cues are necessary when filming is under live sound) from the trainer, who uses body movements, arm and hand signals, or a whip to signal the horse. For example, the trainer may tell the horse to come to him by turning his back; and he may give the cue to stop by turning and facing the horse—usually placing a hand or whip in front of his chest.

Some horse actions are more the result of studio techniques than training. For example, a fierce stallion fight is optically created, although there is a certain amount of combat. Two stallions left together will fight. But injury is minimized by (1) taping the muzzles shut with colored tape that matches the horse's coat color to prevent biting, and (2) using sponge rubber shoes to lessen blows from kicking. Also, fight scenes are filmed at slow speed. Then when the scene is projected on the screen at normal speed, the action appears to be fast and furious.

The American Humane Association has a representative (s) on all sets using animals, making sure that all animals are treated humanely. Besides, trained horses represent a considerable investment, with the result that their free-lance owners will not hazard injury. Moreover, they are well aware that if a horse should hurt himself, he might thereafter refuse to repeat the act. So, a horse fight is stopped if one of the combatants becomes too serious; stunt horses are specially trained to fall and jump off cliffs; and falls at a gallop are performed on mattresses of foam rubber covered with soil.

MOTTLED.—Marked with spots of different colors: dappled, spotted.

MOUNTING AND DISMOUNTING.—See HORSEMANSHIP.

MOUTH.—The mouth is the first part of the alimentary canal. In the horse, it is long and cylindrical. It includes the teeth (both uppers and lowers—24 molars and 12 incisors in the mature horse), the tongue, and three pairs of large salivary glands.

Digestion starts in the mouth. The feed is masticated by the teeth and moistened with saliva. In the mature horse, approximately 85 pounds (10 gallons) of saliva are secreted daily. It wets feedstuffs, thereby making for easier passage down the esophagus. In addition, the saliva contains the enzyme ptyalin, which transforms starch into maltose.

The mouth of the horse differs anatomically and physiologically from the ruminant as follows: Horses have upper incisor teeth, ruminants do not; horses masticate feed with the teeth, ruminants are cud-chewing; horses secrete a larger volume of saliva, and the saliva of the horse contains ptyalin, whereas the saliva of ruminants is enzyme-free.

MOUTHING.—Determining the approximate age of a horse by examining the teeth.
(Also see AGE.)

MUDDER.—A horse that runs well on a track that is wet, sloppy, or heavy.

MUD FEVER.—See SCRATCHES.

MULE.—A cross between the jack (a male of the ass family) on the mare (female of the horse family). The resulting offspring of the reciprocal cross of the stallion mated to a jennet is known as a hinny. The mule and the hinny are indistinguishable.

It has been correctly said that the mule is without pride of ancestry or hope of posterity. He is a hybrid, and, like most hybrids, he is seldom fertile.

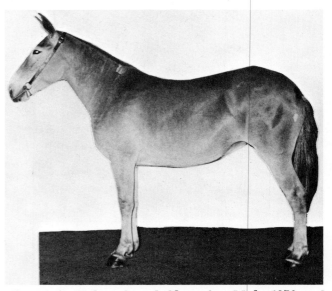

Fig. M-17. Helen, Grand Champion Mule 1970 and 1971 Missouri State Fair. A sorrel mare mule shown by Chipman & Kohl, Perry, Mo. (Courtesy: G. E. Chipman, Green Acres Stock Farm, Perry, Mo.)

The use of the mule in the United States was first popularized by two early American statesmen, George Washington and Henry Clay. The first jack to enter this country, of which there is authentic record, was presented by the Marquis de Lafayette to General Washington in 1787, shortly after the close of the Revolutionary War. Other importations followed; and from that day until mechanization, the hardy mule furnished the main source of animal power for the South. In comparison with the horse, the mule can (1) withstand higher temperatures; (2) endure less experienced labor; (3) better adapt his eating habits to either irregularity or self-feeding with little danger of founder or digestive disturbances; (4) work or stable in lower areas without head injury (the mule lowers his head when the ears touch an object, whereas the horse will throw his head upward under similar conditions); (5) encounter less foot trouble, wire cuts, etc.; and (6) generally maneuver about without harm to himself.

Although the mule resembles his sire, the jack, more than the mare, the desired conformation is identical to that described for the horse; perhaps the one exception is that more stress is placed upon the size, set, and quality of the ear. The most desirable mules must be of good size and draftiness, compact and heavily muscled; must show evidence of plenty of quality; must stand on correct feet and legs; and must be sound. As the natural tendency of the mule is to be lazy and obstinate, an active, energetic disposition is sought.

Mules, donkeys, and hinnys are registered and promoted by the American Donkey and Mule Society, a nonprofit organization. The address of the registry is: 2410 Executive Drive, Indianapolis, Indiana 46241. Also, the Society publishes a quarterly, appropriately called *Mr. Longears.*

MUSEUM OF RACING.—See NATIONAL MUSEUM OF RACING, INC., THE.

MUSIC *(of hounds)*.—The baying of hounds when they are running full pack. It's sweet music to all hunting enthusiasts.

MUSTANG.—Native horse of the Western Plains.
(Also see BREED(S).

MUTATION.—A sudden variation which is later passed on through inheritance and which results from changes in a gene or genes.

MUTTON-WITHERED.—Term used to describe a horse that is low in the withers and heavy in the shoulders.

MUZZLE.—
1. The lower end of the nose which inludes the nostrils, lips, and chin.
2. A protective covering for the nose of a

horse. It is shaped like a bucket, and it may be made of netting, leather, wire mesh, fiberglass, or other material (if solid material is used, ventilation holes must be provided). It is held in position by means of a strap or rope that goes over the head. Muzzles are used on horses which are prone to bite people, or that are addicted to eating dung or their bedding.
(Also see PARTS OF A HORSE—Fig. P-4.)

NAG.—An inferior, aged, or unsound horse.

NAIL IN THE FOOT.—Nail wounds of the hoof are rather common. The horseman should apply first aid, then call a veterinarian if the wound is serious.
(Also see FIRST AID FOR HORSES.)

NAILS.—See SHOEING—Table S-5.

NARRAGANSETT PACER.—This was a fast type of pacer, descended from the indigenous horse of the Narragansett Bay area of Rhode Island, which evolved during the time of the Revolutionary War (1775–1781). During this period, racing was illegal except in Rhode Island.

NATIONAL APPALOOSA PONY.—See BREED(S).

NATIONAL APPALOOSA PONY, INC.—Box 296, Gaston, Indiana 47342. (See Appendix for complete breed registry association list.)

NATIONAL ASSOCIATION OF STATE RACING COMMISSIONERS, THE (NASRC).—As indicated by the name, the NASRC is a nationwide association of State Racing Commissioners banded together for the purposes of (1) informing each other and correlating state programs, and (2) improving and promoting the sport of racing.

ADDRESS.—The National Association of State Racing Commissioners, P. O. Box 4216, Lexington, Ky. 40504.

NATIONAL CHICKASAW HORSE ASSN.—Route 2, Clarinda, Iowa 51232. (See Appendix for complete breed registry association list.)

NATIONAL CUTTING HORSE ASSOCIATION (NCHA).—The NCHA was organized in 1946. Its stated purposes are: To formulate and supervise the rules for competition for cutting horses; to encourage and promote interest in the breeding, training, and competition of the cutting horse; and to assist in the operation of competitive events by providing qualified judges, assistants, etc.

ADDRESS.—National Cutting Horse Association, P. O. Box 12155, Fort Worth, Texas 76116.

NATIONAL MUSEUM OF RACING, INC., THE.—The Museum houses one of the world's greatest collections of equine art, along with trophies, sculptures, and memorabilia of the sport from its earliest days.

Also, the Hall of Fame is located in the same building. In it, the immortals of the sport—horse and human—occupy their places in lasting history.

ADDRESS.—The National Museum of Racing is located directly opposite Saratoga Race Course, America's oldest Thoroughbred racing center, in Saratoga Springs, N.Y.

NATIONAL TROTTING & PACING ASSN., INC.—575 Broadway, Hanover, Pennsylvania 17331. (See Appendix for complete breed registry association list.)

NAVEL CORD, TREATMENT OF.—See FOAL.

NAVEL-ILL.—See NAVEL INFECTION.

NAVEL INFECTION (JOINT-ILL, NAVEL-ILL, Actinobacillosis, streptococcus).—An infectious disease of newborn animals caused by several kinds of bacteria.

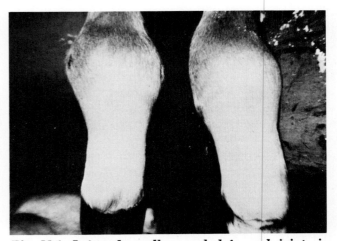

Fig. N-1. Infected, swollen, and deformed joints in foal afflicted with navel infection, or joint-ill. (Courtesy, Dr. V. S. Myers, Jr., V.M.D. Department of Veterinary Surgery and Radiology, University of Minnesota, St. Paul, Minn.)

SYMPTOMS.—Infected animals have loss of appetite; swelling, soreness, and stiffness in the joints; general listlessness; and umbilical swelling and discharge.

TREATMENT.—A veterinarian may give a blood transfusion from the dam to the offspring, or he may administer a sulfa, an antibiotic, a serum, or a bacterin.

PREVENTION.—Practice good sanitation and hygiene at mating and parturition. Feed iodized salt to pregnant mares in iodine-deficient areas. Soon after birth, treat the navel cord of newborn animals with tincture of iodine.

DISCUSSION.—The disease appears throughout the United States. About 50 percent of infected foals die and many that survive have deformed joints. Providing clean quarters for the newborn and painting the navel cord with tincture of iodine are the best preventive measures.
(Also see DISEASES AND PARASITES; FOAL; and HEALTH PROGRAM.)

NAVICULAR BONE.—The smallest of the three bones of the foot. It is located to the posterior junction of the pedal and coronary bone, resting slightly on the coffin bone, but held in place largely by the deep flexor tendon.

(Also see FOOT—Fig. F-20, Parts of the foot; and NAVICULAR DISEASE.)

NAVICULAR DISEASE.—Navicular disease is an inflammation of the small navicular bone and bursa of the front foot. It is often impossible to determine the exact cause of the disease. Affected animals go lame; have a short stubby stride; and usually point the affected foot when standing. Few animals completely recover from the disease. Treatment consists of special shoeing. In cases of persistent and severe lameness, unnerving may be performed by a veterinarian, who can destroy sensation in the foot.

(Also see UNSOUNDNESSES.)

NEAR SIDE.—The left side of a horse. It is the side on which all gear is fastened and unfastened, and it is the side on which the horse is mounted. The custom of working from the left side of the horse evolved quite logically in two ways:

1. In the days when horsemen wore swords, they hung to the left. Hence, the sword would have interfered with the rider by hanging between his legs had he tried mounting from the right.

2. In England, traffic keeps to the left. Therefore, when working around horses the coachman stood on the left side if possible in order to be on the side of the road and out of the line of fire of traffic.

In both the above situations horsemen were most often on the left side of horses: hence, logically it became known as the "near" side, and the right side became the "off" side. With a team of horses, the one on the left is the "near" horse, the one on the right is the "off" horse.

NECK.—The neck should be fairly long. It should be carried high, and it should be slightly arched, lean and muscular, and clean-cut about the throatlatch, with the head well set on. Also, the neck should join neatly to long, oblique, smooth shoulders.

(Also see PARTS OF THE HORSE—Fig. P-4.)

NECK REINING (INDIRECT REIN).—To guide or direct a horse by pressure of the rein on the neck. This is accomplished by carrying the reins, which are held in one hand, to the side towards which it is desired that the horse go. The touch of the reins on the opposite side of the neck tells him to turn. Thereupon, his neck should be arched and his neck and head pointed in the direction of travel.

Neck reining is a Western term and a Western method of using the reins. It is logical that this method of reining should be used on Western horses, because it permits the reins to be held in one hand, thereby freeing the other hand for roping or other work. In Western show-ring classes, the reins must be held in one hand.

In dressage work, this method of reining is called indirect rein.

(Also see INDIRECT REIN.)

NECROSIS.—Death or dying of local body tissue.

NEIGH.—The loud, prolonged call of a horse.

NELSON.—The favorite mount of George Washington.

NEWMARKET.—The center of horse racing in England. Newmarket is the headquarters of the Jockey Club, and the location of two racecourses—the Round Course and the Summer Course. Upward of 2,000 racehorses are trained at Newmarket, and there are a large number of breeding establishments in the area.

NICKING.—See HEREDITY IN HORSES.

NIPPER.—See SHOEING—Table S-5.

NIPPING.—The habit of taking a little nip (bite) at a person is called "nipping." Young horses are playful and curious. Thus, when a hand is placed on a foal's face, his natural response is to use his lips. This procedure can easily lead to nipping. For this reason, when petting a foal always stroke him on the neck or shoulder; don't dab.

Generally, a sharp cuff across the nose of a young horse will cure the nipping habit.

(Also see VICES—Biting.)

NORFOLK TROTTER.—This English breed, which is practically extinct today, was a strong, short-legged, fast trotting animal. The blood of the Norfolk Trotter had much influence on the development of the Hackney breed.

NOSE BAG (FEED BAG).—A bag, usually made of canvas, that is used for feeding a horse. It fits over the muzzle and suspends by a strap or rope that goes over the top of the head.

Fig. N-2. Nose bag in use by a horse in New Delhi, India. This cart horse was stationed near the monument of Mahatma Gandhi. (Photo by A. H. Ensminger)

NOSEBAND.—The noseband is a wide leather band which passes around the nose below the cheekbones. It is used to keep the mouth shut and the bit in position, as a means for attaching the standing martingale, or to enhance the appearance of the bridle. Heavy harness and most riding bridles are equipped with nosebands. The noseband should be adjusted so that it is about one and one-half inches below the cheekbone and loose enough so that two fingers may be placed under it.

NOSE BLEEDING.—Nose bleeding results from a broken blood vessel. Usually it will stop in a short time. Cold compresses may be applied to the outside of the nose and cold water may be syringed up the nostrils. In no case should one attempt to stop bleeding at the nose by plugging the nostrils because a horse cannot breathe through his mouth and will die of suffocation.

NOSTRILS.—The nostrils are the avenues of air intake to the lungs. They should be large, with rosy mucous membrane.

(Also see PARTS OF A HORSE—Fig. P-4.)

NOVICE.—A horse or rider is considered a novice until he has won three first place ribbons in the division in which he is competing, in either American Horse Shows Association or Canadian Horse Shows Association approved shows.

NOVICE CLASSES.—Novice classes are open to novice horses or riders.

NUMBER OF HORSES IN U.S.—United States horse numbers increased with the growth and development of farms; reaching a peak in 1915, at which time there was a record number of 21,431,000 head. In 1920, there were 25,199,552 horses and mules on farms and ranches in the United States and an additional 2,000,000 head in cities.

Mules on farms slowly but steadily increased in numbers for ten years after horses began their decline in 1915, reaching a peak in 1925 at 5,918,000 head. Mule numbers decreased proportionally less than horses because of their great use in the deep South where labor was cheaper and more abundant and the farms smaller in size.

Today, there is much disagreement relative to the U.S. horse population. Part of the confusion stems from the fact that the Census Bureau figures of horses have always been limited to those on farms (and ranches), with no consideration given to those owned by suburbanites. Most population figures fail to reflect the shift in the horse population from farm to town. Then the *coup de grâce* was administered when the census takers discontinued counting horses in 1960; they counted Old Dobbin out with the passing of the draft horse. But they failed to recognize that the light horse was coming up fast; indeed, that the horse was rising to a new and more important position in the fields of recreation and sport.

In 1974, there were an estimated 8.0 million head of horses, mostly light horses, in the United States. Draft animals were the victims of mechanization; farming had changed.

The ten leading states in horse numbers, by rank, are: (1) California, (2) Texas, (3) Illinois, (4) Ohio, (5) New York, (6) Michigan, (7) Washington, (8) Pennsylvania, (9) Oregon, and (10) Oklahoma.

FUTURE OF U.S. HORSE INDUSTRY.— History runs on! Thus, the future of the horse industry, in horse numbers and expenditures, is projected in Figs. N-3 and N-4.

This generation has more leisure time and more money to spend than any generation in history. Currently, the leisure market, in all its aspects, is about $150 billion annually.

But a really big horse boom lies ahead! A shorter work week, increased automation, more suburban and rural living, and the continued recreation and sports surge, with emphasis on physical fitness and the out-of-doors, will require more horses and support more racetracks, shows, and other horse events. It is predicted that we shall have 14 million horses by the year 2000. Economists tell us that leisure-time spending will be the dynamic element in the domestic economy in the years ahead.

NUMBER OF HORSES IN WORLD.—Table N-1 shows the size and density of the important horse countries of the world in 1970–71. As shown, world numbers totaled 66.3 million head. This was far below the 1934–38 prewar figure of 96.4 million head. This decline in numbers since 1938 can be attributed chiefly to mechanization of agriculture in certain areas.

The leading countries in horse numbers, by rank, are: Brazil, United States, U.S.S.R., China, Mexico, Argentina, Poland, Mongolia, Ethiopia, and Yugoslavia.

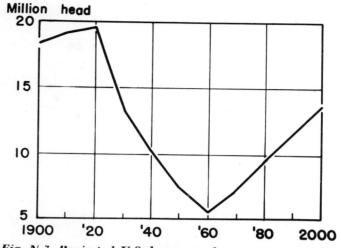

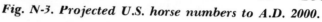

Fig. N-3. Projected U.S. horse numbers to A.D. 2000.

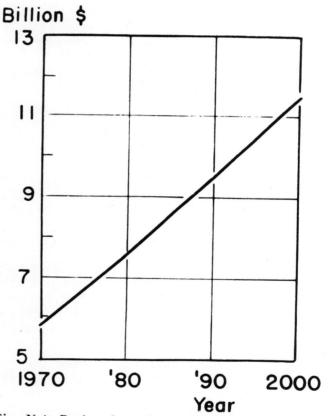

Fig. N-4. Projected total annual expenditures on U.S. horses to A.D. 2000.

Country	No. of Horses[1]	No. of Human Population[2]	Size of Country[2] (sq. mi)	(sq. km)	Horses per Capita	Horses per Sq. Mile	Horses per Sq. Km.
Brazil	9,050,000	98,081,000	3,286,473	8,511,965	.09	2.75	1.06
United States	7,800,000	204,765,770	3,536,855	9,160,454	.03	2.2	.85
U. S. S. R.	7,400,000	245,070,000	8,647,172	22,396,175	.03	.86	.33
China	7,200,000	697,260,000	3,746,453	9,703,313	.01	1.92	.74
Mexico	5,026,000	50,830,000	758,259	1,963,890	.10	6.63	2.56
Argentina	3,600,000	23,550,000	1,079,520	2,795,957	.02	3.3	1.29
Poland	2,570,000	32,750,000	120,664	312,520	.08	21.3	8.22
Mongolia	2,320,000	1,280,000	604,000	1,564,360	1.81	3.84	1.48
Ethiopia	1,415,000	25,900,000	457,256	1,184,293	.55	3.09	1.19
Yugoslavia	1,230,000	20,550,000	98,766	255,804	.60	1.25	.48
WORLD TOTAL	66,312,000	3,631,797,000	135,781,867	351,675,036	.02	.49	.19

[1] *Statistical Yearbook 1972* (New York, United Nations, 1972), pp. 118–126, 1970–71 data

[2] *The 1973 World Almanac* (New York: Newspaper Enterprise Association, Inc., 1972)

NUMBERS, BREED.—See BREED NUMBERS.

NUMNAH.—See SADDLE BLANKET.

NURSING.—See FOAL.

NUTRITIVE NEEDS.—To supply all the needs —maintenance, growth, fitting, reproduction, lactation, and work—the different classes of horses must receive sufficient feed to furnish the necessary quantity of energy (carbohydrates and fats), protein, minerals, and vitamins.

Table N-2 summarizes the pertinent known facts about the nutrient needs of horses. Of course, the nutritive needs vary according to age, weight, use or demands, growth, stage of gestation or lactation, and environment.

(Also see FEEDING HORSES; MINERALS; and VITAMINS.)

NUTRIENT REQUIREMENTS VS. ALLOWANCES.—In ration formulation, two words are commonly used—"requirements" and "allowances." Requirements do not provide for margins of safety. Thus, to feed a horse on the basis of meeting the bare requirements would not be unlike building a bridge without providing margins of safety for heavier than average loads or for floods. No competent engineer would be so foolish as to design such a bridge. Likewise, knowledgeable horse nutritionists provide for margins of safety—they provide for the necessary nutritive allowances. They allow for variations in feed composition; possible losses during storage and processing; day to day, and period to period, differences in needs of animals; age and size of animal; stage of gestation and lactation; the kind and degree of activity; the amount of stress; the system of management; the health, condition, and temperament of the animal; and the kind, quality, and amount of feed—all of which exert a powerful influence in determining nutritive needs.

TABLE N-2

NUTRITIVE NEEDS OF HORSES

Nutrient	Function of Nutrient	Some Deficiency Symptoms	Sources	Comments
Energy—for maintenance, work, reproduction, and conditioning.	Essential for the normal life processes of the horse including body maintenance, reproduction, and lactation. Because energy is necessary for life itself, it is the most important nutrient.	Foals: Slow and stunted growth. Mature horses: Loss of weight, poor condition, and excessive fatigue. Breeding animals: Poor reproduction; failure of some mares to show heat, more services per conception, lowered foal crops, and light weight foals.	Carbohydrates and fats of feeds.	The energy requirements are determined by— <ul><li>Individuality; some horses are hard keepers.</li><li>Size; feed according to approximate body weight.</li><li>Kind, amount, and severity of work; when racing, horses may expend up to 100 times the energy utilized at rest.</li><li>Weather; more energy is needed when it is cold.</li></ul>
Protein—for growth and repair.	Maintenance and building of muscle tissue and bone, including growth of hair and hoofs; development of fetus; growth of young stock; milk production.	Depressed appetite, poor growth, loss of weight, reduced milk production, irregular estrus, and lowered foal crops.	Largely from products remaining after processing rich oil-bearing seeds. Milk by-products should constitute part of protein source for foals.	Common farm grains and grass hays are inadequate as sources of proteins and proteins are of poor quality. There is little bacterial action in the cecum of foals; thus they should receive some high quality proteins such as milk by-products.
Minerals—for that all important 5% of the horse's weight, chiefly the skeleton, and for normal physiological processes.	At Washington State University, generation after generation of rabbits were fed on diets of two different levels of phosphorus. The low phosphorus group (1) was retarded in growth—with (2) 9.8% lower weaning weights, (2) required 12% more matings per conception, and (3) had a 47% lower breaking strength of bones than the rabbits on the high phosphorus diet. There is reason to believe that deficiencies of phosphorus, and the other minerals, affect horses similarly—in growth, reproduction, and soundness.	Unsoundnesses and nutritional deficiency diseases.	Grass hay and farm grains are deficient; thus special mineral supplementation is important. In addition, always give free access to salt.	Excess minerals are expensive; and imbalances may actually be injurious. It is recommended that the proper kinds and amounts of minerals be incorporated in the ration. In addition, horses should be allowed free access to (1) a suitable mineral mix and (2) salt, because of individual animal differences and unusual conditions.

(Continued)

TABLE N-2 (CONTINUED)

Nutrient	Function of Nutrient	Some Deficiency Symptoms	Sources	Comments
Vitamins—for growth, development, health, and reproduction.	The B vitamins are sometimes called the spark plugs or ignition system of the horse.	Single, uncomplicated vitamin deficiencies are the exception rather than the rule. There are no warning signals to tell a caretaker when a horse is not getting enough of a certain vitamin. But a continuing inadequate supply of any one of several vitamins can produce illness which is very hard to diagnose until it becomes severe; at which time it is difficult and expensive, if not impossible to treat. The important thing, therefore, is to insure against such deficiencies ocurring.	Vitamin-rich supplements; and unidentified factors from distiller's dried solubles, fish solubles, dried whey, high quality alfalfa meal, and liver.	Do not shower a horse with mistaken kindness through using shot-gun type vitamin preparations. Instead, the quantity of each vitamin should be based on available scientific knowledge. Cognizance should be taken of the fact that optimum results during the critical periods—early growth, gestation, lactation, and stress (as in racing)—may be dependent upon providing unidentified factors.

OATS.—The leading U.S. horse feed. Oats normally weigh 32 pounds per bushel, but the best horse oats are heavier. The feeding value varies according to the hull content and test weight per bushel.

Because of their bulky nature, oats form a desirable loose mass in the stomach, which prevents impaction.

Oats may be rolled, crimped, or fed whole.

Hulled oats are particularly valuable in the ration for young foals.

Fig. O-1. Oats, the favorite feed for horses. Picture shows head of oat plant. (Courtesy, J. C. Allen and Son, West Lafayette, Ind.)

ODDS *(racing).*—The numbers to the far right of the program page, next to the jockeys' names, indicate the probable odds the horses will pay, as determined by an expert at the beginning of the day. These odds are known as the "morning line." As betting gets underway before each race, these odds will likely change. The amount of money bet on each horse will be shown on the Totalisator and Odds Boards. The program odds (or morning line) for Snuffy may be 8 to 1, but if there is heavy betting on him, these odds may drop to 4 to 1 or 5 to 2 as shown on the Totalisator Board. The odds as shown when the race starts determine the payoffs.

ODDS-ON.—The term used to describe a horse that is likely to win in a race. For example, the "odds-on favorite" in a race.

OFFSET.—A quarter-pivot on the hindquarters, required in many Western reining classes. It must be executed with the horse giving the appearance of doing it easily—without tossing his head, opening his mouth, or otherwise fretting.

OFF SIDE.—The right side of a horse.

OLYMPIC GAMES.—As early as 1450 B.C., the sports-loving Greeks introduced the horse in the Olympic games, in both chariot and horse races. The most celebrated of these events was held at Olympia every fourth year in honor of Zeus. However, because of the scarcity of horses, very few were used in early contests. Classes were divided according to age—and sometimes sex—and the distance of the course was approximately four miles.

For these important events, the Greeks trained both themselves and their horses. The chariot races were even provided with settings to tempt the charioteers to daring deeds. The chariots in use were a low, two-wheeled, narrow-track type of vehicle.

MODERN OLYMPIC GAMES.—The equestrian sport became an Olympic event in the 1912 Games in Stockholm, Sweden. The program in this first modern Olympic Equestrian Games included individual dressage with a maximum of 6 riders per nation; a 3-day event with teams of 4 riders, of which 3 counted toward the team championship; and an individual jumping with 6 riders and a team jumping with 4 riders per nation, of which 3 counted. Except for the addition of team championships in dressage (beginning in 1928) and for only 3 or 4 riders (instead of 6) being allowed in the individual classes, the 1972 version of the equestrian program at the Olympics was virtually the same as the one started in 1912—60 years earlier.

At the 1972 Games in Munich, Germany, the British won the three-day event; West Germany won the individual dressage and the show jumping, although the individual gold medal went to Italy; and the U.S.S.R. won the team dressage.

OPEN BRIDLE.—Bridle without blinds or blinkers covering the eyes. Some bridles are rigged with blinds that shut off vision to the rear and side and a few horses are raced with goggles or "peekaboo" blinds.

OPEN-HOCKED.—Wide apart at the hocks with the feet close together.

OPEN JUMPER.—An open jumper is a horse that is considered suitable to compete in open jumping classes. Such a horse is judged on performance alone; the only requisite is that he be able to jump.

OPEN JUMPING CLASS.—An open jumping class is one that is open to all horses regardless of breed, age, size, experience, or conformation.

OPHTHALMIA.—See MOON BLINDNESS.

OPPOSITION *(reins of).*—See REINS, OPPOSITION.

ORAL.—Given by mouth.

ORGANIZATION CHART.—See MANAGEMENT.

ORIENTAL.—See EASTERN.

ORIENTAL LIGHT-LEGGED HORSE.—See WILD HORSE OF ASIA.

ORIGIN.—See DOMESTICATION AND EAR-LY USE.

ORLOFF TROTTER (ORLOV TROTTER).—A breed of horses originating in the U.S.S.R. in the eighteenth century, principally through the interest of Count Alexis Gregory Orloff Chesminski. Used in the Soviet Union for light work, pleasure driving and riding, exhibition at fairs in various forms of competition including dressage, and extensively in harness racing.

ORNAMENTS (bridle).—Decorative objects on the bridle, commonly worn in parade classes and costume classes, and by most three- and five-gaited horses, and Tennessee Walking Horses, especially where the eyes are set high and the nose long. Such horses wear broad, highly-colored browbands and broad, highly colored nosebands.

In the old days, bridle ornaments were common on driving bridles. In Victorian times, some of the bridle ornaments were very elaborate. They were made of metal, glass, or china, and they had colored flowers or other designs on them. Carriage horses generally wore metal ornaments with the initials or monogram of the owner thereon. United States cavalry horses usually wore copper ornaments with the seal of the U.S. embossed on them.

ORPHAN FOAL.—See FOAL, Raising the Orphan Foal.

OSSELETS.—Osselets, like bucked shins, are primarily an affliction of younger horses and the result of more strain or pressure from training or racing than the immature bone structure can stand. However, osselets are not so common among two-year-olds as bucked shins.

Osselets is a rather inclusive term used to refer to a number of inflammatory conditions around the ankle joints. Generally it denotes a swelling that is fairly well defined and located slightly above or below the actual center of the joint, and, ordinarily, a little to the inside or outside of the exact front of the leg. When touched, it imparts the feeling of putty or mush, and it may be warm to hot. The pain will be in keeping with the degree of inflammation as evidenced by swelling and fever. Afflicted horses travel with a short, choppy stride and show evidence of pain when the ankle is flexed.

Fig. O-2. Osselets on a Thoroughbred mare that was raced too young and too hard; showing inflammatory condition around the ankle joints. (Reproduced with permission of Haileybury Farm and Tampa Tracings, 1971; courtesy, The Wickes, Newville, Pa.)

Standard treatment consists in (1) stopping training at the first sign that the condition is developing, (2) "cooling out," and (3) resting. Firing, or firing followed by blistering, gives very satisfactory results.

(Also see UNSOUNDNESSES, Fig. U-2.)

OSTEOMALACIA.—A failure of mineralization of bone matrix resulting in softening of bone. Osteomalacia occurs in mature horses after bone growth has ceased.

CAUSE.—Lack of vitamin D. Inadequate intake of calcium and phosphorus. Incorrect ratio of calcium and phosphorus.

SYMPTOMS.—Phosphorus deficiency symptoms are: depraved appetite (gnawing on bones, wood, or other objects, or eating dirt), lack of appetite, stiffness of joints, failure to breed regularly, decreased milk production, and an emaciated appearance.

Calcium deficiency symptoms are: fragile bones, reproductive failures, and lowered lactations.

Mature animals are most affected. Usually the acute cases occur during pregnancy and lactation.

DISTRIBUTION AND LOSSES.—Southwestern U.S. is classed as a phosphorus-deficient area, whereas calcium-deficient areas have been reported in parts of Florida, Louisiana, Nebraska, Virginia, and West Virginia.

TREATMENT.—Increase the calcium and phosphorus content of feeds through fertilizing the soils. Select natural feeds that contain sufficient quantities of calcium and phosphorus. Feed a special mineral supplement or supplements. If the disease is far advanced, treatment will not be successful.

PREVENTION.—Feed balanced rations, and allow animals free access to a suitable phosphorus and calcium supplement.

REMARKS.—Calcium deficiencies are much more rare than phosphorus deficiencies in horses.

OUTCROSSING.—See BREEDING HORSES.

OUTLAW.—A horse that is wild and unmanageable, and that cannot be tamed.

OVA.—The female reproductive cells.

OVARY.—The female organ that produces eggs (ova). There are two ovaries.

OVER-AT-THE-KNEES (KNEE-SPRUNG; BUCK-KNEED).—Over at the knees. Standing with the knees too far forward.

OVERCHECK (*check rein*).—A piece of harness (leather or cord) attached to either side of the bit; and run to the pad in harness classes, and to the saddle in riding classes. It is for the purpose of keeping the head up.
(Also see HARNESS—Figs. H-4 and H-5).

OVERFEEDING.—Overfeeding may result in two consequences; if done suddenly it may cause founder (laminitis), if prolonged it will likely result in obesity (too fat). Both are bad.

The main qualities desired in horses are trimness, action, spirit, and endurance. These qualities cannot be obtained in horses that are overfed and fat. The latter is especially true with horses used for racing, where the carrying of any surplus body weight must be avoided.
(Also see FEEDING HORSES—Amount to Feed.)

OVER-REACH.—The hitting of the forefoot with the hind foot.

OVERRUN (*overrun the scent*).—A hunting term. When being pursued, a clever fox may make a very sharp turn, especially to cross a stream, to hop on stones, or to leap on a rail fence and run along for a short distance. The hounds may fail to make the quick turn and continue on in the direction they were going. In such circumstances, the hounds are said to overrun the scent.

OVERSHOT JAW.—The upper jaw protruding beyond the lower jaw. Same as "parrot mouth."

OVULATION.—The time when the follicle bursts and the egg is released.

OVUM.—Scientific Latin name for a single egg.

OWN (*to own the scent*).—Hunting people never say that a hound is baying or barking. Rather, a hound speaks; and they understand his language. Thus, when a hound speaks in a certain way the huntsman knows that he has found the scent. At such time the hound is said "to own the scent" or to honor the scent.

OXBOW STIRRUP.—A large wooden stirrup resembling an oxbow in shape. It is made of a piece of wood bent into a U-shape and held together at the open end of the "U" by a metal bolt long enough to accommodate the stirrup leather.

OXER.—A type of hunting obstacle. It consists of an ordinary hedge about three feet in height with a guardrail set about a yard out from it on one side. If it has a guardrail on both sides, it is called a "double oxer." This is a common type of obstacle in England, but it is rarely seen in the United States except in specially made hunt courses.

P

PACE.—A fast two-beat gait in which the front and hind feet on the same side start and stop simultaneously. The feet rise just above the ground level. There is a split second when all four feet are off the ground and the horse seems to float through the air.

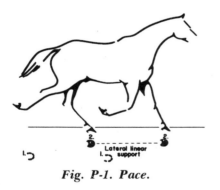

Lateral linear support

Fig. P-1. Pace.

PACER (S).—Correctly speaking, any horse that paces is a "pacer." By common usage, it refers to harness racehorses of the Standardbred breed whose speed gait is the pace.

Pacers and trotters are of similar breeding and type, the particular gaits being largely a matter of training. In fact, many individuals show speed at both the pace and the trot. It is generally recognized, however, that pacers are handicapped in the mud, in the sand, or over rough surface.

(Also see BREED (S)—Table B-2 and STANDARDBRED.)

PACE, STEPPING (OR SLOW PACE).—This is the preferred slow gait for five-gaited show horses. It is a modified pace in which the objectionable side or rolling motion of the true pace is eliminated because the two feet on each side do not move exactly together. Instead, it is a four-beat gait with each of the four feet striking the ground separately. In the take-off, the hind and front feet start almost together, but the hind foot touches the ground slightly ahead of the front foot on the same side, and each foot strikes the ground separately.

PACKHORSE.—A horse used to carry loads on a packsaddle or in baskets (panniers) on the back, as distinguished from a horse used for riding or draft. In ancient times, packhorses were the chief, and often the only, means of transportation for goods. Also, until armies became highly mechanized, packhorses and mules were often used in transporting supplies for armies, particularly over rough terrain.

Today, packhorses find their greatest use by vacationers, hunters, and the U.S. Forest Service, for packing into areas not otherwise easily accessible. Such animals should be surefooted, and should be trained to pack their loads well and with safety.

PAD.—See SADDLE BLANKET.

PADDLING.—Throwing the front feet outward as they are picked up is known as paddling. This condition is predisposed in horses with toe-narrow or pigeon-toed standing positions.

(Also see SHOEING.)

PADDOCK.—1. A small enclosed area, typically adjoining or near a horse stable, and often used as a pasture. (See Fig. P-2.)

2. The enclosure where racehorses are saddled and paraded before a race.

PAINT HORSE, AMERICAN.—See BREED (S).

Fig. P-2. Paddocks enclosed by a practical 5-pole fence, with an open shed in each paddock; at Bitterroot Stock Farm, Hamilton, Montana, owned by Margit Sigray Bessenyey. (Photo by Ernst Peterson, Hamilton, Montana)

PAIR.—Two horses hitched abreast. Also, used in reference to two horses ridden side by side, together as in pair classes.

PAIR CLASSES.—Horse shows have pair classes for many kinds of horses—three-gaited horses, hunters, jumpers, parade horses, and equitation horses. In all pair classes, the horses perform together; hence, manners are important. Additionally, uniformity is stressed in some, and general appearance and uniformity in others.

PALATABILITY.—See FEED.

PALOMINO.—See BREED(S); and COLORS AND MARKINGS OF HORSES.

PALOMINO HORSE ASSOCIATION.—Box 324, Jefferson City, Missouri 65101. (See Appendix for complete breed registry association list.)

PALOMINO HORSE BREEDERS OF AMERICA.—Box 249, Mineral Wells, Texas 76067. (See Appendix for complete breed registry association list.)

PANEL.—In a hunting field, any solid, upright obstacle may be spoken of as a "panel." However, correctly speaking it refers to the "chicken coops" commonly put over wire fences at appropriate intervals in hunting country so that they may be jumped with safety.

(Also see JUMPS (TYPES)—Fig. J-5.)

PARADE HORSES.—Parade Horses are horses of any breed, cross, or color used under elaborate Western, Mexican, or Spanish equipment in Parade Horse classes. They are shown at an animated walk and a parade gait. The latter is a prancing cadenced trot at about five miles per hour.

PARASITES OF HORSES.—Broadly speaking, parasites are organisms living in, on, or at the expense of another living organism. They include fungi, protozoa (or unicellular animals), arthropods (or insects, ticks, and related forms), and helminths (or worms).

Any animal that serves as a residence for a parasite is referred to as a host. In order to complete their life span (cycle), some parasites require only one host while others need more.

While in residence, parasites usually seriously affect the host, but there are notable exceptions. Among the ways in which parasites may do harm are: (1) absorbing food, (2) sucking blood or lymph, (3) feeding on the tissue of the host, (4) obstructing passages, (5) causing nodules or growths, (6) causing irritation, and (7) transmitting diseases. These may result in death of the affected animal; or they may cause large financial loss through stunted growth, lowered production, general unthriftiness, and emaciation. (See Fig. P-3.)

INTERNAL PARASITES.—Some 150 different kinds of internal parasites attack horses throughout the world and probably no animal is ever entirely free of them.

Parasites may be located in practically every tissue and cavity of the body. However, most of them are in the alimentary tract, lungs, body cavity, or bloodstream. Those in the digestive system usually become localized there, but others travel throughout different parts of the body.

The general symptoms of parasitic infection in horses are weakness, unthriftiness, emaciation, tucked-up flanks, distended abdomen, rough coat,

Fig. P-3. Same horse before (upper picture) and after (bottom picture) treatment for internal parasites. Parasites lower the efficiency of mature horses and retard the development of foals. Besides, feed is always too costly to give to parasites. (Courtesy, College of Veterinary Medicine, University of Illinois)

pale membranes in the eyes and mouth, stunted growth in young animals, and in some cases frequent colic and diarrhea. Affected animals usually eat well and their temperature remains normal. But an infected animal always loses some efficiency as a working unit.

Few treatments with only one drug are effective in removing bots and various gastrointestinal worms from horses. Usually, it is necessary to use a combination of drugs. For this purpose, the specific combination is dependent upon the kinds of parasites present in the horses to be treated. It is always wise, therefore, to obtain a definite diagnosis from a veterinarian or veterinary diagnostic laboratory before treatment is given. A veterinarian should always be consulted for safe and effective dosages of the various drugs and treatment schedules.

Trade names of pesticides used to control parasites are mentioned in this book solely to provide specific information. Mention of a trade name does not constitute a guarantee of the product by the author of this book, nor does it imply an endorsement over comparable products that are not named. When any trade-named compound is used, the directions for use given on the label should be followed very carefully.

The common internal parasites of horses and some of the drugs used to treat them are discussed in this book under the alphabetical listing of each parasite.

(Also see HEALTH PROGRAM.)

EXTERNAL PARASITES.—Several kinds of external parasites attack horses. These pests lower the vitality of horses, damage the hair and skin, and produce a generally unthrifty condition.

External parasites also are responsible for the spread of several serious diseases of horses. Equine piroplasmosis (babesiasis) is transmitted by a tick, *Dermacentor nitens.* Mosquitoes *(Culicadae)* are vectors of equine infectious anemia (swamp fever) and equine encephalomyelitis (sleeping sickness).

The common measures used to prevent and control external parasites of horses are practicing good sanitation, good grooming, avoiding a too heavy concentration of horses, and spraying or dusting with insecticides. Flies and lice are the most common external parasites of horses but some of the others can produce more severe injury when they occur.

The common external parasites of horses and approved control measures are discussed in this book under the alphabetical listing of each parasite.

(Also see HEALTH PROGRAM.)

PARERS.—See SHOEING—Table S-5.

PARI-MUTUELS.—This refers to machine-controlled pool betting. The totalisator was invented in France in 1865, by a perfume-shop proprietor named Pierre Oller, who, embittered by a losing streak with the bookies, worked out the idea of the betting pool and began selling tickets over his store counter. His take was 5%; the rest was divided equally among the winners.

Only through the workings of the totalisator can the customer at a racetrack receive the exact amount due him immediately after a race is run. From the moment that a ticket is purchased until it is ready to be cashed in, this giant machine keeps grinding away, tabulating and re-tabulating.

● *What happens to the loser's betting dollar?* —Not all the money that is wagered is returned to bettors. Between 10 and 17 percent goes to the track and state, with the take-out prescribed by law for each state and varying slightly from state to state. On the average, the track and the state divide the take about equally. Roughly, this is what happens to the losing bettor's dollar:

88¢ goes to winning bettors
6¢ goes to the state treasury
6¢ goes to the track, of which—
    3¢ goes to defray taxes
    2¢ for purses and added money for future races
    1¢ to cover salaries, expenses, etc.

PARK HACK.—A horse that is suitable for general riding. In a show, a park hack is required to have easy gaits, good manners, and a showy appearance.

PARK HORSE CLASSES.—Park horse classes are particularly popular with Arabian breeders. According to the American Horse Shows Association *Rule Book,* Arabian park horses are to be shown at the walk, trot, and canter; and are to be judged on brilliant performance, presence, quality, manners, and conformation.

PARK RIDER.—Usually an inexperienced rider who rides in the park for the purpose of "showing off." Typically, park riders dress the part. Unless mounted on a very gentle horse, such a rider is likely to join the "fall club."

PARROT MOUTH (OVERSHOT JAW).—An hereditary imperfection in the way in which the teeth come together. In parrot mouth or overshot jaw, the lower jaw is shorter than the up-

per jaw.
(Also see UNSOUNDNESSES.)

PARTHENON FRIEZE (HORSES).—One of the most famous sculptures in the world is that of the horses on the Parthenon, which dates back to the mid-fifth century B.C. Carved on the top of the outer wall of the Cella of the Parthenon at Athens, it represents the ritual procession of the Pan-Athenaic festival and shows many horses of different types.
(Also see ART, HORSES IN.)

PARTNERSHIPS.—See INHERITANCE AND PARTNERSHIPS.

PARTS OF A HORSE.—In selecting and judging horses, horsemen usually refer to parts rather than the individual as a whole. Nothing so quickly sets a real horseman apart from a novice as a thorough knowledge of the parts and the language commonly used in describing them. Fig. P-4 shows the parts of a horse. (See page 302.)

PARTURITION *(signs of).*—Signs of approaching parturition are as follows: A distended udder, which may be observed 2 to 6 weeks before foaling; shrinkage or falling away of the buttocks' muscles near the tailhead and a falling of the abdomen 7 to 10 days before foaling; filling out of the teats 4 to 6 days before foaling; and appearance of wax on the ends of the nipples 4 to 6 days before foaling. As foaling time draws nearer, the vulva becomes full and loose, milk drops from the teats, and the mare becomes restless, breaks into a sweat, urinates frequently, lies down and gets up, etc. But there are times when all signs fail, so be prepared 30 days in advance of the expected time.

PASO FINO.—See BREED (S).

PASO FINO OWNERS & BREEDERS ASSN., INC.—P. O. Box 764, Columbus, North Carolina 28722. (See Appendix for complete breed registry association list.)

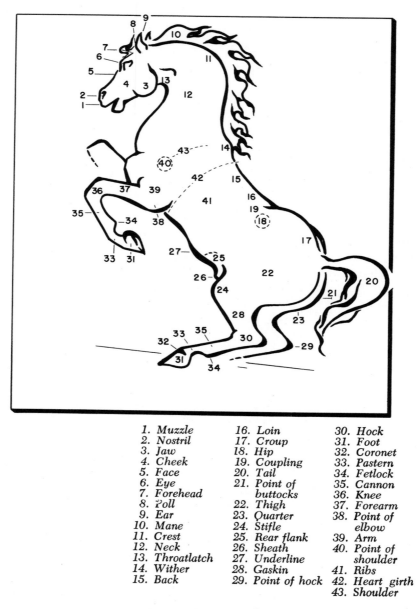

1. Muzzle	16. Loin	30. Hock
2. Nostril	17. Croup	31. Foot
3. Jaw	18. Hip	32. Coronet
4. Cheek	19. Coupling	33. Pastern
5. Face	20. Tail	34. Fetlock
6. Eye	21. Point of	35. Cannon
7. Forehead	buttocks	36. Knee
8. Poll	22. Thigh	37. Forearm
9. Ear	23. Quarter	38. Point of
10. Mane	24. Stifle	elbow
11. Crest	25. Rear flank	39. Arm
12. Neck	26. Sheath	40. Point of
13. Throatlatch	27. Underline	shoulder
14. Wither	28. Gaskin	41. Ribs
15. Back	29. Point of hock	42. Heart girth
		43. Shoulder

Fig. P-4. Parts of a horse.

PASSAGE.—A movement of the *haute école*. This is a slow, cadenced, rather high trot with a fairly long period of suspension, giving the impression that the horse is on springs, or "trotting on air." Also a term for diagonal movement of the horse while facing straight forward, at the walk or trot. (See Fig. P-5.)

PASTERN.—1. That part of the leg between the fetlock joint and the coronary band of the hoof. The pasterns serve as a base of attachment for extensor and flexor tendons; hence they function in locomotion as agents of extension and flexion. The pasterns should slope about 45°; and they should be neither too long nor too short. Ex-

Fig. P-5. White Lipizzan stallion at the Spanish Riding School, Wels, Austria, doing the Passage. (Courtesy, Spanish Riding School)

tremely long pasterns are weak. Very short, straight pasterns increase concussion and produce stilty action.

2. Also, pastern refers to a particular leg mark, where the white extends from the coronet to and including the pastern.

(Also see PARTS OF A HORSE—Fig. P-4; and COLORS AND MARKINGS OF HORSES —Fig. C-10.)

PASTIMES USE.—See USE OF HORSES.

PASTURE BREEDING.—See BREEDING HORSES.

PASTURES.—The great horse breeding centers of the world are characterized by good pastures. Thus, the bluegrass area of Kentucky is known for its lush pastures produced on residual limestone soils. In short, good horsemen, good horses, and good pastures go hand in hand—the latter being the cornerstone of successful horse produc-

tion. Yet, it is becoming increasingly difficult to provide good pastures for many horses, especially for those in suburban areas. Also, it is recognized that many horsemen are prone to overrate the quality of their grass.

In season, there is no finer forage for horses than superior pastures—pastures that are much more than gymnasiums. This is especially true for idle horses, broodmares, and young stock. In fact, pastures have a very definite place for all horses, with the possible exception of animals at heavy work or in training. Even with the latter groups, pastures may be used with discretion. Horses in heavy use may be turned to pasture at night or over the weekend. Certainly, the total benefits derived from pasture are to the good, although pasturing may have some laxative effects and produce a greater tendency to sweat.

In addition to the nutritive value of the grass, pasture provides invaluable exercise on natural footing—with plenty of sunshine, fresh air, and lowered feeding costs as added benefits. Feeding on pasture is the ideal existence for young stock and breeding animals.

But pastures should not be taken for granted. Again and again, scientists and practical horsemen have demonstrated that the following desired goals in pasture production are well with-

Fig. P-6. Standardbred mares and foals on pasture at Hanover Shoe Farm, Hanover, Pennsylvania, the world's largest Standardbred nursery. Good pasture and plenty of shade are important requisites to successful horse production. (Courtesy, The United States Trotting Association)

Fig. P-7. Hungarian mares and foals on pasture at Bitterroot Stock Farm, Hamilton, Montana. Copper magnate Marcus Daly, of Anaconda Copper Co. fame, credited the grasses of Montana's Bitterroot Valley with imparting soundness and stamina to his horses. A half century later, the Hungarian horses owned by Margit Sigray Bessenyey give little reason to dispute her grandfather's claims. (Photo by Ernst Peterson, Hamilton, Montana)

in the realm of possibility:

• To produce higher yields of palatable and nutritious forage.

• To extend the grazing season from as early in the spring to as late in the fall as possible.

• To provide a fairly uniform supply of feed throughout the entire season.

The specific grass or grass-legume mixture will vary from area to area, according to differences in soil, temperature, and rainfall. A complete listing of all adapted and recommended grasses and legumes for horse pastures would be too lengthy for this encyclopedia. However, Table P-1 shows the most important ones by areas. In using this chart, bear in mind that many species of forages have wide geographic adaptation, but sub-species or varieties often have rather specific adaptation. Thus, alfalfa, for example, is represented by many varieties which give this species adaptation to nearly all states. Variety then, within species, makes many forages adapted to the widely varying climate and geographic areas. The county agricultural agent or state agricultural college can furnish recommendations for the area that they serve. See Table P-1 for adapted grasses and legumes, and see Fig. P-8 for areas.

Legume pastures are excellent for horses, as equines are less subject to bloat than cattle or sheep.

Sudan and hybrid Sudans in the growing stage should never be grazed by horses, because of the hazard of cystitis. This disease, which occurs more frequently in mares than in stallions or geldings, is characterized by continuous urination, mares appearing to be constantly in heat, and incoordination in the gait. Animals seldom recover after either the incoordination or the dribbling of urine becomes evident. Apparently hay from Sudan or hybrid Sudans will not produce the same malady.

Horse pastures should be well drained and not too rough or stony. All dangerous places—such as pits, stumps, poles, and tanks—should be guarded. Shade, water, and suitable minerals should be available in all pastures.

Most horse pastures can be improved by fertilizing and management. Also, horsemen need to give attention to balancing pastures nutritionally. Early-in-the-season grasses are of high-water content and lack energy. Mature weathered grass is almost always deficient in protein (being as low as 3 percent or less) and low in carotene. But these deficiencies can be corrected by proper supplemental feeding.

● *Supplementing Early Spring Grass.*—Turning horses on pasture when the first sprigs of green grass appear will usually make for a temporary deficiency of energy, due to (1) washy (high water content) grasses and (2) inadequate forage for animals to consume. As a result, owners are often disappointed in the poor condition of horses.

If there is good reason why grazing cannot be delayed until there is adequate spring growth, it is recommended that early pastures be supplemented with grass hay or straw (a legume hay will accentuate looseness, which usually exists under such circumstances), preferably placed in a rack; perhaps with a high energy concentrate provided, also.

● *Supplementing Dry Pasture.*—Dry, mature, weathered, bleached grass characterizes (1) drought periods and (2) fall-winter pastures. Such cured-on-the-stalk grasses are low in energy, in protein, in carotene, and in phosphorus and perhaps certain other minerals. These deficiencies become more acute following frost and increase in severity as winter advances. This explains the

TABLE P-1

LEGUMES AND GRASSES ADAPTED TO THE 10 AREAS

OF THE 48 CONTIGUOUS STATES 1

Regions of Adaptation (see Fig. P-8)

Legumes	1	2	3	4	5	6	7	8	9	10
Alfalfa	x	x	x	x	x	x	x	x	x	x
Alsike Clover	x	x			x		x		x	
Birdsfoot Trefoil	x	x					x	x	x	
Bur Clover			x	x		x			x	x
Crimson Clover		x	x	x						x
Hop Clover			x							
Kudzu		x	x	x						
Ladino Clover	x	x	x	x	x	x	x	x	x	x
Lespedeza		x	x	x						
Lupine			x							
Persian Clover			x							
Red Clover	x	x	x		x	x	x	x	x	x
Sweet Clover	x	x	x		x	x	x	x	x	x
Vetches	x	x	x	x	x	x	x	x	x	
White Clover	x	x	x	x	x	x	x	x	x	x
Grasses										
Bahia Grass			x	x						
Bermuda Grass		x	x	x				x		x
Big Bluestem	x				x	x		x		
Blue Grama						x				
Blue Panicum						x				
Buffalo Grass					x	x				
Carpet Grass			x	x						
Chewings Fescue									x	
Common Ryegrass	x	x	x	x				x	x	x
Creeping Red Fescue									x	
Dallis Grass			x	x				x		x
Harding Grass								x		x
Indian Grass					x	x				
Kentucky Bluegrass	x	x							x	
Little Bluestem	x				x	x				
Lovegrasses					x	x	x			
Meadow Fescue	x	x				x			x	
Meadow Foxtail	x					x			x	
Millets	x				x	x				
Mountain Bromegrass							x			
Orchardgrass	x	x	x	x			x	x	x	x
Pangola				x						
Perennial Ryegrass	x	x	x	x				x	x	x
Redtop	x	x	x						x	
Reed Canary Grass	x	x							x	x
Rescuegrass			x			x		x		x
Rhodes Grass						x		x		x
Sand Dropseed					x	x				
Side Oats Grama					x	x				
Smooth Bromegrass	x				x		x	x		x
(Continued)										

TABLE P-1 (CONTINUED)

Grasses	1	2	3	4	5	6	7	8	9	10
Soft Chess										x
Tall Fescue	x	x	x	x			x	x	x	x
Tall Oatgrass	x	x					x	x	x	
Timothy	x	x			x		x		x	
Veldt Grass										x
Wheatgrasses					x		x	x		
Yellow Bluestem						x				

1 Adapted from *Pasture—How to Reduce Feed Costs* (Peoria, Illinois: Keystone Steel and Wire, 1958), p. 17.

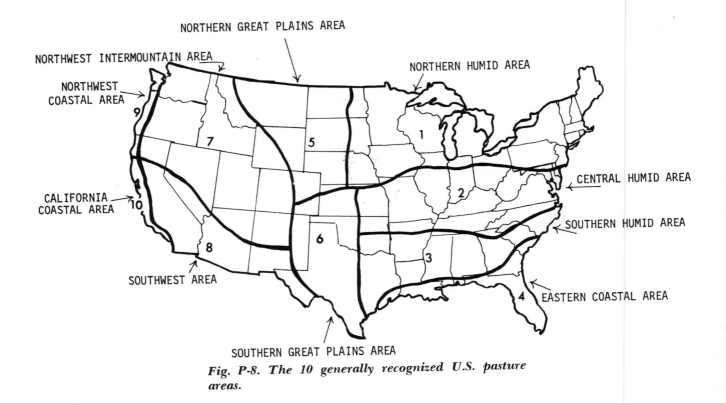

NORTHERN GREAT PLAINS AREA

NORTHWEST INTERMOUNTAIN AREA

NORTHWEST COASTAL AREA

NORTHERN HUMID AREA

CENTRAL HUMID AREA

CALIFORNIA COASTAL AREA

SOUTHERN HUMID AREA

SOUTHWEST AREA

EASTERN COASTAL AREA

SOUTHERN GREAT PLAINS AREA

Fig. P-8. The 10 generally recognized U.S. pasture areas.

often severe loss in condition of horses following the first fall freeze.

In addition to the deficiencies which normally characterize whatever plants are available, dry pasture may be plagued by a short supply of feed.

Generally speaking, a concentrate or supplement is best used during droughts or on fall-winter pastures. However, when there is an acute shortage of forage, hay or other roughage also should be added.

● *Pasture Supplements.*—Horsemen face the question of what supplement to use, when to feed it, and how much of it to feed.

In supplying a supplement to horses on pasture, the following guides should be observed:

● It should balance the diet of the horses to which it is fed, which means that it should supply all the nutrients missing in the forage.

● It should be fed in such a way that each horse gets its proper proportion, which generally means (1) the use of salt blocks, (2) tying up horses during concentrate feeding when more than one animal is fed in a given pasture, or (3) taking them to their stalls at feeding time.

• The daily allowance of the supplement should be determined by (1) the available pasture (quantity and quality), and (2) the condition of the horse.

The results from the use of the supplement, rather than cost per bag, should determine the choice of supplement.

● *Management of Sub-Humid, Humid, and Irrigated Pastures.*—Many good horse pastures have been established only to be lost through careless management. Good pasture management in the sub-humid, humid, and irrigated areas involves the following practices:

• *Controlled grazing.*—Nothing contributes more to good pasture management than controlled grazing. At its best, it embraces the following:

1. *Protection of first year seedings.*— First year seedings should be grazed lightly or not at all in order that they may get a good start in life. Where practical, instead of grazing, it is preferable to mow a new first year seeding about three inches above the ground and to utilize it as hay, provided there is sufficient growth to justify this procedure.

2. *Rotation or alternate grazing.*—Rotation or alternate grazing is accomplished by dividing a pasture into fields (usually two to four) of approximately equal size, so that one field can be grazed while the others are allowed to make new growth. This results in increased pasture yields, more uniform grazing, and higher quality forage.

Generally speaking, rotation or alternate grazing is (1) more practical and profitable on rotation and supplemental pastures than on permanent pastures, and (2) more beneficial where parasite infestations are heavy than where little or no parasitic problems are involved.

3. *Shifting the location of salt, shade, and water.*—Where portable salt containers are used, more uniform grazing and scatter-

ing of the droppings may be obtained simply by the practice of shifting the location of the salt to the less grazed areas of the pasture. Where possible and practical, the shade and the water should be shifted likewise.

4. *Deferred spring grazing.*—Allow 6 to 8 inches of growth before turning horses out to pasture in the spring, thus giving grass a needed start. Anyway, the early spring growth of pastures is high in moisture and washy.

5. *Avoiding close late fall grazing.*— Pastures that are grazed closely late in the fall start late in the spring. With most pastures, three to five inches of growth should be left for winter cover.

6. *Avoiding overgrazing.*—Never graze more closely than two to three inches during the pasture season. Continued close grazing reduces the yield, weakens the plants, allows weeds to invade, and increases soil erosion. The use of temporary and supplemental pastures, may "spell off" regular pastures through seasons of drought and other pasture shortages and thus alleviate overgrazing.

7. *Avoiding undergrazing.*—Undergrazing seeded pastures should also be avoided, because (1) mature forage is unpalatable and of low nutritive value, (2) tall-growing grasses may drive out such low-growing plants due to shading, and (3) weeds, brush, and coarse grasses are more apt to gain a foothold when the pasture is grazed insufficiently. It is a good rule, therefore, to graze the pasture fairly close at least once each year.

• *Clipping pastures and controlling weeds.*—Pastures should be clipped at such intervals as necessary to control weeds (and brush) and to get rid of uneaten clumps and other unpalatable coarse growth left after incomplete grazing. Pastures that are grazed continuously may be clipped at or just preceding the usual haymaking time; rotated pastures may be clipped at the close of the grazing period.

• *Topdressing.*—Like animals, for best results, grasses and legumes must be fed properly throughout a lifetime. It is not sufficient that they be fertilized (and limed if necessary) at or prior to seeding time. In addition, in most areas it is desirable and profitable to top-dress pastures with fertilizer annually, and, at less frequent intervals, with lime (lime to maintain a pH of about 6.5). Such treatments should be based on soil tests, and are usually applied in the spring or fall.

• *Scattering droppings.*—The droppings should be scattered three or four times each year and at the end of each grazing season in order to prevent animals from leaving ungrazed clumps and to help them fertilize a larger area. This can best be done by the use of a brush harrow or chain harrow.

• *Grazing by more than one class of animals.*—Grazing by two or more classes of animals makes for more uniform pasture utilization and fewer weeds and parasites, provided the area is not overstocked. Different kinds of livestock have different habits of grazing; they show preference for different plants and graze to different heights.

• *Irrigating where practical and feasible.*—Where irrigation is practical and feasible, it alleviates the necessity of depending on the weather.

• *Supplementing to provide needed nutrients.*—Although the horse ration should be as economical as possible, condition and results in show, sale, and use are the primary objectives, even at somewhat added expense. Generally, this calls for supplemental feeding on pasture—for providing added energy, protein, minerals, and vitamins.

● *Extending the Grazing Season.*—In the South and in Hawaii, year-round grazing is a reality on many a successful horse establishment. By careful planning and by selecting the proper combination of crops, other areas can approach this desired goal.

In addition to lengthening the grazing season through the selection of species, earlier spring pastures can be secured by avoiding grazing too late in the fall and by the application of a nitrogen fertilizer in the fall or early spring. Nitrogen fertilizers will often stimulate the growth of grass so that it will be ready for grazing ten days to two weeks earlier than unfertilized areas.

PATHOGENIC.—Disease-producing.

PATHOLOGICAL.—Diseased, or due to disease.

PAWING, STALL.—See VICES—Stall Pawing.

PECKING.—Refers to a horse hitting a jump lightly with his front feet.

PEDAL BONE.—See COFFIN BONE.

PEDIGREE.—A record of the ancestry of an animal.

PEDIGREE BREEDING.—Selection on the combined bases of the merits of the individual and the average merits of its ancestry.

PEGASUS.—The word *Pegasus* is of Greek origin, meaning strong. Legend has it that the winged horse, Pegasus, was fashioned from the body of Medusa, daughter of a sea-god who, in her youth, was as mortal as she was beautiful. At his birth, the frisky colt flew to Mount Helicon, where he created a fountain (Horsewell) with one swift blow of his hoof. Using a golden bridle, Bellerophon coaxed the curious animal from his favorite meadow, made him captive, and rode him off. Later, Pegasus unceremoniously dumped his venerable and conceited master and flew into outer space where he became the constellation that bears his name.

PELHAM.—An English curb bit with a bar mouthpiece, straight sidepieces, and four rings for reins. It is used in a pelham bridle for hunters, polo ponies, and pleasure hunters.
(Also see BITS—Fig. B-9.)

PELLETS AS A COMPLETE FEED.—Pelleted feeds may be prepared from concentrates alone, forage alone, or concentrates and roughage combined in a complete ration. The latter will be discussed in this section.

Currently, horsemen are much interested in complete, all-pelleted feed, in which the hay and

Fig. P-9. The pellet (left) has three times the feed value of the baled hay (right). (Courtesy, Albers Milling Company)

grain are combined. Compared to conventional long hay and grain concentrate fed separately, all-pelleted feed has the following advantages:

• It is less bulky and easier to store and handle, thus lessening transportation, building, and labor costs. Pelleted roughage requires one-fifth to one-third as much space as is required by the same roughage in loose or chopped form.

Pelleting prevents horses from selectively refusing ingredients likely to be high in certain dietary essentials; each bite is a balanced feed.

• Pelleting practically eliminates waste; therefore, less pelleted feed is required. Horses may waste up to twenty percent of long hay. Waste of conventional feed is highest where low quality hay is fed or feed containers are poorly designed.

• Pelleting eliminates dustiness and lessens the likelihood of heaves.

• Pellet-fed horses are trimmer in the middle and more attractive because they consume less bulk.

The following points are pertinent to the proper understanding and use of all-pelleted rations:

• One-half inch pellets are preferred for mature horses, and one-fourth inch pellets for weanlings and yearlings. Also, very hard pellets should be avoided; if horses cannot chew them, they will not eat them.

• The ratio of roughage to concentrates should be higher in all-pelleted rations than when long hay is fed. For most horses, the ratio may range

from 60.5 to 69 percent roughage to 31 to 39.5 percent concentrate.

• Any horse feed should form a loose mass in the stomach to assure ease of digestion, fewer digestive disturbances, and less impaction. To this end, in a complete all-pelleted ration, such feeds as oats and barley should be crimped or steam rolled but not finely ground. The roughage should be one-fourth inch chop or coarser. Otherwise, a couple of pounds of long hay may be fed daily to each horse.

• Young horses and horses at heavy work need more energy. They should be fed less roughage and more concentrate.

• When less roughage and more concentrate is fed, horses are likely to be overfed and get too fat if they are idle or at light to medium work. But if the total feed consumption is limited too severely to keep the weight down, the problem of wood chewing is increased because of a lack of physical filling of the digestive tract.

• When the roughage consists of high quality legume hay, a higher percentage of roughage may be used than when all or part of the roughage is grass or other nonlegumes.

• If more energy is needed for racehorses or for young stock on an all-pelleted ration, it can be provided either by increasing the daily allowance of the all-pelleted ration, and/or replacing a portion of the all-pelleted ration with a suitable concentrate or supplement.

• Because waste is eliminated, less all-pelleted feed is required than conventional feed. For a horse at light work, give 14 to 18 pounds of all-pelleted feed daily per 1,000 pounds of body weight. Use a feed that contains 51 to 58 percent total digestible nutrients (TDN). Increase the feed allowance with the severity of work.

• As with any change in feed, the switch to an all-pelleted ration should be made gradually, otherwise such vices as wood chewing and bolting (eating feed too rapidly) may be induced. At first, continue to offer all the long hay the horse wants and slowly replace the grain portion of the conventional ration with the complete pelleted feed. Increase the pelleted feed by 1 to 2 pounds daily and begin gradually lessening the hay. After a few days, the horse usually will stop eating the hay and it can be removed completely from the ration.

• The feces of pellet-fed horses are softer than the feces of those not fed pellets.

Among many horsemen, the feeling persists

that horses fed all-pelleted rations are more likely to chew wood than those fed long hay. This may be true to some degree. But some horses will chew wood regardless of what they are fed. This leads to the conclusion that the way to prevent wood chewing is simply to use metal, masonry, or other nonwood materials for all buildings, fences, and other equipment. Of course, this is not always practical.

Wood chewing can be lessened, although not prevented entirely, through one or more of the following practices:

- Increase the exercise.
- Feed three times a day, rather than twice a day, even though the total daily feed allowance remains the same.
- Spread out the pellets in a larger feed container or place a few large stones about the size of a baseball in the feed container, thereby making the horse work harder and longer to obtain the pellets.
- Provide 2 to 4 pounds of straw or coarse grass hay per animal per day, thereby giving the horse something to nibble on when he is idle.

PELVIC LIMBS.—The pelvic limbs, embracing 40 bones, are the horse's chief means of propulsion forward. The stifle and hock joints will be discussed separately under this heading.

The stifle joint of the horse corresponds to the knee in the human. Excepting for an occasional dislocation of the patella (a condition known as stifled), this joint is not subject to much trouble.

The hock is the most important single joint of the horse, probably being the seat of more serious unsoundnesses than any other part of the body—among them bone spavins, bog spavins, curbs, and thoroughpins. The hock should be wide, deep, flat, clean, hard, strong, well supported, and correctly set with prominent points.

The rear pasterns should be similar to the front ones, although they may be slightly less sloping (a 50° angle being satisfactory for the hind foot).

The set to the hind legs should be such that, when viewed from the rear, a vertical line dropped from the point of the buttock will fall upon the center of the hock, cannon, and foot. When viewed from the side, this vertical line should touch the point of the hock and run parallel with the back of the cannon.

(Also see SKELETON; and LEGS.)

PERCHERON.—See BREED(S).

PERCHERON HORSE ASSOCIATION OF AMERICA.—Route 1, Belmont, Ohio 43718. (See Appendix for complete breed registry association list.)

PERFORMANCE TESTING HORSES.—The breeders of racehorses have always followed a program of mating animals of proved performance on the track. For example, it is interesting to note that the first breed register which appeared in 1791—known as "An Introduction to The General Stud Book,"—recorded the pedigrees of all the Thoroughbred horses winning important races. In a similar way, the Standardbred horse—which is an American creation—takes its name from the fact that, in its early history, animals were required to trot a mile in two minutes and thirty seconds, or to pace a mile in two minutes and twenty-five seconds, before they could be considered as eligible for registry. The chief aim, therefore, of early-day breeders of racehorses was to record the pedigree of outstanding performers rather than all members of the breed.

The simplest type of Progeny Testing in horses consists of the average record or merit of an individual stallion's or mare's offspring. Thus, the offspring of Thoroughbred or Standardbred animals bred for racing may be tested by timing on the track. Less satisfactory tests for saddle horses and harness horses have been devised. However, it is conceivable that actual exhibiting on the tanbark in the great horse shows of the country may be an acceptable criterion for saddle- and harness-bred animals.

PERIODIC OPHTHALMIA.—See MOON BLINDNESS.

PERIOPLE.—The varnish-like substance that covers the outer surface of the wall of the hoof and seals it from excess drying. It is produced by the perioplic ring located at the top of the coronet. A good farrier does not rasp off more of the periople than absolutely necessary.

(Also see FOOT—Fig. F-20 and Table F-5.)

PERUVIAN PASO HORSE.—See BREED (S).

PERUVIAN PASO HORSE REGISTRY OF N.A.—P. O. Box 816, Guerneville, California 95446. (See Appendix for complete breed registry association list.)

PHAETON.—A four-wheeled vehicle of which there are many varieties. The early phaetons were built very high. But those of the nineteenth century were considerably lower and were made in many different shapes and sizes. There was the Pony Phaeton made in 1824 for King George IV. Then in 1828 came the Massive Mail Phaeton driven exclusively by men. Elegant Ladies' Phaetons followed.

Fig. P-10. The Park Phaeton.

pH OF SOIL.—See SOIL pH.

PHOSPHORUS.—See MINERALS.

PIAFFE.—A dressage movement in which the horse does a cadenced trot in place, without moving from the spot. It is the foundation of all high school movements. (See Fig. P-11.)

PICA.—See DEPRAVED APPETITE; and WOOD CHEWING.

Fig. P-11. White Lipizzan stallion at the Spanish Riding School, Wels, Austria, doing the Piaffe. (Courtesy, Spanish Riding School)

PICTURES, MOTION.—See MOTION PICTURE HORSES.

PIEBALD.—Refers to the black-and-white coat color of the Pinto horse.

PIGEON TOE.— (Front toes turned in, heels turned out—opposite of splayfoot) can be helped or corrected by trimming the inner half of the foot more than the outer half.

(Also see FEET (of horse) ; and SHOEING.)

PIG-EYED.—Having small, narrow, squinty eyes, set back in the head; also, having thick eyelids.

PIGGIN' STRING.—A braided rope carried by a rodeo contestant, tucked under his belt or carried in his teeth, and used to tie a bovine's feet together after it is roped.

PILLION.—A type of saddle attached to the back part of an ordinary saddle on which a second person, usually a woman, may ride. Pillions were used extensively in the Middle Ages, prior to the advent of the side-saddle. However, they have been little used since about 1830.

PIN-FIRING.—See FIRING.

PINK COAT (OR HUNTING PINK; SCARLET).—The coat worn by gentlemen members of a hunt. Customarily, it is light scarlet in color, though there are exceptions. They are commonly called "pink," but not because of their color. The name stems from a famous London tailor, named "Pink" or "Pinkie," who named his hunting coats after himself.

PINTO HORSE.—See BREED(S); and COLORS AND MARKINGS OF HORSES.

PINTO HORSE ASSOCIATION OF AMERICA, INC., THE.—P. O. Box 3984, San Diego, California 92103. (See Appendix for complete breed registry association list.)

PINWORMS (Oxyuris equi, Probstmyria vivipara).—Two species of pinworms or rectal worms, frequently are found in horses. Oxyuris equi are whitish worms with long, slender tails. Probstmyria vivipara are so small they are scarcely visible to the eye.

SYMPTOMS.—The symptoms are irritation of the anus and tail rubbing. Heavy infections also may cause digestive disturbances and anemia. Large pinworms are most damaging to horses and may be seen in the feces of heavily infected animals.

TREATMENT.—The common drugs are mebendazole, thiabendazole, trichlorfon, or dichlorvos; or various combinations of trichlorfon, phe-

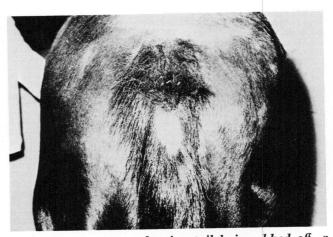

Fig. P-12. Pinworms; showing tail hair rubbed off—a characteristic sign. (Courtesy, Dr. V. S. Myers, Jr., V.M.D., Department of Veterinary Surgery and Radiology, University of Minnesota, St. Paul, Minn.)

nothiazine, piperazine, and thiabendazole. Which drugs to give and dosage should be determined by a veterinarian.

PREVENTION AND CONTROL.—Provide good sanitation and keep animals separated from their own excrement.

DISCUSSION.—Pinworms attack horses throughout the United States.

(Also see DISEASES AND PARASITES; HEALTH PROGRAM; and PARASITES OF HORSES.)

PIROUETTE.—A dressage exercise in which the horse holds his forelegs more or less in place while he moves his hindquarters around them.

PIVOT.—The hind legs form the support and center, like the hub of a wheel, while the front legs turn around, like the spokes.

A horse may be taught to pivot as follows:
- Step 1—Walk him in a small circle, with the circle getting smaller and smaller. Finally, the horse has his hind feet planted and walks around them on his front feet.
- Step 2—Walk about 3 feet from a high fence. Stop; collect the horse; and pivot 180 degrees.

- *Step 3*—Slowly pivot the horse 360 degrees. Then, after he has mastered the technique, speed it up.

PLACE.—To finish second in a race.

PLACENTA.—The membrane by which the fetus is attached to the uterus. Nutrients from the mother pass into the placenta and then through the navel cord to the fetus. When the foal is born, the placenta, commonly called the afterbirth, should be expelled within twelve hours. When the placenta is normal and expelled completely, it should be buried or otherwise disposed of in a sanitary manner.

PLAITING.—See BRAIDING.

PLANTATION WALKING HORSE (TENNESSEE WALKING HORSE).—Horses of this type were first introduced into Tennessee by the early settlers from Virginia and the Carolinas. For many years, the plantation owners of middle Tennessee—men who spent long hours daily in supervising labor from the saddle—selected and bred animals for their easy, springy gaits, good dispositions, and intelligence. Particular stress was placed upon the natural gait known as the running-walk and upon the elimination of the trot. Thus, the three gaits that evolved were: the walk, the running-walk, and the canter. Today, this particular class of horse is largely comprised of one breed, the Tennessee Walking Horse.
(Also see BREED (S)—Table B-2.)

PLATE.—A plain shoe devoid of calks.

PLATER.—A horse that runs in races where the purses are small. The term is derived from early-day racing, especially in England, where races for "cheaper horses" were often run for a piece of silver plate; hence, the name plater. The term is derogatory and denotes an inferior horse.

PLATE, RACING.—See RACING PLATE.

PLEASURE HORSE.—A pleasure horse, of any breeding or color, capable of giving a pleasurable ride. Horse shows provide classes for English pleasure horses, Western pleasure horses, and certain breeds.

PLUG.—A horse of common breeding and poor conformation.

POINT.—The team in back of the leaders in an eight-horse hitch.

POINT FIRING.—See FIRING.

POINTING.—1. Perceptible extension of the stride with little flexion is called pointing. This condition is likely to occur in the Thoroughbred and Standardbred breeds—animals bred and trained for great speed with a long stride. Except in Arabians, pointing is frowned upon.
2. A term used to indicate the pose in standing position where a horse stands on three legs and points with the fourth, usually indicative of lameness.

POINTS.—Black coloration from the knees and hocks down, as in most bays and browns, and in some buckskins, roans, and grays.

POINTS OF A HORSE.—See PARTS OF A HORSE. (See page 302.)

POINT-TO-POINT.—A race or hunt in which the contestants are given certain specified "points" or places to which they must ride. Originally, riders could choose their own course or line so long as they touched base at each of the specified points. Today, many of the courses are laid out and marked by flags.

POISONOUS PLANTS.—Poisonous plants have been known to man since time immemorial. Biblical literature alludes to the poisonous properties of certain plants, and history records that poison-hemlock (made from the plant from which it takes its name) was administered by the Greeks to Socrates and other state prisoners.

No section of the United States is entirely free of poisonous plants, for there are hundreds of them. Also, surprising as it may seem, plants do not readily fall into poisonous and nonpoisonous groups. Some are poisonous only at certain seasons of the year and under other specific conditions. Others are even excellent and nutritious forages providing they do not constitute the sole diet.

The heaviest horse losses from poisonous plants occur on the western ranges because (1) there has been less cultivation and destruction of poisonous plants in range areas, and (2) the frequent overgrazing on some of the western ranges has resulted in the elimination of some of the more nutritious and desirable plants, and these have been replaced by increased numbers of the less desirable and poisonous species. It is estimated that poisonous plants account for 3 to 5 percent of all range animal losses each year; and in some areas more. It is further estimated (*Losses in Agriculture*, Agricultural Handbook No. 291, 1965, Tables 26–30) that poisonous plants cause average annual losses of horses, beef cattle, and sheep of $23,281,000.

The list of poisonous plants is so extensive that no attempt is made herein to discuss them. However, both the horseman and the veterinarian should have a working knowledge of the principal poisonous species in the area in which they operate.

PREVENTING LOSSES FROM POISONOUS PLANTS.—With poisonous plants, the emphasis should be on prevention of losses rather than on treatment, no matter how successful the latter. The following are effective preventive measures:

• Follow good pasture or range management in order to improve the quality of the pasture or range.

• Know the poisonous plants common to the area.

• Know the symptoms that generally indicate plant poisoning, thus making for early action.

• Avoid turning to pasture in very early spring.

• Provide supplemental feed during droughts or after early frost.

• Avoid turning out very hungry animals where there are poisonous plants, especially those that have been in corrals.

• Avoid driving animals too fast when trailing.

• Remove promptly all animals from infested areas when plant poisoning strikes.

• Treat promptly, preferably by a veterinarian.

CONDITIONS THAT INDICATE PLANT POISONING.—Since plants contain many different poisons, there are no general symptoms by which to recognize plant poisoning in animals. It may be suspected, however, if the following conditions prevail:

• If there is sudden onset of obscure illness without visible cause.

• If a number of animals in a herd show acute disorders of the central nervous system or of the digestive tract without fever, but with prostration or rapid loss of weight.

• If there is rapid heart action, stomach and intestinal irritation, general distress, and repeated attempts to void feces.

• If these symptoms are followed by extreme weakness, coma, and collapse, and accompanied by difficult breathing.

It should be recognized, however, that plant poisoning may differ considerably in intensity, depending on (1) the kind and amount of plant eaten, (2) the stage of plant growth, (3) the kind and amount of other feed eaten simultaneously, and (4) the tolerance of the individual animal to the poison.

In addition to these facts, diagnosis is made more complicated because it is difficult to differentiate certain types of plant poisoning from sickness due to chemicals or to certain infectious diseases. Thus, diagnosis had best be left to the skill of a trained veterinarian.

TREATMENT.—Unfortunately, plant-poisoned animals are not generally discovered in sufficient time to prevent loss. Thus, prevention is decidedly superior to treatment.

When trouble is encountered, the owner or caretaker should *promptly* call a veterinarian. In the meantime, the horse should be (1) placed where adequate care and treatment can be given, (2) protected from excessive heat and cold, and (3) allowed to eat only feeds known to be safe.

The veterinarian may determine the kind of poisonous plant involved (1) by observing the symptoms, and/or (2) by finding out exactly what poisonous plant was eaten through looking over the pasture and/or hay and identifying leaves or other plant parts found in the animal's digestive tract at the time of the autopsy.

It is to be emphasized, however, that many poisoned horses that would have recovered had they been left undisturbed have been killed by attempts to administer home remedies by well-meaning but untrained persons.

POLE BENDING.—A popular contest in Western horse shows and in gymkhanas. The horses are required to take a course, threading their way between a row of poles, without knocking any of them over, then turn at the end and come back. This contest provides a test of the speed and maneuverability of the horse.

POLICED.—A term meaning to fall off a horse, synonymous with the term "come a cropper."

POLICE HORSE.—A horse used by a mounted policeman. A rioting crowd is far more afraid of a police horse than of a man armed with a lethal weapon. Thus, it is easier for a policeman to disperse a crowd by riding into them than it is by threatening them with a gun.

In traffic jams, a mounted officer can see over the tops of cars, and, having discovered the cause of the trouble, he can thread his way neatly between the automobiles and straighten out the dilemma. Also, patrol work along shore-lines and in parks is best done by a mounted policeman who does not have to stick to the highway.

The requisites of police horses are generally rather exacting. Many countries or cities require that they be color-matched; for example, all Canadian Mountie horses are black or dark brown, and all New York City police horses are bays. Although they may be of any breed, they are generally of hunter or Thoroughbred type, geldings, 15–2 hands or more in height, around 1200 pounds in weight, 4 to 7 years of age when purchased, level-headed, and possessed of sound feet and legs. Police horses are highly schooled. They

Fig. P-13. The Royal Canadian Mounted Police. (Courtesy, Royal Canadian Mounted Police, Ottawa, Canada)

receive from 1 to 3 years' training before being placed on the "beat."

The Royal Canadian Mounted Police—the "Mounties"—Founded in 1873, has retained horses to do their spectacular Musical Ride. Their proud claim was, and is, that they "always get their man."

POLL.—Top of the head, between and immediately behind the ears.

(Also see PARTS OF A HORSE—Fig. P-4.)

POLL EVIL.—This is an inflamed condition in the region of the poll (the area on top of the neck and immediately behind the ears). It is usually caused by bruising the top of the head. The swelling, which may be on one or both sides, usually contains pus or a straw-colored fluid. At first the affected area is hot and painful, but later the acute symptoms of inflammation subside. Treatment, which should be handled by a veterinarian, consists of establishing proper drainage and removing all dead tissue. In addition to surgery, some veterinarians claim that recovery is hastened by injections of a specially prepared bacterin. Poll evil is slow to yield to treatment, and it may break out again after it is thought to be cured.

(Also see UNSOUNDNESSES.)

POLO.—This is a game of Oriental origin, dating back to 600 B.C. It was first introduced into the U.S. in 1876.

Polo is played by four mounted men on each of two teams. The object is to drive a wooden ball between the opposing team's goal posts. The goals are located at either end of the playing field.

The total length of the field must not exceed 300 yards, and the goals must not be less than 250 yards apart and 8 yards wide. Without side boards the width is 200 yards; with boards it is 160 yards. The goal posts are at least 10 feet high and made of light, easily breakable material. The ball, made of willow or bamboo root, has a diameter of not more than $3\frac{1}{4}$ inches and weighs $4\frac{1}{4}$ to $4\frac{1}{2}$ ounces. The polo mallet is a cane, 48 to 54 inches long (with the length varying according to the individual needs of the play-

ers), with a hand grip at one end and a transverse head (the hitting surface) at the other end. The head is cylindrical or cigar-shaped; $8\frac{1}{2}$ to 9 inches long, $1\frac{5}{8}$ to $1\frac{13}{16}$ inches in diameter, weighs 6 to $7\frac{1}{2}$ ounces; and is made of sycamore, ash, or bamboo.

Spurs (blunt and without rowels) are usually worn. Protective head gear is required. Brown boots, without buckles or projections, are worn. The polo whip is about 40 inches long and flexible. The polo saddle is light and moderately forward. Boots or bandages are required for the pony, and coronet boots are advisable. The pony's tail is usually bandaged to keep long tails from interfering with the polo stick.

The requisites of good polo players are: courage; coolness; aptitude, including a good eye; horsemanship; and team spirit.

The game is played in periods, of $7\frac{1}{2}$ minutes each—called a chukkar, with an interval of 3 minutes between chukkars (and a 5-minute break at half-time). Each time a goal is scored, the team changes ends.

Most games are played on a handicap basis, all players being rated at their worth in goals or minus-goals, with a range of minus 2 to 10.

POLO PONY.—As the name would indicate, polo ponies include that type and class of horses particularly adapted for use in playing the game of polo. At the time the game was first introduced into the United States, there was a decided preference for ponies under 13–2 hands in height. Later, horses up to 14–2 hands were accepted, and more recently horses up to 15–2 and over have been used.

Although very similar to the hunter in type, the polo mount is smaller in size. He must be quick and clever in turning, and he must be able to dodge, swerve, or wheel while on a dead run. He must like the game and be able to follow the ball.

The polo mount is trained to respond to the pressure of the reins on the neck, so that the rider may be free to guide him with only one hand. Up to five or six years are required to complete the schooling of a polo horse, and as many as 4 to 6 mounts may be used by each player in a single game—all of which contributes to the expensiveness of the sport.

Polo ponies are usually of mixed breeding, but

Fig. P-14. Belle of All, one of the most famous polo mounts that ever played at Meadowbrook, Long Island. Note the pronounced Thoroughbred type. Polo ponies must be quick and clever in turning, and they must be able to dodge, swerve, or wheel while on a dead run. (Courtesy, Horse Association of America)

most of them are predominantly Thoroughbred. Type and training, together with native ability and intelligence, are the primary requisites.

POLYUNSATURATED FATTY ACIDS.—The term "polyunsaturated fatty acid" is applied to fatty acids having more than one double bond.

There is no experimental evidence that polyunsaturated fatty acids are either (1) required by horses, or (2) superior to saturated fatty acids.

PONIES FOR DRIVING.—Ponies for driving are of two kinds; namely, (1) harness show ponies, and (2) heavy harness ponies.

The best harness show ponies are vest-pocket editions of fine harness horses; that is, they possess the same desirable characteristics, except that they are in miniature. According to the rules of the American Horse Shows Association, harness show ponies may be of any breed or combination of breeds; the only requisite is that they must be under 12–2 hands in height. Three breeds produce animals that qualify under this category; namely, the Shetland, Welsh, and Hackney.

Heavy harness ponies are, as the name indi-

cates, miniature heavy harness horses—they're under 14–2 hands. Generally they are either pure-bred Hackneys, or predominantly of Hackney breeding.

Fig. P-15. Bolgoed Mighty Atom, Champion Harness Show Pony. This imported grey Welsh Pony stallion stands 46½ inches high. Owned by Hawthorn Farms, Libertyville, Ill. (Courtesy, American Shetland Pony Journal)

PONIES FOR RIDING.—These are children's mounts. In addition to their miniature size, they should possess the following characteristics: (1) gentleness, (2) sound feet and legs, (3) symmetry, (4) good eyes, (5) endurance, (6) intelligence, (7) patience, (8) faithfulness, and (9) hardiness. Above all, they must be kind and gentle in disposition.

Fig. P-16. Pony ridden by Olivia and Anastasia Musgrave of Co. Dublin, Ireland. (Courtesy, Sir Richard Musgrave)

PONY.—A small animal under 14-2 hands high and usually weighing under 900 pounds. Also, it is noteworthy that polo ponies and cowponies are usually referred to as ponies, rather than as horses, even though they may exceed by many inches the 14-2 which is supposed to be the upper limit for a "pony."

Not every small horse is a pony. Some small horses are merely small animals of established light horse breeds. Others are nondescript runts. In ponies, there is a distinct conformation; in miniature, they are either of draft horse, heavy harness horse, or saddle or harness horse type.

Breeding, feeding, care, and management are essentially the same for ponies as for larger light horses. The only differences result from their diminutive size. Most folks are prone to overestimate the amount of work done by a pony, with the result that they overfeed them.

PONY EXPRESS.—The Pony Express was a mail service, operated as a private venture under contract, which carried U.S. mail on horseback from St. Joseph, Missouri, to Placerville, California, in the days before railways or telegraph. It was started in 1861, and it had a brief existence of but 18 months before it was supplanted by a telegraph line. The riders' steeds were, of course, not ponies but fleet horses. The horses were stationed at points 10 to 15 miles apart, and each rider rode 3 to 7 animals successively, covering about 75 miles before passing the pouch to his successor. There were 80 riders, some 420 horses, and 190 relay stations. Riders were paid $25 per week.

The fastest trip ever made was in 7 days and 17 hours, when Lincoln's first inaugural address was carried to the West Coast. But the normal schedule was 8 days, which was about 24 days faster than the schedule of Butterfield's Overland Stage line on the southern route. The maintenance of this schedule through the wilderness, often in blinding snows and howling storms and in the face of Indian dangers, won for the service a fame that has not diminished with the passing of time.

The Pony Express lost money. The average charge for sending a letter during the period was $3, but it cost about $16 per letter to operate the service; thus, the private venture lost $13 per letter, and it is estimated that the Pony Express cost its backers $390,000.

Despite its short life, the Pony Express was credited with many important contributions, not the least of which was its help in keeping East and West joined together during the early crucial days of the Civil War. A 7,200-pound life-size bronze statue of a Pony Express rider and his mount stands in St. Joseph's Civic Center. It was unveiled on April 20, 1940, when the Postal Department honored the riders of the Pony Express with a commemorative postage stamp.

PONY OF THE AMERICAS.—See BREED (S).

PONY OF THE AMERICAS CLUB.—P. O. Box 1447, Mason City, Iowa 50401. (See Appendix for complete breed registry association list.)

POP-EYED.—Refers to a horse whose eyes are generally more prominent or bulge out a little more than normal; also to a horse that is "spooky" or attempts to see everything that goes on.

POPPED KNEE.—Popped knee (so named because of the sudden swelling that accompanies it) is a general term describing inflammatory conditions affecting the knees. It is due either to (1) sprain or strain of one or more of the extensive group of small but important ligaments that hold the bones of the knee in position, or (2) damage to a joint capsule, followed by an increase in the amount of fluid within the capsule and a distention or bulging-out between overlying structure. Of course, faulty conformation of the knees contributes largely to the breaking down of some individuals.

Horses suffering severe popped knees rarely are able to regain a degree of soundness that will allow them to return to the racing form shown before the injury. Thus, the usual cooling applications followed by counterirritant (blistering and firing) treatment are used with varying degrees of effectiveness in the treatment of knee troubles.

POPULATION OF HORSES.—See NUMBER OF HORSES.

PORT.—The upward curve in the center of the mouthpiece of Pelham and Weymouth bits. (Also see BITS—Fig. B-9.)

POSING.—Posing refers to the stance taken by a show horse when not in action. The pose varies according to breed. For example, in a halter class Arabians are not stretched, but American Saddlers are trained to stand with their front legs under them and their hind legs stretched behind them. Other breeds generally stand in a slightly stretched position, somewhat intermediate between these two examples. (Also see CAMP OUT.)

POST.—The starting point of a race.

POST ENTRY.—A last minute entry in a horse show or race. The term stems from racing, where, at one time, the entries were not named until going to the post.

POSTING.—Posting may be described as the rising and descending of the rider with the rhythm of the trot. This action reduces the shock or jar of the trot for both horse and rider. Posting is accomplished by rising easily in the saddle in rhythm at one beat, of the two-beat trot, and settling back at the next beat. In posting, the rider inclines the upper part of the body slightly forward (while at the same time keeping the shoulders back, the chin up, and the legs under the body, with the heels down); supports himself by pressing the knees inward against the horse; and then permits his body to be impelled upward by the thrust of one of the hind legs (the left, for example). The rider remains up during the stride of the other hind leg (the right) and returns nearly to the saddle only to be impelled upward again by the next thrust of the left hind leg. Sitting back in the saddle each time the right forefoot strikes the ground is known as posting on the right diagonal; whereas returning to the saddle when the left fore strikes the ground is known as posting on the left diagonal.

Some competent and experienced equitation instructors report that they prefer to teach post-ing the correct diagonal as follows:

1. Watch the horse's shoulder and knee.
2. Rise in the saddle as the shoulder and knee of the outside foreleg come forward. The rider will then be posting to the outside foreleg or the one nearest the rail.

To change diagonals, the rider should learn to sit one or three or five beats of the trot—preferably one beat; to sit even beats puts the rider back where he was.

The rider should frequently alternate the diagonals used in posting as this makes for greater ease on the horse. When riding in a ring, the rider should post on the outside diagonal so that the work of the hind quarters will be equalized. For correct posting, the stirrups should be sufficiently short to permit the rider to carry most of the weight on the ball of the foot. Only a small portion of the weight should be carried on the inside of the thighs and knees. Correct posting is one of the most difficult phases of riding.

POST-MORTEM.—Examination after death.

POST POSITION.—Refers to race starting position. Beginning with position No. 1 nearest the rail, horses line up at the starting gate according to number. Post positions are drawn by lot in the racing secretary's office, with the owners of the horses taking part in the drawing. The drawing is held on the day before the race, after entries for the following day have closed. The rail position is advantageous, being the "shortest way around," but it is not necessarily an advantage to a slow-breaking horse.

POULTICE.—A soft mass (such as bread, bran, flaxseed, or medicated clay), usually heated and spread on a cloth, for application to sores, inflamed areas, or other lesions. A poultice may be used for the purpose of supplying moist warmth, relieving pain, or acting as a counterirritant or antiseptic.

POUNDING.—A condition in which there is heavy contact with the ground in contrast to the desired light, springy movement.

POWER.—See AUTOMATION VS. MUSCLE POWER.

PREGNANCY SIGNS AND TESTS.—In order to produce as high a percentage of foals as possible and to have them arrive at the time desired, the good horseman will be familiar with the signs of and tests for pregnancy. This is doubly important when it is recognized that a great many mares may either be shy breeders or show signs of heat even when well advanced in gestation.

The signs of pregnancy follow:

• *The cessation of the heat period.*—But it is recognized that this may be difficult to determine and misleading, because some mares will continue to exhibit the characteristic heat symptoms when in foal. Sometimes they show such pronounced signs of heat that they are given the service of a stallion, which often results in abortion.

• *The movement of the living fetus.*—This movement can be seen or felt through the abdominal walls. It will not be possible, however, to use this test until about the seventh month of gestation. Movement of the fetus is most evident the first thing in the morning. This method is not so certain with young maiden mares, as the foal is carried nearer the backbone.

But the absence of external signs of heat in the first weeks after breeding is only 50 to 70 percent accurate, and the movement of the fetus is not evident in early pregnancy. Hence, the need for accurate, quick, and efficient methods of pregnancy diagnosis in the mare has engaged considerable scientific attention for many years. Out of this has evolved a number of different methods for determining whether or not mares are in foal; among them, those which follow.

MANUAL (RECTAL) TEST.—An experienced technician can determine pregnancy (or barrenness) of mares at 98 to 100% accuracy by feeling with the hand through the rectal wall. Normally, the test is made 43 to 45 days after breeding, but pregnancy in maiden mares can be detected within 35 to 40 days following conception. When performed by an experienced veterinarian, the manual test is quite reliable; but it is recognized that only a relatively few veterinarians qualify as experienced.

BIOLOGICAL TESTS.—These tests are based upon detecting either (1) the hormone gonadotrophin (PMS) in mare's blood serum, or (2) the hormone estrogen in mare's urine; using laboratory animals for test purposes.

There are a number of biological tests; among them—

1. *The blood serum test with female rats or mice.*—This test is based upon detecting the hormone gonadotrophin (pregnant mare serum, or PMS) in mare's blood serum, preferably in a blood sample taken 45 to 90 days after service. When injected into immature female rats or mice (usually two test animals are used), PMS causes precocious (early) development of the internal reproductive organs.

The blood serum test may also be made with immature female mice. Forty-eight (48) hours after injection with the blood serum, the mice are painlessly destroyed and the ovaries and womb examined. If the mare from which the blood sample came is pregnant, the reproductive organs of the mice will be noticeably enlarged as compared with normal.

This blood serum test with female rats or mice is considered very sensitive, probably approaching 100 percent accuracy.

2. *The blood serum test with male toads (Bufo).*—This test was developed by Dr. Raymond O. Berry, Texas A & M University. It is based on the fact that the toad emits sperm only (a) when stimulated by amplexus with a female toad, or (b) when stimulated by a gonadotrophic hormone, such as is found in pregnant mare's blood at certain stages. This test may be used on mares that have been bred between 45 and 120 days.

In 1960, the Russian scientist, Samsonova, reported upon a similar test.[1] He used lake frogs (*Rana ridibunda*), the males of which are readily distinguishable.

In comparison with the rat or mouse test, the toad or frog test (a) is much quicker—requiring only 4 hours, and (b) does not necessitate the destruction of the test animal—the same toad or frog may be used for 4 or 5 tests.

3. *The urine test with female rats or mice.*—This test may be used on mares from three months after breeding until termination. Four ounces of urine (and not blood) are collected

---

1. V. M. Samsonova (All-Union Research Institute for Animal Husbandry, U.S.S.R.), *Veterinariya* (1960), 37 (10) : 66.

in a clean bottle and are used as a sample. The urine test is used on spayed, mature female rats or mice. If the mare is pregnant, the estrogen in the urine causes symptoms of heat in the vagina of treated animals.

IMMUNOLOGICAL TESTS.—These tests are based on one of the fundamental concepts of immunology—the antigen to antibody reaction. If an antigen (usually a foreign protein) gains access to the body of an animal, the body responds by producing a specific immune substance, known as an antibody. If the antigen is encountered a second time, the antibody present in the animal's system mops up all the antigen by a coupling reaction. Germs and microbes are examples of antigens; and this mechanism provides one of the body's main defenses for rendering them harmless and preventing disease.

There are a number of immunological tests which utilize the antigen to antibody reaction; among them—

1. *The MIP-Test.*—The MIP-Test (Mare Immunological Pregnancy Test) was developed by Dr. Ronald Chak, D.V.M., Ocala (Florida) Stud Farm, and Mr. Max Bruss, Dorchester Laboratory, Ocala, Florida. This test utilizes the principle whereby pregnant mare serum (gonadotrophin) inhibits the agglutination of gonadotrophin-coated erythrocytes in the presence of gonadotrophin antiserum. The result is the formation of a ring at the bottom of a test tube.

The MIP-Test, which can be run in two hours' time, can determine with virtually 100 percent accuracy equine pregnancy from a blood sample taken 41 to 63 days after the mare is serviced. The MIP-Test Kit contains all the supplies needed for running the test. (The MIP-Test Kit may be secured from the Denver Chemical Manufacturing Co., Stamford, Conn. 06904.)

2. *The Haemagglutination Inhibition (HI) Test.*—In this test, an indicator system is used to establish whether or not any antigen **PMS** is present (i.e., if the mare is pregnant). The indicator consists of sensitized sheep red blood cells which are added to a mixture of serum from the mare under test, an antibody (anti-**PMS**). If **PMS** (antigen) is present, it reacts with the antibody so that the indicator cells are unaffected. On the other hand, when PMS is absent, the antibody is not used up because the antigen is not

there. Intsead, it reacts with the sensitized sheep cells and these clump together, or haemagglutinate. Thus, no clumping (haemagglutination inhibition) means the mare is pregnant, whereas clumping (haemagglutination) indicates that she is barren.

This test is very sensitive and just as accurate as biological tests (with rats or mice). Moreover, it has the following advantages over biological tests: (a) it can be set up and results obtained in 24 hours, whereas biological tests take a minimum of 48 hours; and (b) it does not require a constant supply of rats or mice of the right age.

3. *The Immunoassay for PMSG.*—The Immunoassay for PMSG (pregnant mare serum gonadotrophin), another immunological test, was announced in 1969 by a Johns Hopkins School of Medicine team headed by Dr. H. Lorrin Lau, M.D. This test is sensitive to levels of PMSG (a hormone released during pregnancy) as early as the 21st day and as late as the 282nd day of gestation. It requires only a small sample of blood, and the necessary reagents to conduct it may be stored in a refrigerator.

In addition to determining pregnancy, the Immunoassay for PMSG is, according to Dr. Lau and his associates—the developers of the test—a valuable aid in detecting abnormalities in equine reproduction.

CHEMICAL TEST.—This test involves chemically detecting the hormone, estrogen, in mare's urine from 120 days pregnancy to term.

The addition of concentrated sulfuric or hydrochloric acid to the urine releases the estrogen. It is then taken up in benzene, in which it is very soluble. After the addition of more concentrated sulfuric (or hydrochloric) acid, the solution is allowed to cool thoroughly. If the mare is pregnant (if the test is positive), the solution shows a green fluorescence; if the mare is barren (if the test is negative), there is no fluorescence.

This test is fairly easy to carry out in the laboratory, and it is reliable. However, it cannot be used for early pregnancy detection. It should not be used until 120 days after conception; and, for best results, it should be used 200 to 275 days after breeding at which stage estrogen levels are highest.

PREPOTENCY.—See HEREDITY IN HORSES.

PRESSURE BANDAGES.—See BANDAGE, PRESSURE.

PRICK EARS.—Sharp, pointed ears which are normally directed to the front, and which give an alert and expectant appearance.

PRICKED SOLE.—Descriptive of a foot when a nail has been driven into the sensitive area of the foot, usually the sensitive laminae. The symptoms are extreme lameness and heat in the wall and sole. Treatment should be as follows: Remove the shoe; soak the horse's foot with epsom salts; if the hole can be reached, pare it out and pour iodine into it; apply a flaxseed poultice for several days; and give a tetanus shot.
(Also see FIRST AID FOR HORSES.)

PROCESSING GRAINS.—See FEED.

PRODUCE.—Offspring.

PROFILE.—A horse's head or face as observed from a side view. The profile tells much about the breeding of a horse. A "dished" profile (one with a depression between the forehead and the end of the nose) is indicative of Arabian breeding. A Roman nose indicates coarseness, and possibly draft horse breeding.

PROFIT INDICATORS.—Although profit indicators should vary somewhat according to the establishment, the following barometers will be indicative of how well most horse breeding establishments are doing: (1) percentage foal crop (based on number of mares bred); (2) percentage foal loss from birth to weaning; (3) number of foals produced in lifetime of mare; (4) percentage of breeding difficulty in mares at any one time; and (5) average number of services per conception.

PROGENITOR.—One that originates or precedes; an ancestor.

PROGENY.—Refers to offspring or descendants of one or both parents.

PROPHYLAXIS.—Preventive treatment against disease.

PROTEIN.—Proteins are complex organic compounds made up chiefly of amino acids present in characteristic proportions for each specific protein. This nutrient always contains carbon, hydrogen, oxygen, and nitrogen; and, in addition, it usually contains sulphur and frequently phosphorus. Proteins are essential in all plant and animal life as components of the active protoplasm of each living cell.

Proteins of the animal body are primary constituents of many structural and protective tissues —such as bones, ligaments, hair, hoofs, skin, and the soft tissues which include the organs and muscles. The total protein content of a horse's body ranges from about 10 percent in fat, mature horses to 20 percent in thin, young foals.

Horses of all ages and kinds require adequate amounts of protein of suitable quality; for maintenance, growth, fattening, reproduction, and work. Of course, the protein requirements for growth and reproduction are the greatest and most critical.

A deficiency of proteins in the horse may result in the following deficiency symptoms: depressed appetite, poor growth, loss of weight, reduced milk production, irregular estrus, lowered foal crops, loss of condition, and lack of stamina.

Since the vast majority of protein requirements given in feeding standards meet minimum needs only, the allowances for race, show, breeding, and young animals should be higher.

Because of more limited amino acid synthesis in the horse than in ruminants, plus the fact that the cecum is located beyond the small intestine —the main area for digestion and absorption of nutrients—it is recommended that high quality protein rations, adequate in amino acids be fed to horses. This is especially important for young equines, because cecal synthesis is very limited early in life.

The recommended allowances given in this book under FEEDING HORSES—Table F-3, will meet the requirements for protein plus provide reasonable margins of safety. Some overage in nutrients is important because of variations in feed composition and individual animal differences.

(Also see CECUM SYNTHESIS.)

PROTEIN QUALITY.—Proteins are very complex compounds with each molecule made up of hundreds of thousands of amino acids combined with each other. The amino acids, of which some twenty-three are known, are some-

times referred to as the building stones of proteins. Certain of these amino acids can be made by the animal's body to satisfy its needs. Others cannot be formed fast enough to supply the body's needs and, therefore, are known as essential (or indispensable) amino acids. These must be supplied in the feed. Thus, rations that furnish an insufficient amount of any of the essential amino acids are said to have proteins of poor quality, whereas those which provide the proper proportions of the various necessary amino acids are said to supply proteins of good quality.

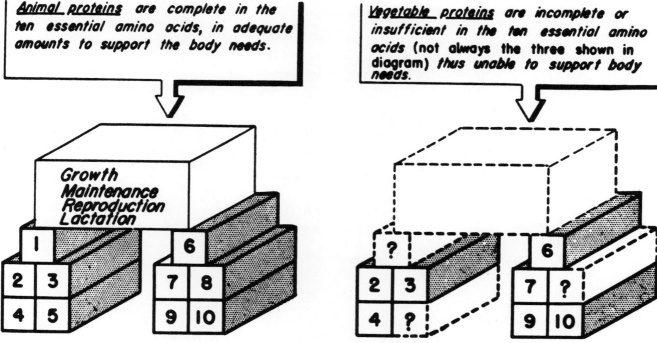

Animal proteins are complete in the ten essential amino acids, in adequate amounts to support the body needs.

Vegetable proteins are incomplete or insufficient in the ten essential amino acids (not always the three shown in diagram) *thus unable to support body needs.*

The Ten Essential Amino Acids:

1. Phenylalanine
2. Tryptophane
3. Leucine
4. Isoleucine
5. Lysine
6. Methionine
7. Valine
8. Histidine
9. Threonine
10. Arginine

Fig. P-17. The amino acids are sometimes referred to as the building stones of proteins. Rations that furnish an insufficient amount of the essential building stones (amino acids) are said to have proteins of poor quality.

PROTEIN SOURCES.—Grass hays and farm grains are low in quality and quantity of proteins. Hence, they must be supplemented with other sources of protein.

In general, proteins of plant origin (linseed meal, cottonseed meal, soybean meal, and peanut meal) are not of as good quality as proteins of animal origin and their by-products (milk by-products, etc.). Because of more limited amino acid synthesis in the horse than in ruminants, plus the fact that the cecum is located beyond the small intestine—the main area for digestion and absorption of nutrients, it is recommended that high quality protein rations, adequate in amino acids, be fed to horses. This is especially important for young equines, because cecal synthesis is very limited early in life.

Fortunately, the amino acid content of proteins from various sources varies. Thus, the deficiencies of one protein may be improved by combining it with another, and the mixture of the two proteins often will have a higher feeding value than either one alone. It is for this reason, along with added palatability, that a considerable variety of feeds in the horse ration is desirable.

PROTEIN POISONING.—Some opinions to the contrary, protein poisoning as such has never been documented. There is no proof that heavy feeding of high protein feeds is harmful provided (1) the ration is balanced out in all other respects; (2) the animal's kidneys are normal and healthy (a large excess of protein in terms of body needs increases the work of the kidneys for the excretion of the urea); (3) any ration change to high protein feed is made gradually, as is recommended in any change in feed; and (4) there is adequate exercise and normal metabolism.

Some horses do appear to be allergic to certain proteins or to excesses of specific amino acids, as a result of which they may develop "protein bumps."

It is recognized that protein in excess of what the body can use tends to be wasted insofar as its specific functions are concerned, since it cannot be stored in any but very limited amounts and must be catabolized. Nevertheless, some wastage of protein in terms of its known functions may be both physiologically and economically desirable in order to (1) maintain the protein reserves, (2) provide an adequate protein-calorie ratio for efficient energy utilization, and (3) assure that protein quality needs are met, despite the marked difference of quality among commonly fed rations. Generally speaking, high protein feeds are more expensive than high energy feeds (feeds high in carbohydrates and fats), with the result that there is the temptation to feed too little of them.

PROTOZOA.—Protozoa are the simplest form of animal life; they consist of only a single cell. There are many classifications of protozoa depending upon their method of reproduction and locomotion and general shape and structure. Since most of them are free-living (occurring in the soil, water, etc.), only a few concern human and animal health. Malaria and amoebic dysentery are examples of devastating human parasitic diseases caused by microorganisms known as protozoa; and Equine Piroplasmosis is an example of a horse parasitic disease caused by protozoan parasites.

PROUD CUT.—A term indicating that a male horse was improperly castrated. A "proud gelding" acts like a stallion, but is infertile.

PROUD FLESH.—The unhealthy tissue which sometimes forms around a wound. If allowed to remain, a large scar will result. For this reason, the veterinarian may prescribe something to burn off proud flesh so that the wound will heal more quickly.

PRZEWALSKY'S HORSE.—The only surviving species of original wild horses—not feral or escaped from domestication—known to exist at the present time is Przewalsky's horse (or the Asiatic wild horse). This is the wild horse discovered by the Russian explorer, Przewalsky, in 1879, in the northwestern corner of Mongolia. It is a small, stockily built, and distinctly yellowish horse, with an erect mane and no forelock. There is usually a dark stripe on the shoulders and down the middle of the back. Like the wild mustang or feral horses of the frontier days, Przewalsky's horses separate into bands, seldom more than forty in number, with a stallion leader in each group. At the present time, it is reported that only three wild bands remain. Fortunately, however, live specimens have been

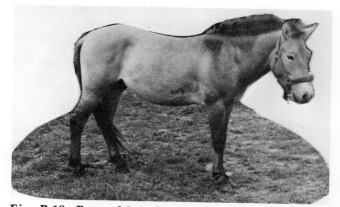

Fig. P-18. Przewalsky's horse, which the author inspected at Janow Podlaski, in Poland. Note that it is small and stockily built, with an erect mane and no forelock. (Photo by A. H. Ensminger)

brought to Europe and America where they are being preserved and propagated successfully in captivity. When crossed on domestic horses, the hybrids are fertile, which proves that Przewalsky's horse is very closely related to the domestic horse.

It is not intended to imply that Przewalsky's horse was the foundation stock of any or all of the present-day improved breeds throughout the world. Rather, this wild horse of Asia is extremely interesting because it is the only one known to have survived the vicissitudes of time.

PUFFS.—Wind galls, bog spavins, or thoroughpins.

PULLED TAIL.—A tail thinned by hairs being pulled.

PULLER (COLD JAWED).—A horse that is hard-mouthed and habitually pulls on the bit as a result of having his mouth spoiled and made insensitive. The "puller" can be cured, but it will take time and patience. The first thing to do is to change riders and/or bits. If he has been ridden with a curb, change to a snaffle. If he has been ridden with a snaffle, try a rubber-mouthed curb or a leather-mouthed bar bit. Sometimes changing to a hackamore will work wonders.

PULLING RECORD.—The world's record in a pulling contest was established at the 1965 Hillsdale County Fair, in Michigan. It is held jointly by Frank Vurckio, Sun Down, N.Y.; and Fowler Bros., Montgomery, Michigan. It was made on a dynamometer (equipment for measuring mechanical power) with a tractive pull of 4,350 pounds (equal to 56,493 pounds, or over 28 tons, on a wagon).

PULSE RATE.—The pulse rate indicates the rapidity of the heart action. Normal for the horse is 32 to 34 per minute.

The pulse of a horse is taken either at the margin of the jaw where an artery winds around from the inner side, at the inside of the elbow, or under the tail. It should be pointed out that the younger, the smaller, and the more nervous the animal, the higher the pulse rate. Also, the pulse rate increases with exercise, excitement, digestion, and high outside temperature.

PUMPKINS, SQUASHES, AND MELONS.—Pumpkins, squashes, and melons are sometimes used as relish for horses. They contain only 6 to 10 percent dry matter; hence, their nutritive value on a wet basis is low in comparison with cereal grains. When fed in the usual amounts, their seeds are not harmful to horses, some opinions to the contrary. However, an entire ration of seeds alone is apt to cause indigestion, because of their high fat content.

(Also see TREATS.)

PUNCTURE WOUNDS.—Nail and rock puncture wounds of the hoof are rather common. Where severe, and especially when the horseman is inexperienced, it is best to call a veterinarian. If a veterinarian is not readily available, or if the horseman is experienced, apply first aid.

(Also see FIRST AID FOR HORSES.)

PUNISHMENT.—See CONTROL OF THE HORSE.

PUREBRED.—An animal descended from a line of ancestors of the same breed but not necessarily registered. This should not be confused with "Thoroughbred," a breed of horses.

PURE BREEDING.—See BREEDING HORS-ES.

PURGATIVE.—See LAXATIVE.

PURSE.—Race prize money to which the owners of horses in the race do not contribute.

Q

QUALITY.—Quality is denoted by clean, flat bone, well-defined joints and tendons, refined head and ears, and fine skin and hair. Good quality in the horse indicates easy keeping and good endurance.

QUARANTINE.—By quarantine is meant the segregation and confinement of one or more animals in the smallest possible area to prevent any direct or indirect contact with animals not so restrained.

Many highly infectious diseases are prevented from gaining a foothold in this country by strict enforcement of local quarantine at points of entry. When an infectious disease outbreak occurs, drastic quarantine must be imposed to restrict movement out of an area or within areas. The type of quarantine varies from one involving a mere physical examination and movement under proper certification to the complete prohibition against the movement of animals, produce, vehicles, and even human beings.

QUARTER *(of the foot).*—1. The side of a horse's foot just in front of the heel.

(Also see FOOT—Fig. F-20.)

2. The rear quarter; below the buttocks.

(Also see PARTS OF A HORSE—Fig. P-4.)

QUARTER BOOT (S) .—This is a flexible boot attached above the coronet which extends down over the hoof. It is designed to protect the quarter of the front heel from the hind toe.

(Also see BOOT; and HARNESS—Figs. H-4 and H-5.)

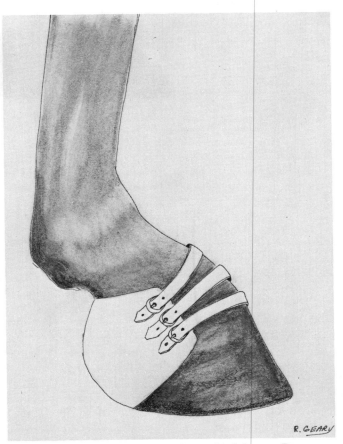

R. GEARY

Fig. Q-1. Quarter boot on a five-gaited horse. Because of the speed at which five-gaited horses are expected to perform at the trot and the rack, they are permitted to wear quarter boots to protect the heels of the front feet, a practice which is forbidden in three-gaited classes.

QUARTER CLIPS.—A triangular upward projection at the side, or quarter, of a horseshoe, used for attachment purposes.

(Also see CLIP.)

QUARTER CRACK (or SAND CRACK) .—A vertical split in the horny wall of the inside of the hoof (in the region of the quarter), which extends from the coronet or hoof head downward, is known as quarter crack or sand crack. It is seldom found in the hind legs. When the crack is on the fore part of the toe, it is called a toe crack. This condition usually results from the hoof being allowed to become too dry and brittle or from improper shoeing. Special shoeing or clamping together of the cracks is the usual treatment. Also, the coronet may be blistered; or a crescent may be burned through the hoof wall over the crack with a hot iron.

[Also see TOE CRACK; UNSOUNDNESSES; and FEET (of horse)]

QUARTER CUTS.

QUARTER CUTS.—Cuts on the quarter of the forefoot caused by striking with the hind foot. Quarter cuts can be prevented by wearing quarter boots and/or by corrective shoeing.

QUARTER HORSES.

QUARTER HORSES.—Quarter racing has become an increasingly popular sport, and appropriately so, for the Quarter Horse breed derived its name and initial fame for extraordinary speed at distances up to a quarter of a mile. Although the great majority of Quarter Horses are used to work cattle and for pleasure purposes, and never appear on the racetrack, the proponents of quarter racing advocate the racetrack as a means of proving animals. Performance, so they contend, is the proof of whether or not a horse can do the job for which he is bred. Thus, quarter racing is used as a breed proving ground for the Quarter Horse. Through it the fundamental quality of speed can be accurately measured and recorded in such a way that the performance of horses in all parts of the country can be compared.

Table Q-1 lists the leading money winning Quarter Horses through 1971. Information pertaining to the origin and characteristics of the Quarter Horse is presented under BREED (S).

The richest race in the world is for two-year-old Quarter Horses. It's the All American Quarter Horse Futurity, run at Ruidoso Downs, New Mexico, each Labor Day. The 1973 race—won by Timets Thinkrich, owned by Frank Vessels, Jr., Los Alamitos Stallion Farm, Los Alamitos, California—paid $330,000 for first money.

QUARTERING.

QUARTERING.—A pattern of grooming in which the blanket is left on. After the head and neck are groomed, the front part of the blanket on one side is folded back and one forequarter groomed; thence the front is replaced, the back part of the blanket on the same side is folded forward, and the hindquarter on the same side is groomed. The same procedure is repeated on the other side. Then the feet and legs are examined. This procedure is followed by some race stables before a workout or race.

QUITTOR.

QUITTOR.—Quittor is a deep-seated running sore at the coronet or hoof head caused by necrosis of the cartilage of the third phalanx. It results in severe lameness. The infection may arise from a puncture wound, corns, and sand cracks; or it may be carried in the bloodstream. Quittor is usually confined to the forefeet, but it sometimes occurs in the hind feet. Drainage and antiseptics may relieve the condition, although surgery by a veterinarian may be necessary.

(Also see UNSOUNDNESSES.)

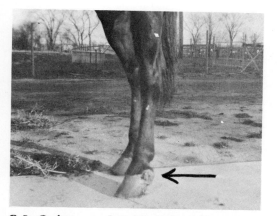

Fig. Q-2. Quittor on left hind foot. Note that this is a running sore at the coronet or hoof head. It causes severe lameness.

TABLE Q-1

LEADING MONEY WINNING QUARTER HORSES, THROUGH 1971

EASY JET, ch.h. 67 by JET DECK	$445,721
LAICO BIRD, br.m. 65 by GOOD BIRD (TB)	435,654
SAVANNAH JR, br.h. 63 by EVERETT JR (TB)	277,003
GO DICK GO, s.h. 64 by LITTLE DICK PRIEST	276,670
MR KID CHARGE, s.c. 69 by KID MEYERS	268,398
KAWEAH BAR, pal. g. 66 by ALAMITOS BAR	241,521
ROCKET WRANGLER, s.c. 68 by ROCKET BAR (TB)	239,890
GOETTA, b.m. 61 by GO MAN GO	233,920
TOP ROCKETT, ch.m. 65 by ROCKET BAR (TB)	217,923
BUNNY BID, s.c. 68 by DOUBLE BID	214,026
THREE OH'S, br.h. 66 by THREE CHICKS	201,715
JET DECK, b.h. 60 by MOON DECK	200,625
TOP LADYBUG, s.m. 64 by TOP DECK (TB)	195,942
MISS THREE WARS, s.m. 67 by THREE CHICKS	181,389
GO DERUSSA GO, s.m. 65 by GO MAN GO	178,221
MR JET MOORE, s.c. 69 by JET DECK	174,803
BAR NONE DOLL, br.m. 63 by MR BAR NONE	166,842
SEA NYMPH, ch.m. 65 by JACKSTRAW (TB)	166,410
CEE BAR DECK, b.g. 63 by SKIP DECK	165,919
JET CHARGER, s.c. 68 by JET DECK	165,318
POKEY BAR, s.h. 59 by THREE BARS (TB)	162,630
TURF'S BEST, blk.h. 65 by REBEL CAUSE	157,330
DECKETTA, s.m. 62 by TOP DECK (TB)	156,761
TONY B DECK, s.c. 68 by JET DECK	155,843

R

RABIES.—See HYDROPHOBIA.

RACEHORSE (S).—The term "racehorse" refers to a horse that is bred and trained for racing. Today, two types of horse races are run: (1) running races (including steeplechase races), and (2) harness races. For the most part, racing is dominated by three breeds. Thus, in running races, it's Thoroughbreds and Quarter Horses; and in harness races, it's Standardbreds. However, on a limited basis, and in a few states, Appaloosa and Arabian Horses are now being raced under saddle.

RACEHORSE FEEDING.—It is recognized that some unsoundnesses may be inherited, others may be due to accident and injury, and still others may be due to subjecting horses to stress and strain far beyond the capability of even the best structure and tissue. However, nutritional deficiencies appear to be the major cause of unsoundnesses.

Racehorses are equine athletes whose nutritive

Fig. R-1. Citation, sensational Thoroughbred, bred and owned by Calumet Farm, shown as a two-year-old. Citation was the first million dollar winner of the Thoroughbred breed, with total earnings of $1,085,760. Running races under saddle are now confined almost exclusively to the Thoroughbred breed. (New York Racing Association Photo)

Fig. R-2. Equine athletes need special rations.

requirements are the most exacting, but the most poorly met, of all animals. This statement may be shocking to some, but it's true for the reasons that follow.

Racehorses are commonly:

• Started in training very shortly past 12 months of age, which is comparable to an adolescent boy or girl doing sweatshop labor.

• Moved from track to track under all sorts of conditions.

• Trained the year around, raced innumerable times each year, and forced to run when fatigued.

• Outdoors only a short time each day—usually before sun-up, with the result that the sun's rays have little chance to produce vitamin D from the cholesterol in the skin.

• Without opportunity for even a few mouthfuls of grass—a rich, natural source of the B vitamins and unidentified factors.

• Fed oats, grass hay, and possibly bran—produced in unknown areas, and on soils of unknown composition. Such an oats-grass hay-bran ration is almost always deficient in vitamins A and D and the B vitamins, and lopsided and low in calcium and phosphorus.

• Given a potion of some concoction of questionable value—if not downright harmful.

By contrast, human athletes—college football teams and participants in the Olympics, for example—are usually required to eat at a special training table, supervised by nutrition experts. They are fed the best diet that science can formulate and technology can prepare. It's high in protein, rich in readily available energy, and fortified and balanced in vitamins and minerals.

It's small wonder, therefore, that so many equine athletes go unsound, whereas most human athletes compete year after year until overtaken by age.

Indeed, high strung and highly stressed, racehorses need special rations just as human athletes do—and for the same reasons; and, the younger the age, the more acute the need. This calls for rations high in protein, rich in readily available energy, fortified with vitamins, minerals, and unidentified factors—and with all nutrients in proper balance.

A racehorse is asked to develop a large amount of horsepower in a period of one to three minutes. The oxidations that occur in a racehorse's body are at a higher pitch than in a draft horse, and, therefore, more vitamins are required. In this connection, it is noteworthy that the late Clyde Beatty, great animal trainer of the circus, sweated off a pound under the stress of every 18-minute performance.

Also, racehorses are the *prima donnas* of the equine world; most of them are temperamental, and no two of them can be fed alike. They vary in rapidity of eating, in the quantity of feed that they will consume, in the proportion of concentrate to roughage that they will take, and in response to different caretakers. Thus, for best results, they must be fed as individuals.

Most racehorse rations are deplorably deficient in protein, simply because they are based on the minimum requirements of little-stressed, slow, plodding draft horses.

During the racing season, the hay of a racehorse should be limited to 7 or 8 pounds, whereas the concentrate allowance may range up to 16 pounds. Heavy roughage eaters may have to be muzzled, to keep them from eating their bedding. A bran mash is commonly fed once a week.

"RACEHORSE HAY," and "RACEHORSE OATS".—Distance lends enchantment! Many horsemen believe not only that there is something magical about certain horse feeds, but that they must be grown in a specific area(s). For example, timothy hay and oats are frequently extolled on the basis that they are grown in certain "name" areas; they are even referred to as "racehorse oats" or "racehorse timothy hay." Such specialty areas may produce superior products, but their feeding value is generally exaggerated far beyond their price, with much of their added cost going for hundreds of miles of transportation and for middlemen.

RACING.—According to some historians, the Greeks introduced horse racing in the Olympic games in 1450 B.C. Also, it is reported that a planned horse race of consequence was run in 1377 between animals owned by Richard II and the Earl of Arundel. The sporting instinct of man being what it is, it is reasonable to surmise, however, that a bit of a contest was staged the first time that two proud mounted horsemen chanced to meet.

The development of horse racing in Britain dates from the seventeenth century, although it is known to have taken place much earlier. Records exist of racing during the Roman occupation; and during the reign of Henry II races took place at Smithfield, which was the great London horse market at the time. But it was in the reign of James I that racing first began to be an organized sport. He took a great liking to Newmarket, where he had a royal palace and a racecourse built. Also, he established public races in various parts of the country.

The famous Rowley Mile Course at Newmarket, the home of English flat racing, is named after Charles II. "Old Riley" was his nickname,

after his favorite hack by that name. Charles II loved racing; he rode in matches, founded races called the Royal Plates, and sometimes adjudicated in the disputes.

The Jockey Club came into existence at Newmarket in 1752, with many rich and influential men among its members. It gradually became the governing body of English racing.

[Also see HARNESS RACEHORSES (Trotters and Pacers); QUARTER HORSES; RUNNING RACEHORSES; STANDARDBRED; and THOROUGHBRED.]

RACING ATTENDANCE.—In 1974, 78,799,936 fans went to Thoroughbred and harness racing. Football (pro and college) ranked second, with 42,910,071 fans; baseball (major and minor leagues) was in a close third place, with an attendance of 41,662,407; and basketball (pro and college) stood fourth, with an attendance of 33,785,097. (Statistics, courtesy of *Triangle Publications, Inc.*)

RACING COLORS.—The Jockey Club assigns colors to racing stables. They may be assigned for one year, or they may be assigned for a lifetime. Sometimes colors are reassigned when no longer in use, but this is not the case with the colors of very famous stables. Jockeys must wear the colors assigned to the stable.

RACING PLATE.—A shoe designed for racehorses. It is light in weight and it grips the track. (Also see SHOEING—Fig. S-9.)

RACING RECORDS.—In running races (Thoroughbreds), Dr. Fager holds the world's record for a mile at 1:32⅕, set at Arlington Park, Chicago, in 1968; and Man O'War set the world's record for 1⅜ mile at 2:14⅕, in 1920. The fastest mile (Dr. Fager) at 1:32⅕ minutes is equal to a speed of 45.4 miles per hour.

In quarter races (Quarter Horses), Trackle Feature set the U.S. Record for a quarter mile (440 yards) at :21.02 in 1969.

In harness racing (Standardbreds), Nevele Pride holds the world's trotting record for a mile at 1:54⅘ minutes, which was established in

1969; and Steady Star set the world's pacing record for a mile at 1:52 minutes in 1971.

(Also see QUARTER HORSES; STANDARDBRED; and THOROUGHBRED.)

RACK.—The rack (formerly, but now incorrectly, called single-foot) is a fast, flashy, unnatural, four-beat gait in which each foot meets the ground separately at equal intervals; hence, it was originally known as the "single-foot," a designation now largely discarded. The rack is easy on the rider but hard on the horse. However, it is without doubt the most popular gait in the American show-ring; being fast, brilliant, and flashy. On the tanbark, great speed at the rack is requested by giving the command, "rack on."

RAFLYN FARMS *(a private registry for Lipizzan horses).*—Route 2, Box 480, Snohomish, Washington 98290. (See Appendix for complete breed registry association list.)

RANGE HORSE.—A horse of nondescript breeding raised and/or used on a ranch in western United States. It is broader than the term "cow pony," for it may include unbroken horses.

RANGERBRED.—The two foundation stallions of the breed came from Turkey. The name Colorado Ranger was selected for the breed to signify that they were bred in Colorado, and that they were bred under range conditions. They are used primarily for stock horses.

RANGY.—Elongated, lean, muscular, of slight build.

RASP.—See SHOEING—Table S-5.

RATCATCHER.—Informal hunting dress, especially a tweed jacket with tan breeches.

RATE *(the hounds).*—A hunting term. The Master or huntsman "rates" his hounds when he scolds or rebukes them, either by voice or whip (thong).

RATION (S).—Correctly speaking, the word "ration" refers to the amount of feed supplied to a horse in a definite period, usually for a day or 24 hours. To most horsemen, however, the word implies the feed or mixture of feeds fed, without limitation to the time in which they are consumed. In this book, the author accedes to the common usage of the word, rather than to dictionary correctness.

Oats, corn, and barley—all farm-grown concentrates—are the grains most commonly used for horses; whereas wheat bran, linseed meal, soybean meal, and cottonseed meal are the favored supplements to the grains. Alfalfa, clover, soybean, timothy, prairie grass, Johnson grass, lespedeza, cereal hays, and dried corn and sorghum fodder constitute the chief forages fed to horses. To be sure, the concentrate and roughage combination used varies in different sections of the United States—home-grown feeds and economy being the primary determining factors. Horses of the West, for example, are fed largely on barley and alfalfa or cereal hay; in the northern Mississippi Valley, the ration consists of oats and corn with timothy or mixed hay for roughage; whereas in the deep South, corn is the leading grain and Johnson grass, lespedeza, and corn fodder the chief roughages.

The addition of a few sliced carrots to the ration and an occasional bran mash, or a small amount of linseed meal, are desirable, particular-

Fig. R-3. Well fed, acrobatic—and nonchalant. (Courtesy, Margit Sigray Bessenyey. Photo by Ernst Peterson)

ly during the wintering period. Also, such feeds may be used in regulating the bowels, on idle days, and at other times as required. Such cooling feeds should also be given to horses whose legs must undergo blistering or firing; for they reduce the tendency toward feverish, inflammatory symptoms. Care must be taken to prevent the animal from getting flabby or washy from too much soft feed while undergoing treatment. Whether the animal is working or idle, the trainer must never relax his vigilant observation nor let his judgment sleep.

Table R-1 contains some suggested rations for different classes of horses. It is merely intended as a general guide. The horseman should give consideration to (1) the quality, availability, and cost of feeds; (2) the character and severity of the work; and (3) the age, individuality, and use of the animal. Under many conditions, it may be more satisfactory to buy a ready-mixed feed.

RAT TAIL.—A tail with a short haircoat.

RATTLERS.—Rattlers (wooden, rubber, or plastic balls) or links of light chain fastened about the pasterns of high-going harness and saddle horses and ponies. Weighted boots are also used to enhance action.

REAR FLANK.—See PARTS OF A HORSE—Fig. P-4.

REARING.—See VICES—Rearing.

REATA.—Spanish for lariat. It is made of rawhide.

RECESSIVE.—A characteristic which appears only when both members of a pair of genes are alike.

(Also see DOMINANT AND RECESSIVE FACTORS.)

RECORD PULL.—See PULLING RECORD.

RECORDS, BREEDING FORMS.—See BREEDING HORSES.

RECORDS, QUARTER HORSE.—See QUARTER HORSES.

RECORDS, STANDARDBRED.—See STANDARDBRED.

RECORDS, THOROUGHBRED.—See THOROUGHBRED.

RECOVERY (after stumbling).—There are two schools of thought as to what to do with the reins when a horse stumbles. Some expert horsemen feel that the reins should remain loose, thereby giving the horse a chance to use his head for balancing in gaining his feet. Other horsemen with equal expertise argue that unless the horse is collected he will continue to go down. The writer's observations lead him to believe that the method used should vary with the horse, and that the horseman will know best which method will work with a particular horse.

RECREATION USE.—See USE OF HORSES.

RECTAL WORMS.—See PINWORMS.

REFUSAL.—When a horse shies out or stops before a jump, it constitutes what is known as a "refusal." The penalty in jumper classes is 3 faults for the first refusal, 6 for the second, and elimination for the third. The penalty in hunter classes is 8 faults for the first refusal, 8 faults for the second refusal, and elimination for the third.

The most common causes for refusals are (1) asking a horse to take a jump for which he has not been sufficiently and properly trained; (2) mishandling by a rider whose hands didn't go with the horse's mouth, with the result that when he thrust his head forward in preparation for a landing, he received a severe blow on the bars of his mouth; and (3) too much schooling,

TABLE R-1

LIGHT HORSE FEEDING GUIDE

Age, sex, and use	Daily allowance	Kind of hay	Suggested grain rations		
			Rations No. 1 (lbs)	Rations No. 2 (lbs)	Rations No. 3 (lbs)
Stallions in breeding season (weighing 900 to 1,400 lb.)	¾ to 1½ lb. grain per 100 lb. body weight, together with a quantity of hay within same range.	Grass–legume mixed; or 1/3 to ½ legume hay, with remainder grass hay.	Oats 55 Wheat 20 Wheat bran 20 Linseed meal 5	Corn 35 Oats 35 Wheat 15 Wheat bran 15	Oats 100
Pregnant mares (weighing 900 to 1,400 lb.)	¾ to 1½ lb. grain per 100 lb. body weight, together with a quantity of hay within same range.	Grass–legume mixed; or 1/3 to ½ legume hay, with remainder grass-hay (straight grass hay may be used first half of pregnancy).	Oats 80 Wheat bran 20	Barley 45 Oats 45 Wheat bran 10	Oats 95 Linseed meal 5
Foals before weaning (weighing 100 to 350 lbs. with projected mature weights of 900 to 1,400 lb.)	½ to ¾ lb. grain per 100 lb. body weight, together with a quantity of hay within same range.	Legume hay	Oats 50 Wheat bran 40 Linseed meal 10	Oats 30 Barley 30 Wheat bran 30 Linseed meal 10	Rations balanced on basis of following assumption: Mares of mature weights of 600, 800, 1,000, and 1,200 lbs. may produce 36, 42, 44, and 49 lbs. of milk daily.
Weanlings (weighing 350 to 450 lb.)	1 to 1½ lb. grain and 1½ to 2 lb. hay per 100 lb. body weight.	Grass–legume mixed; or ½ legume hay, with remainder grass hay.	Barley 30 Oats 30 Wheat bran 30 Linseed meal 10	Oats 70 Wheat bran 15	Oats 80 Linseed meal 20
Yearlings, 2nd Summer (weighing 450 to 700 lb.)	Good, luxuriant pasture (if in training or for other reasons without access to pasture, the ration should be intermediate between the adjacent upper and lower groups).				
Yearlings, or rising 2-year-olds, second Winter (weighing 700 to 1,000 lb.) (Continued)	½ to 1 lb. grain and 1 to 1½ lb. hay per 100 lb. body weight.	Grass–legume mixed; or 1/3 to ½ legume hay, with remainder grass hay.	Oats 80 Wheat bran 20	Barley 35 Oats 35 Bran 15 Linseed meal 15	Oats 80

TABLE R-1 (CONTINUED)

	Roughage	Grain	Concentrate
Light horses at work; riding, driving, and racing (weighing 900 to 1,400 lb.)	Grass hay	Hard use—1¼ to 1 1/3 lb. grain and 1 to 1¼ lb. hay per 100 lb. body weight. Medium use—¾ to 1 lb. grain and 1 to 1¼ lb. hay per 100 lb. body weight. Light use—⅖ to ½ lb. grain and 1¼ to 1½ lb. hay per 100 lb. body weight.	Oats .... 100 Oats .... 70 Corn .... 30 Oats .... 70 Barley 30
Mature idle horses; stallions, mares, and geldings (weighing 900 to 1,400 lb.)	Pasture in season; or grass-legume mixed hay.	1½ to 1¾ lb. hay per 100 lb. body weight.	(With grass hay, add ¾ lb. of a high protein supplement daily.)

Note—With all rations and for all classes and ages of horses, provide free access to separate containers of (1) iodized salt and (2) a mixture of 1 part salt and 2 parts steamed bonemeal or other suitable calcium-phosphorus supplement.

with the result that the horse has "gone sour."

When a horse refuses in a show, he should be given only a short run to bring him up to the jump for the second time, thereby giving him little time in which to consider refusing; also the aids should be used strongly.

In the hunt field when a horse refuses, he should be pulled out of line so as to permit all other riders who are waiting to jump the obstacle to proceed, then the refusing horse should bring up the rear.

REGISTRY ASSOCIATION.—See Appendix I for complete list of breed registry associations.

REGISTRY, OPEN.—Open registry refers to a registry association that has provisions to bring in outside blood—to infuse blood from animals not already registered (or eligible for registry) in the particular association.

Purebreds have been the major factor in horse improvement of the past, and they will continue to exert a powerful influence in the future. But most purebred breeds had their humble beginning from nonpurebreds.

By meeting certain requisites—usually in an Appendix Registry or a Tentative Registry, but with provision to advance to foundation status—there are open registry provisions in the following breeds: American Albino, Appaloosa, Connemara Pony, Morocco Spotted Horse, Palomino, Pinto, Pony of the Americas, Quarter Horse, Standardbred, and Tennessee Walking Horse. Also, the American Shetland Pony Club maintains a special registry for Harness Show Ponies, which are half Shetland and half Hackney or Welsh. In the late thirties, the Morgan Horse Club, Inc., infused American Saddle blood. In recent years, much Thoroughbred blood has been infused into the Quarter Horse breed to improve the racing qualities of certain strains.

Of course, if there is within a given breed some genetic material that excels in the desired trait—speed, endurance, ruggedness, soundness, or whatever the sought-for characteristic—it is possible to select toward it. However, by bringing in outside blood, desired changes may be brought about much more quickly. Time is usually of the essence in a horse breeding program, because it is slow enough at best.

Those breed registry associations that wish to make provision for open registries should carefully conceive and clearly record their objectives and procedures. Outside animals should be required to pass a rigid inspection (individuality and performance) prior to use, and the year of closing the registry should be set far enough ahead to make possible achievement of the goals. Generally speaking, such a program is best accomplished through the use of proved stallions.

REIN, also, CHECK REIN.—See HARNESS—Figs. H-3, H-4, and H-5.

REIN, Indirect.—See INDIRECT REIN.

REINING (A sporting event).—The horse must follow a prescribed course, and is required to demonstrate his proficiency in changing leads, turning, stopping, and backing. He must keep his feet under him at all times while following the various intricate patterns of the contest; and he must rein easily, and back up without undue emotion, fretting, or tail waving.

REINS.—The reins are an intermediary between the rider and the mount; they afford direct contact between the hands and the horse's mouth. The reins regulate the impulsion—slowing, stopping, or backing the horse. The reins, acting through the mouth and the neck, are also used to change direction of travel or to turn the horse to either the right or the left.

The ordinary double bridle has two sets of leather reins, the snaffle and the curb. The snaffle reins are always slightly wider than the curb reins. Also, they are fastened together by a buckle; hence they may be unbuckled to permit the attachment of a running martingale. Curb reins are stitched together.

Hunting bridle reins are frequently braided or rubber-covered, to give a better grip.

Western reins may be made of leather, braided rawhide, cotton, mohair, or synthetic material. They are frequently open at the ends and longer than English reins.

(Also see BRIDLES—Fig. B-66; and HORSEMANSHIP.)

REINS, OPPOSITION.—This refers to the use of the neck rein (indirect rein) in opposition to the plow rein (direct rein). For example, let us assume that the rider wants to keep the forehand stationary and move the hindquarters to the left. He may, in addition to the leg aid, use direct pull on the right rein, and, simultaneously, use the same rein as a neck rein against the horse's neck to prevent it from turning the forehand to the right in response to the direct pull on that rein. Thus, in reality he is using the direct rein in opposition to the indirect rein. The opposition rein reaches its most sophisticated use in dressage work.

REMOUNT SERVICE.—This was a branch of the Quartermaster Corps. of the U.S. Army, established by Act of Congress in 1921, for the purpose of carrying on a horse breeding program to provide sufficient horses of cavalry and artillery types for the Army. On July 1, 1948, it was transferred to the U.S. Department of Agriculture and renamed the Agriculture Remount Service, following which the program was liquidated. At the time of the transfer to the USDA, approximately 700 remount stallions were in service throughout the country.

(Also see WARFARE, HORSES IN.)

REMUDA.—A collection of riding horses at a roundup from which are chosen those used for the day. A relay of mounts.

RENTAL HORSE.—A horse that is available for rental, much like a rental car. The typical rental horse is a sturdy, plodding beast, wise in the ways of inexperienced riders, and without too much spirit. If this were not so, he could not survive and adjust to the treatment (no matter how unintentional) accorded most rental horses. Rental horses are usually rented on an hourly rate basis.

When a rider and a rental stable owner are starting out fresh with each other, they should lay their cards on the table. The rider should give the stable owner an honest evaluation of his riding skills and experience, in order that the owner may select the proper mount for him; and the stable owner should tell the rider, with equal frankness, the characteristics of the mount that is being assigned to him. This will make for a more enjoyable ride and return business for each party. Also, before going on a long ride, it is recommended that the horse first be tried out in the stable arena or corral, thereby making certain that the rider and horse are suited to each other.

REPRODUCTION.—Foals evolve through the process of reproduction. Mares must mate with stallions, or be artificially inseminated, before they can produce young.

Reproduction in horses, or the development of a new equine, results from the union of an egg, or ovum, produced by the mare and a spermatozoon produced by the stallion. These reproductive cells are so small that they can only be seen clearly with a microscope. Each sex cell carries a sample one-half of the inheritance possessed by each parent.

Reproduction is such a delicate and complex process that one wonders that farm animals are so fertile. Yet, it's obvious that more difficulty is experienced in breeding mares than any other kind of livestock. The percentage of mares bred that actually conceive each year will vary from 40 to a high of 85, with an average probably running less than 50; and some of this number will fail to produce living foals. This means that, on the average, two mares are kept a whole year in order to produce one foal. By contrast, nationally, 88% of all beef cows that are bred, calve; 90 to 94% of all ewes, lamb; and 80 to 85% of all sows bred, farrow pigs.

The lower percentage conception in mares than in other classes of livestock is due primarily to the following: (1) research in the field has lagged, (2) an attempt is made to get mares bred in about 4 months instead of 12, and (3) the breeding season has been arbitrarily limited to a period (late winter and early spring) that at its best is only about 50% in agreement with nature.

In the bluegrass country of Kentucky, where there are both good horsemen and as desirable conditions for breeding as can be secured under domestication, 66% foaling is considered as average for the area.

Since regular and normal reproduction are the bases for profit on any horse breeding establishment, it is important that everything possible be done to increase the percent foal crop.

(Also see BREEDING HORSES; and FEED—Reproduction and lactation.)

REPRODUCTIVE ORGANS.—See MARE; and STALLION.

REQUIREMENTS, NUTRITIVE.—See NUTRITIVE NEEDS.

RESEARCH, HORSE.—Other animal industries have long been cognizant of new frontiers possible through research. But horse research has lagged. In 1975, the scientific man years (a man year is defined as one person devoting full time to research for one year) devoted to research on each class of livestock by USDA and college personnel were as follows:

Class of Animal	Scientific Man Years Devoted to Research, in 1975
Beef Cattle	348
Dairy Cattle	308
Poultry	253
Swine	151
Sheep and Wool	79
Horses, Ponies, Mules	25
Laboratory Animals, Pets, Goats, Other Animals	61

There is every reason to believe that today's research will be reflected in a host of tomorrow's advances; that many of today's horse problems will be solved through research. Indeed, horse research should be expanded. More specifically, and among other things, we need to know the following in the horse business:

• We need to know how to modernize rations and effect savings in costs.

• We need to know how to rectify appalling and costly sterility and reproductive failures; 40 to 60 percent of all mares that are bred fail to foal.

• We need to know how (a) to bring mares in heat at will, and (b) to transplant fertilized eggs (Ova transplantation is now being done commercially in cattle.).

• We need to improve artificial insemination.

• We need to know more about the relationship between soil fertility, plant nutrients, and horses.

• We need to know how to provide labor-saving buildings and equipment. Seventy-five percent of horse work is still hand labor, one-third of which could be eliminated by mechanization and modernization.

• We need to know more about automation and integration; how to reap the rewards therefrom.

• We need to know how to control more diseases and parasites.

• We need to know how to increase the durability and useful life of a horse—in racing, in showing, and in breeding.

We must remember, however, (1) that horse research is both slow and costly, and (2) that other industries long have supported research costs liberally with no assistance from the taxpayer, simply including them as a normal part of their operating costs. In addition to individual owners contributing to the support of research programs, the time has arrived when horsemen should review where racing dollars go. Perhaps a liberal proportion of racing revenue which now goes into the treasuries of the thirty states having pari-mutuel betting should be earmarked for horse research, teaching, and extension. Otherwise, there is grave danger of starving "the goose that laid the golden egg."

Finally, it should be emphasized that research can make the information available, but it is still up to each individual—each horseman—to secure and apply the results; "you can lead a horse to water but you can't make him drink."

RESPIRATION.—See BREATHING RATE.

RESTING THE HORSE.—In endurance or trail rides, experienced horsemen rest their mounts in two ways: (1) by frequent change of gait—from walk to trot, and trot to walk; and (2) by getting off and leading a horse about five minutes out of each hour. Also, during the noon hour the rider removes the saddle, rubs the horse down, and waters and feeds him.

On a hunt, after the horse has exerted himself and during a check, the rider should dismount and walk his horse to cool him out.

"Never sit a standing horse" is old and sound advice, whatever the ride. Also, a rub down following work is as restful to a horse as to a human being.

RESTRAINING.—The horse is big and strong. Hence, means of restraining him are necessary from time to time. The essential features of such methods and equipment are: (1) thorough restraint of the animal, without the hazard of injury, and (2) convenience and protection of the operator. Fig. R-4 shows various means of restraining a horse.

REWARDS.—The training of a horse is based on a system of rewards and punishment. Rewards differ according to the circumstances. They may include relaxing of the reins, relaxing of the pressure of the legs, a pat on the shoulder, or a word of praise. Sometimes it is well to give a little sugar or a bit of a carrot as a reward or treat. It should be recognized, however, that feeding treats from the hand is apt to promote a tendency toward nipping, especially in ponies.

(Also see CONTROL OF THE HORSE; and TREATS.)

RIBBED-UP.—Said of a horse on which the back ribs are well arched and incline well backwards, bringing the ends closer to the point of the hip and making the horse shorter in the coupling.

RIBS.—There are usually eighteen pairs of ribs in the horse, but a nineteenth rib on one side or both is not at all rare. Eight pairs are known as true ribs, joining the segments of the sternum or breastbone; whereas the remaining 10 pairs are floating, merely overlapping and being attached to each other. The seventh and eighth ribs are longest, with the back ribs much shorter.

A capacious chest and middle, which is desirable in all horses, is obtained through long, well-sprung ribs. Such a structural condition allows for more room for the vital internal organs, and experienced horsemen know that such horses eat better and stand up under more hard work.

(Also see SKELETON; and PARTS OF A HORSE—Fig. P-4.)

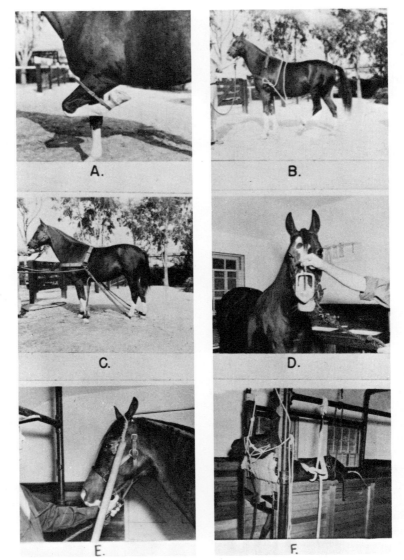

Fig. R-4. *Various means of restraining a horse: A, knee strap; B, side sling; C, casting harness; D, humane nose twitch; E, ear twitch; and F, stocks.*

RICKETS.—Rickets is a disease of growing foals, and other animals, characterized by a failure of growing bone to ossify, or harden, properly.

CAUSE.—Lack of calcium, phosphorus, or vitamin D; or an incorrect ratio of the two minerals.

SYMPTOMS.—Enlargement of the knee and hock joints, and the animal may exhibit great pain when moving about. Irregular bulges (beaded ribs) at juncture of ribs with breastbone, and bowed legs.

DISTRIBUTION AND LOSSES.—Worldwide. It is seldom fatal.

TREATMENT.—If the disease has not advanced too far, treatment may be successful by supplying adequate amounts of vitamin D, calcium, and phosphorus, and/or adjusting the ratio of calcium to phosphorus.

PREVENTION.—Provide (1) sufficient calcium, phosphorus, and vitamin D, and (2) a correct ratio of the two minerals.

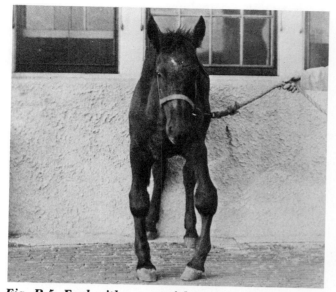

Fig. R-5. Foal with severe rickets. Note the enlarged joints and crooked legs. Rickets may be caused by a lack of calcium, phosphorus, or vitamin D; or by an incorrect ratio of the two minerals. (Courtesy, Department of Veterinary Pathology and Hygiene, College of Veterinary Medicine, University of Illinois)

REMARKS.—Rickets in foals is not uncommon in Central and South America.

RIDGELING.—A ridgeling is a horse with at least one testicle in the abdomen (not descended). Such a horse is difficult to geld, and often retains the characteristics of a stallion. Ridgelings are frequently used as teasers, to test the response of a mare prior to breeding—to determine if a mare is in heat and ready to breed.

RIDING A HORSE.—See HORSEMANSHIP.

RIDING CLUBS.—Today, there is a rise in rural living. Some folks are moving to the country because they seek serenity and tranquility, or they want to get away from smog and pollution. Others desire a better place for their children. Still others are motivated because of a common love for horses. The latter are demanding, and they will get, uncommon facilities for horse care. The horse community of the future will be an Equine Country Club. These elite horse centers

will be financed in different ways—by individual ownership and promoters, through closed membership and dues, or with investment capital raised through public offerings. Some will be "chains," just like motels, supermarkets, and whatnot. The architectural design will differ. But most of them will have stalls and corrals, indoor and outdoor arenas, riding rings, bridle paths and trails, and a lodge or clubhouse. Adjacent acreage for privately owned homes will be available in some cases.

A pleasant and varied social life will be centered around equine activities—including horse shows, trail rides, gymkhanas, etc. Most of them will have on their staffs top professionals who will give riding instruction and train horses. These equine centers will be attractive and well kept.

Equine Country Clubs, along with the suburban-owned horses which persist, will demand the maximum in convenience feeds and the minimum amount of manure and pollution.

RIDING ETIQUETTE.—Riding etiquette, or courtesy, is much like good etiquette anywhere else. There are certain rules that should be observed in group rides.

(Also see HORSEMANSHIP—Rules of Good Horsemanship.)

RIDING HABIT.—See CLOTHES FOR RIDERS.

RIDING HORSES.—Riding horses have many and varied uses, but, as the name indicates, they are all ridden. They may have a very definite utility value, as is true of stock horses, or they may be used chiefly for purposes of recreation and sport. For the latter use, training, manners, and style are of paramount importance, although durability and efficiency are not to be overlooked in any horse.

RIDING SCHOOLS.—For greatest enjoyment, one should learn to ride correctly. It is an unfortunate truth that many people think they can ride if only they can stick on a horse. Although these same people may pay well for instruction in golf, swimming, tennis, and other sports, it never occurs to them that a competent riding master may be essential in their learning to ride correctly.

Equitation is a very difficult subject to teach. In the first place, no two horses nor two riders are alike. Then there is hardly any limit to the types of available equipment, and there are the different gaits; and, in addition, riding to hounds and riding on a city bridle path present entirely different problems. Moreover, riding cannot be taught by merely reading a set of instructions. It can be mastered only after patient practice under a competent instructor. The amateur, therefore, should be under no illusions about achieving horsemanship and horsemastership merely through reading a book.

It must be recognized also that there are many schools of riding, and each riding master will proceed along different lines. Yet, the end result will always be the same—training the rider to get the maximum pleasure with the least exertion to himself and his mount. Regardless of the method of instruction, the first requisite is that of instilling confidence in the amateur. Confidence is usually obtained through first becoming familiar with the horse and equipment and then by riding a gentle and obedient horse at the walk in an enclosed ring, while keeping the mount under control at all times.

(Also see HORSEMANSHIP.)

RIDING STABLE.—A stable which performs one or more of the following services: gives riding lessons, rents horses, and/or boards horses.

(Also see INCENTIVE BASIS FOR THE HELP; and RIDING SCHOOLS.)

RIGGING.—The exterior leather trappings of a Western saddle.

RIGHT LEAD.—Right front foot and right rear lead on the canter.

RIGOR MORTIS.—Stiffening of the body after death.

RINGBONE.—Ringbone is a bony growth on the pastern bone generally of the forefoot, although occasionally the hind foot is affected. The condition usually causes a lameness, accompanied by a stiff ankle. This condition generally follows severe straining, blows, sprains, or improper shoeing. Treatment consists of the application of cold water bandages for temporary relief. For more permanent relief, veterinarians sometimes resort to blistering, firing, or severing of the nerve leading to the area. The condition is thought to be hereditary.

(Also see UNSOUNDNESSES.)

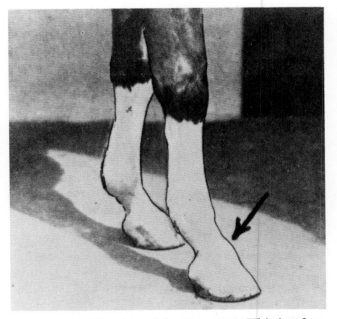

Fig. R-6. Ringbone on right front foot. This is a bony growth on the pastern bone. Note the bulging effect approximately one inch above the coronary band. (Courtesy, USDA)

RINGER.—A horse that is passed off under false identity, with the idea of entering him in a race below his class where he is almost certain to win. In the early 1920's, the most common camouflage for a ringer was a coat of paint—hence the terms "dark horse" and "horse of another color." Formerly, the ringer's nemesis was rain; today, it is the lip tattoo system of The Jockey Club, for each horse in every major racing meet must be tattooed.

RINGS *(indoor and outdoor).*—Rings have no standard or required specifications for size, type of construction, or maintenance.

For most purposes, a ring 125 x 250 feet will suffice. However, many good show-rings are either smaller or larger than this. For example, the ring of the famous Devon Horse Show, which is often used for jumpers, is 150 x 300 feet. But the ring at the Spanish Riding School in Vienna is only 59 x 180 feet.

The surface of a show-ring must be resilient and firm to assure proper footing, and it also must be free of dust. In outdoor rings, proper drainage and a good track base are necessary for all-weather use. A ring can be drained by (1) locating it high enough for water to drain away from it, and (2) installing, when necessary, drainage tile or perforated steel pipe underneath the track, with the perforations on the bottom side of the pipe.

Fig. R-8. Indoor arena in Rex C. Cauble's Cutter Bill Championship Arena (named after Cutter Bill, the World Champion Cutting Horse), Denton, Texas. This working arena is 360 feet long and 80 feet wide. It is illuminated with Mercury Vapor lights. The floor is made of 4 inches of sand over a hard clay base. (Courtesy, Quarter Horse Journal*)*

Fig. R-7. Jumps in the attractive ring at Ribbonwood Arabian Ranch, Mountain Center, Calif. (Photo by Miss Gloria Rawcliffe)

Fig. R-9. The ring at the Spanish Riding School is resilient and dust-free. The surface consists of a mixture of ⅔ sawdust and ⅓ sand, which is sprinkled with water at intervals to keep down the dust. (Courtesy, Spanish Riding School, Wels, Austria)

The track usually will be firm if it is covered with a mixture of organic matter and dirt or sand. For example, the ring at the Spanish Riding School is covered with a mixture of ⅔ sawdust and ⅓ sand. It is sprinkled with water at intervals to keep down the dust.

In many indoor rings in the United States, 6 to 8 inches of tanbark are used on a dirt base. Unless tanbark is watered frequently, it will pulverize and give poor footing. Some rings are covered 18 to 24 inches deep with shavings or sawdust mixed with dirt or sand. Other rings are covered with approximately 9 inches of wood shavings, 2 inches of sawdust, and 4 inches of sand all mixed together and oiled. Salt may be

added because it holds moisture when wetted down and reduces dust.

In outdoor rings, organic matter for resilience is sometimes provided by seeding rye or other small grain on the track during the off-season and disking under the green crop.

No matter how good the construction, a show-ring must be maintained. It must be smoothed and leveled, holes must be filled, and when it gets too hard, the ground must be broken. A flexible, chain-type harrow is recommended for show-ring maintenance.

Besides ring size, construction, and maintenance, other factors to be considered are (1) ring layout to facilitate reversing a performance class in a ring that has turf or other decorative material in the center; (2) attractiveness of the ring; (3) spectator seating capacity, comfort, and visibility; (4) nearby parking; and (5) handling the crowd.

RINGWORM.—This is a contagious infection of the outer layers of skin caused by an infestation of microscopic fungi.

SYMPTOMS.—Round, scaly areas almost devoid of hair appear mainly in the vicinity of eyes, ears, side of the neck, or root of the tail. Mild itching usually accompanies the infection.

TREATMENT.—Clip the hair from the infected skin areas. Soften skin crusts with warm soap and water and remove them if desired. Let infected areas dry and then paint them with weak tincture of iodine every 3 days or treat them with a mixture of one part salicylic acid and 10 parts alcohol every 3 days until the infection clears up.

PREVENTION AND CONTROL.—Isolate infected animals. Disinfect everything that has been in contact with infected animals, including curry combs and brushes. Practice strict sanitation.

DISCUSSION.—Ringworm attacks horses throughout the United States, primarily as a stable infection. It is unsightly and infected animals may have considerable discomfort, but economic losses are low.

(Also see DISEASES AND PARASITES; HEALTH PROGRAM; and PARASITES OF HORSES.)

RIOT (RIOTOUS).—When hounds hunt any animal or bird other than their intended quarry, they are said to riot. Riotous hounds of a pack are undisciplined hounds.

RISLING.—See RIDGELING.

ROACH BACKED.—Arched-backed, razor-backed.

ROACHED MANE.—A mane that has been cut short and tapered so that it stands upright. It is not as short as a clipped mane.

ROAD HACK.—A horse shown under saddle whose outstanding gait is speed at the trot.

ROADSTERS.—The sport of showing a roadster originated in the horse and buggy era. It was founded upon the desire to own an attractive horse that possessed the necessary speed to pass any of its rivals encountered upon the city or country thoroughfares.

*Fig. R-10. Saint Nick, Standardbred shown here as a roadster to buggy. (Courtesy, **Saddle and Bridle**)*

In the show-ring, roadsters are generally shown in either or both (1) roadster to bike, or (2) roadster to buggy classes. (In many of the larger shows, a roadster appointment class is provided. Appointments are listed in the A.H.S.A. *Rule Book*.) Roadster to buggy classes are hitched singly or in pairs. Some shows also provide a class or classes for roadsters under saddle. In all divisions—whether shown to bike or buggy, or under saddle—entries must trot; pacing is barred.

Originally, roadster classes included animals of both Standardbred and Morgan extraction. In recent years, however, the Morgan has developed more in the direction of a saddler, leaving the roadster classification almost exclusively to the Standardbred.

In addition to possessing the usual Standard-bred characteristics, particular stress is placed in roadster show classes upon the manners, style, and beauty of conformation, combined with speed. In striking contrast to heavy-harness classes, the roadster is shown hitched to very light vehicles permitting fast travel.

Custom decrees that roadsters shall enter the ring at a jog, and work the wrong way (clockwise) of the track first. After jogging for a brief time, usually the judge asks that they perform at the road gait, then jog again (all clockwise of the ring). Then, in succession, the judge asks them to reverse, jog, road gait, and turn on or trot at speed. Lastly, they are called to the center of the ring for inspection in a standing position; at which time the judge usually tests their manners by asking each driver to back his horse.

ROAN.—See COLORS AND MARKINGS OF HORSES.

ROARER.—A wind-broken animal that makes a loud noise in drawing air into the lungs.

ROARING (whistling).—An animal that whistles or wheezes when respiration is speeded up with exercise is said to be a "roarer." Within recent years a surgical operation has been perfected which when properly performed is successful in about 70 percent of the cases so treated.

(Also see UNSOUNDNESSES.)

RODEO.—The word "rodeo" originated in the days of unfenced ranges, in the 1870s. Following the roundup, in which cowboys from many ranches came together to handle cattle and be paid off, they usually provided their own entertainment by staging informal contests in riding, roping, bulldogging, etc. Today, formal rodeos are sporting events, with prize money offered to the winners.

The word *rodeo* is of Spanish origin; it comes from the verb *rodear,* which means to surround. Professionals and Westerners pronounce the word ro'deo, with the accent on the first syllable. Easterners usually use the old Mexican pronunciation with the accent on the last syllable—they say rō day'o.

The first rodeo with paying spectators was held on July 4, 1886, in Prescott, Arizona. Around 1900, rodeo began to merge with Wild West Shows, staging a combination circus and carnival devoted to Western lore. Competition and cost caused the demise of the Wild West Show, but rodeo survived and grew in popularity.

Today, rodeo is a multi-million dollar business. Over 3,000 rodeos are held annually. Most of the large ones are sanctioned by one of two professional associations: The Rodeo Cowboy's Association, and the International Rodeo Association. In the West, many of the colleges and high schools have rodeo teams.

Eight regular events in professional rodeo are used to determine the national championships: bareback bronc riding, barrel racing, bull riding, calf roping, saddle bronc riding, steer roping, steer wrestling, team roping, etc.

(Also see the alphabetical listing of each event.)

RODEO COWBOYS ASSOCIATION, INC.—2929 West 19th Ave., Denver, Colo. 80204

ROLLBACK.—A rollback is a turnaround in place, in which the horse pivots on his rear feet to reverse his direction. It's like the military drill, "To the rear—march."

A horse may be trained to do a rollback as follows: Starting with the walk and trot, stop and pivot in both directions. Then go into a short lope, stops, pivots, and kicks out into a short lope. Finally, crowd the horse and speed up the complete rollback.

After the horse is trained, the rollback can be done this way: (1) stop, (2) give the horse some rein so that he can regain his balance, (3) pull the rein diagonally for a 180-degree pivot, and (4) push off into a lope.

If done properly, the rollback is coordinated, smooth, and easy for the rider to stay on the horse. If uncoordinated, it's rough and difficult for the rider to stay on.

ROLLER.—A surcingle, or form of girth, used to hold a blanket in place.

ROLLERS, RATTLERS.—Wooden balls on a cord, encircling a horse's pastern to give the horse more action.

ROLLING.—Excessive lateral shoulder motion, characteristic of horses with protruding shoulders, is known as rolling.

ROLLING UP.—A practice that originated in the German cavalry. It is used when a horse refuses to leave the stable or another horse(s), or to perform some other desired act. Rolling up consists in making a horse turn rapidly in short circles (in one direction), then moving out in the desired direction.

ROMAL.—A braided rawhide terminating in a single or double tapered strap, usually between 3 and 4 feet long. It is attached to the end of closed, braided rawhide reins. In some Western classes, the American Horse Shows Association *Rule Book* permits the rider to hold romal or end of split reins to keep them from swinging and to adjust the position of the reins provided it is held at least 16 inches from the reining hand.

ROMAN-NOSED.—Refers to a horse having a profile that is convex from poll to muzzle. It is opposite to the "dished" profile of the classic Arabian head. A Roman nose is more common in horses of draft breeding than in light horses. Also, it is characteristic of the Criollo, the cow pony of South America, and of some animals of the Lipizzan breed.

ROPE BURNS.—Rope burns are the result of improper tying and picketing. Generally, they happen as a result of tying the horse with a rope so long that he wraps it around his back pastern. The skin is rubbed off, and the injury heals very slowly. Hence, the animal is laid up for some time. The wound should be kept clean and ointment applied daily.

ROPE-WALKING.—See WINDING OR ROPE-WALKING.

ROSETTES.—A bridle ornament. Some riding bridles need rosettes to keep the throatlatch and headpiece in their proper positions where they pass through the ends of the browbands.

(Also see ORNAMENTS.)

ROUNDUP.—The roundup consists in collecting together horses or cattle for purposes of branding, treating for parasites, separating out for breeding, and marketing.

Fig. R-11. A horse roundup. (Courtesy, **The Western Horseman***)*

ROUNDWORM, LARGE.—See ASCARIDS.

ROUNDWORMS.—Roundworms, or nematodes, are unsegmented worms, usually cylindrical and elongated in shape and with tapered ends. They may be free-living or parasitic, and they vary greatly in size. Some are barely visible to the naked eye; others are a foot in length and as thick as an ordinary lead pencil.

The forms of infection by nematodes vary a great deal. The worms enter a variety of locations outside of the intestinal tract and wander, apparently aimlessly, in various organs and cavities, sometimes dying there.

Roundworms are among the most important parasites of man and animals. They suck blood, carry disease, excrete toxins, disturb digestion and respiration, and generally cause emaciation. Ascarids are an example, (see ASCARIDS).

(Also see DISEASES AND PARASITES; and PARASITES OF HORSES.)

RUBBER PADS.—Horses that are used on hard roads, such as police horses, are sometimes shod with rubber pads under the shoes, with tar and oakum placed between the pad and the sole of the horse's foot.

Horses used on turf, or on terrain other than paved roads, are better off without pads of any kind. Also, prospective buyers should be wary of buying a horse that is shod with rubber pads, because rubber pads are sometimes used in pathological shoeing to correct navicular disease or some other foot trouble.

RUBBING DOWN.—Horses that are worked or exercised should be rubbed down, both before leaving the stable and immediately upon their return. Heated, wet, or sweating animals should be handled as follows:

1. Remove the equipment as fast as possible, wipe it off, and put it away.

2. Remove excess perspiration with a sweat scraper; then rub briskly with a grooming or drying cloth to dry the coat partially. The rubbing cloth can be made from old toweling or blankets. It should be about 18 to 24 inches square.

3. Blanket and walk the horse until cool.

4. Allow a couple of swallows of water every few minutes while cooling out.

A good rubdown promotes circulation, relieves fatigue and overexertions, and prevents soreness. To assure that the horse will be rubbed thoroughly and that no body part will be missed, follow a definite order. This may differ according to individual preference.

RUG.—A heavy wool blanket sometimes used for horses.

RUN.—See GALLOP.

RUNAWAY (BOLTING).—A horse out of control. Most runaways are caused by the rider. The most common causes of runaways are: (1) inexperienced riders venturing out of the ring and into the open spaces before they are ready; and (2) a rider on a bridle path or trail rushing up to the horse in front of him.

When a runaway occurs, the rider should reach forward on one side and take hold of the rein as close to the bit as possible, then pull (with a seesaw motion) the horse's head to the side.

An experienced rider can usually stop a runaway horse by collecting him. This is accomplished by a rhythmic lifting of the head, and, consequently, a lifting of the front end. This is effective because a horse cannot run at top speed unless he can thrust his nose out and throw his center of balance forward.

RUNNING MARTINGALE.—See MARTINGALES.

RUNNING-OUT.—When a horse skirts around an object instead of jumping it, either when jumping in the show-ring or steeplechasing, it is known as "Running Out."

RUNNING RACEHORSES.—Racehorses used for running (an extended gallop) under the saddle are now confined almost exclusively to two breeds, Thoroughbreds and Quarter Horses. Also, the Thoroughbred breed (including both purebreds and crossbreds) has been used widely for other purposes; especially as polo mounts, hunters, and cavalry horses. Quarter Horses are the cow pony of the West.

Although trials of speed had taken place between horses from the earliest recorded history, the true and unmistakable foundation of the Thoroughbred breed, as such, traces back only to the reign of Charles II, known as the "father of the British turf."

Although the length of race, weight carried, and type of track have undergone considerable variation in recent years, the running horse always has been selected for speed and more speed at the run. The distinguishing characteristics of the running horse, as represented by the Thoroughbred, are the extreme refinement, oblique shoulders, well-made withers, heavily-muscled rear quarters, straight hind legs, and close travel to the ground.

Quarter Horse running races are increasing in importance. Also, Appaloosa and Arabian running races have been approved in a few states.

RUNNING WALK.—The running walk is a slow, four-beat gait, intermediate in speed between the walk and rack. The hind foot oversteps the front foot from a few to as many as 18 inches, giving the motion a smooth gliding effect. It is characterized by a bobbing or nodding of the head, a flopping of the ears, and a snapping of the teeth in rhythm with the movement of the legs. The running walk is easy on both horse and rider. It is the all-day business gait of the South and is executed at a speed of 6 to 8 miles per hour. This is a necessary gait in Plantation Walking Horses.

RUSHING *(jumps)*.—A characteristic of jumping horses whose training has been too hurried. Such a horse rushes rather than refuses because he associates the first alternative with the least pain. Rectifying the situation will require much time and patience. The horse should be placed in the hands of a competent horseman, who will make a fresh start over low hurdles until he regains his confidence.

S

SACKING.—To slap a horse with a sack or saddle blanket as a part of gentling and training.

SADDLE (S).—Horses were ridden long before there were saddles. The "horsecloth" was first used about 800 B.C., but the use of saddles with trees did not exist until the fourth century A.D. Ancient horsemen took particular pride in their saddles. To them, they were much more than something to throw on a horse's back. They were

symbolic of the culture and art of the period. The author of this book, who was accorded the rare privilege of studying and photographing the cultural relics of China, was fascinated with two saddles that he saw in a Peking Museum, (see Fig. S-1).

Fig. S-1. Two ornate saddles of the Ching Dynasty, (1644–1911), made of leather covered with gold and inlaid with precious stones. These saddles are on display in The Palace Museum (formerly called the Forbidden City). The grounds of The Palace Museum cover 178 acres, of which 37 acres are under roof.

English and Western saddles are the two most common types, but individual styling within the types may vary considerably.

ENGLISH SADDLE.—English saddles include the flat types that are modified specifically for pleasure riding, training, racing, jumping, or polo. The English saddle (Fig. S-2) is characterized by its relatively flat seat and its generally light weight.

The following points should be remembered about English saddles:

• When an English saddle is used on a show horse, use a white web or linen girth.

• A saddle blanket usually is not necessary with an English saddle.

• For English pleasure riding or showing, use an English saddle and a double bit or Pelham bridle.

• For hunting and jumping, use a forward seat English saddle and a hunting snaffle or Pelham bit.

WESTERN SADDLE.—A Western saddle (Fig. S-3) is the common saddle used by cowboys and western stockmen. The essential features are a steel, light metal, or wooden tree; a pommel, topped by a horn for roping, and a cantle (the height of the pommel and cantle vary according to the uses to which the saddle is to be put and the personal preference of the rider); a comparatively deep seat; heavy square or round skirts; a double cinch, usually, but a single cinch may be used; and heavy stirrups that may be hooded or open. A Western saddle is designed to give comfort for all-day riding and provide enough strength to stand up under the strain of calf roping. The average Western saddle weighs 35 to 40 pounds.

Additional pertinent facts about Western saddles are:

• They're used for Western riding of all kinds, both work and pleasure.

• Western saddles are utilitarian. They're designed to provide all-day comfort, and the horn is a convenient and secure post around which the lariat can be tied or quickly wound when handling cattle.

• The design of Western saddles—especially height of pommel and cantle—is determined by use and personal preference.

Westerners take pride in their saddles. To them they're much more than something to throw over a horse's back, or to use in working cattle. They're symbolic of the development of the range, of trailing, and of the transition from the Texas longhorn to the prime bullock. Most makes and styles of Western saddles are accorded meaningful names, with such selections suggestive of their historical significance, their construction, and/or their use.

To reputable manufacturers and proud owners alike, the names of Western saddles are symbols of service, pledges of integrity, and assurances of courage, character, and wisdom.

SADDLEBAG.—A large bag or pouch of leather or canvas carried hanging from one side of a saddle. Commonly a pair of saddlebags is carried, united by a band or strap, and so hung that the weight is evenly distributed.

SADDLE BLANKET (or NUMNAH, PAD, or CORONA).—With English saddles, saddle blankets are usually not necessary when the saddle is thoroughly cleaned after each ride, when the rider uses a balanced seat, and when the mount is properly groomed. When kept clean and when properly used, however, a blanket will usually prevent a sore back. For this reason, even with

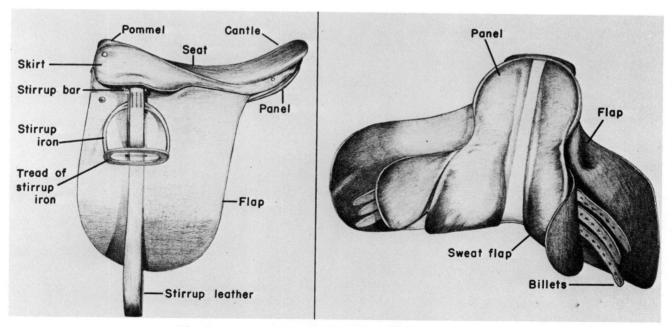

Fig. S-2. An English saddle: A, upright position; B, the underside.

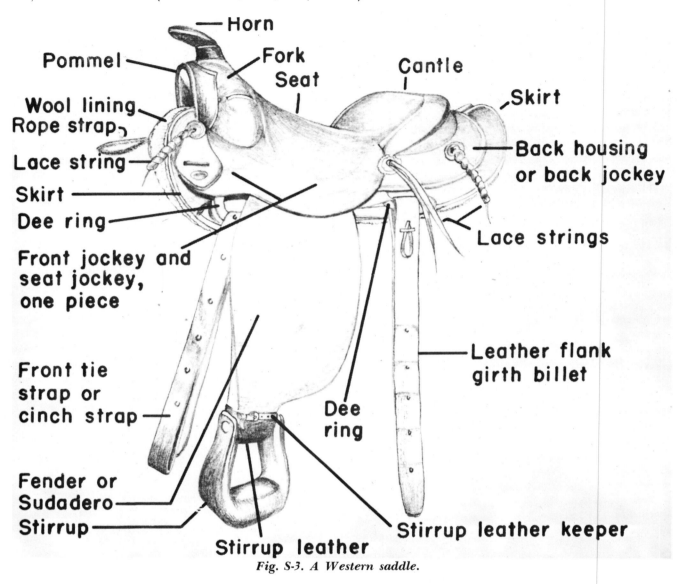

Horn

Pommel

Fork
Seat

Cantle

Skirt

Wool lining
Rope strap

Back housing
or back jockey

Lace string

Skirt

Dee ring

Lace strings

Front jockey and
seat jockey,
one piece

Front tie
strap or
cinch strap

Dee
ring

Leather flank
girth billet

Fender or
Sudadero
Stirrup

Stirrup leather keeper

Stirrup leather

Fig. S-3. A Western saddle.

English saddles, many good horsemen always insist on the use of a saddle blanket.

A saddle blanket or corona is almost always used with Western saddles.

Felt, mohair, or pad blankets that are adapted to the various types of saddles may be secured. Many good horsemen even prefer a folded Navajo blanket, with a hair pad inside. The corona is a blanket cut to the shape of the saddle and has a large colorful roll around the edge that is quite showy for use with a stock saddle.

The saddle pad or blanket should be placed well forward on the horse's neck and then slid back into position so as to smooth down the hair. It should come to rest smoothly and in such manner that two and one-half to four inches of it will show in front of the saddle. After being used, the blanket or pad should be hung up to dry. It then should be brushed thoroughly to eliminate hair and dried sweat.

SADDLEBRED.—Another term for the American Saddle Horse breed.

SADDLE BRONC RIDING *(a rodeo event)*.—The horse has a modified saddle and a halter to which is attached one rein which the cowboy must hold in one hand only. The contestant must stay on the bronc for 8 to 10 seconds, depending on the event, in order to qualify.

SADDLE CLASSES.—Horse shows offer saddle classes for every breed except the Hackney. The requirements are slightly different for each breed. Hence, anyone planning to exhibit should familiarize himself with the American Horse Shows Association *Rule Book*.

(Also see PARK HACK; PARK HORSE CLASSES; and SADDLE HORSES—THREE- AND FIVE-GAITED.)

SADDLE HORSE (SADDLER).—A horseman's term for the American Saddle Horse breed.

(Also see SADDLE HORSES; THREE- AND FIVE-GAITED; and BREED (S)—Table B-2.)

SADDLE HORSES, THREE- AND FIVE-GAITED.—Long after the development of the New England town, the opening up of roads along the eastern seaboard, and the development of the buggy and the popularity of the roadster type of horse, the states of Virginia, West Virginia, Kentucky, Tennessee, and Missouri still consisted of large plantations under the ownership of southern gentlemen. Roads were few and far between, and travel was largely on horseback over the most natural paths that could be found. Thus, there was need for a horse that would carry the plantation owners with dignity befitting their station in life and with the least distress possible to both rider and horse. As the plantation owners rode over their broad estates, easy gaits were a necessity. Such was the need, and out of this need arose the beautiful American Saddle Horse.

Animals qualifying as either three- or five-gaited saddle horses in the Saddle Horse Division as described by the American Horse Shows Association are generally of American Saddle Horse breeding, a truly American creation. Occasionally, however, animals of the other light horse breeds are trained to execute the five gaits. It must also be remembered that the vast majority of American horses of all breeds are of the three-gaited variety and that only a relatively small proportion of these animals are ever exhibited. Instead, most of the three-gaited horses are used for utility purposes and pleasure riding.

The gaits of the three-gaited horses are: the walk, the trot, and the canter. In addition to performing these same gaits, the five-gaited horse must possess a slow gait and the rack. The slow gait may be either the running-walk, foxtrot, or stepping pace (slow pace); but for show purposes only the stepping pace is accepted. In the show-ring, generally the judge requests that five-gaited horses execute the gaits in the following order: the walk, the trot, the slow gait, the rack, and the canter.

Whether an animal is three-gaited or five-gaited is primarily a matter of training. Custom decrees that three-gaited horses be shown with their manes roached or clipped short and their tails clipped or sheared for a short distance from the base; whereas five-gaited horses are shown with flowing manes and full-length tails. Also, because of the speed at which five-gaited horses are expected to perform at the trot and the rack, they are permitted to wear quarter boots to protect the heels of the front feet, a practice which is forbidden in three-gaited classes.

Fig. S-4. A weanling American Saddle Horse filly. Whether an animal of American Saddle Horse breeding is three-gaited or five-gaited is primarily a matter of training. (Courtesy, American Saddle Horse Breeders Association)

Both three- and five-gaited horses are shown under saddle; and each may be shown in combination classes, in which they must perform both in harness and under saddle. Also, five-gaited horses (but not three-gaited horses) may be shown in a third division; namely, in fine harness classes.

In combination classes, the entries enter the

ring hitched to an appropriate four-wheeled vehicle, with the saddle and bridle hidden in the back of the rig. The judge works the class both ways of the ring, then lines them up in the center for inspection and backs each horse in order to test his manners. Next the judge orders that the entries be unhitched, unharnessed, saddled, bridled, and worked under saddle both ways of the ring. Finally, the horses are again lined up in the center of the ring, and each animal is backed under saddle.

A fine harness horse is exactly what the name implies—a fine horse presented in fine harness. The entire ensemble is elegant, and represents the ultimate in grace and charm.

Fine harness horses are penalized if driven at excessive speed. Combination horses, especially five-gaited ones, should be driven at a more speedy trot than fine harness horses.

In addition to executing the gaits with perfection, both three- and five-gaited animals should possess the following characteristics:

• *Superior conformation,* in which the principal requirements are:
   • Graceful lines obtained through a fairly long, arched neck; short, strong back and loin with a good seat; a nicely turned croup; a smartly carried, flowing tail; and a relatively long underline.
   • A shapely and smart head.
   • Nicely sloping shoulders and pasterns.
   • Symmetry and blending of all parts.
   • Quality, as evidenced by a clean-cut, chiseled appearance throughout, and soundness.
   • Style, alertness, and animation, sometimes said to be comparable to that of a "peacock."

• *Perfect manners,* which include form, training, and obedience—those qualities that make for a most finished performance.

• *Superior action,* including an elastic step, high action, and evidence of spirit and dash.

SADDLER (SADDLE HORSE).—Another term for the American Saddle Horse breed.

SADDLE SEAT.—When riding a three- or five-gaited horse, at all gaits and either on the bridle path or in the show-ring, the rider assumes the show or park seat—sitting erect and well back in the saddle (leaving a space of at least a hand's breadth between the back of the jodhpurs and the cantle). The ball of the foot rests directly over the stirrup iron; knees are in; heels are lower than the toes; and the hands and reins are in such position that the horse will carry his head high and his neck arched. In this position, the body is easily erect and balanced on a base consisting of seat, thighs, knees, and stirrups; the chest is high and just forward of the true vertical; and the back is hollow, the waist relaxed, the head erect, and the shoulders square.

(Also see HORSEMANSHIP—Figs. H-24 and H-25.)

SADDLE, SIDE.—A lady's old fashioned saddle which may be seen in an occasional show-ring class. With a side saddle, the lady sits with both limbs to one side, usually toward the left or near side.

SADDLE SORE.—A sore caused by misfitting saddle or one that has been put on incorrectly. They occur most frequently at the withers and on the spine under the cantle, although sores on either side of the spine are not uncommon. Common treatment consists in bathing the sore with an antiseptic solution and applying methylene blue. The horse should be rested until the sore is completely healed.

SADDLING THE MOUNT.—Regardless of the type of saddle—English or Western—it should be placed on the horse's back so that the girth (In English saddles, it's a girth; in Western saddles, it's a cinch.) will come about four inches to the rear of the point of the horse's elbow.

When first adjusted, the girth should be loose enough to admit a finger between it and the horse's belly. After tightening the saddle, it is always a good practice to "untrack" the horse—that is, to lead him ahead several paces before mounting. This procedure serves two purposes: First, if the horse is the kind that "blows up" so that he cannot be cinched snugly, the "untracking" will usually cause him to relax; and second, if a horse has any bad habits, he will often get them out of his system before the rider mounts.

After the horse has been ridden a few minutes, the girth should always be re-examined and tightened if necessary. The saddle should always be cinched tightly enough so that it will not turn when the horse is being mounted, but not so tight as to cause discomfort to the horse.

The length of stirrups will depend upon the type of riding. It may vary from very short on running horses to quite long on stock horses. The stirrup leather on English saddles should always be turned so that the flat side of the leather comes against the leg of the rider.

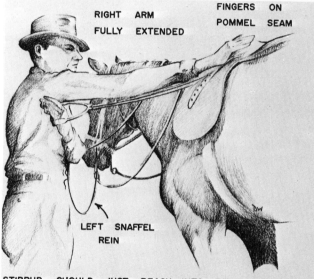

RIGHT ARM FULLY EXTENDED — FINGERS ON POMMEL SEAM

LEFT SNAFFEL REIN

STIRRUP SHOULD JUST REACH INTO RIGHT ARMPIT....... ADJUST ACCORDINGLY........ REVERSE ARM ARRANGEMENT WHEN ADJUSTING RIGHT OR OFF STIRRUP

Fig. S-5. Method of checking the stirrup straps of an English saddle for proper length.

For correct posting, in English riding, the stirrup straps or stirrup leathers must be adjusted to the right length. If stirrups are too short, posting will be high and exaggerated. For English riding, the stirrups can be adjusted to the approximate correct length before mounting by making them about one inch shorter than the length of the rider's arm with fingers extended. When the rider is sitting in the saddle, with the legs extended downward and the feet out of the stirrups, the bottom of the stirrup iron should touch just below the ankle bone. For Western riding, the length of stirrups may be considered

as about right when there is approximately a three-inch clearance between the saddle tree and the crotch of the mounted rider standing in the stirrups.

SAFETY.—No horse is a pleasure unless he is safe and handled safely. Most of the accidents that the writer has known about have been with gentle horses, and most of them have been the fault of a human, and not a horse. Here are some safety rules:

• *Work from the left.*—Always saddle or harness a horse from his left (near side), and remove tack on the same side.

• *Announce your presence.*—Do not walk up behind a horse unannounced. Speak to him so that he will know you are approaching. Remember that horses cannot see behind them, and that they instinctively kick to protect their blind spot.

• *Keep calm and collected.*—Never shout or beat a horse; it will only make matters worse.

• *Don't wrap the lead rope or reins around any part of your body.*—Horses do spook, and they are big and strong. Hence, to have a horse tied to your body is asking for trouble.

• *Walk to the left of your horse when leading him.*—Walk along the left side of your horse; never in front.

• *Don't tie a horse with the bridle reins.*—When tying a horse, use a strong halter and lead rope, and tie him high and rather close to the object (tie post). Never tie a horse with the bridle reins.

• *Don't leave a halter on a horse that is turned to pasture.*—Although a haltered horse is usually easier to catch, there is the hazard of him getting caught on some object and not being able to get free.

• *Slow down on treacherous footing.*—Slow to a walk when on pavement, ice, bridges, etc.

• *Don't mount in a low building or near fences.*—Many a head has been cracked and a leg cut by violating this rule. So, always be in the clear when mounting.

• *Check tack; make sure it is in good condition.*—Especially check your girth, cinch straps, curb chain and reins to make sure that they are in good condition.

• *Don't tease; don't let the horse nibble.*—Remember that a nibbling horse sometimes bites.

• *Keep your head in the clear when bridling.*

—A horse may throw his head to avoid the bit. Hence, keep your head in the clear, otherwise he may hit you.

SALES, ALL-TIME TOP.—Horsemen and students frequently like to refer to the great sales in history of the many breeds. A summary of the all-time top horse sales follows; with the individual sales given in Table S-1, and the consignment sales given in Table S-2. (See pp. 364–366.)

The all-time top of any individual sale was established in 1973 by Secretariat, a Thoroughbred stallion, when he sold at private treaty to a syndicate for $6,080,000.

(Also see AUCTIONS.)

SALIVA TEST.—The testing of saliva of a racehorse for the presence of drugs or narcotics (stimulant or sedative). Such doping is forbidden by law.

(Also see DOPING.)

SALT.—See MINERALS.

SALT DEFICIENCY.—Horses are most likely to develop signs of salt deficiency when worked hard in hot weather. Horses deprived of salt tire easily, stop sweating, and exhibit muscle spasms.

CAUSE.—Lack of salt (sodium chloride).

SYMPTOMS.—Loss of appetite, pica, retarded growth, loss of weight, a rough coat, lowered production of milk, and a ravenous appetite for salt.

DISTRIBUTION AND LOSSES.—Worldwide.

TREATMENT.—Salt-starved animals should be gradually accustomed to salt; slowly increase the hand-fed allowance until the animals may be safely allowed free access to it.

PREVENTION.—Provide plenty of salt at all times, preferably by free-choice feeding.

REMARKS.—Common salt is one of the most essential minerals for grass-eating animals and one of the easiest and cheapest to provide. Excess salt intake can result in toxicity.

TABLE S-1

ALL-TIME TOP INDIVIDUAL SALES[1]

Breed	Year of Sale	Identity of Animal	Sex	Price	How Sold	Seller	Purchaser
American Paint Horse	1966	Yellow Mount	Stallion	$ 10,000	Private Treaty	Jack Bruns, Muleshoe, Texas	Mr. and Mrs. S. H. Williamson, Iowa Park, Texas
	1967	Dual Image	Stallion	15,000	Private Treaty	J. R. Archer, Corpus Christi, Texas	Larry Swain, San Antonio, Texas
	1968	Baldy Raider	Stallion	15,000	Private Treaty	Jim Smoot, Gainesville, Texas	Richard Harris, Atlanta, Georgia
	1969	Diablo Cochise	Stallion	6,500	Private Treaty	Lester Bloomenstiel, Baton Rouge, La.	Ed Pike, Lakeland, Florida
	1970	Music Maker	Stallion	15,000	Private Treaty	Forrest Williamson, Arkansas City, Kansas	Kay Neal, Logan, Oklahoma
	1971	Ceasar Bar's Dinero	Stallion	10,000	Private Treaty	Joe Denman, Fort Worth, Texas	Harley Webb, Arlington, Texas
American Saddle Horse	1947	Beau Fortune	Stallion	50,000	Private Treaty	Teater and Reesler, Skokie, Chicago, Illinois	Crebilly Farm, West Chester, Pa.
	1947	The Invasion	Gelding	23,000	Auction	T. A. Walsh, Jr., Omaha, Neb.	Mrs. Jane Gordon, Malvern, Pa.
(Continued)	1958	Delightful Society	Mare	30,000	Auction	Louis Greaspoon, St. Louis, Mo.	Donald Decker, Omaha, Neb.

Breed	Year of Sale	Identity of Animal	Sex	Price	How Sold	Seller	Purchaser
	1960	Stonewall Imperial	Gelding	26,500	Auction	Candy Shaffer Stable	Julianna Schmuts, Louisville, Ky.
	1960	Skyrocket	Stallion	17,000	Auction	Candy Shaffer Stable	F. R. Sullivan, Orange, N. J.
	1962	Legal Tender	Gelding	30,000	Auction	T. N. Wood, Harvey's Lake, Pa.	Crabtree Stables, Simpsonville, Kentucky
	1965	Radiation	Mare	40,000	Auction	Tom Moore	Patent Leather Farms, Inc. of Wartrace, Tenn. & Bartow, Fla.
	1969	So Exciting	Mare	29,500	Auction	Greystone Manor Stables, Lancaster, Pennsylvania	Charles Eoff, Indianapolis, Ind.
	1970	Bellissima	Mare	50,000	Auction	Knolland Farms	Meadowbrook Farm, Ft. Wayne, Indiana
	1971	Supreme Spirit	Stallion	100,000	Private Treaty	Tom Moore	Grape Tree Farm
	1972	Supreme Melissa	Filly	21,000	Auction	Tattersalls for Julianne Schmutz, Glenview, Ky.	Grape Tree Farm
Appaloosa	1960	Hanogie	Mare	6,300	Auction	Carey Appaloosa Ranch, Denver, Colorado	Paul Johnson, Cascade, Colorado
	1961	Top Hat	Stallion	9,000	Auction	Ace Hopper, Plainview, Texas	W. F. Hicks, Ft. Worth, Texas
	1961	Tinker Bell Day	Mare	10,000	Private Treaty	Ed Hulseman, Red Bluff, Calif.	W. F. Sandercock, Dixon, Calif.
	1964	Quinta's Flying String	Colt	17,500	Auction	Quinta Dispersal, Napa, Calif.	Myrtle Brown, Arbuckle, Calif.
	1966	Chic Appeal	Stallion	15,500	Auction	Leo Marsters, Payette, Idaho	Dale Rumsey, Phoenix, Arizona
	1967	Sutter's Show Boy	Stallion	44,000	Auction	Robert Heilmann, Grass Valley, California	Partnership, Fiddlestix Farm, Grass Valley, California
	1968	Hawkeye F-3035	Stallion	17,000	Auction	A-9 Farms	Unknown
	1969	Top Scat	Stallion	11,000	Auction	Mr. Rutherford	B. Backenburg
	1970	Heza Prince	Stallion	8,000	Auction	Tom Davenport	Wayne & Lois Wyant
	1971	Rocketeer	Stallion	40,000	Auction	Darrell Dalton	Tom Connelly, Huntsville, Texas
Arabian	1961	Indriffnant	Mare	7,900	Auction	Al-Marah Arabian Horse Farm, Washington, D. C.	A. M. Work, Portland, Ore.
	1969	Naborr 25472	Stallion	150,000	Auction	Anne McCormick, Scottsdale, Arizona	Tom Chauncey and Wayne Newton, Phoenix and Prescott, Ariz.
	1969	Pallada	Mare	25,000	Auction	McCormick Arabians, Scottsdale, Arizona	Mrs. Marianne Hannah, Mountain Center, California
	1971	Silhouette	Mare	56,000	Auction	Lasma Arabians, Scottsdale, Arizona	Dr. Howard Kale, Belleview, Washington

(Continued)

TABLE s-1 (CONTINUED)

Breed	Year of Sale	Identity of Animal	Sex	Price	How Sold	Seller	Purchaser
	1971	The Judge	Stallion	30,000	Auction	Lasma Arabians, Scottsdale, Arizona	Dr. James Cary, Houston, Texas
Belgian	1917	Farceur	Stallion	47,500	Auction	Wm. Crownover, Hudson, Iowa	C. G. Good, Ogden, Iowa
Clydesdale	1911	Baron of Buchlyvie 11263	Stallion	47,500	Auction	J. Kilpatrick, Craigie Mains, Ayr., Scotland	Wm. Dunlop, Dunure Mains, Ayr, Scotland
Palomino	1966	Shoshoni Bar	Stallion	2,100	Auction	Bent Arrow Ranch, Broken Arrow, Oklahoma	Richard G. Williams LaCross, Wisconsin
	1967	Mr. Kickapoo Bars	Stallion	3,350	Auction	Bent Arrow Ranch, Broken Arrow, Oklahoma	Paul Dick, Mt. Hope, Kansas
	1968	Golden Shoofly	Mare	2,850	Auction	Bent Arrow Ranch, Broken Arrow, Oklahoma	Hancock Ranch, Tupelo, Miss.
	1969	Instant Blonde	Mare	5,100	Auction	Bent Arrow Ranch, Broken Arrow, Oklahoma	Senator Peltier, Louisiana
	1970	Bo-Beep Bos'n Bar Towell	Mare Mare	2,500 2,500	Auction Auction	Bent Arrow Ranch, Broken Arrow, Oklahoma	C. D. Fitzwilliam, Texas
	1971	Palomino Dream	Stallion	12,250		King Ranch Quarter Horse Sale	
Pony of the Americas	1960	Hand's Ta-Ma-Naus T-828	Weanling Colt	2,500	Auction	Boomhower & Barrett	Robert Gatner
	1967	GR's Big Creek's Dandy T-5524	Yearling Filly	2,100	Auction	Ed Merfeld	Milford & Mary Lammers
	1967	Tomahawk's Big Creek 2547	Stallion	2,755	Auction	Ed Merfeld	John Ludtke
	1970	S.D.'s Flashy Maiden T-7452	Mare	2,500	Auction	Golden Rod Pony Farm	Seven Brook Pony Farm
	1970	Apache Scout	Gelding	2,000	Auction	Scott Stoltzfus	Andrea Lockner
	1971	Hi Vue's Sister	Weanling Filly	2,075	Auction	Howard Victor	Ray & Phyllis Franken
Quarter Horse	1949	Geronimo	Stallion,	20,000	Auction	J. R. Bell, Canoga Park, Calif.	A. R. Levis, Henderson, Colorado
	1952	N. R. Paul A P-19	Stallion	30,000	Private Treaty	R. Q. Sutherland, Kansas City, Missouri	Gordon Wheeler, Riverside, California
	1954	Miss Panama	Mare	8,000	Auction	Grace Ranch	Art Pollard
	1957	Poco Tom	Stallion	10,200	Auction	Volney Hildreth, Fort Worth, Texas	Waldo Haythorne, Ogallala, Nebraska
	1957	Kip Mac	Gelding	5,500	Auction	Volney Hildreth, Fort Worth, Texas	George Glascock, Cresson, Texas
(Continued)	1957	Paulyanna	Mare	10,400	Auction	R. Q. Sutherland, Overland Park, Kansas	J. J. Davidson, Albuquerque, New Mexico

TABLE s-1 (CONTINUED)

Breed	Year of Sale	Identity of Animal	Sex	Price	How Sold	Seller	Purchaser
	1958	Skipity Scoot	Stallion	12,100	Auction	T. E. Connolly, San Francisco; F. Azevedo, Colsa, California	J. P. Davidson, Albuquerque, New Mexico
	1958	Pailalika	Mare	10,200	Auction	Pinehurst Stables, Houston, Tex.	Charles Coates, Chappel Hill, Texas
	1959	King Glo	Stallion	50,000	Auction	J. O. Hankins, Rocksprings, Tex.	C. E. Boyd, Sweetwater, Texas
	1960	Go Man Go	Stallion	125,000	Private Treaty	J. B. Ferguson, Wharton, Texas	F. Vessels, Los Alamitos, Calif., and W. H. Peckham, Richmond, Texas
	1960	Cee Bars Jr.	Colt	12,000	Auction	John Askow, Fayette, Arkansas	Ross Inman, Lamar, Colorado
	1960	Josie's Bar	Mare	37,200	Auction	E. L. Gosselin, Edmond, Okla.	Frank Vessels, Los Alamitos, California
	1961	Vandy II	Stallion	40,000	Auction	Paul Lomax, Skiatook, Okla.	Hadan Livestock Co., Camarillo, California
	1961	Three Deep	Mare	20,000	Auction	Sam Steiger, Prescott, Arizona	Jay Scott, Littleton, Colorado
	1962	Robin Reed	Stallion	120,000	Private Treaty	Roy D. Barnes, Denver, Colorado	Chapparal Racing Stables, Wildorado, Texas
	1963	Bar Depth	Stallion	100,000	Private Treaty	Lester Goodson, Houston, Texas	Truman Johnson, Riverside, California
	1963	Moolah Bar	Mare	45,000	Auction	Mawson Estate, Lompoc, Calif.	Red Bee Ranch, Wichita, Kansas
	1964	Leo Bar	Stallion	60,000	Auction	Lou Kosloff's Flying K Ranch	Don Brokaw, Apple Valley, Calif.
	1964	Scoop Bam	Mare	50,000	Auction	Gill Cattle Co., Tucson, Arizona	Red Bee Ranch, Wichita, Kansas
	1965	May Moon	Mare	46,000	Auction	Belsby Ranch, Fresno, Calif.	Edd Richards, Dinuba, Calif.
	1966	Rocket Bar	Stallion	400,000	Private Treaty	George Kaufman, Modesto, Calif.	W. H. Peckham, Richmond, & S. F. Henderson, Odessa, Texas
	1967	Go Josie Go	Mare	66,000	Auction	A. O. Phillips, Plano, Texas	Burnett Estates, Fort Worth & Clarence Scharbauer Jr., Midland, Texas
	1968	Miss Gold Angel	Mare	87,000	Auction	Oakdale, California	Ray Marler, Ontario, Oregon
	1969	Nother Brother	Stallion	142,500	Private Treaty	Spencer Childers, Fresno, Calif.	Professional Group, Ogden, Utah
	1971	Go Galla Go	Mare	127,500	Auction	C. W. Cascio, Tom Neff, Sunland Park, New Mexico	J. R. Adams, Guymon, Okla.
	1971	Speed Scene	Yearling Colt	100,000	Auction	Tom Neff, Ruidoso, New Mexico	Lorna Call, Salt Lake City, Utah
Shetland Pony (Continued)	1950	Hillswicks Oracle	Stallion	4,300	Auction	Mrs. Volney Diltz, Des Moines, Iowa	W. P. Atkinson, Oklahoma City, Oklahoma

TABLE s-1 (CONTINUED)

Breed	Year of Sale	Identity of Animal	Sex	Price	How Sold	Seller	Purchaser
	1950	Dunrovin Larigo Flame	Mare	1,750	Auction	Gene Lowrey, Nebraska City, Nebraska	C. R. Donley, Anadarko, Okla.
	1953	Little Masterpiece	Stallion	7,500	Auction	V. Diltz, Des Moines, Iowa and P. Carlile, Parny, Okla.	Sam Taylor, Genmantown, Tenn.
	1953	C—Jo's Toppy	Mare	6,000	Auction	Cliff and Jo Teague, Sherman, Texas	I. B. Greene, Ridgeway, Illinois
	1954	Dora's Candy Lue	Mare	10,000	Auction	Verne Brewer, Gainesville, Tex., and R. D. Peterson, Templeton, Texas	L. W. Smith, Tulia, Texas
	1954	Little Masterpiece	Stallion	25,000			Don Vestal, Parker, Colorado
	1957	C—Jo's Topper	Stallion	56,000	Auction	C—Jo Pony Farm, Sherman, Tex.	Syndicate of five: Boseman, Loewus, Frey, Casemore, and Blair, from Louisiana
	1957	Dainty Doll	Mare	12,500	Auction	Mrs. E. A. Barnes, Lafayette, Ind.	Clark McKelvex, Euless, Texas
	1958	Supreme's Bit of Gold	Stallion	85,000	Auction	T. P. Parker, Valley View, Texas	Happy Valley Pony Farm, Bloomfield, Iowa
	1958	Valley Springs Golden Fleece	Mare	33,000	Auction	Ike Bozeman, Zachary, Louisiana	Paul Loewer, Branch, Louisiana
	1960	Captain Topper	Stallion	56,500	Auction	Vern Brewer, Gainesville, Texas	Miss Patricia Burton, Dryden, Michigan
	1961	Atkinson's Hillswicke Bonny Cindy	Mare	14,500	Auction	Vern Brewer, Gainesville, Texas	C. C. Bales
	1962	Happy Valley's Red Christopher	Stallion	6,500	Auction	Happy Valley Pony Farm	J. W. McClelland
	1963	Pierre Cody's Black Crystal	Mare	3,000	Auction	H. P. Kilkelly	Joe Finn
	1964	Ponyland's Globetrotter	Stallion	2,800	Auction	Wm. Seekamp	L. B. Andersen
	1965	Larigo's Dark Magic	Stallion	5,000	Auction	Heyl Pony Farm	Paul Kitck
	1966	Holiday Edition	Mare	2,000	Auction	Burnidge Bros.	C. Elwood Thompson
	1967	Defender's Rambler	Stallion	4,000	Auction	John Hughes	Pat Butts
	1968	Tamerlane's Golden Rose	Mare	5,000	Auction	Burnidge Bros.	Tom Wells
	1969	Sunny Acres Billy Jack	Stallion	5,000	Auction	Elmer Williams	Roy Strawhacker
	1970	Wait & See's Delight	Mare	725	Auction	Ben Edwards	George Hart

(Continued)

TABLE s-1 (CONTINUED)

Breed	Year of Sale	Identity of Animal	Sex	Price	How Sold	Seller	Purchaser
	1971	Paladin's Lamplighter	Gelding	685	Auction	Jim Spurrier	W. W. Wetenkamp
	1973	Little Man	Stallion	4,750	Auction	J. R. Matthews, Great Mills, Maryland	Mr. & Mrs. Delmer Moody Belton, Missouri
Standardbred	1889	Axtell	Stallion	105,000	Private Treaty	C. W. Williams Independence, Iowa	W. P. Ijame, Terre Haute, Ind., J. W. Conley, Chicago, Ill., and Fred Morgan, Detroit, Mich.
	1890	Director	Stallion	75,000	Private Treaty	Monroe Salisbury, Pleasanton, California	A. H. Moore, Philadelphia, Pa.
	1891	Arion	Stallion	125,000	Private Treaty	Leland Stanford, Palo Alto, Calif.	J. M. Forbes, Milton, Mass.
	1896	Anteeo	Stallion	60,000	Private Treaty	S. A. Brown, Kalamazoo, Mich.	H. S. Henry, Morrisville, Pa.
	1903	Dan Patch	Stallion	60,000	Private Treaty	M. E. Sturgis, New York, N. Y.	M. W. Savage, Minneapolis, Minnesota
	1947	Algiers	Stallion	70,000	Auction	E. J. Baker, St. Charles, Illinois	C. F. Gaines, and Mrs. H. W. Nichols, Lexington, Kentucky
	1949	Nibble Hanover	Stallion	100,000	Private Treaty	D. W. Bostwick, Shelburne, Vt.	Hanover Shoe Farms, Hanover, Pennsylvania
	1951	Tar Heel	Stallion	125,000	Auction	W. N. Reynolds, Est., Winston, Salem, N. C.	Hanover Shoe Farms, Hanover, Pennsylvania
	1955	Adios	Stallion	500,000	Private Treaty		Hanover Shoe Farms, Hanover, Pennsylvania
	1956	Good Time	Stallion	116,000	Private Treaty		Castleton Farm, Lexington, Ky.
	1957	Demon Hanover	Stallion	500,000	Private Treaty	R. Critchfield, Wooster, Ohio	(Syndicate) to be located at Walnut Hall Farm, Conerail, Ky.
	1957	Queen of Diamonds	Mare	30,000	Auction	Wallace McKenzie, Diamond, Ohio	H. Beever, St. Joseph, Missouri
	1958	Adios	Stallion	500,000	Private Treaty	Hanover Shoe Farms, Hanover, Pennsylvania	Syndicate
	1958	Dancer Hanover	Colt	105,000	Private Treaty	Hanover Shoe Farms, Hanover, Pennsylvania	Syndicate headed by S. Dancer, New Egypt, N. J.
	1959	Dancer Hanover	Colt	200,000	Private Treaty	Syndicate	Hanover Shoe Farms, Hanover, Pennsylvania
	1960	Adios Butler	Stallion	600,000	Private Treaty	Paige West, Snow Hill, Md.; A. Pellio, Scarsdale, N. Y.	Syndicated owners retained 20 shares
	1960	Mon Mite	Yearling Colt	81,000	Auction	Walnut Hall Farm, Conerail, Kentucky	K. D. Owen, R. D. Ricketts, R. Thomas, Houston, Texas

(Continued)

TABLE s-1 (CONTINUED)

Breed	Year of Sale	Identity of Animal	Sex	Price	How Sold	Seller	Purchaser
	1961	Jamin	Stallion	800,000	Private Treaty	Mme. Leon Lory-Roederer, France	Syndicate headed by Stanley Tananbaum, Yonkers Raceway
	1962	Painter	Stallion	130,000	Auction	Hunter Hill Farm, Cambridge City, Indiana	Two Gaits Farm, Castleton Farm, Marson, Indianapolis, Ind.
	1963	Safe Mission	Stallion	52,000	Auction	Almahurst Farm, Lexington, Ky.	Gilberto Melzi, Milan, Italy
	1964	Sprite Rodney	Mare	92,000	Auction	Eaton Ridge Farm, Lexington, Kentucky	Hanover Shoe Farms, Hanover, Pennsylvania
	1964	Effrat Hanover	Yearling Colt	65,000	Auction	Hanover Shoe Farms, Hanover, Pennsylvania	Comanche Stable
	1964	Speed	Yearling Colt	65,000	Auction	Walnut Hall Stud Farm, Lexington, Kentucky	Castleton Farm, Lexington, Ky.
	1965	Speedy Streak	Yearling Colt	113,000	Auction	Castleton Farm, Lexington, Ky.	Gainesway Farm, Lexington, Ky.
	1966	Bret Hanover	Stallion	2,000,000	Private Treaty	Richard Downing, Shaker Heights, Ohio	Castleton Farm, Lexington, Ky.
	1966	Brad Hanover	Yearling Colt	100,000	Auction	Hanover Shoe Farms, Hanover, Pennsylvania	Lehigh Stables, New Egypt, N. J.
	1967	Bart Hanover	Yearling Colt	105,000	Auction	Hanover Shoe Farms, Hanover, Pennsylvania	Rose Hild Farm and Egyptian Acres Stable
	1968	Nevele Bigshot	Yearling Colt	115,000	Auction	Hanover Shoe Farms, Hanover, Pennsylvania	Nevele Acres
	1969	Dexter Hanover	Yearling Colt	125,000	Auction	Hanover Shoe Farms, Hanover, Pennsylvania	T. A., A. W. & Mildred Dexter; A. Schmidt; Apache Stable
	1970	Miracle Tip	Yearling Colt	117,000	Auction	Castleton Farm, Lexington, Ky.	Messenger Stables and Cliff Baker Ranch
	1971	Good Humor Man	Yearling Colt	210,000	Auction	Stoner Creek Stud	Vernon Goshneaur
Tennessee Walking Horse	1964	Perfection's Carbon Copy	Stallion	125,000	Private Treaty	Rodgers, Binns, Raney & Welle	George L. Lenox
	1966	Triple Threat	Stallion	130,000	Private Treaty	Kreskie & Wright	Gotlob Koenig
	1968	Ace's Sensation	Stallion	100,000	Private Treaty	Beech & Hale	R. Randall Rollins
	1970	Ebony's Black Market	Stallion	100,001	Private Treaty	Beech & Hale	Dr. Harold McIver
Thoroughbred	1912	Rock Sand	Stallion	150,000	Private Treaty	August Belmont II	Syndicate
	1915	Tracery	Stallion	265,000	Private Treaty	August Belmont II	Senor Ungue, Argentina

(Continued)

TABLE s-1 (CONTINUED)

Breed	Year of Sale	Identity of Animal	Sex	Price	How Sold	Seller	Purchaser
	1922	Whiskaway	Stallion	125,000	Private Treaty	H. P. Whitney	Charles W. Clarke
	1925	Friar Rock	Stallion	130,000	Private Treaty	J. E. Madden	W. R. Coe
	1927	Hustle On	Colt	70,000	Auction	Himyar Stud	W. R. Coe
	1928	New Broom	Colt	75,000	Auction	Mr. T. J. Regan	Eastland Farm Syndicate
	1943	Pericles	Colt	66,000	Auction	A. B. Hancock	William Helis
	1945	Stardust	Stallion	448,000	Private Treaty	H. R. H. Aga Kahn	Syndicate of English Breeders
	1945	Sayajirao	Colt	117,000	Auction	Sir Eric Ohlson	Maharajah of Baroda
	1946	Bois Roussel	Stallion	320,000	Private Treaty	Peter Beatty	Prince Aly Kahn & Syndicate
	1947	Stepfather	3-yr. Colt	200,000	Auction	Louis B. Mayer	Harry M. Warner
	1947	Honeymoon	Mare in training	135,000	Auction	Louis B. Mayer	Harry M. Warner
	1947	Busher	Mare in training	135,000	Auction	Louis B. Mayer	Harry M. Warner
	1948	The Phoenix	Stallion	640,000	Private Treaty	Frederick Meyer (Ireland)	Syndicate of English Breeders
	1948	Algasir	Gelding in training	106,000	Auction	Est. A. C. Ernst	Mrs. F. Ambrose Clark
	1948	Busher	Mare	150,000	Private Treaty	Louis B. Mayer	Mrs. E. N. Graham
	1949	Nasrullah	Stallion	372,000	Private Treaty	Joseph McGrath	Syndicate
	1951	Say Blue	Mare	72,000	Auction	Coldstream Stud	Henry H. Knight
	1953	Tulyar	Stallion	700,000	Private Treaty	H. R. H. Aga Kahn	Irish National Stud
	1953	Lithe	Mare	85,000	Auction	Hal Price Headley	J. S. Phipps
	1954	Polynesian	Stallion	560,000	Private Treaty	Mrs. P. A. B. Widener, II	Ira Dryman & Syndicate
	1954	Nalur (Nasrullah-Lurline B)	Colt	86,000	Private Treaty	Clifford Mooers	F. S. Adams & Syndicate
	1954	Festoon	Mare	105,840	Auction (Newmarket)	Est. Lord Dewar	A. B. Askew
	1955	Nashua	Stallion	1,251,200	Sealed Bid	Est. Wm. Woodward, Jr.	Leslie B. Combs II & Syndicate
	1955	Tulsan (Nasrullah-In Bloom)	Colt	80,000	Auction	Dr. Zolie Asbury	Forrest H. Lindsay
	1955	No Strings	Mare	60,500	Auction	Henry H. Knight	Mrs. Parker B. Poe

(Continued)

Breed	Year of Sale	Identity of Animal	Sex	Price	How Sold	Seller	Purchaser
	1956	Swaps (½ int. retained by Ellsworth, then sold in 1957 to Galbreaths)	Stallion	2,000,000	Private Treaty	Rex Ellsworth	Mr. & Mrs. John W. Galbreath
	1956	Rise 'N Shine (Hyperion-Deodora)	Colt	87,000	Auction	Taylor Hardin	Mrs. M. E. Lunan
	1956	Segula	Mare	126,000	Auction	Woolwine Syndicate	Stavros Niarchos
	1956	Sometime Thing (Idun-Royal Charger)	Filly in training	100,000	Auction	A. S. Vanderbilt	Whitney Stone
	1957	Round Table	Stallion	175,000	Private Treaty	A. B. Hancock, Jr.	Travis Kerr
	1957	Law and Order (Nasrullah-In Bloom)	Colt	65,000	Auction	Dr. Eslie Asbury	King Ranch
	1958	Turn-To	Stallion	1,400,000	Private Treaty	Harry F. Guggenheim	Syndicate
	1958	Gallant Man	Stallion	1,333,333	Private Treaty	Ralph Lowe	Syndicate
	1958	Top Charger (Royal Charger-Popularity)	Colt	65,000	Auction	Spendthrift Farm	Leslie Combs and Mrs. John M. Olin
	1959	Ribot	Stallion	1,350,000	Private Treaty (5-yr. lease)	Razza Dormello-Olgiata	John W. Galbreath
	1959	Royal Dragoon (Royal Charger Grecian Queen)	Colt	80,000	Auction	Leslie Combs II	C. G. Raible
	1959	Globemaster (Heliopolis-No Strings)	Colt	80,000	Auction	James L. Wiley	Penowa Farms
	1959	Highland Fling (Nashua-Bella Figura)	Mare / Filly	80,000 / 59,000	Auction / Auction	Philip Godfrey / Leslie Combs II	Keswick Stable / W. Haggin Perry
	1960	Tom Fool	Stallion	1,750,000	Private Treaty	Greentree Stud	Syndicate
	1960	Bally Ache	Stallion	1,250,000	Private Treaty	Leonard Fruchtmon	Syndicate
	1960	Pashmina (Nashua-Beau Jet)	Colt	75,000	Auction	Leslie Combs II	John M. Olin
	1960	Royal Native	Filly in training	250,000	Private Treaty	P. L. Grissom	Wm. B. McDonald

(Continued)

TABLE s-1 (CONTINUED)

Breed	Year of Sale	Identity of Animal	Sex	Price	How Sold	Seller	Purchaser
	1960	(Royal Charger-Thataway)	Filly	60,000	Auction	Leslie Combs II	Mrs. John M. Olin
	1961	Hasty Road	Stallion	1,330,000	Private Treaty	Hasty House Farm	Syndicate
	1961	Hail to Reason	Stallion	1,085,000	Private Treaty	H. Jacobs	Syndicate
	1961	Swapson (Swaps-Obedient)	Colt	130,000	Auction	Leslie Combs II	John M. Olin
	1961	Honey's Gem	Mare	137,000	Auction	E. Janss Jr. & Dr. J. K. Robbins	Frank C. Bishop Syndicate
	1961	Firey Angel (Nashua-Beau Jet)	Filly	70,000	Auction	Leslie Combs II	Maine Chance Farm
	1962	Shirley Jones	Mare in training	105,000	Auction	Brae Burn Farms	Mrs. J. O. Burgwin
	1962	Sunset Glow	Mare	60,000	Auction	Est. Ira Drymon	Caper Hill Farm
	1962	Polylady	Filly in training	120,000	Auction	Est. W. Alton Jones	Mrs. John W. Galbreath
	1962	(Swaps-Auld Alliance)	Filly	83,000	Auction	Keswick Stables	Robeby Stable
	1963	(Swaps-Blue Star II)	Colt	85,000	Auction	Stonereath Farm	Penowa Farm
	1963	Flanders Field	Mare	66,000	Auction	Robert Courtney, Agent	Desi Arnaz
	1963	(Nashua-Grecian Queen)	Filly	55,000	Auction	Spendthrift Farm	C. W. Engelhard
	1964	Gun Bow	Stallion	1,000,000	Private Treaty	Gedney Farms	Syndicate
	1964	One Bold Bid (Bold Ruler-Forget Me Not)	Colt	170,000	Auction	Warner L. Jones Jr.	Mrs. Harry W. Morrison
	1964	La Dauphine	Mare	177,000	Auction	Leslie Combs II and John W. Hanes	Charles H. Wacker III
	1964	Treasure Chest	Filly in training	70,000	Auction	Ocala Stud Farm	Dave Shaer
	1965	Tom Rolfe	Stallion	1,600,000	Private Treaty	Raymond Guest	A. B. Hancock Jr. Syndicate
	1965	Package of Prove It, Olden Times, Candy Spots	Stallions	3,750,000	Private Treaty	Rex Ellsworth	Syndicate
	1965	Hail to All	Stallion	1,500,000	Private Treaty	Ben Cohen	Syndicate
	1965	Fleet Nasrullah	Stallion	1,050,000	Private Treaty	E. B. Johnson	Syndicate

(Continued)

TABLE s-1 (CONTINUED)

Breed	Year of Sale	Identity of Animal	Sex	Price	How Sold	Seller	Purchaser
	1965	Father's Image	Stallion	1,000,000	Private Treaty	J. M. Olin	Syndicate
	1965	Devil's Tattoo	Colt in training	71,000	Auction	Edith Marienhoff & Judge Louie Bandel	Catherine Tyne Potter
	1966	Graustark	Stallion	2,400,000	Private Treaty	John W. Galbreath	Syndicate
	1966	Kauai King	Stallion	2,160,000	Private Treaty	M. Ford	Syndicate
	1966	Restless Wind	Stallion	1,280,000	Private Treaty	Llangollen Farm	Syndicate
	1966	Royal Gunner	Stallion	1,260,000	Private Treaty	M. Ford	Syndicate
	1966	Creme Dela Creme	Stallion	1,200,000	Private Treaty	Bwamalson Farm	Syndicate
	1966	(Bold Ruler-La Dauphine)	Colt	200,000	Auction	Leslie Combs II	Frank McMahon
	1966	Berlo	Mare	235,000	Auction	Est. Wm. duPont	John E. duPont
	1966	Admiring	Filly in training	310,000	Auction	Bieber-Jacobs Stable	C. W. Engelhard & Robeby Stable
	1966	(Sailor-Levee)	Filly	177,000	Auction	Morven Stud	C. W. Engelhard
	1967	Buck Passer	Stallion	4,800,000	Private Treaty	Ogden Phipps	Syndicate
	1967	Raise a Native	Stallion	2,625,000	Private Treaty	Harbor View Farm	Syndicate
	1967	(Raise a Native-Gay Hostess)	Colt	250,000	Auction	Leslie Combs II	Frank McMahon
	1967	Quill	Mare	365,000	Auction	John A. Bell, et al.	A. B. Hancock Jr. Agent
	1967	(Bold Ruler-Blue Norther)	Filly	190,000	Auction	Mrs. Wm. R. Hawn	John E. duPont
	1968	Reine Enchanteur	Filly	405,000	Auction	Mrs. Julian G. Rogers	W. P. Rosso
	1968	Successor	Stallion	1,050,000	Private Treaty	Wheatley Stable	Flag Is Up Farm
	1969	Too Bald	Mare	225,000	Auction		Charles Engelhard
	1969	Ribot's Fan	Filly	175,000	Auction	Cain Hoy Stable	Robert J. Kleberg, Jr., King Ranch
	1969	Terlago	Colt	220,000	Auction	Mrs. Wallace Gilroy	Moon Bloodstock Agency
	1970	Gerating	Mare	125,000	Auction	Lee Eaton	Heerman Bloodstock Agency
	1970	Hip #127	Stallion	510,000	Auction	Spendthrift Farm	Frank McMahon, Vancouver, B. C.
	1970	Affectionately	Filly	256,000	Auction	Hirsch Jacobs	John W. Jacobs
	1971	Nijinsky	Stallion	5,440,000	Private Treaty	Windfield Farm	Syndicate

(Continued)

TABLE s-1 (CONTINUED)

Breed	Year of Sale	Identity of Animal	Sex	Price	How Sold	Seller	Purchaser
	1971	Section	Mare	160,000	Auction	Edward B. Benjamin	J. Elliot Burch, agent
	1971	Parida	Mare	160,000	Auction	Bieber-Jacobs Stable	Mrs. Marcia Grumberg, agent
	1972	What a Treat	Mare	450,000	Auction	George D. Widener	
	1972	Casque Grise	Colt	235,000	Auction	Fasig-Tipton, Co.	Mrs. Marion du Pont Scott
	1973	Secretariat	Colt	6,080,000	Private Treaty	Meadow Stable	Syndicate
	1973	Riva Ridge	Colt	5,120,000	Private Treaty	Meadow Stable	Syndicate

1 Several of the breed registry associations, and others, provided information that is reported in this table. To each of those who contributed, the author is most grateful.

Breed	Year of Sale	Number of Animals	Average Price	Seller
American Paint	1962	10	$ 525	Texas Paint Horse Auction
	1963	23	550	Texas Paint Horse Auction
	1964	40	625	Broken Arrow Horse Farm
	1965	45	675	Broken Arrow Horse Farm
	1966	50	650	Broken Arrow Horse Farm
	1967	16	687	California Paint Horse Club
	1968	42	670	Broken Arrow Horse Farm
	1969	20	914	California Autumn Haze Sale
	1970	37	650	Michigan Paint Horse Club
	1971	19	1,066	Kansas Paint Horse Club
Appaloosa	1967	19	2,071	G. Newman and W. Pruitt
	1968	54	1,211	Texas Appaloosa Horse Club
	1969	45	906	North-Eastern Appaloosa Sale
	1970	58	1,150	North-Eastern Appaloosa Sale
	1971	43	2,678	Jedd Van Kampen (Top O'the World Sale)
Arabian	1961	36	3,332	Al-Marah Arabian Horse Farm, 700 River Road, Washington, D.C.
	1969	48	8,203	McCormick's Arabians, Scottsdale, Arizona
	1971	27	22,775	Lasma Arabians, Scottsdale, Arizona
Palomino	1966	9 (colts) 24	1,450 1,000	Bent Arrow Ranch, Broken Arrow, Okla.
	1967	40	1,100	Bent Arrow Ranch, Broken Arrow, Okla.
	1968	40	1,015	Bent Arrow Ranch, Broken Arrow, Okla.
	1969	72	1,031	Bent Arrow Ranch, Broken Arrow, Okla.
	1970	77	874	Bent Arrow Ranch, Broken Arrow, Okla.
	1971	68	1,064	Bent Arrow Ranch, Broken Arrow, Okla.
Paso Fino	1971	30	1,780	Hacienda de Cupido
Pony of the Americas	1971	150	468	Breed Promotion Sale
Quarter Horse	1948	34	1,208	Circle JR-Bellwood Ranch, Corona, Calif.
	1951	10	1,477	Grace Ranch, Tucson, Arizona
	1952	36	1,255	Jinkens Bros., Fort Worth, Texas
	1954	53	1,635	Three D Stock Farm, Arlington, Texas
	1955	25	1,358	King Ranch, Kingsville, Texas
	1956	26	1,598	R. L. Underwood, Wichita Falls, Texas
	1957	44	3,401	R. Q. Sutherland, Overland Park, Kansas
	1958	29	3,403	Pinehurst Stables, Houston, Texas
	1959	51	5,806	J. L. Taylor, Chino, California

(Continued)

Breed	Year of Sale	Number of Animals	Average Price	Seller
	1960	66	7,042	E. L. Gosselin (and guests), Edmond, Okla.
	1961	25	4,104	King Ranch, Kingsville, Texas
	1968	130	4,167	Ruidosa Downs, New Mexico
	1971	51	10,722	Ruidosa Downs, New Mexico
	1972	22	3,179	King Ranch, Kingsville, Texas
Shetland Pony	1953	139	889	Southwestern Shetland Breed, Promotion Sale
	1956	133	1,611	National Breed Promotion Sale
	1957	22	7,935	C. C. Teague Consignment to Perry Carlile Sale, Perry, Oklahoma
	1958	120	4,935	Lowery Dispersal Sale at Perry Carlile Sale, Perry, Oklahoma
	1960	59	4,345	Vern Brewer Production Sale, Gainesville, Texas
	1961	141	537	National Breed Promotion Sale
	1962	80	300	National Breed Promotion Sale
	1963	117	200	National Breed Promotion Sale
	1964	51	275	National Breed Promotion Sale
	1965	81	227	National Breed Promotion Sale
	1966	97	251	National Breed Promotion Sale
	1967	71	165	National Breed Promotion Sale
	1968	57	186	National Breed Promotion Sale
	1969	58	168	National Breed Promotion Sale
	1970	41	187	National Breed Promotion Sale
	1971	29	180	National Breed Promotion Sale
Standardbred	1952	36 (all ages)	14,850	W. N. Reynolds, Disposal, Harrisburg, Pa.
	1952	15 (yearlings)	6,533	Harrisburg, Pennsylvania
	1956	847	2,376	Harrisburg, Pennsylvania
	1958	867 (yearlings)	2,901	Harrisburg, Pennsylvania
	1959	922	3,498	Standardbred Horse Sales Company
	1960	44	10,750	Walnut Hall Stud Farm, Lexington, Ky.
	1961	125	9,013	Hanover Shoe Farms, Hanover, Pa.
	1962	32	11,925	Walnut Hall Stud Farm, Lexington, Ky.
	1963	20	13,385	Walnut Hall Stud Farm, Lexington, Ky.
	1964	28	12,393	Walnut Hall Stud Farm, Lexington, Ky.
	1965	159	10,672	Hanover Shoe Farms, Hanover, Pa.
	1966	77	11,170	Castleton Farm, Lexington, Kentucky
	1967	188	12,137	Hanover Shoe Farms, Hanover, Pa.
	1968	177	18,204	Hanover Shoe Farms, Hanover, Pa.

(Continued)

Breed	Year of Sale	Number of Animals		Average Price	Seller
	1969	165		15,228	Hanover Shoe Farms, Hanover, Pa.
	1970	89		15,067	Castleton Farm, Lexington, Kentucky
	1971	32		17,922	Stoner Creek Stud Farm
Thoroughbred	1946	415	(yearlings)	9,912	Keeneland Summer Sales
	1947	60	(race horses)	25,830	Louis B. Mayer (Dispersal)
		436	(yearlings)	6,827	Keeneland Summer Sales
	1949	9	(broodmares)	44,222	Est. Crispin Oglebay
	1950	42	(2-yr.-olds)	14,410	Louis B. Mayer
	1951	48	(broodmares)	20,635	Coldstream Stud
	1952	47	(yearlings)	14,526	Almahurst Farm (Henry H. Knight)
	1953	302	(yearlings)	9,746	Keeneland Summer Sales
	1954	344	(yearlings)	9,940	Keeneland Summer Sales
		20	(broodmares)	26,955	Keeneland Summer Sales
	1955	68	(broodmares)	15,232	Henry H. Knight
		346	(yearlings)	11,174	Keeneland Summer Sales
		55	(weanlings)	6,609	Henry H. Knight
	1956	219	(yearlings)	10,133	Saratoga Yearling Sales
	1957	235	(yearlings)	11,789	Keeneland Summer Sales
	1958	357	(yearlings)	9,615	Keeneland Summer Sales
	1959	303	(yearlings)	11,664	Keeneland Summer Sales
	1960	303	(yearlings)	11,844	Keeneland Summer Sales
	1961	298	(yearlings)	14,177	Keeneland Summer Sales
	1962	273	(yearlings)	12,993	Keeneland Summer Sales
	1963	275	(yearlings)	14,191	Keeneland Summer Sales
	1964	212	(yearlings)	17,763	Saratoga Yearling Sales
	1965	25	(broodmares)	40,615	J. W. Hanes & Leslie Combs II
		282	(yearlings)	17,973	Keeneland Summer Sales
	1966	257	(yearlings)	19,535	Saratoga Yearling Sales
		72	(mixed)	39,842	Foxcatcher Gaines
	1967	255	(yearlings)	22,145	Saratoga Yearling Sales
	1968	248	(yearlings)	30,671	Keeneland Summer Sales, Lexington, Ky.
	1969	299	(yearlings)	25,699	Keeneland Summer Sales, Lexington, Ky.
	1970	262	(yearlings)	30,153	Keeneland Summer Sales, Lexington, Ky.
	1971	333	(yearlings)	31,775	Keeneland Summer Sales, Lexington, Ky.
	1972	40	(mixed)	83,930	George D. Widener
	1973	350	(yearlings)	56,514	Keeneland Summer Sales, Lexington, Ky.

SAND CRACK.—See QUARTER CRACK.

SARAPE (SERAPE).—A woolen blanket, often of bright geometric patterns, worn by Spanish-American men as a cloak or poncho.

SARCOPTIC MITES.—See MITES.

SAVVY.—To understand; to be knowledgeable about.

SCAB OR SCABIES.—See MITES.

SCALDS (BURNS).—An injury to the skin or flesh caused by hot liquid, by steam, or by irritating chemicals. Scalds and burns are not to be confused with galls, which are sores on the hide caused by harness or saddle.

In scalds, the long hair remains attached to the injured part. Thus, unless the scalded area is very small, professional help should be obtained because it will be necessary to clip the hair away from the injured area in order to permit the application of a suitable dressing to the skin.

[Also see BURNS (SCALDS); and GALLS.]

SCALPER.—See HARNESS—Fig. H-4.

SCALPING.—That condition in which the hairline at the top of the hind foot hits the toe of the forefoot as it breaks over.

SCHOOLING (TRAINING).—Training and developing the natural characteristics in a horse is known as schooling.

If the offspring of Man O'War and six of the fastest mares to grace the tracks had merely worked on laundry trucks until six years old and if they then suddenly—without training or other preparation—had been placed upon a racetrack, the immediate results would have been disappointing. Their natural aptitude in conformation and breeding would not have been enough.

Schooling and training would still have been necessary in order to bring out their inherent ability. No horse—whether he be used for saddle, race, or other purposes—reaches a high degree of proficiency without an education.

On the other hand, it must be emphasized that it is equally disappointing to spend time and money in educating a colt for purposes to which he is not adapted. It is difficult, for example, to train a Hackney as a five-gaited park hack, and it is equally unsatisfactory to school a born Standardbred to the high action of the heavy harness horse.

Although the word *schooling* is used more frequently by trainers of jumpers than by other horsemen, no horse of any class or breed comes to his high degree of proficiency without schooling. To be sure, they must have the natural aptitude to begin with, but that is not sufficient to get the best out of them.

(Also see DRESSAGE; and HORSEMANSHIP.)

SCORECARD.—A horse must conform to the specific type that is needed for the function he is to perform. Secondly, he should conform to the characteristics of the breed that he represents. The use of a scorecard is a good way to make sure that no part is overlooked and a proper value is assigned to each part.

A scorecard is a listing of the different parts of an animal, with a numerical value assigned to each part according to its relative importance. Also, breed characteristics may be considered in a scorecard. A horse scorecard suitable for all breeds is given in Table S-3 (See page 368.)

SCORING.—Preliminary warming up of horses before the start. The horses are turned near the starting point and hustled away as they will be in the race.

SCOTCH COLLAR.—Housing over the collar of draft show harness.

SCOURING (DIARRHEA).—Scouring or diarrhea in foals may be associated with infectious diseases or may be caused by unclean surround-

HORSE SCORECARD					
Characteristics	Points or Percent	Name or Number of Horse	Name or Number of Horse	Name or Number of Horse	Name or Number of Horse
BREED TYPE .... Animals should possess the distinctive characteristics of the breed represented, including— *Color:* *Height at maturity:* *Weight at maturity:*	15				
FORM .... *Style and beauty:* Attractive, good carriage, alert, refined, symmetrical, and all parts nicely blended together *Body:* Nicely turned; long well-sprung ribs; heavily muscled. *Back and loin:* Short and strong, wide, well muscled, and short coupled. *Croup:* Long, level, wide, muscular, with a high-set tail. *Rear quarters:* Deep and muscular. *Gaskin:* Heavily muscled. *Withers:* Prominent, and of the same height as the high point of the croup. *Shoulders:* Deep, well laid in, and sloping about a 45-degree angle. *Chest:* Fairly wide, deep, and full. *Arm and forearm:* Well muscled.	35				
FEET AND LEGS .... *Legs:* Correct position and set when viewed from front, side and rear. *Pasterns:* Long, and sloping at about a 45-degree angle. *Feet:* In proportion to size of horse, good shape, wide and deep at heels, dense texture of hoof. *Hocks:* Deep, clean-cut, and well supported. *Knees:* Broad, tapered gradually into cannon. *Cannons:* Clean, flat, with tendons well defined.	15				
HEAD AND NECK .... Alertly carried, showing style and character. *Head:* Well proportioned to rest of body, refined, cleancut, with chiseled appearance; broad, full forehead with great width between the eyes; ears medium sized, well carried, and attractive; eyes large and prominent. *Neck:* Long, nicely arched, clean cut about the throatlatch, with head well set on, gracefully carried.	10				
QUALITY .... Clean, flat bone; well-defined and clean joints and tendons, and fine skin and hair.	10				
ACTION .... *Walk:* Easy, springy, prompt, balanced, a long step, with each foot carried forward in a straight line; feet lifted clear of the ground. *Trot:* Prompt, straight, elastic, balanced, with hocks carried closely, and high flection of knees and hocks.	15				

(Continued)

Characteristics	Points or Percent	Name or Number of Horse	Name or Number of Horse	Name or Number of Horse	Name or Number of Horse
DISCRIMINATION: Any abnormality that affects the serviceability of the horse.					
DISQUALIFICATION: In keeping with breed registry or show regulations.					
TOTAL POINTS OR PERCENT	100				

ings. Any of the following conditions may bring on diarrhea: contaminated udder or teats; nonremoval of fecal matter from the digestive tract; fretfulness or temperature above normal in the mare; an excess of feed affecting the quality of the mare's milk; cold, damp bed; or continued exposure to cold rains. As treatment is not always successful, the best practice is to avoid the undesirable conditions.

Some foals scour during the foal heat of the mare, which occurs between the seventh and ninth day following foaling.

Diarrhea is caused by an irritant in the digestive tract that should be removed if recovery is to be expected. Only in exceptional cases should an astringent be given with the idea of checking the diarrhea; and such treatment should be prescribed by the veterinarian.

If the foal is scouring, the ration of the mare should be reduced, and a part of her milk should be taken away by milking her out at intervals.

SCRAPER.—A metal or wooden, slightly concave, tool shaped like a hook at the upper end and used with one hand for scraping sweat and liquid from the body. Also, a thin metal strip with handles affixed at either end, used with both hands for scraping sweat and liquid from the body.

SCRATCH.—To withdraw a horse from a race after he has been entered.

SCRATCH (by cowboy).—The action of a cowboy when he spurs a horse by keeping his feet moving in a kicking motion alternately forward and backward.

SCRATCH (to start from).—The term "to start from scratch" refers to a race without handicaps. The phrase dates from U.S. colonial days when races were informal affairs, usually taking place on a village road. The customary starting line was "scratched" across a dirt road and all horses started on even terms; hence they "started from scratch."

SCRATCHES (CRACKED HEEL, GREASE HEEL or MUD FEVER).—Scratches or grease heel is a mange-like inflammation of the posterior surfaces of the fetlocks, most frequently confined to the hind legs. The usual causes are: wet, muddy, and filthy surroundings; failure to dry legs that have become wet from slush, rain, or washing; pasterns not thoroughly cleaned by grooming; and short clipping of hair on back of the pasterns. It is most prevalent during wet, cold weather.

Treatment consists of placing the affected animal in clean quarters, clipping closely all hair on the affected areas, cleaning with mild soap and water, and applying astringent, antiseptic substances at regular intervals.

(Also see UNSOUNDNESSES.)

SCREWWORM.—Screwworms are the larvae of the blow fly, Cochliomyia hominivorax (Callitroga americanum). The maggots of the screwworm fly require living flesh of animals on which to feed.

SYMPTOMS.—Symptoms include loss of appetite, unthriftiness, and lowered activity.

TREATMENT.—The application of coumaphos (Co-Ral) or ronnel (Korlan) in keeping with manufacturer's directions will provide relief.

PREVENTION AND CONTROL.—Area-wide screwworm eradication by sterilizing pupal-stage screwworms with X-rays or gamma rays has been most effective. Try to keep animals from wounding themselves and protect any wounds that do occur. Schedule castrations in winter when flies are least numerous and active.

DISCUSSION.—Screwworm appears mostly in the South and Southwest where it may cause 50 percent of the normal annual livestock losses. The screwworm has been eradicated from the Southern United States east of the Mississippi River.

(Also see DISEASES AND PARASITES; HEALTH PROGRAM; and PARASITES OF HORSES.)

SCROTUM.—The sac-like pouch that suspends the testicles outside the male animal.

SCRUB.—A low-grade animal.

SEAT.—See HORSEMANSHIP.

SECONDARY INVADERS.—Infective agents which attack after a primary organism has established an infection.

SECOND HORSEMAN.—A hunting term referring to the groom who, in the middle of the day, brings a fresh horse for his Master to ride as he continues the hunt. Following the exchange, the horse that started in the morning is taken home.

SECRETARIAT.—See BREED (S)—Fig. B-45; and TRIPLE CROWN.

SECRETARY *(hunt).*—The Hunt Secretary is responsible for keeping the books and making himself useful in many other ways.

SEEDY TOE.—The condition in which the wall at the front part of the foot separates from the sensitive laminae, producing a hollow space. It may cause lameness, which is usually due to sand or dirt getting into the cavity and causing irritation.

Treatment is seldom effective in uniting the parts. But the condition can be helped by putting on a shoe with a broad toe clip; by filling in between the clip and the separation with tar and oakum; by keeping the hoof soft with occasional poultices; and by blistering the coronet at intervals to stimulate the growth of horn.

SELECTING AND JUDGING HORSES.—Relatively few horses are inspected and evaluated by experienced judges. Most of them are bought by persons who lack experience in judging but who have a practical need for the animal and take pride in owning a good horse. Before buying a horse, an amateur should get the help of a competent horseman.

HOW TO SELECT A HORSE.—When selecting a horse, the buyer must first decide what kind of horse he needs. This means that he must consider the following points:

• The mount should be purchased within a price range that the buyer can afford.

• The amateur or child should have a quiet, gentle, well-broken horse that is neither headstrong nor unmanageable. The horse should never be too spirited for the rider's skill.

• The size of the horse should be in keeping with the size and weight of the rider. A small child should have a small horse or pony, but a heavy man should have a horse of the weight-carrying type. Also, a tall man or woman looks out of place if not mounted on a horse of considerable height.

• Usually the novice will do best to start with a three-gaited horse and first master the three nat-

Fig. S-6. The mount should be selected carefully for the individual rider—keeping in mind (1) the purchase price that the rider can afford, (2) the skill of the rider, (3) the size of the rider, and (4) the type of work to be performed.

ural gaits before attempting to ride a horse executing the more complicated gaits.

• Other conditions being equal, the breed and color of horse may be decided on the basis of preference.

• The mount should be suited to the type of work to be performed.

After deciding on the kind of horse needed and getting an ideal in mind, the buyer is ready to select the individual horse. Selection on the basis of body conformation and performance is the best single method of obtaining a good horse. Of course, when animals are selected for breeding purposes, two additional criteria should be considered. These are (1) the record of the horse's progeny if the animal is old enough and has reproduced, and (2) the animal's pedigree. Also, show-ring winnings may be helpful.

Proficiency in judging horses necessitates a knowledge of: (1) the parts of a horse, (2) the proper value assigned to each part (a score card may be used for this purpose), (3) blemishes and unsoundnesses, (4) ways to determine age, (5) the gaits, and (6) colors and markings.

(Also see AGE; BLEMISHES AND UNSOUNDNESSES OF HORSES; COLORS AND MARKINGS; GAITS; PARTS OF A HORSE; and SCORE CARD.)

OTHER CONSIDERATIONS IN BUYING A HORSE.—In addition to desirable qualities in conformation, there should be style and beauty,

balance and symmetry, an abundance of quality, an energetic yet manageable disposition, freedom from vices, good wind, suitable age, freedom from disease, and proper condition. The buyer should also be on the alert for possible misrepresentations. As each of these factors should receive careful consideration when buying a horse, they will be discussed separately.

STYLE AND BEAUTY.—This has reference to the attractiveness with which the horse displays himself at all times. Good carriage of the head, active ears, an alert, active disposition, and beauty of conformation are factors contributing to the style of the horse. This quality is especially important in heavy harness, fine harness, and saddle horses.

BALANCE AND SYMMETRY.—Balance and symmetry refers to the harmonious development of all parts. With the full development of all important parts, which are nicely blended together, the horse will present an attractive appearance.

QUALITY.—Quality is denoted by clean, flat bone, well-defined joints and tendons, refined head and ears, and fine skin and hair. Good quality in the horse indicates easy keeping and good endurance.

AN ENERGETIC YET MANAGEABLE DISPOSITION.—Both sexes and all types of horses should at all times display energetic yet manageable dispositions. The disposition of a horse, whether good or bad, is usually considered as being a product of both inheritance and environment. Regardless of the cause of a nasty disposition, one should avoid purchasing such an animal. Superb manners and disposition are especially important in all types of pleasure horses.

FREEDOM FROM VICES.—Although not considered as unsoundnesses, such stable vices as cribbing, weaving, tail rubbing, kicking, stall-walking and stall-trotting, and halter-pulling do detract from the value of a horse. But vices are not confined to actions in the stall. Some horses object to taking a bit in their mouths; others are touchy about the ears; still others jump when an attempt is made to place a saddle or harness on their backs. Any of these traits is objectionable.

GOOD WIND.—Good wind is imperative. Defects of wind may be easily detected by first moving the animal at a rapid gait for some distance, then suddenly bringing him to a stop and listening in near proximity to the head. Unsound animals are usually noisy in breathing.

SUITABLE AGE.—The horse is usually considered as being in his prime between the ages of three and eight. Since younger horses are still growing and becoming hardened, many two- and three-year-olds do not stand up under heavy racing or other use. Although a horse's market value begins to depreciate when he reaches his eighth year, he may be useful in performing certain services until he is well over twenty years old.

FREEDOM FROM DISEASES.—In transporting a horse, there is always a possible exposure to the many ills to which he is subject. Sometimes these prove to be of sufficiently serious nature as to make working impossible at a time when the animal is most needed; and occasionally they even prove fatal. It must also be remembered that such diseases as contracted may very likely spread to the other horses on the farm and even in the community, thus exposing them to the same risk.

CONDITION.—Both productive ability and endurance are lowered by either a thin, run-down condition or an overfat and highly fitted condition. A good, vigorous, thrifty condition is conducive to the best work and breeding ability, and horses so fitted attract the eye of the prospective buyer. However, extremes in feeding and lack of exercise are to be avoided in purchasing a horse for either work or breeding. It must be remembered that fat will cover up a multitude of defects. In buying valuable mares or stallions, the purchaser should insist on having a health certificate signed by a licensed veterinarian. Such examination should also show that the reproductive organs are normal and healthy.

MISREPRESENTATIONS.—The inexperienced man is especially likely to encounter misrepresentations as to age, soundness, vices, and the training and working ability of the horse. Perhaps knowing the seller as well as the horse is the best preventative of this sort of thing.

SELENIUM POISONING (ALKALI DISEASE).—Generally this is a chronic disease, which results from ingesting too much selenium.

CAUSE.—Consumption of plants grown on soils containing selenium.

SYMPTOMS.—Loss of hair from the mane and tail in horses. In severe cases, the hoofs slough off, lameness occurs, feed consumption decreases, and death may occur by starvation.

DISTRIBUTION AND LOSSES.—In certain regions of western U.S.—especially certain areas in South Dakota, Montana, Wyoming, Nebraska, Kansas, and perhaps areas in other states in the Great Plains and Rocky Mountains. Also, in Canada.

TREATMENT.—Although arsenic has been shown to counteract the effects of selenium toxicity, there appears to be no practical method of treating other than removal of animals from affected areas.

PREVENTION.—Abandon areas where soils contain selenium, because crops produced on such soils constitute a menace to both animals and man.

REMARKS.—Chronic cases of selenium poisoning occur when animals consume feeds containing 8.5 ppm of selenium over an extended period; acute cases occur on 500 to 1,000 ppm. The toxic levels of selenium are in the range of 2.27–4.54 mg/lb. of feed.

SELF-COLORED.—A term applied to the mane and tail when they are the same color as the body coat.

SELF-FEEDING.—Self-feeding refers to the practice of keeping feed before animals at all times, as opposed to feeding given quantities at certain times of the day. Self-feeding of horses is usually limited to the use of either a salt-protein block, a salt-feed mix in meal form, or a high roughage ration consisting of chopped hay and grain mixed (and unpelleted). A few caretakers do self-feed high energy rations but, sooner or later, they usually founder a horse.

SELL AT HALTER.—Sold with no guarantee except the title.

SEMEN.—Sperm mixed with fluids from the accessory glands.

SERAPE (SARAPE).—See SARAPE.

SERUM, BLOOD.—The clear portion of blood separated from its more solid elements.

SERUMS.—Serums, also known as immune blood serum or immune serum, are obtained from the blood of animals (often horses) that have developed a solid immunity from having received one or more doses of infectious organisms. They do not contain any organisms, either dead or alive. Serums are used for the protective nature of the antibodies that they contain, which stop the action of an infectious agent or neutralize a product of that agent. They give a passive immunity. Among the serums that have proved successful are those for tetanus and anthrax.

SERVICEABLY SOUND.—Said of a horse that has nothing wrong that will materially impair its value for the intended use.

SESAMOID FRACTURES.—The sesamoids are two pyramid-like bones that form a part of the fetlock or ankle joints (on both front and rear legs) and articulate with the posterior part of the lower end of the cannon bone. They lie imbedded in ligaments and cartilage which form a bearing surface over which the flexor tendons glide.

The fracture of these fragile little bones is more frequent than has been supposed.

SET-TAIL.—A high-carried tail which is fashionable for three- and five-gaited horses of the American Saddle Horse breed and for Tennessee Walking Horses. To set a tail the two large muscles that are used to pull the tail down are cut or "nicked" and the tail is held upward (usually by ropes that go through pulleys and are attached to weights) until the wound has healed and the muscles have lengthened. Then the tail is put into a device made of iron and covered with wool. This is attached to a surcingle usually by four straps (a back strap, two side straps, and a strap extending between the horse's legs to the belly of the surcingle). In this contraption the tail assumes the waterfall form.

With anesthesia, the operation can be performed with little pain to the horse. Also, the use of antibiotics has alleviated much of the disfigurement that formerly resulted from infections and crude surgery in cutting the tail.

SEX CELLS.—The egg and the sperm, which unite to create life. They transmit genetic characteristics from the parents to the offspring.

SEX CHARACTER.—Sex character is indicated by the head and neck in particular. The head and neck should show boldness and masculinity in the stallion and refinement and femininity in the broodmare.

SEX DETERMINATION.—The sex of an animal is determined by chromosomes. The mare has a pair of similar chromosomes (called X chromosomes), whereas the stallion has a pair of

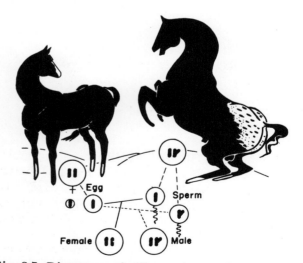

Fig. S-7. Diagrammatic illustration of the mechanism of sex determination in horses, showing how sex is determined by the chromosomal makeup of the individual.

unlike sex chromosomes (called X and Y chromosomes).

The pairs of sex chromosomes separate out when the germ cells are formed. Thus, each of the ova or eggs produced by the mare contains the X chromosome; whereas the sperm of the stallion are of two types, one-half containing the X chromosome and the other one-half the Y chromosome. Since, on the average, the eggs and sperm unite at random, it can be understood that half of the progeny will contain the chromosomal makeup XX (females) and the other one-half XY (males).

(Also see HEREDITY IN HORSES.)

SHADBELLY.—A special cut of hunting coat somewhat similar to a cutaway. It is usually worn with a top hat, rather than a derby, and it is more dressy than the ordinary hunting coat.

(Also see **CLOTHES FOR RIDERS.**)

SHADE FOR HORSES.—A shade should be provided for horses that are in the hot sun. An unshaded horse standing in an air temperature of 100° F. has to dispose of enough heat in a 10-hour period to bring 9 gallons of ice water to the boiling point.

The most satisfactory horse shades are (1) oriented with a north-south placement, (2) at least 12 to 15 feet in height (in addition to being cooler, high shades allow a mounted rider to pass under), and (3) open all around.

SHADOW ROLL.—See HARNESS—Fig. H-5.

SHAFT.—See HARNESS—Figs. H-4 and H-5.

SHAMPOOING THE HORSE.—Shampooing will make the horse look better and feel better. Horses like to be clean. In the wild state, they cleaned themselves frequently by rolling and taking dust baths. They do the same thing when turned into a corral.

Shampooing (1) cleans the animal—it removes the dirt, stains, and sweat that cannot be removed by grooming; (2) makes for a fine haircoat with a good sheen; and (3) keeps the skin smooth and mellow.

Formerly, there was strong prejudice against washing horses; perhaps stemming from the use of old-fashioned, harsh detergents and strong soaps, followed by poor rinsing. But "baths" are good for horses, just as they are good for people; and horses like to be shampooed.

Shampoo the horse as frequently as necessary, as determined by soiling, work, and weather conditions. For example, always wash him following use on a sloppy, muddy ring, trail, or track—when he comes back covered with mud from head to tail; or after using him when it's hot and muggy, and he's all lathered up with sweat.

In preparation for shampooing, (1) groom the horse carefully; (2) secure the animal for washing either by having someone hold him by the shank or by tying; and (3) have shampoo concentrate, warm water, buckets, and sponges available.

● *Step 1.—Wet* the animal thoroughly all over with water alone. For this purpose, fill one bucket with warm water (and refill it as necessary), then apply the water to the horse by means of a large sponge which may be dipped into the bucket as fast and frequently as desired.

To assure that the horse will be washed thoroughly and that no body parts will be missed, follow a definite order. This may differ somewhat according to individual preference, but the following procedure is most common: Start with the head, wetting between the ears and on the foretop (but do not get water in the ears; either hold them down or shut them off with the hand as the head is washed), over the face and cheeks, and around the eyes, muzzle, and nostrils.

Thence, proceed to the left side. While carrying the bucket in your left hand and holding the sponge in your right hand, with long strokes wet the neck, withers, shoulder, back, side, and croup. Return to the front, and with sponge in left hand, wash the chest. Return the sponge to the right hand and wash under the elbow and down the foreleg. Then, take the sponge in the left hand, set the bucket down as near as possible, and sponge the belly thoroughly. Hold onto the hind leg on the outside above the hock (this precaution will keep a restive horse from pawing, kicking, or stepping on your foot) while sponging the sheath (of stallions and geldings) and the inside of the hind leg down to the hoof.

Station yourself to the left of the horse near the hind leg, facing to the rear. Set the bucket nearby. Take the sponge in the right hand and wash behind the hind legs and in the groove between the thighs. Since many horses fuss about this operation, be careful so as to avoid getting kicked or stepped on.

Hold up the tail with the left hand and wash under it with the right hand. The tail is best washed by sponging with plenty of water at the tail head, then putting the full length of the tail into the bucket of water, lifting the bucket to the bone and sloshing the tail around in the water. Set the bucket down, grip the tail near the top and draw the squeezed sponge down the full length of the hair; then give the tail a snap from side to side to swish out the water that is left.

After wetting the near (left) side and the rear end, get a bucket of fresh water. Then, while holding the bucket in your right hand and the sponge in your left hand, wet the off (right) side of the horse in the same order as described above, starting with the neck.

● *Step 2.—Shampoo* the horse. Put in a bucket or other suitable container shampoo concentrate and water in the amounts and proportions recommended on the shampoo label, then stir it vigorously with your hand to form suds. Sponge the shampoo solution over the animal, following exactly the same procedure and order as outlined for wetting. Scrub against the hair with the sponge and your hands until a rich, thick lather covers all parts.

● *Step 3.—Rinse* the horse with warm water, using either a bucket and sponge or a hose (if the horse is used to the latter), following the procedure and order given in Step 1. Rinse thoroughly.

● *Step 4.—Scrape* with a sweat scraper held snugly against the hair to remove excess water, using long sweeping strokes and following the procedure and order given in Step 1, except do not scrape the head and legs.

● *Step 5.—Dry* with a clean dry sponge or coarse towel, squeezing it out at intervals; following the procedure and order given in Step 1.

● *Step 6.—Blanket* the horse and walk him until he is completely dry.

● *Step 7.—Apply a coat dressing* if desired.

SHAWNEE.—The Shawnee Trail was a famous early-day cattle trail which stretched from Texas to the windswept town of Baxter Springs, Kansas,

and which peaked in 1870, following the Civil War.

SHEATH.—See PARTS OF A HORSE—Fig. P-4.

SHETLAND PONY.—See BREED (S).

SHIRE.—See BREED (S).

SHOE BOIL (or CAPPED ELBOW).—Shoe boil is a soft, flabby swelling caused by an irritation at the point of the elbow, hence the common name "capped elbow." The two most common causes of this unsoundness are injury from the heel calk of the shoe and injury from contact with the floor. Affected animals may or may not go lame, depending upon the degree of inflammation and the size of the swelling. If discovered while yet small, shoe boil may be successfully treated by daily applications of tincture of iodine and the use of the shoe boil boot or roll. The latter is strapped about the pastern in such manner as to keep the heel from pressing upon the elbow while the horse is in a recumbent position. For treatment of large shoe boils, surgery by a veterinarian may be necessary, but such treatment is not always successful. Some horsemen report good results from the use of ligature which is passed around the neck of the swelling and tightened each day until circulation is stopped and the whole mass sloughs off.

(Also see UNSOUNDNESSES.)

SHOEING.—Shoeing is the art of making, fitting, and filing shoes to the feet of a horse.

Horseshoeing is a time-honored profession. In the Golden Age of the horse, which extended from the Gay Nineties to the mechanization of American agriculture, every school boy knew and respected the village blacksmith who plied his trade "under the spreading chestnut tree."

Horses should be shod when they are to be used on hard surfaces for any period of time. Also, shoes may be used to change gaits and action, correct faulty hoof structure or growth, and protect the hoof from such conditions as corns, contraction, or cracks, and aid in gripping the track. Shoes should be made to fit the foot, not the foot

Fig. S-8. Don Canfield, noted farrier, plying his trade. (Photo by A. H. Ensminger)

to fit the shoe. Reshoe or reset at 6- to 8-week intervals. Shoeing should be done either by a professional shoer, or by a person who has taken sufficient instruction from a master of the art.

It is not necessary that horse owners and managers be expert farriers. Yet, they should be knowledgeable relative to (1) anatomy and nomenclature of the foot (see FOOT), (2) what constitutes proper stance and motion, and how to correct some common faults through trimming, (3) the basic horseshoeing tools and how to use them, (4) how to recognize good and faulty shoeing, (5) kinds of shoes, and (6) treatment of dry hoofs. Today, every horseman would do well to take basic farrier intsruction under a Master Farrier, not from the standpoint of becoming a professional farrier, but to the end that they may become finished horsemen.

COMMON FAULTS, AND HOW TO CORRECT THEM.—Table S-4 describes the common faults and tells how to correct them through proper trimming.

HORSESHOEING TOOLS, AND HOW TO USE THEM.—Horses are shod to protect the foot from breaking and wearing away faster than the growth of the horn. Also, shoes may be used to change gaits and action, to correct faulty hoof structure or growth, and to protect the hoof itself from such conditions as corns, contraction, or cracks. When properly done, shoes should interfere as little as possible with the physiological functions of the different structures of the foot or with the gaits of the horse.

Just as do-it-yourself wood workers, mechanics, and whatnot usually have a shop and some tools, so the horseman should have certain basic horseshoeing tools, and know how to use them. Table S-5 may be used as a guide in selecting tools.

KINDS OF SHOES.—A number of factors should be considered when selecting the shoes for a given horse; among them:

• *The proper size.*—The shoe should fit the foot, rather than any attempt being made to trim the hoof to fit the shoe.

• *Front vs. hind shoes.*—Front shoes are more nearly circular and wider at the heels than hind shoes.

• *The individual horse.*—His weight, the shape and texture of his hoof, and the set of his legs should be considered.

• *The use to which the horse is put, and the kind of ground surface.*—A plain shoe or a rim shoe is satisfactory for most horses used for pleasure, cutting, roping, barrel racing, polo, and jumping; whereas racing plates, to aid in gripping the track, are needed on running horses. Also, there are many corrective shoes, a few of which are listed in Table S-6. (See page 379.)

Shoes may be either hand-made or ready-made (factory-made). The latter are becoming increasingly popular because they (1) require a minimum of work, and (2) are ideal for the do-it-yourselfer. Both steel and aluminum shoes are available. Fig. S-9 shows four common types of horseshoes.

TABLE S-4

COMMON FOOT FAULTS, AND HOW TO CORRECT THEM

Fault	How it Looks	How to Trim
Splayfoot	Front toes turned out, heels turned in.	Trim the outer half of the foot.
Pigeon-toed	Front toes turned in, heels turned out, the opposite of splayfoot.	Trim the inner half of foot more heavily; leave the outer half relatively long.
Quarter crack	Vertical crack on side of hoof.	Keep the hoof moist, shorten the toes, and use a corrective shoe.
Cocked ankles	Standing bent forward on fetlocks—most frequently the hind ones.	Lower the heels to correct. However, raising the heels makes for more immediate horse comfort.
Contracted heels	Close at the heels.	Lower the heels and allow the frog to carry more of the weight, which tends to spread the heels apart.

A. Racing plate.

B. Hot shoe.

C. Rim shoe.

D. Ready-made shoe.

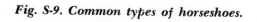

Fig. S-9. Common types of horseshoes.

Tools	Use
Anvil	As a block to shape shoes, and as the farrier's work bench.
Forge	To heat steel or shoes in preparation for shaping them for the horse being shod.
Vise	To finish shoes, and to hold metal.
	To remove dirt and trim excess frog and sole from the foot. The hook on the end is used to trim the frog and clean the crevice between the bar and frog.
Nippers or Parers	To trim the wall of the hoof and other parts that are too hard for the knife. There is hardly any limit to the sizes and descriptions of these items; some are one-sided, others are two-sided.
Hoof Level	To determine the angle of the hoof relative to the ground surface.
Clinch Cutter	To cut clinches prior to pulling shoes.
Rasp	To level the foot after trimming; one side is coarse, and the other side fine.
Driving Hammer	To drive nails into the hoof.
Hardy	As a wedge in the anvil hole, in cutting steel of the desired length and in cutting off shoes.
Hammers	To shape shoes. Various kinds of hammers may be used.
Tongs	To hold hot metal.
Nails	Assorted sizes of nails are available for different types of horseshoes.
Apron	To protect the horseshoer from sparks, from cuts that might otherwise be inflicted by slips of the knife or rasp, and from possible nail injury of nervous horses.

TABLE S-6

SOME CORRECTIVE SHOES, AND THEIR USE

Kind of Corrective Shoe	Purpose or Use
The bar shoe	To apply pressure to the frog of the foot, or to relieve pressure on any part of it.
The rocker toe shoe	For use on horses that stumble, that forge, or that have ringbone or sidebone.
The squared toe shoe with trailer	For cow-hocked horses.
The lateral extension toed shoe	For horses that either toe out or toe in.

HOW TO RECOGNIZE GOOD AND FAULTY SHOEING.—The following check list may be used as a means by which to evaluate the shoeing job, whether plied by yourself or a professional farrier:

1. As Viewed from the Front.—

Yes No
☐ ☐ Are the front feet the same size, the toes the same length, and the heels the same height?
☐ ☐ Is the foot in balance in relation to the leg?
☐ ☐ Is the foot directly under the leg, is the axis of the foot in prolongation to the axis of the upper leg bones, and is the weight of the body equally distributed over the foot structure?

2. As Viewed from the Side.—

Yes No
☐ ☐ Does the axis of the foot coincide with the axis of the pastern?
☐ ☐ Does the slope of the wall from the coronet to the lower border parallel the slope of the pastern?
☐ ☐ Has the lower outer border of the wall been rasped?
☐ ☐ Does the conformation of the foot and the type of shoe used warrant the amount of rasping done?

3. As the Height and Strength of Nailing Are Inspected Closely.—

Yes No
☐ ☐ Do the nails come out of the wall at the proper height and in sound horn?
☐ ☐ Are the nails driven to a greater height in the wall than necessary?
☐ ☐ Is the size of the nail used best suited for the size and condition of the foot and the weight of the shoe?
☐ ☐ Are the clinches of sufficient thickness where the nail comes out of the wall to insure strength?
☐ ☐ Are the clinches smooth and not projecting above the surface of the wall?

4. As the Outline and Size of the Shoe Are Scrutinized.—

Yes No
☐ ☐ Is the toe of the shoe fitted with sufficient fullness to give lateral support to the foot at the moment of breaking over and leaving the ground?
☐ ☐ Are the branches of the shoe from the bend of the quarter to the heel fitted full-

(Continued)

er than the outline of the wall to provide for expansion of the foot and normal growth of horn between shoeing periods?

☐ ☐ Are the heels of the shoe of sufficient length and width to cover the buttresses?

☐ ☐ Are the heels finished without sharp edges?

☐ ☐ Does the shoe rest evenly on the bearing surface of the hoof, covering the lower border of the wall, white line, and buttresses?

☐ ☐ Is the shoe concaved so that it does not rest upon the horny sole?

☐ ☐ Are the nail heads properly seated?

☐ ☐ Is the shoe the correct size for the foot?

☐ ☐ Will the weight of the shoe provide reasonable wear and protection to the foot?

☐ ☐ Have the ragged particles of the horny frog been removed?

SHOEING, COLD.—See COLD-SHOEING.

SHORT-COUPLED (COUPLED).—Describes a horse having a short distance (usually not more than four fingers' width) between the last rib and the point of the hip.

SHOULDER.—The area above and in front of the forelegs. A sloping shoulder (about a 45° angle) is desired. Such a shoulder is usually associated with sloping pasterns and springy, elastic action.

(Also see PARTS OF A HORSE—Fig. P-4.)

SHOULDER-IN.—A movement on two tracks. The horse's hind feet travel along a straight track parallel to the rail or wall, while the front feet make a track approximately one foot away from the rail or wall. As he tracks in this manner, the horse bends his spine in an even curve from the poll to the tail in an arc directed away from the rail or wall.

SHOW.—1. Finishing third in a race.

2. Also, a racing ticket which is good if the horse finishes first, second, or third.

SHOW-RINGS.—See RINGS.

SHOWS, HORSE.—Horse shows have increased in recent years, on all levels—local, state, and national. Also, they have grown in terms of quality and prize money as is evidenced in Table S-7, based on figures provided by the American Horse Shows Association.

In addition to spectator entertainment, horse shows stimulate improved breeding, for winning horses (and their relatives) bring good prices.

The American Horse Shows Association (A.H.S.A.) regulates the rules and schedules of all the big shows. Recognized shows include all regular shows, local shows, combined training events, and dressage competitions which are members of the A.H.S.A.

SHOWING A HORSE.—To have success in showing horses, an exhibitor must know the rules of the class and the correct showing techniques.

IN HAND (HALTER, OR BREEDING CLASSES).—The terms "in hand," "halter," or "breeding classes" refer to classes in which the horses are shown in hand (led into the ring wearing only halter or bridle). The halter or bridle should be clean, properly adjusted, and fitted with a fresh-looking lead. If the horse is shown wearing a bridle, the exhibitor should not jerk on the reins hard enough to injure the mouth.

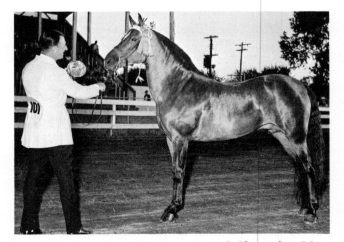

Fig. S-10. Lippitt Dusky Kate, Grand Champion Morgan Mare, owned by Mrs. Willard K. Denton, Mt. Kisco, N. Y. (Courtesy, Morgan Horse Club, Inc.)

TABLE S-7

GROWTH OF HORSE SHOWS

Year	AHSA Sanctioned Shows (no.)	Major Shows (over 50% of Divisions with "A" Rating) (no.)	Prize Money ($)
1959	425	142	1,453,322
1968	825	275	2,879,280
1970	945	315	3,297,650
1974	1258	405	4,987,649

The following practices are recommended for showing in hand, or at halter.

• Train the horse early.

• Groom the horse thoroughly.

• Dress neatly for the show.

• Enter the ring promptly and in tandem when the class is called. Line up at the location indicated by the ringmaster or judge unless directed to continue around the ring in tandem.

● Stand the horse squarely on all four feet with the forefeet on higher ground than the hind feet if possible. The standing position of the horse should vary according to the breed. For example, Arabians are not stretched, but American Saddlers are trained to stand with their front legs straight under them and their hind legs stretched behind them. Other breeds generally stand in a slightly stretched position, somewhat intermediate between these two examples. When standing and facing the horse, hold the lead strap or rope in the left hand 10 to 12 inches from the halter ring. Try to make the horse keep his head up.

• Unless the judge directs otherwise, the horse should first be shown at the walk and then at the trot. Move the horse as follows:

1. Reduce the length of the lead strap or rope by a series of "figure 8" folds or by coils held in the left hand. Hold the upper part of the lead strap or rope in the right hand and lead from the left side of the horse. If the horse is well-mannered, give him 2 to 3 feet of lead so he can keep his head, neck, and body in a straight line as he moves forward. But keep the lead taut so the horse is always under control. Do not look back.

2. The exhibitor should keep the horse's head up and briskly move him forward in a

Fig. S-11. *Correct method of leading when showing "in hand."*

straight line for 50 to 100 feet as directed.

3. At the end of the walk, turn to the right. That is, the exhibitor should turn the horse away from himself and walk around the horse. If the horse is turned toward the exhibitor, the horse is more likely to step on the exhibitor. Make the turn in as small a space as practical, and as effortless as possible. When showing at the trot, bring the horse to a walk and move him slightly in the direction of the exhibitor before turning.

4. The exhibitor should lift his knees a little higher than usual when he is showing in the ring.

5. Trail the horse with a whip if it is permitted and desired. Most light horses are given early training by trailing with the whip but usually they are shown without this aid. If a "trailer" is used, he should follow at a proper

distance. The distance should not be so near he might get kicked but not so far he would be ineffective. The trailer should keep the animal moving in a straight line, avoid getting between the judge and the horse, and always cross in front of the horse at the turn.

• Walk the horse down about 50 feet and walk back; then trot down about 100 feet and trot back. To save time, the judge may direct that horses be walked down and trotted back, which is a proper procedure. After the horse has been walked and trotted, stand him promptly in front of the judge. After the judge has made a quick inspection, move to the location in the line indicated by the ringmaster or judge.

• Keep the horse posed at all times; keep one eye on the judge and the other on the horse.

• When the judge signals to change positions, the exhibitor should back the horse out of line, or if there is room, turn him to the rear of the line and approach the new position from behind.

• Try to keep the horse from kicking when he is close to other horses.

• Keep calm; a nervous showman creates an unfavorable impression.

• Work in close partnership with the horse.

• Be courteous and respect the rights of other exhibitors.

• Do not stand between the judge and the horse.

• Be a good sport; win without bragging and lose without complaining.

PERFORMANCE CLASSES.—Performance classes for horses are so numerous and varied that it is not practical to describe them here. Instead, the showman should refer to the official *Rule Book* of the American Horse Shows Association and to the rules printed in the programs of local horse shows.

SHOW OR SALE, FITTING FOR.—Each year, many horses are fitted for shows or sales. In both cases, a fattening process is involved, but exercise is doubly essential.

For horses that are being fitted for shows, the conditioning process is also a matter of hardening, and the horses are used daily in harness or under saddle. Regardless of whether a sale or a show is the major objective, fleshing should be obtained without sacrificing action or soundness or without causing filling of the legs and hocks.

Fig. S-12. Five-gaited World Grand Champion, Yorktown. (Courtesy, Mrs. Jean McLean Davis, Oak Hill Farm, Harrodsburg, Ky.)

In fattening horses, the animals should be brought to full feed rather gradually, until the ration reaches a maximum of about 2 pounds of grain daily for each 100 pounds of live weight. When on full feed, horses make surprising gains. Daily weight gains of 4 to 5 pounds are not uncommon. Such animals soon become fat, sleek, and attractive. This is probably the basis for the statement that "fat will cover up a multitude of sins in a horse."

Although exercise is desirable from the standpoint of keeping the animals sound, it is estimated that such activity decreases the daily rate of gains by as much as 20 percent. Because of the greater cost of gains and the expense involved in bringing about forced exercise, most feeders of sale horses limit the exercise to that obtained naturally from running in a paddock.

In comparison with finishing cattle or sheep, there is more risk in fattening horses. Heavily fed horses kept in idleness are likely to become blemished and injured through playfulness, and there are more sicknesses among liberally fed horses than in other classes of stock handled in a similar manner.

In fitting show horses, the finish must remain firm and hard, the action superb, and the soundness unquestioned. Thus, they must be carefully fed, groomed, and exercised to bring them to proper bloom.

Horsemen who fit and sell yearlings or younger animals may feed a palatable milk replacer or commercial feed to advantage.

SHYING.—See VICES—Shying.

SICKLE-HOCKED.—Very crooked in the hind leg, usually light of bone, and cut in under the hock. Such a conformation is predisposed to curbiness.

SIDEBONES.—Sidebones are ossified lateral cartilages immediately above and toward the rear quarter of the hoof head. They occur most commonly in the forefeet. Lameness may or may not be present. The condition may occur on one or both sides of the foot, or on one or both front feet. This is perhaps the most common unsoundness of the feet of horses.

Sidebones may be partially or entirely of genetic origin; or the condition may result from running or working horses on pavement or other hard surface. Sidebones may also develop following sprains, cracks, quittor, or other injuries. Treatments vary and are not always successful. Temporary relief from fever and soreness can usually be obtained through the application of cold-water bandages. Veterinarians sometimes apply blistering agents, fire, or sever the nerve leading to the area; but the "nerving" operation has fallen into disfavor among most horsemen and racing officials.

(Also see UNSOUNDNESSES.)

SIDE GALLOP.—A gallop done on two tracks; that is, the hind feet and forefeet make two parallel tracks, usually about one foot apart. Of course, the horse must lead with the inside forefoot; hence, the outside forefoot cannot cross over in front of the leading foot.

The side gallop is sometimes used (1) to slow down a jumper when he attempts to rush a jump, or (2) to break a horse of the habit of bolting or running away.

SIDE SADDLE.—See SADDLE, SIDE.

SIDE STEP.—See TRAVERSE.

SIGNALS.—This usually refers to certain cues given by the rider in addition to the aids. For example, the rider of a gaited horse may touch the middle of the top of the crest as a signal to trot.

(Also see AIDS.)

SILAGE.—Well-preserved silage of good quality, free from mold and not frozen, affords a highly nutritious succulent forage for horses during the winter months. As horses are more susceptible than cattle or even sheep to botulism or other digestive disturbances resulting from feeding poor silage, none but choice, fresh silage should ever be fed.

Various types of silages may be fed successfully to horses, but corn silage and grass-legume silage are most common. If the silage contains much grain, the concentrate allowance should be reduced accordingly.

Fine as the silage may be, it should not be used as the only roughage for horses. Usually it should be fed in such quantity as to replace not more than one-third to one-half of the roughage ration, considering that ordinarily one pound of hay is equivalent to approximately three pounds of wet silage. This means that the silage allowance usually does not exceed ten to fifteen pounds daily per head for mature animals, although much larger amounts have been used satisfactorily in some instances. Silage is especially suited for the winter feeding of idle horses, broodmares, and growing foals.

SILKS.—The colored caps and shirts which jockeys and drivers of harness horses wear. They serve to identify the stable, as each stable has its own racing colors.

SINGLE-FOOT.—The rack was formerly called single-foot. Use of the word single-foot is now obsolete, and considered incorrect.

(Also see RACK.)

SIRE.—The male parent. A term used when speaking of a horse's parentage.

SISTERS.—See BROTHERS.

SIT-FAST.—A hard and painful swelling on the back of a horse, caused by the pressure of an ill-fitting saddle. A lump first forms, and, if there has been an old wound, a dry scabby skin forms over it. The only solution is surgery, which is usually successful.

SIZE (of horse).—When reference is made to the size of a horse, it means his height in hands (each hand is four inches). The average height of each breed is given under BREED (S)—Table B-2.
(Also see MEASURING HORSES.)

SIZE OF HORSE INDUSTRY.—See MAGNITUDE OF HORSE INDUSTRY.

SKELETON OF THE HORSE.—The skeleton of the horse consists of 205 bones, as follows:

Vertebral column	54
Ribs	36
Sternum	1
Skull (including auditory ossicles)	34
Thoracic limbs	40
Pelvic limbs	40
Total	205

(See Figs. S-13, S-14, and S-15.)

SKEWBALD.—Refers to coat color other than black—such as bay, brown, or chestnut—combined with white.

SKIMMED MILK, DRIED, AND DRIED BUTTERMILK.—As the names indicate, these products are dehydrated skim milk and buttermilk, respectively. They contain less than 8 percent moisture, and average 32 to 35 percent protein. One pound of dried skimmed milk or dried buttermilk has about the same composition and feeding value as 10 pounds of their liquid forms.

Dried skimmed milk (or buttermilk) is especially valuable for young equines; for creep feeding until past weaning.

SKINNER.—1. A term, now seldom used, meaning that the animal's chief value was for what its hide would bring.
2. In the days of multiple-hitches of mules and horses, the driver was called a "skinner." This was particularly true of mule drivers, who were known as "mule skinners."

SKOWRONEK.—A famous, gray Arabian stallion bred at Volhynia in Poland and foaled in 1909. Skowronek was imported to England and eventually acquired by Lady Wentworth. He had great influence on modern Arabians, both in England and in the U.S.

SKULL.—The skull encloses the brain and the most important organs of sense. It consists of thirty-four bones, mostly flat, which yield and overlap at points of union at the time of birth, thus making for greater ease of parturition.

The size of the head should be proportionate to the size of the horse, and the shape true to the characteristics of the breed or type represented. Thus, the Thoroughbred possesses a broad forehead, with the face gradually tapering from the forehead to the muzzle, giving the animal an intelligent and alert expression.

The lower jaw should always be strong and well defined, with good width between the branches so as not to compress the larynx when the neck is flexed.

The mature male horse has 40 teeth, and the female 36. Animals of each sex possess 24 molars or grinders and 12 incisors or front teeth. In addition, the male has 4 tushes or pointed teeth, and sometimes these occur in females.

The young animal, whether male or female, has 24 temporary or milk teeth. These include 12 incisors and 12 molars.
(Also see SKELETON.)

SLAB-SIDED.—Flat-ribbed.

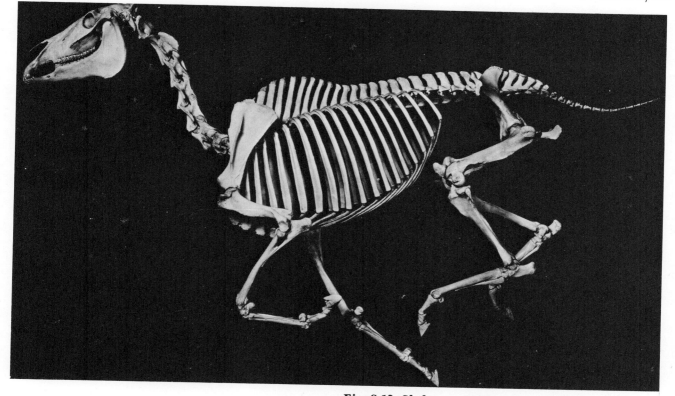

Fig. S-13. Skeleton of the famous American racehorse Sysonby, showing action at the run. This illustration shows how the bones act as levers as (1) the hind legs are drawn up beneath the body, then moved forward preparatory to straightening out and propelling the horse forward with a long stride typical of great running horses, and (2) the front legs sustain a tremendous jar as the horse lands. The run is a four-beat gait where the feet strike the ground separately; first one hind foot, then the other hind foot, then the front foot on the same side as the first hind foot, then the other front foot which decides the lead. (Courtesy, The American Museum of Natural History, New York, N.Y.)

Fig. S-14. Skeleton of horse and man. It can be seen that: (1) the knee joint in the horse is the counterpart of the wrist joint in man; (2) the stifle joint in the horse is the counterpart of the knee joint in man; and. (3) the hock joint in the horse is the counterpart of the ankle joint in man. (Courtesy, The American Museum of Natural History, New York, N.Y.)

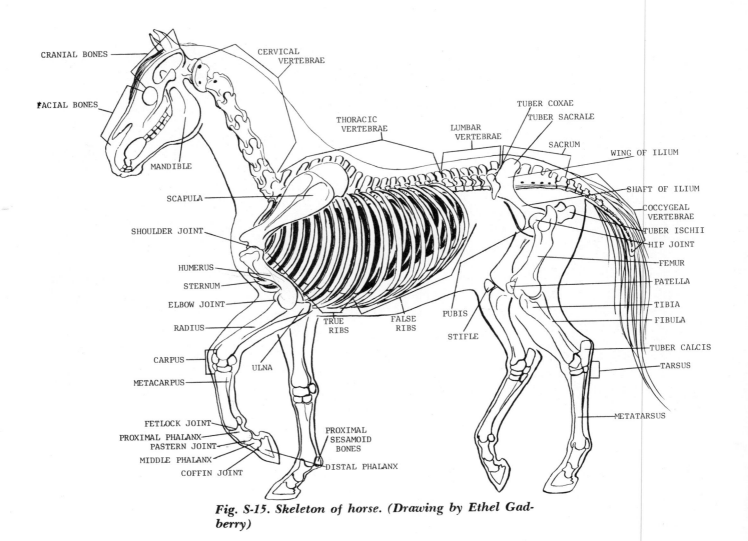

CRANIAL BONES

CERVICAL VERTEBRAE

FACIAL BONES

THORACIC VERTEBRAE

TUBER COXAE

TUBER SACRALE

LUMBAR VERTEBRAE

SACRUM

MANDIBLE

WING OF ILIUM

SCAPULA

SHAFT OF ILIUM

SHOULDER JOINT

COCCYGEAL VERTEBRAE

TUBER ISCHII

HIP JOINT

HUMERUS

FEMUR

STERNUM

PATELLA

ELBOW JOINT

TIBIA

RADIUS

FIBULA

TRUE RIBS

FALSE RIBS

PUBIS

STIFLE

TUBER CALCIS

CARPUS

ULNA

TARSUS

METACARPUS

FETLOCK JOINT

METATARSUS

PROXIMAL PHALANX

PASTERN JOINT

PROXIMAL SESAMOID BONES

MIDDLE PHALANX

COFFIN JOINT

DISTAL PHALANX

Fig. S-15. Skeleton of horse. (Drawing by Ethel Gadberry)

SLEEPING SICKNESS (ENCEPHALOMYELI-TIS).—See ENCEPHALOMYELITIS.

SLIDING STOP.—The quick stop executed by a Western horse. When properly done, the rider's reining hand is low, the horse's head is low and his front feet are near the ground. Most judges prefer a stop with three or four feet on the ground, rather than the more spectacular two hind-leg stop. If the stop is on three feet, one forefoot is up slightly, ready to turn or roll back either way. Most expert Western horsemen don't like a sliding stop with both front feet up in the air because the horse is not balanced and can fall over backward.

It takes months of training to get a horse to do the sliding stop right. First he should be stopped at the walk, then the trot, next the short lope, and finally when wide open.

In executing the sliding stop, the Western rider uses his aids as follows: (1) squeezes with his legs, (2) says "Ho," (3) sits back deep in the saddle, and (4) pulls up on the reins. The leg pressure is to alert the horse. Throwing the rider's weight back, when properly timed, drives the horse's hind feet up under him. The reins are pulled no harder than necessary, then the pressure is released so that the horse can use his head to maintain his balance.

Proper timing is important. The rider squeezes when the lead foot is off the ground and the hind feet are getting ready to come off. As his hind feet come up, he shifts his weight back and starts making contact with the horse's mouth. He does not jerk, for jerking hurts the horse's mouth, and makes his head fly up and his mouth gape open. Another important thing relative to timing is this: If the rider "applies the brakes" when the horse is stretched out and his front feet are in the air, he forces the horse to throw all his weight on his front feet and he'll bounce.

The really good sliding stop is performed with rhythm and balance, and is easy and smooth.

Fig. S-17. *Slobbering. This shows a horse undergoing profuse salivation due to eating clover hay heavily laden with the fungus, Rhizoctonia leguminicola. (Courtesy, Jurgen von Bredow, Edgewood, Md.)*

Fig. S-16. *A good stop. Note that the reining hand is low, the horse's head is low, and three of the feet are on the ground.*

SLIPPER.—A light temporary shoe is called a slipper.

SLOBBERING.—Horsemen have long associated the feeding of red clover hay with slobbering. But they didn't know why. In 1962, University of Wisconsin workers reported that a fungus, *Rhizoctonia leguminicola*, which caused black patch disease of red clover, is the cause, rather than the clover plant itself. (See Fig. S-17.)

SLOPING SHOULDERS.—Shoulders properly angulated and laid back.

SLOW PACE.—See STEPPING PACE.

SMALL INTESTINE.—See INTESTINE.

SMOKY EYE.—A whitish-clouded eye. (Also see WALL EYE.)

SMOOTH.—Unshod, "barefoot."

SMOOTH COAT.—Short, hard, close-fitting coat of hair.

SMOOTH-MOUTHED.—No cups in the teeth. Indicates a horse is 12 years of age or older.

SNAFFLE (BIT).—The first type of bit to which historians make reference. It was developed by the early Greek horsemen. The snaffle is the most widely used of all bits, and the bit usually used when starting a horse in training.

(Also see BITS—Fig. B-9.)

SNIP.—A white mark between the nostrils or on the lips.

(Also see COLORS AND MARKINGS OF HORSES—Fig. C-9.)

SNORTER.—An excitable horse.

SODIUM CHLORIDE (SALT).—See MINERALS.

SOFT.—Easily fatigued.

SOIL ANALYSIS.—For the horseman who produces his own grass and/or hay, a soil analysis can be very helpful; for example, (1) the phosphorus content of soils affects plant composition, (2) soils high in molybdenum and selenium affect the composition of the feeds produced, (3) iodine deficiency areas are important in horse nutrition, and (4) other similar soil-plant-animal relationships are important.

No analysis is any better than the sample taken. So, make sure that you get a representative sample of soil. Ask your County Agent (Farm Advisor) how to take the samples and where to send them. Some Colleges of Agriculture make soil analyses at nominal cost.

(Also see FEED.)

SOIL, pH OF.—The pH of a soil is an expression of its acidity or alkalinity, with number 7.0 being considered as neutral. A pH below 7.0 means that the soil is acid, and a pH above 7.0 means that the soil is alkaline. The most favorable pH range for plant growth is generally considered to lie between 6.0 and 7.5.

SOLID COLOR.—Having no white markings.

SORE SHINS.—See BUCKED SHINS.

SORGHUMS, GRAIN (MILO; KAFIR).—The grain sorghums—which include a number of varieties of earless plants, bearing heads of seeds—are assuming an increasingly important role in American agriculture. New and higher-yielding varieties have been developed and become popular. As a result, more and more grain sorghums are being fed to horses.

Kafirs and milos are among the more important sorghums grown for grain. Other less widely produced types include sorgo, feterita, durra, hegari, kaoliang, and shallu. These grains are generally grown in regions where climatic and

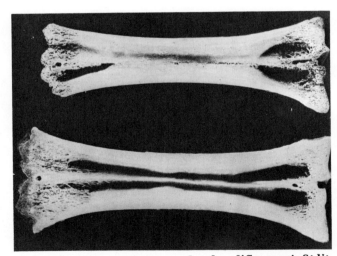

Fig. S-18. Soil nutrients made the difference! Split bones from two animals of similar breeding and age. Small, fragile, pitted bone (top) obtained from animal pastured on belly-deep grass grown on weathered soil low in mineral content. Big, rugged, strong bone (bottom) from animal grown on moderately weathered, but highly mineralized soil. (From Animal Science, by Dr. M. E. Ensminger)

Fig. S-19. A Texas kafir crop. Kafir is usually threshed. (Courtesy, USDA, Soil Conservation Service)

soil conditions are unfavorable for corn.

Like white corn, the grain sorghums are low in carotene (vitamin A value). Also, they are deficient in other vitamins, and in proteins and minerals.

For horses, the sorghums should be steam rolled or ground coarsely.

SORING.—The use of caustic liquid (called "scooter juice"), chains, or shackles to make the fore ankles of a Tennessee Walking Horse sore is called soring. This process, along with (1) feet seven inches or more in length and (2) training, enhances the running-walk gait.

Soring is now illegal. In 1970, a federal law was passed banning the practice; and the U.S. Department of Agriculture implemented the law in 1972. U.S.D.A. regulations provide fines up to $2,000 and six months' imprisonment for anyone engaged in the practice of horse soring to produce special gaits in the show-ring. Also, the American Horse Shows Association *Rule Book*, Tennessee Walking Horse Division, states:

Horses that have raw or bleeding sores in the pastern or coronet areas must be disqualified by the judge for the balance of the show and the owners, trainers, and riders are subject to further penalty under the provisions of Rule III, Part I, Sec. 7.

SORREL (CHESTNUT).—A horse that is red in color.

(Also see COLORS AND MARKINGS OF HORSES.)

SOUND.—Said of a horse free from injury, flaw, mutilation, or decay; also one that is guaranteed free from blemishes and unsoundnesses.

SOUNDNESS.—The horse should be serviceably sound, and in the young animal there should be no indication of defects in conformation that may predispose unsoundnesses. The horseman must first know and recognize the normal structure and function before attempting to determine unsoundnesses.

(Also see BLEMISHES; and UNSOUNDNESS-ES.)

SOYBEAN MEAL.—Soybean meal, processed from the soybean, is the most widely used protein supplement in the United States. It is the ground residue (soybean oil cake or soybean oil chips) remaining after the removal of most of the oil from soybeans. The oil is extracted by either of three processes: (1) the expeller process, (2) the hydraulic process, or (3) the solvent process. Although a name descriptive of the extraction process must be used in the brand name, well-cooked soybean meal produced by each of the extraction processes is of approximately the same feeding value.

Soybean meal normally contains 41, 44, or 50 percent protein, according to the amount of hull removed; and the proteins are of better quality than the other protein-rich supplements of plant origin. It is low in calcium, phosphorus, carotene, and vitamin D.

Soybean meal is satisfactory as the only protein supplement to grain for mature horses, providing a high quality ground legume is incorporated in the ration and adequate sources of calcium and phosphorus are provided. For foals, it is best that a dried milk by-product be included.

SPACE REQUIREMENTS FOR BARNS.—See BUILDINGS.

SPACE REQUIREMENTS FOR EQUIPMENT. —See EQUIPMENT, FEED AND WATER.

SPACE REQUIREMENTS FOR FEED AND BEDDING.—See BUILDINGS—Table B-11.

SPACE REQUIREMENTS FOR SERVICE PASSAGES.—See BUILDINGS—Table B-10.

SPACE REQUIREMENTS FOR STALLS AND SHEDS.—See BUILDINGS—Table B-9.

SPADE (BIT).—The spade bit is a Western bit which was brought to this continent by the Spanish conquistadores. Its effectiveness stems from the spade, or spoon, which rises from the center of the mouthpiece like the port of a Weymouth

Curb Bit. The spoon exerts pressure on the mouth.

(Also see BITS—Fig. B-10.)

SPANISH-BARB.—See BREED (S).

SPANISH-BARB BREEDERS ASSOCIATION.—Box 7479, Colorado Springs, Colo. 80907. (See Appendix for complete breed registry association list.)

SPANISH MUSTANG.—See BREED (S).

SPANISH MUSTANG REGISTRY, INC., THE.—Rt. 2, Box 74, Marshall, Texas 75670. (See Appendix for complete breed registry association list.)

SPANISH RIDING SCHOOL (VIENNA RIDING SCHOOL).—The Spanish Riding School, at Vienna, Austria, was founded by Emperor Maximilian in 1565. By 1572, it was known as the "Spanish Riding Stable," due to the use of horses of Andalusian descent; attested to by paintings on the walls of the rooms showing spotted horses, similar in color to our Appaloosas and Pony of the Americas.

The Lipizzan breed—named after the town of Lipizza, one time site of the old Hapsburg stud farm—was started back in 1565 (the same year that the Spanish Riding School was started) by Emperor Maximilian, who assembled white animals of Arabian and Spanish breeding. Foals of the Lipizzan breed are brown or gray at birth, but turn completely white at four to six years of age.

The entire interior of the riding hall at the Spanish Riding School is decorated in unrelieved white with one exception—a heroic-sized painting of Emperor Charles VI shown on a Lipizzan stallion, placed in the Emperor's box at the end of the hall. It was under his rule that the hall was completed. Much architectural sculpture is in evidence in the panelled ceilings, from which hang immense crystal chandeliers, and in the columns which support the upper and lower galleries that surround the 180-ft. long, 59-ft. wide, and 56-ft. high ring. It's a sparkling setting for the stately

Fig. S-20. Lipizzan stallion about to kick out in Capriole movement. (Courtesy, Spanish Riding School, Wels, Austria)

white horses and their scarlet-coated riders!

It's easy to picture the glamorous and varied festivities that went on in this magnificent hall in days of old—the tournaments; the carousels; the fancy-dress festivals of Empress Maria Theresa; the majestic concert with Beethoven conducting over one thousand musicians; and the Austrian parliament assembled there in 1848.

Toward the close of World War II, the Spanish Riding School and the Lipizzan breed were threatened with extinction by both the German and Russian armies. In desperation, the school heads appealed to excavalryman George S. Patton whose tanks were dashing across Austria in the spring of 1945. After observing a special exhibition of the historic white horses, the horse fancier General agreed to preserve and protect the entire herd as a part of European culture. To this end, the Spanish Riding School and its horses were moved to Wels, Austria, near Salzburg.

Anyone liking perfection, nonhorselovers as well as horselovers, will be thrilled by the truly amazing accomplishments of these superbly-trained Lipizzan horses. The precision is almost unbelievable. The most difficult movements are done with ease and grace; among them, the Capriole, one of several intricate movements resembling the leaping, twisting, fighting, and frolicking of high-spirited horses in pasture.

SPANISH WALK AND TROT.—This is an artificial movement in which the horse, in turn, lifts each forefoot, very high, then extends it forward and holds it out for a perceptible pause before returning it to the ground. It is a four-beat gait, meaning that each foot takes off from and strikes the ground at a separate interval. Also, the horse must move forward a uniform distance with each step.

The Spanish trot is similar to the Spanish walk, although the hind feet are lifted somewhat higher than at the walk.

The Spanish walk and trot are not included in any of the recognized national or international dressage competitions; nevertheless, they are great crowd pleasers.

The preliminary training for the Spanish walk is done from the ground. The trainer usually induces the horse to raise, extend, and lower one foot after the other by means of light taps of the whip. Simultaneously, the horse must be taught to progress forward. When the animal fully understands what is expected of him, the trainer mounts and continues the training.

SPAVIN.—There are three kinds of spavins—blood spavin, bog spavin, and bone spavin (or jack spavin), all of which appear in the hock area.

(Also see BLOOD SPAVIN; BOG SPAVIN; BONE SPAVIN; and UNSOUNDNESSES.)

SPAYED MARE.—A desexed equine female. Occasionally, this type of surgery is performed in order (1) to remove diseased ovaries, or (2) to suppress heat in the hope that the spayed mare will perform or race better.

SPEAK (hounds).—A hunting term. Hounds do not bark—they speak.

SPECK IN EYE.—A spot in the eye, but not covering the pupil. It may or may not impair the vision.

(Also see FEATHER IN EYE.)

SPEED.—The rate of travel of a horse. It varies according to individuals and gaits. On the average, it is about as follows:

Gait	Rate Per Hour (miles)
Walk	4
Trot	9
Canter	12
Running Walk	7
Foxtrot	9
Rack	20
Extended gallop (in racing)	40

(Also see RACING RECORDS.)

SPEEDY CUTTING.—A condition of a horse at speed in which a hind leg above the scalping mark hits against the shoe of a breaking-over forefoot. In trotters, legs on the same side are involved; in pacers, diagonal legs are involved. In some cases, a good farrier can correct the trouble by making a very slight change in the level of the foot or the weight of the shoe. Unless corrective shoeing works, the horse prone to speedy cutting should wear boots as a protection.

SPERM, SPERM CELL.—Male sex cell produced in the testicles.

SPLAYFOOT.— (Front toes turned out, heels turned in) can be helped or corrected by trimming the outer half of the foot.

(Also see SHOEING.)

SPLENIC FEVER.—See ANTHRAX.

SPLINTS.—Splints are abnormal bony growths found on the cannon bone, usually on the inside surface, but occasionally on the outside. They are most common on the front legs. When found on the hind cannon, they are generally on the outside. Splints may enlarge and interfere with a ligament and cause irritation and lameness. Their presence detracts from the appearance of the animal, even when there is no lameness. When found on young horses, they often disappear. Point firing, blistering agents, and tincture of iodine have been employed with variable success in treating splints. (See Fig. S-21.)

(Also see UNSOUNDNESSES.)

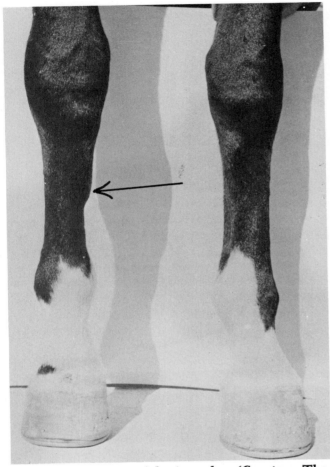

Fig. S-21. Splints on right front leg. (Courtesy, **The Western Horseman)**

SPOOKY.—Nervous.

SPOON.—The projection, for exerting pressure on the mouth, which rises from the center of the mouthpiece of a spade bit, much like the port of a Weymouth Curb Bit. The spoon may vary from less than an inch to two or more inches in length.

(Also see BITS—Fig. B-10.)

SPORTS USE.—See USE OF HORSES.

SPRAINS (STRAINS).—Sprains (or strains) may affect muscles, tendons, and ligaments. When muscles or tendons are involved, it is commonly called strain; when it's a ligament, it's called sprain. Although muscle strains may occur they may be regarded as rare. Actually, most so-called "muscle sprains" are tendon sprains. In the horse, the term "sprain," or "strain," when applied to tendon or ligament infers that there is a state of laceration of the fibers of the part involved, this being more or less complete. It may be what is termed "stretched," but if it is stretched to the limit it is fairly safe to assume that laceration has occurred.

A strain is caused by overstress. The greatest strain-producing gait is the gallop, particularly when the horse tires as at the end of a race at which time the muscles tire and the strain comes on the tendons.

The earliest and most frequent symptom of sprain is lameness, accompanied by local swelling. There is pain on pressure and the affected part is usually warmer than the corresponding one on the normal limb.

• *Treatment of sprain (involving a ligament).*—In mild sprain, treatment is relatively unimportant and is designed mostly toward prevention of pain. In moderate sprain, the critical factor in treatment is protection in order to permit repair. In severe sprain where the ligament is ruptured, emphasis must be placed on drawing the cut edges of the ligament together in order to assure a ligament of normal length and strength, along with adequate rest.

• *Treatment of strain (involving muscles or tendons).*—Treatment of simple strain consists of relieving the acute condition by injection of a local anesthetic and corticoids. Local heat and protection against movement which causes pain are additional methods of therapy. Treatment of violent strain involves immobilization by means of a plaster cast, with or without surgery.

SPRINTER.—A horse who performs best at distances of a mile or under.

SPROUTED GRAIN.—See HYDROPONICS.

SPURS.—A U-shaped metal implement with a pointed or rowel-tipped projection, first used by the Assyrians. Spurs are secured to the heels of the horseman and used to convey commands to the horse; not simply to make him go faster. The good horseman takes pride in never putting a mark on his horse with his spurs.

There are different types of spurs for different uses—hunting, racing, Western riding, etc. Also, the designs are numerous and neck lengths vary with fashion.

SQUASHES.—See PUMPKINS, SQUASHES, and MELONS.

STABLE.—See STALL.

STABLE FLY.—See FLIES.

STABLE MANAGEMENT.—The following stable management practices are recommended:
• Remove the top layer of clay floors yearly; replace with fresh clay, then level and tamp. Keep the stable floor higher than the surrounding area so the floor will stay dry.
• Keep stalls well lighted.
• Use properly constructed hay racks to lessen waste and contamination of hay. Do not have hay racks in maternity stalls.
• Scrub concentrate containers as often as necessary and always after feeding a wet mash.
• Remove excrement and wet or soiled material from the bedding daily, and provide fresh bedding.
• Practice strict stable sanitation to prevent fecal contamination of feed and water.
• Lead foals when taking them from the stall to the paddock and back as a way to further their training.
• Restrict the ration when horses are idle, and provide either a wet bran mash the evening before an idle day or turn idle horses to pasture.
• Provide proper ventilation at all times by means of open doors, windows that open inwardly from the top, or stall partitions slatted at the top.
• Keep stables in repair at all times to lessen injury hazards.

STABLE VICES.—See VICES.

STAG.—A male horse that was castrated after reaching maturity.

STAGECOACH.—A heavy, enclosed, four-wheeled vehicle, usually drawn by four horses, formerly used for making regular trips between stations and carrying passengers and goods.

Fig. S-22. Stagecoach.

STAGGERS.—See BLIND STAGGERS.

STAKE HORSE.—A stake horse is one good enough to compete in a Stake Race.

STAKE RACE.—A stake race, short for sweepstake, is just what the name implies. Each owner puts up an equal amount of money (nominating fees, fees for keeping them eligible, and starting fees) and the winner takes all. Also, the track usually puts up added money. Actually, few stake races are run on a winner-take-all basis; rather, the money is divided between the first four horses.

STAKING OUT A HORSE (TETHERING).—To restrain a horse with a rope or chain so that it can range or graze only within the radius allowed.

Unless a horse is accustomed to being staked out, he is likely to get tangled up in the rope and get a severe rope burn. Staking out training should begin early in life—with the young foal. The writer has observed that staking out horses (and other animals) is rather common in most parts of the world, and that they are accustomed to the practice from birth.

Staking out is usually accomplished by means of a metal pin or stake (for driving into the ground) with a swivel head to which a 20- to 30-foot rope or chain is attached. There is less hazard of the horse getting entangled if the stake is three or four feet high.

STALL.—Space or compartment in which an animal is placed or confined. It may be a straight stall with the animal tied at the front end (a tie-stall) or a compartment with the animal loose inside (a box-stall). Most horsemen prefer box stalls because they allow the horse more liberty, both when standing or lying down.

Fig. S-23. Box stalls in the stable of Mr. and Mrs. C. G. Furlong, Ojai, Calif. (Courtesy, Sunset Magazine*)*

Adequate quarters (in either box- or tie-stall) for a horse should be: (1) ample in size and height for the particular type of animal; (2) properly finished and without projections; (3) dry with good footing; (4) equipped with suitable doors; (5) provided with ample windows for proper lighting; (6) well ventilated; (7) cool in summer and warm in winter; (8) equipped with suitable mangers, grain containers, watering facilities, and mineral boxes; and (9) easy to keep clean.

The following features are particularly important in stalls:

• *Floors.*—A raised clay floor. Remove the top layer each year, replace with fresh clay, and level and tamp. A quarter or half-moon concrete apron poured just inside the stall door will alleviate pawing and lessen the frequency of filling and leveling of a clay floor.

• *Concrete footings.*—Concrete footings and foundation walls are recommended as they are both durable and noncorrosive. The foundation should be a minimum of 8″ high, so as to be above the manure level.

• *Ceiling height.*—A ceiling height of eight to nine feet is recommended, although there is no harm if it is higher.

• *Walls.*—The inside of the stall should be boarded up to a height of about five feet, using either (1) durable plywood of adequate thickness and strength, or (2) two-inch, hard lumber, (such as oak) placed horizontally. Hollow concrete blocks encourage stall kicking; hence, when used, they should either be filled with concrete or lined with wood. Above five feet, and extending up to a minimum of seven feet (or even to the ceiling), stall partitions or fronts may be slatted, preferably with metal, to allow for air circulation and companionship with other horses.

• *Doors.*—Stall doors may be either (1) full sliding type suspended by overhead rollers or rails, or (2) the swinging dutch type, with the top part swinging down or to the side.

• *Weather protection over stall doors.*—This is important. It can be easily and simply achieved by an overhanging roof.

(Also see BUILDINGS—Space requirements—Table B-9.)

STALLION.—By definition, a stallion is a male horse four years old or over; in Thoroughbreds, five years old or over.

The stallion should be a purebred animal, a good representative of the breed selected, and a superior individual in type and soundness. If he is an older horse with progeny, the progeny should be of uniformly high quality and of approved type and soundness.

Based on U.S. averages over many years, only half (50%) of the mares bred in the U.S. con-

Fig. S-24. The stallion. (Courtesy, Albers Milling Co.)

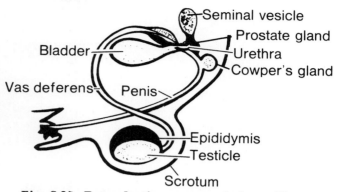

Fig. S-25. Reproductive organs of the stallion.

ceive. In any one mating, perhaps half the fault can be attributed to the stallion—the rest is due to the mare. But since a stallion is responsible for breeding several mares in a given season, it is most important that any deficiencies pertaining to him, whatever they are, be rectified. To this end, it is recommended that the care and management of the stallion be in keeping with approved practices. Additionally, each stallion should be studied as an individual, and his care, feeding, exercise, and handling should be varied accordingly.

REPRODUCTIVE ORGANS OF THE STALLION.—The stallion's functions in reproduction are (1) to produce the male reproductive cells, the sperm, or spermatozoa, and (2) to introduce sperm into the female reproductive tract at the proper time. Fig. S-25 is a schematic drawing of the reproductive organs of the stallion.

The two testicles are the primary sex organs of the stallion. They produce the sperm and a hormone called testosterone, which regulates and maintains the male reproductive tract in its functional state and is responsible for the masculine appearance and behavior of the stallion.

Sperm are produced in the inner walls or surface of the seminiferous tubules, which are a mass of minute, coiled tubules. These tubules merge into a series of larger ducts that carry the sperm to a coiled tube called the epididymis. The epididymis is the place where the sperm are stored and where they mature, or ripen.

The testicles and epididymides are enclosed in the scrotum, the chief function of which is thermoregulatory. The scrotum maintains the testicles at temperatures several degrees cooler than the rest of the body.

From the epididymis, the sperm move through a tube, the vas deferens, into the urethra. The urethra has a dual role. It carries urine from the bladder through the penis and sperm from the junction with the vas deferens to the end of the penis.

Along the urethra are the accessory glands. These are the prostate, the seminal vesicles, and cowper's gland. Their fluids nourish and preserve the sperm and provide a medium that transports the sperm. The fluids and sperm combined are called semen.

CARE AND MANAGEMENT OF THE STALLION.—The following points are pertinent to the care and management of the stallion.

QUARTERS.—The most convenient arrangement is a roomy box-stall that opens directly into a two- or three-acre pasture.

FEEDING.—The ration exerts a powerful effect on sperm production and semen quality. Successful breeders adhere to the following rules:
• Feed a balanced ration, giving particular attention to proteins, minerals, and vitamins.
• Regulate the feed allowance because the stallion can become infertile if he gets too fat. Also, increase the exercise when the stallion is not a sure breeder.
• Provide pasture in season as a source of both nutrients and exercise.

EXERCISE.—Allow the stallion the run of a sizeable pasture but also provide additional, unhurried exercise either under saddle or hitched to a cart; by longeing; or by leading.

GROOMING.—Groom the stallion daily to make him more attractive and to assist in maintaining his good health and condition.

AGE AND SERVICE.—Limit the mature stallion to not more than two services per day, one early in the morning and the other late in the afternoon; allow one day of rest each week.

The number of hand matings per year for stallions of different ages should be limited as follows: 2 years old, 10 to 15; 3 years old, 20 to 40; 4 years old, 30 to 60; mature horses, 80 to 100; and over 18 years old, 20 to 40. Limit the 2-year-olds to two to three services per week; the 3-year-olds to one service per day; and the 4-year-olds or over to two services per day. A stallion may remain a vigorous and reliable breeder up to 20 to 25 years of age.

There are breed differences. Thus, when first entering stud duty, the average 3-year-old Thoroughbred should be limited to 20 to 25 mares per season, but a Standardbred of the same age may breed 25 to 30 mares. A 4- to 5-year-old Thoroughbred should be limited to 30 to 40 mares per season, but a Standardbred of the same age may breed 40 to 50 mares.

FERTILITY OF THE STALLION.—Any stallion of breeding age that is purchased should be a guaranteed breeder; this is usually understood among reputable breeders.

The most reliable and obvious indication of potency is a large number of healthy, vigorous foals from a season's service. As an added protection, or in order to follow the horse during the midst of a heavy breeding program, a microscopic examination of the semen may be made by an experienced person. As the stallion dismounts from service, some of the semen is collected in a sterilized funnel by holding the penis over the plugged funnel. A sample of the semen is then strained through sterile gauze, and a small amount is placed on a slide for examination. A great number of active sperm cells is an indication, although not definite assurance, that the stallion is fertile. Some establishments make a regular practice of making such a microscopic ex-

amination twice each week during the breeding season. If it is desired to examine a stallion's semen after the breeding season or when a mare is not in season an artificial vagina may be used. When an entire ejaculate is available for study, the four main criteria of quality are: (1) semen volume, (2) spermatozoan count, (3) progressive movement, and (4) morphology.

If the stallion is a shy breeder or lacks fertility although one is certain that the feed and exercise have been up to standard, masturbation should be suspected. Some horses are very hard to catch in the act, but generally masturbation can be detected by (1) the shrinkage of the muscles over the loin, and (2) the presence of dried semen on the abdomen or on the back of the front legs. Once this practice is detected or even suspected, corrective measures should be taken. Stalling and turning the horse out where he can see other horses will help in some instances; also, giving the horse more sunshine, grass, and outdoor exercise is helpful. Another method consists in obtaining a plastic stallion ring of the proper size (they may be obtained from most breeder's supply houses in sizes to fit any horse) and fitting it snugly over the penis just back of the glans. It should be of such size that it will neither come off nor slide up the penis, yet loose enough that it does not interfere with normal circulation. The ring is removed when the horse is washed for breeding, and replaced after service. Also, it should be removed and cleaned weekly when the horse is not used for breeding. Another very effective adaptation of the same idea is the "bird cage" type of stallion ring; in addition to having a ring, this type is made to encompass completely the end of the penis.

STALLION BREEDING CONTRACT.— The stallion breeding contract should always be in writing; and the higher the stud fee, the more important it is that good business methods are practiced. Neither "gentlemen's agreements" nor "barn door records" will suffice.

A breeding contract is binding on the parties who sign it. Thus, the contract should be carefully read and fully understood before it is signed. The contract should be executed in duplicate for each mare, one copy to be retained by each party. (See sample stallion breeding contract.)

BREEDING CONTRACT

This contract for the breeding season of_____made and entered into by and between_____
                              (year)   (owner of stallion)
_____, _____, hereinafter designated stallion owner, and
                              (address)

_____, _____, hereinafter designated
        (owner of mare)   (address)
mare owner.

This contract covers—

   The stallion,_____, whose service fee is $_____; $_____ of which
                              (name of stallion)
is paid with this contract and the balance will be paid before the mare leaves_____.
                                                                              (name of farm or ranch)
and

   The mare, _____, reg. no. _____, by_____
                        (name of mare)   (sire)
out of_____, age_____, color_____.
                                                        (dam)
The mare owner agrees that—

   Upon arrival, the mare will (a) be halter broken, (b) have the hind shoes removed, and (c) be accompanied by a health certificate signed by a veterinarian, certifying that she is healthy and in sound breeding condition.

   Stallion owner will not be responsible for accident, disease, or death to the mare, or to her foal (if she has a foal).

   Stallion owner may, at his discretion, have his veterinarian (a) check and treat the mare for breeding condition or diseases, and (b) treat her for parasites if needed, with the expenses of such services charged to the mare owner's account and paid when the mare leaves the farm or ranch.

   He will pay the following board on his mare at the time the mare leaves the farm or ranch: Feed and facilities $_____ per day.

   Should the mare prove barren, or should the foal die at birth, he will send notice of same, signed by a licensed veterinarian, within 5 days of such barren determination or death.

   Should he fail to deliver the above mare to the stallion owner's premises on or before_____,
                                                                                            (date)
stallion owner shall be under no further obligation with respect to any matter herein set forth.

   This contract shall not be assigned or transferred. In the event the mare is sold, any remaining unpaid fee shall immediately become due and payable and no refund shall be due anyone under any circumstances.

The stallion owner agrees that—

   He will provide suitable facilities for the mare and feed and care for her in a good and husbandman-like manner.

   Mare owner will not be responsible for any disease, accident, or injury to stallion owner's horses.

   A live foal is guaranteed—meaning a foal that can stand up alone and nurse.

The stallion owner and mare owner mutually agree that—

   This contract is not valid unless completed in full.

   Should the above named stallion die or become unfit for service, or should the above named mare die or become unfit to breed, this contract shall become null and void and money paid as part of this contract shall be refunded to mare owner.

   Should the mare prove barren, or should the foal die at birth, with certification of same provided to stallion owner within the time specified, the stallion owner has the option either to (a) rebreed the mare the following year, or (b) refund the $_____ portion of the breeding fee, thereby cancelling this entire contract.

   The mare will not receive more than_____covers during the breeding season, and she will not be
                                          (number)
bred before_____, 19_____, or after _____, 19_____.

_____   _____   _____
   (date)   (signature, mare owner or rep.)   (address)

_____   _____   _____
   (date)   (signature, stallion owner or rep.)   (address)

STALLION STATIONS.—Recently, there has been a trend toward grouping ten to twenty stallions on a breeding farm, commonly referred to as a Stallion Station. This development has been especially strong in the Thoroughbred, Standardbred, and Quarter Horse breeds.

These highly specialized breeding establishments have the following advantages:

• It makes it convenient for an owner wishing to breed several mares to avail himself of the selection of a number of stallions.

• It is more practical to employ expert personnel to handle the breeding operations.

• It usually makes for superior facilities for this specialized purpose.

• It generally results in a higher percentage of in-foal mares, earlier conception, and more efficient use of the stallion—primarily due to more expert management; examination, and medication if necessary; and improved facilities.

As with all good things, there may be, and sometimes are, disadvantages, such as the following:

• The hazard of spreading contagious diseases is increased where there is a great concentration of horses, thus requiring extreme cleanliness and precautions.

• There is considerable expense in operating a highly specialized service of this kind.

• There is difficulty in obtaining a battery of really outstanding sires.

Fig. S-26. Laboratory at Westerly Stud, Santa Ynez, Calif. (Courtesy, **The Thoroughbred of California***)*

STALLION ENROLLMENT LAWS.—At one time, twenty-two states had stallion enrollment laws, enacted to bring about the improvement of horses and mules through the control of the public service stallions and jacks. With the decline in horse and mule numbers, some states repealed these laws; others have been lax in enforcing them. Also, the National Stallion Board was legally liquidated several years ago.

The first stallion law was passed by the legislature of Wisconsin in 1906. In 1907, Minnesota and Iowa enacted similar laws. Other states soon followed suit. Although the laws varied considerably between states, all had similar objectives. They were designed to accomplish one or more of the following things:

1. To prevent false representation as to breeding.

2. To bar heritably unsound and diseased horses.

3. To label unsound horses and jacks.

4. To eliminate the inferior sire, whether he be scrub, grade, or purebred.

STALL KICKING.—See VICES—Stall kicking.

STALL PAWING.—See VICES—Stall pawing.

STALL WALKING.—Stall walking refers to the stable vice characterized by the horse making circular trips around the stall for hours at a time. Nervousness and excess energy are the primary causes.

STANDARDBRED.—Nevele Pride established the world's trotting record for a mile at 1:54 4/5 in 1969. Steady Star set a new world's pacing record for a mile at 1:52 in 1971. Table S-8 lists the leading money-winning trotters, whereas Table S-9 lists the leading money-winning pacers. Information pertaining to the origin and characteristics of the Standardbred is presented under BREED (S). (See Fig. S-27.)

STANDARD JACK AND JENNET REGISTRY OF AMERICA.—300 Todds Road, Lexington, Kentucky 40511. (See Appendix for complete breed registry association list.)

STANDARD QUARTER HORSE ASSN.—4390 Fenton, Denver, Colorado 80212. (See Appendix

TABLE S-8

LEADING MONEY-WINNING TROTTERS THROUGH 1971

	Horse	Total Money Won	Racing Years	Owner
1.	Une De Mai	$1,425,955	1967–71	Pierre De Montesson
2.	Fresh Yankee	1,150,530	1965–71	Duncan A. MacDonald
3.	Roquepine	956,161	1963–69	Henri P. Levesque
4.	Su Mac Lad	885,095	1956–65	I. W. Berkemeyer
5.	Nevele Pride	873,238	1967–69	Nevele Acres and Louis Resnick
6.	Speedy Scot	650,909	1962–65	Castleton Farm
7.	Duke Rodney	639,408	1960–66	Patrick and Elizabeth Di Gennaro
8.	Tidalium Pelo	638,597	1966–71	Roger Lemarie
9.	Elaine Rodney	610,685	1959–68	Santipasta Stable
10.	Dayan	549,224	1968–71	Adonis Stable
11.	Tornese	546,404	1955–61	Sebastian and Salvatore Manzoni
12.	Carlisle	544,136	1965–69	L. S. Lloyds, Mary E. Miller and Martha D. Hempt
13.	Noble Victory	522,391	1964–66	K. D. Owen
14.	Grandpa Jim	501,008	1966–71	Trainor Acres

TABLE S-9

LEADING MONEY-WINNING PACERS THROUGH 1971

	Horse	Total Money Won	Racing Years	Owner
1.	Rum Customer	$1,001,548	1967–71	Kennilworth Farm and Louis and Connie Mancuso
2.	Cardigan Bay	1,000,837	1959–68	Cardigan Bay Stable and I. W. Berkemeyer
3.	Bret Hanover	922,616	1964–66	Richard Downing
4.	Laverne Hanover	868,470	1968–71	Thomas W. Murphy, Jr.
5.	Overcall	783,948	1965–69	Helen R. Buck
6.	Albatross	741,549	1970–71	Albatross Stable
7.	Henry T. Adios	706,698	1960–64	Derrico Stable
8.	Romeo Hanover	658,505	1965–67	Lucky Star Stable and Morton Finder
9.	Fulla Napoleon	582,279	1967–70	Red Sheep Stable
10.	Bye Bye Byrd	554,257	1957–61	Mr. and Mrs. R. C. Larkin
11.	Best Of All	548,899	1966–68	Samuel Huttenbauer
12.	Irvin Paul	548,518	1958–61	Abraham Wilsker and Charles King
13.	Adios Butler	509,844	1958–61	Adios Butler Syndicate
14.	Nardin's Byrd	507,341	1966–69	Trader Horn, Inc.

Fig. S-27. Greyhound, Standardbred harness race-horse, in action. With a stride exceeding 27 feet, Greyhound was often referred to as the "Silver Groomed Flyer." Trotters and pacers are of similar breeding and type, the particular gaits being largely a matter of training. Today, harness racehorses are almost exclusively of the Standardbred breed. (Courtesy, United States Trotting Association)

for complete breed registry association list.)

STANDING HALTER.—Similar to a martingale, it is a strap that runs from the girth to a tight halter on the horse's head. It helps keep the horse from throwing its head up and going into a break.

STANDING MARTINGALE.—See MARTINGALES.

STAR.—Any white mark on the forehead located above a line running from eye to eye.

(Also see COLORS AND MARKINGS OF HORSES—Fig. C-9.)

STAR AND STRIPE.—Head marking which includes both star and stripe.

(Also see COLORS AND MARKINGS OF HORSES—Fig. C-9.)

STAR GAZER.—A horse that holds its head high in an awkward position.

STAR, STRIPE AND SNIP.—All three head marks; i.e., star, stripe and snip.

(Also see COLORS AND MARKINGS OF HORSES—Fig. C-9.)

STARTING.—In starting the horse, the rider should simultaneously invoke the use of the natural aids. He should tighten the reins slightly to awake the mount to attention, bring slight pressure with the inner calf muscles, and incline the body forward. Finally, as a last resort, he may use, judiciously, one or more of the artificial aids.

STARTING GATE.—A mechanical, removable barrier at the race track used to assist the starter in securing a fast start. It was first used in Great Britain in 1900.

STATE COMMERCIAL FEED LAWS.—See FEED.

STAYER.—A horse that can perform well over a distance—a mile and a half, or farther.

STEEPLECHASER.—A horse used in cross-country racing which includes jumps.

STEEPLECHASING AND HURDLE RACING.—The steeplechase, an event two to four miles long with 10 to 30 jumps or hurdles, is a combination of running (on the turf) and jumping. It is of European origin. Steeplechasing has not captured the fancy of the general racing public at major tracks in the United States. Most steeplechasing in this country today is conducted at hunt-racing meetings.

Some of the larger American tracks have steeplechase courses inside the flat-racing oval, and present one steeplechase or hurdle event during each racing program. Tracks with courses for jumpers are Saratoga, Pimlico, Delaware Park, Belmont Park, Suffolk Downs, and Aqueduct. Nearly all tracks in Canada—more closely akin to Britain, where jumping is very popular—feature steeplechasing and hurdle racing.

Hurdle racing, technically, is over a flat course with movable hurdles, while steeplechasing is run over fixed hazards—hedges, water pools, etc.

The most famous steeplechase in the world is the annual Grand National at Aintree, England. The course is four miles and 856 yards long, and is gruelling to negotiate. In 1928, for example, 42 horses started in the Grand National and only two finished. The jumps are not the only thing which causes the pile-ups. The scramble to get safely over the first jump, in a large field, leads to many casualties, and fatigue brings others down.

The Maryland Hunt Cup, which is run on the course at Glyndon, Maryland, is the most notable American steeplechase. It was founded in 1894. English jockeys have looked askance at its stiff timber fences. To a man, they have tactfully declined an opportunity to ride the course. On a green hillside overlooking a natural amphitheater at Glyndon, ardent followers of the chase gather each spring for the Maryland Hunt Cup. It is the only race on the day's card, and the cup is the only prize.

Fig. S-28. L'escargot, great Irish Steeplechaser. Winner on both sides of the Atlantic; in Ireland and England, and in the United States. (Courtesy, Pegasus Ltd., Dublin, Ireland)

STEER ROPING (*a rodeo event*).—This event has come to the arena from the Western range where cowboys must work the cattle by roping them for branding, dehorning, and doctoring.

Steer roping horses either perform for the head roper or for the heeler. The head roper ropes the head of the steer, at which moment his horse immediately turns his rear end toward the steer and makes the rope taut; thence the heeler ropes the heels of the steer. Both horses pull in opposite directions, stretching the steer out so that it can be rolled over on its side. Next, the head roper dismounts and ties the legs of the animal so that it cannot get up.

Steer roping horses must be trained to turn around and pull on the rope. Their training consists in "logging"; that is, driving the horse with long lines while he pulls a log or other similar object on the ground. He must be taught to pull but also to stand still and keep tension on the rope to the object being dragged.

STEER WRESTLING (BULLDOGGING; *a rodeo event).*—In steer wrestling, the rider must overtake the steer, jump off his horse onto the head of the animal, and twist it to the ground so that all four feet are in the same direction.

STEPPING PACE (or **SLOW PACE**).—This is the preferred slow gait for five-gaited show horses. It is a modified pace in which the objectionable side or rolling motion of the true pace is eliminated because the two feet on each side do not move exactly together. Instead, it is a four-beat gait with each of the four feet striking the ground separately. In the take-off, the hind and front feet start almost together, but the hind foot touches the ground slightly ahead of the front foot on the same side, and each foot strikes the ground separately.

STERILE.—A term used to designate a stallion that is infertile.

STERILITY.—See MARE; and STALLION—Fertility of the stallion.

STERNUM.—The sternum or breastbone of the horse is composed of eight segments, the whole of which is shaped somewhat like a canoe. There are indentures in the sides for the reception of the cartilages extending from the ribs.

(Also see SKELETON.)

STIFLE.—The joint immediately behind the rear flank. The stifle joint in the horse is the counterpart of the knee joint in man.

(Also see PARTS OF A HORSE—Fig. P-4.)

STIFLED.—The stifle corresponds to the knee in man. A horse is said to be stifled when the patella (or kneecap) slips out of place and temporarily locks in a location above and to the inside of its normal location. Technically, this condition is known as dorsal patellar fixation. Sometimes it is possible to place the patella back in normal position manually. However, the most effective treatment is surgery, known as medical patellar desmotomy, which consists of the removal of one of the ligaments which attach to the patella.

(Also see UNSOUNDNESSES.)

STIMULANTS.—Whiskey or brandy are sometimes used as stimulants in cases of collapse or chill. However, the administration of any liquid to a horse is risky business and should be left to a professional.

(Also see DRENCHING.)

STIRRUPS.—That part of the saddle into which the rider's foot is placed. Heavy wooden stirrups, either hooded or open, are used on Western saddles, whereas light stirrups are usually used on English saddles.

Although the Greeks were accomplished horsemen as early as 500 B.C., the use of saddles and stirrups at that time was unknown. Stirrups appear to have been first used in the second century A.D., by the dreaded Huns of Attila.

(Also see SADDLES.)

"STOCKED UP" (SWOLLEN LEGS; FILLED LEGS).—See SWOLLEN LEGS.

STOCK HORSES.—Stock horses constitute the largest single class of light horses of this country; there are approximately 500,000 of them in use in the seventeen range states. They are the cow ponies of the West.

Usually, stock horses are of mixed breeding. Most generally they are descended from the Mustang—the feral horse of the United States. Subsequently, Mustang mares were mated to sires of practically every known light horse breed—especially Quarter Horses and Thoroughbreds. Stallions of the other breeds have also been used. Such grading-up has improved the size, speed,

Fig. S-29. A stock horse in action. Stock horses constitute the largest single class of light horses in this country. (Courtesy, Quarter Horse Journal)

and perhaps the appearance of the cow pony, but most horsemen will concede that no amount of improved breeding will ever produce a gamer, hardier, and more durable animal than the Mustang. In addition to being game and hardy, the stock horse must be agile, sure-footed, fast, short coupled, deep, powerfully muscled, durable, and must possess good feet and legs. Above all, the cowboy insists that his pony be a good companion and that he possess "cow sense."

STOCKING.—White extending from the coronet to the knee, and when the white includes the knee, the mark is called a full stocking.

(Also see COLORS AND MARKINGS OF HORSES—Fig. C-10.)

STOCKING (HALF).—White extending from the coronet to the middle of the cannon.

(Also see COLORS AND MARKINGS OF HORSES—Fig. C-10.)

STOCKING (Stocked up).—The term applied to swelling of the lower part of the legs, particularly the hind legs. It comes on when the animal stands in the stable. Usually, the condition can be relieved by exercise, massage, and laxative feeds.

STOCK SADDLES.—See SADDLES—Western saddle.

STOMACH.—The stomach is the enlarged part of the alimentary canal which lies between the esophagus and the small intestine. It holds 8 to 16 quarts (but it functions best at two-thirds capacity); and it secretes gastric juices by which proteins and fats are broken down.

At the time of eating, feed passes through the horse's stomach very rapidly—so much so that feed eaten at the beginning of the meal passes to the intestine before the last part of the meal is completed.

Some basic differences between the stomach of the horse and the stomach of the ruminant are:

The ruminant has four compartments (rumen, reticulum, omasum, and the abomasum or true stomach), whereas the horse has one.

The stomach capacity of the horse is much smaller—8 to 16 quarts for the mature horse as opposed to about 200 quarts for the mature cow. Because of its small stomach, if a horse is fed too much roughage, labored breathing and quick tiring may result. Actually the horse's stomach is designed for almost constant intake of small quantities of feed, (such as happens when a horse is out grazing on pasture) rather than large amounts at one time.

Without feed, the horse's stomach will empty completely in twenty-four hours, whereas it takes about seventy-two hours (three times as long) for the ruminant's stomach to empty.

There is comparatively little microbial action in the stomach of the horse, but much such action in the stomach (rumen) of the ruminant.

STOMACH WORMS (Habronema spp., Trichostrongylus axei).—A group of parasitic worms that produces inflammation of the stomach.

SYMPTOMS.—Horses suffer loss of condition and severe gastritis. Sometimes, the larvae of large stomach worms are partially responsible for the skin disease of horses called summer sores.

TREATMENT.—Probably the best drug to use for Habronema spp. is carbon disulfide. Dosage and administration should be determined by a veterinarian. No drugs have been tested adequately against Trichostrongylus axei, the small stomach worm.

PREVENTION AND CONTROL.—Provide good sanitation, proper manure disposal, and fly control.

DISCUSSION.—Stomach worms attack horses throughout the United States. Wasted feed and lowered efficiency are the chief losses.

(Also see DISEASES AND PARASITES; HEALTH PROGRAM; and PARASITES OF HORSES.)

STONE IN THE FOOT.—Stone puncture wounds are rather common, probably with the object lodged between the shoe and frog or bar. If no hoof pick is available, it can be dislodged by hammering with another stone or by means of a metal English stirrup. Always remove a stone by driving it in the direction of the toe rather than toward the heel, because it is easy to inflict injury on the structure of the hoof by forcing an instrument into the heel. Usually, the horse will go sound once the stone is removed. However, if there is a puncture wound, treatment may be necessary.

(Also see FIRST AID FOR HORSES—Wounds.)

STOPPING.—The rider stops the horse by pulling back on the reins in slow and repeated movements, by releasing the pressure the instant the animal shows signs of obedience, and by repeating the action as often as necessary to bring him to a dead stop. At the same time, the rider, without standing up, puts his weight evenly into both stirrups and leans slightly backward.

STRAIGHT SHOULDER.—A condition resulting from overstressing a muscle or tendon.
(Also see SPRAINS.)

STRAIN.—A condition resulting from overstressing a muscle or tendon.
(Also see SPRAINS.)

STRANGLES.—See DISTEMPER (STRANGLES).

STRAW (FOR BEDDING).—Cereal straw (wheat, barley, oats, or rye) is the most common type of horse bedding in Central and Western United States. When chopped, straws are more absorbent. Cut straw, from comparable material, will absorb twenty-five percent more water than long straw. But chopped straw may be dusty. Sometimes horses eat straw bedding. When the latter happens, it may be necessary to use such products as shavings or peat moss, or to muzzle the animal.

(Also see BEDDING.)

STRAY.—An animal that has wandered into a herd.

STRESS.—This refers to any physical or emotional factor to which the horse fails to make a satisfactory adaptation. Stress may be caused by excitement, temperament, fatigue, shipping, disease, heat or cold, nervous strain, number of horses together, previous nutrition, breed, age, or management. Race and show horses are always under stress; and the more tired they are and the greater the speed, the greater the stress. Also, the greater the stress, the more exacting the nutritive requirements.

STRETCHING.—Saddle and harness horses are taught to stand or pose in a stretched position when standing. This practice originated with ladies' harness horses before the advent of the automobile; and there was a very practical reason for it. A horse that is stretched cannot move forward or backward until he collects himself. Hence, such a pose tended to insure that the horse or horses stood still while milady stepped into her phaeton or Victoria.

The stretched position of the horse will vary according to the breed. For example, when shown in hand, American Saddlers are stood with their front legs straight and their hind legs back, whereas Arabians are not stretched. Other breeds are usually stood in a slightly stretched position; somewhat intermediate between these two examples.

STRIDE.—The distance covered by one foot when in motion. Greyhound, great Standardbred trotter, had a stride of more than 27 feet.

STRIKING.—Sometimes this vice occurs in fearful or mean horses. When the attendant does something that the horse doesn't like, he reacts with a sudden slap of one or both front feet. If this action is accompanied by a leap forward, watch out!

STRINGHALT.—Stringhalt is characterized by excessive flexing of the hind legs. It is most easily detected when backing a horse. The condition may be cured or greatly relieved by a surgical operation on the lateral extensor tendon. An incision is made over the tendon on the outside of the leg just below the hock, and about two inches of the tendon is removed.

(Also see UNSOUNDNESSES.)

STRIPE.—A narrow white marking that extends from about the line of the eyes to the nostrils.

(Also see COLORS AND MARKINGS OF HORSES—Fig. C-9.)

STRONGYLES, LARGE AND SMALL (Strongylus spp. and OTHERS).—There are about 60 species of strongyles. Three kinds are large worms that grow up to 2 inches long. The rest are small and some are barely visible to the eye. Large strongyles are variously called bloodworms (Strongylus vulgaris), palisade worms, sclerostomes, and red worms.

SYMPTOMS.—Infected horses have lack of appetite, anemia, progressive emaciation, a rough haircoat, sunken eyes, digestive disturbances including colic, a tucked-up appearance, and sometimes posterior paralysis and death. Collectively these symptoms indicate the disease known as strongylosis. Harmful effects are greatest in young animals. One species of large strongyles (Strongylus vulgaris) may permanently damage the intestinal blood vessel wall and cause death at any age.

TREATMENT.—Use mebendazole; thiabendazole; phenothiazine + piperazine; phenothiazine + piperazine-1-carbodithioic acid; dithiazanine + piperazine; trichlorfon; or dichlorvos. The decision as to which drugs to use and the dosage level should be made by a veterinarian.

Fig. S-30. Horse with strongyle infection. (Courtesy, Department of Veterinary Pathology and Hygiene, College of Veterinary Medicine, University of Illinois)

PREVENTION AND CONTROL.—Gather manure daily from pastures and barns and store it in a pit 2 to 3 weeks. Rotate pastures and avoid moist pasture and over-stocking.

DISCUSSION.—Strongyles attack horses throughout the United States wherever horses are pastured. Attacks of strongyles result in loss of feed due to feeding the worms, lowered work efficiency, ratarded growth of young animals, lowered breeding efficiency, and death in severe infections.

(Also see DISEASES AND PARASITES; HEALTH PROGRAM; and PARASITES OF HORSES.)

STRONGYLOIDES.—See THREADWORM.

STUD.—1. A male horse (stallion) kept for breeding.

2. An establishment or farm where animals are kept for breeding.

STUD BOOK.—The registry in which each breed of horses is recorded is known as the Stud Book.

STUD FEES.—Fees which the owner collects for a stallion's breeding services. Generally stud fees are on the basis of guaranteeing a live foal, which means that the foal must stand and nurse; otherwise, the stud fee is either refunded or not collected, or the stallion owner agrees to rebreed the mare the following year; according to the stipulations in the contract (see STALLION—Stallion Breeding Contract).

There is a wide range in stud fees, depending on the popularity of the stallion. The service fee on an unknown stallion may be as low as $50, or less. The Arabian stallion *Naborr, which sold for $150,000 in 1969, has been standing at a fee of $10,000. With syndicated stallions, a common rule of thumb is that the stud fee is one-fourth each syndicate share. On this basis, it may be conjectured that the stud fee of Secretariat (1973 Triple Crown Winner, and world record $6,080,000 horse) would be $47,500 (32 shares at $190,000 each; hence $190,000 ÷ 4 = $47,500).

STUMBLING.—When a horse trips and falls to his knees (usually no further), it is known as stumbling. Stumbling is usually caused by poor shoeing, faulty conformation, unsoundness, rundown condition, fatigue, poor horsemanship, and/or lack of balance. Additionally, some horses just don't seem to care; they travel so close to the ground that they will stumble on relatively level ground. Whatever the cause, a horse is more apt to stumble when at the walk than at a trot or canter, simply because he is more relaxed when walking and less "on the bit."

Stumbling is a hazard to both the rider and the horse; hence, it should be corrected if at all possible. Moreover, one should not knowingly buy a stumbling horse. If there are scars on the knees, stumbling should be suspected; and the cause should be determined.

STUMP SUCKING.—See VICES—Cribber.

STYLE.—This refers to the attractiveness with which the horse displays himself at all times. Good carriage of the head, active ears, an alert, active disposition, and beauty of conformation are factors contributing to the style of the horse. This quality is important in show horses.

(Also see SELECTING HORSES.)

SUBCUTANEOUS.—Under the skin.

SUBSTANCE.—A combination of good bone, muscularity, and width and depth of body. These characteristics are important because they are indicative of hardiness, ruggedness, and stamina.

SUCKLING.—A foal that is not weaned.

SUDAN.—Sudan and hybrid Sudans in the growing stage should never be grazed by horses, because of the hazard of cystitis. This disease, which occurs more frequently in mares than in stallions or geldings, is characterized by continuous urination, mares appearing to be constantly in heat, and incoordination in the gait. Animals seldom recover after either the incoordination or the dribbling of urine become evident. Apparently, hay from Sudan or hybrid Sudans will not produce the same malady.

SUFFOLK.—See BREED (S).

SUGAR AND HONEY.—The horse has a "sweet tooth"; or at least he readily cultivates a taste for sweets. Hence, when added to the ration, sugar and honey make for a "sweet feed," or appetizer. For this reason, small amounts (usually about five percent) of sugar or honey are sometimes added to the concentrate mixtures of racehorses, show horses, and finicky eaters. Once a horse becomes accustomed to a sweet feed, it is difficult to eliminate it from the ration; in fact, if the sweets are suddenly deleted, the horse may refuse to eat altogether. Thus, if for any reason sweets must be taken out of the ration, the change should be very gradual.

Also, sugar cubes are a good and convenient reward, provided too many of them are not used and the tendency of nipping or biting is avoided.

Some trainers add 1 to 2 pounds of high quality glucose (sugar) to the ration of racehorses on the morning of the race, as a source of readily available energy.

(Also see TREATS.)

SULFA DRUG (SULFONAMIDE).—A synthetic organic drug which has the ability to inhibit the growth of, or to destroy, microorganisms.

SULKY OR BIKE.—Light racing rig with bicycle-type wheels used in harness races. The sulkies weigh from 29 to 37 pounds, and usually have hardwood shafts, although aluminum and steel sulkies have been introduced recently.

(Also see HARNESS—Figs. H-4 and H-5; and VEHICLES, HORSE-DRAWN.)

SUNFLOWER MEAL.—The development of high oil-yielding varieties by Russian scientists has stirred worldwide interest in the use of sunflowers as an oil seed crop. Some of these varieties yield over fifty percent oil.

Sunflower meal (forty-one percent protein or better) can be used as a protein supplement for horses provided (1) it is good quality, and (2) care is taken to supply adequate lysine, for sunflower meal is low in this amino acid. When incorporated in well-balanced rations, properly processed sunflower meal of good quality may supply up to one-third of the protein supplement of horses.

SUPPLING EXERCISES (for the horse, and for the rider).—This refers to exercises designed to make for greater flexibility. Such exercises will improve both the horse and the rider.

Suppling will improve the balance of a horse and make him more flexible and more obedient to the will of the rider. Among the various suppling exercises recommended for the horse are: bending his neck, raising and lowering his head, bending his croup, and carrying his legs further under him than nature intended.

A good horseman is characterized by his ability to regain his balance when the horse swerves, bucks, or makes some other sudden motion. Among the suppling exercises recommended to improve the flexibility of the rider are: bending forward and touching the toes while the horse is in motion, raising the hands high in the air, rotating the head and rotating the body from the hips, lying back until the head rests on the croup, and turning completely around in the saddle. In addition to making for a more flexible rider, such suppling exercises instill confidence in timid riders.

SUPPORTIVE TREATMENT.—Treatment of individual symptoms of a disease where diagnosis is obscure or where a specific treatment has not been established.

SURCINGLE.—A belt, band, or girth passing around a horse's body behind the withers.

SURREY.—A four-wheeled carriage, with a straight, or nearly straight, bottom.

SUSPENDER.—See HARNESS—Figs. H-4 and H-5.

SUSPENSORY LIGAMENT SPRAIN.—The suspensory ligament is situated over the back of the leg and passes over the fetlock or ankle joint, both in the fore and hind legs. Its principal function is to support the fetlock. This ligament is frequently the object of severe strain; the swelling begins just above the ankle and extends obliquely downward and forward over the sides of the ankle. Should the injury be further up on the leg, the exact location at first may appear obscure as the ligament is covered by the flexor tendons.

When the suspensory ligament is affected, the swelling will be found right up against the bone. If it is the flexor tendons that are involved, the swelling will be further back near the surface on the back of the leg.

The front legs are more frequently affected than the hind legs; except in the Standardbred breed, where suspensory ligament injury most commonly occurs in the hind legs.

SWAMP FEVER.—See EQUINE INFECTIOUS ANEMIA (SWAMP FEVER).

SWAN NECK.—A long, slim, swanlike neck.

"SWAP HORSES IN MIDSTREAM".—Upon being congratulated when renominated for the presidency, Lincoln said: "I do not allow myself to suppose that either the convention or the league have concluded to decide that I am either the greatest or the best man in America, but rather they have concluded it is not best to swap horses while crossing the river, and have further concluded that I am not so poor a horse that they might not make a botch of it in trying to swap." One historian of that period credited the utterance to a Dutch farmer; and H.L. Mencken reports that the phrase was used some twenty-four years earlier.

SWAYBACKED.—Having a decided dip in the back. Also termed "easy-backed" and "saddle-backed."

SWAYING.—A vacillating motion, particularly in the hindquarters, is known as swaying. Such a deviation from normal stride or movement is meaningful to a horseman. It may indicate kidney trouble or intestinal trouble (such as poisoning or a twisted gut). When a horse is swaying the veterinarian should be called at once.

SWEATING.—Perspiration, or sweating, is the natural result of normal exercise in warm weather or excessive exercise in any temperature. Horses that are soft, and not in condition, will sweat more than others. Also, nervous horses will often sweat even when they're in good condition.

Sweating should be used as a guide to the amount of work that a horse can stand; when sweating becomes excessive, it's time for a rest. Also, the salt lost in sweating during warm weather should be replaced; otherwise, the animal may suffer from heat exhaustion. A horse that is hot and sweaty should be cooled out gradually and allowed to drink only a little water at a time.

Any sudden breaking out in sweat that is not due to exercise is reason for concern. It may be a sign of either azoturia or of "tying up." Likewise, sudden cessation of sweating while a horse is hard at work is a sign of trouble. A veterinarian should be called when such warning signals appear.

SWEAT SCRAPER.—A half-moon-shaped strip of metal or wood to which a handle is attached. This article is useful for the quick removal of the outer layer of excessive sweat following a workout. The edge may have a projecting rubber piece attached, the use of which avoids damage to body prominences and tender spots.

SWEENEY.—A depression in the shoulder due to atrophied muscles is known as sweeney. Sweeney is caused by nerve injury. No known treatment will restore the nerve, but it is possible to fill in the depression by injecting irritants into the affected area.

(Also see UNSOUNDNESSES.)

SWEEPSTAKES.—A race in which the winner takes all.

SWEET FEED.—See FEED, SWEET.

SWING TEAM.—The middle team in a six-horse hitch, or the team in front of the wheelers in an eight-horse hitch.

SWOLLEN LEGS (FILLED LEGS; "STOCKED UP").—Although this term is not scientific, it is well understood by horsemen to mean a condition in which there is more or less swelling of the legs. The legs return almost to normal with exercise, then "fill" again after the animal has been in the stable for some time. The best treatment is the application of cotton-wadding bandages immediately after the horse returns from work, and hand-rubbing. It is evident that efforts should be made to prevent the occurrence, and to lessen the amount of the swelling because it interferes with the blood supply to the swollen part. Before the horse is taken out again, the cotton-wadding bandages should be removed, and the legs should be hand-rubbed.

SYMMETRY.—Symmetry is usually used along with the word "balance." Balance and symmetry refer to the harmonious development of all parts. With the full development of all important parts, which are nicely blended together, the horse will present an attractive appearance.

SYNDICATED HORSES.—Reduced to simple terms, a syndicated horse is one that is owned by several people. Most commonly, it's a stallion; although an expensive yearling or broodmare is sometime syndicated. Also, any number of people can form a syndicate. However, there is a tendency to use the term "partnership" where two to four owners are involved, and to confine the word "syndicate" to a larger group of owners.

Each member of the syndicate owns a certain number of "shares," depending on how much he purchased or contributed. It's much like a stock market investor, who may own one or several shares of General Electric, IBM, or some other company. Sometimes one person may own as much as half-interest in a horse. Occasionally, half-shares are sold.

Generally speaking, the number of shares in a stallion is limited to the number of mares that may reasonably be bred to him in one season—usually 30 to 35 with Thoroughbred stallions.

Fig. S-31. The syndicated stallion, Nashua, with Mr. Leslie B. Combs II (left), Spendthrift Farm. Mr. Combs has probably contributed more than any other person to stallion syndication. When he syndicated Nashua, he sold all but one share of a total of 32, each at $39,100 (for a total of $1,251,200), over the telephone one afternoon; and the only reason that the one share was not sold until the next morning was that he couldn't reach one of his regular clients on the telephone the previous afternoon. (Courtesy, Spendthrift Farm)

In a syndication, liability is mutually shared; that is, all parties are mutually or fully responsible for the liabilities of the syndicate. However, the syndicate is not liable for personal, as distinct from syndicate, debts. Syndicate agreements may be written in practically any form desired by the partners. For example, the services of a syndicated sire and the expenses for his keep may be shared according to shares (investment) just as contributions to any other partnership in the form of capital, labor, and management may be shared in any proportions.

WHY AND HOW OWNERS SYNDICATE.— The owner of a stallion that has raced successfully usually has the opportunity to choose between: (1) continuing as sole owner of the horse, and standing him for service privately or publicly, or (2) syndicating him. In recent years, more and more owners of top stallions have elected to syndicate. The most common reasons for so doing are:

• The stallion owner does not have a breeding farm or an extensive band of broodmares.

• The owner believes that the stallion under consideration may not nick well with many of his mares; or perhaps the stallion is closely related to the mares.

• The owner has need for immediate income.

• Syndicating spreads the risk, should the stallion get injured or die, or prove unsuccessful as a sire.

The owner may arrange the syndication himself, usually with competent legal advice; or, if preferred, the syndication can be turned over to a professional manager, who will generally take a free share as his organization fee.

The following pointers are pertinent to successful syndication of stallions:

● *Check fertility.*—Before syndicating, it is a good idea to check the fertility by test-mating to a cold-blooded (draft) mare. Of course, if the stallion is still racing, and has not been retired to stud, this is impossible.

● *Establish stud fee.*—A common rule of thumb is that each syndicate share is worth four times the stud fee. Hence, if it is decided that the stallion under consideration will command a $5,000 stud fee, each share would be worth $20,000. If thirty shares are involved, the horse would have a value of $600,000 for syndication purposes.

● *Determine time of payment.*—In most cases, payment is due upon the signing of the syndicate contract, although some contracts (1) allow 30, 60, or 90 days, or (2) provide that the price of a share may be paid on the installment plan over a two- or three-year-period.

● *Put it in writing.*—Syndication agreements should be clear, detailed, and in writing.

SYRINGE (S).—A syringe is a device used to inject fluids into or withdraw from the body. They come in many sizes. Syringes should always be kept sterile, and used only under the supervision of a veterinarian.

T

TACK.—Tack includes all articles of gear, or equipment, that are used on or attached to riding and driving horses. Each horse should have his own saddle, bridle, halter, and lead shank so they can be adjusted to fit.

For greatest enjoyment, a horseman should have the proper tack and clothing and learn to ride correctly.

Superior quality tack usually is cheaper in the long run.

(See alphabetical listing of different tack items.)

TACK, CARE OF.—Good tack is expensive and should have good care. If it is properly cared for, it will last for years.

Ideally, each article should be cleaned thoroughly every time it is used on a horse. However, the owner or caretaker of pleasure horses may not have time to do this. A busy person, therefore, should clean the vital parts after each use and then thoroughly clean all tack once a week. After each use, the underside of the saddle and the inside of the bridle should be cleaned; the bit should be washed; and the pad or blanket, if used, should be brushed after it has dried out and before it is reused.

All tack used on race and show horses should be thoroughly cleaned after each use.

Proper cleaning of tack will:

• Extend the life of leather and metal.

Fig. T-1. Cleaning the saddle. (Courtesy, **Western Horseman,** *Colorado Springs, Colorado)*

- Make leather soft and pliable.
- Help keep the horse comfortable. He will get fewer saddle and harness sores than he will from dirty, crusted, or stiff leather and less irritation and infection than he will from a rusty, moldy, or dirty bit.
- Assure that minor tack defects are noticed and repaired before they become serious. This lessens the likelihood of breaking a rein or line, girth, girth strap, stirrup leather, or other vital part.
- Give pride and pleasure in the ownership and use of tack; the horse, rider or driver, and tack will all look good.

EQUIPMENT FOR CLEANING.—The following items of cleaning equipment are commonly used:

- A saddle rack on which to clean the saddle. Preferably, the rack should be designed to hold the saddle with either the seat up or the bottom up so both sides can be easily cleaned.
- A bridle rack, peg, or hook on which to hang the bridle for cleaning.
- A rack for cleaning harness, if harness is used.
- A bucket for warm water.

- Three sponges, preferably, although one sponge is enough if it is rinsed properly—one sponge for washing off sweat and dirt, another for applying leather preservative or glycerine soap, and a third for occasional application of neat's-foot or similar oil.
- A chamois cloth for drying off leather.
- About a yard of cheese cloth for applying metal polish.
- A flannel rag for polishing.
- Saddle soap or castile soap for cleaning.
- A leather preservative or glycerine soap for finishing.
- Neat's-foot or similar oil.
- Metal polish.
- Petroleum jelly.

HOW TO CLEAN.—To assure that all parts of all articles of tack are properly cleaned, some practical order of cleaning should be followed. Any order that works is satisfactory.

Once a week all leather should be washed with saddle soap or castile soap as described in the section on washing the saddle and then neat's-foot oil or other leather dressing should be lightly applied. Do not use too much oil; it will darken new leather and soil clothing.

Wooden parts of equipment may be sanded, varnished, and waxed whenever necessary.

The following order of cleaning is suggested for the saddle, bridle, and saddle pad or blanket:

- *The saddle.*—Clean the saddle as follows:
1. Remove the girth and clean it first, the same way the rest of the saddle is cleaned.
2. Turn the saddle upside down and wash the panel (the part of the saddle that touches the horse's back) and the gullet (the underside center of the saddle). Use a sponge that has been wetted in warm water and wrung out to apply saddle soap to the leather. Rub the leather well to work up a stiff lather that will remove sweat and dirt before it hardens. Wash until clean.
3. Turn the saddle over and wash the rest of it the same way.
4. Dry the saddle with chamois.
5. Dampen a clean sponge slightly and apply leather preservative or glycerine soap without suds to all parts of the saddle.

- *The bridle.*—Clean the bridle as follows:
1. Wash the bit in warm water.
2. Clean the leather parts the same way the

saddle was cleaned.

3. Use a cheesecloth to apply metal polish to all metal parts of the bridle and then use a flannel cloth to polish them. If the bridle is not to be used for several days, clean and dry the bit and then apply a light coat of petroleum jelly to keep it from pitting or rusting.

● *The blanket or pad.*—Clean blankets and pads as follows:

1. Hang up or spread out blankets and pads to dry.

2. When dry, brush off hair and dried sweat.

● *After cleaning.*—Handle tack as follows after cleaning:

1. Store all tack in a cool, dry place.

2. Hang the bridle on its rack so all parts drape naturally without bending.

3. Put the saddle on its rack.

4. Cover the saddle, bridle, and harness (if harness is used).

● *The vehicle.*—Carts, sulkies, buckboards, and viceroys should be kept clean at all times. If vehicles are to be used in the show-ring, they should be washed a few hours ahead. Then apply metal polish to chrome, and wipe enamel wood finish with soft, dry flannel. Upholstering should be brushed, vacuumed, or washed—according to the material.

TACK ROOM.—Place for storage of bridles, saddles, other equipment, and accessories used in horseback riding. Also a display room for pictures, prizes, ribbons, trophies, and the like.

Fig. T-2. Tack room of Dwight Murphy's San Marcos Ranch, Santa Ynez Valley, Calif. Note the large natural color paintings by Nicholas S. Ferfires, depicting the different costumes and saddles of riders and the beautiful silver decorated saddles used in parades on the noted Palominos of San Marcos Ranch. (Photo by John H. Williamson, Arcadia, Calif.)

TACK APPOINTMENTS.—This refers to the specific types of tack required in certain horse show classes. For information relative to the appointments required in each class, the exhibitor should refer to the *Rule Book* of the American Horse Shows Association or the show catalog.

TACKLE, BREAKING.—See BREAKING TACKLE.

TAG.—One of the many games that may be played on horseback. The person who is "it" should be required to tag the rider, not the horse. There are many variations and kinds of tag. In Chinese tag, the one who is tagged must keep one hand on that place until he tags someone else. In cross-tag, if a rider passes between the chaser and the one being chased, the chaser must leave his original quarry and pursue the new one. Beginners should play tag at the walk; intermediate riders may play it at the trot; whereas advanced riders may play it at a gallop.

TAIL.—The horse's tail is the appendage at the end of the spine, consisting of an average of eighteen coccygeal vertebrae. Nature ordained certain breed differences in tails. Also, custom has decreed that certain breeds be clipped and sheared in distinct haircuts and hair styles. Some of these differences, natural and artificial, follow.

Hackneys.—Hackneys are docked, which means that a part of the solid portion of the tail is removed. This fashion dates to the Gay Nineties, when, driven by ladies, bob-tailed Hackneys attached to high-seated rigs made a dashing picture as they pranced down the avenue. The tails were docked because, so the argument went, it wasn't safe for a woman to drive a horse whose tail was long, because some horses panic if they get their tail over the lines.

American Saddle Horses and Tennessee Walking Horses.—The tails of American Saddlers and Tennessee Walkers are set by cutting the two large muscles that pull the tail down, followed by putting the tail in a contraption known as a tail-set. Also, wigs (false tails) are frequently used on such horses. The objective is to get the much sought waterfall form of tail seen in American Saddlers and Tennessee Walkers. The practice of setting the tails of animals of these two breeds arose from the thinking that high-set natural tails and strong backs go together; hence, by setting tails man has attempted to improve on nature.

Quarter Horses.—The tails of Quarter Horses are shortened to about hock length and shaped by pulling. Some ropers claim that this keeps the tail off the rope. Perhaps, too, Quarter Horse enthusiasts wish to avoid any possibility of having their mounts identified with broomtails (wild horses, which usually have long and full tails). Whatever the reason, most western stock horses of all breeds are accorded a similar trim.

Thoroughbreds.—Thoroughbreds and their kin (hunters, jumpers, and polo ponies) are supposed to have fine, thin tails; hence, if nature fails, man applies the comb.

(Also see GROOMING A HORSE—Fig. G-3.)

TAIL (*banged or thinned*).—A tail is banged if the hair is cut off in a straight line below the dock; it is thinned if it is shortened; and it is thinned and tapered if the hairs are pulled and broken.

TAILBOARD (S).—A tailboard is a board projecting from the wall of the stall high enough to strike the rubbing horse at the point of the buttock (the point that sticks farthest out behind), instead of the tail. It should extend around the entire stall, including the door. Tailboards are almost always needed for horses that wear tail-sets. But they need not be installed for other horses unless the need arises.

SPECIFICATIONS.—A 2" x 12" plank, securely bracketed to project 12 inches out from the wall.

TAIL FEMALE.—The female, or bottom line of a pedigree.

TAIL MALE.—The sire line, or top line, in a

pedigree.

TAIL RUBBING.—See VICES—Tail Rubbing.

TAIL-SET.—A crupper-like contrivance, with a shaped section for the tail, which brings the tail high so that it can be doubled and tied down, to give it an "arch" and extremely high carriage; but a tail so set must first be "nicked" to give such results. The set is worn most of the time while the horse is in the stable, and until a short time before the horse is to be shown. Horses with "set" tails are usually "gingered" before entering the ring, in order to assure high tail carriage while being shown.

TAKEOFF.—The rise or leap from the ground in making a jump. There are two schools of thought relative to who should determine take-off—the horse, or the rider. Some expert jumpers feel that the horse should be allowed to do what comes naturally—that he should be permitted to make his own decision. Others of equal expertise argue that the rider knows best. Caprilli, the great Italian master who introduced forward-seat riding to the world, insisted that the rider should signal for the takeoff. Other proponents of signalling clinch their argument by pointing out that, unless signalled, many horses tend to take off too close or too far from the obstacle. Perhaps, knowingly or unknowingly, most good rider-horse combinations use a team approach—together they determine the takeoff.

TALLY-HO.—The cry sounded by hunters upon sighting the fox as it breaks from cover.

TANDEM.—Said of two horses, one hitched in front of the other. This hitch originated in hunting countries where the meets were often some distance and the horseman wished to get to the hunt without tiring his hunter. So, he hitched his hunter in the lead, where he trotted along with slack traces, while a plodding wheeler pulled the cart with a large box or crate of hounds under a high seat. It is noteworthy that driving tandem is far more difficult than driving two horses as a team, because the driver has little control over the leader.

As the use of tandem hitches became stylish, classes for them were included in horse shows. Today, there are tandem horse show classes for Hackneys or Hackney Ponies, to be shown to a suitable two- or four-wheeled vehicle. The wheel pony must be of proper size for the shafts and possess substance and power; the lead pony is smaller and notable for brilliance of action, beauty, and smartness. Also, there are tandem classes for hunters under saddle, in which the pair of hunters work single file.

TAPADERA.—A long, decorative covering over the stirrup used in parade classes.

TAPEWORMS (*Anoplocephala magna, A. perfoliata, Paranoplocephala mamillana*).—*Anopacephala perfoliata* is the most common and most damaging of the three species of tapeworms found in horses.

SYMPTOMS.—Heavy infections may cause digestive disturbances, loss in weight, and anemia.

TREATMENT.—Traditional treatments are areca nut, kamala, and oleoresin of male fern; no modern effective drugs have been developed for treatment of tapeworm infections in horses.

PREVENTION AND CONTROL.—Provide good sanitation and husbandry, proper manure disposal, and clean bedding.

DISCUSSION.—Tapeworms attack horses throughout the northern part of the United States. Losses are primarily in wasted feed and retarded growth.

(Also see DISEASES AND PARASITES; HEALTH PROGRAM; and PARASITES OF HORSES.)

TARPAN.—Though now extinct, the Tarpan—a small dun-colored, genuine wild species of horse—was formerly abundant everywhere in southern Russia and Central Asia. These animals were hated by the farmers because they devoured their crops and especially because the Tarpan stallions constantly recruited domestic mares for their wild bands. For these reasons, they were killed off by the Russians, finally being completely exterminated by the year 1870.

TATTERSALL.—1. A gaily colored vest worn for riding and hunting.

2. Also, Tattersall refers to the famous sales conducted by a Blood Stock Agency in England.

TATTOO.—See IDENTIFICATION.

TAXES, INCOME.—The tax information that follows pertains specifically to horsemen, so that they may be aware of the implications involved, and so that they may take steps to avoid certain pitfalls. Also, horsemen are admonished to consult a competent tax advisor before embarking upon any sizeable horse operation.

CASH VS. ACCRUAL METHOD.—There are two standard methods of reporting, the cash basis and the accrual basis. Most horsemen use the cash basis, in which income is reported when it is actually received and expenses are recorded when actually paid. It does not include the value of products sold or services performed for which payment was not actually available during the taxable year. In addition to being simple and easy, the cash basis has the advantage of allowing the horseman partially to control his income for tax purposes by timing year-end payment of expenses.

From a management standpoint, however, the accrual basis is preferred because it more nearly reflects the income of a particular period. Under it, income is accounted for when it is earned and expenses are recorded when incurred rather than when paid. Also, the accrual basis necessitates that complete annual inventories be kept, with taxes paid on increases of inventory, and deductions made for any decreases in inventory.

On large horse establishments, it is recommended that both record systems be used—the cash basis for tax purposes, and the accrual basis for management purposes. A competent accountant can set up such a system with the same set of records simply by adding a few memo accounts that are removed at the end of the year when closing the books for tax purposes.

HOBBY OR BUSINESS?—The first real hazard, and one which should be avoided unless it really applies, is that participation in the horse business—whether in breeding, racing, training, and/or showing—may be regarded by the Internal Revenue Service (IRS), as indulgence in a hobby or diversion rather than a true business venture, with the result that any losses accruing therefrom are disallowed in their entirety. This should cause no concern to those who derive their entire living from the horse business or to those successful horsemen who normally operate at a profit. Rather, it is the person of independent means, or one who is profitably engaged in another enterprise or other enterprises, who is likely to be challenged when he or she has an unbroken string of loss years accruing from breeding, racing, and/or showing operations. Also, IRS does not automatically take cognizance of the fact that breeding programs designed to develop a new breed of horses, or even to build up a herd, take many years. It is essential, therefore, that the horseman establish a profit-making motive and a reasonable chance of achieving this aim. Then, he must conduct his operations in a businesslike manner throughout, and refrain from anything that may cause his actions even to be suspicioned as pursuit of a hobby rather than the conducting of a business.

In breeding, racing, training, and/or showing horses, a fine line often separates a hobby from a business. Moreover, a hobby sometimes turns out to be a profitable venture to the point that the taxpayer may turn it into a business.

It is important to the taxpayer that the facts and circumstances support the premise that he entered into the activity with the *intent* of making a profit. The regulations list different factors which are relevant, no one of which is conclusive or exclusive in making a determination. These factors are:

● History of income or losses.

● High ratio of expenses to receipts, or a declining loss ratio.

● Amount of occasional profits or losses, and their relation to the amount of investment and value of the assets used in the activity.

● Cause of the losses.

● Success of the taxpayer in carrying on other activities.

- Financial status of the taxpayer.
- Time and effort expended by taxpayer in the horse activity.
- Expertise of the taxpayer or his consultant.
- Manner in which the taxpayer carries on the activity.
- Reasonableness of the expectation of profit by the taxpayer.
- Expectation of appreciation of value of assets used.
- Elements involved of personal pleasure or recreation.
- Personal pleasure derived is not conclusive of hobby.

In addition to the items listed above, a review of decided cases produces the following additional important elements for consideration:

- Lack of any other occupation.
- Lack of recreational facilities and absence of social functions at the business location.
- Good, complete, accurate, and separate records of the business and finances.
- Membership and active participation in breed organizations.
- Advertising to develop a market for surplus horses.
- Preparation of cost studies and comparison with trade averages to implement changing methods for better financial results.
- Continuous budgets, and income and expense projections, to move toward lower losses and larger profits.
- Culling of undesirable animals.
- Boarding of horses if it will help generate more income.
- Racing or showing in order to earn purses and premiums and to advertise the business.
- Making additional capital investments and improvements if they may be expected to increase income.
- Finally, if you are satisfied that you cannot make a profit, quit.

It is emphasized that the matter of *intent* is paramount. Generally speaking, taxpayers who meet, to a reasonable degree, the above points can, if necessary, prove to the courts their "intent to show a profit from a business venture."

Proof of *intent* is especially difficult if (1) the taxpayer is wealthy and over a period of years has sustained heavy losses sufficient to put an average horseman out of business, or (2) there is some interest connected with the horse enterprise of greater importance in the taxpayer's scheme of life than making a profit. Indeed, these two points tend to indicate an expensive hobby, rather than a business.

PROFIT 2 YEARS OUT OF A CONSECUTIVE 7 YEARS.—The horseman is expected to make a profit 2 years out of the 7 consecutive years; that is, there will be a presumption in favor of the taxpayer if this situation prevails. Otherwise, he will likely be challenged by the Internal Revenue Service, and the venture may be classed as a hobby.

The government has the burden of proof that the activity is not a business if the taxpayer makes a profit in any 2 years out of a consecutive 7 years; otherwise, the burden is still upon the taxpayer.

HOLDING PERIOD (TIME OWNED) ON BOUGHT HORSES.—To be eligible for capital gain treatment, purchased (or gift) horses, including racing and show horses, must be held 24 months. (Cattle must be held 24 months, also. Swine and sheep need be held only 12 months.)

RAISED HORSES.—Raised horses for cash method taxpayers have a "zero" tax basis. Hence, all proceeds on disposition of eligible animals are a gain to be treated as capital gain.

CAPITAL GAIN.—Since capital gain is not taxed nearly so heavily as ordinary income, it behooves horsemen to report the maximum thereunder permitted by law. For an individual horseman with up to $50,000 long-term capital gain, the tax rate is 25%; for over $50,000 it is 35%. For corporations, capital gain tax is 30%.

LIMITATION ON LOSSES.—Under the 1976 Tax Reform Law, the $25,000 limitation was eliminated and the amount of loss that a horseman can deduct from nonhorse income was limited to the amount that he has "at risk." The "at risk" is interpreted to mean that the horseman will be limited to his out-of-pocket dollar investment, plus contracts or loans for monies or property put into the horse business that carries his personal liability or responsibility.

If the loss in any year is less than the amount "at risk," the full amount of the loss is deductible and the "at risk" amount is reduced by the loss deducted. The reduced "at risk" amount is then carried over to the next year to determine any limit deductions lost under that year.

If the loss is greater than the amount "at risk," the deductible loss is limited to the amount "at risk" at the end of the year. The amount "at risk" is reduced to "0." In this case, the nondeductible portion of the loss is carried over to the next year and is available for deduction then, if not prevented by application by the "at risk" rule.

HORSES OF DIFFERENT SEXES CANNOT BE EXCHANGED "TAX-FREE."—Horses of different sexes are not considered "like kind" and cannot be exchanged on a tax-free basis. Neither do geldings qualify as "like kind" for exchange for stallions. However, mares for mares, and stallions for stallions, are eligible for "tax-free" exchange.

STUD AND TRAINING FEES DEDUCTIBLE.—Both stud fees and training fees are tax deductible in the year paid by a cash basis taxpayer.

ASSET DEPRECIATION RANGES (ADR).—A horseman can select the period of time over which he can depreciate his horse, from an ADR range of 8 to 12 years.

RECAPTURE OF DEPRECIATION ON.—Depreciation on horses bought (horses raised have no depreciation basis for a horseman on a cash basis) for breeding and racing purposes is subject to depreciation recapture as are all other similar business assets. Thus, gain realized on the sale of such horses is taxed at ordinary income rates to the extent of depreciation claimed or allowable on such animals after 1969; and the remainder of the gain, if any, is taxed as capital gain, provided the holding period of two years has been satisfied.

The following example will serve to illustrate how Recapture of Depreciation works:

Example: A mare is purchased for $2,000 in July, 1969. Depreciation in 1969 is $600 and 1970 depreciation is $375. The mare is sold in early 1971 for $1,750. How much of the depreciation is treated as ordinary income, and how much as capital gain?

Answer: The total depreciation of $975 gives an adjusted tax basis of $1,025 ($2,000–$975). The gain on sale is $725 ($1,750–$1,025). The post-1969 depreciation portion of the $725 gain, $375, is treated as ordinary income and the remaining pre-1970 depreciation of $350 is treated as a capital gain.

APPRAISAL, SALVAGE, AND DEPRECIATION.—If the "useful" life guidelines issued by the Treasury are followed, the taxpayer will not be challenged. They are:

Buildings . . . . 25 years
Machinery and equipment . . . . 10 years
Breeding and work horses . . . 8–12 years

Definitions of "appraisal, salvage, and depreciation" as applied to horses follow:

Appraisal refers to the act of establishing the worth of the horse.

Salvage refers to the remaining value, if any, of an animal after it has served its intended purpose—for example, at the end of usefulness as a breeding animal, or at the end of a racing or showing career.

Depreciation refers to the amortization or write-off of the cost of a horse over the period of its useful life.

In each of the above, the horseman, or the specialist to whom such matters are entrusted, should apply rates which he can justify.

On purchased animals, the price paid establishes value for depreciation purposes. Inherited or gift horses can also be depreciated, with their value established by a qualified appraiser or on the basis of current sales of similar animals. Raised horses cannot be depreciated for the cost of raising them has been deducted as an annual expense.

Breeding animals have no appreciable salvage value at the end of their reproductive life. On the other hand, the salvage value of a racehorse that is retired to stud is a matter of opinion.

Depreciation figures on horses are difficult to come by, and they vary according to source, use, and breed. Unfortunately, no adequate scientific study of the actual average useful life of horses for racing, showing, and breeding purposes has been undertaken. Moreover, the Internal Revenue Service has not stipulated any depreciation rates other than suggesting that horses used for breeding or work purposes should have an 8- to 12-year life.

The accounting firm of Owens, Potter and Hisle, Lexington, Kentucky, which specializes in accounting for horse establishments, has developed Table T-1 as a depreciation guide of the useful lives of race and breeding horses.

The author suggests that the depreciation schedule on show horses be the same as those given for racehorses in Table T-1.

Horsemen have claimed and been allowed rates widely at variance with the figures given in Table T-1. For example, some owners claim depreciation on yearlings from date of acquisition, whereas others date it from the time they are placed in training; but such practices might prove difficult to defend in a well-fought tax case. If

the return is filed in a district where there are few horsemen, the examiner may fail to challenge the method simply because he is unfamiliar with the peculiarities of the industry. Inconsistent practices are likely to continue unless the horse industry itself takes initiative and accumulates factual studies, made by an independent agency, which horsemen can present. Without doubt, the results of such a research study would more than justify the cost.

Any one of the following three methods may be used in computing depreciation of horses:

1. *The straight-line method,* in which annual depreciation on the horse is determined by dividing its purchase price when acquired, less its estimated salvage value, if any, by the total number of years of useful life remaining (see Table T-1). For example, according to Table T-1, a racehorse acquired at age three has an expected useful race life of four years. Hence, a depreciation of 25 percent would be taken each year un-

TABLE T-1

HORSE DEPRECIATION GUIDE 1

Age When Acquired	Years of Useful Life Remaining		
	Racehorses	Broodmares	Stallions
1	6		
2	5		
3	4		
4	3	10	10
5	3	9	9
6	2	9	9
7	2	8	8
8	2	7	7
9		7	7
10		6	6
11		5	5
12		5	5
13		5	5
14		4	4
15		4	4
16		4	4
17		3	3
18		3	3
19		2	2
20		2	2
21		2	2

1 From *The Blood Horse* (Dec. 2, 1967) p. 3747; with the permission of Mr. John C. Owens and Mr. Rex B. Potter, of the firm of Owens, Potter and Hisle, Lexington, Kentucky.

der the straight-line method.

The following example will serve to illustrate how the straight-line method works:

Example: A mare costing $8,000 was purchased at age four, at which age she also dropped her first foal. For purposes of computing depreciation, it is estimated that she has 10 more years of useful life remaining (Table T-1).

Further, it is estimated that her salvage value at the end of this period (at age 14) will be $100. How much depreciation may be taken each year by the straight-line method?

Answer: $8,000 — $100 = $7,900, the depreciation which may be taken over a 10-year period; hence—

100 ÷ 10 = 10%, annual percentage write-off

$7,900 x 10% = $790, annual dollars write-off.

2. *The declining balance method,* in which the largest depreciation is taken during the early years of life, and a gradually smaller allowance is taken in later years. The amount of depreciation taken each year is subtracted before figuring the next year's depreciation, so that the same depreciation rate is applied to a smaller or declining balance each year. The maximum rate under this method may not exceed twice the rate that would be used under the straight-line method. For example, if *new* tangible property has an estimated useful life of 5 years remaining, the depreciation rate under the straight-line method is 20 percent; but under the declining balance system, depreciation may be figured at any rate that does not exceed 40 percent.

Horses that are purchased are usually considered *"used property,"* and, therefore, limited to 150 percent of the straight-line rate. Salvage value is not deducted before figuring depreciation under this method, but depreciation must stop when the unrecovered cost is reduced to salvage value.

3. *The sum of the years-digit method,* in which a different fraction is applied each year to the basis of the property less its estimated salvage value. The denominator, or bottom of the fraction, which remains constant, is the total of the numbers representing the years of useful life of the horse. For example, if the useful life is 5 years, the denominator is 15 (1 plus 2, plus 3, plus 4, plus 5, equals 15). The numerator, or top of the fraction, is the number of years of life remaining at the beginning of the year for which the computation is made. For the first year of an estimated 5-year life, the numerator would be 5, the second year 4, etc. Thus, for a horse with a useful life of five years, the fraction to be applied to the cost minus salvage to figure depreciation for the first year is $5/15$; the fraction for the second year is $4/15$, etc.

In addition to the 3 months of depreciation given above, there's Section 179, "bonus" depreciation. This permits the taxpayer to write off 20 percent of the cost, or portion of the cost, of a purchased horse during the first taxable year for which a depreciation deduction is allowable, provided (1) the horse has an estimated useful life of at least six years, (2) the horse was acquired from an unrelated person, and (3) the maximum write-off is $2,000 for the year, or $4,000 on a joint return. This "bonus" depreciation applies to both new and used property; hence, young broodmares, young stallions, and purchased yearlings put into training will so qualify.

Before a horseman adopts any method of depreciation, competent tax assistance should be sought. Many factors must be considered.

RECAPTURE OF CERTAIN FARMLAND EXPENDITURES.—This rule is for the purpose of alleviating the practice of purchasing a farm or ranch with the intention of engaging in land development and speculation through (1) deducting land improvement costs against nonfarm income, and (2) selling the improved land in a few years and claiming capital gains on the profit. It applies to land that has been held less than 10 years and pertains to deductions for land improvement—for soil and water conservation and land clearance. The Act stipulates that—

1. If held for 5 years or less, deductions for land improvement will be recaptured as ordinary income and at 100 percent.

2. If held longer than 5 years, but less than 10 years, the percentage is scaled down 20 percent per year in excess of 5 years. The following example shows how it works:

A taxpayer acquired land in 1970 and sells in 1978. In 1972, taxpayer expended

$30,000, in land improvements. Hence, the recapture will be 40 percent, or $12,000 ($30,000 x 40%) because the land was sold in the eighth year following purchase. This means that $12,000 of the total expenditures will be recapturable and taxed as ordinary income.

IN THE EVENT OF A COURT CASE.—In the event of a court case, it is usually advisable that the taxpayer appear in person and testify, rather than expect that his attorney and accountant handle the matter entirely. This is especially important from the standpoint of establishing intent, for no one knows the original intent better than the owner. Additionally, it is usually advisable that the testimony of recognized experts in the field be used to substantiate the fact that there was, or is, a reasonable expectation of making a profit. However, whether or not the taxpayer and/or experts testify in a particular case should be left to the decision of the lawyer, for nothing is worse for the taxpayer than not giving the lawyer free rein to develop the case.

TEAM ROPING *(a rodeo event)*.—This involves two contestants roping each end of a running steer.

TEASER.—A horse, usually a stallion or a ridgeling, used to test the response of a mare prior to breeding, or used to determine if a mare is in heat and ready to breed.

TEETH, STRUCTURE OF.—The tooth consists of an outside cement and a second layer of a very hard enamel followed by the dentine and a center known as the pulp. The enamel passes up over the surface of the teeth and extends inward, forming a pit. The inside and bottom of the pit, which is blackened by feed, constitutes the "mark" or "cup." As the rims of these cups disappear through wear, two distinct rings of enamel remain, one around the margin of the tooth and the other around the cup. With wear, the cups become smaller—first more oval or rounding in shape, then triangular and more shallow, and they finally disappear completely.

Further wear on the table or grinding surface of the tooth exposes the tip of the pulp canal or cavity in the center of the tooth. The exposed tip of this canal, which appears between what is left of the cup and the front tooth, is known as the "dental star." The gradual wearing and disappearance of the cups according to a rather definite pattern in period of time enables the experienced horseman to judge the age of an animal with a fair degree of accuracy up to twelve years. (See Fig. T-3.)

(Also see AGE.)

TEETH, TAMPERED (OR "BISHOPED").—Occasionally, unscrupulous horsemen endeavor to make the amateur a victim of their trade tricks, especially through tampering with the teeth. As very young horses increase in value to a certain stage, the milk teeth are sometimes pulled a few months before they would normally fall out. This hastens the appearance of the permanent teeth and makes the animal appear older.

"Bishoping" is the practice of artificially drilling, burning, or staining cups in the teeth of older horses in an attempt to make them sell as young horses. The experienced horseman can detect such deception because the ring of enamel that is always present around the natural cup cannot be reproduced. This makes the practice more difficult than counterfeiting money. Moreover, the slanting position and triangular shape of the teeth of an older animal cannot be changed. An experienced horseman should always be called upon to make an examination if there is any suspicion that the teeth have been tampered with.

(Also see AGE.)

TEMPERAMENT.—Refers to the horse's suitability for the job it is to perform.

TEMPERATURE.—Normal rectal temperature for the horse is 100.5°F., with a range of 99 to 100.8° F.

Every horseman should provide himself with an animal thermometer, which is heavier and more rugged than the ordinary human thermometer. The temperature is measured by inserting the thermometer full length into the rectum,

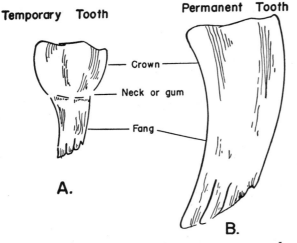

Temporary Tooth   **Permanent Tooth**   **Sectional Views**

— Crown —
— Neck or gum —
— Fang —

A.   B.

Cup
Cement
Central enamel
Ivory
Pulp
Enamel

5 yrs.
9 yrs.
15 yrs.
20 yrs.

C.

Fig. T-3. The horse's tooth. A, temporary lower pincher tooth; B, permanent lower pincher tooth. Temporary or milk teeth are smaller and much whiter than permanent teeth, and constricted at the gum line (neck). C, longitudinal section of a permanent lower middle pincher tooth; and cross-sections of permanent lower middle pincher teeth at different age levels. These drawings show why, with advancing age, the teeth of a horse (1) slant out toward the front, (2) change in wearing surface as noted in the cross sectional shape, (3) change in shape of cups and in the time of disappearance of the cups, and (4) change in appearance and shape of the dental star. (Drawing by R. F. Johnson)

where it should be left a minimum of three minutes. Prior to inserting the thermometer, a long string should be tied to the end.

One Centigrade (C.) degree is $\frac{1}{100}$ the difference between the temperature of melting ice and that of water boiling at standard atmospheric pressure.

One Fahrenheit (F.) degree is $\frac{1}{180}$ of the difference between the temperature of melting ice and that of water boiling at standard atmospheric pressure.

To Change	To	Multiply by
Degrees Centigrade	Degrees Fahrenheit	9/5 and add 32
Degrees Fahrenheit	Degrees Centigrade	Subtract 32, then multiply by 5/9

TENDONS.—Fibers (of connective tissues) arranged in parallel bundles which attach muscles to bones.

TENNESSEE WALKING HORSE.—See BREED(S).

TENNESSEE WALKING HORSE BREEDERS' AND EXHIBITORS' ASSOCIATION OF AMERICA.—Box 286, Lewisburg, Tennessee 37091. (See Appendix for complete breed registry association list.)

TERRETS.—The two rings attached to driving harness through which the driving reins pass.

(Also see HARNESS.)

TESTICLE.—A male gland which produces sperm. There are two testicles.

TETANUS (LOCKJAW).—Chiefly a wound-infection disease caused by a powerful toxin, more than 100 times as toxic as strychnine, that is liberated by the bacterium *Clostridium tetani,* an anaerobe.

SYMPTOMS.—This disease usually is associated with a wound. First sign of tetanus is a stiffness about the head. Animals often chew slowly and weakly and swallow awkwardly. The third

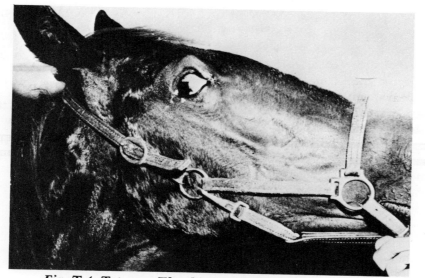

Fig. T-4. Tetanus. The third eyelid is shown protruding over the forward surface of the eyeball (called "haws")—a characteristic symptom. (Courtesy, Dr. V. S. Myers, Jr., V.M.D., Department of Veterinary Surgery and Radiology, University of Minnesota, St. Paul, Minn.)

or inner eyelid protrudes over the forward surface of the eyeball. The slightest noise or movement causes sick animals to have violent spasms. Usually sick animals remain standing until close to death. All ages are susceptible.

TREATMENT.—Place sick animals under the care of a veterinarian and keep them quiet. Good nursing is important. If given early in the disease, massive doses of antitoxin, 100,000 to 200,000 units or more, may be effective. Also, tranquilizers will reduce the extent and severity of muscular spasms, and antibiotics will help.

PREVENTION.—Under the direction of a veterinarian, give tetanus toxoid in two doses at 6-week intervals, followed by a booster injection annually. If premises are unsanitary, all surgery should be accompanied with tetanus antitoxin.

DISCUSSION.—Tetanus is worldwide, but in the United States it occurs most frequently in the South. Death occurs in over half of the affected cases.

(Also see DISEASES AND PARASITES; and HEALTH PROGRAM.)

TETHERING.—See STAKING OUT A HORSE.

THERAPY.—Treating disease.

THICK WIND.—Difficulty in breathing is known as thick wind.
(Also see UNSOUNDNESSES.)

THIGH.—The area below the croup and above the gaskin; to the outside of each of the rear quarters. It should be muscular and well turned.
(Also see PARTS OF A HORSE—Fig. P-4.)

THONG.—The lash of the whip.

THORACIC LIMBS.—This includes all the bones of the foreleg; namely, the scapula, humerus, radius and ulna, seven or eight carpal bones, cannon bone and two splint bones, two sesamoid bones, large pastern bone, small pastern bone, navicular bone, and coffin bone. The correctness of these bones determines the action and consequent usefulness and value of the animal. Since the front feet support about 60 percent of the horse's weight and are subject to great concussion, they should receive careful attention.

The scapula, humerus, radius, and ulna are enclosed in heavy muscles which move them; whereas the parts of the leg below the knee are motivated by long tendons.

The carpal bones collectively comprise the knee of the horse, which corresponds to the wrist in man. The knee should be broad, deep, straight, clean-cut, strongly supported, and free from soft fluctuating swellings. The cannons should be wide, flat, and clean with large, sharply defined, cord-like tendons.

The degree of slope of the pasterns is closely associated with that of the shoulders, and moderate slope (about 45°) to these parts of the anatomy—the scapula and large and small pastern bones—is desirable. Oblique shoulders and pasterns aid in producing elastic springy action and absorb concussions or jars much better than short, straight pasterns and straight shoulders—thereby lessening the possibility of an unsoundness.

The set to the front legs should also be true. When viewed from the front a vertical line dropped from the point of the shoulder should fall upon the center of the knee, cannon, pastern, and foot. When viewed from the side, a vertical line dropped from the center of the elbow joint should fall upon the center of the knee and fetlock and strike the ground just back of the hoof. (Also see LEGS; and SKELETON.)

THOROUGHBRED.—Table T-2 gives the track records for Thoroughbreds at some of the more popular American distances, whereas Table T-3 lists the leading money-winners. Information pertaining to the origin and characteristics of the Thoroughbred is presented under Breed(s).

THOROUGHBRED RACING ASSOCIATION (T.R.A.).—The T.R.A. was formed in 1942 for the purpose of promoting the business of racing of Thoroughbred horses in the United States, and to coordinate and enforce the rules of racing throughout the country. All of the major racetracks of the United States are members of the T.R.A.

ADDRESS.—Thoroughbred Racing Association, 5 Dakota Drive, Suite 210, Lake Success, New Hyde Park, New York 11040.

THOROUGHPIN.—Thoroughpin is a puffy condition in the web of the hock. It can be determined by movement of the puff, when pressed, to the opposite side of the leg. Treatment consists of applying pressure and massaging, but these may not always be successful.
(Also see UNSOUNDNESSES.)

THREADWORM (*Strongyloides westeri*).—Threadworms are also known as strongyloides.

SYMPTOMS.—Threadworms attack foals, causing diarrhea. The worms disappear by the time foals are 6 months old.

TREATMENT.—Thiabendazole is effective in removing threadworms.

PREVENTION AND CONTROL.—Provide good sanitation and clean, dry bedding.

DISCUSSION.—These worms are common where there is a concentration of foals. Losses are primarily in stunted growth and unthriftiness.

THREE-DAY EVENT (COMBINED TRAINING, OR HORSE TRIALS).—The first three-day event was introduced at Badminton, Gloucestershire, in England, in 1949, following the Olympic Games held in England the previous year. It was designed to assist in the selection of horses and riders to represent Great Britain at the Olympic Games in Helsinki in 1952. The test consists of the following: first day, dressage; second day, endurance, roads and tracks, steeplechase, and cross-country; third day, show jumping.

Success in three-day events is determined by the strength and courage of the horse, closely coupled with the spirit and tact of the rider. (See Fig. T-5.)

THREE-GAITED SADDLE HORSES.—See SADDLE HORSES, THREE- AND FIVE-GAITED.

TABLE T-2

WORLD TRACK RECORDS FOR THOROUGHBREDS

Distance	Horse	Age	Weight	Track	Date	Time
1–4	Big Racket	4	114	Hipodromo de las Americas, Mexico City, Mexico	February 5, 1945	:20⅘
2 1–2f	Tie Score	5	115	Hipodromo de las Americas, Mexico City, Mexico	February 5, 1946	:26⅘
3–8	Atoka	6	105	Butte, Montana	September 7, 1906	:33½
3 1–2f	Joe Blair	5	115	Juarez, Mexico	February 5, 1916	:39
	Deep Sun	7	120	Shenandoah Downs, Charles Town, West Virginia	July 11, 1959	:39
1–2	Tamran's Jet	2	118	Sunland Park, Sunland, New Mexico	March 22, 1968	:44⅘
	Crimson Saint	2	119	Oaklawn Park, Hot Springs, Arkansas	April 1, 1971	:44⅘
	Mighty Mr. A.	3	116	Sportsman's Park, Cicero, Illinois	November 1, 1971	:44⅘
	Thief of Bagdad	5	114	Sportsman's Park, Cicero, Illinois	November 5, 1971	:44⅘
4 1–2f	Kathryn's Doll	2	111	Turf Paradise, Phoenix, Arizona	April 9, 1967	:50⅖
	Dear Ethel	2	114	Miles Park, Louisville, Kentucky	July 4, 1967	:50⅖
5–8	Zip Pocket	3	122	Turf Paradise, Phoenix, Arizona	April 22, 1967	:55⅖
5 1–2f	Zip Pocket	3	129	Turf Paradise, Phoenix, Arizona	November 19, 1967	1:01⅗
5 3–4f	Fighting Fox	4	126	Empire City, Yonkers, New York	July 8, 1939	1:07⅖
	Doublrab	4	130	Empire City, Yonkers, New York	July 18, 1942	1:07⅖
3–4 T*	Gelding, by Blink Broken Tendril	3	123	Brighton, England	August 6, 1929	1:06⅕
	Zip Pocket	2	120	Turf Paradise, Phoenix, Arizona	December 4, 1966	1:07⅖
	Vale of Tears	6	120	Ak-Sar-Ben, Omaha, Nebraska	June 7, 1969	1:07⅖
6 1–2f	Turbulator	5	120	Longacres, Seattle, Washington	August 16, 1970	1:14
7–8	Triple Bend	4	123	Hollywood Park, Inglewood, California	1972	1:19⅘
	Native Diver	6	126	Hollywood Park, Inglewood, California	May 22, 1965	1:20
1	Dr. Fager	4	134	Arlington Park, Arlington Heights, Illinois	August 24, 1968	1:32⅕
1m70y	Drill Site	5	115	Garden State Park, Cherry Hill, New Jersey	October 12, 1964	1:38⅘
T	Pass the Brandy	7	114	Arlington Park, Arlington Heights, Illinois	July 25, 1970	1:38⅘
1 1–16	Swaps	4	130	Hollywood Park, Inglewood, California	June 23, 1956	1:39
1 1–8 T	Pink Pigeon	4	116	Santa Anita Park, Arcadia, California	March 27, 1969	1:45⅘
1 3–16	Fleet Bird	4	123	Golden Gate Fields, Albany, California	October 24, 1953	1:52⅗
T	Star Envoy	4	111	Hialeah Park, Hialeah, Florida	March 18, 1972	1:52⅗
1 1–4 T	Quilche	6	115	Santa Anita Park, Arcadia, California	February 23, 1970	1:58
1 3–8 T	Quilche	6	115	Hollywood Park, Inglewood, California	April 25, 1970	2:11⅗
1 1–2 T	Fiddle Isle	5	124	Santa Anita Park, Arcadia, California	March 21, 1970	2:23
1 9–16	Lone Wolf	5	115	Keeneland, Lexington, Kentucky	October 31, 1961	2:37⅗
1 5–8	Swaps	4	130	Hollywood Park, Inglewood, California	July 25, 1956	2:38⅕
1m5½f	Distribute	9	109	River Downs, Cincinnati, Ohio	September 7, 1940	2:51⅗
1 3–4 T	Swartz Pete	6		Alexandra Park, Auckland, New Zealand	January 1, 1966	2:50⅘
1 7–8 T	El Moro	8	116	Delaware Park, Wilmington, Delaware	July 22, 1963	3:11⅘
2 T	Polazel	3		Salisbury, England	July 8, 1924	3:15
2m40y	Winning Mark	4	107	Thistledown, Cleveland, Ohio	July 20, 1940	3:29⅖
2m70y	Iberis	4	122	Hawthorne, Cicero, Illinois	October 15, 1969	3:30⅗
2 1–16	Midafternoon	4	126	Jamaica, Jamaica, Long Island, New York	November 15, 1956	3:29⅗
2 1–8T	Ceinturion	5	119	Newbury, England	September 29, 1923	3:35
2 3–16	Santiago	5	112	Narragansett Park, Pawtucket, Rhode Island	September 27, 1941	3:51⅕
2 1–4 T	Dakota	4	116	Lingfield, England	May 27, 1927	3:37⅗
2 3–8	Wiki Jack	4	97	Tijuana, Mexico	February 8, 1925	4:15
2 1–2	Miss Grillo	6	118	Pimlico, Baltimore, Maryland	November 12, 1948	4:14⅗
2 5–8	‡Worthman	5	101	Tijuana, Mexico	February 22, 1925	4:51⅖
2 3–4	Shot Put	4	126	Washington Park, Homewood, Illinois	August 14, 1940	4:48⅘
2 7–8	††Bosh	5	100	Tijuana, Mexico	March 8, 1925	5:23
3	Farragut	5	113	Agua Caliente, Mexico	March 9, 1941	5:15
3 3–8	Winning Mark	4	104	Washington Park, Homewood, Illinois	August 21, 1940	6:13
4	Sotemia	5	119	Churchill Downs, Louisville, Kentucky	October 7, 1912	7:10⅘

(Continued)

T Turf course. Santa Anita Park turf course distances are partially downhill except 1⅛ m. *3–4 mile course at Brighton started on a hill and to within one-third of a mile from the finish was down grade. ‡Track heavy. ††Track sloppy.

TABLE T-2 (CONTINUED)

(Straight Course)

Distance	Horse	Age	Weight	Track	Date	Time
1–4	Red Jones	7	126	Cranwood Race Course, Warrensville Heights, Ohio	October 21, 1958	:21⅕
	Wandering Boy	6	118	Turf Paradise, Phoenix, Arizona	December 5, 1965	:21⅕
	Bekky's Star	2	115	Sunland Park, Sunland, New Mexico	February 12, 1968	:21⅕
2 1–2f	Meditacao	2	113	Hipodromo de las Americas, Mexico City, Mexico	April 2, 1970	:26⅖
3–8	King Rhymer	2	118	Santa Anita Park, Arcadia, California	February 27, 1947	:32
1–2	Sonido	2	111	Hipodromo La Rinconada, Caracas, Venezuela	June 28, 1970	:44⅖
4 1–2f	The Pimpernel	2	118	Belmont Park, Elmont, New York	May 17, 1951	:49⅘
	Reneged	2	118	Belmont Park, Elmont, New York	June 7, 1955	:49⅘
5–8 T	Indigenous	4	131	Epsom Downs, Epsom, England	June 2, 1960	:53⅗
5 1–2f	Delegate	7	113	Belmont Park, Elmont, New York	October 10, 1951	1:01⅗
3–4	Vestment	2	115	Belmont Park, Elmont, New York	October 15, 1954	1:07⅘
6 1–2f	Porter's Mite	2	119	Belmont Park, Elmont, New York	September 17, 1938	1:14⅖
	Native Dancer	2	122	Belmont Park, Elmont, New York	September 17, 1952	1:14⅖
§Abt7–8	High Strung	2	122	Belmont Park, Elmont, New York	September 15, 1928	1:19
7–8 T	First Edition	4	126	Hurst Park, Hampton Court, England	May 25, 1926	1:20
1 T	Alizarene	4	120	Chepstow, England	June 28, 1949	1:32⅗
1 1–4	Banquet	3	108	Monmouth Park, New Jersey	July 17, 1890	2:03¾

T Turf course. § 165 feet short of 7–8 mile.

1 "f" stands for furlong. A furlong is a racing distance of ⅛ mile, or 40 rods, or 220 yards, or 201.17 meters. "y" stands for yards. "m" stands for mile. Where no special designation is made, distance is in miles. For example, 1–4 means one-fourth mile.

TABLE T-3

Horse	Total Money Won	Racing Years	Owner
Kelso	1,977,896	1959–1966	Mrs. Richard duPont
Round Table	1,749,869	1956–1959	Thavis Kerr
Buckpasser	1,462,014	1965–1967	Ogden Phipps
Allez France	1,330,967	1972–	Mrs. Allen Manning
Secretariat	1,316,778	1972–1973	Helen (Penny) Tweedy
Nashua	1,288,565	1954–1956	William Woodward, Jr.
Carry Back	1,241,165	1960–1963	Jack Price
Dahlia	1,234,655	1972–	N. B. Hunt
Damascus	1,176,781	1966–1968	Mrs. Thomas Bancroft
Cougar II	1,162,725	1970–1973	Mrs. Mary F. Jones
Susan's Girl	1,111,802	1971–	Fred W. Hooper
Fort Marcy	1,109,791	1966–1971	Paul Mellon
Citation	1,085,760	1947–1951	Calumet Farm
Forego	1,036,678	1972–	Mrs. Martha Gerry
Native Diver	1,026,500	1961–1967	Mr. & Mrs. L. K. Shapiro
Riva Ridge	1,009,727	1971–	Meadow Stable
Dr. Fager	1,002,642	1966–1968	Tartan Farm

Fig. T-5. Yorick, winner of three-day event in Ireland. (Courtesy, Pegasus Ltd., Dublin, Ireland)

THRIFTY CONDITION.—Healthy, active, vigorous.

THROAT.—The throat, or throttle, is the place of juncture of the head and neck. The throat should be clean-cut, with a good throttle; neither too angular nor too thick. The portion of the horse's neck around which the throatlatch passes is known as the throatlatch.

THROATLATCH.—See PARTS OF A HORSE —Fig. P-4.

THROMBOSIS.—The coagulation of the blood or the deposition of a fibrinous clot within the heart or blood vessels is known as thrombosis. It may occur within the heart, in the arteries, or in the veins. Venous thrombosis is more common than arterial.

The symptoms vary, depending on the type and severity of the obstruction. Upon being exercised, weakness and collapse of the hind legs may occur. The horse sinks to the ground, but following rest he recovers and is able to move again. There is no cure.

THRUSH.—Thrush is a disease of the frog, commonly of the hind feet, caused by a necrotic fungus characterized by a pungent odor. It causes a deterioration of tissues in the cleft of the frog or in the juncture between the frog and bars; and it produces lameness. If not treated, it can be serious. The presence of thrush is indicative of unsanitary conditions in the animal's stall. Most cases will respond to trimming away of the affected frog, sanitation, and the use of an antiseptic. Every horseman has his favorite thrush remedy; among them are calomel, creolin, iodine, bichloride of mercury, formalin, and carbolic acid.

(Also see UNSOUNDNESSES.)

TICKS.—Several kinds may be found on horses. The most common ones are the winter tick, *Dermacentor albipictus;* the lone star tick, *Amblyomma americanum;* and the spinose ear tick, *Otobius megnini.*

SYMPTOMS.—The symptoms are lowered vitality and itching; animals rub and scratch infested parts.

TREATMENT.—To control winter and lone star ticks, use the same treatments that are used for lice. For the control of spinose ear ticks, apply a 5 percent coumaphos dust inside the ears, or spray inside the ears with an aerosol bomb containing 2.5 percent ronnel. Repeat treatments as necessary.

PREVENTION AND CONTROL.—Treatment with insecticides will control ticks on horses and protect them against reinfestation for several weeks.

DISCUSSION.—Ticks appear mostly in the South and West. They reduce vitality of horses and may spread piroplasmosis and African horse-sickness.

(Also see DISEASES AND PARASITES; HEALTH PROGRAM; and PARASITES OF HORSES.)

TIE.—To attach or fasten by use of a halter and a shank. Always use a strong halter and a strong lead rope. Tie to a sturdy object and high and close enough to alleviate any hazard of the horse getting his foot over the rope.

(Also see TYING THE HORSE.)

TIE DOWN.—A Standing Martingale is sometimes called a tie down.

(Also see MARTINGALES.)

TIE ROPE.—See HALTER SHANK (TIE ROPE).

TIMOTHY.—Timothy is the preferred hay by most horsemen. Although it may be grown alone, it is commonly seeded in mixtures with medium red or alsike clover.

Timothy is easy to harvest and cure. However, in comparison with hay made from the legumes, it is low in crude protein and minerals, particularly calcium.

As with all other forages, the feeding value of timothy is affected by the stage of growth of the plants at the time of cutting. With increasing maturity, (1) the percentage of crude protein decreases, (2) the percentage of crude fiber increases, (3) the hay becomes less palatable, and (4) the digestibility decreases. However, delaying cutting until timothy has reached the full bloom stage, or later, usually results in the highest yields. When both yield and quality are considered, the best results are obtained when timothy is cut for hay at the early bloom stage.

TOE.—See FOOT—Parts of the Foot, Fig. F-20.

TOE CRACK.—A vertical split in the horny wall of the hoof on the forepart of the toe. (See Fig. T-6.)

(Also see QUARTER CRACK.)

TOE WEIGHT.—A metal weight (knob) fitted to a spur previously placed on the front hoof to induce a change or balance in motion. Used extensively in the training and racing of harness horses.

TONGS.—See SHOEING—Table S-5.

TONGUE-LOLLER.—A horse whose tongue hangs out.

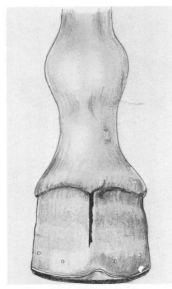

Fig. T-6. Toe crack.

TONGUE SWALLOWING (GURGLING; CHOKING UP).—A choking up most commonly observed the latter part of a race, or after its finish. The exact nature of the trouble has not been established, but it seems that fatigue plays a part. It is probable that the tongue is not swallowed. Horses which suffer from this condition have an abnormally flabby and mobile soft palate, which appears to be at the root of the trouble. It is most common in steeplechasers and distance flat racers; and it has been observed in hunters.

TONIC.—A drug, medicine, or feed designed to stimulate the appetite.

The "hoss doctor"—along with fads, fables, and trade secrets—is ever present. His products and sales pitch are reminiscent of the "medicine man" of old. He enjoys a flourishing business pawning off on unsuspecting horsemen a myriad of tonics.

Generally speaking, claims are made for increased growth, improved breeding, better development, more speed, and increased stamina; and the feeding directions call for a cup or for 3 or 4 tablespoonsful per horse daily.

But such "horse practitioners" are not entirely to blame. Many owners insist on some kind of treatment. Like the ulcer patient who had to go to six different doctors before he could find one who would tell him that he could have a cocktail, they'll keep going until they get it. Especially when a horse "starts down," they'll grasp for straws. In such frantic moments, they'll buy and try almost any formula for which claims are made, completely oblivious to the facts (1) that distilled water might do just as much good—and far less harm, and (2) that they are buying losing tickets with their eyes wide open.

Horsemen are also great imitators. They'll single out some great horse, and, in one way or another, find out what it's getting. Then, they'll get some of the "same stuff" and use it from then 'til doomsday. The writer has known them to pay $50 for a gallon of a mysterious concoction, in a green jug, made in some little hamlet in Kentucky. Of course, the fallacy of such imitation—of feeding what the "great horse" got—is that the "name" horse might have been even greater had it been fed properly, and that there must be a reason why there are so few truly great horses. Also, the following searching question might well be asked: Why do many horses start training in great physical shape, only to slow down and lose appetite, and be taken out of training for some rest?

There is no panacea in the horse business. Success cannot be achieved through witchcraft or old wives' tales; some merely achieve despite such handicaps. Instead, it calls for the combined best wit, wisdom, and judgment of science, technology, and practical experience.

The horse of today cannot be fed as it was yesterday and be expected to perform as the horse of tomorrow! Scientific feeding, including the necessary quantities and relationships of minerals and vitamins, is necessary.

If the horse's appetite is poor and its coat dull, and if the animal appears lethargic, the owner should seek the counsel of a veterinarian and/or a nutritionist. Among the tonics which may be prescribed, and which may be helpful under certain conditions when fed as directed, are:

1. *Fowler's solution.*—To stimulate appetite and increase bloom, administered as follows: A tablespoonful of the solution given daily for ten days, then omitted for ten days, then fed again for ten days. But remember that Fowler's solution is an arsenic compound. Remember, too, that arsenic is a cumulative poison. Hence, it should only be fed under the direction of a veterinarian.

2. *Molasses.*—Molasses is palatable, and cane molasses is a good source of certain trace minerals. At least five percent molasses can be added

with benefit to most horse rations.

3. *Zinc.*—Research with cattle has shown that supplementing the ration with 50 to 100 ppm of zinc will improve the haircoat. Obviously, zinc is necessary for the development of skin and hair. Since beautiful haircoats are important in horses, fortifying the daily ration with 50 to 100 ppm of zinc should improve the haircoat if the zinc in the feed is on the low side.

TOPLINE.—A desirable topline is one with a short, strong back and loin, with a long, nicely turned and heavily-muscled croup, and a high, well-set tail. Also, the withers should be clearly defined and of the same height as the high point of the croup.

TOTAL DIGESTIBLE NUTRIENT (TDN) SYSTEM.—Total digestible nutrients (TDN) is the sum of the digestible protein, fiber, nitrogen-free extract, and fat x 2.25.

Back of TDN values are the following steps:

1. *Digestibility.*—The digestibility of a particular feed for a specific class of stock is determined by a digestion trial. It is made by determining the percentage of each nutrient in the feed through chemical analysis; giving the feed to the test animal for a preliminary period, so that all residues of former feeds will pass out of the digestive tract; giving weighed amounts of the feed during the test period; collecting, weighing and analyzing the feces; determining the difference between the amount of the nutrient fed and the amount found in the feces; and computing the percentage of each nutrient digested. The latter figure is known as the digestion *coefficient* for that nutrient in the feed.

2. *Computation of percent digestible nutrients.* —Digestible nutrients are computed by multiplying the percentage of each nutrient in the feed [protein, fiber, N-free extract (NFE), and fat] by its digestion coefficient. The result is expressed as digestible protein, digestible fiber, digestible NFE, and digestible fat. Thus, for corn the digestible nutrients could be estimated as shown in Table T-4. (See page 428.)

3. *Computation of total digestible nutrients.*— To approximate the greater energy value of fat, the percentage of digestible fat is multiplied by

TABLE T-4

COMPUTATION OF DIGESTIBLE NUTRIENTS OF CORN

Total % of Nutrient in Feed	Digestion Coefficient / 100	=	% Digestible Nutrient	
			Digestible Nutrient	
			(%)	(lb.)
9.3% protein	X $\frac{67}{100}$	=	6.2 (protein)	6.2
1.9% fiber	X $\frac{39}{100}$	=	0.7 (fiber)	0.7
70.1% nitrogen-free extract (NFE)	X $\frac{85}{100}$	=	59.6 (NFE)	59.6
3.9% ether extract (fat)	X $\frac{85}{100}$	=	3.3 (fat)	3.3

2.25. Hence, for the preceding sample of corn, the TDN may be calculated as follows:

	%		%
Digestible protein	6.2 x 1	=	6.2
Digestible crude fiber	0.7 x 1	=	0.7
Digestible NFE	59.6 x 1	=	59.6
Digestible ether extract (fat) . .	3.3 x 2.25	=	7.4

73.9% TDN, or

73.9 lb. TDN/100 lb. corn

4. *Animal requirements or feeding standards.*—In the TDN system, the feed requirements (energy) of farm animals are given as pounds of total digestible nutrients.

ADVANTAGES AND DISADVANTAGES OF THE TDN SYSTEM.—The main advantage of the TDN system is that it has been used a long time and many people are acquainted with it.

The main disadvantages of the TDN system are:

1. It is based on physiological fuel values for humans and dogs. These do not apply to ruminants. The factors of 1 for protein, crude fiber and nitrogen-free extract, and 2.25 for fat are not always constant.

2. It overevaluates high fiber feeds (roughages) in relation to low fiber feeds (concentrates) when fed for high rates of production, due to the higher heat loss per pound of TDN in the case of the high fiber feeds.

3. It does not measure energy in energy units.

4. It does not measure all losses of energy from the body.

TOTALISATOR.—The mechanical "brains" of the pari-mutuel system.

TOTE BOARD.—The indicator board of the totalisator on which is flashed all pari-mutuel information before or after a race.

TOUT.—A low-order con man who peddles tips, betting systems, etc. to the unwary racegoer.

TOXEMIA.—A condition produced by the presence of poisons (toxins) in the blood.

TOXOIDS (or ANATOXINS).—A toxoid is a "tamed" toxin. Some bacteria, such as those that cause tetanus, produce powerful poisons or toxins. These are the substances that actually cause the damage; the bacteria themselves may produce only very mild symptoms. The same toxin is formed when the bacteria are grown in the laboratory, but it is then treated chemically. It loses the poisonous or toxic properties but still retains the power to stimulate the body cells; they form the appropriate antibody (antitoxin). Among toxoids is tetanus toxoid.

TRACE MINERALS.—See MINERALS.

TRACES.—The parts of a harness which run from the collar to the single-tree.
(Also see HARNESS.)

TRAIL.—The trail was the mode of transportation of its day. There were no trucks, and there were no iron rails and brass-banded steam engines puffing across the prairies. Transportation on four good legs was the only way in which to get from hither to yon. Snake-like lines of plodding, bellowing herds became part of the American scene, and, subsequently, of the literature, folklore, and art.

TRAILER, VAN, AND TRUCK SHIPMENTS.—Trailers, vans, and trucks have the distinct advantage of door-to-door transportation; that is, loading from in front of one stable and unloading in front of another.

The trailer is usually a one- or two-horse unit, which is drawn behind a car or truck. Generally speaking, this method of transportation is best adapted to short distances—less than 500 miles. Horses are trailered to shows, races, endurance rides, breeding establishments, to new owners,

from one work area to another on the range; in fact, it may well be said that today's horses are well traveled.

The van or van-like trailer is a common and satisfactory method of transportation where three to eight horses are involved. There is hardly any limit to the kinds of vans, ranging from rather simple to very palatial pieces of equipment.

Most experienced horse shippers frown upon shipping horses in an open truck.

(Also see TRANSPORTING HORSES.)

Fig. T-7. Front view of a horse in a trailer, showing animal properly blanketed, double tied, and with hay in the manger. Trailers are a very popular means of transporting one or two horses. (Courtesy, USDA)

Fig. T-8. Horse van of Gem State Stables, Thoroughbreds, Tipton, California. (Courtesy, Velma V. Morrison)

TRAIL-RIDE.—A term given to a cross-country ride. Trail rides are becoming more popular every year. (See Fig. T-9.)

TRAINING.—There are as many successful ways to train horses as there are to train children. The writer has observed several top professional train-

Fig. T-9. An Arizona trail ride. (Courtesy, **The West-ern Horseman)**

ers. Each used a different technique, yet all end-ed up with the same result—a champion. Most of them follow the basic principles given herein.

Fig. T-10. People need horses and horses need people. Train them together. (Courtesy, Dean Kenney, Blue Ribbon Ranch, Culver City, Calif.)

● *The Foal* (daily lessons of 15 to 30 min-utes each, for 7 to 10 days).—If the foal is trained early in life, it will be a better disciplined, more serviceable horse. Give it one lesson at a time, and in sequence; that is, be sure the pupil mas-ters each learning experience before it is given the next one.

Put a well-fitted halter on the foal when it is 10 to 14 days old. When it has become accus-tomed to the halter, in a day or so, tie it secure-ly in the stall beside the mare. Try to keep the foal from freeing itself from the rope or from becoming tangled up in it.

Leave the foal tied 15 to 30 minutes each day for 2 or 3 days. Groom the animal carefully while it is tied. Rub each leg and handle each foot so that the foal becomes accustomed to hav-ing its feet picked up. After it has been groomed, lead it around with the mare for a few days and then lead it by itself. Lead it at both the walk and the trot. Many breeders teach a foal to lead simply by leading it with the mare from the stall

Fig. T-11. Teaching the foal to lead. After the foal has been gentled to a halter, a nonskid loop slipped over the hindquarters will teach him to move forward promptly.

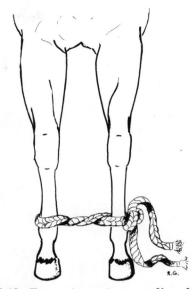

Fig. T-12. Front feet of a yearling hobbled with a large, soft cotton rope. This training lesson is designed to teach the young horse to stand still (as if tied) and not get excited if he gets caught in a fence.

to the paddock and back again.

At this stage of the training, be sure the foal executes your commands to stop and go as soon as you give them. When halted, make it stand in show position—squarely on all four legs with its head up.

Use all your patience, gentleness, and firmness in training the foal. Never let your temper get the best of you.

● *The Yearling* (daily lessons of 30 minutes each, repeated until each learning experience is mastered).—The horse learns by repetition. Thus, teach only one thing at a time, and repeat it in the same manner daily until mastered; then proceed to the next learning experience. Teach the yearling the following, in order:

1. *Teach "whoa" and his name.*—The yearling should be taught that "whoa" means stop. Always give the command, then call his name, as "Whoa, Duke."

2. *Hobble him.*—Next the young horse should be hobbled; first the two front feet, then "sideline" (tie a front foot and a hind foot on the same side together). Hobbling is for the purpose of teaching the horse to stand still (as if tied) and not get excited if he gets caught in a fence. Many a valuable horse has mutilated himself for lack of this kind of training.

3. *Put the saddle blanket on* (repeat for 2 days).—Gently put the saddle blanket on the young horse's back, and move it from head to tail, until he is not afraid of having an object on his back.

4. *Saddle him (repeat for 5 or 6 days).*—Next, ease a saddle on him. Put it on and off several times. Then tighten the girth moderately and lead him around.

Thus, the gentling of the yearling is for the purposes of teaching him the meaning of the word "whoa"; to stand patiently when hobbled or caught in a wire fence; and to get used to the saddle blanket and the saddle. After a few days of gentling like this, the yearling may be turned to pasture for a time.

● *At Eighteen Months of Age* (each lesson 30 minutes daily, repeated until mastered).—At eighteen months of age, the young horse should receive additional training, with each step mastered before moving on to the next. The trainer should always be gentle, but firm; and should not make a pet out of the horse. Let him know who is boss. When he must be punished for wrongdoing, use the whip—one time only; and do so immediately after the horse commits the act. Never discipline a horse by gouging him with spurs. When he does well, reward him by stroking his neck or shoulder and calling his name: "That's a good boy, Duke."

1. *Teach him to drive, turn, stop, and back up; by using plowlines.*—Tie the stirrups together under the horse, then run plowlines through

Fig. T-13. When the horse is approximately 18 months of age, use plowlines to teach him to drive, turn, stop, and back up.

them. Stand behind the horse and use the plowlines to drive, turn, stop, and back up.

2. *Teach the horse to flex his neck and set his head.*—This may be accomplished either by (1) tying the reins to the stirrups or (2) using rubber reins made from strips of old inner tube. Then turn the young horse loose in the corral or training ring for 30 minutes (he can't hurt himself).

3. *Use the bosal; ride him; introduce leg pressure.*—During the first few months of riding, use a bosal; it will alleviate the hazard of hurting his mouth with bits. Do some light riding; introduce leg pressure.

● *At Two Years of Age* (each lesson 30 minutes daily, repeated until mastered).—The two-year-old is ready for the following advanced training:

1. *Teach the aids.*—Mount the horse and put him in motion by use of the aids—the legs, hands and reins, and voice (see AIDS). After riding him for 5 or 6 days at the walk and trot, move him into the lope or canter; always on the proper lead—a right foot lead when going clockwise, a left foot lead when moving counter-clockwise.

2. *Teach him to back.*—From the ground,

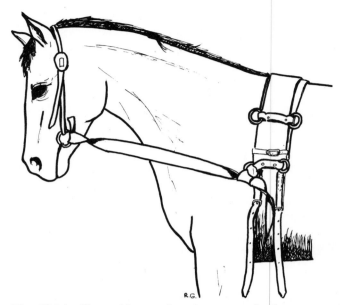

Fig. T-14. About 18 months of age, teach the young horse to flex his neck and set his head. This shows rubber reins, made from strips of an old inner tube, being used for this purpose.

teach the horse to back. Hold the reins near the bosal or bit; push back (push and release) and command "Back, Duke." If necessary, push on his shoulder and/or switch him on the forelegs. Next, mount the horse and, from his back, teach him to stop and back up. If he won't back when you're mounted, have a friend stand in front of him and switch him back while you pull (pull and release) on the reins and command "Back, Duke." Backing teaches the horse to get his feet under him, which is essential for pivots and sharp turns.

3. *Pivot.*—Each time the horse is stopped and backed up, pause for a few seconds, then collect him (with the reins, and apply a little leg pressure) and pivot (see PIVOT). Always teach the young horse to turn on his hind feet; pull him back until his hind feet are under him, then pull diagonally on the reins.

4. *Sliding stop.*—Teach the horse to make a proper sliding stop—to "stick his tail in the ground" (see SLIDING STOP).

Some good horsemen train horses on the longe line—that light strap of webbing or leather 30 feet long (see LONGE). For example, when the writer visited the Spanish Riding School of Vienna, where the famed Lipizzaner stallions perform, he learned that all basic training—the gaits, leads, stops, rollbacks, etc.—is given on the longe. Starting at age four, they work these horses from the ground for one year before they are ever mounted.

Fig. T-15. Superbly trained white Lipizzan stallion at the Spanish Riding School, Wels, Austria, doing the Courbette. The horse leaps forward on his hind legs in several bounds, the number determined by his agility, with his forelegs drawn in and not touching the ground. (Courtesy, Spanish Riding School)

The only exception to use of the longe line in training is a roping horse; because, when on the end of a rope, a roping horse is taught to run straight back from the trainer, rather than around him.

(Also see SCHOOLING.)

TRAITS, UNDESIRABLE.—Undesirable traits occur in all animals, and horses are no exception. They may show up in coat color, bone structure or body conformation, temperament, physiological systems, performance, longevity, and reproduction. Some are of great practical importance; others may be considered good or bad according to preference of the owner or the use to which the horse is put. For example, a certain color may be preferred by one person, but discriminated against by another. Likewise, the owner of a rodeo string may want horses with temperaments that make for good buckers, whereas such unruly dispositions have no place in animals intended for pleasure riding.

TRAKEHNEN (TRAKEHNER).—A breed of horses which originated in Germany, beginning with a planned breeding program set up by William I, King of Prussia, in 1732. The Trakehner breed stems from Thoroughbreds and Arabians. It is a beautiful and good tempered breed. They possess strong backs and good action, and they stand about 16 hands high at maturity.

TRANSPORTING HORSES.—Horses can be transported by trailer, van, truck, rail, boat, or plane. Most horses are transported in a one- or two-horse trailer drawn behind a car or truck. The requisites for good motor transportation, regardless of type, are as follows:

• *Provide good footing.*—The floor of the vehicle should be covered with heavy coco matting made for the purpose; with sand covered with straw or other suitable bedding material; or with rubber mats. Clean the floor covering at frequent intervals while in transit to avoid ammonia and heat.

• *Drive carefully.*—Drive at a moderate, constant speed as distinguished from fast or jerky driving, which causes added stress and tiring. If weather conditions make the roads unsafe, the vehicle should be stopped.

• *Make nurse stops.*—Nurse stops should be made at about 3-hour intervals when mares and foals are transported together.

• *Provide proper ventilation.*—Provide plenty of fresh air without drafts.

• *Teach horses to load early in life.* —When horses will be transported later in life, they should be accustomed to transportation as youngsters before they get too big and strong. This can be done by moving them by trailer from one part of the farm to another.

• *Provide health certificate and statement of ownership.*—A health certificate signed by a licensed veterinarian is required for most interstate shipments. Foreign shipments must be accompanied by a health certificate that has been ap-

Fig. T-16. Trailer transporting.

proved by a government veterinarian. This takes several days. Branded horses must be accompanied by a brand certificate, and all horses should be accompanied by a statement of ownership.

• *Schedule properly.*—Schedule the transportation so that animals will arrive on time. Show, sale, and race animals should arrive a few days early.

• *Have the horses relaxed.*—Horses ship best if they are relaxed and not overtired before they are moved.

• *Clean and disinfect public conveyance.*—Before using any type of public conveyance, thoroughly clean and disinfect it. Steam is excellent

for this purpose. Remove nails or other hazards that might cause injury.

• *Have a competent caretaker accompany horses.*—Valuable horses should not be shipped in the care of an inexperienced person.

• *Use shanks except on stallions.*—When animals are tied, use a ⅝-inch cotton rope shank that is 5 feet long and has a big swivel snap at the end. Chain shanks are too noisy. Always tie the shank with a knot that can easily and quickly be released in case of an emergency.

• *Feed lightly.*—Allow horses only a half feed of grain before they are loaded for shipment and at the first feed after they reach their destination. In transit, horses should be given all the good quality hay they will eat, preferably alfalfa, to keep the bowels loose, but no concentrates should be fed. Commerical hay nets or homemade burlap containers may be used to hold the hay in transit, but they should not be placed too high.

• *Water liberally.*—When transporting horses, give them all the fresh, clean water they will drink at frequent intervals unless the weather is extremely hot and there is danger of gorging. A tiny bit of molasses may be added to each pail of water, beginning about a week before the horses are shipped, and the addition of molasses to the water may be continued in transit. This prevents any taste change in the water.

• *Pad the stalls.*—Many experienced shippers favor padding the inside of the vehicle to lessen the likelihood of injury, especially when a valuable animal is shipped. Coco matting or a sack of straw properly placed may save the horse's hocks from injury.

• *Take along tools and supplies.*—The following tools and supplies should be taken along in a suitable box: pinch bar, hammer, hatchet, saw, nails, pliers, flashlight, extra halters and shanks, twitch, canvas slapper or short piece of hose, pair of gloves, fork and broom, fire extinguisher, and medicine for colic and shipping fever provided by a veterinarian.

• *Check shoes, blankets, and bandages.*—Whenever possible, ship horses barefoot. Never allow them to wear calked shoes during a long shipment. They may wear smooth shoes. In cool weather, horses may be blanketed if an attendant is present in case a horse gets entangled. The legs of racehorses in training should be bandaged to keep the ankles from getting scuffed or the tendons bruised. Bandages are not necessary on breeding stock except for valuable stallions and young animals. When bandages are used, they should be reset often.

• *Be calm when loading and unloading.*—In loading and unloading horses, always be patient and never show anger. Try kindness first; pat the horse and speak to him to reassure him. If this fails, it may be necessary to use one of the following techniques:

• Sometimes the use of the twitch at the right time is desirable, especially if the horse is tossing his head about.

• When a horse must be disciplined, a canvas slapper or a short rubber hose can be used effectively; these make noise without causing much hurt.

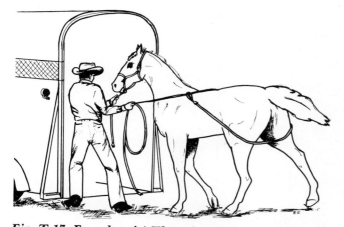

Fig. T-17. Easy does it! Throwing a loop over the rear quarters will move the problem horse forward and into the trailer.

• If a horse gets very excited and is about to break out, dash a bucket of water in his face; usually he will back off and calm down.

• A nervous, excitable horse may be calmed by a tranquilizer, which should be administered by a veterinarian.

• If a horse will not move or is kicking, grab his tail and push it over his back. In this position, he cannot kick but can be pushed along.

• *Control insects.*—In season, flies and other insects molest animals in transit. When necessary, use a reliable insecticide to control insects. Follow directions on the container label.

(Also see AIR TRANSPORTATION; and TRAILER, VAN, AND TRUCK SHIPMENTS.)

TRAPPY.—A short, quick, choppy stride; a tendency of horses with short, straight pasterns and straight shoulders.

TRAVELER.—The favorite mount of General Lee.

TRAVERSE OR SIDE STEP.—This is a lateral movement of the animal to the right or left as desired, without moving forward or backward. This trick will often assist in (1) lining up horses in the show-ring, (2) opening and closing gates, and (3) taking position in a mounted drill or a posse.

TREATS *(for horses).*—Horses are fed a great variety of treats. On a government horse breeding establishment in Brazil, the author saw a large and well-manicured vegetable garden, growing everything from carrots to melons, just for horses. Also, trainers recognize that most racehorses, which are the *prima donnas* of the equine world, don't "eat like a horse"; they eat like people—and sometimes they're just as finicky. Their menus may include a choice of carrots or other roots, fruit, pumpkins, squashes, or melons, sugar or honey, and innumerable other goodies.

Ask the average horseman why he feeds treats to his horse and you'll get a variety of answers. However, high on the list of reasons will be (1) as appetizers; (2) as a source of nutrients and as conditioners; (3) as rewards; (4) as a means of alleviating obesity (dieting the horse); or (5) folklore.

TREATS AS APPETIZERS.—If a horse doesn't eat his feed, it won't do him any good. Hence, feed consumption is important.

Sooner or later, a horseman is bound to get one of those exasperating equines that just refuses to clean up his feed. Perhaps he'll eat a few bites, then stop; or maybe he won't even touch the stuff. Sometimes this happens to race and show horses that started training in great physical shape, only to lose appetite and have to be taken out of training for rest.

Lots of things can cause finicky eaters; among them, (1) stress and nervousness, (2) an unpalatable and monotonous ration, (3) nutritional deficiencies, (4) poor health, and (5) lack of exercise. Whatever the cause, the condition(s) making for poor feed consumption should be rectified—if it can be determined, and if it is within the power of the caretaker to correct it. Additionally, there should be incorporated in the ration something that the horse really likes—such as carrots or other roots; molasses, sugar, or honey; or sliced fruit.

But treats can be overdone. Hence, a horse should not be permitted to eat too much of any treat, simply because he likes it. In this respect, horses are like boys and girls. If given a choice between candy and a well-balanced diet, most youngsters will take the candy. Yet, few parents or doctors would be so foolish as to permit a child to eat unlimited candy.

TREATS AS A SOURCE OF NUTRIENTS.—Sometimes folks, and even nutritionists, overlook the fact that, when evaluated on a dry matter basis, high-water-content tubers, fruits, and melons have almost the same nutrient value as the cereal grains. This becomes apparent in the following table which gives the energy value on a moisture-free basis of several horse treats compared with barley, corn, oats, and timothy.

TABLE T-5

Feed	Water	Dry Matter	Energy Value (TDN)	
			As Fed	Moisture Free Basis
	(%)	(%)	(%)	(%)
Barley	10	90	77	85
Corn	10	90	80	90
Oats	11	89	68	76
Timothy hay, mature . .	14	86	41	48
Apples	82	18	13	74
Carrots	88	12	10	82
Melons	94	6	5	80
Potatoes	79	21	18	85
Sugar beets	87	13	10	77

Generally speaking, horse treats are not a good buy when evaluated on a cost per unit of nutrient content (protein, energy, etc.) basis. This becomes obvious when it is realized that it takes nearly 7 pounds of carrots to equal 1 pound of oats in energy value; primarily because of the difference in water content of the two feeds. Occasionally, such products as carrots are in surplus or not suited for human consumption. At such times, they may be available for as little as $2 to $3 per ton, in which case they are a good buy in comparison with grains. Even then, it is best that they not replace more than 10 to 20 percent of the normal grain ration. For the most part, however, treats are fed to horses because they possess qualities that cannot be revealed by a chemical analysis—because of their values as appetizers, in aiding digestion, and as conditioners.

TREATS AS REWARDS.—The training of horses is based on a system of rewards and punishment. This doesn't mean that the horse is fed a tidbit each time he obeys, or that he is beaten when he refuses or does something wrong.

But horses are big and strong; hence, it's best that they want to do something, rather than have to be forced. Also, too frequent or improper use of such artificial aids as whips, spurs, reins, and bits makes them less effective; worse yet, it will likely make for a mean horse.

Horses appreciate a pat on the shoulder or a word of praise. However, better results may be obtained by working on an equine's greediness—his fondness for such things as carrots or a sugar cube. Also, treats may be used effectively as rewards to teach some specific thing such as posing, or to cure a vice like moving while the rider is mounting; but this should not be overdone.

TREATS TO ALLEVIATE OBESITY.— Horses are equine athletes; hence, they should be lean and hard, rather than fat and soft. Obese horses should be avoided because (1) they lack agility, (2) excessive weight puts a strain on the musculo-skeletal system, (3) it lowers fertility in broodmares and stallions, (4) fat horses are prone to founder, and (5) overweight horses are more susceptible to azoturia.

Such watery feeds as carrots and melons are filling, but low in calories. This becomes obvious when it's realized that (1) it takes more than 8 pounds of fresh carrots to produce 1 pound of dried product, and (2) it takes nearly 7 pounds of carrots or over 13 pounds of melons to furnish as much energy as 1 pound of oats. Thus, when used as a "salad" for the horse, carrots or melons are as effective as slenderizers for equines as they are for humans.

TREATS FOR FOLKLORE REASONS.— Among the bagful of horsemen's secrets, sometimes the claim is made that apple cider will prolong life, increase vigor, and improve sex drive, fertility, and reproduction. However, there isn't a shred of evidence, based on studies conducted by a reputable experiment station, to substantiate such claims. Of course, it's good to have faith in something; and, too, nature is a wonderful thing. It is estimated that 70 to 80 percent of all horses with afflictions would recover even without treatment.

(Also see CARROTS AND OTHER ROOTS; PUMPKINS, SQUASHES, AND MELONS; SUGAR AND HONEY.)

TREE.—The foundation of the saddle, which may be made of steel, light metal, or wood. Western saddle trees are covered with heavy rawhide, over which the exterior leather, horn, and undercovering (usually sheepskin) are added.

English saddle trees are light and are usually strengthened by steel strips, especially across the front and back.

TRIGGER.—The mount of Roy Rogers, well-known Western entertainer. (Also see MOTION PICTURE HORSES.)

TRIMMING FEET.—See FEET.

TRIPLE BAR JUMPS.—Three bars of increasing height with a wide spread. According to the *Rule Book* of the American Horse Shows Association, the bars must have a minimum height of three feet, and the difference in height of the bars must be at least nine inches. The horse must take all three bars at a leap. In case of a tie, either the distance between bars may be increased or the height may be raised.

TRIPLE CROWN.—The annual classic stakes for three-year-olds; the Kentucky Derby (the first Saturday in May), the Preakness Stakes (usually about two weeks later), and the Belmont Stakes (early in June) are the three points of the Triple Crown. Weights for each race are the same: 126 pounds for all horses, with a 5-pound allowance for fillies.

Fig. T-18. Secretariat, 1973 Triple Crown Winner— the first Triple Crown Winner in 25 years. Secretariat, winner of $1,316,778, was bred and raced by Helen (Penny) Tweedy, Meadow Stud, Doswell, Virginia. (Photograph by J. Noye, Versailles, Ky.)

Through 1973, only nine colts have won the Triple Crown:

1919—Sir Barton	1941—Whirlaway
1930—Gallant Fox	1943—Count Fleet
1935—Omaha	1946—Assault
1937—War Admiral	1948—Citation
1973—Secretariat	

The English equivalent of the Triple Crown includes the Epsom Derby, The St. Leger Stakes, and the Two Thousand Guineas.

TROIKA.—The word "troika" is a Russian word meaning trio or three. A troika hitch is a three-horse combination team hitched to a vehicle; e.g., a carriage, wagon, sleigh, or sled. The carriage is the vehicle of common use and it is known as a charaban. It is a light four-wheeled two-passenger vehicle with an elevated seat for the driver.

Fig. T-19. Troika pulled by three magnificent Orloff Trotters, a gift from The Soviet Union to Mr. Cyrus Eaton of Ohio. (Courtesy, Mr. Eaton.)

TROJAN HORSE.—The gigantic, hollow, wooden horse filled with soldiers and used by the Greeks for gaining entrance into Troy during the Trojan War. It insured the conquest of the City of Troy.

TROT.—This is a natural, rapid, two-beat, diagonal gait in which a front foot and the opposite hind foot take off and strike the ground simultaneously. There is a brief moment when all four feet are off the ground and the horse seems to float through the air.

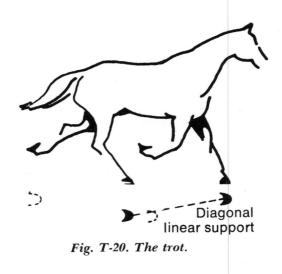

Fig. T-20. The trot.

TROTTERS.—A Standardbred horse whose speed gait is the trot is known as a trotter.

Trotters and pacers are of similar breeding and type, the particular gait being largely a matter of training.

(Also see BREED (S) —Table B-2; and STANDARDBRED.)

TUB-CART.—See GOVERNESS CART.

TUCKED-UP.—Having the belly under the loin. Refers also to a small-waisted horse. Differs from "herring-gutted" and similar conditions, in that a horse may be "tucked-up" temporarily due to hard work, lack of water, lack of bulk in the diet, etc. Also, called "gaunted-up" or "ganted-up."

TURF.—1. A track or course for horse racing.

2. The sport or business of horse racing.

3. A close-growing, well-knit, usually fine-leafed growth of grass.

TURNING.—In turning, the rider must pull the rein on the side toward which it is desired that the horse shall go; at the same time he must slacken off the pressure on the opposite side. Simultaneously, more weight is shifted to the stirrup on the side of the turn. Adequate rein pressure should be applied, but it is not necessary to jerk or pull hard.

TURNING OUT TO GRASS.—A hunting term referring to the practice of turning a horse out to grass, or resting him, at the close of the hunting season. If there are no rocks, his shoes may be removed. With good fences, good grass, and protection from internal and external parasites, such a change in pace and environment is beneficial to the horse.

When a horse is brought in after being on grass, he must be conditioned before hunting.

TUSHES.—Four pointed teeth in the mature male horse. These are located between the incisors and molars. Females do not have tushes as a rule.

(Also see AGE—Table A-1.)

TWITCH.—A rope run through the end of a stick, used on the horse's upper lip; it is tightened by twisting in order to attract the horse's attention so it will stand still.

Fig. T-21. Twitch.

TWO TRACK.—A movement in which the hind legs follow a separate track from that made by the forelegs; that is, the hind feet and the forefeet make two parallel tracks, usually about one foot apart. This movement may be done either by following the outer edge of the arena or by cutting diagonally across the arena.

TYING THE HORSE.—Horses should be tied by a halter shank or tie rope, attached to the halter. Never, never tie a horse by the bridle reins. Some additional cautions are: Never tie a horse so long that his forefeet will get over the rope; and never tie a horse so that the halter shank will slip down on the post and exert a downward pull on the horse.

If a horse has a tendency to get his foot over his halter shank when tied in the stall, run the shank through the ring and attach a weight to the end. The weight will keep the halter shank short, yet permit the horse to pull the shank to its full length when he desires to do so.

Fig. T-22. A properly tied horse. Note sturdy halter; strong lead rope; and horse tied high and reasonably close to a sturdy object.

"TYING UP" SYNDROME.—The "tying up" syndrome has been observed increasingly in recent years, particularly among racehorses, horses in endurance trials, and other horses in heavy exercise or training. It is characterized by muscle rigidity and lameness affecting the muscles of the croup and loin, accompanied by pain, disinclination to move, a variable temperature, and brownish colored urine.

Tying up differs from physiologic muscle fatigue in the conspicuous absence of hardness of muscle in the fatigue syndrome.

Some authorities feel that tying up and azoturia are one and the same, differing only in intensity. Both conditions result from exertion and present similar clinical signs and lesions. However, unlike azoturia, tying up seldom is characterized by kidney damage or high mortality.

Tying up appears to be more prevalent in mares than in geldings or stallions, more prevalent in young animals that are in high condition when put in training, and more prevalent following transportation of horses in vans or trailers. Yet, there are exceptions; tying up does occur in older animals and among those that have been in training for some time.

The cause is unknown, although it does seem to be associated with nervousness.

Affected animals usually recover in a short time. Treatment should be by a veterinarian. Among the specific treatments used are calcium borogluconate solution, insulin, thiamine, corticosteroids, tranquilizers, and selenium. The number of treatments within itself indicates a lack of basic knowledge and agreement relative to the disease.

Fig. T-23. Horses vary in size and use. The Shetland Pony foal (left) is thought to have descended from the small, shaggy, wild stock of northern Europe; whereas the draft horse (right) is thought to have descended primarily from the ponderous, wild black horse of Flanders. (Courtesy, Iowa State University)

TYPE.—Type may be defined as an ideal or standard of perfection combining all the characteristics that contribute to the animal's usefulness for a specific purpose.

TYPES AND CLASSES OF HORSES.—Horses may be classified as draft horses, light horses, or ponies, according to size, build, and use. Draft horses are used for drawing heavy loads, and light horses and ponies are used for recreation and sport.

In no class of animals have so many diverse and distinct types been developed as in the horse. The descendants of the Oriental light-legged horse have, for generations, been bred and used for riding and driving purposes—first as the chariot and riding horses of Egypt, Greece, and Arabia; later as the running horse of England; and finally for purposes of recreation and sport in the United States and throughout the world. In due time, further refinements in breeding light horses were made, and these animals were adapted for more specific purposes. In this manner, light horses specifically adapted to the purposes enumerated in Table T-6 have evolved.

In attempting to produce animals to meet these specific purposes, new breeds of light horses have been developed. In certain cases, however, the particular use or performance is so exacting that only one breed appears to be sufficiently specialized; for example, in running races the Thoroughbred is used almost exclusively, and harness races are now synonymous with the Standardbred breed.

TABLE T-6

LIGHT HORSE SUMMARY

Type	Primary Use	Breeds
Riding Horses	Three-gaited saddle horses	American Albino Horse American Paint Horse American Saddle Horse Andalusian Appaloosa Arabian Galiceno Hungarian Horse Missouri Fox Trotting Horse Morgan Horse Morocco Spotted Horse Palomino Paso Fino Peruvian Paso Horse Pinto Horse Quarter Horse Thoroughbred Ysabella
	Five-gaited saddle horses Walking horses	American Saddle Horse Tennessee Walking Horse
	Stock horses	Grades, crossbreds, or following purebreds: American Buckskin American Mustang American Paint Horse Appaloosa Arabian Chickasaw Hungarian Horse Morgan Horse Pinto Horse Quarter Horse Spanish Mustang Thoroughbred
	Polo mounts	Grades, crossbreds, and purebreds of all breeds, but predominantly of Thoroughbred breeding.
	Hunters and Jumpers	Grades, crossbreds, and purebreds of all breeds, but predominantly of Thoroughbred breeding.
	Ponies for riding	American Gotland Horse Connemara Pony Pony of the Americas Shetland Pony Welsh Pony

(Continued)

TABLE T-6 (CONTINUED)

Type	Primary Use		Breeds
Racehorses[1]	Running racehorses		Thoroughbred
	Harness racehorses (trotters and pacers)		Standardbred
	Quarter racehorses		Quarter Horse
Driving Horses	Heavy harness horses		Hackney
	Fine harness horses		American Saddle Horses (predominantly, although other breeds are so used)
	Roadsters		Standardbred
	Ponies for driving: 1. Harness show ponies 2. Heavy harness ponies		Hackney Shetland Pony Welsh Pony

1. In a few states, Appaloosa and Arabian horses are also being raced under saddle.

U

UNDERLINE.—See PARTS OF A HORSE—Fig. P-4.

UNDERPINNING.—The legs and feet of the horse.

UNDERSHOT JAW.—An hereditary imperfection in the way in which the teeth come together. In undershot jaw, the lower jaw is longer than the upper.

UNICORN.—An unusual three-horse hitch with two horses hitched as a pair and a third hitched in front of the pair.

UNITED STATES TROTTING ASSN.—750 Michigan Ave., Columbus, Ohio 43215. (See Appendix for complete breed registry association list.)

UNNERVED (DENERVED).—The nerve leading to the foot is sometimes severed on a horse suffering from navicular disease. An unnerved horse is unsound. They're barred from racing, and they're unsafe for jumping.

UNSOUNDNESSES.—Unsoundnesses include those more serious abnormalities that affect the serviceability of the horse. Unsoundnesses may be caused by any one or various combinations of the following: (1) an inherent or predisposing weakness; (2) subjecting the horse to strain and stress far beyond the capability of even the best structure and tissue; (3) accident or injury; and (4) nutritional deficiencies, particularly minerals. Unsoundnesses that can be definitely traced to the latter three causes should not be considered as hereditary. Unless one is very positive that they are not hereditary, however, serious unsoundnesses should always be regarded with suspicion in the breeding animal. Probably no unsoundness is actually inherited, but the fact that individuals may inherit a predisposition to an unsoundness through faulty conformation cannot be questioned.

The accompanying outline and figures (Table U-1, and Figs. U-1 and U-2) show the body locations of the common blemishes and unsoundnesses. As noted, the great preponderance of troubles affect the limbs.

(Also see discussion of each unsoundness under its alphabetical listing.)

OUTLINE OF UNSOUNDNESSES.—

TABLE U-1

I. Head:
    1. Blindness
    2. Moon blindness
       (periodic ophthalmia)
    3. Parrotmouth and under-
       shot jaw
    4. Poll evil

II. Withers and shoulders:
    1. Fistulous withers
    2. Sweeney

III. Front limbs:
    1. Bowed tendons
    2. Calf-kneed
    3. Cocked ankles
    4. Knee-sprung
    5. Ringbone
    6. Shoe boil
    7. Splints
    8. Wind-puffs

    9. Contracted feet
   10. Corns
   11. Founder or laminitis
   12. Navicular disease
   13. Quarter crack or sand crack   } Front Feet
   14. Quittor
   15. Scratches or grease heel
   16. Sidebones
   17. Thrush

IV. Rear limbs:
    1. Cocked ankles
    2. Ringbone
    3. Stifled
    4. Stringhalt
    5. Wind-puffs

    6. Blood spavin
    7. Bog spavin
    8. Bone spavin or jack   } Hocks
    9. Capped hock
   10. Curb
   11. Thoroughpin

   12. Contracted feet
   13. Corn
   14. Founder or laminitis
   15. Quarter crack or sand crack   } Hind Feet
   16. Quittor
   17. Scratches or grease heel
   18. Thrush

V. General:
    1. Heaves
    2. Hernia or rupture
    3. Roaring
    4. Thick wind

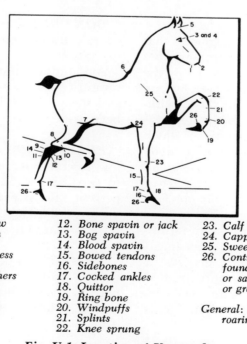

1. *Undershot jaw*
2. *Parrot mouth*
3. *Blindness*
4. *Moon Blindness*
5. *Poll evil*
6. *Fistulous withers*
7. *Stifled*
8. *Thoroughpin*
9. *Capped hock*
10. *Stringhalt*
11. *Curb*

12. *Bone spavin or jack*
13. *Bog spavin*
14. *Blood spavin*
15. *Bowed tendons*
16. *Sidebones*
17. *Cocked ankles*
18. *Quittor*
19. *Ring bone*
20. *Windpuffs*
21. *Splints*
22. *Knee sprung*

23. *Calf kneed*
24. *Capped elbow*
25. *Sweeney*
26. *Contracted feet, corns, founder, thrush, quarter or sand crack, scratches or grease heel.*

General: heaves, hernia, roaring, thick wind.

Fig. U-1. Location of Unsoundnesses.

Fig. U-2. Most common causes, ranked in order, for retiring horses from the track: (1) bowed tendons, (2) knee injury, (3) osselets, (4) bucked shin, (5) splint, (6) fractured sesamoid, (7) fractured fibula, (8) sand crack, and (9) suspensory ligament.

UREA.—Urea is a white, crystalline, odorless, nonprotein nitrogen powder having the formula N_2H_4CO, and containing 46.6 percent nitrogen. It is synthesized in quantities in chemical plants that produce anhydrous ammonia by fixing some of the nitrogen from the air; some of the ammonia gas is combined with gaseous carbon dioxide to produce the white, crystalline, solid urea which is quite stable. Considerable urea is used as a feed for ruminants.

UREA FOR HORSES.—It is recognized that horses frequently consume urea-containing cubes and blocks intended for cattle and sheep, particularly on the western range. Moreover, it appears that mature horses are able to do so without untoward effects. The latter observation was confirmed in one limited experiment[1] in which four horses consumed an average of 4.57 pounds per day of a urea-containing supplement, or 0.55 lb./head/day of feed urea (262%), for five months. Also, the Louisiana Station[2] did not find urea detrimental or toxic to horses when it constituted up to five percent of the grain ration, with up to 0.5 lb. per day of urea consumed. There are reports, however, of urea toxicity in foals, in which bacterial action is more limited than in older horses. Also, most state feed control laws limit the sale of urea-containing feeds to ruminants.

—————————
1, Veterinary Medicine (Dec. 1963), 58 (12) : 945–46.
2, "Non-Toxicity of Urea Feeding to Horses," Veterinary Medicine/Small Animal Clinician (Nov. 1965) .

URINALYSIS.—See DOPING.

URINARY CALCULI (GRAVEL, STONES, WATER BELLY).—Concretions formed within the urinary tract by precipitation of salts normally excreted in the urine.

CAUSE.—Unknown, but there is a higher incidence when there is: A high potassium intake, an incorrect Ca-P ratio, or a high proportion of beet pulp or grain sorghum in the ration.

SYMPTOMS.—Frequent attempt to urinate, dribbling or stoppage of the urine, pain and renal colic. Usually only males affected, the females being able to pass the concretions. Bladder may rupture, with death following. Otherwise, uremic poisoning may set in.

DISTRIBUTION AND LOSSES.—Worldwide. Affected animals seldom recover completely.

TREATMENT.—Once calculi develop, dietary treatment appears to be of little value. Smooth muscle relaxants may allow passage of calculi if used before rupture of bladder.

CONTROL.—Provide abundant water. Increase water consumption by including 5 to 10% salt in the ration.
Ammonium chloride has been used as a control measure with cattle (1¼ to 1½ oz./head/day) and sheep (0.5% level of ration), but it has not been widely successful.

PREVENTION.—Avoid high phosphorus and low calcium. Keep the Ca:P ratio between one to two parts of Ca to one part of P. One to two percent salt in the concentrate ration may help (using the higher levels in the winter when water consumption is normally lower).

REMARKS.—Calculi are stone-like concretions in the urinary tract which almost always originate in the kidneys. These stones block the passage of urine.

U.S. EQUESTRIAN TEAM (U.S.E.T.).—Prior to the liquidation of the U.S. Cavalry in 1949, it furnished and subsidized the equestrian teams that represented the nation. Today, the U.S. Equestrian Team is financed by gifts, and, except for the dressage horses which are owned by their riders, the team horses are lent or donated by interested supporters.

The office and training grounds are at Gladstone, N.J., at Hamilton Farms, the estate of the James Cox Brady family. There are forty-eight stalls, plus an indoor riding hall.

Screening trials are held in different sections of the U.S., and the top riders are invited to come to Gladstone *at their own expense* for further training. Candidates for the screening trials must be sixteen years of age or older, U.S. citizens, and possess an amateur license.

USES OF HORSES.—The horse was first used as a source of food. Records dating back some 25,000 years ago reveal that, prior to their domestication, these animals were hunted by Paleolithic (Old Stone Age) man. Following domestication, mares were milked for human food—a practice still followed in certain parts of the world. Next, in period of time, man used the horse to wage war. About 1500 B.C., Pharaoh pursued the Israelites to the Red Sea, using chariots and horses; and The Great Horse of medieval times was the knight's steed. As early as 1450 B.C., the sports-loving Greeks used the horse in the Olympic games, in both chariot and horse races. The use of horses in pulling loads and tilling the soil was a comparatively recent development. The improved roads that the Romans constructed during Caesar's campaigns, beginning about 55 B.C., were largely instrumental in encouraging the breeding of horses for use in transportation—for drawing heavy loads. However, there is no evidence to indicate that the horse was used in Europe to draw the plow prior to the tenth century, and few of them replaced oxen as the main source of agricultural power until the end of the eighteenth century.

Ironical as it may seem, the development of manufacturing and commerce was responsible for both the rise and fall of the horse and mule industry in the United States. The early growth of American industry created a large need for horses to transport the raw and manufactured goods and to produce needed agricultural products for those people who lived in the cities and villages. However, the relentless wheels of progress steadily lifted from the horse his role in both agriculture and war.

Today, the horse is used primarily for recreation and sport.

(Also see TYPES AND CLASSES OF HORSES.)

URTICARIA (NETTLE RASH; HIVES).—This is a skin disorder in which round elevations or swellings appear on the skin at various parts of the body. As a rule they disappear in a very short time. The swellings appear very suddenly and

Fig. U-3. Uses of horses.

vary in size from that of a pea up to several inches. It occurs more frequently in young horses than in adults. It may be seen in stabled horses that are at rest, but which are still receiving their working diet. Also, it is frequently seen when horses are first turned to pasture.

In most instances the condition disappears spontaneously. But it is always wise to give antihistamines as soon as possible, and to repeat for the following two days. Adrenalin, given in doses from 4 to 8 cc. subcutaneously, is also effective. In some cases the lesions may persist for 3 to 4 days. The affected horse should always be kept in a box stall and given a laxative diet (one containing considerable wheat bran).

VACCINATION.—Vaccination may be defined as the injection of some agent (such as a bacterin or vaccine) into an animal for the purpose of preventing disease.

In regions where a disease appears season after season, it is advised that healthy susceptible animals be vaccinated before being exposed and before there is a disease outbreak. This practice is recommended not only because it takes time to produce an active immunity but also because some animals may be about to be infected with the disease. The delay of vaccination until there is a disease outbreak may increase the seriousness of the infection. In addition, a new outbreak will "reseed" the premises with the infective agent.

In vaccination, the object is to produce in the animal a reaction that in some cases is a mild form of the disease.

It is a mistake, however, to depend on vaccination alone for disease prevention. One should always insure its success by the removal of all interfering adverse conditions. It must also be said that varying degrees of immunity or resistance result when animals are actively immunized. Individual animals vary widely in their response to similar vaccinations. Heredity also plays a part in the determination of the level of resistance. In addition, nutritional and management practices play an important part in degrees of resistance displayed by animals.

VACCINES.—Usually vaccines are defined as suspensions of live microorganisms (bacteria or virus) or microorganisms that have had their pathogenic properties removed but their antigenic properties retained. Vaccines are purposely administered to produce a mild attack of disease, thus stimulating the resistance of that animal to that specific disease, often resulting in permanent immunity. Vaccines are employed mainly in the prevention rather than in the curing of disease. For example, anthrax vaccine is used to prevent anthrax.

Great care must be exercised in the preparation, storage, and administration of vaccines. Since the improper use of them may result in disease outbreaks, it is strongly recommended that a veterinarian be consulted about their use.

VAULTING.—Vaulting on the back of a moving horse began with the Romans as a part of their basic riding instruction. In Medieval Europe it was also used in training knights in the art of horsemanship. Also, the Cossacks and the American Indians were noted for their ability at vaulting.

Today, vaulting as a sport is particularly popular with children's groups. It has its strongest support in Germany, where most riding schools have vaulting classes for juniors.

Modern vaulting is performed on the back of a cantering horse, controlled on the longe line of the instructor. The horse is usually equipped with a leather vaulting surcingle and longed in a snaffle bridle with side reins to keep its neck straight and steady.

The following six basic exercises are compulsory in competition: (1) the riding seat, (2) the keel and flag, (3) the mill, (4) the flank, (5) the free stand, and (6) the scissors. A team consists of eight members, each of whom must perform all exercises, for which a score ranging from zero to ten is given on the basis of form, grace, and precision. At the end of the individual exercises, the team is given five to seven minutes in which to present a free-style program.

Besides being an interesting spectator event, vaulting develops courage, rhythm, balance, grace, and feeling for the movements of the horse. Riding instructors report that vaulting is particularly valuable for timid children. With the constant vaulting on and off and getting used to having the horse move on at the canter, the children gain confidence.

Although every rider may not be active enough to vault on a moving horse, all riders should learn to vault off at all gaits as training to fall properly. They should always try to land facing in the direction in which the horse is moving, with their feet together, their knees slightly bent, and their weight even on the balls of both feet. (Also see CIRCUS HORSE.)

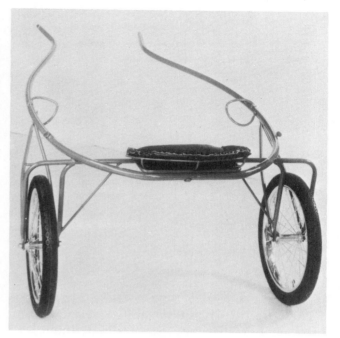

Fig. V-2. Racing sulky.

Fig. V-1. Free-stand vaulting.

Fig. V-3. Pony sulky. (Courtesy, Walden Photos, Inc.)

VEHICLES, HORSE-DRAWN.—Prior to the advent of improved roads and automobiles, the horse was used to draw vehicles, most of which originally evolved to meet practical needs, following which they were embellished to meet individual tastes.

Fig. V-4. Buckboard wagon.

Fig. V-5. Horse training cart.

APPROPRIATE HORSE-DRAWN VEHICLES

There was the dignified family carriage with a fringe on top; the buckboard with its jump seat —the pick-up truck of grandfather's time; the governess cart, with its door at the rear and two seats facing each other; the high two-wheeled dog cart, for transporting hounds to the hunt; the high seated rig of the society matron; the old-fashioned-top buggy of the country doctor; and the roadster of the young gallant.

Even hitches evolved for practical reasons. Tandem driving, for example, was originated by the hunting men of Old England. Wishing to spare their hunting mount as they traveled to and from the meet, these ingenious huntsmen devised the method of driving him ahead; where he trotted between slack traces, while the horse to the rear did all of the work.

It is noteworthy, therefore, that most horse vehicles of today are of historical significance; indeed, they are reminiscent of the horse and buggy era.

VENEZUELAN EQUINE ENCEPHALOMYE-LITIS (VEE).

—In 1971, an outbreak of Venezuelan Equine Encephalomyelitis (VEE) was reported in Texas. This was the first time the disease had occurred in the United States.

VEE is an infectious virus disease of the central nervous system of horses, causing mortality as high as 80 to 90 percent. The disease also may attack humans. The symptoms of VEE in horses are similar to those in the common eastern and western types of encephalomyelitis. In humans the infection usually produces a mild to severe respiratory illness with severe frontal headaches and high fever. Children usually are affected more severely than adults. VEE is generally not fatal in humans but some deaths have been reported.

VEE was first diagnosed in Venezuela in 1936 and was reported in several South and Central American countries before the outbreak occurred in the United States.

VEE is transmitted by mosquitoes and other insects. There is also a possibility of contact transmission between horses. Rodents are susceptible to VEE and may be reservoirs of the virus in the natural spread of the disease.

In 1971, a program to control the spread of VEE was initiated. It included spraying to control mosquitoes and the vaccination of horses.

(Also see DISEASES AND PARASITES; and HEALTH PROGRAM.)

VENTILATION.—See ENVIRONMENTAL CONTROL—Ventilation.

VERTEBRAL COLUMN.—It is considered that there is an average of 18 coccygeal (tail) vertebrae. In addition, the vertebral column consists of 7 cervical (neck) vertebrae, 18 dorsal (back), 6 lumbar (loin), and 5 sacral (croup) vertebrae.

In horses of the correct conformation, the lower line of the dorsal vertebrae (commonly referred to as the backbone) is arched slightly upward. The degree to which the backbone is arched in different horses varies greatly. If the arch is extreme, the animal is referred to as "roach backed"; whereas if the backbone sags very markedly, the animal is known as "sway backed." Either of these conditions represents a weakness in conformation and is objectionable.

Desired height at the withers and proper topline are obtained through variation in the length of the spinous processes which project upward from the vertebrae. Thus, the structure at this point is of especial importance in the saddle horse, determining the desirableness of the seat.

There is a close correlation between the length of the individual vertebrae and the length of the component parts of the entire animal. Thus, an animal with long vertebrae has a long neck, back, loin, croup, and tail. Within limits, length is desired. For example, the longer neck on a saddle horse gives the desired effect of "much horse in front of the rider." On the other hand, a very long back and loin are objectionable, denoting lack of strength. Apparent length of back may be alleviated by having a sloping shoulder, with the upper end joining the back at the rear part of the withers.

(Also see SKELETON.)

VESICULAR STOMATITIS.—A contagious disease of the mouth caused by a virus.

SYMPTOMS.—Blisters and rawness appear mainy on the tongue but also on the inner surfaces of the lips, angles of the mouth, and the gums. There is considerable salivation. Symptoms appear in 2 to 5 days after exposure.

TREATMENT.—Make the animal as comfortable as possible and provide plenty of water and soft feed.

CONTROL.—None.

PREVENTION.—None. No vaccination is available.

DISCUSSION.—The disease may affect fifty percent of the animals on the premises.

(Also see DISEASES AND PARASITES; and HEALTH PROGRAM.)

VETERINARIAN.—One who treats diseases or afflictions of animals medically and surgically; a practitioner of veterinary medicine or surgery.

U.S. veterinarians are trained in eighteen colleges of veterinary medicine, scattered across the country. Their standards are high; their entrance requirements are discriminating, and their training is rigorous. Following graduation, veterinarians must pass an examination and secure a license in order to practice in the state of their choice, as is required of medical doctors and lawyers.

Unfortunately for horse owners, the vast majority of veterinarians specialize in small animals —they become cat and dog doctors. However, with increased horse numbers and values, more and more veterinarians are becoming equine practitioners, in which the top ones "do alright" financially.

Since horses are in most instances quite valuable, when disease is encountered they merit the best of care that a competent veterinarian can accord them.

The equine veterinary practitioners of America are banded together in the American Association of Equine Practitioners, the headquarters address of which is—Route 5, 14 Hillcrest Circle, Golden, Colorado 80401.

Also, most American veterinarians are members of the American Veterinary Medical Association, whose headquarters address is—600 S. Michigan Avenue, Chicago, Ill. 60605.

VICEROY.—A lightweight, cut-under, wire-wheeled show vehicle with curved dash, used for some heavy harness classes, and especially for Hackney Ponies, Shetlands, and Harness Show Ponies.

(Also see VEHICLES, HORSE-DRAWN.)

VICES.—Most vices stem from either confinement and lack of exercise or incompetent handling. Once acquired they are difficult to cope with or to correct. The common ones are:

● *Biting.*—This refers to a horse that sinks his teeth into another horse or into a person. Biting may be caused by a horse, especially a foal, being teased and allowed to nip. Also, sensitive or thin-skinned horses frequently bite when they are being girthed up or groomed under the stomach, because it hurts.

Many different cures may be used for biting, each with varying degrees of success. A foal that nips can usually be cured by a sharp cuff on the nose or a whack with the whip. Where biting is due to the grooming hurting the skin, the use of a soft brush minimizes the desire to bite; this, along with re-education, will usually be effective. With a confirmed old nipper, it is best to keep a halter on him so that whenever he is approached he can be held at a safe distance. Also, always watch the ears of a known nipper; when you see them go back, speak sharply to him and let him know that he will be disciplined if he goes further. But never punish him unless he misbehaves. If everything else fails to cure a confirmed biter, a muzzle may be used as a last resort.

● *Bolting.*—Bolting is the name given to the habit that ravenous horses have of eating too fast. This condition may be controlled by adding chopped hay to the grain ration or by placing some large, round stones, as big or bigger than baseballs, in the feed box.

● *Bucking.*—Bucking takes several forms, but in all cases the horse stands on its forelegs and kicks up its hind legs. Bucking before or during a gallop is usually due to excitement. "Fly-bucking," in which the head is kept high and the horse kicks out either to the side or behind, is generally observed only in highly schooled horses, in response to perplexity. When bucking to dismount a rider, the horse springs with quick leaps, arches his back, and descends with his forelegs rigid and his head held as low as possible. The latter type of bucking is an evasion and originates because of poor handling and fear.

Bucking can be cured through regular exercise by a good horseman, with consistent rewards and punishment to reinforce the desired reaction to signals and to increase the horse's confidence. Of course, good bucking horses are in demand in rodeos.

● *Cribber (wind sucking, stump sucking).*—A horse that has the vice of biting or setting the teeth against some object, such as the manger, while sucking air is known as a cribber. This causes a bloated appearance and hard keeping; and such horses are more subject to colic. The common remedy for a cribber is a strap buckled around the neck in a way that will compress the larynx when the head is flexed, but that will not cause any discomfort when the horse is not indulging in the vice. A surgical operation to relieve cribbing has been developed and used with some success.

● *Halter Pulling.*—Halter pulling is the act of pulling back on the halter rope when the horse is tied to an object. Once a halter-tied horse breaks loose, he is a potential halter puller ever after.

Halter pulling is usually a man-made vice, caused by tying the horse too low, too short, or so long that he gets a foot over the tie rope. Also, it may result when a horse has been tied to a pole or tree at the proper height but so loosely that the rope slides down on the pole or tree. At other times, the horse may be tied with a halter or rope that is too light or flimsy, or tied too closely to something terrifying, with the result that he pulls back in fright and breaks the rope.

The number of times required to make a horse into a confirmed halter puller will vary according to the first traumatic experience and the temperament of the horse. One bad experience may make a confirmed halter puller that is hard to break.

There are many methods of breaking a halter puller. Either a rope under the tail, or a rope around the belly, so arranged that it will tighten up when the horse flies back and breaks his halter, appears to be very successful; and there is no danger of serious injury from the use of either method.

● *Kicking.*—When a horse kicks hard, he lowers his head, raises his croup, and thrusts his hind legs backward. Kicking at other horses or at persons may be either aggressive or self-defensive. Occasionally, unusual excitement or injury will cause the so-called gentle horse to kick.

Timid horses are most likely to become kickers. The best way to prevent the kicking vice from developing is never to frighten a horse from behind. Always speak when you approach a horse from the rear; and avoid like the plague someone charging up from behind. When a horse kicks another horse, the best cure is immediately to give him a good whack with the whip.

Kicking at walls is usually a sign of lack of exercise and boredom. Also, hollow concrete blocks encourage stall kicking; some horses like the sound emitted by kicking it. Hence, when such blocks are used for stall walls they should either be filled or lined with wood.

A true kicker appears to have no other motive than the satisfaction of striking something or somebody with his hind feet. Fortunately, few horses are born kickers.

● *Rearing.*—Rearing is the act of standing up on the hind legs. In rearing, the horse moves his hind legs some distance under his body, throws his head up, and uses all four legs (particularly the hind ones) to propel his front end upward. The confirmed rearer can be felt to balance himself and prepare for the act.

Rearing is employed to evade forward action, and it may be an act of resistance to the rider. Habitual rearing is usually a sign of fear, caused by a poor rider. Most any horse can be made to rear if he is kicked, whipped, and jerked at the same time.

When the forefeet of a rearing horse leave the ground, the rider should immediately release pressure on the reins and lean forward over the side of his neck (never put your head on top of his neck, for you are apt to get hit as he comes up). Then the minute the horse is on all fours again, the rider should urge him forward, so as to avoid a repetition of the violent act.

Rearing is dangerous, because the horse may fall over backward on the rider. Hence, every effort should be made to break the animal of the vice. Two approaches may be used: (1) put a better rider on his back, and (2) restore his confidence.

● *Shying.*—Shying is the tendency to turn around and run away from something—usually unfamiliar objects, traffic, or an unusual crowd. Shying may also be caused by defective vision or hearing, nervousness, or playfulness. Once a horse starts shying at an object, or at a particular place on a road or trail, he may continue to do so for no apparent reason.

The rider should develop the habit of being on the constant alert for frightening objects and make every effort to keep the horse moving past them. Firm use of the aids, particularly the legs, is the best cure. Also, when the horse shys, the rider should attempt to calm him by speaking to him in a soothing voice ("You're all right, Duke"), and by stroking his neck. Above all, the more frightened the horse becomes the more quiet and calm should be the rider.

● *Stall pawing.*—Stall pawing is frequently encountered in horses that stand in stalls for long periods of time, without exercise. It appears, therefore, that it is caused largely by confinement and boredom. Prevention is largely a matter of giving the horse ample room and exercise.

With all their virtues, it is recognized that clay floors lend themselves to stall pawing. A concrete apron of quarter-moon design (with the concave arc facing the door so that it will catch the pawing foot) in each stall near the doorway will prevent horses from digging a hole in a clay floor at this point. This arrangement is particularly desirable in barns for yearlings, as they are likely to fret around the door.

● *Tail rubbing.*—Persistent rubbing of the tail against the side of the stall or other objects is objectionable. The presence of parasites may cause animals to acquire this vice. Installation of a tail board or electric wire may be necessary in breaking animals of this habit. A tail board is a board projecting from the wall of the stall high enough to strike just below the point of the buttock (instead of the tail) of the rubbing horse.

● *Weaving.*—A rhythmical swaying back and forth while standing in the stall is called weaving. The prevention and cure are exercise, with ample room and free from stress.

● *Other vices.*—Other vices that are often difficult to cope with and which detract from the value of the animal are: balking, backing, striking with the front feet, a tendency to run away, and objection to harnessing, saddling and grooming. Many of these vices originate with incompetent handling. This is especially true in older animals, thus lending credence to the statement, "You can't teach an old horse new tricks."

(Also see SELECTING HORSES.)

VICTORIA.—A low, four-wheeled, open carriage for two, partly protected with a top, and with a raised seat in front for the rider. Opinions differ as to the origin of the Victoria. It appears, however, that it was named after Queen Victoria of England, who first used it when she was Princess, then later when she was Queen. The Victoria could be drawn by one or two horses.

Fig. V-6. The Victoria.

VIRUSES.—Viruses may be defined as disease-producing agents that (1) are so small that they cannot be seen through an ordinary microscope (they can be seen by using an electron microscope), (2) are capable of passing through the pores of special filters which retain ordinary bacteria, and (3) propagate only in living tissue. They are generally classified according to the tissues they invade, although this is a very arbitrary method, as some viruses invade many tissues.

Viruses cause over 30 diseases of animals, including equine sleeping sickness—all of which are highly contagious. Virus diseases are often complicated by the presence of secondary bacterial invaders. In some cases, a virus is unable to produce a disease in the absence of so-called secondary bacteria.

VITAMINS.—Largely through the trial and error method, it was discovered that specific foods were helpful in the treatment of certain illnesses. In 1747, Lind, a British naval doctor, showed that the juice of citrus fruits (now known to be high in vitamin C) was a cure for scurvy. More than a century later—in 1897—it was concluded that the disease beri-beri was common to a diet of polished rice (deficient in vitamin B_1). Also, at a very early date, the Chinese used a concoction as a remedy for night blindness. And cod-liver oil was used in treating or preventing rickets long before anything was known about the cause of the disease.

Finally, in 1912, Funk, a Polish scientist working in London, first referred to these nutrients as "vitamines" (later the "e" was dropped; hence, the word vitamin). The actual existence of vitamins, therefore, has been known less than seventy-five years, and only within the last few years has it been possible to see or touch many of them in pure form. Previously, they were mysterious invisible "little things" known by their effects. In fact, most of the present knowledge relative to the vitamin content of both human foods and animal feeds came through studies with animals.

VITAMINS FOR THE HORSE.—Certain vitamins are necessary to the growth, development, health, and reproduction of horses. Deficiencies of vitamins A and D are sometimes encountered.

Also, indications are that vitamin E and some of the B vitamins (riboflavin and perhaps thiamine) are required by horses. Further, it is recognized that single, uncomplicated vitamin deficiencies are the exception rather than the rule.

High-quality, leafy, green forages plus plenty of sunshine generally give horses most of the vitamins they need. Horses get carotene (which the animal can convert to vitamin A) and riboflavin from green pasture and green hay not over a year old. Horses get vitamin D from sunlight and sun-cured hay.

A lack of one or more vitamins in a horse ration may be more serious than a short supply of grain and hay. Unfortunately, there are no warning signals to tell a caretaker when a horse is not getting enough of certain vitamins. A continuous shortage of any one of several of them can produce illness which is very hard to diagnose until it becomes severe; at which time it is difficult and expensive—if not too late. The important thing, therefore, is to insure against such deficiencies occurring.

Presently available information indicates that the vitamin allowances recommended in Table V-1 will meet the minimum requirements for horses and provide a reasonable margin of safety.

A capsuled discussion of each of the vitamins follows.

VITAMIN A.—Severe deficiency of vitamin A may cause night blindness, reproductive difficulties, poor or uneven hoof development, difficulty in breathing, incoordination, and poor appetite. There is also some evidence that deficiency of this vitamin may cause or contribute to certain leg bone weaknesses. When vitamin A deficiency symptoms appear, the horseman should add a stabilized vitamin A product to the ration.

Vitamin A is not synthesized in the cecum; thus, it must be provided in the feed, either (1) as vitamin A, or (2) as carotene, the precursor of vitamin A.

There should be adequate vitamin A, but excesses are to be avoided. Exorbitant amounts are costly and wasteful, and they may even be harmful. The latter caution is based on some indications that too high levels of vitamin A over an extended period of time appear to be harmful to man and some animals.

For a 1,000-pound horse, 50,000 USP of vitamin A per day are recommended.

TABLE V-1

RECOMMENDED ALLOWANCES OF VITAMINS

Kind of Vitamin	Daily Allowance per 1,000-Pound Horse[1]	Allowance per ton of Finished Feed (hay and grain combined) [2]
Vitamin A . . . . . . .USP	50,000	4,000,000
Vitamin D_2 . . . . . .USP	7,000	560,000
Vitamin E . . . . IU	200	16,000
Choline . . . . mg	400	32,000
Pantothenic acid . . . . . mg	60	4,800
Niacin . . . . mg	50	4,000
Riboflavin . . . . . . mg	40	3,200
Thiamin (B_1) . . . . . mg	25	2,000
Vitamin K . . . . mg	8	640
Folic acid . . . . mg	2.5	200
Vitamin B_{12} . . . . . . mcg[3] . . .	125	10,000

1. This is based on an allowance of 25 pounds of feed per 1,000-pound horse per day, or 2.5 pounds of feed per 100 pounds of body weight.

2. Where hay is fed separately, double this amount should be added to the concentrate.

3. Micrograms.

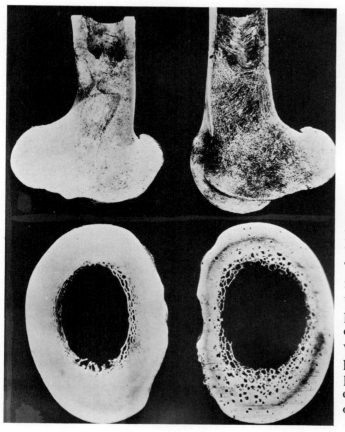

Fig. V-7. Vitamin A made the difference! Upper: On the right is shown the sagittal section of the distal end of the femur of a vitamin A-deficient horse compared to normal bone (left). Lower: On the right is shown the cross section of the cannon bone from a vitamin A-deficient horse compared to normal bone (left). (Courtesy, California Agricultural Experiment Station)

Measurement of Vitamin A Potency.—The vitamin A potency (whether due to the vitamin itself, to carotene, or to both) of feeds is usually reported in terms of I.U. or U.S.P. units. These two units of measurement are the same. They are based on the growth response of rats, in which several different levels of the test product are fed to different groups of rats, as a supplement to a vitamin A-free diet which has caused growth to cease. A U.S.P. or I.U. is the vitamin A value for rats of 0.30 microgram of pure vitamin A alcohol, or of 0.60 microgram of pure beta-carotene. The carotene or vitamin A content of feeds is commonly determined by colorimetric or spectroscopic methods.

Vitamin A Deficiency (Night Blindness and Xerophthalmia)—A vitamin A deficiency in horses may develop if dried, poor-quality roughage is fed for a prolonged period.

CAUSE.—Vitamin A deficiency.

SYMPTOMS.—Night blindness, the first symptom of vitamin A deficiency, is characterized by faulty vision, especially noticeable when the affected animal is forced to move about in twilight in strange surroundings.

Xerophthalmia develops in the advanced stages of vitamin A deficiency. The eyes become severely affected, and blindness may follow.

DISTRIBUTION AND LOSSES.—Worldwide.

TREATMENT.—Treatment consists of correcting the dietary deficiencies.

PREVENTION.—Provide good sources of carotene (vitamin A) through green, leafy hays; silage; lush, green pastures; yellow corn or green and yellow peas; whole milk; fish oil; or add stabilized vitamin A to the ration.

VITAMIN D.—Foals sometimes develop rickets because of insufficient vitamin D, calcium, or phosphorus. This can be prevented by exposing the animal to direct sunlight as much as possible, by allowing it free access to a suitable mineral mixture, or by providing it with good-quality sun-cured hay or luxuriant pasture grown on well-fertilized soil. In northern areas that do not have adequate sunshine, many horsemen provide the foal with a vitamin D supplement.

For horses, both D_2 (the plant form) and D_3 (the animal form) are equally effective, so there is no need to use some of each.

With vitamin D, as with vitamin A, there is need for adequacy without harmful excesses. Too much vitamin D may harm a horse. In 1964, Dr. Robert E. Cooke, Director of Pediatrics at Johns Hopkins Hospital, reported evidence that the consumption of high levels of vitamin D by pregnant mothers may cause mental retardation, changes in the bony structure of the face, and effects upon the aortic valve of the hearts of babies. Admittedly, research on the subject with horses is needed.

The vitamin D requirement is less when a proper balance of calcium and phosphorus exists in the ration. A vitamin D level for horses of about one-seventh the level of vitamin A appears to be about right; or about 7,000 U.S.P. daily.

VITAMIN E.—Horses seem to require vitamin E. Most practical rations contain liberal quantities of it, perhaps enough except under conditions of work stress or reproduction, or where there is interference with its utilization. Rather than buy and use costly vitamin E concentrates indiscriminately, add them to the ration only on the advice of a nutritionist or veterinarian.

There is experimental evidence that vitamin E improves the fertility of both mares and stallions, and that it prevents and corrects anhidrosis (dry, dull haircoat).

Stowe, of the University of Kentucky, reported that daily doses per mare of 100,000 U.S.P. units of vitamin A and 100 I.U. of vitamin E, beginning one month prior to the breeding season and continuing for three months, improved conception rate by 64%.

Anhidrosis (dry coat) in horses—a condition showing dull haircoat, elevated temperature, high blood pressure, and labored breathing—has been successfully treated by the oral administration of 1,000 to 3,000 I.U. of vitamin E daily for one month.

The requirements for vitamin E are influenced by interrelationships with other essential nutrients; increased by the presence of interfering substances, and spared by the presence of other substances that may be protective or that may assume part of its functions. The addition of approximately 130 I.U. of vitamin E per day to most rations should be adequate.

CHOLINE CHLORIDE.—Choline is a metabolic essential for building and maintaining cell structure and in the transmission of nerve impulses. Choline deficiency has been produced in rats, dogs, chickens, pigs, and other species. Slow growth is a nonspecific symptom.

The dietary requirement for choline depends on the level of methionine (an amino acid) in the ration. Also, it is noteworthy that all naturally occurring fats contain some choline; however, normal horse feeds are low in fat. Hence, the addition to the ration of about two-thirds of the recommended choline allowance (400 mg per day is the recommended allowance for a 1,000-pound horse) is indicated.

PANTOTHENIC ACID.—Intestinal synthesis of pantothenic acid has been found to occur in all species studied. In the case of the horse, such synthesis appears to be sufficiently extensive to meet body needs, at least in part. Hence, the addition to the ration of about five-sixths of the recommended allowance of pantothenic acid should be adequate.

NIACIN (NICOTINIC ACID).—Some evidence indicates that niacin is synthesized by the horse. Also, the horse can convert the essential amino acid tryptophan into niacin. Hence, it is important to make certain that the ration is adequate in niacin; otherwise, the horse will use tryptophan to supply niacin needs. Niacin is widely distributed in feeds; fermentation solubles and certain oil meals are especially good sources. Only a modest addition of niacin to the ration is indicated.

VITAMIN B_2 (RIBOFLAVIN).—A deficiency of riboflavin may cause periodic ophthalmia (moon blindness), but it is known that lack of this vitamin is not the only factor in producing this condition. Sometimes moon blindness follows leptospirosis in horses and it may be caused by a localized hypersensitivity or allergic reaction. Periodic ophthalmia caused by lack of riboflavin may be prevented by feeding green hay and green pasture, supplying feeds high in riboflavin, or by adding crystaline riboflavin to the ration at the rate of 40 mg per horse per day.

VITAMIN B_1 (THIAMINE).—A thiamine deficiency has been observed in horses fed on poor quality hay and grain. Although sufficient thiamine may be synthesized in the digestive system, the amount absorbed may not always meet the full requirements. Other vitamins of the B complex may be essential. Healthy horses usually get enough of them either in natural rations or by synthesis in the intestinal tract. When neither green pasture nor high-quality dry roughage is available, B vitamins may be provided by adding to the ration distillers dried solubles, dried brewers yeast, or animal liver meal.

Vitamin B_1 is synthesized in the lower gut of the horse by bacterial action, but there is some doubt as to its sufficiency.

Vitamin B_1 is required for normal carbohydrate metabolism. Since carbohydrate metabolism is increased during physical exertion, it is important that B_1 be available in quantity at such times. Hence, the addition to the ration of 25 mg of B_1 per horse per day is the recommended allowance.

VITAMIN K.—When vitamin K is deficient, the coagulation time of the blood is increased and the prothrombin level is decreased. This is the main justification in adding this vitamin to the ration of the horse.

FOLIC ACID.—Folic acid is widely distributed in horse feeds. Hence, it is unlikely that a dietary source is required; although a small amount may be in the nature of cheap insurance.

VITAMIN B_{12}.—It has been reported that horses in poor nutritional condition showing anemia respond to the administration of vitamin B_{12}. An allowance of 125 mcg of B_{12} per day is recommended. The addition of enough B_{12} to supply half of this total will probably be adequate insurance in most horse rations.

VITAMIN B_6 (PYRIDOXINE).—There is no evidence that deficiencies of vitamin B_6 occur in horses on commonly fed rations; and it is not expected that deficiencies should occur in view of the widespread distribution of vitamin B_6 in feedstuffs.

BIOTIN.—There is substantial intestinal synthesis of biotin in all animal species studied, including man. Also, biotin is widely distributed in all feeds. Hence, there is no present evidence that it should be added to horse feeds.

PARA AMINOBENZOIC ACID.—Evidence that it performs essential functions in otherwise complete rations is lacking.

ASCORBIC ACID (VITAMIN C).—A dietary need for ascorbic acid is limited to man, the guinea pig, and the monkey. Hence, there is no need to add this vitamin to horse rations.

UNIDENTIFIED FACTORS.—Since the U.S. foal crop is only around fifty percent, and since horses under stress (racing, showing, etc.) frequently become temperamental in their eating habits, it is obvious that there is room for improvement in the ration somewhere along the line. Perhaps unidentified factors are involved.

Unidentified factors include those vitamins which the chemist has not yet isolated and identified. For this reason, they are sometimes referred to as the vitamins of the future. There is mounting evidence of the importance of unidentified factors for animals, including man. Among other things, they lower the incidence of ulcers in man and swine. For horses, they appear to increase growth and improve feed efficiency and breeding performance when added to rations thought to be complete with regard to known nutrients. The anatomical and physiological mechanism of the digestive system of the horse, plus the stresses and strains to which modern horses are subjected, would indicate the wisdom of adding unidentified factor sources to the ration of the horse. Unidentified factors appear to be of special importance during breeding, gestation, lactation, and growth.

Three highly regarded unidentified factor sources are: whey solubles, corn fermentation solubles, and dehydrated alfalfa meal.

VIXEN.—A female fox.

VOICE.—The voice is one of the aids used in riding, but it should be used correctly. First, it should be realized that a horse does not comprehend words as symbols used in meaningful combinations. However, he is aware of and responds to the inflections and subtleties in the voice. Thus, a calm, soothing voice—like, "Easy, Duke" —can impart confidence to the timid horse. A complimentary tone—like, "Good boy, Duke"— along with a stroke(s) on the neck, may be used as a reward for a job well done. A sharp tone will often be sufficient rebuke to prevent a horse from misbehaving. Generally speaking, horses like to be talked to. A calm, continuous voice has carried many an inexperienced rider through a bad spot.

Never cluck to a horse. Good horsemen look upon a clucker as both rude and uninformed. Besides, it may startle other horses.

The Huntsman uses his voice to cheer and rate the hounds. Experienced members of the club can judge from the combination of his voice and the horn what the hounds are doing, even though they cannot be seen. Usually the words used by the Huntsman are as indistinguishable as those of a tobacco auctioneer, but the tone and voice, along with the sequence of the notes emitted, make very clear what's going on.

WALK.—The walk is a natural, slow, flatfooted, four-beat gait. A four-beat gait is one in which each foot leaves and strikes the ground at separate intervals. The walk should be springy, regular, and true.

Triangular support
Fig. W-1. The walk.

WALKING HORSES.—This particular class of horses is largely comprised of one breed: the Tennessee Walking Horse.

Horses of this type were first introduced into Tennessee by the early settlers from Virginia and the Carolinas. For many years, the plantation owners of middle Tennessee—men who spent long hours daily in supervising labor from the saddle—selected and bred animals for their easy, springy gaits, good dispositions, and intelligence. Particular stress was placed upon the natural gait known as the running-walk and upon the elimination of the trot. Thus, the three gaits that evolved in the walking horse (also called Plantation Walking Horse) were: the walk, the running-walk, and the canter.

In animals of this type, the head is somewhat low in carriage, and at the running-walk there is a characteristic nodding of the head. Sometimes there is also a flopping of the ears and a

Fig. W-2. A Tennessee Walking horse. (Courtesy, Albers Milling Company)

snapping of the teeth while the animal is in this rhythmic movement. Walking horses are also noted for their wonderful dispositions. Their easy gaits and a superb disposition make them an ideal type of horse for the amateur rider or the professional or society person who rides infrequently.

WALKING HORSE SEAT.—When in motion, the position should be natural, coordinated, and graceful. From the side view, a straight line can be drawn perpendicular to the ground through the rider's head, neck, shoulder, hip, and ankle. The rider's toe should never be any more forward than his knee, thereby keeping his center of balance directly above his feet and ankles. The upper arms should fall naturally from the shoulders toward the hip bones, and should be flexible, never clutched to the body, extended forward, or spread away from the body. The hands should be in a comfortable waist-level position, depending on how and where the horse carries his head. The use of the hands should be smooth and gradual, without jerking or pumping at any of the gaits, or jerking on the reins when parked.

(Also see HORSEMANSHIP—Fig. H-26.)

WALK-OVER.—When only one horse remains in a field for a race, other contestants having been withdrawn, the horse that accepts the challenge need only gallop from start to finish to go into the record as the winner and take home the stakes and half of the added money. This is only possible today in stakes events wherein nomination, elegibility, and starting fees have been paid. If overnight races or allowance races do not fill, or attract enough entries to make a field allowing betting in the win, place, and show pools, the race is cancelled and a substitute race arranged. Walk-overs are rare occurrences today, and they are usually limited to weight-for-age races where other owners feel that they have no chance at equal weight with a particular horse. The last walk-over of note occurred in 1948 when Citation had only Eddie Arcaro, his jockey, in the saddle to contend with in the Pimlico Special. With only a gallop required of him, Citation had other ideas and ran the mile and three sixteenths in 1:59 4/5 which was only three and one fifth seconds slower than the record for the race and faster than Shut Out or Challedon had previously run to win against competition.

WALK-TROT HORSE.—A three-gaited horse is frequently referred to as a walk-trot horse. Its three gaits are: the walk, the trot, and the canter.

WALL (of hoof).—This is the shell and wearing surface of the foot. It extends vertically from the edge of the hair around the front and sides of the foot, then turns in upon itself at the heel, forming the bar which extends forward toward the center. The wall protects—there is no feeling in it until the area of the coronary band is reached.

(See FOOT—Parts of the foot, Fig. F-20—Table F-5.)

WALL-EYE.—Also termed glass, blue, china, or crockery eye; refers to lack of color (lack of pigment in the iris) in a horse's eye. Such eyes are unattractive, nevertheless they are functional.

WALTZING.—The waltz, as performed in the circus by the high school horse, is very pretty. Actually, it is merely an alternation of pivot on quarters and pivot on forehand. If a horse is perfectly trained to respond to the aides, it is an easy matter to teach him to waltz.

WARBLES.—Warbles or grubs are not nearly so common in horses as in cattle. However, when they get onto horses they can inflict considerable pain and damage.

The warble fly likes warm weather and appears in the summertime. The eggs are laid at the base of the hairs on the lower part of all four legs of the horse. There they hatch out into minute larvae which penetrate the skin and migrate throughout the body until they eventually arrive at the back, frequently just under the saddle area. They appear as small painful lumps under the skin of the back. In cattle, the mature larvae pass out through the skin to develop into a new generation of flies. But in the horses the larvae often die under the skin producing either an abscess or a fistula. When this happens they must be removed by surgical means. Even after surgery, a painful sore remains which may take considerable time to heal sufficiently for the horse to be put back to work.

Prevention in the horse is almost impossible unless nearby cattle are treated against the fly.

WARFARE, HORSES IN.—Unfortunately, not long after domestication of the horse, man used him for waging war. About 1500 B.C., Pharaoh pursued the Israelites to the Red Sea, using chariots and horses (Exodus 14:7). This would seem to imply that the Egyptian army used horses, both as cavalry and to draw vehicles.

During the glamorous days of the knight in armor, horses of size, strength, and endurance were essential. The Great Horse of medieval times was the knight's steed. Usually stallions were used. Often the knight and his armor weighed 350 to 425 pounds. During the Crusades and for several centuries after, the clad-in-armor type of warrior relied upon sheer weight to beat down the enemy.

The deeds of great warriors, mounted on their favorite chargers, were long perpetuated in marble or bronze. Every school boy vividly associates Alexander the Great with his charger, Bucephalus; Napoleon with his famous horse, Marengo; the Duke of Wellington with his favorite mount, Copenhagen; George Washington, receiving the surrender of Cornwallis' army at Yorktown, with his handsome mount, Nelson; and General Grant with his horse, Jack.

Though declining in numbers and considered old fashioned by those persons who are enthralled by the speed of the machine age, the horse—man's good friend and stout companion through the ages—dramatically proved his worth again and again on the field of battle and on our farms during World War II.

Once the bulwark of armies—its numbers often deciding the issue of conflict—the horse in World War II was practically jeeped, tanked, and trucked out of his long-held place of importance in military history. Despite the unparalleled mechanization, however, horses played an indispensable role on many fronts during the great struggle for freedom. It is an old cavalry axiom that a horse can go wherever a man can travel, a feat which even the Army's famous little jeep could not accomplish.

The use of horses in World War II reached its greatest proportions in the Russian Army. Long famous for its Cossacks and centuries of cavalry tradition, Russia had, in 1940, about 200,000 horses in cavalry and 800,000 more in artillery, draft, and pack. It is also estimated that the U.S.S.R. had two mounted armies available for combat. The Russian cavalry is credited with playing a decisive role in the defense of both Moscow and Stalingrad—striking swift, devastating blows, then quickly withdrawing and melting into the forests and countryside. The full story of the role played by the Russian Cossacks may never be known.

Germany and Japan also recognized the place of the horse in modern warfare. According to the most reliable sources available, the Germans at one time had 50,000 horses for cavalry use and approximately 910,000 draft and pack animals. The Japanese—constantly building up their horse units in China, where large areas were prohibitive to motor vehicles—probably had a cavalry force of 50,000 horses with an additional 300,000 in use for draft and pack purposes.

The United States Army had relatively few horses during World War II—only about 25,000 for cavalry use and 12,000 for draft and pack—but these units performed magnificently in combat. The 26th Cavalry fought a brilliant delaying action on Luzon; and both horses and mules were used in the Burma and Italian campaigns, which were conducted through jungles and over mountains where no vehicle of any sort could go.

On the civilian front, the contributions of horses and mules, though less spectacular than on the field of battle, were nonetheless substantial. Though statistics show a continued gradual but steady decline in horse and mule numbers throughout the war years, perhaps figures alone do not tell the true story. With the rationing of critical rubber and gasoline, the diverting of iron and steel to war production, and the consequent

Fig. W-4. Pack horse and men climbing a rugged terrain in World War II. (U.S. Army Photograph)

Fig. W-3. Pack mules and "mule skinners" in service in World War II. Again and again, horses and mules dramatically proved their worth on the field of battle. (U.S. Army Photograph)

shortage of equipment—all resulting in a scarcity of mechanized power—there is little doubt that the horses and mules on farms in the United States were utilized to the maximum to help carry the major load of farm production.

During the five war years, 1941 to 1945, the total number of horses on farms declined 13.5 percent below the average of 1936 to 1940.

The Remount Service, which was established by Act of Congress in 1921, was transferred to the United States Department of Agriculture on July 1, 1948, following which the program was liquidated. At the time of the transfer, approximately 700 remount stallions were in service throughout the country.

WARM-BLOODED (HOT-BLOODED).—A term referring to Eastern or Oriental blood, especially Arabian.

WARM-UP, WARMING UP.—The process or routine of graduated exercise until the horse is properly conditioned for a strenuous effort.

WARTS.—Warts on horses are a nuisance, especially during the summer when flies seek them out for special attention. The persistant irritation of fly bites makes the animal restless and bad tempered. When the weight of the warts causes them to hang down, they are known as papillomas.

It is now fairly well established that warts are caused by viruses. Although the viruses have not yet been identified, vaccines can be prepared against them.

TREATMENT.—Even the smallest wart or group of warts should be treated without delay. If the infection becomes widespread, the veterinarian can send off a sample of the wart tissue and have what is called an autogenous vaccine prepared against the virus. When the wart is persistant or in a vital area of the horse's anatomy, such as the genitals, the veterinarian may have to remove it surgically. Papillomas and warts can be tied off so that the blood supply is stopped, by use of a rubber ring or elastrator. However, when this method is used the horse must always be injected against tetanus since the wound caused by the rubber ring provides an ideal place for the growth of the tetanus germ.

WATER.—Horses should have ample quantities of clean, fresh, cool water. They will drink 10 to 12 gallons daily; the amount depends on weather, amount of work done, and rations fed.

Free access to water is desirable. When this is not possible, horses should be watered at approximately the same times daily. Opinions vary among horsemen, as to the proper times and method of watering horses. All agree, however, that regularity and frequency are desirable. Most horsemen agree that water may be given before, during, or after feeding.

Frequent, small waterings between feedings are desirable during warm weather or when the animal is being put to hard use. Do not allow a horse to drink heavily when he is hot, because he may founder; and do not allow a horse to drink heavily just before being put to work.

(Also see EQUIPMENT, FEED AND WATER.)

WATER FOUNTAINS.—A water fountain is a bowl (usually metal) equipped with a paddle which opens a valve. These devices are excellent for providing clean, fresh water for the horse. The bowl is easily removed and cleaned; and the horse very quickly learns to press the paddle, thereby opening the valve. In either very cold climates or very hot climates, it is important that the bowl be equipped with proper drainage, and that all pipes leading to the bowl be properly insulated. Water fountains, of which there are many brands, are carried by most tack shops and by most feed stores that handle horse feed.

(Also see EQUIPMENT, FEED AND WATER.)

WATERING OUT.—This is a racehorse term, applicable to both running horses and harness horses. When a horse is brought in from the track, after a race or workout, he is usually hot and sweaty. The trainer throws a cooler over him, gives him a few sips of water to quench his thirst, then walks him. After five minutes or so, he gives him another mouthful of water, then continues the walk. This process is continued until the horse is cooled out and has had all the water he wants. When the horse has his fill of water, he is said to be "watered out."

WEANING.—See FOAL—Weaning.

WEANLING.—The period in the life of a young equine from weaning (about six months of age) to one year of age.

(Also see FEEDING; and Foal.)

Fig. W-5. A weanling. (Courtesy, Margit Sigray Bessenyey. Photo by Ernst Peterson, Hamilton, Mont.)

WEAVING.—See VICES—Weaving.

WEIGHT.—The weight of horses varies widely between breeds, between individuals, and according to age and condition. Although the weight is best determined by placing the animal on properly balanced scales, Table W-1 will serve as a useful guide.

TABLE W-1
HORSE WEIGHT CHART

Breed of Horse	Weanling Weight	Yearling Weight	Small Adult Weight	Average Adult Weight	Large Adult Weight
	(lb.)	(lb.)	(lb.)	(lb.)	(lb.)
American Paint Horse	500	750	975	1,150	1,350
American Saddle Horse	400	700	1,000	1,100	1,200
Appaloosa	500	750	1,000	1,100	1,250
Arabian	400	675	850	975	1,175
Belgian	650	1,350	1,800	2,000	2,400
Morgan Horse	400	675	950	1,050	1,150
Mules	300	500	750	1,000	1,250
Percheron	600	1,200	1,700	2,000	2,200
Pinto	400	700	1,000	1,100	1,200
Pony of The Americas	150	350	400	700	900
Quarter Horse	500	750	975	1,150	1,350
Shetland Pony	125	300	375	500	550
Standardbred	500	750	900	1,050	1,225
Tennessee Walking Horse	400	700	950	1,050	1,250
Thoroughbred	400	625	885	975	1,215
Welsh Pony	150	300	500	600	700

1. From a study made by the author. These are estimated average figures, on a nationwide basis. Naturally, weight will vary between individuals and according to condition.

WEIGHTS AND MEASURES.—See METRIC SYSTEM.

WEIGHTS AND MEASURES OF FEED.—In calculating rations and mixing concentrates, it is usually necessary to use weights rather than measures. However, in practical feeding operations it is often more convenient for the horseman to measure the concentrates. Table W-2 will serve as a guide in feeding by measure. (See page 472.)

WELSH PONY.—See BREED (S).

WELSH PONY SOCIETY OF AMERICA.—P. O. Drawer A, White Post, Virginia 22663. (See Appendix for complete breed registry association list.)

WESTERN CHUNK.—See FARM CHUNK.

WESTERN ENCEPHALITIS.—See ENCEPHALOMYELITIS.

WESTERN HORSE.—The term "Western horse" refers to all types, breeds and crosses of horses, both wild and domesticated, found in the western states. (See Fig. W-6.)

WESTERN PLEASURE CLASSES.—This class is especially appealing to women and junior riders. It is primarily a walk, trot, and canter class. It is designed to demonstrate the horse's unruffled disposition, quick response to changing gaits, and proper lead.

TABLE W-2

WEIGHTS AND MEASURES OF COMMON FEEDS

Feed	Approximate Weight	
	(lb. per quart)	(lb. per bushel)
Alfalfa meal	0.6	19
Barley	1.5	48
Beet pulp (dried)	0.6	19
Brewers grain (dried)	0.6	19
Buckwheat	1.6	50
Buckwheat bran	1.0	29
Corn, cracked	1.6	50
Corn, husked ear	——	70
Corn, shelled	1.8	56
Corn meal	1.6	50
Corn-and-cob meal	1.4	45
Cottonseed meal	1.5	48
Cowpeas	1.9	60
Distillers grain (dried)	0.6	19
Fish Meal	1.0	35
Gluten feed	1.3	42
Linseed meal (new process) . .	0.9	29
Linseed meal (old process) . . .	1.1	35
Meat scrap	1.3	42
Molasses feed	0.8	26
Oat middlings	1.5	48
Oats	1.0	32
Oats, ground	0.7	22
Peanut meal	1.0	32
Rice bran	0.8	26
Rye	1.7	56
Soybeans	1.8	60
Tankage	1.6	51
Velvetbeans, shelled	1.8	60
Wheat	1.9	60
Wheat bran	0.5	16
Wheat middlings, standard . . .	0.8	26
Wheat screenings	1.0	32

Fig. W-6. Western horses. Note the various types, breeds, and crosses. (Courtesy, **The Western Horseman***)*

WESTERN RIDING CLASS.—A Western Riding Class is conducted over a prescribed course to test the all-around disposition and ability of a ranch horse. The horse is required to perform the usual ranch chores over trails; and to give a quiet, comfortable, pleasant ride in the open country, through and over obstacles.

WESTERN SADDLE.—See SADDLES—Western saddle.

WESTERN SEAT.—When using a stock saddle and riding Western style, the rider should sit straight, keep the legs fairly straight—or bent slightly forward at the knees—and rest the balls of the feet on the stirrup treads with the heels down. The left hand with the reins should be carried in a relaxed manner slightly above and ahead of the horn. The right hand should be placed on the thigh, or it may be dropped loosely down the side, or held about waist high without resting it on anything. In cutting horses or in barrel racing, the left hand may rest on the saddle horn. "Sitting" the saddle is required at all gaits. Neither posting the trot (jog) nor standing in the stirrups at the trot or gallop (lope) is accepted in Western style riding. Because speed and agility are frequently required of stock horses, a firm seat and superior balance are important.

(Also see HORSEMANSHIP—Seat.)

WESTERN TACK.—The gear used on Western horses.

(Also see BITS; BRIDLES; and SADDLES.)

WEYMOUTH (BIT, BRIDLE).—A Weymouth bit is an English curb bit. It usually has a moderate port, straight shanks, or side pieces, and is provided with lip-strap loops.

A Weymouth bridle is an English double-bitted (consisting of curb and snaffle), double-reined bridle used in showing three- and five-gaited horses.

(Also see BIT—Fig. B-9; and BRIDLES—Fig. B-66.)

WHEAT.—The total annual U.S. wheat tonnage is second only to corn. However, because it is produced mainly for the manufacture of flour and other human foods, it is generally too high in price to feed to horses. When the price is favorable, however, it may be used for horses. It should be mixed with a more bulky feed in order to prevent colic.

Compared with corn, wheat is higher in protein and carbohydrates, lower in fat, and slightly higher in total digestible nutrients. Wheat, like white corn, is deficient in carotene.

Since the kernels are small and hard, wheat should be steam rolled or crushed.

WHEAT BRAN.—Wheat bran is the coarse outer covering of the wheat kernel. It contains a fair amount of protein (averaging about 16 percent), a good amount of phosphorus, and is laxative in action. Bran is valuable for horses because of its bulky nature and laxative properties. It may be fed as a wet mash.

WHEELERS.—The team on the pole or tongue, hitched directly in front of a rig or wagon in a four or more horse hitch.

WHEY, DRIED (MILK SUGAR FEED).—Dried whey is derived from drying whey from cheese manufacture. It is high in lactose (milk sugar), containing at least 65 percent, and rich in riboflavin, pantothenic acid, and some of the important unidentified factors. One pound of dried whey contains about the same nutrients as 13 to 14 pounds of liquid whey.

WHEY-PRODUCT, DRIED.—When a portion of the lactose (milk sugar) which normally occurs in whey is removed, the resulting dried residue is called dried whey-product. According to the Association of American Feed Control Officials, the minimum percent of lactose must be prominently declared on the label of the dried whey-product. Dried whey-product is a rich source of the water-soluble vitamins.

WHINNY.—A horse's call of pleasure and expectancy.

WHIP.—An instrument or device of wood, bone, plastic, leather, fiberglass, metal, or combination thereof with a loop or cracker of leather or cord at the upper end; used for disciplining or goading an animal. Sometimes a required accessory when driving in a horse show. Also, one who handles a whip expertly, one who drives a horse in harness other than racing, or one who "whips in" or manages the hounds of a hunt club.

WHIPCORD (CLOTH).—A strong, durable cloth, with a more pronounced rib than gabardine. It is used for riding coats or breeches.

"WHIP" IN THE U.S. SENATE.—The term "whip" is derived from the British fox hunting term "whipper-in," the Huntsman's principal assistant whose job is to keep the hounds from leaving the pack. In the United States Senate, the principal job of the whip is to round up the party's Senators for important votes and to try to make sure that they vote in keeping with the wishes of the party leaders.

WHISTLING.—See ROARING.

WHITE.—See COLORS AND MARKINGS OF HORSES.

WHITE HEELS.—Where both heels are white, inside and outside.

(Also see COLORS AND MARKINGS OF HORSES—Fig. C-10.)

WHITE INSIDE HEEL.—Where the inside heel only is white.

(Also see COLORS AND MARKINGS OF HORSES—Fig. C-10.)

WHITE LINE.—The union between the sole and the wall of the foot.

WHITE OUTSIDE HEEL.—Where the outside heel only is white.

(Also see COLORS AND MARKINGS OF HORSES—Fig. C-10.)

WHITE WORMS.—See ASCARIDS.

WHOA.—The command to stop; stand. When repeated softly, means to slow down, but may also mean attention.

WILD HORSE OF ASIA.—The wild horses of Asia, sometimes referred to as the Oriental light-legged horses, were of Asiatic origin, tracing to a wild horse (now extinct) of the Asiatic deserts. Historic evidence indicates that this group of horses gave rise to most of the swift and slenderly built breeds of modern times. The Arabian, the Barb, and the Turk are all descendants of these animals; and, in turn, the Thoroughbred originated from these stocks.

WILD HORSE OF EUROPE.—The European wild horse, sometimes referred to as the European forest type, continued to live in the forests of Germany and Scandinavia until the beginning of recorded history; and wild horses are believed to have lived in the Vosges Mountains on the western border of Alsace until the year of 1600. One of the pagan practices of the ancient German tribes was the sacrifice of horses and the eating of their meat at religious feasts. To this day one may find a relic of horse worship in the horse skulls set on the gables of houses and barns in southern Germany.

The European wild horse was the wild black horse of Flanders. This was a stocky animal that possessed considerably more size and scale than the Oriental type. This draft type was native to western Europe at the time of the Roman invasion. It was the forerunner of the Great War Horse of the Middle Ages. The latter, in turn, fathered the modern draft breeds.

Not all wild horses of Europe were large, however, for small, shaggy animals were native to northern Europe. They were strong and hardy and required less feed than other types of horses. These animals are thought to be the progenitors of the Shetland Pony.

WIN.—A racing ticket which is good only if the horse wins.

WIND.—Good wind refers to good breathing—breathing that is not noisy. Defects of wind may be easily detected by first moving the animal at a rapid gait for some distance, then suddenly bringing him to a stop and listening in close proximity to the head.

WINDGALL.—See WIND-PUFFS.

WINDING OR ROPE-WALKING.—A twisting of the striding leg around in front of the supporting leg so as to make contact in the manner of a "rope-walking" artist is known as winding or rope-walking. This condition most often occurs in horses with very wide fronts.

WINDOWS.—Windows provide natural lighting and are desirable in a horse barn. They should be located high enough to prevent drafts from blowing directly on the horse; and, preferably, they should open inward. Also, they should be protected, so that the horse will not break them or cut himself.

WINDPIPE (TRACHEA).—The windpipe, or trachea, is the main trunk of the system of tubes by which air passes to and from the lungs. In the horse, it averages about 30 to 32 inches long and about 2 to 2½ inches in diameter. The windpipe should be well defined and of adequate size to permit intake of sufficient oxygen.

WIND-PUFFS (OR WINDGALL).—Windgalls or "puffs" are an enlargement of the fluid sac (bursa) located immediately above the pastern joints on the fore and rear legs. They are usually the result of too fast or hard road work, especially on hard surfaces. Treatment consists of applying cold packs followed by liniments or sharp blistering agents. Firing or draining by a veterinarian may be in order, but experienced horsemen report that in many cases no permanent benefit results from such treatment.

(Also see UNSOUNDNESSES.)

WIND SUCKING.—See VICES—Cribber.

WINDY, OR WIND-BROKEN.—Said of an animal that whistles or roars when exerted.

WINGING.—An exaggerated paddling, particularly noticeable in high-going horses.

WINKERS.—See BLINKERS.

WISPING.—Wisping is the rubbing down of a horse with a "wisp" of straw, hay, or other similar vegetation. It is one of the best ways in which to remove sweat and partially dried mud from a horse.

WITHERS.—The top of the shoulders. The withers should be rather clearly defined and of the same height as the hips. Good withers and oblique shoulders make for a better seat in riding horses.

(Also see PARTS OF A HORSE—Fig. P-4.)

WOBBLES (EQUINE INCOORDINATION).—This condition is seen in young horses under two years of age, particularly in Thoroughbreds, with a higher incidence in colts than in fillies. It is characterized by incoordination in the hind limbs. In some cases, the forelegs are also affected with the weaving, drunken gait being accentuated by swaying of the head and neck. The cause of the disease is not known. Some authorities feel that it may be linked with accidents to the spine during foaling, which ultimately cause pressure on the spinal cord.

WOLF TEETH.—Normally, a mature male horse has 40 teeth and a mature female has 36 teeth. Quite commonly, however, a small, pointed tooth known as a "wolf tooth" may appear in front of each molar in the upper jaw, thus increasing the total number of teeth to 42 in the male and 38 in the female. Less frequently, two more wolf teeth in the lower jaw increase the total number of teeth in the male and female to 44 and 40, respectively.

(Also see AGE.)

WOOD CHEWING.—Horses, particularly those confined to stalls or lots, frequently chew wood —they eat up their stalls or fences and the bark of trees. This condition is usually caused by one or more of the following conditions:

● *Boredom,* because they have nothing to do. The more limited the exercise, and the more quickly they consume their feed, the greater the unoccupied time available and the consequent boredom. By contrast, little *Eohippus* (the dawn horse of fifty-eight million years ago) was a denizen of the swamp. Later, through evolution, he became a creature of the prairies. Although his natural habitat shifted during this long predomestication period, until man confined him, he gleaned the feeds provided by nature. Inevitably, this occupied his time and provided exercise.

● *Nutritional inadequacies,* which may be due to (a) a deficiency of one or more nutrients, (b) an imbalance between certain nutrients, or (c) objection to the physical form of the ration—for example, it may be ground too finely.

● *Psychological stress and habit,* which contribute to the behavior of horses, and which have been accentuated by the unnatural environment to which man has subjected them.

Whatever the reason(s) for wood chewing, the suspected causative factor(s) should first be rectified. When and where needed, the exercise should be stepped up; the eating time should be prolonged, and the interval between feedings shortened; nutritional deficiencies, imbalances, and physical form of ration should be corrected; and stress should be minimized. Even after these conditions have been rectified, it may be disconcerting to find that wood chewing, and perhaps various other forms of pica, persist among certain horses—perhaps due to habit. Thus, in the final analysis, there is only one foolproof way in which to prevent wood chewing; namely, to have no wood on which they can chew—to use metal, or other similar materials, for fences and barns. (Also see DEPRAVED APPETITE.)

WORK.—See FEED—Work.

WORK HORSES.—As with light horses, similar distinct types—though fewer in number—evolved in the draft horse. From the ponderous beast of Flanders, used as foundation stock, the Great War Horse of the Middle Ages was developed; the Great War Horse, in turn, served as the forerunner of the draft horse of commerce and agriculture. Further and eventual refinement through breeding and selection adapted the draft animals to many and diverse uses, most of which have subsequently passed into oblivion with mechanization.

Fig. W-7. High-quality draft horses drawing a plow. (Courtesy, Horse Association of America)

Although marked differences in size and weight exist between draft animals, all possess a deep, broad, compact, muscular form suited to the pulling of a heavy load at the walk. A detailed description of a draft type of animal is as follows: He should have plenty of size, draftiness, and substance. The head should be shapely and clean-cut,

the eyes large and clear, and the ears active. The chest should be especially deep and of ample width. The topline should include a short, strong back and loin, with a long, nicely turned, and well-muscled croup, and a well-set tail. The middle should be wide and deep, and there should be good depth in both fore and rear flanks. Muscling should be heavy throughout, especially in the forearm and gaskin; the shoulder should be sloping; the legs should be straight, true, and squarely set; the bone should be strong and flat and show plenty of quality. The pasterns should be sloping and the feet should be large and have adequate width at the heels and toughness in conformation. With this splendid draft type, there should be style, balance, and symmetry; an abundance of quality; an energetic yet manageable disposition; soundness; and freedom from disease. The action should be straight and true, with a long, swift, and elastic stride both at the walk and the trot.

WORKING COW HORSE (*a sporting event*).—This event combines reining ability and simulates numerous jobs which are common to everyday ranch life. The horse must display superior reining skill when starting, stopping, turning, changing leads, and making a sliding stop; and he must travel in smooth, even gaits. Also, the horse must work cows.

WORLD NUMBERS.—See NUMBER OF HORSES IN WORLD.

WORLD WAR II, HORSES AND MULES IN.—See WARFARE, HORSES IN.

WOUNDS.—See FIRST AID FOR HORSES.

WRANGLER.—One who rounds up and saddles range horses.

WRANGLING.—Rounding up range horses.

Y

YEARLING.—A young horse between the ages of one and two years.

(Also see FEEDING HORSES—Feeding yearlings; and TRAINING—The yearling.)

YEAST.—Yeast is a microscopic, one-celled plant of the same family as the mushroom. There are hundreds of different kinds of yeasts, just as there are many species of grasses. However, based on their particular functions or contributions to the ration as vitamin products, yeast and yeast products may be classified roughly into the following two groups:

● *Yeast products used chiefly as a source of B vitamins and protein.*—This group includes brewers dried yeast, torula dried yeast, grain distillers dried yeast, and molasses distillers dried yeast.

● *Irradiated dried yeast.*—This is yeast that has been exposed to ultraviolet light, and which may be used as a source of vitamin D for four-footed animals.

Yeast is high in protein, averaging about 44.9 percent. From the standpoint of quality, it is among the best of the plant proteins, but not as good as the animal proteins. It is deficient in methionine. Whether or not yeast is used as a protein supplement in animal rations should be determined solely by its price relationship to other protein supplements.

Yeast is high in the B vitamins. Also it may contain an unidentified factor or factors. Usually yeast is used at levels of two to five percent of the ration in supplying B vitamins.

Yeast contains considerable ergosterol, which, when exposed to ultraviolet light, produces vitamin D. After having been subjected to ultraviolet light, it is known as irradiated yeast. Irradiated yeast is usually considered a practical source of vitamin D.

YSABELLA.—See BREED (S).

YSABELLA SADDLE HORSE ASSOCIATION, INC.—c/o Prairie Edge Farm, Route 3, Williamsport, Indiana 47993. (See Appendix for complete breed registry association list.)

Z

ZINC.—See MINERALS.

ZONING.—Horsemen need to take a hard look at many existing, and some proposed, zoning laws. In recent years, the greatest expansion of light horses has been in suburban areas; on high-priced land, under relatively confined conditions, where most, if not all, feed is brought in, and where neighbors are close. However, zoning laws and other restrictions are making it difficult, and often impossible, to maintain horses in such areas; and bridle trails and other facilities are either disappearing or becoming more restrictive.

ZOOLOGICAL CLASSIFICATION OF THE HORSE.—In the zoological scheme, the horse is classed as *Equus caballus.* He is distinguished from asses and zebras, other members of the genus *Equus,* by the longer hair of the mane and tail and the presence of the "chestnut" on the inside of the hind leg.

Dogwood and horses in Maryland. Hungarian Horses, owned by Margit Sigray Bessenyey, Indian Head, Maryland. (Photo by Ernst Peterson, Hamilton, Mont.)

On pasture. Hungarian mares and foals at Bitterroot Stock Farm, Hamilton, Mont., owned by Margit Sigray Bessenyey. (Photo by Ernst Peterson, Hamilton, Mont.)

Appendix I

BREED REGISTRY ASSOCIATIONS

A BREED REGISTRY ASSOCIATION consists of a group of breeders banded together for the purposes of (1) recording the lineage of their animals, (2) protecting the purity of the breed, (3) encouraging further improvement of the breed, and (4) promoting interest in the breed. A list of the horse breed registry associations is given in Appendix I, beginning on page 470.

APPENDIX I

BREED REGISTRY ASSOCIATIONS

Class of Animal	Breed	Association	Address
Light Horses:	American Bashkir Curly	American Bashkir Curly Registry	Box 453, Ely, Nevada 89301
	American Creme Horse	American Albino Association	Box 79, Crabtree, Oregon 97335
	American Mustang	American Mustang Association, Inc.	P. O. Box 338, Yucaipa, California 92399
	American Paint Horse	American Paint Horse Association	P. O. Box 13486, Ft. Worth, Texas 76118
	American Part-Blooded (Morgans, American Saddle Horses, Standard-breds, Hackneys, Tennessee Walking Horses, Quarter Horses.)	American Part-Blooded Horse Registry	4120 S. E. River Drive, Portland, Oregon 97222
	American Saddle Horse	American Saddle Horse Breeders Assn.	929 S. Fourth Street, Louisville, Kentucky 40203
	American White Horse	American Albino Assn.	Box 79, Crabtree, Oregon 97335
	Andalusian	American Andalusian Assn.	P. O. Box 1290, Silver City, New Mexico 88061
	Appaloosa	Appaloosa Horse Club, Inc.	P. O. Box 8403, Moscow, Idaho 83843
	Arabian—purebred	Arabian Horse Registry of America, Inc.	3435 S. Yosemite, Denver, Colorado 80231
	Buckskin	American Buckskin Registry Assn.	P. O. Box 1125, Anderson, California 96007
		International Buckskin Horse Assn., Inc.	P. O. Box 357, St. John, Indiana 46373
	Chickasaw	Chickasaw Horse Assn., Inc., The	P. O. Box 8, Love Valley, N. C. 28677
		National Chickasaw Horse Assn.	Route 2, Clarinda, Iowa 51232
	Cleveland Bay	Cleveland Bay Assn. of America	Middleburg, Virginia 22117
	Galiceno	Galiceno Horse Breeders Assn., Inc.	111 E. Elm Street, Tyler, Texas 75701
	Hackney	American Hackney Horse Society	P. O. Box 174, Pittsfield, Illinois 62363
	Hanoverian	American Hanoverian Society	809 W. 106th Street, Carmel, Indiana 46032
	Hungarian	Hungarian Horse Assn.	Bitterroot Stock Farm, Hamilton, Montana 59840
	Lipizzan	American Lipizzan Horse Registry	P. O. Box 415, Platteville, Wisconsin 53818
	Missouri Fox Trotting Horse	Missouri Fox Trotting Horse Breed Assn., Inc.	P. O. Box 637, Ava, Missouri 65608
	Morab	Morab Horse Registry of America	P. O. Box 143, Clovis, California 93612

(Continued)

BREED REGISTRY ASSOCIATIONS (CONTINUED)

Class of Animal	Breed	Association	Address
Light Horses:	Morgan	American Morgan Horse Assn., Inc.	Box 1, Westmoreland, New York 13490
	Morocco Spotted Horse	Morocco Spotted Horse Co-operative Assn. of America	Route 1, Ridott, Illinois 61067
	Palomino	Palomino Horse Assn., Inc., The	P. O. Box 324, Jefferson City, Missouri 65101
		Palomino Horse Breeders of America	Box 249, Mineral Wells, Texas 76067
	Paso Fino	American Paso Fino Horse Assn., Inc.	Mellan Bank Bldg., Room 3018 525 William Penn Place, Pittsburgh, Pa. 15219
		Paso Fino Owners & Breeders Assn., Inc.	P. O. Box 764, Columbus, North Carolina 28722
	Peruvian Paso	American Assn. of Owners & Breeders of Peruvian Paso Horses	P. O. Box 2035, California City, California 93505
		Peruvian Paso Horse Registry of N.A.	P. O. Box 816, Guerneville, California 95446
	Pinto	Pinto Horse Assn. of America Inc.	P. O. Box 3984, San Diego, California 92103
	Quarter Horse	American Quarter Horse Assn.	Box 200, Amarillo, Texas 79105
		Standard Quarter Horse Assn.	4390 Fenton, Denver, Colorado 80212
	Rangerbred	Colorado Ranger Horse Assn., Inc.	7023 Eden Mill Road, Woodbine, Maryland 21797
	Spanish-Barb	Spanish-Barb Breeders Assn.	P. O. Box 7479, Colorado Springs, Colorado 80907
	Spanish Mustang	Spanish Mustang Registry Inc., The	Route 2, Box 74, Marshall, Texas 75670
	Standardbreds	United States Trotting Assn.	750 Michigan Avenue, Columbus, Ohio 43215
		National Trotting & Pacing Assn., Inc.	575 Broadway, Hanover, Pennsylvania 17331
	Tennessee Walking Horse	Tennessee Walking Horse Breeders Assn. of America	P. O. Box 286, Lewisburg, Tennessee 37091
	Thoroughbred	Jockey Club, The	300 Park Avenue, New York, New York 10022
	Trakehner	American Trakehner Assn., Inc.	P. O. Box 268, Norman, Oklahoma 73069
	Ysabella	Ysabella Saddle Horse Assn., Inc.	c/o Prairie Edge Farm, Route 3, Williamsport, Indiana 47993

(Continued)

BREED REGISTRY ASSOCIATIONS (CONTINUED)

Class of Animal	Breed	Association	Address
Half-Breds:	Half-bred Thoroughbreds: Foals by registered Thoroughbred stallions and out of mares not registered in The American (Jockey Club) Stud Book, or in the Arabian Stud Book.	American Remount Assn. (The Half-Thoroughbred Registry) [1]	Box 1066, Perris, California 92370
	Half-bred Arabian: 1. In the Half-Arabian Stud Book: Foals by registered Arabian stallions and out of mares that are not registered in either the American (Jockey Club) Stud Book or The Arabian Stud Book. 2. In the Anglo-Arab Stud Book: (a) Foals by registered[2] Thoroughbred stallions and out of registered Arabian mares. (b) Foals by registered Arabian stallions and out of registered Thoroughbred mares. (c) Foals by registered Thoroughbred[2] or Arabian stallions and out of registered Anglo-Arab mares. (d) Foals by registered Anglo-Arab stallions out of registered Thoroughbred, Arabian, or Anglo-Arab mares.	International Arabian Horse Association	224 E. Olive Ave., Burbank, California 91503

(Continued)

1. Formerly the Half-Bred Stud Book operated by The American Remount Association, but now a privately owned registry.
2. Thoroughbred stallions registered in either The American (Jockey Club) Stud Book, the General Stud Book (English) or the French Stud Book are accepted.

BREED REGISTRY ASSOCIATIONS (CONTINUED)

Class of Animal	Breed	Association	Address
Ponies:	Connemara Pony	American Connemara Pony Society	R. D. 1, Hoshiekon Farm, Goshen, Connecticut 06756
	Gotland Horse	American Gotland Horse Assn.	R. R. #2, Box 181, Elkland, Missouri 65644
	National Appaloosa Pony	National Appaloosa Pony, Inc.	Box 296, Gaston, Indiana 47342
	Pony of the Americas	Pony of the Americas Club	P. O. Box 1447, Mason City, Iowa 50401
	Shetland Pony	American Shetland Pony Club	P. O. Box 435, Fowler, Indiana 47944
	Walking Pony	American Walking Pony Assn.	Route 5, Box 88, Upper River Road, Macon, Georgia 31201
	Welsh Pony	Welsh Pony Society of America	P. O. Drawer A, White Post, Virginia 22663
Draft Horses:	Belgian	Belgian Draft Horse Corporation of America	P. O. Box 335, Wabash, Indiana 46992
	Clydesdale	Clydesdale Breeders' Association of the United States	Rt. 3, Waverly, Iowa 50677
	Percheron	Percheron Horse Association of America	Route 1, Belmont, Ohio 43718
	Shire	American Shire Horse Association	6960 Northwest Drive, Ferndale, Washington 98248
	Suffolk	American Suffolk Horse Association, Inc.	672 Polk Blvd., Des Moines, Iowa 50312
Jacks, Jennets and Donkeys:	Donkeys, Mules, and Hinnys	American Donkey and Mule Society Inc.,	2410 Executive Drive, Indianapolis, Indiana 46241
	Miniature Donkeys	Miniature Donkey Registry of the United States, Inc.	1108 Jackson St., Omaha, Nebraska 68102
	Jacks and Jennets	Standard Jack and Jennet Registry of America	300 Todds Road, Lexington, Kentucky 40511

Appendix II

BREED MAGAZINES

THE HORSE BREED MAGAZINES publish news items and informative articles of special interest to horsemen. Also, many of them employ field representatives whose chief duty is to assist in the buying and selling of animals.

In the compilation of the list herewith presented (see Appendix II), beginning on page 475, no attempt was made to list the general livestock magazines of which there are numerous outstanding ones. Only those magazines which are chiefly devoted to horses are included.

Breed	Publication	Address
General	*American Horseman*	257 Park Ave. South, New York, New York 10010
	Arizona Horseman, The	61 E. Columbus, Phoenix, Arizona 85012
	Capital Horseman	14405 W. 52nd Ave., Arvada, Colo. 80002
	Chronicle of the Horse, The	Middleburg, Va. 22117
	Corral, The	Box 151, Medina, Ohio 44256
	Hoof and Horn	P. O. Box "C," Englewood, Colorado 80110
	Horse and Horseman	34249 Camino Capistrano, Capistrano Beach, Calif. 92624
	Horse and Rider	Box 555, Temecula, California 92390
	Horse Lover, The	651 Brannan St., San Francisco, Calif. 94107
	Horse Show	527 Madison Ave., New York, N. Y. 10022
	Horse World	Box 588, Lexington, Ky. 40501
	Horseman	5314 Bingle Rd., Houston, Texas 77018
	Horseman's Review	Rt. 1, Box 12, Monroe Center, Illinois 61062
	Horsemen's Gazette	R. R. 1, Badger, Minnesota 56714
	Horsemen's Journal	Suite 317, 6000 Executive Blvd., Rockville, Maryland 20852
	Horsemen's Yankee Pedlar	2805 Boston Rd., Wilbraham, Mass. 01095
	Lariat, The	12675 S. W. First Street, Beaverton, Oregon 97005
	Maryland Horse, The	Box 4, Timonium, Md. 21093
	National Horse Journal, The	P. O. Box 927, Toronto 5, Ontario, Canada
	Northeast Horseman	P. O. Box 131, Hampden, Maine 04444
	Practical Horseman	19 Wilmont Mews, West Chester, Pennsylvania 19380
	Southern Horseman, The	Box 5735, Meridian, Miss. 39301
	Tack n' Togs	P. O. Box 67, Minneapolis, Minn. 55440
	Trail Rider, The	P. O. Box 397, Chatsworth, Ga. 30705
	Turf and Sport Digest	704 Norwood Dr., Pasadena, California 91105
	Western Horseman, The	P. O. Box 7980, Colorado Springs, Colorado 80933
American Saddle Horse	*National Horseman*	Box 4067, Baxter Station, Louisville, Kentucky 40204
	Saddle and Bridle	2333 Brentwood Blvd., St. Louis, Mo. 63144
Appaloosa	*Appaloosa News*	Box 8403, Moscow, Idaho 83843
	Appy, The	15039 Rock Creek Rd., Chardon, Ohio 44024
Arabian	*Arabian Horse, The*	1777 Wynkoop St., Suite 1, Denver, Colorado 80202
	Arabian Horse News	P. O. Box 2962, Denver, Colorado 80201
(Continued)	*Arabian Horse Times, The*	819 E. Elm Ave., Waseca, Minnesota 56093

APPENDIX II

BREED MAGAZINES (CONTINUED)

Breed	Publication	Address
	Arabian Horse World	815 San Antonio Rd., Palo Alto, California 94303
Morgan	*Morgan Horse, The*	Box 1, Westmoreland, New York 13490
Paint	*Paint Horse Journal, The*	Box 13486, Fort Worth, Texas 76118
Palomino	*Palomino Horses*	Box 249, Mineral Wells, Tex. 76067
Peruvian Paso Horse	*Peruvian Horse Review*	P. O. Box 816, Guerneville, California 95446
Pinto	*Pinto Horse, The*	910 W. Washington, San Diego, California 92103
Pony of Americas	*Pony of Americas Club Official Magazine*	Box 1447, Mason City, Iowa 50401
Quarter Horse	*Quarter Horse Digest*	Gann Valley, S. D. 57341
	Quarter Horse Journal	Box 9105, Amarillo, Tex. 79105
Shetland Pony	*American Shetland Pony Journal*	Box 435, Fowler, Indiana 47944
Spanish Barb	*Spanish Mustang Registry, Inc. Newsletter, The*	Route 2, Box 74, Marshall, Texas 75670
Standardbred	*Harness Horse, The*	P. O. Box 1831, Harrisburg, Pa. 17105
	Highpoint Bulletin	Box 1179, Santa Rosa, Calif. 95402
	Hoof Beats (U.S. Trotting)	750 Michigan Ave., Columbus, Ohio 43215
Tennessee Walking Horse	*Nashville Tennessean*	1100 Broad, Nashville, Tennessee 37201
	Voice of the Tennessee Walking Horse	Box 6009, Chattanooga, Tenn. 37401
	Walker, The	P. O. Box 286, Lewisburg, Tennessee 37091
	Walking Horse Report	P. O. Box 619, Shelbyville, Tenn. 37160
Thoroughbred	*Arizona Thoroughbred, The*	3723 Pueblo Way, Scottsdale, Ariz. 85251
	Backstretch, The	19363 James Couzens Hwy., Detroit, Mich. 48235
	Blood Horse, The	Box 4038, Lexington, Ky. 40504
	British Columbia Thoroughbred, The	4023 E. Hasting St., North Burnaby, B.C., Canada
	Florida Horse, The	Box 699, Ocala, Fla. 32670
	Oregon Thoroughbred Review	1001 N. Schmeer Rd., Portland, Oregon 97217
	Thoroughbred of California, The	201 Colorado Place, Arcadia, California 91006
	Thoroughbred Record, The	Box 11788, Lexington, Kentucky 40511
	Washington Horse, The	13470 Empire Way So., Seattle, Wash. 98178
Welsh Pony	*Welsh Pony World*	4531 Dexter St., N. W., Washington, D. C. 20007
Donkeys and Mules	*Mr. Longears*	100 Church St., Amsterdam, New York 12010

Appendix III

HORSE BOOKS

Without claiming that either all or the best horse books are listed, the books listed in Appendix III, beginning on page 478, are recommended as the kind that will provide valuable reference material for the horseman's bookshelf and enhance the home library.

APPENDIX III

HORSE BOOKS

Title of Book	Author(s)	Publisher
American Cowboy, The; Pub. 1955	Joe B. Frantz and Julian Ernest Choate, Jr.	University of Oklahoma Press, Norman, Okla.
American Horse Breeding; Pub. 1953	Herbert H. Reese	Borden Publishing Co., Los Angeles, Calif.
Anatomy and Physiology of Farm Animals; Pub. 1965	R. D. Frandson	Lea & Febiger, Philadelphia
Anatomy of the Domestic Animals, The; Pub. 1953	S. Sisson and J. D. Grossman	W. B. Saunders Company, Philadelphia, Pa.
And Miles to Go; Pub. 1967	Linell Smith	Little, Brown and Company, Boston & Toronto
Appaloosa Horse, The; Pub. 1957	Haines, et al.	R. C. Bailey Printing Co., Lewiston, Idaho
Arab Breeding in Poland; Pub. 1969	Edward Skorkowski	Your Pony, Columbus, Wisconsin
Art & Science of Horseshoeing, The; Pub. 1970	R. Gordon Greeley	J. B. Lippincott Company, Philadelphia and Toronto
Beginner's Guide to Horses, The	Carol R. Melcher	A. S. Barnes and Company, Inc., Cranbury, N.J.
Biography of the Tennessee Walking Horse; Pub. 1960	Ben A. Green	The Parthenon Press, Nashville, Tenn.
Bit by Bit; Pub. 1965	Diana Tuke	J. A. Allen & Co., Ltd., London, England
Black Beauty; Pub. 1970	Anna Sewell	Collins; London and Glasgow
Book of the Horse, The; Pub. 1970	Paul Hamlyn	The Hamlin Publishing Group Limited; London, New York, Sydney and Toronto
Breeding and Rearing of Jacks, Jennets and Mules, The; Pub. 1902	L. W. Knight, M.D.	The Cumberland Press, Nashville, Tenn.
Breeding the Racehorse; Pub. 1964	F. Tesio	J. A. Allen & Company, London, England
Breeding Thoroughbreds; Pub. 1946	J. F. Wall	Charles Scribner's & Sons, New York, N. Y.
Complete Horseshoeing Guide, The; Pub. 1968	Robert F. Wiseman	University of Oklahoma Press, Norman, Okla.
Cowboys, The; Pub. 1973	William H. Forbis	Time-Life Books, New York, N.Y.
Dealing with Horses; Pub. 1969	J. F. Kelly	Arco Publishing Co., Inc., New York, N.Y.
Diseases of the Horse; Pub. 1942	U.S.D.A.	U. S. Government Printing Press Office, Washington, D.C.
Disorders of the Horse	Elsie Hanauer	A. S. Barnes and Company, Inc., Cranbury, N.J.
Duke's Physiology of Domestic Animals; Pub. 1970	Melvin J. Swenson	Comstock Publishing Associates, Ithaca, N.Y.
Elegant Carriage, The; Pub. 1969	Marylian Watney	J. A. Allen & Co., 1 Lower Grosvenor Place, London, England
Elements of Farrier Science; Pub. 1966	D. M. Canfield	Enderes Tool Co., Inc., Albert Lea, Minn.
Encyclopedia of the Horse, The; Pub. 1973	Edited by Lt. Col. G. E. G. Hope and G. N. Jackson	The Viking Press, New York, N.Y.
English Pleasure Carriages; Pub. 1971	William Bridges Adams	Adams & Dart, 40 Jay Street, Bath, Somerset, England

(Continued)

Title of Book	Author(s)	Publisher
Equestrian Sport in Five Continents (in English and other languages); Pub. 1963	Editorial Staff: Ernest Alfred Sarasin	Federation Equestrian International, FEI, Germany
Equine Medicine & Surgery; Pub. 1963	Edited by J. F. Bone, et al.	American Veterinary Publications, Inc., Santa Barbara, Calif
Every Horse Owner's Cyclopedia; Pub. 1871	J. H. Walsh	Porter & Coates, Philadelphia, Pa.
Famous Horses of America; Pub. 1877		Porter & Coates, Philadelphia, Pa.
Feeding Ponies; Pub. 1968	William C. Miller	J. A. Allen & Co., Ltd., London, England
Feeding the Horse; Pub. 1969		The Blood-Horse, Lexington, Ky.
First Aid Hints for the Horse Owner; Pub. 1971	Lt. Col. W. E. Lyon	Collins, St. James Place, London, England
Genetic Principles in Horse Breeding; Pub. 1970	John F. Lasley	John F. Lasley, Columbia, Mo.
Genetics of the Horse; Pub. 1971	William E. Jones and Ralph Bogart	Caballus Publishers, East Lansing, Mich.
Great Ones, The; Pub. 1970	Editor: Kent Hollingsworth	The Blood-Horse, Lexington, Ky.
Grooming Horses; Pub. 1971	R. W. Collins	The Blood-Horse, Lexington, Ky. 1959; re-printed, under special arrangement, by The Thoroughbred Record Co., Inc. 1971.
Grooming Your Horse	Neale Haley	A. S. Barnes and Company, Inc., Cranbury, N.J.
Hagan's Infectious Diseases of Domestic Animals; Pub. 1973	Dorsey William Bruner and James Howard Gillespie	Comstock Publishing Associates, Ithaca, N.Y.
Harper's Encyclopedia for Horsemen; Pub. 1973	Louis Taylor	Harper & Row, Publishers, New York
History of American Jacks and Mules; Pub. 1971	Frank C. Mills	Hutch-Line, Inc., Hutchison, Kansas
History of Horse Racing, The; Pub. 1972	Roger Longoigg	Stein and Day, New York, N.Y.
History of The Arabian Horse Club Registry of America, Inc., The; Pub. 1950	Albert W. Harris	The Arabian Horse Club Registry of America, Inc., Chicago, Ill.
History of the Percheron Horse, A; Pub. 1917	Compiled by: Alvin Howard Sanders	Breeders Gazette Print, Chicago, Ill.
History of Thoroughbred Racing in America, The; Pub. 1965	W. H. Robertson	Prentice-Hall, Inc., Englewood Cliffs, N.J.
Horse, The; Pub. 1969	J. M. Kays	A. S. Barnes and Company, Inc., Cranbury, N.J.: Thomas Yoseloff Ltd., London, England
Horse, The; Pub. 1913	Issac Phillips Roberts	The Macmillan Company, London, England
Horse, The; Pub. 1972	Peter D. Rossdale	The California Thoroughbred Breeders Association, Arcadia, Calif.
Horse America Made, The; Pub. 1961	Louis Taylor	American Saddle Horse Breeders Association, Louisville, Ky.
Horse Breeding and Stud Management; Pub. 1971	Henry Wynmalen	J. A. Allen & Co., Ltd., Lower Grosvenor Place, London, England
Horse-Breeding Farm, The; Pub. 1973	Larryann C. Willis	A. S. Barnes and Company, Inc., Cranbury, New Jersey 08512
Horse Buyer's Guide, The; Pub. 1973	Jeanne K. Posey	A. S. Barnes and Company, Inc., Cranbury, N.J.

(Continued)

Title of Book	Author(s)	Publisher
Horse Owner's Vet Book, The; Pub. 1973	E. C. Straiton	J. B. Lippincott, Co., Philadelphia and New York
Horse Psychology; Pub. 1969	Moyra Williams	A. S. Barnes and Company, Inc., Cranbury, N.J.
Horse Science Handbook, Vol. 1, 1963 Vol. 2, 1964 Vol. 3, 1966	Edited by: M. E. Ensminger	Agriservices Foundation, Clovis, Calif.
Horse Shows; Pub. 1956	A. N. Phillips	The Interstate Printers & Publishers, Danville, Ill.
Horse Today & Tomorrow?, The; Pub. 1972	Harald Lange and Kurt Jeschko	Arco Publishing Company, Inc., New York, N.Y.
Horseman's Encyclopedia, The; Pub. 1963	Margaret Cabell Self	Arco Publishing Company, Inc., New York, N.Y.
Horseman's Handbook on Practical Breeding, A; Pub. 1950	J. F. Wall	Thoroughbred Bloodlines, Camden, S. C.
Horseman's Scrapbook in Verse and Prose, A; Pub. 1954	D. J. Kays	Long's College Book Company, Columbus, Ohio
Horseman's Short Course (proceedings); Pub. 1968	Staff	Washington Horse Breeders Ass'n., Seattle, Wash.
Horseman's Tax Guide; Pub. 1963	John O. Humphreys	The Blood Horse, Lexington, Ky.
Horsemanship; Pub. 1963	**Mrs. A. William Jasper**	Boy Scouts of America, New Brunswick, N.J.
Horsemanship and Horsemastership; Pub. 1962	Edited by: Gordon Wright	Doubleday & Company, Inc., Garden City, N.Y.
Horses; Pub. 1961	G. G. Simpson	Oxford University Press, New York, N.Y.
Horses; Pub. 1953	M. C. Self	A. S. Barnes and Company, Inc., Cranbury, N.J.
Horses and Americans; Pub. 1939	Phil Strong	Frederick A. Stokes Company, New York, N.Y.
Horses and Horsemanship; Pub. 1969	**M. E. Ensminger**	The Interstate Printers & Publishers, Danville, Ill.
Horses and Horsemanship; Pub. 1970	Louise Evelyn Walraven	A. S. Barnes and Company, Inc., Cranbury, N.J.
Horses and Horsemanship Through the Ages; Pub. 1969	Luigi Gianoli	Crown Publishers, Inc., New York, N.Y.
Horses, Horses, Horses; Pub. 1969	M. E. Ensminger	M. E. Ensminger, Clovis, Calif.
Horses, Horses, Horses; Pub. 1970	Suzanne Wilding	Van Nostrand Reinhold Company, New York, N.Y.
Horses in America; Pub. 1971	Francis Haines	Thomas Y. Crowell Company, New York, N.Y.
Horses of Today, Their History, Breeds and Qualifications; Pub. 1956	H. H. Reese	Wood & Jones, Pasadena, Calif.
Horses: Their Breeding, Care and Training	Heather Smith Thomas	A. S. Barnes and Company, Inc., Cranbury, N.J.
Horses, Their Selection, Care and Handling; Pub. 1943	Margaret Cabell Self	A. S. Barnes and Company, Inc., Cranbury, N.J.
Horseshoeing; Pub. 1966	A. Lungwitz	Oregon State University Press, Corvallis, Oregon
"Hosses"; Pub. 1927	Charles Wright Gray	Garden City Publishing Co., Inc. Garden City, New York
How to Buy a Race Horse; Pub. 1968	Alex Bower	Cromwell Bookstock Agency, Lexington, Ky.
Introduction to the Wonderful World of Horses, An; Pub. 1968	Roundup, Inc.	Roundup, Inc., McHenry, Ill.

(Continued)

Title of Book	Author(s)	Publisher
Judging Manual for American Saddlebred Horses; Pub. 1973	Prepared by: John Foss	American Saddle Horse Breeders Assn., Louisville, Ky.
Keep Your Own Pony	Geodge Wheatley	A. S. Barnes and Company, Inc., Cranbury, N.J.
Kellogg Arabians, The; Pub. 1958	Herbert H. Reese and Gladys Brown Edwards	Borden Publishing Co., Los Angeles, Calif.
Kingdom of the Horse, The; Pub. 1969	Hans-Heinrich Isenbart and Emil Martin Buhrer	Time-Life Books, U.S., et al.
Know About Horses; Pub. 1961	Harry Disston	The Devin-Adair Company, New York, N.Y.
Know Your Pony	Daphne Machin Goodall	A. S. Barnes and Company, Inc., Cranbury, N.J.
Laboratory Guide to Parasitology With Introduction to Experimental Methods; Pub. 1971	Ralph W. Macy and Allen K. Berntzen	Charles C. Thomas, Springfield, Ill.
Lame Horse, The	James R. Rooney	A. S. Barnes and Company, Inc., Cranbury, N.J.
Lameness in Horses; Pub. 1967	O. R. Adams	Lea & Febiger, Philadelphia, Pa.
Law and Your Horse, The; Pub. 1971	Edward H. Greene	A. S. Barnes and Company, Inc., Cranbury, N.J.; Thomas Yoseloff Ltd., London, England
Leg at Each Corner, A; Pub. 1963	Norman Thelwell	E. P. Dutton & Co., Inc., New York, N.Y.
Light Horse Breeds, The; Pub. 1960	John W. Patten	A. S. Barnes and Company, Inc., Cranbury, N.J.
Manual of Horsemanship of The British Horse Society and The Pony Club, The; Pub. 1968	The British Horse Society and the Pony Club	The British Horse Society, Warwickshire, England
Mare Owner's Handbook; Pub. 1971	Edited by: Tex Rogers	Cordovan Corporation, Houston, Texas
Mares, Foals and Foaling; Pub. 1959	Friedrich Andrist	J. A. Allen & Co., Lower Grosvenor Place, London, England
Pathology of Domestic Animals, Vols. 1 and 2; Pub. 1970	K. V. F. Jubb and Peter C. Kennedy	Academic Press, New York and London
People With Long Ears; Pub. 1970	Robin Borwick	Cassell & Co., Ltd., London, England
Percheron Horse, The; Pub. 1886	M. C. Weld	O. Judd Co., New York, N.Y.
Personality of the Horse, The; Pub. 1963	Edited by: Brandt Aymar and Edward Sagarin	Bonanza Books, New York, N.Y.
Points of the Horse; Pub. 1969	Capt. M. Horace Hays	Arco Publishing Co., Inc., New York, N.Y.
Practical Dressage for Amateur Trainers	Janice M. Ladendorf	A. S. Barnes and Company, Inc., Cranbury, N.J.
Practical Horse Breeding and Training; Pub. 1942	Jack Widmer	Charles Scribner's Sons, New York, N.Y.
Practical Light Horse Breeding; Pub. 1936	J. F. Wall	The Monumental Printing Co., Baltimore, Md.
Proceedings of the First International Conference on Equine Infectious Diseases; Pub. 1966	Edited by: John T. Bryans, et al.	The Grayson Foundation, Lexington, Ky.
Progress in Equine Practice; Pub. 1966	Edited by: E. J. Catcott, et al.	American Veterinary Publications, Inc., Santa Barbara, Calif.
Racehorse in Training, The; Pub. 1925	William Day and Alfred J. Day	Cassell and Company, Ltd.; London, New York, Toronto, and Melbourne
Saddle Up!; Pub. 1970	Charles E. Ball	J. B. Lippincott Company, Philadelphia, Pa., and New York

(Continued)

Title of Book	Author(s)	Publisher
Saddlery; Pub. 1963	E. Hartley Edwards	A. S. Barnes and Company, Inc., Cranbury, N.J.
Selecting, Fitting and Showing Horses; Pub. 1963	J. E. Nordby and H. E. Lattig	The Interstate Printers & Publishers, Danville, Ill.
Shetland Pony, The; Pub. 1959	L. Frank Bedell	The Iowa State University Press, Ames, Iowa
Shetland Pony, The; Pub. 1965	Maurice C. Cox	A. and C. Black Ltd., London, England
Spanish Riding School, The; Pub. 1972	Hans Handler	McGraw-Hill Book Co., Ltd. Maidenhead, England.
Stable Management & Exercise; Pub. 1971	M. Horace Hayes	Stanley Paul & Co., Ltd., London, England
Steeplechasing; Pub. 1970	John Hislop	J. A. Allen & Co., Ltd., Lower Grosvenor Place, London, England
Stud Managers Course Intermittent years since 1951	Lectures	Stud Managers Course, Lexington, Ky.
Stud Manager's Handbook, The; beginning with Vol. 1 in 1965, and annually to date.	Edited by: M. E. Ensminger	Agriservices Foundation, Clovis, Calif.
Studies on Reproduction in Horses; Pub. 1959	Dr. Y. Nishikawa	Japan Racing Association, Tokyo, Japan
Summerhays' Encyclopaedia for Horsemen; Pub. 1966	Compiled by R. S. Summerhays	Frederick Warne and Co. Ltd., London and New York
Tales of the King's Horses; Pub. 1958	Lloyd Rosenvold and Doris Rosenvold	Rosenvold Publications, Montrose, Canada
Thelwell's Riding Academy; Pub. 1967	Norman Thelwell	E. P. Dutton & Co., Inc., New York, N.Y.
Thoroughbred Bloodlines—an elementary study; Pub. 1935	John F. Wall	Monumental Printing Company, Baltimore, Md.
Thoroughbred Racing Stock; Pub. 1938	Lady Wentworth	Charles Scribner's Sons, New York, N.Y.
Thoroughbreds I Have Known	Richard Stone Reeves Juno Cole Weyer	A. S. Barnes and Company, Inc., Cranbury, N.J.
Top Form Book of Horse Care; Pub. 1966	Frederick Harper	Popular Library, New York, N.Y.
Touch of Greatness, A; Pub. 1945	C. W. Anderson	The Macmillan Company, New York
Training Horses for Races; Pub. 1926	Capt. G. W. L. Meredith	Constable and Company, Ltd., London, England
Training Tips for Western Riders; Pub. 1960	L. N. Sikes with Bob Gray	The Texas Horseman, Houston, Texas
Training the Arabian Horse; Pub. 1961	Herbert H. Reese	The Cruse Publishing Company, Inc., Fort Collins, Colo.
Training the Quarter Horse Jumper; Pub. 1968	H. Patricia Levings	A. S. Barnes and Company, Inc., Cranbury, N.J.; Thomas Yoseloff, Ltd., London, England
Training Thoroughbreds; Pub. 1961	Preston M. Burch	The Blood-Horse, Lexington, Ky.
Trotting Horse of America, The; Pub. 1871	Hiram Woodruff	University Press; Welch, Bigelow, & Co., Cambridge, Mass.
TV Vet Horse Book	TV Vet	Farming Press Ltd., Fenton House Wharfdale Road, Ipswich, Suffolk, England
Understanding and Training Horses; Pub. 1964	A. James Ricci	J. B. Lippincott Company, Philadelphia and New York
Using the American Quarter Horse; Pub. 1958	L. N. Sikes with Bob Gray	The Saddlerock Corporation, Houston, Texas

(Continued)

Title of Book	Author(s)	Publisher
Veterinary Medicine; Pub. 1969	D. C. Blood and J. A. Henderson	The Williams and Wilkins Co., Baltimore, Md.
Veterinary Notes for Horse Owners; Pub. 1972	Capt. M. Horace Hays	Arco Publishing Co., Inc., New York, N.Y.
Veterinary Notes for the Standardbred Breeder	Dr. W. R. McGee	United States Trotting Assn., Columbus, Ohio
Veterinary Parasitology; Pub. 1968	Geoffrey Lepage	Charles C. Thomas, Springfield, Ill.
Western Equitation, Horsemanship and Showmanship; Pub. 1973	Dwight Stewart	Vantage Press, Inc., New York, N.Y.
Western Horse, The; Pub. 1967	J. A. Gorman	The Interstate Printers & Publishers, Danville, Ill.
Wild Horse of the West, The; Pub. 1945	Walker D. Wyman	University of Nebraska Press, Lincoln, Nebraska
World of Horses, The; Pub. 1969	Judith Campbell	The Hamlyn Publishing Group Limited; London, New York, Sydney and Toronto
World of Pinto Horses, The; Pub. 1970	Edited by: Roxanne D. Greene	The Pinto Horse Association of America, Inc., San Diego, Calif.
Young Horseman's Handbook, Volumes 1–9; Pub. 1961	Harry Disston	The Jarman Press, Charlottesville, Va.
Your Horse, A Veterinary Book; Pub. 1967	A Sporting Life Publication	The Sporting Life Long Acre, London, England

Appendix IV

COLLEGES OF AGRICULTURE

Horsemen can obtain a list of available bulletins and circulars, and information regarding horses, by writing to their State Agricultural College. A list of the State Agricultural Colleges (Land Grant institutions have an *) follows in Appendix IV, beginning on page 485.

State	Address
Alabama	*Auburn University, Auburn. Tuskegee Institute, Tuskegee.
Alaska	*University of Alaska, Palmer.
Arizona	*University of Arizona, Tucson. Arizona State University, Tempe.
Arkansas	*University of Arkansas, Fayetteville. Arkansas State University, State College.
California	*University of California, Davis. California State Polytechnic College, San Luis Obispo. California State Polytechnic College, Kellogg-Voorhis, Pomona. California State University, Chico. California State University, Fresno.
Colorado	*Colorado State University, Fort Collins.
Connecticut	*University of Connecticut, Storrs.
Delaware	*University of Delaware, Newark.
Florida	*University of Florida, Gainesville. Florida A & M University, Tallahassee.
Georgia	*University of Georgia, Athens.
Hawaii	*University of Hawaii, Honolulu.
Idaho	*University of Idaho, Moscow.
Illinois	*University of Illinois, Urbana. Southern Illinois University, Carbondale. Illinois Normal University, Normal. Western Illinois University, Macomb.
Indiana	*Purdue University, Lafayette.
Iowa	*Iowa State University, Ames.
Kansas	*Kansas State University, Manhattan.
Kentucky	*University of Kentucky, Lexington. Berea College, Berea. Murray State University, Murray. Western Kentucky University, Bowling Green.
Louisiana	*Louisiana State University, University Station, Baton Rouge. Francis T. Nicholls State College, Thibodaux. Grambling College, Grambling. McNeese State College, Lake Charles. Northeast Louisiana State College, Monroe. Northwestern State College of Louisiana, Natchitoches. Southeastern Louisiana College, Hammond. Southern University and A & M College, Baton Rouge. University of Southwestern Louisiana, The, Lafayette.
Maine	*University of Maine, Orono.
Maryland	*University of Maryland, College Park.
Massachusetts	*University of Massachusetts, Amherst.
Michigan	*Michigan State University, East Lansing. Michigan Emmanual Missionary College, Berrien Springs.

(Continued)

State	Address
Minnesota	*University of Minnesota, St. Paul.
Mississippi	*Mississippi State University, State College.
Missouri	*University of Missouri, Columbia.
Montana	*Montana State University, Bozeman.
Nebraska	*University of Nebraska, Lincoln.
Nevada	*University of Nevada, Reno.
New Hampshire	*University of New Hampshire, Durham.
New Jersey	*Rutgers, The State University, New Brunswick.
New Mexico	*New Mexico State University, University Park.
New York	*Cornell University, Ithaca.
North Carolina	*North Carolina State University, Raleigh. Agricultural and Technical College of North Carolina, Greensboro. Pembroke State College, Pembroke.
North Dakota	*North Dakota State University, Fargo.
Ohio	*Ohio State University, Columbus.
Oklahoma	*Oklahoma State University, Stillwater. Panhandle A & M College, Goodwell.
Oregon	*Oregon State University, Corvallis.
Pennsylvania	*Pennsylvania State University, State College. Delaware Valley College of Science and Agriculture, Doylestown.
Puerto Rico	*University of Puerto Rico, Rio Piedras.
Rhode Island	*University of Rhode Island, Kingston.
South Carolina	*Clemson University, Clemson.
South Dakota	*South Dakota State University, University Station, Brookings.
Tennessee	*University of Tennessee, Knoxville. Middle Tennessee State University, Murfreesboro. Tennessee A & I State University, Nashville. Tennessee Technological University, Cookeville.
Texas	*Texas A & M University, College Station. Abilene Christian College, Abilene. Prairie View A & M College, Prairie View. Sul Ross State College, Alpine. Texas A & I University, Kingsville. Texas Technological College, Lubbock.
Utah	*Utah State University, Logan. Brigham Young University, Provo.
Vermont	*University of Vermont, Burlington.
Virginia	*Virginia Polytechnic Institute, Blacksburg. Virginia State College, Petersburg.
Washington	*Washington State University, Pullman.
West Virginia	*West Virginia University, Morgantown.
Wisconsin	*University of Wisconsin, Madison. University of Wisconsin, River Falls.
Wyoming	*University of Wyoming, Laramie.

(Continued)

IN CANADA

Province	Address
Alberta	University of Alberta, Edmonton.
British Columbia	University of British Columbia, Vancouver.
Manitoba	University of Manitoba, Winnipeg.
Nova Scotia	University of Nova Scotia, Truro.
Ontario	University of Guelph, Guelph.
Quebec	Macdonald College, St. Anne de Bellevue.
Saskatchewan	University of Saskatchewan, Saskatoon.